A Spiritual Exposition of Revelations of Jesus Christ

© Oghenovo A. Obrimah

December 2019

Kindle Direct Publishing

All Rights Reserved

The text of this publication or any part thereof may not be reproduced or transmitted in any form or by any means electronic or mechanical, including photocopying, recording, storage in an information retrieval system or otherwise without prior written permission of the Copyright Owner.

ISBN: 978-165-256-1989

Contents

CHAPTER 1

Preface

When most people, Christian or non-Christian think about revelations that were entrusted to Apostle John by our Lord Jesus Christ, revelations that are preserved for us in the Book of Revelation, they think APOCALYPSE, think judgment, think the end of the world. While they associate Apocalypse with triumph of good over evil, it is unlikely that they see Apocalypse as triumph of the LOVE OF GOD. For some non-Christians who have become aware of the Book of Revelation, the main question on their mind is:

> How exactly can a loving God promise His creation - mankind - an unavoidable doomsday?

THE TRUTH OF THE MATTER?

> Doomsday is not inevitable, is not unavoidable.

Whether or not we end up at doomsday lies in the hands not of sincere Christians, but in the hands of pretense Christians and non-Christians. I am guessing I just shocked you. I am not, however, merely aiming for shock value. On the contrary, I aim to provide you with concrete Scriptural evidence that all who preach or teach an unavoidable doomsday either are sincerely mistaken, or are charlatans (false prophets) seeking not only to subvert those who truly have faith in Jesus Christ, but also to misrepresent Christianity to the rest of the world.

> If Christians are represented as praying for, and desiring destruction of their neighbors merely because they, their neighbors choose not to pray to Jesus Christ, is it any wonder that some non-Christians think Christians consider themselves superior to everyone else?

Reality of False Prophets 1 *Persons, false prophets, or otherwise, who teach that Christians desire destruction of neighbors who do not believe in Jesus Christ, do so for formenting of hatred against Christians.*

But is it possible that false prophets are able to infiltrate the Church, and substitute their self conceived falsehoods for true knowledge of The Father and Son?

Well then, let us consider the evidence from Jesus Christ Himself in *Matthew 7:15-16; 24:11, 24-26*; and from apostles of the Lord Jesus Christ in *2Peter 2:1-3*; 1John 4:1; *Galatians 5:22-23*; and Colossians 3:12-14.

Beware of false prophets, who come to you in sheep's clothing, but inwardly they are ravenous wolves. YOU WILL KNOW THEM BY THEIR FRUITS. Do men gather grapes from thornbushes or figs from thistles?

Then many false prophets will rise up and deceive many.

For false Christs and false prophets will rise and show great signs and wonders to deceive, if possible, even the elect. See, I have told you beforehand. Therefore if they say to you, 'Look, He is in the desert!' do not go out; or 'Look, He is in the inner rooms!' do not believe it.

But there were also false prophets among the people, EVEN AS THERE WILL BE FALSE TEACHERS AMONG YOU, who will secretly bring in destructive heresies, even denying the Lord who bought them, and bring on themselves swift destruction. And many will follow their destructive ways, BECAUSE OF WHOM THE WAY OF TRUTH WILL BE BLASPHEMED. By covetousness they will exploit you with deceptive words; for a long time their judgment has not been idle, and their destruction does not slumber.

Beloved, do not believe every spirit, but test the spirits, whether they are of God; because MANY FALSE PROPHETS HAVE GONE OUT INTO THE WORLD.

But the fruit of the Spirit is *love*, joy, *peace*, patience, *kindness*, goodness, faithfulness, gentleness, *self control*; against such there is no law.

Put on then, as God's chosen ones, holy and beloved, *compassion*, kindness, *lowliness*, meekness, and *patience*, forbearing one another and, if one has a complaint against another, forgiving each other; as the Lord has forgiven you, so you also must forgive. And above all these put on love, which binds everything together in perfect harmony.

Why is it that Apostle Peter declares certainty of presence of false teachers among those who profess faith in Jesus Christ?

First, given *pastors* and/or *evangelists* can make lots of money off receipts of tithes and offerings from unsuspecting believers who are swayed by oration, miracles, or both, in presence of the lure of money, that is, covetousness, and gravitation of people towards capacity for oration, as opposed to preaching of the gospel in simple words, and in the power of a changed life, there always is an incentive for charlatans (*false prophets*) to place themselves among believers in the name of Jesus Christ.

Love of Truth 1 *If you love oration, miracles, and swelling feelings of emotion more than you love the truth, you stand the risk of entrusting your soul not to Jesus Christ, but to false prophets.*

Second, the devil has an interest in arrival at the outcome that there are not any Christians who arrive at the spiritual reality that man can, in presence of the LOVE OF GOD, THE GRACE of The Lord Jesus Christ, FELLOWSHIP OF THE BLOOD of Jesus Christ, and FELLOWSHIP OF THE HOLY SPIRIT overcome *self, sin,* the *world,* and the devil. It is not only 'overcoming', however, that is evidence for reality of the person of Christ. If all Christians do is overcome self, sin, the world, and the devil, they do not provide any evidence for pragmatism of a life of faith in the name of Jesus Christ. When mature believers in Christ overcome, and in addition, demonstrate capacity for good works that benefit not only the Church, but society at large, they demonstrate reality of the resurrection of Jesus Christ. If the devil can succeed at leading believers in the name of Jesus Christ astray, believers do not overcome, and do not arrive at good works that reveal spiritual reality of the person of Jesus Christ to the world. You see then that with so much at stake, it is unlikely that the Church is not always under attack of infiltrations from false prophets. In a parable recorded for our benefit in Matthew 13:24-30, Jesus alluded to this reality. In the parable, Jesus sows good seed into His kingdom. While men slept, however, which is to be interpreted as, '*during a time during which the Church lost it's spiritual vigilance,*' His enemy, the devil sowed tares among the good seed and went on his way.

Love of Truth 2 *If you willfully cling to any sin or weakness of which you are convicted by the Holy Spirit, you become susceptible to deceptions of false prophets.*

Third, as is well articulated by Apostle Peter, some false prophets come into the Church only so THE WAY OF TRUTH WILL BE BLASPHEMED. In their demonstration of character that is antithesis of the LOVE OF CHRIST, this while they are leaders in Church, they aim to turn people away from the good news of our Lord Jesus Christ.

Love of Truth 3 *If you induce non-Christians to arrive at the impression that faith in Jesus Christ renders you superior, an attitude that, in entirety, is contrary to teachings of Jesus Christ, you aid false prophets whose desire is blaspheming (ridiculing) of the good news of Christ.*

The key to avoiding the deception of false prophets?

Testing of new teachings, such as you are about to encounter in this book, for arrival at ascertainment of truthfulness. But then, how exactly will testing for truthfulness be effective if you have not, yourself, chosen to live by the truth, and by nothing but the truth? In respect of importance of *love of the truth*, and *knowledge of the truth*, Apostle Paul and our Lord Jesus Christ declare as follows in 2Thessalonians 2:9-11, and John 8:31-32.

> The coming of the lawless one is according to the working of Satan, with all power, signs, and lying wonders, and with all un-righteous deception among those who perish, *because they did not receive the love of the truth, that they might be saved.* And for this reason God will send them strong delusion, that they should be-lieve the lie, that they all may be condemned who did not believe the truth but had pleasure in unrighteousness.

> Then Jesus said to those Jews who believed Him, "If you abide in my word, you are my disciples indeed. *And you shall know the truth,* and THE TRUTH SHALL MAKE YOU FREE.

Friend, through Apostle Paul, the Holy Spirit declares that whenever peo-ple do not love the truth, they arrive at pleasure in unrighteousness. We arrive then at the inference that absence of love for truth, or rejection of truth is evident in love for evil and unrighteousness. Each of evil, and un-righteousness are done to fellow men. In presence of this insight, we arrive at the conclusion that A PERSON WHO LOVES THE TRUTH BELIEVES THAT:

✠ All men are created equal in intrinsic worth by one God;[1]

✠ That God is Love; and that

---

[1]Later on in this missive, I will address the spiritual reality that, while all men are equal in intrinsic worth, they can differ with respect to merits that they acquire.

✠ God commands all men to, in their love for one another, demonstrate reverence for His eternal power and deity.

The Scriptural Evidence?

If someone says, "I love God," and hates his brother, he is a liar; for he who does not love his brother whom he has seen, how can he love God whom he has not seen? And this commandment we have from Him: THAT HE WHO LOVES GOD MUST LOVE HIS BROTHER ALSO (1John 4:20-21).

Love of Truth 4 *The Scriptures declare that it is those who love the truth who arrive at knowledge of the truth - who arrive at true spiritual freedom. If you do not love the truth, Scriptures declare that you eventually will have to choose a delusion, in which to believe.*

Love of Truth 5 IF YOU LOVE THE TRUTH, YOU BELIEVE THAT ALL MEN ARE CREATED EQUAL BY ONE GOD, AND THAT THIS GOD IS LOVE, AND THAT THIS GOD COMMANDS ALL MEN TO, IN THEIR LOVE FOR ONE ANOTHER, DEMONSTRATE REVERENCE FOR HIS ETERNAL POWER AND DEITY.

What then is the evidence that Armageddon is not inevitable, is a conditional outcome that is chosen by those who, regardless or not, of profession of faith in Jesus Christ, refuse to love their fellow men?

Well then, let us listen to Christian Scriptures (Isaiah 45:18; Psalms 115:15-16; Matthew 5:5).

For thus says the Lord, who created the heavens (He is God!), WHO FORMED THE EARTH and made it (He established it; He did not create it a chaos, HE FORMED IT TO BE INHABITED!): "I am the Lord, and there is no other."

May you be blessed by the Lord, who made heaven and earth! The heavens are the Lord's heavens, but THE EARTH HE HAS GIVEN TO THE SONS OF MEN.

BLESSED ARE THE MEEK, FOR THEY SHALL INHERIT THE EARTH.

The consensus? The Father of our Lord Jesus Christ created the earth to be inhabited, to be filled with people who are MEEK IN SPIRIT, that is, people who are *not* PROUD, *not* RACIST, *not* BIGOTED, and NON-TRIBALISTIC. Unless He does not have any choice, and this only because man opposes His purpose of keeping the earth inhabited, The Father seeks to maintain His promise that He has given the earth to man.

Friend, Jesus is not appearing a second time because people refuse to accept Him as Lord and Savior. Jesus will appear a second time for salvation of those who truly love Him, only because there is wickedness and evil targeted at those who, irrespective of the deity to whom they pray, walk in love towards their fellow man.

> Do you think that I assert a heresy, that Jesus cares more about whether people pray to Him, as opposed to whether they love their neighbor?

> Well then, let us listen to Jesus Christ Himself, and in the Old Testament, The Father of The Lord Jesus Christ.

> When you spread out your hands, I will hide My eyes from you; EVEN THOUGH YOU MAKE MANY PRAYERS, I WILL NOT HEAR. Your hands are full of blood. Wash yourselves; make yourselves clean; remove the evil of your doings from before My eyes; CEASE TO DO EVIL, LEARN TO DO GOOD; seek justice, rebuke the oppressor, defend the fatherless, plead for the widow (Isaiah 1:15-17).

> Not every one who is saying to me Lord, lord, shall come into the reign of the heavens; but he who is doing the will of my Father who is in the heavens. Many will say to me in that day, Lord, lord, have we not in thy name prophesied? and in thy name cast out demons? and in thy name done many mighty things? and then I WILL ACKNOWLEDGE TO THEM, THAT - I NEVER KNEW YOU; DEPART FROM ME, YOU WHO PRACTICE LAWLESSNESS! (Matthew 7:21-23).

Reality of False Prophets 2 *It is unequivocal from the preceding two Scriptures that prayer is not the way to the heart of Jesus and His Father, our Father in the Heavens.*

Reality of False Prophets 3 *A person who practices lawlessness is a person who refuses to submit to God's revelation of Himself as Love, and God's demand that man walk in love towards all of his or her fellow men. False Prophets encourage people in lawlessness.*

> If you love me, keep my commandments (John 14:15).

> A new commandment I give to you, that you love one another; as I have loved you, that you also love one another. BY THIS ALL WILL KNOW THAT YOU ARE MY DISCIPLES, IF YOU HAVE LOVE FOR ONE ANOTHER (John 13:34-35).

Friend, our Lord Jesus Christ declares that God having appeared in form of man on earth (2Corinthians 5:19), declares that a man's love for God now is evident only in demonstration of love towards other men. In presence of plethora of religions claiming to be paths to God, God declares that He no longer will accept people on basis of some religious beliefs, declares that it is actions that will demonstrate whether or not a person truly has love for God.

Love of Truth 6 *Friend, God, Father of Jesus Christ declares that He is not impressed by directioning of prayers towards His person, declares that the minimum to which a person must attain if he or she is to be minimally accept-able to Him as a person who cares for His deity and eternal power is, without exception, love for each and every fellow man.*

> The Lord Jesus Christ is not appearing a second time because He is angry that people do not want to receive Him as Lord and Savior.

> Rather, He appears a second time only because those who love others are mistreated and He has to honor His promise to deliver them from evil.

Why then the Revelations Entrusted to Apostle John?

Revelations entrusted to Apostle John are for encouragement of those who repose faith in the name of Jesus Christ (Christians), and those who demonstrate love for God via their commitment, without exception, to love for their fellow man. In the revelations, The Lord Jesus Christ promises that those who are courageous in their decision to love, *no matter what,* receive glorious rewards. In this respect, if anyone labels a fellow man or woman to be less than a man or woman, with objective of sidestepping the demand of love from God, let he or she know that the seed sown shall be manifest only in his or her own life. The declaration of The Father in this respect?

> He who digs a pit will fall into it, and a stone will come back upon him who starts it rolling (Proverbs 26:27).

Simultaneously, revelations that are entrusted to Apostle John serve as a warning to those who seek to test Father, Son, and Holy Spirit. Ever since the Lord Jesus Christ ascended back to the heavens there are those who think that if they mistreat Christians, and Jesus does not physically appear for their salvation, that they prove Jesus is not real. This belief of course does not have any basis in reality. In the revelations given to Apostle John, The Lord Jesus Christ warns the world that persecution of those who have faith in Jesus Christ (Christians) ALWAYS will be costly, for those

who choose to trouble Christians will, themselves, receive trouble from The
Father (2Thessalonians 1:6).

> But what then about all of those timelines in the Book of Revela-
> tion?

Well, in that respect, let us consult The Lord Jesus Christ (Matthew
24:36), and the Book of Revelation itself (Revelation 3:3; 16:15).

> And concerning that day and the hour no one hath known -
> not even the messengers of the heavens - except my Father only.

> Remember then what you received and heard; keep that, and
> repent. If you will not awake, I will come like a thief, and you will
> not know at what hour I will come upon you.

> Lo, I am coming like a thief! Blessed is he who is awake, keep-
> ing his garments that he may not go naked and be seen exposed.

Love of Truth 7 *Friend, Jesus Himself declares, both while He was on earth,
and in revelations entrusted to Apostle John, that regardless of all of the
prophecies about His coming, that no one can, on basis of those prophecies,
predict the timing of His Second Coming.*

Reality of False Prophets 4 *Anyone who purports to predict timing of the
Second Coming of Christ either is sincerely mistaken in his or her motives, or
is a false prophet. If a person loves Christ, he or she believes the assertion by
Jesus that timing of His Second Coming cannot be deciphered.*

Suppose we take to heart the assertion, by Jesus Himself that timing of
His Second Coming will surprise even those who have faith in His name.

> How are those who believe in Jesus to prepare for His Second
> Coming?

> Exactly what actions and attitudes are recommended if Chris-
> tians are to be prepared for the Second Coming of Jesus Christ
> (1Thessalonians 5:2,4-5,6-9)?

> For you yourselves know well that the day of the Lord will come
> like a thief in the night. But you are not in darkness, brethren, for
> that day to surprise you like a thief. For you are all sons of light
> and sons of the day; we are not of the night or darkness.

So then let us not sleep, as others do, but let us keep awake and be sober. For those who sleep, sleep at night, and those who get drunk are drunk at night. BUT, SINCE WE BELONG TO THE DAY, LET US BE SOBER, AND PUT ON THE BREASTPLATE OF FAITH AND LOVE, AND FOR A HELMET THE HOPE OF SALVATION. For God has not destined us for wrath, but to obtain salvation through our Lord Jesus Christ.

Christian Scriptures are very clear. If Christians seek to be prepared for the second coming of Jesus Christ, they continue to walk in love, continue to walk in faith (the belief that God has given us life, and this life is in His Son Jesus Christ), and they continue to hope in The Father for their salvation.

NOTE THEN WHAT IS NOT INCLUDED IN PREPARATION FOR THE SECOND COMING OF JESUS CHRIST, WHICH IS, ATTENTION TO TIME-LINES OF ANY PROPHECY.

Does the preceding Scripture stand in isolation? Well, let us consider Romans 13:11-14, and 2Peter 3:10-14.

Besides this you know what hour it is, how it is full time now for you to wake from sleep. For salvation is nearer to us now than when we first believed; night is far gone, the day is at hand. LET US THEN CAST OFF THE WORKS OF DARKNESS AND PUT ON THE ARMOR OF LIGHT; let us conduct ourselves becomingly as in the day, not in reveling and drunkenness, not in debauchery and licentiousness, not in quarreling and jealousy. BUT PUT ON THE LORD JESUS CHRIST, AND MAKE NO PROVISION FOR THE FLESH, TO GRATIFY IT'S DESIRES.

And it will come - the day of the Lord - as a thief in the night, in which the heavens with a rushing noise will pass away, and the elements with burning heat be dissolved, WHAT KIND OF PERSONS DOTH IT BEHOVE YOU TO BE IN HOLY BEHAVIORS AND PIOUS ACTS? waiting for and hasting to the presence of the day of God, by which the heavens, being on fire, shall be dissolved, and the elements with burning heat shall melt; and for new heavens and a new earth according to His promise we do wait, in which righteousness doth dwell; WHEREFORE, BELOVED, THESE THINGS WAITING FOR, BE DILIGENT, SPOTLESS AND UNBLAMEABLE, BY HIM TO BE FOUND IN PEACE.

Apostle Paul admonishes Christians to put on the armor of light, which in Ephesians 6:10-18 is made up of:

✠ The Helmet of Salvation

✠ The Breastplate of Righteousness

✠ The equipment of the Gospel of Peace

✠ The Belt of Truth

✠ The Shield of Faith

✠ The Sword of the Spirit

✠ Prayers and Supplications in the Spirit, in which always there are Thanksgivings

Apostle Peter recommends holy behaviors, and pious actions, recommends diligence at being spotless, at being unblameable, and in peace with God and man.

> When it comes to preparing for the second coming of Jesus Christ, not even in the Book of Revelation are those who trust in Jesus Christ, those who love His name advised to focus on prophetic timelines.

> The only consistent admonition? Walking in Faith, Hope, and Love, which are the only qualities that survive into eternity (1 Corinthians 13:13). Only those in whom Jesus finds Faith in Himself, Hope in the sharing of His glory, and Love for God and fellow man are not taken by surprise at Second Coming of Jesus Christ.

Reality of False Prophets 5 *If you seek to prepare for the Second Coming of Christ via paying of attention to timelines, the warnings from Jesus, and the advice from the apostles both declare that you will be taken by surprise.*

Love of Truth 8 *If you seek to be prepared for the Second Coming of Christ, what you need are, faith in Jesus Christ, Love for God and fellow man, and the hope of acquiring the character and essence of Jesus Christ. Remember, however, that the Second Coming of Christ is necessary only if pretense Christians and non-Christians who love evil refuse to walk in love towards genuine Christians, and non-Christians who choose to love their fellow man.*

> Well then, if timelines provided in the Book of Revelation do not have any bearing on preparation for the Second Coming of Christ, what exactly is the point of all of the timelines in the Book of Revelation?

Friend, you are puzzled precisely because you have been led astray by prophets or teachers who either are sincerely wrong in their expositions of the Book of Revelation, or who have entered the Church as false prophets, teachers, or apostles.

Love of Truth 9 *The Book of Revelation provides unambiguous evidence in the very last chapter that none of the events depicted in the entire book relate directly to the Second Coming of Jesus Christ.*

How is this possible?

Well, in the very last chapter of the Book of Revelation, and in the last two verses, Jesus Himself declares that the Book of Revelation does not say anything about timing of His Second Coming.

Are you positively Shocked?

So was I when, upon my searching of the Book of Revelation for arrival at right interpretation of the truth (2Timothy 2:15), I happened upon this revelation. In presence of such a declaration by Jesus Himself, clearly the Book of Revelation is not entrusted to Christians as a timeline for the Second Coming of Jesus Christ.

Love of Truth 10 BY ASSERTION OF THE LORD JESUS CHRIST HIMSELF, THE BOOK OF REVELATION HAS NOTHING WHATSOEVER TO SAY ABOUT TIMING OF HIS SECOND COMING. *Since Jesus has declared that no one is able to figure out timing of His Second Coming, His assertion that the visions entrusted to Apostle John do not say anything about timing of His Second Coming cannot be asserted to be surprising. But then, just about every 'attempt at interpretation' of the Book of Revelation says, otherwise, that is, contradicts the declaration by The Lord Jesus Himself, yet is unambiguously wrong. This, however, is the problem with 'attempts at interpretation', which is, they do not necessarily coincide with spiritual revelations. This book is not an attempt at interpretation of the Book of Revelation. Quite the contrary, via spiritual revelation arrived at in the Holy Spirit, this book articulates, for your benefit, spiritual realities that are essence of the Book of Revelation.*

The words by Jesus Himself at end of the Book of Revelation?

He saith - who is testifying these things - Yes, I come quickly! Amen! Yes, be coming, Lord Jesus! The grace of our Lord Jesus Christ is with you all. Amen.

Friend, if at the end of the Book of Revelation, Jesus Himself declares that His Second Coming resides in the future, and Apostle John affirms same in his response to words spoken by Jesus, we safely and unambiguously conclude that everything written in that very last chapter - *Revelation ch. 22* - does not relate directly to the Second Coming of Christ. We also immediately arrive at the inference that all of the timelines that are recorded in the Book of Revelation have nothing to say about timing of the Second Coming of Christ. In presence of this realization, we arrive at the inference that when Apostle John declares in Revelation 21:1 as follows:

> And I saw a new heaven and a new earth, for the first heaven
> and the first earth did pass away, and the sea is not any more,

that he does not refer to the Second Coming of Jesus Christ. We arrive then at a puzzle, which is, if arrival of a new heaven and a new earth does not coincide with the Second Coming of Jesus Christ, what exactly does it mean that Apostle John saw a new heaven and a new earth?

> Friend, this book provides you with the first spiritually sound revelation of true meaning of a new heaven, new earth, and new Jerusalem. Naturally, this devolves into a discussion of entirety of the Book of Revelation.

In Mathematics, there is a principle referred to as 'REDUCIO AD ABSURDUM', that is, 'PROOF BY CONTRADICTION'. Whenever a principle is established via demonstration of *Reducio Ad Absurdum*, a mathematician starts off with the opposite assumption, then using formal tools of Mathematics, establishes that the opposite must be true. Let us then apply the principle of *Reducio Ad Absurdum* to contents of the Book of Revelation. In the Gospels, and in the Book of Revelation, Jesus declares that knowledge of timelines do not enable prediction of timing of His Second Coming. Regardless of any and all timelines that are found in Scriptures, except they maintain righteousness by faith in living of their daily lives, Jesus and His original apostles assert His Second Coming will catch even those who genuinely repose faith in Jesus by surprise. So then, we assumed feasibility of the opposite, and commenced our investigations in the very last chapter of the Book of Revelation. Right away, we arrived at the inference that none of the events recorded in the Book of Revelation coincide with the Second Coming of Jesus Christ. Using the principle of *Reducio Ad Absurdum* then, we confirm that timelines, which are provided in the Book of Revelation, do not relate to the Second Coming of Christ. If this conclusion is robust, there must be evident, in the Book of Revelation, alternate rationales for all of the timelines that are entrusted, by revelation, to Apostle John. For completeness of the proof then, we require alternate rationales for all of the timelines that are provided in the Book of Revelation. Importantly, we must be able to link all of those timelines to arrival of NEW HEAVENS, NEW EARTH, AND THE NEW JERUSALEM in Revelation 21:1. We also must arrive at an alternate spiritual explanation for NEW HEAVENS, NEW EARTH, AND THE NEW JERUSALEM that is consistent with all of the rest of Christian Scriptures, and that simultaneously is not contingent on a Second Coming of Jesus Christ. Then, much as Mathematicians, we will be able to close with the acronym, QED. This book is about all of the rest of that proof, about all of the discussions that enable completeness of the proof, that enable arrival at **QED**. As with any mathematical proof, there are several intermediate steps to navigate, terms to clarify, and intermediate statements to establish. As you navigate every single chapter of this book with me, I believe you either will discover something new, or find new fodder for an existing belief.

> But is it possible to apply mathematical rigor to exposition of matters that inherently are metaphysical, that is, spiritual in their very essence?

Friend, in matters that, in their very essence, are metaphysical, is there not any demand for consistency and logical progression? If the metaphysical or spiritual is not required to satisfy principles of rationality, do we not consign faith to domain of irrationality, as such infer that religion is rooted in cognitive dissonance? If, as already is well validated, God has provided us with a universe that functions on principles of rationality, how exactly can He provide us with a metaphysical or spiritual world whose principles deviate from demands of rationality?

Faith AND Rationality 1 *A Loving God and Father who provides us with a physical universe that operates by principles of rationality - gravity, relativity, potential energy, kinetic energy etc. - cannot remain a Loving God and Father if, simultaneously, He demands cognitive dissonance if we are to be at peace with, or in relationship with Him.*

Prophetic Word 1 *Combined, and understood properly, visions entrusted to Apostle John by The Lord Jesus Christ - He, who along with His Father, Our Father in the Heavens, is Creator of the physical universe in which we live - must be assumed to conform with principles of rationality.*

Prophetic Word 2 *Faith in Jesus Christ satisfies principles of rationality, yet incorporates two metaphysical components, namely, faith in the resurrection, and High Priestly ministry of Jesus Christ.*

Faith AND Rationality 2 *Throughout this book, and the accompanying book, 'TRUE SANCTIFICATION', I have provided some evidence in support of rationality of faith in Jesus Christ. For a detailed exposition of what it means to have faith in the name of Jesus Christ, see my book, 'IN JESUS NAME'.*

The exposition you are about to encounter in this book is, in entirety metaphysical and spiritual, in fact more so than books that are 'attempts at interpretation' of the Book of Revelation. Regardless, all of the interpretation is internally consistent, fits together perfectly. While it is possible for an articulation to be internally consistent, yet consistently wrong, this is possible only when consistency is not arrived at via imposition of an external validating agent. I assure you that internal consistency of the metaphysical, equivalently spiritual exposition in this book is inferred in context of imposition of validation from Books of the Bible, other than the Book of Revelation.

Prophecy Principle 1 *This exposition of the Book of Revelation is, in entirety metaphysical, equivalently, spiritual, perhaps more so than any and all books that are attempts at interpretation of the Book of Revelation. Using validators of internal consistency from all other Books of the Bible, the exposition is shown to be perfectly internally consistent, and progressively logical. Much then as the physical world operates by laws of rationality - gravity, relativity, potential energy, kinetic energy etc. - so also metaphysical revelations from The Lord Jesus Christ satisfy principles of rationality.*

The *Book of Revelation* can be divided into three integrated parts that fit together like a puzzle. Revelation *chs. 1 through 6, chs. 8 through 9, & chs. 15 through 16* are, for the most part, BIG PICTURE chapters. Let us refer to these chapters as BIG PICTURE I. Revelation *ch. 7* is an INTERLUDE CHAPTER, as such can be grouped into BIG PICTURE I. Revelation *chs. 10 through 14, & 17 through 20* are, for the most part, *Detail Chapters*. Let us refer to these chapters as DETAIL CHAPTERS. Finally, Revelation *chs. 21 & 22* are, for the most part, Big Picture chapters, as such can be delineated, BIG PICTURE II.

Absent exposition of BIG PICTURE I, it is difficult, perhaps impossible to correctly articulate BIG PICTURE II. Absent exposition of DETAIL CHAPTERS, you likely do not arrive at any confidence in exposition of BIG PICTURE I. In light of structure of the Book of Revelation, *Chapters 1 through 10, 12, & 14* of this book are expositions of BIG PICTURE I; *Chapters 11 & 13* contain exposition of the DETAIL CHAPTERS. *Chapters 15 through 20* contain exposition of BIG PICTURE II, as such facilitate a return to the Big Picture. Importantly, and as must be expected of a credible exposition, the exposition in *Chapters 1 through 10, 12, & 14* ties in perfectly into the exposition in *Chapters 15 through 20*. The exposition in Chapters 11 & 13 further ties in perfectly into the big picture established in *Chapters 1 through 10, 12, & 14*.

Faith AND Rationality 3 *Scientific articles commence with the* BIG PICTURE *(Abstract and Introductory Section), then delve into the* DETAILS, *then end with a* CONCLUDING SECTION *that reiterates the Big Picture. By this principle, the organization of the Book of Revelation by Apostle John, which was arrived at in context of guidance of the Holy Spirit is, in entirety, scientific, as such rational.*

WHY DOES THIS BOOK SPEND A LOT MORE TIME ON THE BIG PICTURE ASPECTS OF THE PUZZLE, IN RELATION TO THE DETAIL ASPECTS?

The spiritual truths or realities that are entrusted to Apostle John by The Lord Jesus Christ are, for the most part, truths that, in their very essence, are eternal. The details that are included, which are bounded by timelines, are included primarily for your benefit and mine, with objective that in presence of evidence for materialization of the eternal truths in time and history, you and I have confidence that the eternal truths remain in force. In this respect, I point out that whereas 'attempts at interpretation' of the Book of Revelation make it appear that the *Beasts of Revelation*, the *Mark of the Beast*, the *Great Whore*, and *Apocalypse* are central to the visions entrusted to Apostle John, in this revelational exposition of those visions, these matters only are part of the details.

> I believe you begin to infer uniqueness of the exposition that you are about to encounter.

For ease of those who already are familiar with treatments of highlighted matters - the *Beasts of Revelation*, the *Mark of the Beast*, the *Great Whore*, and *Apocalypse*, I have delineated, in the *Table of Contents* where exactly these matters are articulated. Given exposition of highlighted matters occurs in context of expositions of BIG PICTURE I, however, it is important that you, the reader, visit those pages (in *Chapter 11*) only subsequent to completion of a reading of *the first section* of BIG PICTURE I (*Chapters 1 through 10*). In this respect, note that the exposition of the Book of Revelation that you are about to read does not find any evidence for the widely held notion that it is possible for persons who genuinely have faith in Jesus Christ to be physically or spiritually left behind. If you, prior to taking up of a reading of Chapter 11, take time to study BIG PICTURE I (*Chapters 1 through 10*) you will understand exactly why the 'LEFT BEHIND' teaching is a misinterpretation of visions that are recorded for us in the Book of Revelation.

> I am confident that by the time you turn the last page of this book, you will have arrived at agreement with me on spiritual essence of timelines and imagery that are provided in the Book of Revelation.

Necessity of alternate rationales for timelines that are provided in the Book of Revelation is as spiritual, as it is mathematical. If the timelines do not have any alternate spiritual meaning, all of the Book of Revelation is an exercise in spiritual hubris. We know, however, that the God who is Father of The Lord Jesus Christ does not do anything merely for show, that whatever He does is infused with His goodness, is done only because it is necessary. With the Holy Spirit as Guarantor, I promise that by the time you complete reading of this book, you will have arrived at an understanding of true spiritual meaning of timelines and spiritual imagery that are provided in the Book of Revelation. Much more importantly, you will arrive at discovery of true essence of the Book of Revelation, essence you have yet to encounter in any and all attempts at interpretation of the Book of Revelation. As a primer, by the time you complete reading of this book, you will have arrived at a better understanding of your place in Christ, of your place in the Church, of, inclusive of separation of Church and State, relations Jesus desires will subsist between Church and State, and how exactly interactions between yourself, the Church, and the State relate to the spiritual reign of our Lord and Savior Jesus Christ.

Love of Truth 11 THERE ARE SPIRITUAL TRUTHS THAT ARE IMMENSE IN THEIR SPIRITUAL VALUE THAT ARE EMBODIED IN REVELATIONS ENTRUSTED TO APOSTLE JOHN BY OUR LORD JESUS CHRIST. THIS BOOK UNEARTHS THESE SPIRITUAL TRUTHS FOR YOUR SPIRITUAL BENEFIT, FOR THE SPIRITUAL BENEFIT OF THE CHURCH, AND FOR SPIRITUAL BENEFIT OF ALL OF MANKIND.

Acknowledgements

I received Jesus as Lord and Savior in 1990. Shortly after this, in my spirit, I heard - not audibly, rather via a distilling into my spirit, *which is how The Father seeks to commune with us* - the Holy Spirit directing that I was not, at that time to attempt to understand the Book of Revelation. Having grown up in a church that had invested a lot of resources into interpretation of the Book of Revelation, I assumed this restraint meant I was to lean on others for understanding of the visions entrusted to Apostle John. In obedience to the Holy Spirit, while I have read the entire New Testament of Christian Scriptures through at the very least, 10 *times*, at time of writing, I have read the Book of Revelation through no more than three times. The first time I read the Book of Revelation was in 2016; the second time was in 2018; upon my third reading in 2019, the Holy Spirit distilled into my spirit that I was to write up revelations provided to me on true meaning of the visions that were entrusted to Apostle John. This book that you now read is outcome of my obedience to inspiration of The Holy Spirit.

The first revelation provided me by The Holy Spirit that is foundational to spiritual success of this endeavor was on importance of the CHRISTIAN BYZANTINE EMPIRE - the empire founded by *Emperor Constantine* in *325 AD*, whose glory as the greatest civilization of it's time lasted until at the very least, 1204 AD when it's capital, CONSTANTINOPLE was sacked by fellow Christians - the crusaders of the Fourth Christian Crusade. The Christian Byzantine Empire, which also was the EASTERN ROMAN EMPIRE, was founded on a righteous premise on part of *Constantine the Great*, that is, on the desire to build a civilization on secular laws that are founded on principles of Christianity. This was the only spiritual insight that I received from my first reading of the Book of Revelation in 2016. This insight is key for arrival at a spiritually sound exposition of the messages of our Lord Jesus Christ to the seven churches in Asia (*Revelation chs. 2 & 3*). I discuss the messages of our Lord Jesus Christ to the seven churches in Chapter 5.

On my second reading, I arrived at an important insight, which was, the word 'Angel' is not in the ancient texts, is an assumption on part of interpreters of the Bible that messengers who are mentioned in celestial visions must be celestial beings. The Holy Spirit, and Christian Scriptures make clear that this assumption on part of the interpreters is erroneous. In every instance in which the word ANGEL occurs in the Book of Revelation, the word translated 'Angel' actually means no more than 'MESSENGER', meaning the entity in question could be 'a man' or 'a celestial being'. In neither instance, however - man or celestial being - does the word messenger connote an entity with wings. Within this context, with each of Moses and Elijah in the heavens with our Lord Jesus Christ, each of Moses or Elijah could be referred to as messengers. In addition, a man on earth could be referred to as a messenger. In Christian Scriptures, entities with wings are referred to either as *Cherubim* or *Seraphim*. I have articulated this revelation, which is crucial for arrival at a proper understanding of the visions, in Chapter 4.

Consequent on my third reading in course of the first quarter of 2019, The Holy Spirit bid me organize my thoughts on spiritual insights that I had acquired in course of all of my readings of the Book of Revelation. It was in course of this exercise, and the acknowledgement in my spirit that all was not yet clear to me that The Holy Spirit provided me with the next piece of the puzzle, which is, the key to the NUMEROLOGY OF THE FATHER (*true spiritual symbolism of numbers that are utilized repeatedly in the visions*) that lies at the core of all of the visions recorded in the Book of Revelation. I have articulated this revelation, which also is crucial for a right understanding of the visions, in Chapter 6. Subsequent to this revelation, the rest of the revelations would arrive thick and fast. Next, was the realization that the words 'PRESENCE' and 'COMING' do not mean exactly the same thing. The core of the evidence that establishes existence of a difference between these two spiritual terms is domiciled in Chapter 3, but revisited and extended in Chapters 18 and 19.

The next major revelation, subsequent to which all else would be fine tuned in course of my writing was the realization that prophecies can become useless, that is, can fail (1Corinthians 13:8). I always had wondered at this assertion by Apostle Paul. With help of The Holy Spirit, I have arrived at the understanding, and the understanding is crucial for a right understanding of the visions in the Book of Revelation. In this respect, The Holy Spirit guided me to the realization that prophecies in the Book of Revelation are incorporative of God's responses to man's actions, with outcome while all prior 'attempts at interpretation' of the visions assume only one outcome - *Apocalypse, and the Second Coming of Christ* - I was guided to discern three possible outcomes, and a single spiritual system that is set in place for guidance of each and every one of those three feasible outcomes. I have articulated the evidence from Scriptures that prophecies can fail in Chapter 2. The evidence for the three possible outcomes, all of which are outcomes of God's responses to man's choices on earth, and ONE OF WHICH DOES NOT INDUCE A SECOND COMING OF CHRIST is domiciled in Chapter 9. As precursors to Chapter 9, Chapters 7 and 8 provide evidence that 'things' (events or prophecies) that are yet to come always are possible only because of the things that always are, only because of the things that do not change. So then, all of the discussion of 'things to come' in the Book of Revelation are predicated on The Father's declaration that,

I am the Lord, I do not change (Malachi 3:6);

on the declaration that our Lord Jesus Christ,

Is the same yesterday, today, and forever (Hebrews 13:8);

and on the validating declaration by our Lord Jesus Christ that:

I am the Alpha and the Omega - the Beginning and End - the First and the Last (Revelation 22:13).

Robert Young (1822 TO 1888)

In *1862*, The Father, Son, and Holy Spirit inspired a self taught man, ROBERT YOUNG to come up with a '*Literal*' translation of the Bible. The term, *Literal* here is to be interpreted as a '*word-for-word*' translation that does not introduce any *perceived* understanding of intended meaning of the words.

Robert Young lived much of an ordinary life. But then, so it is with many who do great exploits for The Father in a world within which the Church has learnt to respect *grandeur of the world* more than *spiritual anointing of The Father*.

The *Young's Literal Translation (YLT)* of the Bible, which you might never have heard of, is a spiritual gift given to you and I, by The Father, Son, and Holy Spirit, a spiritual gift made possible by love and obedience of Robert Young.

Every spiritual gift that exists in the body of Christ is made possible by love and obedience of a son of God. We know of course that this was initiated by our Lord Jesus Christ, the only begotten Son of God.

In a perfect Church, interpretation of words that are inspired by The Holy Spirit, words that come to us in Scriptures, is dichotomized from any perceptions of what it is the words are designed to convey, with outcome, 'TRANSLATION' from either of *Hebrew*, Aramaic, or *Greek* to English is dichotomized from 'INTERPRETATION' of meaning of words that now are rendered in English.

ROBERT YOUNG BELIEVED YOU AND I OUGHT TO KNOW THE EXACT WORDS WRITTEN IN THE SCRIPTURES. ROBERT YOUNG LOVED BOTH PEOPLE, AND TRUTH.

The only translation of the Bible, which enables us dichotomize 'what is written', from attempts at interpretation of 'what is written' is the *Young's Literal Translation (YLT)* of the Bible. Without all of the literal translations in the *YLT*, this spiritual work of love - A SPIRITUAL EXPOSITION OF REVELATIONS OF JESUS CHRIST - would be impossible.

Wherever they may be, I hope descendants of ROBERT YOUNG realize how great a work their ancestor, ROBERT YOUNG has wrought for God.

YOU AND I OWE A DEBT OF GRATITUDE TO THE FATHER THAT ROBERT YOUNG LOVED THE FATHER ENOUGH TO EMBARK ON THE JOURNEY THAT PRODUCED THE YOUNG'S LITERAL TRANSLATION OF THE BIBLE.

Benediction

I commend you to the Love of The Father, the grace of The Lord Jesus Christ, and the Fellowship of the Holy Spirit, and pray that you embark on your reading with a heart willing to hear from your only teacher, The Holy Spirit, whom The Father has provided for teaching you of all things, for guiding you into discernment of what is truth.

In Jesus Name. Amen.

Sincerely,

Oghenovo A. Obrimah, PhD

Declarations

All Scripture quotations either are from the 'New King James Version' (*NKJV*), 'Revised Standard Version' (*RSV*), the 'Darby' Bible, the 'New International Version' (*NIV*), or 'Young's Literal Translation' (*YLT*) of the Bible.

With exception of instances within which brackets are included in a Scripture Verse, whether they be *italicized* or **boldened**, any words rendered in brackets in context of enumeration of biblical text are included by the author in spirit of an *Amplified Reading* of the Bible.

This book is a companion book to three other books. My 2016 publication titled, In Jesus Name, 382 pgs. published by *Createspace* and available for sale on *Amazon.com*, my 2019 publication titled, 'True Sanctification' (*480 pgs.*), also available for sale on *Amazon.com*, and my book, 'Divine Meritocracy'.

This book will leave you in awe of the *Love*, Justice, Mercy, *Thoughtfulness*, Patience, and Righteousness of The Father and The Lord Jesus Christ. You might be so much in awe, you are besides yourself, do not even know what exactly to do next. Right at that point, while spiritually you remain in fellowship with The Father, Son, and Holy Spirit, my books, 'In Jesus Name', and 'True Sanctification' help bring you back to earth for pursuit of all of the righteous purposes expected of you by Father, Son, and Holy Spirit. IN JESUS NAME discusses, in detail, the resources made available to you by Father, Son, and Holy Spirit, and how exactly to go about acquiring said resources for enhancement of your spiritual welfare. TRUE SANCTIFICATION discusses responsibilities that are expected of you, if you are to maintain and experience increase in the resources that you acquire from Father, Son, and Holy Spirit. My book, 'Divine Meritocracy' distills some of the most salient truths enunciated in TRUE SANCTIFICATION in context of a uniquely distinctive perspective that cannot itself be found in TRUE SANCTIFICATION. If you have a degree in Theology or Religion, or have interest in those formal facets of Christian experience (I personally am constrained by the Holy Spirit to only care about teachings that enable practical Christian living, teachings that enable people better understand how to live fulfilled as Christians, and how to be revelations of Christ to the world), you will find DIVINE MERI-TOCRACY, which itself is focused on practical Christian living, equivalently, *organization of Christian society*, truly fascinating. I assure you that the pragmatic spiritual knowledge that you acquire from each of these books, for which you pay a finite amount in dollars, is infinite, priceless.

I do not cover the subject matter of this book in any other medium. I have, however, addressed some of the *side material* contained in this book in various blog posts available on my *Medium*© social media page, which is located at *@oghenovoobrimah*. While I have, in some instances, referred the reader to such related posts, such instances are too numerous for individual citation. I encourage the reader to visit *my Medium*© *social media page*, both for insights into topics that lie outside of the scope of this treatise, but also for arrival at additional insights on some of the *side material* that I cover in this book.

In some instances, I have had to refer to events in history. The reference historical text that I have adopted is authored by reputable professors from different universities who collaborated to author a comprehensive reference text on history of the world, from ancient times to the present day. The Editor of the reference text, *Prof. J. Whitney Hall* is a Professor at Yale University who has a museum of history named after him at Yale University, as such has significant reputation. In so far as my belief in reputation of the professors is concerned, this relates only to discussions of historical events, not discussions of origins of life on earth, a matter about which no one can acquire reputation, for all only can philosophize over the scientific evidence for origins of life. I of course am a creationist who believes in intentional design as essence of life in the universe. Wherever the citation, '*HWE*' is encountered, it refers to the reference historical text. The bibiliographical reference for the historical text is:

> *History of the World: Earliest Times to the Present Day*, 2015, Hall, J.W. (ed.), World Communications Group, Bridgewater CT.

If you seek to reach out to me, there are several ways to achieve this objective. First, you can click on one of my blog posts on *Medium.com*, then scroll down to the bottom and respond to me, but with choice of a '*private note*', as opposed to a publicly viewable response. My Medium address is *@oghenovoobrimah*.

If you choose to send an e-mail, please title it: '*On A Spiritual Revelation*', and send it to *oobrimah@hotmail.com*. If you choose to reach me on twitter via private message, my twitter account information is: *@oobrimah*.

If your concerns are generic to the subject matter of this book, as such could be helpful to other readers, you can reach me at my Amazon.com author page located at: *https://www.amazon.com/author/oghenovoobrimah.*

CHAPTER 2

Important Principle: Prophecies Can Fail

It perhaps sounds outlandish, yet the righteous principle that prophecies can fail is well articulated in Christian Scriptures. First, fulfillment of prophecies, which truly emanate from God, but that are consequences for human behavior inherently are conditioned on man's response to said prophecies. If you are familiar with the story of Jonah the Prophet (perhaps as popularized in that children's movie about '*pirates who go sailing, but who do not do anything*'), you are aware that The Father truly sent Jonah to Nineveh with a prophecy that seemed not to be fulfilled. The prophecy went as follows (Jonah 3:4):

> Yet 40 days, and Nineveh shall be overthrown.

But then what happened? From the king to the least significant person in the kingdom of Nineveh, everyone repented, put on rags, dust, and ashes. So, what did The Father do in response? Well, should a just, righteous, and merciful God destroy people who declare that they are repentant of their sins? And what were those sins (Jonah 1:1-2)?

> Now the word of the Lord came to Jonah the son of Amittai, saying, "Arise, go to Nineveh, that great city, and cry against it; for their wickedness has come up before me."

IN THE WORDS OF THE PIRATES WHO DON'T DO ANYTHING?

> The Father was going to punish Nineveh because Ninevites spent all of their time slapping one another and stealing fish.

1

As always, The Father sought to punish Nineveh not for refusal to acknowledge Him as their God, but for refusal to acknowledge import of His existence, for refusal to consider their fellow man worthy of dignity on basis of the fact that he or she also is created by the same God. The Father sought to punish Nineveh because Ninevites were evil in their dealings with one another, and in their dealings with other cities.

The response of the king of Nineveh reveals that the king understood import of the message borne by Jonah. In Jonah 3:8-9 we have the following words spoken by the king of Nineveh.

> But let man and beast be covered with sackcloth, and let them cry mightily to God; yea, let every one turn from his evil way and from the violence which is in his hands. Who knows, God may yet repent and turn from his fierce anger, so that we perish not?

So then, I am guessing you agree that it would not have been a godly thing for The Father to disregard the show of repentance, and proceed with destruction of the people of Nineveh. So then, Nineveh was spared, was not, as prophesied by Jonah, destroyed in 40 days.

But did the people of Nineveh truly change their ways? Turns out not; turns out the ragging, and the ashes, and the dust all was out of fear of the wrath of The Father.

Prophetic Lessons 1 *Whenever people repent out of fear of repercussions for their evil actions, typically, the repentance does not last, does not result in true reformation. Repentance that transforms into true reformation always is predicated on the acknowledgment that wrong actions inherently are wrong.*

Eventually, by *612 BC*, Nineveh had been razed to the ground by Babylon and her allies (*HWE*, pg. 51). This eventual destruction of Nineveh is prophesied in Zephaniah 2:13. Zephaniah was a prophet who prophesied in the days of Josiah, son of Amoz, king of Judah who ruled Judah from *640 to 609 BC*. The Babylonians and Ninevites were cousins, but Nineveh having the upper military hand had been mistreating the Babylonians (*HWE*, pgs. 47-51). Jonah was a prophet during the reign of Jeroboam, king of Israel, son of Joash, king over both Judah and Israel, who reigned from about *781 to 741 BC*, periods during which Ninevites were mistreating their cousins, the Babylonians. In aggregate, Nineveh's mistreatment of Babylon spans at the very least *1208* through *612 BC*, a total of, at the very least *596* years. Eventually, the Babylonians grew strong enough to, with help of other allies, such as the Chaldeans take on Nineveh and win. The famous king Nebucchadnezzar (*604 to 562 BC*) who sacked Judah and it's capital Jerusalem, because much like Ninevites, God's own people refused to love what is good and hate what is evil, arose in Babylon subsequent to the sacking of Nineveh (*HWE*, pg. 51).

Prophecy Principle 2 *Whenever prophecy relays judgments from The Father, and people who are targets of the judgments repent of their sins, if the line of The Father's mercy has yet to be crossed, the prophecy can fail, yet the prophet is genuinely sent of The Father.*

Now then, consider king Hezekiah and his response to a prophecy from The Father, a prophecy borne to him by prophet Isaiah, the prophet who so experienced the glory of God, he was entrusted with visions of the sufferings and glory of our Lord Jesus Christ (*Isaiah Chapters 6, 53, 54, & 61*). The story is told in Isaiah Chapter 38. As the story goes, Hezekiah fell very sick. For background, up until this time, Hezekiah had been a good king, the only king to have gotten all of Judah together for celebration of the *Feast of Unleavened Bread* and the *Passover* since the times of king Solomon (2Chronicles 30:26). So then, The Father sent word to Hezekiah through prophet Isaiah that he would die from his illness, as such was to put his house in order. On receipt of the message from The Father, Hezekiah turned his face toward the wall of his bed chamber and cried out to The Father, enumerating the fact that his heart had been true to The Father. Prophet Isaiah still was in the courts of the palace when The Father sent word to him that he should go back to Hezekiah and let him know that He had changed His mind, and was adding 15 more years of life to Hezekiah.

King Hezekiah was so happy to be alive, he invited emissaries from Babylon to observe all of the shields of gold and silver that king Solomon had made many years back, artifacts of tremendous monetary and sentimental value to the people of Judah. The word that the emissaries took back to Babylon was so enticing, King Nebuchadnezzer would later invade Judah, such that conquest of Judah would become the signature victory of his reign as monarch over Babylon. That being said, it is important to note that King Nebuchadnezzar was raised up to invade Judah by The Father Himself as discipline for His people's unwillingness to treat each other right.

As it turns out, king Hezekiah did not make good use of his last 15 years, such that The Father had to send him a rebuke, again through prophet Isaiah (Isaiah Chapter 39). The lesson?

Spiritual Insight 1 *If you are going to ask The Father for more years of life, it is best not to focus on what you already have achieved, best to frame the request in context of what you believe still remains to be achieved; this way your eyes and heart remain focused on righteous objectives, as opposed to your own self.*

But the righteous principle in respect of prophecy that fails?

Prophecy Principle 3 *Whenever a prophecy arrives from The Father, your response to the prophecy reveals the state of your heart towards God, as* *such, conditional on your response, the prophecy can fail. This is another interpretation of Prophecy Principle 1.*

How then the words of our Lord Jesus Christ Himself? In Matthew 11:13, and Luke 16:16, The Lord Jesus Christ declares:

> For all the prophets and the law prophesied until John.

> The law and the prophets are till John; since then the reign of God is proclaimed good news, and every one doth press into it.

In the immediately preceding Scripture verses, Jesus declares that any prophecy uttered in the Old Testament that genuinely was from The Father, but that does not relate to any of John's work, His ministry, and the preaching of the good news of Jesus Christ, failed at timing of commencement of John's ministry. The Old Covenant having now passed away, and the New Covenant being now ushered in (at that point in time), every prophecy whose meaning and relevance depended on continuation of the Old Covenant automatically had failed. Given all of the failing prophecies now were superseded by better promises, clearly, the prophecies failed for the good of us all.

The evidence, and then the righteousness principle?

> Therefore my brethren, you also have become dead to the law through the body of Christ (*prophecies that pertain to the Old Covenant are dead*), that you may be married to another - to Him who was raised from the dead (*only prophecies that relate to faith in Jesus Christ matter now*), that we should bear fruit to God (Romans 7:4).

> But as it is, Christ has obtained a ministry which is as much more excellent than the old as the covenant He mediates is better, since IT IS ENACTED ON BETTER PROMISES. For if that first covenant had been faultless, there would have been no occasion for a second (Hebrews 8:6-7).

Paraphrase of Hebrews 8:6-7?

> The Old Covenant been faulty, and having been done away with implies imperfectness of the prophecies that were attached to it. We have exchanged these imperfections for promises and prophecies that are better, that are more perfect. Promises and prophecies that now are ours in context of the New Covenant are better, are more perfect because they depend in entirety only on what Jesus has done, all of which is perfect.

Prophecy Principle 4 *Prophecies can fail because the covenant under which they were uttered is nullified, is superseded by a new covenant. Since the prophecy fails because an old covenant is superseded by a new and better covenant, you and I ought to rejoice that prophecies uttered under the nullified covenant fail to materialize.*

The devil and evil men are aware of prophecies that The Father has declared in respect of the future. If you are not aware, know this, there are men who study Christian Scriptures only because they seek to prove they are able to thwart whatever it seems is prophesied to transpire in future. Such people delight in fulfillment of prophecies that they think benefit them, and work actively towards frustration of prophecies that seem to be detrimental to their welfare. In order to thwart such men, The Father can allow a prophecy that delights the hearts of evil men to fail. In such cases, evil men delight in the prophecies because they perceive fulfillment of the prophecy to be more detrimental to welfare of the righteous. In the decision to allow the prophecy fail, The Father looks out for the welfare of those who love righteousness, for the welfare of those who delight in the name of The Lord Jesus Christ. This in part is the reason The Father refuses to disclose the timing of second coming of The Lord Jesus Christ (Matthew 24:36, 44). This is the reason the second coming of Christ is placed in context of normal affairs of this life - work, marriage, feasting etc. (Matthew 24:36-44). In this respect, consider the following words.

> And if those days had not been shortened (*if the prophecy had not been mitigated*), no human being would be saved; but for the sake of the elect (*for the welfare of the righteous*) those days will be shortened (Matthew 24:22).

Prophecy Principle 5 *Prophecies will fail (e.g., time will be shortened) if their failing enables The Father protect those who trust in the name of the Lord Jesus Christ.*

Last but not the least, prophecies will fail if and when church bodies on this earth transform into what they really ought to be, which is the spiritual body of Christ, as such arrive at what the Holy Spirit defines as perfection. In this respect, consider the following Scripture.

> The Love doth never fail; AND WHETHER THERE BE PROPHE-CIES, THEY SHALL BECOME USELESS; whether tongues, they shall cease; whether knowledge, it shall become useless; FOR IN PART WE KNOW, AND IN PART WE PROPHECY; and WHEN THAT WHICH IS PERFECT MAY COME THEN THAT WHICH IS IN PART SHALL BECOME USELESS; and now there doth remain faith, hope, love - these three; and the greatest of these is Love (1Corinthians 13:8-10,13).

And He gave some as apostles, and some as prophets, and some as proclaimers of good news, and some as shepherds and teachers, unto the perfecting of the saints, for a work of ministration, for a building up of the body of the Christ, TILL WE MAY ALL COME TO THE UNITY OF THE FAITH AND OF THE RECOGNITION OF THE SON OF GOD, to a perfect man, to a measure of the stature of the fullness of the Christ (Ephesians 4:11-13).

In the immediately preceding Scriptures, the Holy Spirit declares, through Apostle Paul that when the Church arrives at perfection, that some prophecies given to us under the New Covenant will become useless, that is, will cease to be of any relevance.

In the same Scripture, the Holy Spirit declares that we arrive at perfection when all of the body of Christ arrives at *unity of the faith*, and of the *recognition of the Son of God*, to *a measure of the stature of the fullness of The Lord Jesus Christ*. This assertion means several things. First, UNITY OF THE FAITH implies absence of any material differences in interpretation of Christian Scriptures. Second, UNITY OF RECOGNITION OF THE SON OF GOD means we all agree as to who Jesus is, and all that Jesus has done for us, such that, in a spiritual sense, we arrive at the same 'recognition' of The Lord Jesus Christ. Third, ARRIVAL AT A MEASURE OF THE STATURE OF THE FULLNESS OF CHRIST implies, with the minimum known only to The Father, that all attain to some minimum realization of the spiritual image of Christ, a realization that is representative of, yet not necessarily identical to of all of His fullness.

Spiritual Insight 2 *In the military, 'Lieutenant Generals', 'Major Generals', 'Brigadier Generals', and 'Generals' all are Generals. So then, Lieutenant Generals, Major Generals, and Brigadier Generals all are* REPRESENTATIVE *of what it means to be a General,* YET ARE NOT IDENTICAL *to the highest possible realization of a General.*

Spiritual Insight 3 *The difference between 'Lieutenant Generals', 'Major Generals', Brigadier Generals', and 'Generals'?* MERITS.

Naturally, attainment to a measure of the stature of the fullness of Christ will first be achieved by some, who then share their knowledge, experience, and revelations with others, so they also are able to attain to same spiritual stature in Christ. In presence of stated three perfections, which embody a PERFECT MAN, the Holy Spirit declares that some of the prophecies given to us in the Book of Revelation will become useless.

Note, however, the conditionality. The prophecies fail only if that which is perfect arrives. Who is responsible for ensuring that, '*that which is perfect*' arrives? Those whom The Father has placed in the body of Christ as apostles, prophets, evangelists, and shepherds & teachers, and those to whom they are given as gifts by Christ, namely all those who profess faith in the name of Jesus Christ. You see then that the matter lies in the hands of all who genuinely profess faith in our Lord and Savior Jesus Christ. If we seek Utopia of which attainment to a measure of the stature of our Lord Jesus Christ is representative, the matter lies in entirety in our hands. If those given as gifts do not do their part, we do not attain to unity of perfection. If those to whom the gifts are given refuse to heed teachings designed for their perfections, we do not attain to unity of perfection. The Father, the Lord Jesus Christ, and the Holy Spirit already have done their part, and continue to do their part. If we do not attain to perfection, it only will be because church bodies refuse to become what they ought really to be, which is, the body of Christ.

And what is a well defined measure of the perfection to which those who profess faith in Jesus Christ are supposed to attain?

> He who is saying, 'I have known him,' and his command is not keeping, a liar he is, and in him the truth is not; and whoever may keep his word, TRULY IN HIM THE LOVE OF GOD HATH BEEN PERFECTED; in this we know that in him we are. He who is saying in Him he doth remain, ought according as He walked also himself so to walk (1John 2:4-6).

> God no one hath ever seen; if we may love one another, God in us doth remain, and HIS LOVE IS HAVING BEEN PERFECTED IN US (1John 4:11-12).

> Blessed is the God and Father of our Lord Jesus Christ, who did bless us in every spiritual blessing in the heavenly places in Christ, according as He did choose us in Him before the foundation of the world, FOR OUR BEING HOLY AND UNBLEMISHED BEFORE HIM, IN LOVE (Ephesians 1:3-4).

In 1John 2:4-6; & 4:11-12, the Holy Spirit declares through Apostle John that we are perfected when the Love of God that is poured into us through the Holy Spirit is perfected. In this respect, perfection means our living out of the Love of Christ is unblemished, that is, without spot or stain (Ephesians 1:3-4).

Spiritual Insight 4 *Love that is without spot or stain, love that is unblemished, is love that has the quality of the Love of Christ, as such is demonstrated without partiality to all men.*

If those who profess faith in Christ love with the Love of Christ, as such love without partiality, love cuts across denominations, transcends all minor disagreements. Disagreements become minor and inconsequential, because all are willing to submit their differences of interpretation of Scripture to common discussion, and are willing to accede to the most spiritually articulate revelation of Christian Scripture. I note here that the most spiritually articulate revelations of Christian Scripture are backed up by evidence for newness of life, by evidence of lives that reflect the power and love of Christ to the world.

WHY MUST THIS BE THE CASE?

He who is having my commands, and is keeping them, that one it is who is loving me, and he who is loving me shall be loved by my Father, and I will love him, and will manifest myself to him (John 14:21).

Love of Truth 12 *It is normative that The Lord Jesus Christ and The Holy Spirit do not reveal revelational truths to those who refuse to walk in newness of life, to those who refuse to be perfected in the love of Christ.*

Upon arrival at the perfection of love that is evinced in unity of the faith, and of recognition of the Son of God, denominations transform into organizational convenience, as opposed to walls that divide. Upon attainment to such a spiritual stature, White believers love Black believers like they are just as White as they are, and vice versa. Believers do not see themselves as Asian, White, Black, or Hispanic; rather we all see ourselves as the same, as epitomes of Christ to a fallen world. When these sorts of attitudes, character, and essence become ubiquitous and pervasive, the Church will have arrived at perfection.

Friend, if you are reading this in 2019, and you have any doubts as to the fact that the Church has been moving away from, as opposed to moving towards perfection, you, my friend, are in need of eyesalve for your eyes.

Will the Church ever arrive at perfection of Love? Right now, with all of the divisions, denominational walls, and politicization of Church, perfection of the Church seems way in the far flung future. But, if we refuse to believe that it is possible, it never will come to pass. But if enough believe, and pray, and work for it, and if others respond, and all lay aside their egos, and all seek the face of Christ genuinely, arrival at perfection is possible.

Prophecy Principle 6 *Prophecies will fail if church bodies, which ought to be representative of the body of Christ, but which can become tainted with lusts of the world, and the pride of life, arrive at perfection of Love.*

"With God nothing will be impossible (Luke 1:37)."

The Earth God Has Given to Men

The Book of Revelation reveals the sorts of events that will transpire on earth if church bodies do not transform into the body of Christ, or if church bodies transform into the body of Christ, and evil men decide not to live at peace with the body of Christ. In the scenario within which the Church refuses to transform into the body of Christ, Jesus appears to save those who wait eagerly for His salvation. With all of the divisions in the Church body at the present time, and all of the self and love of money, it would seem that we are in the sort of equilibrium within which we expect an appearing of our Lord and Savior Jesus Christ.

How exactly will it all turn out? And should we assume that it must turn out a certain way?

Well, The Father's objective remains as it has been since advent of our Lord Jesus Christ, namely believers in Christ as priests and kings, ushering in the reign of our Lord Jesus Christ, yet living as ordinary citizens, who like any other citizens are honored for their contributions to well being of society. So long as the world celebrates those who have faith in Jesus Christ for the good that they manifestly contribute to the well being of society, the will of The Father is done on earth as it is in heaven. To be celebrated for contributions to well being of society is not, however, a demand on society, for this exactly is how society is supposed to relate to all men, namely to celebrate what is good, and deter or punish what is evil. You see then, that regardless of the deity to which men choose to pray, that The Father merely demands that Love, which embeds absence of partiality or discrimination, and commitment to justice, be essence of interactions between all men.

We arrive then at the inference that The Father's will straddles your individuality, His expectations in respect of the Church, and His expectations in respect of society. While judgments of men follow on their actions, and while judgments of churches or societies also follow on their actions, GRAND JUDGMENTS THAT ALTER PATHS OF CHURCHES OR SOCIETIES cannot occur in exactly the same time frame as judgments for specific actions. This is evident in the normative that grand judgments that alter paths of churches or societies accrue from all of the specific individual judgments that transpire over some period of time. That churches and societies experience grand judgments from The Father is evident in Revelation Chapters 2, 3, and 19, and in the following Scripture (1Peter 4:17-18).

For the time has come for judgment to begin with the household of God; and if it begins with us, what will be the end of those who do not obey the gospel of God? And "if the righteous man is scarcely saved, where will the impious and sinner appear?"

In respect of grand judgments, the division of the descendants of Jacob into two nations, JUDAH and ISRAEL was a grand judgment from The Father that separated the more stubborn of the descendants - the ten tribes that exclude Judah and Simeon - from the less stubborn of the descendants - Judah and Simeon. Similarly, conquest and exile of Judah to Babylon was a grand judgment from The Father that altered the path of an entire nation. Concerning feasibility of grand judgments that alter paths of a church or society, The Father declares as follows in 2Chronicles 7:14.

> If my people who are called by my name will humble themselves, and pray and seek my face, and turn from their wicked ways, then I will hear from heaven, and will forgive their sin and heal their land.

> Then the word of the Lord came to Solomon, saying: "Concerning this temple which you are building, if you walk in My statutes, execute My judgments, keep all of My commandments, and walk in them, then I will perform My word with you, which I spoke to your father David. And I will dwell among the children of Israel (*then my Glory will reside in the temple that you build, see 1Kings 8:10-11*), and will not forsake My people Israel (1Kings 6:11-13)."

Necessity of Grand Judgments 1 *When The Father stops hearing prayers because a church or society has given itself over to wickedness, this is arrival at a grand judgment. Absent repentance and reformation of such a church or society, The Father declares that the people will not find healing for consequences of their sins.*

So then, would The Father root determination of grand judgments in time, or much like His governance of the heavens with immutable laws, such as laws of gravity and relativity, would He establish some inviolate principle for arrival at grand judgments of churches and societies? Clearly, within such an aegis, changes to paths of churches and nations are rooted either in predetermined amounts of time, or in some other immutable principle that is established by The Father.

Friend, all of the revelations that are recorded for us in the Book of Revelation relate to The Father's principles for management of GRAND JUDGMENTS on this earth. In this respect, given evolution of time must be rooted in consequences for actions that are just and righteous, or actions that are evil, The Father has instituted a spiritual system for guidance of evolution of time and events on earth. Delineation of this spiritual system, and provision of empirical evidence that is rooted in timelines, empirical evidence, which those of us in these times can examine for validation, or non-validation is essence of all of the Book of Revelation. The spiritual system in question, resolves into New Heavens, New Earth, and the New Jerusalem.

Necessity of Grand Judgments 2 *Revelations that were entrusted to Apostle John by our Lord Jesus Christ all relate to delineation of the spiritual system that has been instituted by The Father for arrival at grand judgments of churches and societies, with outcome events and time are guided by the instituted spiritual system.*

The spiritual system instituted by The Father and The Son evolves conditional on about five factors:

✠ man's choices;

✠ natural consequences of man's choices that are pre-specified by The Father;

✠ The Father's punishments for evil, which are pre-specified;

✠ The Father's rewards for righteousness, which also are pre-specified;

✠ Sovereign unanticipated interventions on part of The Father.

MAN'S CHOICES ARE SEGMENTED INTO TWO CLASSES:

♣ choices by the Church, which is supposed to be the body of Christ, but can become apostate; and

♣ choices by civil governments of nations of the earth.

But does our Lord Jesus Christ desire to, or interact with civil governments of nations?

Well then, let us hear the Scriptures on the matter.

For those ruling are not a terror to the good works, but to the evil; and dost thou wish not to be afraid of the authority? that which is good be doing, and thou shalt have praise from it, FOR OF GOD IT (CIVIL AUTHORITY) IS A MINISTRANT TO THEE for good; and if that which is evil thou mayest do, be fearing, for not in vain doth it bear the sword; for of God it is a ministrant, and avenger for wrath to him who is doing that which is evil (Romans 13:3-4)

In the Book of Revelation, our Lord Jesus Christ demonstrates that the nations (civil governments) will not be justified on basis of choices of the Church, only can be justified by their choices in respect of good versus evil. When a civil government rewards evil with good, and good with evil, it is judged by The Lord Jesus Christ. Correspondingly, when a civil government rewards good with good, and evil with evil, it earns rewards from The Father.

The Book of Revelation makes clear that the Church cannot be justified by choices that occur within civil governments, only can be justified by her response to commands of her Lord and Savior Jesus Christ. In this respect, the demands on the Church differ from those placed on the nations. While the nations only are judged on basis of the choice between good and evil, the Church is judged on basis of her willingness to be transformed into a perfect man, that is, into a measure of the stature of the fullness of Christ. You see then that demands placed on the Church are of a more spiritual nature than demands placed on nations, that is, civil governments.

I ask that you be patient, that you patiently assess the evidence that I present, that you attempt as much as possible to disabuse your mind of what you think you already know, that you approach the teachings in this book with true humility of mind, yet with reasoning, intelligence, and guidance of the Holy Spirit. I do not ask that you not ponder, for to demand such is to characterize myself as a Charlatan; rather I ask that you be willing to consider that all you previously thought you knew about the Book of Revelation could be wrong. I already have provided you with a litmus test for your willingness to consider that what you previously thought was right is wrong, which is, concrete evidence that NEW HEAVENS, NEW EARTH, AND THE NEW JERUSALEM do not have anything to do with the Second Coming of Christ. My plea that you patiently consider what you are about to read then is rooted in evidence, not any hand waving, or demand for thoughtlessness.

Prophecy Principle 7 *There is not any hand waving in this book. This book is all reasoning, evidence, and illumination of the Holy Spirit.*

As additional supporting evidence for your willingness to consider that your prior understanding of the Book of Revelation is extremely flawed or wrong, consider the following declarations by Apostle Paul in Galatians 4:21-22, 25-26, and Philippians 3:20.

> Tell me, you who desire to be under the law, do you not hear the law? For it is written that Abraham had two sons: the one by a bondwoman, the other by a freewoman. For this Hagar is Mount Sinai in Arabia (THE BONDWOMAN), and corresponds to Jerusalem which now is, and is in bondage with her children - but the Jerusalem above (IN THE HEAVENS) is free, which is the mother of us all.

> For our citizenship is in the heavens, whence also a Savior we await - the Lord Jesus Christ.

In the preceding texts, Apostle Paul makes very clear that Christians are not to consider the earthly Jerusalem to be their mother, are to consider themselves to be birthed by the heavenly Jerusalem. This is not to mean that Christians should not care about Jews - clearly, regardless of deity to which people choose to pray, those of us who believe in the name of Jesus Christ are called to love all men. Rather, Apostle Paul declares that Christians are not to consider themselves to be spiritually linked with the earthly Jerusalem, which along with her children, remain in bondage of spiritual decay that is brought into the world by sin. Since only our Lord Jesus Christ sets free from the bondage of sin (THERE IS NOT SALVATION IN ANY OTHER NAME, BUT THE NAME OF JESUS - Acts 4:12), we are unable to set the earthly Jerusalem free. The only way that the earthly Jerusalem can be set free is if the Jews are grafted into the heavenly Jerusalem that sprouted out from the earthly Jerusalem, and that is birthed by our Lord Jesus Christ. In this respect, Apostle Paul declares as follows in Romans 11:23, 26-27, and defines the COMMONWEALTH OF (SPIRITUAL) ISRAEL as follows in Ephesians 2:12-13,19-20.

> And they also, if they do not continue in unbelief (*the bondage is spiritual, not physical, requires arrival at faith in Christ on part of the Jews*), will be grafted in (INTO THE HEAVENLY JERUSALEM), for God is able to graft them in again. AND SO ALL ISRAEL WILL BE SAVED, as it is written: "The Deliverer will come out of Zion, and He will turn away ungodliness from Jacob; For this is my covenant with them, when I take away their sins."

> Remember that you were at that time separated from Christ, alienated from the COMMONWEALTH OF ISRAEL, and strangers to the covenants of promise, having no hope and without God in the world. But now in Christ Jesus you who once were far off have been brought near in the blood of Christ. So then you are no longer strangers and sojourners, but you are fellow citizens with the saints and members of the household of God, built upon the foundation of the apostles and prophets, Christ Jesus Himself being the chief cornerstone.

> Most of preceding interpretations of the Book of Revelation have an important role for the Middle East, for the earthly Jerusalem. It is clear from Christian Scriptures outside of the Book of Revelation that any, and all such interpretations are wrong.

Prophecy Principle 8 *The Holy Spirit is very clear that spiritually speaking, Israel, that is, the* COMMONWEALTH OF ISRAEL *comprises of all those, Jew or Gentile, who receive Jesus as Lord and Savior. The gospel then no longer has any ties to the physical nation of Israel.*

Prophecy Principle 9 *Any interpretation of the Book of Revelation that has a place for the* EARTHLY JERUSALEM *is a misinterpretation of prophecies provided for our benefit by our Lord Jesus Christ. For us, believers in the name of Jesus Christ, our mother is the* HEAVENLY JERUSALEM.

Prophecy Principle 10 *Since the Jews only can be spiritually grafted into the heavenly Jerusalem -* COMMONWEALTH OF ISRAEL *- by faith, there is not any attempt at physical liberation of the earthly Jerusalem that accords with faith in Jesus Christ.*

Prophecy Principle 11 THE BOOK OF REVELATION IS NOT ABOUT THE SECOND COMING OF JESUS CHRIST, OR ABOUT THE EARTHLY JERUSALEM. CLEARLY THEN, THERE IS DEMAND FOR A NEW REVELATIONAL INTERPRETATION OF PROPHECIES RECORDED FOR OUR BENEFIT IN THE BOOK OF REVELATION.

If you are to arrive at a new understanding of the Book of Revelation, you must be willing to open your mind, not such that you do not reason over the new interpretation, but such that you are like a new wineskin that can receive new wine. In this respect, our Lord Jesus Christ declares as follows in Matthew 9:17.

> Nor do they put new wine into old wineskins, or else the wineskins break, the wine is spilled, and the wineskins ruined. But they put new wine into new wineskins, and both are preserved.

Prophecy Principle 12 *This new spiritual understanding of the Book of Revelation is birthed for your benefit and mine by The Father, Son, and Holy Spirit.*

At the end of the day, I do not ever demand that you take my word for interpretation of the revelations provided to Apostle John. All that I ask of you as you read is that you take the time to ponder or meditate over the teaching, over the reasonings or interpretations, and over the supporting evidence with help of the Holy Spirit. So then, there are lessons to learn, there are teachings that will enhance your walk with Christ, and teachings that help you arrive at a better understanding of your place in the world, in relation to the Church, and in relation to the nations. Let us get on with it then to the glory of The Father, Son, and Holy Spirit.

In Jesus Name. Amen.

CHAPTER 3

Dichotomizing 'Presence' from 'Coming'

If you are to arrive at a clear understanding of essence of visions that were entrusted to Apostle John by our Lord Jesus Christ, we must clear out some confusion of terminology. The first 'confusion of terminology' that we tackle is the substitution, in the interpretive translations of the Bible (*NKJV, RSV, NIV etc.*) of the word, 'COMING' for what, in the original languages was penned as 'PRESENCE'. In the original languages of Christian Scriptures, the word 'PRESENCE' is not the same as the word, 'COMING'. Rather unfortunately, and for unintentional arrival at some confusion, the *NKJV, RSV, NIV*, and other interpretive translations of Christian Scriptures sometimes interpret the word, PRESENCE as COMING.

Why did the scholars do this?

Presence is Spiritual 1 *They, much as most Christians, assumed the term 'Presence' of Jesus Christ referred to the 'Second Coming' of Jesus Christ.*

> We are, Always, in the Presence of Christ

In all of it's usages in the New Testament, the word, 'PRESENCE', refers to a spiritual, as opposed to a physical presence. In presence of this usage, the word 'presence' does not imply a physical appearance by the Lord Jesus Christ. All of the Scriptural evidence for the difference between the words, 'PRESENCE', and 'COMING' come from the *Young's Literal Translation (YLT)* of the Bible, a translation that is not interpretive (*that does not attempt to impose an understanding on the original text*), that merely translates words in the original languages to their equivalents in English.

First, we establish the following commonality to all of the translations, literal, or interpretive, which is, Christian Scriptures unequivocally declare that, spiritually, we are in the Presence of The Father, and our Lord Jesus Christ.

Some Initial Scriptural Evidence?

For we are not as the many, adulterating the word of God, but as of sincerity - but as of God; IN THE PRESENCE OF GOD, IN CHRIST we do speak (2Corinthians 2:17).

For what is our hope, or joy, or crown of rejoicing? are not even ye BEFORE OUR LORD JESUS CHRIST IN HIS PRESENCE? for ye are our glory and joy (1Thessalonians 2:19-20).

And you the Lord cause to increase and to abound in the love to one another, and to all, even as we also to you, to the establishing your hearts blameless in sanctification before our God and Father, IN THE PRESENCE OF OUR LORD JESUS CHRIST with all His saints (1Thessalonians 3:12-13).

All of the Scriptures cited declare very clearly that we are in the presence of our Lord Jesus Christ.

The Confusion?

Presence is Spiritual 2 *While all interpretive translations of 2Corinthians 2:17 correctly render* IN THE PRESENCE OF GOD, *as* 'IN SIGHT OF GOD', *or* 'BEFORE GOD', *in 1Thessalonians 2:19, the RSV renders* 'IN THE PRESENCE OF OUR LORD JESUS?', 'BEFORE OUR LORD JESUS AT HIS COMING?' *Further, in 1Thessalonians 3:12-13, all of NKJV, RSV, NIV, and the Darby Bible translate,* 'IN THE PRESENCE OF OUR LORD JESUS CHRIST' *as,* 'AT THE COMING OF OUR LORD JESUS CHRIST'.

If we focus on the original text (the literal translation), the very last Scripture links IN THE PRESENCE OF OUR LORD JESUS CHRIST with *'establishment of our hearts blameless in sanctification'*. Giving it is unequivocal that sanctification only occurs while we are in this life, the presence of our Lord Jesus Christ is, very clearly and unambiguously associated with our time here on earth. We arrive then at unambiguous evidence that being in the presence of our Lord Jesus Christ is not associated with a physical translation to heaven, but with our sanctification here on earth.

The interpretive translations render the word that, in the original language means *'sanctification'*, *'holiness'*. If holiness is attained to at the Second Coming of Christ, as such does not have to be established on earth prior to the Second Coming of Christ, we arrive at the inference that either of the literal or interpretive translations can be right.

WELL THEN, WHAT DO THE SCRIPTURES SAY (HEBREWS 12: 14, NKJV, RSV, NIV, DARBY, YLT)?

Pursue peace with all people, and holiness, without which no one will see the Lord (*NKJV*).

Strive for peace with all men, and for the holiness without which no one will see the Lord (*RSV*).

Make every effort to live in peace with all men and to be holy; without holiness no one will see the Lord (*NIV*).

Pursue peace with all, and holiness, without which no one shall see the Lord (*Darby*).

Peace pursue with all, and the separation (holiness), apart from which no one shall see the Lord (*YLT*).

Presence is Spiritual 3 *All of the interpretive translations agree with the YLT, declare that sanctification and holiness both occur here on earth. Given The Lord Jesus Christ has explicitly declared that He never again will set foot on this earth (Matthew 24:23-27), we conclude that the YLT is right, the interpretive translations, flawed.*

Presence is Spiritual 4 *So then, we conclude that all of the Scriptures cited (2Corinthians 2:17; 1Thessalonians 2:19; 1Thessalonians 3:12-13) refer to the* SPIRITUAL PRESENCE OF CHRIST, *not a Physical Second Coming of Christ.*

For additional concreteness, while we are in the presence of our Lord Jesus Christ, where exactly are we located, here on earth, or in the heavens?

THE SCRIPTURAL EVIDENCE?

If, then, ye were raised with the Christ, the things above seek ye, where the Christ is, on the right hand of God seated, the things above mind ye, not the things upon the earth, for ye did die, and your life hath been hid with the Christ in God; when the Christ - our life - may be manifested, then also we with Him shall be manifested in glory. PUT TO DEATH, THEN, YOUR MEMBERS THAT ARE UPON THE EARTH - whoredom (fornication), uncleanness, passion, evil desire, and the covetousness, which is idolatry (Colossians 3:1-5).

But, ye came to Mount Zion, and to a city of the living God, to the heavenly Jerusalem, and to myriads of messengers, to the company and assembly of the first-born in heaven enrolled, and to God the judge of all, and to spirits of righteous men made perfect, and to a mediator of a new covenant - Jesus, and to blood of sprinkling, speaking better things than that of Abel! See, may ye not refuse Him who is speaking, for if those did not escape who refused him who upon earth was divinely speaking - much less we who do turn away from Him who speaketh from heaven (Hebrews 12:22-25).

In Colossians 3:1-5, while we mind things that are heavenly or spiritual, which in Colossians 3:12 are inclusive of: *kindness*, meekness, and *patience*, we maintain this perspective while living here on earth, as such put to death the *lusts of the flesh (*such as fornication*)*, the *lusts of the eyes* (such as, covetousness), and the *pride of life* (evil desire) - *1John 2:15-16.*

Presence is Spiritual 5 *Clearly, heavenly mindedness, which consists in cultivation of virtues of our Lord Jesus Christ, as opposed to a desire to go to heaven, is compatible with life on earth.*

Hebrews 12:22-24 makes clear that, while you and I remain here on earth, as such hear from the blood of Jesus Christ, which speaks from heaven, you and I are assembled at the heavenly Mount Zion, to a city of the living God, the heavenly Jerusalem. We hear what the blood of Jesus speaks because, spiritually we are in assembly with The Father, The Son, The Holy Spirit (who is embodied in The Son - *2Corinthians 3:17; Revelation 5:6*), and the blood of Jesus Christ. For concreteness, within context of this spiritual assembly, we are in fellowship with:

✠ The Father, who is God and Judge of all, but who yet has committed all judgment to our Lord Jesus Christ (John 5:22).

✠ Our Lord Jesus Christ, the mediator of the New Covenant between man and God (Hebrews 8:6; 1John 2:1).

✠ The Blood of Jesus Christ, the blood without which neither you nor I can be cleansed from our sins (1John 1:7). If we are unable to be cleansed from our sins, we cannot become the righteousness of God (2Corinthians 5:21), meaning while we can be forgiven of our sins, we cannot be reconciled to God (Romans 5:10-11). The importance of the Blood for our sanctification is evident in the spiritual truth that we are in fellowship not only with Jesus, but with the blood of Jesus (1Peter 1:2).

✠ Myriads of Messengers who are ministering spirits to all who are heirs of salvation.

✠ Spirits of Righteous Men made Perfect. You and I have fellowship with spirits of Apostles Peter, James, John, Paul etc., men whose spirits were perfected via their fellowship with The Father, Son, and Holy Spirit. We do not become these men, we simply have fellowship with their spirits, meaning we can receive strength and illumination via fellowship with their spirits, which are in Christ (Colossians 3:1-3).

✠ **The First-born Enrolled in Heaven** are all those whose names not only are enrolled in the Lamb's Book of Life, but who also are the first to do something for The Father. ABRAHAM, *'Father of Faith'*, MOSES, *'the most truly humble man'*, SAMSON, *'the single handed deliverer'*, GIDEON, *'the first man to win a war without any weapons'*, and the ORIGINAL 12 APOSTLES (excluding Judas Iscariot, and including Apostle Paul) likely are some of those who make up this group.

Prophecy Insight 1 *If you have received Jesus as Lord and Savior, you have come to the spiritual assembly that is depicted in Hebrews 12:22-24. You then are* IN THE PRESENCE OF CHRIST *by fiat decree of The Father. If you actualize this spiritual reality in your life, if the fellowship of Jesus, and His Father, and His blood becomes spiritual reality in your life, you become sanctified, arrive at a* PERFECT MAN, *at a measure of the stature of the fullness of Christ. .*

Friend, the evidence is unambiguously clear that when the Scriptures declare that we are in the presence of The Father, and of our Lord Jesus Christ, that it declares our lives are represented in the presence of Father and Son in the heavenly Jerusalem, meaning, spiritually we are in the presence of Father and Son in the heavens. IS THIS CONSISTENT WITH OUR SANCTIFICATION HERE ON EARTH? Absolutely, for the blood of Jesus Christ is applied to us in the presence of The Father and The Son, such that spiritually speaking, our cleansing occurs in the heavens, then is manifested in our lives here on earth. If it is true that our cleansing first transpires spiritually in the heavens, then manifests here on earth, there must be some sort of mechanism at work. The mechanism at work is as follows. In context of sanctification, it is the LOVE OF GOD that is perfected in us, with outcome we grow spiritually, only because, first we receive a fresh infusion of the Love of God that increases each of the *quality* (PURITY), and *capacity* of our love. Given the command for the increase of the Love of God in our lives comes from the heavens, that is, from our Father in Heaven, all sanctification that truly transpires on earth emanates from a *pronouncement* (saying) of The Father that transpires in the heavens. When The Father decrees increase to our love, the blood of Jesus is applied for our benefit, we receive grace that we have yet to merit, and The Holy Spirit supplies us with fresh grace, that is, fresh infusion of the Love of The Father, of the Love of Christ. Hallelujah!!!

The Scriptural Evidence?

And hope (*the hope of becoming like Christ in Love*) does not disappoint us, because GOD'S LOVE HAS BEEN POURED INTO OUR HEARTS THROUGH THE HOLY SPIRIT which has been given to us (Romans 5:5).

He who is saying, 'I have known him,' and his command is not keeping, a liar he is, and in him the truth is not; and whoever may keep his word, TRULY IN HIM THE LOVE OF GOD HATH BEEN PERFECTED; in this we know that in him we are. He who is saying in Him he doth remain, ought according as He walked also himself so to walk (1John 2:4–6).

God no one hath ever seen; if we may love one another, God in us doth remain, and HIS LOVE IS HAVING BEEN PERFECTED IN US (1John 4:11–12).

Blessed is the God and Father of our Lord Jesus Christ, who did bless us in every spiritual blessing in the heavenly places in Christ, according as He did choose us in Him before the foundation of the world, FOR OUR BEING HOLY AND UNBLEMISHED BEFORE HIM, IN LOVE (Ephesians 1:3–4).

Spiritual Insight 5 *Christian Scriptures are unequivocal, it is The Love of Christ, which itself is received from God, that is perfected in context of the process of Sanctification. Holiness itself is defined as perfection in Love, as such only can be attained to by those who receive the Love of God.*

Why then the Grace of our Lord Jesus Christ?

Law came in, to increase the trespass, but where (*awareness of*) sin increased, GRACE (*the Love of God, which is not merited*) ABOUNDED ALL THE MORE, so that, as sin reigned in death, grace also might reign through (*love for*) righteousness (*in the hearts of those who believe*) to eternal life through Jesus Christ our Lord (Romans 5:20–21).

Let us therefore come boldly to the throne of grace (*the throne on which sits our Father in Heaven, He who dispenses unmerited favor*), THAT WE MAY OBTAIN MERCY AND FIND GRACE to help in time of need (Hebrews 4:16).

But we are bound to give thanks to God always for you, brethren beloved by the Lord, because God from the beginning chose you for salvation through sanctification by the Spirit and belief in the truth, to which He called you by our gospel, for the obtaining of the glory (*Essence*) of our Lord Jesus Christ (2 Thessalonians 2:13–14).

Spiritual Insight 6 *Why is it that we need to obtain mercy? Always, the grace that we need for overcoming, is grace for which, on basis of our own merits alone, we do not yet qualify. All of our overcoming then is made possible by the merits of our Lord Jesus Christ, by access to grace (power) that He earned for us, but for which we are yet to qualify.*

Spiritual Insight 7 *It is our commitment to living of the Life of Christ, that is, to demonstrations of the Love of Christ* IN ALL OF OUR INTERACTIONS *that induces pronouncements of increase to our Love from The Father. How then to attract pronouncements of increase to our Love from The Father? That, friend, is essence of my book,* 'TRUE SANCTIFICATION'.

The Evidence that our sanctification commences with God, that it all commences in the heavens?

I planted, Apollos watered, but GOD WAS GIVING GROWTH; so that neither is he who is planting anything, nor he who is watering, but He who is giving growth - God (1Corinthians 3:6-7).

Let no one beguile you of your prize, delighting in humble-mindedness and in worship of the messengers, intruding into things he hath not seen being vainly puffed up by the mind of his flesh, and not holding the head, from which all the body - through the joints and bands gathering supply, and being knit together - MAY INCREASE WITH THE INCREASE OF GOD (Colossians 2:18-19).

And increase ye (*first*), in grace (*unmerited favor*) and in the knowledge of our Lord and Savior Jesus Christ; to him is the glory both now, and to the day of the age! Amen (2Peter 3:18).

Spiritual Insight 8 *It is unequivocally true. Spiritual growth that transpires in context of our sanctification, equivalently, in context of perfection of the Love of Christ in us commences with a fiat decree from The Father. The Father is not partial; all who merit the fiat decree that enables the next infusion of the* LOVE OF GOD *of which they are desirous receive a fresh infusion of the* GRACE OF GOD.

AN IMPORTANT WORD OF ADMONITION: The Father will not tolerate even one hatred from those who seek to be sanctified. It will take only one hatred that is cherished against another for a believer in Christ to be disqualified from receipt of fresh infusion of the Love of Christ.

Some Additional Supporting Scriptures?

And to Him who is able to guard you, not stumbling, AND TO SET YOU IN THE PRESENCE OF HIS GLORY UNBLEMISHED, IN GLAD-NESS, to the only wise God our Savior, is glory and greatness, power and authority, both now and to all the ages! Amen (Jude 1:24-25).

Therefore, we also having so great a cloud of witnesses set around us, EVERY WEIGHT having put off, and the closely besetting sin, through endurance may we run the contest that is set before us, looking to the author and perfecter of faith - Jesus, who over-against the joy set before Him - did endure a cross, shame having despised, on the right hand also of the throne of God did sit down (Hebrews 12:1-2).

Presence is Spiritual 6 *A person who is unblemished and without spot is not lacking in any particular, is, in entirety, perfected in the Love of Christ. If you desire pronouncements of increases to your love from The Father, you must be willing to give up EVERY weakness and sinful tendency that is pointed out by The Holy Spirit. The Father will not compromise this standard.*

Presence is Spiritual 7 *Only those who are willing to give up EVERY weakness and sinful tendency arrive at a PERFECT MAN, arrive at being presented by The Father, with gladness, to all who are assembled in the heavenly Jerusalem as a new revelation of the glory of Christ.*

Is there a 'Presence of Christ' on Earth to Anticipate?

Already, we have established that the word translated, 'COMING' in each of 2Corinthians 2:17; 1Thessalonians 2:19; 1Thessalonians 3:12-13 ought really to be interpreted, 'PRESENCE'. We have established then, that we are in the Presence of Christ. We further have established that, while all who believe in Christ are in the Presence of Christ, it is those who allow the Love of Christ to be perfected in them that are presented by The Father, with gladness to all of the hosts of heaven as revelations of the glory of Christ.

Next, we ask the question, "While spiritually we are in the Presence of Christ - and this always - is it simultaneously the case that we expect some distinct manifestation of the Presence of Christ on earth?" As always, for an answer we turn to the Scriptures.

For this to you we say in the word of the Lord, that we who are living - WHO DO REMAIN OVER TO THE PRESENCE OF THE LORD - may not precede those asleep (1Thessalonians 4:15).

And we ask you, brethren, IN REGARD TO THE PRESENCE OF OUR LORD JESUS CHRIST, and of our gathering together unto Him, that ye be not quickly shaken in mind, nor be troubled, neither through spirit, neither through word, neither through letters as through us, as that the day of Christ hath arrived (2Thessalonians 2:1-2).

Be patient, then, brethren, TILL THE PRESENCE OF THE LORD; lo, the husbandman doth expect the precious fruit of the earth, being patient for it, till he may receive rain - early and latter; be patient, ye also; establish your hearts, because THE PRESENCE OF THE LORD HATH DRAWN NIGH (James 5:7-8).

This first knowing, that there shall come in the latter end of the days scoffers, according to their own desires going on, and saying, WHERE IS THE PROMISE OF HIS PRESENCE? for since the fathers did fall asleep, all things so remain from the beginning of creation (2Peter 3:3-4).

In all of the preceding verses, the word, 'PRESENCE', is consistently interpreted as 'COMING' by the *NKJV, RSV, NIV*, Darby Bible, and other translations of the Bible. Given all of the texts refer to the Presence of our Lord Jesus Christ on this earth at some time in future, clearly, as at the timing of writing by Apostle Paul, the Presence of Jesus Christ still was in the future. That the presence of Jesus Christ on earth must be spiritual is evident in the warning from Jesus in Matthew 24:23-27 that He never again will in future manifest on this earth physically.

Then if any one may say to you, LO, HERE IS THE CHRIST! OR HERE! YE MAY NOT BELIEVE; for there shall arise false Christs, and false prophets, and they shall give great signs and wonders, so as to lead astray, if possible, also the chosen. Lo, I did tell you beforehand. If therefore they may say to you, Lo, in the wilderness He is, ye may not go forth; lo, in the inner chambers, ye may not believe; for as the lightning doth come forth from the east, and doth appear unto the west, SO SHALL BE ALSO THE PRESENCE OF THE SON OF MAN (Matthew 24:23-27).

Presence is Spiritual 8 *If Jesus declares His Presence on earth, yet warns that He will not be physically present on earth, Jesus declares, rather unequivocally that His Presence will, at some point, arrive on earth, and that His Presence will be spiritual, not physical.*

Presence is Spiritual 9 *The word, PRESENCE in Matthew 24:23-27 is again translated COMING in all other translations of Christian Scriptures. Given Jesus explicitly excludes a physical appearance, clearly, THE WORD 'COMING' is not as appropriate as the word, 'PRESENCE'.*

The Reign of Jesus Christ Precedes His Coming

We already have unambiguously established that, at the end of the Book of Revelation, our Lord Jesus Christ declares His Coming, equivalently, Second Coming still to be in the future (Revelation 22:20). Consistent with location in future of the Coming of our Lord Jesus Christ, in all of the Book of Revelation, wherever the word 'COMING' is applied to our Lord Jesus Christ (Revelation 1:4,8; 4:8; & 11:17), His Coming always is in the future. While the Coming of Jesus Christ unambiguously is stated to be in the future at end of the Book of Revelation, simultaneously, the Book of Revelation declares that the REIGN of our Lord Jesus Christ on earth commences prior to His Coming, that is, prior to His Second Coming. The relevant Scripture is, Revelation 11:15-17.

> And the seventh messenger did sound, and there came great voices in the heaven, saying, The kingdoms of the world did become those of our Lord and of His Christ, and He shall reign to the ages of the ages! and the twenty and four elders, who before God are sitting upon their thrones, did fall upon their faces, and did bow before God, saying, "We give thanks to Thee, O Lord God, the Almighty, WHO ART, AND WHO WAST, AND WHO ART COMING, because THOU HAST TAKEN THY GREAT POWER AND DIDST REIGN; AND THE NATIONS WERE ANGRY, and thine anger did come, and the time of the dead, to be judged, and to give the reward to thy servants, to the prophets, and to the saints, and to those fearing thy name, to the small and to the great, and to destroy those who are destroying the land."

Consider the following sequence of events depicted subsequent to sounding of the trumpet by the seventh messenger.

1. The Coming of Christ still is in the future.

2. The kingdoms of the world did become those of our Lord and of His Christ.

3. Christ takes up His great power and begins to reign. Given HIS COMING STILL IS IN THE FUTURE, and given He did already begin to Reign, it is unequivocal that REIGN PRECEDES COMING. Further, if He Reigns, but His Presence is lacking, clearly we arrive at a misnomer. It is safe to infer then that Commencement of the Reign of Jesus Christ coincides with Arrival of His Presence. We shall go on to validate this inference.

4. The nations became angry, and the anger of Christ is aroused, and the anger is vented on the nations. Since the nations are on earth,

the Reign of Jesus Christ must also be on earth. We shall render this inference more concrete.

5. The dead are judged, and those who are good and alive are rewarded with good by our Lord Jesus Christ. Those who destroy the land, that is, the earth are destroyed.

6. Yet, at this point in time, the Coming of Jesus - the Second Coming - still is delineated to be in future.

In the discussion to follow, in the interpretive translations, but with restriction to the Gospels only, the word, 'REIGN' in the original text is, rather inaccurately, interpreted as, 'KINGDOM'. I have provided an extensive discussion of spiritual implications of the inaccurate rendition in my book, 'True Sanctification'. Suffice it here to say that while *reign* implies that you, a believer in Christ, have opportunity to reign with Christ, the word *kingdom* implies you merely are a citizen of the kingdom of Christ. Clearly, there is a difference. While I do not provide all of the renditions, all of the interpretive translations agree, in Revelation 5:9-10, that the saints reign with Christ on earth. The 'rendered' additional evidence from the interpretive and literal translations that you are able to reign with Christ (2Timothy 2:12)?

> If we endure, we shall also reign with Him. If we deny Him, He also will deny us (*NKJV*).

> If we endure, we shall also reign with Him; if we deny Him, He also will deny us (*RSV*).

> If we endure, we will also reign with Him. If we disown Him, He will also disown us (*NIV*).

> If we endure, we shall also reign together; if we deny, He also will deny us (*Darby*).

> If we do endure together - we shall also reign together; if we deny Him, He also shall deny us (*YLT*).

Prophecy Insight 2 *In presence of the internal contradiction that is evident within the interpretive translations, a contradiction that is evident in the fact that arrival at membership of the kingdom of God is free, is conditional only on grace that is received by faith (Ephesians 2:8), it is unequivocal that the literal rendition, 'REIGN' is intent of words of Jesus Christ.*

For avoidance of any doubt whatsoever, where exactly does this reign of our Lord Jesus Christ transpire, and what exactly is the nature of this reign?

And when He took the scroll, the four living creatures and the twenty-four elders fell before the Lamb, having each one harps and golden vials full of perfumes, which are the prayers of the saints, and they sing a new song, saying, "Worthy art thou to take the scroll, and to open the seals of it, because thou wast slain, and didst redeem us to God in they blood, out of every tribe, and tongue, and people, and nation, AND DIDST MAKE US TO OUR GOD KINGS AND PRIESTS, AND WE SHALL REIGN UPON THE EARTH (Revelation 5:9-10)."

The law and the prophets are till John; since then the reign of God is proclaimed good news, and every one doth press into it (Luke 16:16).

And having been questioned by the Pharisees, when the reign of God doth come, He answered them, and said, The reign of God doth not come with observation; nor shall they say, Lo, here; or lo, there; for lo, THE REIGN OF GOD IS WITHIN YOU (Luke 17:20-21).

Jesus answered and said to him, verily, verily, I say to thee, if any one may not be born from above, he is not able to see the reign of God (John 3:3).

Jesus answered, verily, verily, I say to thee, if any one may not be born of water, and the Spirit, he is not able to enter into the reign of God (John 3:5).

THE SPIRITUAL REALITIES, AS OUTLINED IN THE PRECEDING VERSES:

✠ The reign of Jesus Christ occurs here on earth.

✠ The reign is spiritual - only those who are born of God are able to see it, that is, only those who are born of God perceive it's reality.

✠ The reign of God is within us, again implying it is spiritual.

✠ Those who are wise seek to press into the reign of God.

✠ For arrival at functioning as kings and priests unto the Lord Jesus Christ, only those who are born of water and the Spirit are able to enter into the reign of God.

Presence is Spiritual 10 *The* REIGN OF GOD, *equivalently, the* REIGN OF OUR LORD JESUS CHRIST, *equivalently, the* PRESENCE OF CHRIST *occurs here on earth; is spiritual; is perceived only by those who are born of God; and entry into it is attained only by those who allow themselves to be born anew of water and the Holy Spirit.*

Presence is Spiritual 11 *Revelation 11:15-17 makes clear that, at timing of the revelations entrusted to Apostle John, that the* PRESENCE OF CHRIST, *equivalently, the* REIGN OF CHRIST *still was in the future. With Apostle John as the Apostle who survived all other apostles, we arrive at confirmation for assertions in 1Thessalonians 4:15; 2Thessalonians 2:1; James 5:7-8); and 2Peter 3:3-4 that, at timing of their writings, the* PRESENCE OF CHRIST *had yet to be realized.*

Presence is Spiritual 12 *The Apostles all declare that they were filled with the Holy Spirit, yet were in expectation of the* PRESENCE OF CHRIST. *We arrive then at an extremely important truth and realization, which is, until arrival of the Presence of Christ, to be filled with the Holy Spirit was not the same thing as to have the Presence of Christ, or to be in the Reign of God. As you go along in this book, you will arrive at knowledge of timing of arrival of the Reign of Christ, with outcome that in this dispensation, to be filled with the Holy Spirit implies participation in the Reign of Christ.*

Presence is Spiritual 13 *Those who are born from above see the Reign of God, equivalently, see the* PRESENCE OF CHRIST. *Those who are born of water and the Spirit enter into the Reign of God, that is, have the presence of Christ within them. Clearly, 'TO SEE' is not the same as 'TO ENTER'. As we go along, you will discover the difference between those who 'see', and those who 'enter' into the reign of God.*

'In the Presence of Christ' is not tantamount to 'In The Reign of Christ'

As we already have seen, to be IN THE PRESENCE OF GOD is to be in spiritual assembly on Mount Zion, that is, in the Heavenly Jerusalem with The Father, our Lord Jesus Christ, the blood of our Lord Jesus Christ, ministering spirits, the spirits of just men made perfect, and all of the first born that are enrolled in heaven.

When it comes to the REIGN OF CHRIST, our Lord Jesus Christ states emphatically, that His Reign will transpire in our spirits, in our inner man; that if we attain to His Reign, we arrive at some spiritual realization of His Presence in our spirit.

Prophecy Insight 3 *In presence of characterization of what it means to be in the* PRESENCE OF CHRIST, *and what it means to be in the* REIGN OF CHRIST, *clearly, to be in the Presence of Christ is not tantamount to entering into the Reign of Christ.*

The Reconciliation?

All who believe in Christ are in the PRESENCE OF CHRIST. Only those whom The Father presents in the spiritual assembly in the New Jerusalem as having become a PERFECT MAN enter into the REIGN OF CHRIST. We arrive then at the inference that to receive Jesus as Lord and Savior is not tantamount to entering into the Reign of Christ. In light of stated inference, only the subset of those who believe who go on to attain to a Perfect Man, which hopefully turns out to be everyone who believes in the name of Christ, enter into the Reign of Christ. Consistent with the declaration of the Apostles that, in their time, the Reign of Christ remained in the future, our Lord Jesus Christ states as follows in respect of His disciples, and defines eternal life as follows.

> And Peter said, "Lo, we left all, and did follow thee;" And He said to them, verily I say to you, that there is not one who left house, or parents, or brothers, or wife, or children, for the sake of the Reign of God, who may not receive back manifold more in this time, and in the coming age, life age-during (eternal life) - Luke 18:28-30.

> And this is the life age-during, that they may know thee, the only true God, and Him whom thou didst send - Jesus Christ (John 17:3).

Prophecy Insight 4 *Our Lord Jesus Christ is emphatic. His Reign having not arrived in time of His Apostles, they would not have opportunity to know Him or His Father in some personal sense, as such would not arrive at eternal life until after death, that is, until the next age. Note, however, that they were in the Presence of Christ, and experienced filling of The Holy Spirit. Note also that The Holy Spirit taught them about what would be experienced in context of the Reign of Christ, and conditions for entering into the Reign of Christ. Regardless, until their death, they did not arrive at participation in the Reign of Christ.*

Prophecy Insight 5 LET Φ *(pronounced, 'phi') be the set consisting of all those who believe in the name of Jesus Christ. It is mathematical fact that, with '$\subseteq$' denoting subset, that $\Phi \subseteq \Phi$; that is,* A SET IS A SUBSET OF ITSELF; *meaning it is possible for all those who have faith in the name of Jesus Christ to become part of the Reign of Jesus Christ.*

The Supporting Evidence?

> Wherefore, the rather, brethren, be diligent to make steadfast your calling and choice, for these things doing, YE MAY NEVER STUMBLE (*ye become perfect*), for so, richly shall be superadded to you the entrance into the age-during Reign of our Lord and Savior Jesus Christ (2Peter 1:10-11).

Prophecy Insight 6 *The evidence is unequivocal. Only the subset of those who profess faith in Christ, who go on to attain to a PERFECT MAN are ushered into the age-during Reign of our Lord and Savior Jesus Christ. You and I ought to pray that all who believe exert effort for making it into the REIGN OF CHRIST.*

Prophecy Insight 7 *If the Reign of our Lord Jesus Christ already has arrived, you have opportunity to be ushered in, this while yet you are alive. If, as was the case with the Apostles, the Reign of Jesus Christ still was in the future, it was subsequent to physical death that you were ushered into the Reign of Jesus Christ.*

Prophecy Insight 8 *To not be ushered into the REIGN OF CHRIST is not necessarily to be lost, is not necessarily equivalent to losing of salvation. More on this later in Chapter 8.*

What then about the Coming of Christ?

Outside of the Book of Revelation, in the original text, the Coming of Christ is explicitly discussed in only seven Scriptures, three of which are restatement, of three Scriptures that are recorded in the Book of Matthews, in the other Gospels. The Scriptures are: Matthew 16:27-28; Matthew 24:30-31; Matthew 26:64; Mark 13:26; Mark 14:62; Luke 21:27; and Acts 2:20. The three Scriptures in the Book of Matthew, and the Scripture in the Book of Acts are, respectively:

> For, the Son of Man is about to come in the glory of His Father, with His messengers, and then He will reward each, according to His work. Verily I say to you, there are certain of those standing here who shall not taste of death till they may see the Son of Man COMING IN HIS REIGN (Matthew 16:27-28).

> And then shall appear the sign of the Son of Man in the heaven; and then shall all the tribes of the earth smite the breast, and THEY SHALL SEE THE SON OF MAN COMING UPON THE CLOUDS OF THE HEAVEN, with power and much glory; and He shall send His messengers with a great sound of a trumpet, and they shall gather together His chosen from the four winds, from the ends of the heavens unto the ends thereof (Matthew 24:30-31).

> Jesus saith to him, Thou hast said; nevertheless I say to you, hereafter ye shall see the Son of Man sitting on the right hand of the power, and COMING UPON THE CLOUDS, of the heaven (Matthew 26:64).

The sun shall be turned to darkness, and the moon to blood, before THE COMING OF THE DAY OF THE LORD - the great and illustrious (Acts 2:20).

The wording of MATTHEW 16:27-28 somewhat is ambiguous, because in reality, Matthew refers to two different events, namely the REIGN OF CHRIST, and the SECOND COMING OF CHRIST. The right interpretation of the verse, which is consistent with all of our pre-existing inferences is:

'the Coming of Christ transpires in context of His Reign.'

HOW DO WE KNOW THIS?

Well, combined, Revelation 22:12,20; 19:6,11-16; & 11:15-17 establish that the reward of Christ aligns with His Second Coming, and occurs subsequent to commencement of His reign. For fulfillment of the prophecy that someone alive would witness His reign, while in vision, in Revelation 19:6, 11-16, Apostle John witnessed the coming of our Lord Jesus Christ in His reign.

And lo, I come quickly, and my reward is with me, to render to each as his work shall be (Revelation 22:12).

And I heard as the voice of a great multitude, and as the voice of many waters, and as the voice of mighty thunderings, saying, ALLELUIA! BECAUSE REIGN DID THE LORD GOD - THE ALMIGHTY. And I saw the heaven having been opened, and lo, a white horse, and He who is sitting upon it is called Faithful and True, and in righteousness doth He judge and war, and His eyes are as a flame of fire, and upon His head are many diadems (a crown with diadems) - having a name written that no one hath known, except Himself, and He is arrayed with a garment covered with blood, and His name is called, THE WORD OF GOD. And the armies in the heaven were following Him upon white horses clothed in fine linen - white and pure (Revelation 19:6,11-16).

Presence is Spiritual 14 *The Book of Revelation clearly declares that timing of reward from our Lord Jesus Christ aligns with timing of His coming (Revelation 22:12, 20), and occurs subsequent to commencement of His reign, as such people 'see the Son of Man COMING IN HIS REIGN (Revelation 19:6,11-16; 11:15-17).'*

Presence is Spiritual 15 *Combined, Matthew 16:27-28, Revelation 22:12,20, and Revelation 19:6,11-16 establish dichotomy of events characterized as COMING OF CHRIST, and the REIGN (PRESENCE) OF CHRIST; demonstrate that the two events have been confused, have rather unconsciously, yet wrongly been collapsed into one single event.*

MATTHEW 24:30-31 declares that those who are reaped by Jesus Christ are gathered not from the earth, but from one end of the heavens to the other, meaning those reaped are not on earth. Well, who are those located in the heavens?

> Not every one who is saying to me, Lord, Lord, shall come into the reign of the heavens (*the reign of God*); but he who is doing the will of my Father who is in the heavens - Matthew 7:21.

Presence is Spiritual 16 *In Matthew 24:30-31, Apostle Matthew reiterates the spiritual reality that the Coming of Christ serves for reaping those who already are participating in the reign of the heavens, those who already are participating in the reign of God.*

Presence is Spiritual 17 *Matthew 26:64 and Acts 2:20 do not provide any contradictions to either of Matthew 16:27-28, or Matthew 24:30-31.*

Let us denote times that preceded arrival of the Presence of Christ, the ANTECEDENT AGE, and the age ushered in by arrival of the Presence of Christ, the PRESENCE AGE. The discussion in Chapter 5 introduces you to evolution of time from the ANTECEDENT AGE, which is made up of the Churches in *Ephesus, Smyrna, Pergamum, Thyatira, Sardis*, and *Philadelphia*, to arrival of the PRESENCE AGE in context of the *Church in Laodicea*. The discussion elucidates essence of the PRESENCE OF CHRIST, and how exactly this induces spiritual realities that are not available in context of the ANTECEDENT AGE. Given the Book of Revelation does not address the COMING OF CHRIST, there is nothing much more to add to discussion of that event, except to provide a discussion of meaning of 'coming with the clouds'. In view of all that still is in need of establishment in order for that discussion to be properly understood and placed in context, I have delayed that discussion until *Chapter 18*. I encourage you to check your curiosity, such that, at the very least you complete reading of *Chapters 1 through 11* prior to checking out of meaning of 'coming with the clouds' in *Chapter 18*.

In light of all of the evidence, clearly, the focus of the Book of Revelation is on spiritual implications of the REIGN OF CHRIST for your individual self, the Church, and the Nations, and for interactions that subsist between yourself, the Church, and the Nations. Clearly then, the Book of Revelation relates to how exactly you, I, the Church, and the Nations are able to make the most of life here on earth in context of the Reign of Christ. In presence of this inference, clearly, the Book of Revelation is not about how to prepare for going to heaven to be with Christ, in actuality provides us with revelations that enable us make the most of our time here on earth.

Prophecy Interpretation 1 *The Book of Revelation provides revelations that enable us make the most of our time on earth. We have then that the traditional directive to Christians that they not be comfortable with living on earth*

*is not from our Lord Jesus Christ, stems from misunderstandings of the Book
of Revelation. In the Book of Revelation, the Lord Jesus Christ declares emphatically and unambiguously that He has left you, and I, and the Church
on earth precisely so we can make the most of the time; precisely so we can
demonstrate His Reign on Earth.*

Someone then may say, "but do the Scriptures not declare that we are to
focus our minds on the things above, and not on the things of this earth?"
This is true, and I already have cited one of the relevant Scripture texts,
which is, Colossians 3:1-4.

> But what exactly do the Scriptures imply by the command to set
> the mind on heavenly, as opposed to earthly things?

Using the follow-up texts to Colossians 3:1-4, and with intent of some
parsimony of rendition of the follow-up Scriptures, Apostle Paul continues
on as follows:

> PUT TO DEATH, THEN, YOUR MEMBERS THAT ARE UPON THE EARTH
> - WHOREDOM, UNCLEANNESS, PASSION, EVIL DESIRE, AND THE COV-
> ETOUSNESS, WHICH IS IDOLATRY (Colossians 3:5).

Apostle Paul continues with the discussion of things that are upon the
earth in Colossians 3:6-8. It is unambiguously clear, however, from Colossians 3:5 that, in the declaration that you are not to set your heart on things
upon the earth, that Apostle Paul refers essentially to avoidance of the *lusts
of the flesh*, the *lust of the eyes*, and the *pride of life* (1John 2:15-17).

Spiritual Insight 9 *The declaration that faith in Jesus Christ should not be
associated with a dwelling of the mind on things upon the earth is in entirety
spiritual, has nothing whatsoever to do with 'not living of life to it's fullest', or
'not becoming wealthy' in context of business activities or professions that are
pursued in righteousness of Christ.*

> What then does it mean to set the mind on things above, on
> things in the heavens?

> Put on, therefore, as choice ones of God, holy and beloved, bow-
> els of mercies, kindness, humble-mindedness, meekness, long-
> suffering, and above all these things, have love, which is a bond
> of the perfection, and all whatever ye may do in word or in work,
> do all things in the name of the Lord Jesus - giving thanks to the
> God and Father, through Him (Colossians 3:12,14,17).

As is evident, setting of the mind on things above consists in entirety of a focus on demonstration of the character and essence of Christ to the world in words or in work. Clearly, with work included as context for glorifying Christ, in essence, Apostle Paul is declaring that the Lord Jesus Christ expects that you will not abdicate principles of love in your dealings that occur in context of work. Work then is recommended, with outcome it is the character, which you display at work, that is focus of the admonition from Apostle Paul.

Spiritual Insight 10 *Heavenly mindedness is evident not in your unwilling-ness to make the most of your time here on earth for production of wealth via righteous applications of your abilities, which by the way, are God given (Deuteronomy 8:18), but with the expectation that The Father expects you will not abandon the character of Christ in your dealings that transpire in context of work.*

Spiritual Insight 11 *That work is noble in context of faith in Christ is evident in the declaration in 2Thessalonians 3:10, which declares, "If any one is* NOT WILLING TO WORK, *neither let him eat."*

Before we get into all of the big picture and details of the revelations that are recorded for our spiritual benefit in the Book of Revelation, there remain some preliminary matters to get out of the way. In this respect, in the very next Chapter you discover that the word, 'ANGEL' does not exist anywhere in the original text of Christian Scriptures.

CHAPTER 4

Who Are The 'Messengers' of the Book of Revelation?

The word translated, 'angel' in most translations of the Bible actually literally means 'messenger'. While the word 'messenger' seems not to have grandeur or dignity in today's vocabulary of english and today's society, this was not the case in ancient times. In ancient times, Daniel, who was a Counselor to king Nebucchadnezzer of Babylon could be sent to another kingdom as an *emissary*, equivalently, as a *messenger* of the king of Babylon.

> In ancient times, a messenger simply was a person in whom trust was reposed who bore a message from one royal personage to another.

> In presence of importance of 'Trust', messengers were persons who were held in high esteem by their royals.

In this chapter, I demonstrate beyond any doubt whatsoever a truth that you may find shocking, which is, the word 'ANGEL' does not occur, not even once, in the original text of Christian Scriptures. In every instance of occurrence of the word, Angel, the literal translation of the word is, 'MESSENGER'.

Love of Truth 13 *If you do a search of the YLT for the word, 'Angel', the word does not occur, not even once, in the literal word-for-word translation of the original text.*

First, I reiterate that I am not by this truth claiming that you have been deceived, or that there has been an attempt at deceiving you. The most rational rationalization for the inaccuracy probably resides in the assumption, on part of the interpretive translations that a messenger from God must, of necessity, be *a celestial being*, a being that is grandiose in his or her grandeur. In this respect, I note that the word 'MESSENGER' can imply a being having wings. More generally, however, the word 'MESSENGER' does not imply a being having wings. Whenever Christian Scriptures refers explicitly to beings who have wings, and who serve God, they are referred to as either of *Cherubim* or *Seraphim*. In this respect, consider the following description in Ezekiel 10:20-22.

> It is the living creature that I saw under the God of Israel by the river Chebar, AND I KNOW THAT THEY ARE CHERUBS. Four faces are to each, AND FOUR WINGS TO EACH, and the likeness of the hands of man is under their wings. As to the likeness of their faces, they are the faces that I saw by the river Chebar, their appearances and themselves; each straight forward they go.

Prophecy Principle 13 *Shocking but true; the word* ANGEL *does not exist in Christian Scriptures. The word translated* 'ANGEL' *means* 'MESSENGER', *essentially,* 'MESSAGE BEARER'. *Wherever beings with wings are described in Christian Scriptures, they are referred to as Cherubs or Seraphs. Prior to sin finding room in him, Satan was an anointed Cherub (Ezekiel 28:14).*

A Man Can Be A Messenger

The original text of Christian Scriptures makes clear that 'man' can be designated a messenger from The Father. In this respect, consider Haggai 1:13.

> And Haggai, MESSENGER OF JEHOVAH, IN MESSAGES OF JEHOVAH, speaketh to the people, saying: "I am with you, an affirmation of Jehovah."

Concerning John the Baptist and our Lord Jesus Christ, Jehovah declares as follows in Malachi 3:1.

> Lo, I am sending MY MESSENGER, and he (JOHN THE BAPTIST) hath prepared a way before me, and suddenly come in unto His temple doth the Lord whom ye are seeking, even the MESSENGER OF THE COVENANT (OUR LORD JESUS CHRIST), whom ye are desiring, Lo, He is coming, said Jehovah of Hosts.

Concerning His functioning in capacity of a message bearer, our Lord Jesus Christ declares as follows in John 7:28.

> Jesus cried, therefore, in the temple, teaching and saying, "Ye have both known me, and ye have known whence I am; and I have not come of myself, BUT HE WHO SENT ME IS TRUE, whom ye have not known; and I have known Him, because I am from Him, and He did send me.

Concerning the fact that messengers can be men, Jehovah and Apostle Paul declare as follows in Ezekiel 30:9, and Galatians 4:14.

> In that day go forth do MESSENGERS from before me in ships, to trouble confident Cush, and there hath been great pain among them, as the day of Egypt, for lo, it hath come.

> And my trial that is in my flesh ye did not despise nor reject, but as a MESSENGER of God ye did receive me - as Christ Jesus (Galatians 4:14).

The corresponding translation of Galatians 4:14 in the *NKJV*?

> And my trial which was in my flesh you did not despise or reject, but you received me as an ANGEL of God, even as Christ Jesus.

Spiritual Insight 12 *When Christian Scriptures declare that some believers have entertained messengers unawares (Hebrews 13:2), they can be referring to men bearing messages from The Father.*

Spiritual Insight 13 *Whenever Christian Scriptures declare that people do not know the time of their inspection or visitation from God (Luke 19:41-44), or that there is a day of inspection (Job 10:12; Isaiah 10:3, 60:17; Jeremiah 23:12, 46:21; Hosea 9:7; 1Peter 2:11-12), messengers sent to inspect or to visit can be men bearing messages from The Father.*

Prophecy Principle 14 *Whenever the Book of Revelation refers to messengers, the beings in question need not have wings. It might not be easy, but when you read the Book of Revelation, every time you encounter the word 'MESSENGER' or 'ANGEL', remind yourself that it does not necessarily imply a being with wings.*

A spiritual entity who can disappear can be a messenger

While it is eminently clear that messengers can be men, they equally can be ministering spirits, spiritual beings who live in the heavens, but who manifest on earth for the good of mankind. Clearly, some of these ministering spirits are people that resurrected with Christ on the third day, who then invisibly ascended to heaven with Him (Matthew 27:51-53; Ephesians 4:8).

How do we know this for a fact?

And Jesus answering said to them, ye go astray, not knowing the Writings, nor the power of God; for IN THE RISING AGAIN they do not marry, nor are THEY given in marriage, but ARE AS MESSENGERS OF GOD IN HEAVEN (Matthew 22:30).

Beware! - ye may not despise one of these little ones, for I say to you, that THEIR MESSENGERS IN THE HEAVENS do always behold the face of my Father who is in the heavens (Matthew 18:10).

And the messenger of Jehovah putteth forth the end of his staff which is in His hand, and cometh against the flesh, and against the unleavened things, and the fire goeth up out of the rock and consumeth the flesh and the unleavened things - AND THE MESSENGER OF JEHOVAH HATH GONE FROM HIS EYES. And Gideon seeth that He is a messenger of Jehovah, and Gideon saith, Alas, Lord Jehovah! because that I have seen a messenger of Jehovah face to face! (Judges 6:21-22).

And it cometh to pass, in the going up of the flame from off the altar toward the heavens, that THE MESSENGER OF JEHOVAH GOETH UP IN THE FLAME OF THE ALTAR, and Manoah and his wife are looking on, and they fall on their faces to the earth, and the messenger of Jehovah hath not added again to appear unto Manoah, and unto his wife, then hath Manoah known that He is a messenger of Jehovah. And Manoah saith unto his wife, "we certainly die, for we have seen God (Judges 13:20-22)."

Matthew 22:30 clearly establishes that when The Father raises people from the dead, they become messengers to Him in the heavens. Clearly, messengers that are in the heavens consist, in part, of people, such as Moses, who believed in God, died, then were resurrected from the dead. This truth further is evident in passages from the Book of Judges, which establish that MESSENGERS who live in the heavens can have the form of a man, such that only upon their supernatural disappearance are people able to discern that they are ministering spirits sent from The Father. We conclude then that The Father having adopted the form that He subsequently endowed on man as His physical image, that His messengers have the same form.

Prophecy Principle 15 MESSENGERS *can be men who are body, soul, and spirit, and who live on earth, or can be spiritual beings - ministering spirits - who live in the heavens in presence of The Father.*

Prophecy Principle 16 *The* MESSENGERS *of the seven churches in Revelation Chapters 2 and 3 likely are ministering spirits, who, like our Lord Jesus Christ, took up human existence for a season for actualization of purposes of*

The Father on earth. These messengers fight for the gospel, but consistent with The Father's decision to give man power of choice, are not allowed to force their will on man. Like our Lord Jesus Christ, messengers fight for the gospel with their spiritual giftings.

Is there any Scriptural evidence in support of the feasibility that messengers of the seven churches of Revelation Chapters 2 and 3 are ministering spirits who take up human form, who act as agents for Christ on earth, and reside on earth for a season?

> Have ye not known that we shall judge MESSENGERS? why not then the things of life (1Corinthians 6:3).

Spiritual Insight 14 *If those who reign with Christ will judge messengers, it only can be in context of affairs that transpire on this earth. We have then, that much as our Lord Jesus Christ judges the messengers of the seven churches in Revelation Chapters 2 and 3, so also judgment of messengers can be consigned to those who reign with Christ.*

The messages of our Lord Jesus Christ in Revelation Chapters 2 and 3 are directed to the messengers of the churches. Our Lord Jesus Christ makes clear that He deems the messengers responsible for spiritual state of the Churches. Where the messengers are not at fault, the Lord Jesus Christ directs any spiritual ire (spiritual indignation) towards specific persons or groups within a Church. We discuss these messages, their spiritual imports, and their timelines in the very next Chapter.

Prophecy Principle 17 *The messages from our Lord Jesus Christ to the seven churches of Revelation Chapters 2 and 3 are, first and foremost, directed at the messengers of the seven churches. Where the messengers are not blemished in any way, but yet there are things amiss, the Lord Jesus Christ directs His ire at specific persons or groups within a Church.*

Prophecy Principle 18 *Our Lord Jesus Christ declares that, typically the spiritual health of followers can be deduced from the spiritual health of their leaders. So then, spiritual quality of leadership of Churches is of significant importance. If leaders are in good spiritual health, followers that are in bad spiritual health make the choice not to listen to their leaders.*

> Of the hospitality be not forgetful, for through this unawares certain did entertain messengers (Hebrews 13:2).

CHAPTER 5

Messages to the Seven Churches

A careful reading of Revelation Chapter 1 reveals that the Book of Revelation can be broken up into three parts, namely:

✠ What John had seen - these relate in entirety to the messages to be sent to the seven churches - Revelation Chapters 2 & 3.

✠ The things that are - meaning the things that do not change, that always will be - Revelation Chapters 4 & 5.

✠ The things that are about to come after these things - the rest of the Book of Revelation.

The Evidence?

I was in the Spirit on the Lord's Day, and I heard behind me a great voice, as of a trumpet, saying, "I an the Alpha and the Omega, the First and the Last," and, "What thou dost see (WHAT YOU ALREADY SEE), write in a scroll, and send to the seven assemblies (churches) that are in Asia: to Ephesus, and to Smyrna, and to Pergamos, and to Thyatira, and to Sardis, and to Philadelphia, and to Laodicea (Revelation 1:10-11)."

And when I saw Him, I did fall at His feet as dead, and He placed His right hand upon me, saying to me, "Be not afraid; I am the First and the Last, and He who is living, and I did become dead, and lo I am living to the ages of the ages. Amen! And I have the keys of the Hades and of the Death. Write the things that thou hast seen (WHAT NEEDS TO BE SENT TO THE SEVEN CHURCHES), and the things that are, and the things that are about to come after these things (Revelation 1:17-19)."

Clearly, the phrases,

"What thou dost see (WHAT YOU ALREADY SEE), write in a scroll, and send to the seven assemblies (churches) that are in Asia - Revelation 1:11,

AND

"Write the things that thou hast seen, and the things that are, and the things that are about to come after these things (Revelation 1:19),"

indicate, in sense of progression of the visions, that Apostle John had been moved beyond the visions that make up the 'messages to the seven churches' to two new sets of visions - the things that are, and the things that are to come after these things.

Background

It was only at timing of the reading of the Book of Revelation during which the Holy Spirit inspired me to write this book that my eyes opened to the fact that all seven churches in Revelation Chapters 2 and 3 are located in Asia. I always never in prior readings had noticed this fact. Out of the seven churches, only two are explicitly mentioned in Paul's Epistles, namely the Churches at Ephesus and Laodicea. While Apostle Paul mentions that he wrote an Epistle to the Church in Laodicea, the Epistle did not survive. With the condition of the Laodicean Church as depicted in Revelation Chapter 3, that perhaps is no wonder.

Is there any chance Laodiceans read the Epistle from Paul, got upset, and tore it all up? Well, who knows?

The Epistle to the Church in Ephesus? Ecclesiastical. Beautiful.

In terms of an entire Epistle, as I elucidate in Chapter 18 of my Book, 'TRUE SANCTIFICATION', the Epistle to the Ephesians is Apostle Paul both at his most ecclesiastical in inspiration, yet with some of the most beautiful prose that subsist in all of Christian Scriptures. In Chapters 1 and 3 (Ephesians 1:1-15; Ephesians 3:14-21) of the Book of Ephesians, Apostle Paul writes two of the longest, yet absolutely coherent and beautiful sentences that you will find in any book. A sentence that lists things can be long;

this, however, never is a test of difficulty of constructions of English vocabulary. When a sentence that strings ideas is long, yet turns out to be beautifully constructed, however, the outcome always is beautifully prosaic. EVER TRIED WRITING A VERY LONG SENTENCE? Well, then, you know how hard it is to produce a long sentence that is totally coherent, yet easy to read and comprehend. The Epistle by Apostle Paul to the Church in Colossae, which also is located in Asia, is as Ecclesiastical as that to the Ephesians, a testament to the glory and pre-eminence of our Lord Jesus Christ, but not quite as beautifully prosaic as the Epistle to the Ephesians. With respect to practical applications of the Ecclesiastical revelations, the Epistle to the Colossians provides truths not extensively enunciated in Ephesians.

Spiritual Insight 15 *When Churches, such as those at Ephesus and Colossae, are filled with sincere believers who do not need to be reprimanded for wrong attitudes or behaviors, it is easier for the Holy Spirit to direct the spirit of an Apostle towards revelations that are Ecclesiastical.*

Spiritual Insight 16 *If you seek prayers that are ecclesiastical in their essence, that are reachings of the spirit and soul towards The Father, The Lord Jesus Christ, and the Holy Spirit, read the Epistle of Apostle Paul to the Ephesians.*

Rather unfortunately, by the timing of Apostle John's visions on the Isle of Patmos, the Church in Ephesus had left it's first love, was no longer as fervent as was the case during the time of Apostle Paul, who by that time had given his life for sake of the gospel. Given Apostle Paul intimates that he still was alive at the destruction of the second temple and Jerusalem by Roman General Titus in 70 AD (1Thessalonians 2:16), Apostle Paul likely was executed during the reign of a *'Flavian'* Emperor, that is, by any of Emperors *Vespasian*, *Titus*, or *Domitian*. In this respect, the tradition that he was executed by Emperor Nero, who ruled over the Roman Empire from 54 to 68 AD (*HWE*, pg. 131) cannot be held to be true. Given Apostle Paul was in Athens at timing of penning of the First Epistle to the Thessalonians (1Thessalonians 3:1), and given this must have been post 70 AD (1Thessalonians 2:16), and given he must have been under house arrest and released prior to the destruction of Jerusalem (*the temple had yet to be destroyed at timing of his arrest*), in presence of certainty of only two Epistles that are written post 70 AD (1&2 Thessalonians), and a maximum of three (with perhaps, inclusion of Galatians, which also could have been penned prior to his arrest), the evidence indicates Apostle Paul likely was executed for the sake of the Gospel under *Emperor Vespasian (69-79 AD)*, who, having had to fight for the Emperorship, may have, shortly after the destruction of Rome, executed Apostle Paul to please segments of Roman society who, otherwise, might have been rebellious. Given *Emperor Domitian (81-96 AD)* is, of the three Flavian Emperors, the emperor that is known for unwarranted cruelty, however, it is not impossible that Apostle Paul was executed in context of the reign of Emperor Domitian. Within this context, Apostle Paul would have been physically visiting local churches of interest, as such would not have had any need for writing of any new epistles; or perhaps it could be the case that those writings duplicate truths already enunciated in the other 14 Epistles, as such are, intentionally, not preserved for us by the grace of God.

Given almost all of the seven churches in Revelation Chapters 2 and 3 had something specific to which they had to attend, something that was in need of improvement, it perhaps is the case that the Church in Colossae had maintained it's spirituality, as such was not in need of a rebuke from our Lord and Savior Jesus Christ. Consistent with this possibility, COLOSSAE is ancient site of what would become the capital of the first Christian Civilization, the CHRISTIAN BYZANTINE CIVILIZATION, equivalently, EASTERN ROMAN EMPIRE founded by Emperor Constantine in *325 AD*. Modern day Turkey is founded on what used to be Constantinople. While the WESTERN ROMAN EMPIRE floundered in darkness of strife and war between *325 AD* and the invasion by Muslims of the Byzantine Empire between *673 & 726 AD*, the Byzantine Empire, which functioned on civil law founded on Christian principles, but which was secular in that so long as they were willing to abide by law and order, it welcomed all peoples, was a beacon of light, knowledge, and prosperity for the then known world (*HWE*, pgs. 164-165). Consider that historians agree that the Western Roman Empire crumbled no later than *467 AD* (*HWE*, pg. 137), meaning it collapsed prior to birth of Islam about *612 AD*. It is testament to strength of the Byzantine Empire that Constantinople was encircled by Muslim Jihadists for *10 years* (*716 to 726 AD*), yet the attack eventually was beaten back, and a truce reached in the 750s AD that lasted about 300 years (*HWE*, pgs. 165-166). During those years, the Byzantine Empire would remain strong, yet some chinks would begin to appear. Regardless, rejection of authority of papal Rome in *867 AD*, which was the spiritually right decision, for the body of Christ ultimately is responsible to Christ only, was an important milestone. With respect to milestones, the Council of Nicaea, which preserved the doctrine of God as Father, Son, and Holy Spirit was convened by Constantine in Constantinople in *325 AD*. During the eighth century, the Byzantine Church rejected statues of Christ as items of worship, but allowed religious drawings. Allowance of religious drawings, and too much of a focus on sacraments, liturgy, and symbolism ultimately would weaken spiritual strength of the Byzantine Church. Given the Byzantine Church was way healthier than it's Western Cousin, which was ruled over by papal Rome, however, much remained to be celebrated. In essence, from institution of the first Pope in *590 AD* to the sacking of Constantinople by the Turks in *1453 AD*, only the Byzantine Church could be considered truly Christian. The Church Body in the former Western Empire was no more than it's backslidden cousin. In wake of the demise of the Roman Empire, in the desire to maintain worldly pomp and splendor, the

Church in the former Western Empire deliberately embraced dilution of the Good News of our Lord Jesus Christ.

Love of Truth 14 *If you place* LOVE OF MONEY *or* POLITICAL RELEVANCE *ahead of* LOVE FOR CHRIST, *and demonstration of the Love of Christ, it is guaranteed that your Love for Christ will falter (Luke 16:13), such that, absent repentance and reformation, you lose all of the love that you genuinely had in your heart for Christ.*

Historical Spiritual Nugget 1 *Emperor Constantine established Constantinople, and the Christian Byzantine Civilization primarily because Rome would not abandon it's pantheon of idols. Having converted to Christianity in 312 BC, Emperor Constantine sought a fresh start that would be characterized by civil laws and societal interactions that are founded on the* 'LOVE OF GOD'.

Prophecy Principle 19 *Establishment of Constantinople by Emperor Constantine was fulfillment of prophecy in the Book of Revelation. Evidence for this assertion to follow, albeit, not immediately.*

While historians assume Constantine established Constantinople for his own hubris or sinful pride, the evidence clearly disagrees, for regents who act in sinful pride do not care much for people over whom they rule. Historians agree, however, that people who, at that time could be referred to as 'PEASANTS' did not have it better in any part of the world than they had it in the immediacy of Constantinople. In this respect, for much of the history of the Byzantine Empire, land farmed by peasants were directly owned by the Emperor, and could not be bought at any price by anyone else (*HWE*, pg. 168). In return, whenever necessary, peasants sent a family member to fight in the Emperor's wars. In ancient times, typically this meant no more than one man of fighting age - father or son - from each household. Since peacefulness of the society in those times required maintenance of an army, this was not oppression, this reasonably was the best deal for peasants; under the specified deal, they got to keep 100 percent of whatever they produced off of their land. This was better than FEUDALISM that was practice of Western Europe, a system within which peasants kept only a proportion - certainly less than 50 percent - of whatever they produced off of their land, and yet could be forced into military service by any of rich barons or lords who owned their lands.

Historical Spiritual Nugget 2 *If a pudding tastes great and nourishes the body, it only could have been prepared with good ingredients.*

Historical Spiritual Nugget 3 *If Emperor Constantine cared about the common people, ensuring laws were put in place for protection of their welfare, he could not simultaneously have established Constantinople out of personal hubris.*

So then, are the seven churches merely about that time, or also about some progression in time?

Consistent with some other interpretations of the Book of Revelation, I believe the Churches are prophetic about time. I provide, however, an important new spiritual insight, which is, there exists an important spiritual difference between the time of the first six churches - EPHESUS, SMYRNA, PERGAMUM, THYATIRA, SARDIS, & PHILADELPHIA, and the time spanned by the Church in LAODICEA. More about this, later on in this chapter. First, however, I delineate spiritual importance of focus of our Lord Jesus Christ on Churches that are located in Asia. In this respect, I provide a reminder that the BYZANTINE (CHRISTIAN) EMPIRE, equivalently, the *Eastern Roman Empire*, which had Constantinople as it's capital, was located in Asia, and plays a part in timeline of the seven churches.

The Seven Churches: Why Asia?

Let us backtrack somewhat to the ministry of our Lord and Savior Jesus Christ. Our Lord Jesus Christ declared that He was sent only to the lost house of Israel (Matthew 15:24), that it would be His disciples who would carry the gospel to the rest of the world (Matthew 28:18-20). So then, until persecution forced the disciples out of Jerusalem, who then went everywhere spreading the fragrance that is the gospel (good news) of our Lord and Savior Jesus Christ, the gospel was preached first to the Jews. In spirit of spreading of the gospel to the rest of the world, twice Apostle Paul desired to preach the gospel in Asia, but initially he was forbidden of the Holy Spirit (Acts 16:6). Eventually, he would preach the gospel in Ephesus with much success, yet in context of great opposition. In this respect, Apostle Paul declares in 1Corinthians 16:8-9; 15:32, and Luke the Physician asserts in Acts 19:10.

> But I will stay in Ephesus until Pentecost, for a wide door for effective work has opened to me, and there are many adversaries.

> What do I gain if, humanly speaking, I fought with wild beasts at Ephesus? If the dead are not raised, "Let us eat and drink, for tomorrow we die."

> This continued for two years, so that all the residents of Asia heard the word of the Lord, both Jews and Greeks.

Why was Apostle Paul so desirous of preaching the gospel in Asia?

You might not be aware of this, but many groups in Asia are descendants of Abraham. You see, subsequent to passing of Sarah, Abraham married another wife, by name Keturah (Genesis 25:1), and in addition, had concubines

(Genesis 25:6). Abraham had six additional children with Keturah, and additional children via his concubines. Given the promise from The Father was to Isaac alone, Abraham sent all of his other children EASTWARD, that is, towards ASIA, away from Isaac. While we do not have a record of modern day descendants of Abraham, clearly many groups in Asia are descendants of Abraham. So then, Apostle Paul was eager to preach the gospel in Asia, to descendants of Abraham. Until the Jews, as a group of people, chose to reject the gospel, however, the Holy Spirit would not allow Apostle Paul to preach the gospel in Asia. In this respect, we have the following words in Acts 18:5-6.

> When Silas and Timothy arrived in Macedonia, Paul was occupied with preaching, testifying to the Jews that the Christ was Jesus. And when they opposed and reviled him, he shook out his garments and said to them, "YOUR BLOOD BE UPON YOUR HEADS! I am innocent. FROM NOW ON I WILL GO TO THE GENTILES."

Almost immediately after this declaration by Apostle Paul, the Holy Spirit allowed Apollos to preach the gospel in Ephesus eloquently (Acts 18:24-25). Apollos was helped by Aquila and Priscilla (Acts 18:26-28), and shortly was joined by Apostle Paul himself (Acts 19:1), who would end up spending two years in Ephesus (Acts 19:1-10).

Prophecy Insight 9 *Once the Jews, as a collective, rejected the gospel, The Father turned His attention to preaching of the gospel to the other biological descendants of Abraham. The Father would provide these other biological descendants of Abraham opportunity to become proponents of the gospel of our Lord Jesus Christ. Asia would have opportunity to be a sort of spiritual capital for the Christian Church.*

Prophecy Insight 10 *In the establishment of Constantinople as capital of the Christian Church by Constantine the Great in 325 AD, The Father, Son, and Holy Spirit provided the other biological descendants of Abraham with the opportunity to become part of the foundation of the Christian Church.*

Why would The Father Provide Asia with such an Opportunity?

In so far as spiritual rights are concerned, The Father having characterized Himself as the God of Abraham, Isaac, and Jacob (Exodus 3:16), within context of nations or tribes on the earth, the Jews are the firstborn of The Father. This is evident in the fact that, in so far as earthly lineage is concerned, Jesus was a Jew, a descendant of Abraham, Isaac, and Jacob (*Matthew Ch. 1*). Until they officially opposed preaching of the gospel by Apostle Paul, note 'OPPOSED PREACHING OF THE GOSPEL', not 'REFUSED TO BELIEVE', the Jews enjoyed spiritual preference with The Father. In this respect, consider the following Scripture.

And concerning the rising again of the dead, did ye not read that which was spoken to you by God, saying, "I AM THE GOD OF ABRAHAM, AND THE GOD OF ISAAC, AND THE GOD OF JACOB?" God is not a God of dead men, but of living (Matthew 22:31-33).

And Abraham saith unto God, O that Ishmael may live before Thee; and God saith, Sarah thy wife is certainly bearing a son to thee, and thou hast called his name Isaac, and I HAVE ESTAB-LISHED MY COVENANT WITH HIM, FOR A COVENANT AGE-DURING, to his seed after him. As to Ishmael, I have heard thee; lo, I have blessed him, and made him fruitful, and multiplied him, very ex-ceedingly; twelve princes doth he beget, and I have made him be-come a great nation; and MY COVENANT I ESTABLISH WITH ISAAC, whom Sarah doth bear to thee at this appointed time in the next year (Genesis 17:18-21).

Once the Jews, as a collective, opposed preaching of the gospel, they lost their right of priority, equivalently, the right of the first born with God. Next in line, however, for consideration as anchors for preaching of the gospel would not be the Gentiles, but rather all of the other children of Abraham, who as we already have discussed were sent by Abraham towards Asia. So then, once the Jews opposed preaching of the gospel, which primarily had been focused on them, the door was thrown wide open for preaching of the gospel to all men. Priority of consideration as anchors would fall, however, on other descendants of Abraham. As we shall see, the other descendants of Abraham, and the Gentiles all would go on to fail as anchors for preaching of the Gospel, with outcome preaching of the Gospel would become anchored on spiritual presence of our Lord Jesus Christ on this earth.

Prophecy Interpretation 2 *Whatever biological preferences existed in con-text of dichotomy of genealogy that subsists between the Jews, other descen-dants of Abraham, and Gentiles all now are obviated.* CHRIST IS ALL, AND IN ALL *(Colossians 3:11). While this truth was a spiritual reality at timing of it's penning by Apostle Paul prior to 100 AD, it would take The Father, Son, and Holy Spirit until the time of the Church in Laodicea (timing to be discovered later on in this chapter) to fully establish spiritual reality of* 'CHRIST IS ALL, AND IN ALL' *for your benefit and mine.*

Why necessity of time for arrival at full spiritual reality of 'Christ is all, and in all?'

Well, friend, much as politicians hate to lose power, neither of the Jews, nor the other descendants of Abraham, nor some specific groupings of Gentiles were willing to give up their preferential spiritual rights without a fight. For destruction of all resistance, The Father, Son, and Holy Spirit demonstrated that each of these groups of people were no better than any other group of people on face of the earth. In this respect, consider the following words by Apostle Paul who, himself, as a Roman citizen, 'learned person' - essentially a holder of a PhD, and Pharisee was, prior to his conversion, a member of the preferred class.

> For consider your call, brethren; not many of you were wise according to worldly standards, not many were powerful, not many were of noble birth; but GOD CHOSE WHAT IS FOOLISH IN THE WORLD TO SHAME THE WISE, God chose what is weak in the world to shame the strong, God chose what is low and despised in the world, even things that are not, to bring to nothing the things that are, SO THAT NO HUMAN BEING MIGHT BOAST IN THE PRESENCE OF GOD (1Corinthians 1:26-29).

> He is the source of your life in Christ Jesus, whom God made our wisdom, our righteousness and sanctification and redemption; therefore, as it is written, "LET HIM WHO BOASTS, BOAST OF THE LORD (1Corinthians 1:30-31)."

Necessity of Grand Judgments 3 *For destruction of all resistance, The Father, Son, and Holy Spirit demonstrated that infilling of the Holy Spirit, which is a meritocracy, can produce believers who are more meritorious than either of descendants of Abraham, or Gentiles, such as Greeks or Romans who considered themselves a preferred class.*

> "How could man choose to resist The Father, Son, and Holy Spirit, you perhaps wonder?"

Well then, consider that with perfect knowledge that God exists, and is his creator, that the *'adversary'* (*YLT*), or *Satan* (*other translations*), who also is known as *the 'devil'* (John 13:27; Revelation 2:9; Revelation 12:9; 20:2), who himself had stood in presence of God as a COVERING CHERUB, chose to rebel against The Father (Ezekiel 28:14-15). How much more men who always can come up with excuses as to rationales for their resistance to The Father?

THE MOST FAVORED EXCUSE?

> We are not convinced that this is the real truth. How do we know this is the real truth?

WHEN A PERSON WHO FEELS THAT HIS OR HER PREFERENTIAL STATUS IS STRIPPED, EVINCES DOUBTS ABOUT TRUTH, THERE EXISTS A HIGH LIKELIHOOD THAT HE OR SHE MERELY 'REACTS' WITH THE EMOTIONS, THAT HE OR SHE DOES NOT 'RESPOND' WITH HIS OR HER INTELLIGENCE.

Necessity of Grand Judgments 4 *So then, The Father, Son, and Holy Spirit take up the fight, demonstrate that there no longer are any spiritually preferred classes on face of the earth, declare that relationship with God is equitable to all, and that closeness to God is outcome of a meritocracy, outcome of qualification for infilling of the Holy Spirit, equivalently, qualification for infilling of the Love of God.*

The Scriptural Evidence that while salvation and access to the Holy Spirit is offered freely by God, that infilling of the Holy Spirit is predicated on merit?

> And this having said, He breathed on them, and saith to them, RECEIVE THE HOLY SPIRIT (John 20:22).

> Then opened He up their understanding to understand the Writings, and He said to them - thus it had been written, and thus it was behoving the Christ to suffer, and to rise out of the dead the third day, and reformation and remission of sins to be proclaimed in His name to all the nations, beginning from Jerusalem: and ye - ye are witnesses of these things. And, lo, I do send the promise of my Father upon you, but ye - ABIDE YE IN THE CITY OF JERUSALEM TILL YE BE CLOTHED WITH POWER FROM ON HIGH (Luke 24:45-49).

> Therefore do not be unwise, but understand what the will of the Lord is. And do not be drunk with wine, in which is dissipation; but be filled with The Spirit (Ephesians 5:17-18).

In order for the disciples of our Lord Jesus Christ to receive baptism of the Holy Spirit, they had to obey the Lord Jesus Christ, had to, absent knowledge of exactly how long, commit themselves to waiting in Jerusalem. The command from our Lord Jesus Christ was to ensure that upon receipt of the Holy Spirit at Pentecost, they would be in a position to preach to large crowds of Jews that were gathered from around the world for celebration of Jewish feasts. Qualification for a filling, as opposed to a receiving of the Holy Spirit then, always has been predicated on obedience to our Lord Jesus Christ. In this respect, Ephesians 5:17-18 links the doing of the will of The Father, and infilling of The Holy Spirit.

Spiritual Insight 17 THE INFILLING OF THE HOLY SPIRIT IS THE NEW SPIRITUAL MERITOCRACY. *The will of The Father is that we love one another with the Love of our Lord Jesus Christ (John 13:34-35). ROMANS 5:5 explicitly declares that it is through the Holy Spirit that we receive the LOVE OF GOD. Since Love does not do any harm to a neighbor (Romans 13:10), and gives glory to God, that is, actively demonstrates love towards neighbors (Galatians 6:10), a meritocracy that is grounded in infilling of the Holy Spirit never can devolve* *into oppression, always maintains equality of all before God, always main-tains,* CHRIST IS ALL, AND IN ALL *(Colossians 3:11). Within context of infilling of the Holy Spirit, the most meritorious become leaders and examples (1Peter 5:3), not rulers or masters, and are honored for their loving leadership (1Peter 5:17).*

FOR A MORE DETAILED DISCUSSION OF THE INTERRELATIONSHIP BETWEEN EQUALITY OF CHRISTIANS, MERITOCRACY OF INFILLING OF THE HOLY SPIRIT, SANCTIFICATION, AND THE DEMAND OF LOVE FROM THOSE WHO HAVE FAITH IN THE NAME OF JESUS CHRIST, CHECK OUT MY BOOK, 'TRUE SANCTIFICATION'.

A Foretaste of the Revelations to Follow

First, the spiritual evidence from the message to the seven churches. If you read the messages to the Churches in Ephesus, Smyrna, Pergamum, Thyatira, Sardis, and Philadelphia, the messages from our Lord Jesus Christ are directed in entirety to the messenger of that specific church, that is, to the spirit allowed to take up human form that is representative of that church. The evidence for spirits taking up human form? Well, first, evidence that the devil took up human form, then evidence from our Lord Jesus Christ, then the generic evidence.

> You are of your father the devil, and the desires of your father you want to do. He (*Cain*) was a murderer from the beginning, and does not stand in the truth, because there is not truth in him. When he speaks a lie, he speaks from his own resources, for he is a liar and the father of it (John 8:44).

> "How that God (*who is a Spirit, John 4:24*) was in Christ - a world reconciling to Himself, not reckoning to them their trespasses...(2Corinthians 5:19)."

> And the day is, that sons of God (*who also must be spirit*) come in to station themselves by Jehovah, and there doth come also the Adversary in their midst (Job 1:6).

> Seeing then, the children have partaken of flesh and blood (only spirits are not already flesh and blood), He Himself (JESUS) in like manner did take part of the same, that through death He might destroy him having the power of death - that is, the devil and might deliver those, whoever, with fear of death, throughout all their life, were subjects of bondage (Hebrews 2:14-15).

In all of the messages to the first six churches, admonitions from Jesus are directed at the entire church body, or segments that are teaching falsehoods and heresies, not at individuals. The message to the last Church,

LAODICEA deviates from this pattern. In the message to Laodicea, the admonition turns personal as follows in Revelation 3:20.

> Behold, I stand at the door and knock; IF ANY ONE HEARS MY VOICE AND OPENS THE DOOR, I will come in to him and eat with him, and he with me.

The key here is the terminology 'ANY ONE', and the invitation to non-intermediated spiritual fellowship with our Lord Jesus Christ. In these words, our Lord Jesus Christ declared that the gospel now no longer would have any physical headquarters or capital, or be administered by any messengers, that the gospel would become in entirety a spiritual matter of the heart, exactly as He had declared in John 4:24 that believers in His name would worship in spirit and in truth. Direction of His invitation to 'ANY ONE' reinforces the phrase "THAT WHOSOEVER BELIEVES IN HIM SHOULD NOT PERISH BUT HAVE EVERLASTING LIFE" *in John 3:16.*

Prophecy Insight 11 *Relative to the other six Churches, it is only in context of the message to the Church in Laodicea that individuals receive invitation to personal fellowship with our Lord Jesus Christ.*

Prophecy Interpretation 3 *The messages to the seven Churches unequivocally declare that the* PRESENCE OF CHRIST *arrived in context of the time spanned by the Church in Laodicea.*

> Does this then imply that prior to the time of the Church in Laodicea, that believers did not have fellowship with Christ?

Well, let us ask two interrelated questions, which are: IS THE HOLY SPIRIT GOD IN HIS VERY ESSENCE? and IS THE HOLY SPIRIT JESUS CHRIST?

The answers to these two questions are Yes, and No. Based on these answers, while the Holy Spirit brings to believers all of the essence of The Father, this does not, in of itself induce fellowship with either of The Father or The Son. So then, those who believed in Christ in the time of Apostle Paul could be filled with the Holy Spirit, yet not to be able to attain to fellowship with the Lord Jesus Christ. Given it was all who are filled with the Holy Spirit at that time that were unable to arrive at fellowship with Jesus Christ, this was not their fault, and there is not any partiality with God. For concreteness, I proffer a few Scriptural texts, which prove that to be filled with the Holy Spirit does not imply fellowship of Father and Son.

> Because three are who are testifying in the heaven, The Father, The Word, and The Holy Spirit, and these - the three - are one (1John 5:7).

One body and one Spirit, according also ye were called in one hope of your calling; one Lord, one faith, one baptism, one God and Father of all, who is over all, and through all, and in you all (Ephesians 4:4-6).

But I tell you the truth; it is better for you that I go away, for if I may not go away, the Comforter (Holy Spirit) will not come unto you, and if I go on, I will send Him to you (John 16:7).

However, when He, the Spirit of truth, has come, He will guide you into all truth; for He will not speak on His own authority, but whatever He hears He will speak; and He will tell you things to come. HE WILL GLORIFY ME, FOR HE WILL TAKE OF WHAT IS MINE AND DECLARE IT TO YOU. All things that The Father has are Mine. Therefore I said that He will take of Mine and declare it to you (John 16:13-14).

And the fruit of the Spirit is: Love, joy, peace, long-suffering (patience), kindness, goodness,, faith, meekness, temperance: against such there is no law (Galatians 5:22).

All things were delivered to me by my Father, and none doth know The Son, except The Father, nor doth any know The Father, except the Son, and he to whom The Son may wish to reveal Him (Matthew 11:27).

He who is having my commands, and is keeping them, that one it is who is loving me, and he who is loving me shall be loved by my Father, and I WILL LOVE HIM, AND WILL MANIFEST MYSELF TO HIM (John 14:21).

For through Him (*our Lord Jesus Christ*) we both (*Jew and Gentile*) have access by one Spirit to The Father (Ephesians 2:18).

And this is the life age-during, that they may know Thee, the only true God, and Him whom thou didst send - Jesus Christ (John 17:3).

✠ THE PRECEDING VERSES ESTABLISH THE FOLLOWING IMPORTANT, AND CRUCIAL POINTS.

♣ The *first three Scriptures* establish that while The Father, The Word (*who manifests as the Son of God*), and Holy Spirit are one in essence, that is, equal in essence, they are three separate individual entities, all of whom are Spirit. Importantly, all emanated out of The Father, with outcome there only is one God, and Father of us all. In human words and understanding, one can say that, much as a cell in the body '*self divides*', that is, *mestasizes* for replication of it's very self, The Father mestasized Himself, such that out of Himself came The Word, and out of The Word came The Holy Spirit. Since the mestasization must produce a replica, The Word also is God in essence, but not in priority. If The Father created all of life, as such ultimately is source of '*the cell*', clearly, The Father must have capacity for mestasization.

♣ In the very next Scripture (the 4th), The Lord Jesus Christ emphasizes that The Holy Spirit will receive from Him and give to us. So then, absent spiritual fellowship with Jesus Himself, we are able to attain to gifts that have been made possible for us by The Father and The Son. THIS IS AN EXTREMELY CRUCIAL POINT.

♣ The 5th Scripture lists the *fruit of The Spirit*. The Holy Spirit also brings to us *manifestations of the Spirit*. It is unequivocally implied, however, that the manifestations of The Spirit (1Corinthians 12:7-11) do not include all of the GIFTS from Jesus Christ (Ephesians 4:7-11), meaning some gifts are received only if a believer arrives at fellowship with Jesus Christ. This distinction again, is of extremely crucial importance. The gifts that only are received from our Lord Jesus Christ directly are the gifts of *Apostleship* (cf. Paul's introductions of himself in most of his Epistles); *Proclamation of Good News (Evangelism)*; the combo of *Sherpherd & Teacher*; and *Powers*. As you will discover later on in this book, responses of the Church to ministry of believers whom The Lord Jesus Christ attests as having these gifts serve as evidence for The Father's judgments as to willingness of the Church to be perfected in His Love. For a thorough discussion of manifestations of The Holy Spirit, and Gifts from our Lord Jesus Christ, see my book, 'TRUE SANCTIFICATION'.

♣ The 6th and 7th Scriptures declare that only The Father can authorize a revelation of His Son, and only The Son can usher a believer into the Presence of The Father. This establishes the spiritual reality that fellowship with The Holy Spirit is not tantamount to fellowship with Father and Son. The Holy Spirit brings to us the gifts of The Father and Son (*cf. Luke 11:13; Matthew 7:11*), but does not Himself reveal The Father and Son to us.

♣ The 8th Scripture declares that only those who are in the Holy Spirit are able to know Christ, and that only Christ provides access to The Father (John 14:6). This of course again, is an extremely crucial point, meaning only those who qualify, in context of their fellowship with The Holy Spirit are able, in the self same Holy Spirit, to arrive at knowledge of Christ, and The Father. One of the confusions of non-Christians is the assumption that when Jesus declares that He is the only way to The Father, that He speaks of salvation. In the declaration that He is the only way to The Father, in actuality, Jesus declares that, absent relationship with Him, none can arrive at experiential knowledge of The Father.

♣ The 9th Scripture rounds it out, declares that only those who qualify, in The Holy Spirit, who then arrive at fellowship with The Son, and The Father, who then receive revelations of The Son and The Father, as such arrive at experiential knowledge of The Son and The Father, arrive at life that is age during, at life that is eternal. These persons who arrive at life that is age-during are the ones to whom The Father entrusts any LOVE PROJECTS that He seeks to implement in cooperation with Civil Society. As you will discover later on in this book, responses of Civil Society to Love Projects that do not demand that they repose faith in Jesus Christ are, for good or evil, adapted to their judgment, and serve as evidence for The Father's responses to Civil Society or Government. For more on The Father's Love Projects, check out my book, 'TRUE SANCTIFICATION'.

Spiritual Insight 18 *Friend, the Scriptures declare that while the Holy Spirit is God in essence (1John 5:7), and while the Holy Spirit teaches you about Christ, and reproduces character of Christ in you, and brings to you gifts and manifestations from Christ, that for arrival at a personal revelation of Jesus Christ,* ONLY THE SON CAN INTRODUCE YOU TO HIMSELF, AND TO THE FATHER. *This work, revelations of The Son and The Father to those who, in the Holy Spirit qualify, The Father and our Lord Jesus Christ have reserved for themselves.*

Prophecy Insight 12 *In the Book of Revelation, our Lord Jesus Christ Himself declares that He did not commence the work of revealing Himself to men, and bringing men into knowledge of Himself and The Father until the time of the Church in Laodicea.*

What else is implied by arrival of the Presence of Christ in context of the time spanned by the Church in Laodicea?

In the revelations entrusted to Apostle John, our Lord Jesus Christ declared that whereas people had needed to hear the gospel from another person in order to arrive at faith in Him, commencing with the time of the Church in Laodicea, for those who are able to hear His voice, that is, those who have desire to know God, it would become possible that, absent any contact with any preacher of the gospel, that their hearts can be drawn to Christ. Not only this, subsequent to such persons being drawn to Christ, absent contact with any teachers or preachers, such persons who are drawn to Christ would be able to learn of Christ, and become like Christ, because Christ Himself would fellowship with them via agency of the Holy Spirit.

Prophecy Insight 13 *Apostle Paul is a type of all of those believers who, in context of arrival of the* PRESENCE OF CHRIST, *would have opportunity to be drawn to and taught directly by Christ.*

The Supporting Scriptural Evidence?

For there is no difference between Jew and Greek, for the same Lord of all is rich to all those calling upon Him, for every one - whoever shall call upon the name of the Lord, he shall be saved. How then shall they call upon Him in whom they did not believe? and how shall they believe on Him of whom they did not hear? AND HOW SHALL THEY HEAR APART FROM ONE PREACHING? and how shall they preach, if they may not be sent? according as it hath been written, "How beautiful the feet of those proclaiming good tidings of peace, of those proclaiming good tidings of the good things!" (Romans 10:12-15).

Having gone, then, disciple all the nations, (baptizing them - to the name of the Father, and of the Son, and of the Holy Spirit, teaching them to observe all, whatever I did command you), and lo, I am with you all the days - till the full end of the age (Matthew 28:19-20).

For I am not ashamed of the good news of the Christ, for it is the power of God to salvation to every one who is believing, both to Jew first, and to Greek (Romans 1:16).

And I, if I may be lifted up from the earth, WILL DRAW ALL MEN UNTO MYSELF (John 12:32).

For this is the covenant that I make, with the house of Israel, after those days, an affirmation of Jehovah, I have given my law in their inward part, and on their heart I do write it, and I have been to them for God, and they are to me for a people. AND THEY DO NOT TEACH ANY MORE EACH HIS NEIGHBOR, AND EACH HIS BROTHER, SAYING, 'KNOW YE JEHOVAH', FOR THEY ALL KNOW ME, from their least unto their greatest, an affirmation of Jehovah; For I pardon their iniquity, and of their sin I make mention no more (Jeremiah 31:33-34).

Which He wrought in Christ, having raised Him out of the dead, and did set Him at His right hand in the heavenly places, far above all principality, and authority, and might, and lordship, and every name named, NOT ONLY IN THIS AGE, BUT ALSO IN THE COMING ONE (Ephesians 1:20-21).

And He said to them, verily I say to you, that there is not one who left house, or parents, or brothers, or wife, or children, for the sake of the reign of God, who may not receive back manifold more in this time, and IN THE COMING AGE, LIFE AGE-DURING (Luke 18:29-30).

Friend, Apostle Paul, who himself is a type of those who receive revelation of the Person of Christ directly from the Spirit of our Lord Jesus Christ, declares that in context of his time, for arrival at faith, people needed to hear the preaching of the gospel. He declares then that the preaching of the gospel is the power of God unto salvation. Prophetically, however, our Lord Jesus Christ declares that absent a preacher, He will draw all men to Himself. The Father adds that all men will have opportunity to be taught directly by Himself, The Son, and The Holy Spirit. You see then that the age of Christ is divided into two - THE AGE OF THE PREACHING OF THE GOSPEL; and THE AGE OF THE PRESENCE OF CHRIST.

Prophecy Insight 14 *All those who were faithful in context of the age of the preaching of the gospel received eternal life in context of the age of the* PRESENCE OF CHRIST - *the age that was to come (Luke 18:29-30).*

By this, the Holy Spirit declares that if you are in fellowship with Christ, you simultaneously are in fellowship with the spirits of Apostles Paul, Peter, James, John, Abraham, Isaac, Jacob, and every believer who was faithful to Christ in context of the age of the preaching of the gospel.

The Supporting Evidence (a Scripture you already have seen)?

But, ye came to Mount Zion, and to a city of the living God, to the heavenly Jerusalem, and to myriads of messengers, to the company and assembly of the first-born in heaven enrolled, and to God the judge of all, AND TO SPIRITS OF RIGHTEOUS MEN MADE PERFECT, and to a mediator of a new covenant - Jesus, and to blood of sprinkling, speaking better things than that of Abel!

Presence is Spiritual 18 *The spirits of the apostles are spirits of just men made perfect. Given we are assembled with all of such spirits, without any conscious realization on our part, we may be receiving help from spirits of apostles. When you study the Scriptures, and suddenly arrive at an insight,* *perhaps one of Apostle Paul's Epistles, it just may be the spirit of Apostle Paul, the spirit that was there when the words were inspired by The Holy Spirit, who provides you with the much needed enlightenment.*

Prophecy Insight 15 *In light of Hebrews 12:22-24, Apostles Paul, Peter, James, John etc. all attained to eternal life on commencement of the age of the PRESENCE OF CHRIST. The age of the PRESENCE OF CHRIST (more evidence to follow) having arrived, you and I have opportunity to attain to eternal life while we are here on earth, for eternal life consists in fellowship with Father and Son that translates into knowledge of Father and Son (John 17:3).*

I have entered assertions about essence of the messages to the seven Churches, and provided some preliminary evidence for presence of some spiritual dichotomy between the first six Churches, and the last Church, the Church in Laodicea. On then now to, the detailed evidence for the assertions, and discussion of timelines and/or symbolisms embedded in messages to each of the seven Churches.

The Message to the Church in Ephesus

The Church in Ephesus was mature. In presence of their maturity, Apostle Paul could delve into matters that are 'meaty', as opposed to matters that, spiritually speaking, are for children. In this respect, let us juxtapose Apostle Paul's words to the Churches at Corinth and Ephesus.

In his writings to the Church in Corinth, Apostle Paul describes believers in the Church in Corinth as follows in 1Corinthians 1:4,7; 3:1-4; then describes those who are ready for 'meaty' teachings in Hebrews 5:13-14.

> I give thanks to God always for you because of the grace of God which was given you in Christ Jesus, so that YOU ARE NOT LACKING IN ANY SPIRITUAL GIFT, as you wait for the revealing of our Lord Jesus Christ.

> But, I brethren, could not address you as spiritual men, but as men of flesh, as BABES IN CHRIST. I FED YOU WITH MILK, NOT SOLID FOOD; for you were not ready for it; and even yet you are not ready, FOR YOU ARE STILL OF THE FLESH. For while there is jealousy and strife among you, are you not of the flesh and BEHAVING LIKE ORDINARY MEN? For when one says, "I BELONG TO PAUL," and another, "I BELONG TO APOLLOS," are you not merely men?

> For everyone who partakes only of milk is unskilled in the word of righteousness, for he is a babe. But solid food belongs to those who are of full age (TO THOSE WHO ARE SPIRITUAL, WHO ARE MATURE), that is, those who by reason of use have their senses exercised to discern both good and evil (*only those who care to discern*

the nature of their actions - good versus evil - become mature in Christ).

Clearly, while the Church in Corinth was richly blessed with spiritual gifts, it simultaneously was deficient in the LOVE OF GOD, in the LOVE OF CHRIST. Regardless then, of manifestations of the Holy Spirit, the Church in Corinth was full of babes in Christ, for to not realize superiority of Love as defining characteristic of faith in Christ, and to not seek to excel in Love is to be as a babe in Christ. It is for this reason that Apostle Paul engages in a rich discussion of spiritual gifts in 1Corinthians *ch. 12*, and concludes 1Corinthians *ch. 12*, and launches into 1Corinthians *ch. 13* as follows:

Are all apostles? Are all prophets? Are all teachers? Do all work miracles? Do all speak with tongues? Do all interpret? But earnestly desire the higher gift. AND I WILL SHOW YOU A STILL MORE EXCELLENT WAY (1Corinthians 12:29-31).

"If with the tongues of men and of messengers I speak, AND HAVE NOT LOVE, I HAVE BECOME BRASS SOUNDING, OR A CYMBAL TIN-KLING; and if I have prophecy, and know all secrets, and all the knowledge, and if I have faith, so as to move mountains, AND HAVE NOT LOVE, I AM NOTHING (*1Corithians 13:1-2*)..."

Spiritual Insight 19 *You can manifest spiritual gifts, such as speaking in tongues, or speaking a prophecy, or utterance of knowledge and wisdom, yet be no more than a babe in Christ.*

Spiritual Insight 20 *If you do not care to discern the true nature of your motives and actions - whether they are good (stem out of 'LOVE OF GOD' that creates healthy love for your self, with outcome you love your self as you are loved by God, and arrive at pure motives and loving actions in relation to others) or evil (whether they stem out of sinful pride, covetousness, envy, jealousy, rivalry, emulation etc., with outcome your love for your self is a function of what you see in others, or what others achieve), you are unable to arrive at maturity in Christ.*

Spiritual Insight 21 *It is the* LOVE OF CHRIST *that defines a person as having the* SPIRIT OF CHRIST. *Jesus declared this clearly when He said, "By this, all men will know that you are my disciples, if you have Love one for another (John 13:35)."*

What then about the Church in Ephesus?

Blessed is the God and Father of our Lord Jesus Christ, who did bless us in every spiritual blessing in the heavenly places in Christ, according as He did choose us in him before the foundation of the world, FOR OUR BEING HOLY AND UNBLEMISHED BEFORE HIM, IN LOVE.

Because of this I also, HAVING HEARD OF YOUR FAITH IN THE LORD JESUS, AND THE LOVE TO ALL THE SAINTS, do not cease giving thanks for you, making mention of you in my prayers, that the God of our Lord Jesus Christ, the Father of glory, may give to you a spirit of wisdom and revelation in the recognition of Him.

It is straightforwardly clear from the immediately preceding verses that the disciples in Ephesus understood the 'MEAT' of the gospel, understood that love is essence of the gospel. So then, their faith was evident in their love. Love was not abstract, love was evident in midst of the believers in Ephesus. Yet also they had the spiritual gifts. But they understood that walking in love was more important than a desire for manifestation of spiritual gifts. Rationality of superiority of love as evidence for knowledge of Christ is straightforwardly evident in the fact that while love that is sincere always is representative of Christ, people have been known to fake gifts of healings. Where gifts of healing have been genuine, they have been known to be demonstrated out of hubris of self aggrandizement, that is, out of sinful pride, as opposed to out of love for Christ.

Prophecy Insight 16 *Prior to passing on of Apostle Paul to glory, the Church in Ephesus was a model of the Love of God.*

Spiritual Insight 22 *Apostle Paul declares that only those whose faith already work by love (Galatians 5:6) are able to receive a spirit of wisdom and revelation in the recognition of The Lord Jesus Christ.*

With the foregoing in mind, you are able to better appreciate the judgment of our Lord Jesus Christ in the following words recorded in Revelation 2:4-5.

BUT I HAVE THIS AGAINST YOU, THAT YOU HAVE ABANDONED THE LOVE YOU HAD AT FIRST. Remember then from what you have fallen, repent and do the works you did at first. If not, I will come to you and remove your lampstand from it's place, unless you repent.

For understanding of importance and context of the warning from our Lord Jesus Christ that He would "*remove the lampstand of the Church in Ephesus from it's place*", consider where Jesus stands while He speaks with Apostle John in Revelation 1:20; 2:1.

The secret of the seven stars that thou hast seen upon my right hand, and the seven golden lamp-stands: the seven stars are messengers of the seven assemblies, and THE SEVEN LAMP-STANDS THAT THOU HAST SEEN ARE SEVEN ASSEMBLIES.

To the messenger of the Ephesian assembly write: These things saith He who is holding the seven stars in His right hand, WHO IS WALKING IN THE MIDST OF THE SEVEN LAMP-STANDS - the golden.

Prophecy Interpretation 4 *Friend, Jesus warned the Church in Ephesus that if it did not reform, He would no longer walk in the midst of it. By this, Jesus warned the assembly in Ephesus that consequences of disobedience would be withdrawal of the Holy Spirit from the Church.*

Prophecy Interpretation 5 *In the message to the Church in Ephesus, which, for a specific period of time, is representative of the Church in Asia, our Lord Jesus Christ provides warning that He can withdraw His Spirit from the Church.*

The Time Element of the Church in Ephesus

For an arrival at an understanding of the time element, it is important to enumerate all that remained right within the Church in Ephesus, namely (Revelation 2:2-3, 6):

✠ Good Works.

✠ Good Labor that is not wearied.

✠ Endurance.

✠ Non-tolerance for evil persons - for persons who do not have faith (2Thessalonians 3:2), that is, persons who refuse to believe that all men, male or female are created in the image of God, as such are deserving of love.

✠ Showing up of fake claims to apostleship for what they truly are, falsehoods.

✠ Hatred for the works of the Nicolaitans, for which Christ also has hatred.

It is clear that there was much that remained good within the Church in Ephesus. Given demonstrations of the LOVE OF GOD are the most excellent virtue of discipleship to Christ, however, what had become lacking, LOVE, was primary in it's essence.

For timing of the transition from the Church in Ephesus to the next Church, the *Church in Smyrna*, we rely on a specific prediction concerning the *Church in Smyrna* that identifies timing of transition of the CHURCH IN EPHESUS to the *Church in Smyrna*. This is satisfaction of the principle that is referred to in Mathematics as *Backward Induction Compatibility (BIC)*. In so far as it relates to establishment of timelines, BIC demands that the end date for a preceding Church coincide with the beginning date for the immediately sequel Church. The only robust approach to inferring the end date for a preceding Church then, is identification of the beginning date for the Church that is immediately sequel.

Prophecy Principle 20 *In what follows, for identification of the end date for a preceding Church, we first infer the beginning date for the immediately sequel Church. This is application of the Mathematical principle of* BACKWARD INDUCTION COMPATIBILITY (BIC).

In Revelation 2:10, persecution that subsists for 10 days against the disciples of Christ is prophesied by our Lord Jesus Christ. The prophecy principle for interpretation of *'lengths of day that pertain to affairs of man'* is 'A DAY FOR A YEAR' (Numbers 14:34; Ezekiel 4:6). This means the Church in Smyrna would experience persecution for 10 *years* in man's time. It is important to note here that 'A DAY OF JESUS CHRIST', equivalently, 'A DAY WITH THE LORD', which can be a thousand years (2Peter 3:8) refers to affairs that are God's not man's. So, when affairs pertain, in entirety, to man, a prophetic day is equivalent to a year of time. When there is reference to God's agenda, as to a day of Jesus Christ, a day is as a thousand years. It is important to keep this distinction in perspective.

Prophecy Principle 21 *In the application of revelations provided by The Father, Son, and Holy Spirit in the Old Testament, or books of the New Testament, other than the Book of Revelation, for interpretation of prophecies entrusted to Apostle John, we arrive at an important feature of predictions that have robustness, which is, there exist inputs outside of the predictions, such as the* 'A DAY FOR A YEAR' *principle, that subsist independent of the predictions, but yet are necessary for understanding of the predictions.*

Prophecy Principle 22 *Interpretation of prophecies entrusted to Apostle John require inputs from other Books of the Bible, with outcome the Book of Revelation serves as an augmentation of all of the Literature (other Books) that preceded it. We see then that The Father, Son, and Holy Spirit are Mathematicians, ensure that there are assumptions necessary for interpretation that are not within control of the prophecies or the prophet.* IN MATHEMATICS, THIS IS REFERRED TO AS A MODEL THAT DOES NOT ASSUME IT'S INTENDED OBJECTIVE.

The fulfillment of the prophecy?

In *303 AD*, Emperor Diocletian (*284 to 305 AD*) of Rome outlawed Christianity by royal edict (*HWE*, pg. 136). Diocletian went on to die in *305 AD*, resulting in a struggle for emperorship of Rome between Licinius, co-emperor of Rome with CONSTANTINE THE GREAT, Emperor of Rome (*306 to 337 AD*). While Licinius continued to persecute Christians under the edict enacted by Diocletian, in *312 AD*, Constantine the Great converted to Christianity and began to fight for protection of Christians. By *324 AD*, Licinius had been executed, and Constantine became sole emperor over all of Rome. In 324 AD, Constantine issued an edict affirming that no one was to be persecuted for not wanting to become a Christian. Christians were to tolerate non-Christians, not persecute them as they had suffered under Diocletian and Licinius.

Prophetic Lessons 2 *Wherever there truly is The Spirit of Christ in rulers, there is tolerance for all faiths. Intolerance only is demonstrated in response to evil, and love for doing of evil to fellow man.*

> From Diocletian's edict in 303 to conversion of Constantine the Great to Christianity in 312 AD is exactly 10 years. Since the persecution would transpire subsequent to commencement of time of the Church in Smyrna, timing of commencement of the Church must precede 303 AD. It is safe then to place commencement of the time of the Church in Smyrna at commencement of the reign of Diocletian, which is, 284 AD.

Prophecy Insight 17 *Given the Church in Smyrna is the only Church not having any defect of any kind, it must have been the faithfulness of the Church in Smyrna that induced persecution from Diocletian. We have then that righteousness of the Church in Smyrna must have angered Diocletian himself. It is safe then to place ending of the time of the Church in Ephesus, and commencement of timing of the Church in Smyrna at about 284 AD. We know for a fact, however, that the time of the Church in Smyrna commenced no later than 302 AD.*

The Promise to those in any of the assemblies who respond rightly to chastisement of our Lord Jesus Christ, who overcome desires of the flesh, sin, the world, evil persons, and the devil?

> He who is having an ear - let him hear what the Spirit saith to the assemblies: To him who is overcoming - I will give to him to eat of the tree of life that is in the midst of the paradise of God (Revelation 2:7).

Prophecy Principle 23 *The timeline of the* CHURCH IN EPHESUS *is from time of Apostle John (about 100 AD) to no later than 302 AD, but yet could have ended by 284 AD.*

The Lesson for us today?

Prophetic Lessons 3 *If you seek to eat of the tree of life that is in the midst of the paradise of God, you must aspire to, and arrive at capacity for demonstration of the Love of God in every facet of your life on earth - at home, at work, to neighbors, to fellow believers, in context of physical assemblies of God's people for spiritual fellowship, and at play.*

The Message to the Church in Smyrna

Glory to our Lord Jesus Christ. In the message to the CHURCH IN SMYRNA (Revelation 2:8-11), our Lord Jesus Christ does not reveal any weaknesses or sins, of which the Church was in need of repentance. Consistent with preceding assertions then, persecution that is endured by the Church in Smyrna is outcome of faithfulness of the Church to Christ. For the persecution to come, which already we have discussed, however, there is provision of encouragement.

The Most Important Insight?

In absence of any weaknesses or sins within the Church in Smyrna, our Lord Jesus Christ reveals that the *Church in Ephesus*, which is, the immediately preceding Church, repented of it's sins, regained it's first Love. The Church in Smyrna then was a purified version of the Church in Ephesus, which perhaps explains onset of persecution by Emperor Diocletian.

The Timeline for the Church in Smyrna?

For arrival at the timeline for the CHURCH IN SMYRNA, we again turn to discussion of the next Church, the *Church in Pergamum*. In Revelation 2:13, concerning the *Church in Pergamum*, our Lord Jesus Christ declares:

> I have known thy works, and where thou dost dwell - where the throne of the Adversary is - and thou dost hold fast my name, and thou didst not deny my faith, even in the days in which Antipas was my faithful witness, who was put to death beside you, where the Adversary doth dwell.

We know from Ezekiel 28:11-19, that the king of Tyre was representative of the devil, meaning the devil, who has made himself an adversary to those who have faith in Jesus Christ, has his spiritual capital in the region of Tyre, which is located in Asia. We have then that, spiritually speaking, the Church in Pergamum is located in the heart of Asia. Given the Church in Smyrna was persecuted by Diocletian, while the Church in Smyrna physically was located in Asia, it's spiritual influence resided primarily within the heart of the Roman Empire, that is, in Western Europe; hence, onset of persecution from Emperor Diocletian. In this respect, it is unlikely that persecution arrives on basis of spiritual influence in regions of Asia, a region to which Emperorship of Rome was, to a large extent, inured. Given Constantine the Great established CONSTANTINOPLE in Asia as capital of a Christian Empire in 325 AD, with outcome the spiritual influence of the Church shifted from Western Europe to Asia, we have that the time of the CHURCH IN SMYRNA is relatively short, does not extend beyond 324 AD. We also arrive at the inference that the time of the CHURCH IN PERGAMUM commenced 325 AD.

Prophecy Principle 24 *The timeline of the Church in Smyrna is 284 (or no later than 302) to 324 AD.*

The Lesson for us today?

Prophetic Lessons 4 *It is a good thing to find God's people through the ages responding to loving chastisement of our Lord Jesus Christ for arrival at true repentance, revival, and reformation. Without reformation of the* CHURCH IN EPHESUS, *the* CHURCH IN SMYRNA, *the immediately sequel Church, could not have been found to be faithful to our Lord Jesus Christ.*

Prophetic Lessons 5 *Our Lord Jesus Christ encourages you to be faithful unto death, to not allow persecution derail your faith, for only those who are faithful unto death attain to the crown of life, only they are not hurt by the second death (Matthew 10:39; 16:25).*

The Message to the Church in Pergamum

As we already have inferred, the time of the CHURCH IN PERGAMUM began in 325 AD with merging of Church and State in founding of *Constantinople* as capital of the CHRISTIAN BYZANTINE EMPIRE. A matching of the historical records to warnings and admonitions proffered by our Lord Jesus Christ implies the Church in Pergamum lasted until the eighth century AD, that is, until sometime after the invasion, and stalemating of the invasion by Islam, an invasion that lasted from about *673 to 726 AD*.

Sometime in the 750s AD, controversy rocked the Church in Byzantium in the sense of rightness of worship of images that are crafted out of wood (*HWE*, pg. 167), stone, metal etc., worship, which The Father declares to be idolatry. Worship of spiritual images is idolatry because our Lord Jesus Christ is image of the invisible God, The Father. Simultaneously, those of us who repose faith in Christ are the image of Christ (Colossians 1:12-15). If those of us who have faith in Jesus Christ are the image of Christ, how can it be right that, simultaneously we make drawings or images of Christ, or any other person and bow to such images? When we refuse to acknowledge that we are the image of Christ, and begin to adore paintings and sculptures that attempt to represent Christ, we degrade the image of Christ in us, engage in idolatry.

The spiritual support in the Scriptures (Colossians 1:12-15; Galatians 4:19; Romans 8:29)?

Giving thanks to the Father who did make us meet (qualify us) for the participation of the inheritance of the saints in the light, who did rescue us out of the authority of the darkness, and did translate us into the reign of the Son of His love, in whom we have the redemption through his blood, the forgiveness of the sins, WHO IS THE IMAGE OF THE INVISIBLE GOD, FIRST-BORN OF ALL CREATION.

My little children, with whom I am again in travail UNTIL CHRIST BE FORMED IN YOU!

Because whom He did foreknow, He also did foreappoint, CONFORMED TO THE IMAGE OF HIS SON, that He might be first-born among many brethren.

Where there is not Greek and Jew, circumcision and uncircumcision, foreigner, Scythian, servant, freeman - but the all and in all - Christ (Colossians 3:11).

Spiritual Insight 23 *If we are representatives of Christ to the world, with outcome Christ is in us, is formed in us, with outcome we acquire the glory of Christ (2Thessalonians 2:14), it is impossible that it can be right that we make drawings and statues of Christ, and bow to them.*

The Timeline for the Church in Pergamum?

In Revelation 2:14-15, our Lord Jesus Christ lists weaknesses and sins of the CHURCH IN PERGAMUM as whoredom (*sex with several different partners*), idol-sacrifices (*sacrifices to idols*), and holding to the teaching of the Nicolaitans. In presence of evidence for a fight against idolatry in the 750s AD within the Christian Byzantine Empire, which was located in Asia, it would seem that the Church in Pergamum lasted at the very least until the latter part of the eighth century AD.

Using the words of our Lord Jesus Christ that are directed to the next Church, the *Church in Thyatira*, and the historical facts, we are able to confirm that the time of the Church in Pergamum lasted until about 1095 AD. This is evident as follows. In the message to the *Church in Thyatira*, which still is located where the Adversary dwells (Revelation 2:24), that is, in Asia, our Lord Jesus Christ is not happy that the Church in Thyatira tolerates the woman Jezebel as a teacher, a teacher who leads believers astray to whoredom and eating of idol-sacrifices (Revelation 2:20-23). It is apparent from adoption of the word, 'TOLERATE' as relationship between the CHURCH IN THYATIRA and JEZEBEL that Jezebel is, in reality, not part of the Church in Thyatira, is an external influence that is tolerated by the Church. In 1095 AD, in spite of the decision to reject authority of papal Rome over Churches located within the Christian Byzantine Empire, the Emperor of the Christian Byzantine Empire requested help from papal Rome against Muslim hordes who were being restless in the extremes of the Empire. By this time, worship of religious images already was in full swing within enclaves of Papal Rome, with outcome that whereas such worship had been banned within the Byzantine Empire in the 750s AD, it now would be reintroduced by the guests who had been invited in to provide military help for the Byzantine Empire. We conclude then that the Church in Pergamum commenced in 325 AD and ended sometime prior to 1095 AD. The discussion to follow of the timeline for the CHURCH IN THYATIRA, which will require discussion of the timeline for the immediately sequel church, the Church in Sardis, will establish the end of the time of the CHURCH IN THYATIRA to be about 1055 AD.

Prophecy Principle 25 *The timeline of the Church in Pergamum is 325 to 1055 AD.*

Was the Church in Pergamum Truly a Christian Empire?

With the Church in Pergamum lasting for about 730 years, that is, from *325 to 1055 AD*, if the Byzantine Empire truly was a Christian Empire, what evidence is there in support of the belief that the Byzantine Empire functioned on Christian principles? In this respect, consider the following quotes from page 168 of *HWE*.

> "The economic strength of the Byzantine Empire rested, first, upon the *maintenance of a free peasantry* who worked imperial lands in return for military service."

> "EVERY EFFORT WAS MADE TO PROTECT THE FREE SMALL FARMER, the backbone of armed service. Governors of themes were forbidden to own lands within their jurisdiction or to marry into local families. Imperial laws attempted to prevent the purchase of land by wealthy land owners."

> "No aspect of Byzantium's life better illustrates the wealth of the Empire than the public architecture of the city of Constantinople. The great church of St. Sophia, erected by Justinian between *532 and 537 AD*, remains a world landmark."

Prophecy Principle 26 *The most important characteristic of a Christian Empire is protection of the weak from aggression and exploitation, and provision of opportunity for self actualization. When such are in place, beauty of architecture attests to presence of skills endowed by The Father in response to civil laws that are righteous, both in their motives, and in their implementation.*

Prophecy Principle 27 *Note that at timing of completion of the edifice for honor of The Father that is christened, the* CHURCH OF ST. SOPHIA, *there did not exist any other organized religion in competition with Christianity - Islam would not emerge as a system of beliefs until, at the very least, 612 AD, that is, for another 75 years. It is normative then, that the desire to glorify Christ in the erection of the beautiful edifice that is the* CHURCH OF ST. SOPHIA *cannot be attributed to a spirit of competition with any other organized form of religion.*

The Lesson for us today?

In Revelation 2:16, our Lord Jesus Christ declares that if those in the CHURCH IN PERGAMUM who are caught up in idolatry, whoredom, and teaching of the Nicolaitans do not reform, He would come and fight against them. So long as the messenger to the CHURCH IN PERGAMUM did his part, warned the believers in question about their behavior, there would not be any adverse consequences for the faithful in the CHURCH IN PERGAMUM.

Prophecy Insight 18 *When leaders of the Church are faithful to their calling, that is, are good examples to the rest of the Church; are leaders who reward actions and attitudes that are loving, good, and righteous; are leaders who declare evil to be what it really is, that is, evil; and leaders who correct, reprimand, and punish evil in the sense of not rewarding those who love evil with rewards that ought to be reserved for those who are loving, good, and righteous, or who make every effort to exclude those who are evil from the assembly, leaders and those who are faithful in the Church never are punished by our Lord Jesus Christ for perversions of those who profess the name of Christ, but who yet choose and love evil.*

The qualities of the messenger, and the faithful believers in the Church in Pergamum, which secured this mercy from The Lord Jesus Christ?

✠ Good works

✠ Holding fast to the name of Jesus Christ

✠ Not denying the faith of Jesus Christ

✠ Loving Jesus to the death

The promise of our Lord Jesus Christ to those who overcome (Revelation 2:17)?

> He who is having an ear - let him hear what the Spirit saith to the assemblies: To him who is overcoming, I will give to him to eat from the hidden manna, and will give to him a white stone, and upon the stone a new name written, that no one knew except him who is receiving it.

Prophecy Interpretation 6 *If you seek to be considered faithful to Jesus, you will not abandon your faith, merely because your neighbor had to give his or her life for the sake of the name of Jesus Christ. You recognize that sometimes the blood of martyrs is seed for the victory to be won for good of the faith, for good of the next generation, and for redounding of praise to the glory of our Lord and Savior Jesus Christ.*

Prophetic Lessons 6 *Whenever, as is evident in our values, decisions, and actions, the Love of God is restored in our spirits and it leads to persecution, we are to rejoice in the salvation of our Lord and Savior Jesus Christ, for the persecution will serve to usher in the glory of our Lord Jesus Christ. The persecution of the* CHURCH IN SMYRNA *led to the birth of the* CHURCH IN PERGAMUM, *a Church that continued to walk in the Love of Christ.*

The Message to the Church in Thyatira

As already highlighted in course of the discussion of the message to the *Church in Pergamum*, the time of the CHURCH IN THYATIRA commenced no later than 1095 AD. The signature event? The Emperor of the Byzantine Empire requested for help from papal Rome, this subsequent to dissociation of the Byzantine Church from papal Rome in 867 AD. The rationale for the request? After 300 years of somewhat peaceful cohabitation with Muslims on outskirts of it's borders, The Emperor feared Muslims were getting skittish, did not think Constantinople and the Byzantine Empire could handle yet another invasion by Islamic Jihadists.

In 1096, crusaders began arriving within the Byzantine Empire. The crusade was successful, resulted in recapture of Jerusalem in 1099. Consider, however, that in the decision to recapture Jerusalem from Muslims, contrary to Scriptures, and as already elucidated, the Church declared the earthly Jerusalem to have spiritual relevance for the Christian faith. In the declaration of Jerusalem to have spiritual, as opposed to mere historical significance for Christians, out of fear, the Byzantine Church arrived at an error, arrived at a partnership with a cousin Church, which itself, in *867 AD*, had declared to be apostate. So then, what happened, the Byzantine Empire had to cede some territory to people from it's cousin Church, who then naturally brought along with them their devotion to worship of images, their devotion to idolatry. Here then was source of chagrin of our Lord Jesus Christ, that is, whereas the Byzantine Church did not itself teach idolatry, by virtue of it's partnership with the papal Church, it now did not have any other choice, but to tolerate teaching of idolatry within it's domain. Consistent with elucidated history, whenever Scriptures use a woman as a type, righteous or evil, a woman always signifies a Church. We see then that the Church in Thyatira, equivalently, The Byzantine Church is chastised for allowing another Church, papal Rome to begin teaching of idolatry within it's domains. We find then fulfillment of the words of our Lord Jesus Christ that while the CHURCH IN THYATIRA did not itself teach idolatry, it would begin to tolerate a teacher of idolatry, namely papal Rome.

Prophecy Interpretation 7 *In the decision to partner with it's cousin Church out of fear, a cousin Church, which it already had recognized to be apostate, The* CHURCH IN THYATIRA *had to tolerate teaching of idolatry by it's cousin Church, papal Rome. Combined, characterization of the* CHURCH IN THYATIRA *by our Lord Jesus Christ, and the historical evidence enable establishment of a timeline for the* CHURCH IN THYATIRA.

Consistent with bringing in of 'unChristlike' behaviors into it's domain, some of the peoples in the countryside of the Byzantine Empire were alienated by behaviors of crusaders who were wont to take supplies from the people by force (*HWE*, pg. 205). The tolerance for idolatry would go on to induce whoredom and a spirit of partying, which, as we well know, go hand-in-hand (1Corinthians 10:7-8).

> Friend, wherever there is idolatry there always is debauchery and whoredom (sexual immorality). The two are inextricably linked together.

Prophecy Insight 19 *It is unambiguously clear that the* CHURCH IN THYATIRA *is the Church in existence between 1095 and 1099 AD, the years during which the Byzantine Empire hosted help from papal Rome for recapture of Jerusalem from Muslims in context of the First Crusade.*

In the overextending of itself for establishment of the kingdom of Jerusalem in *1099 AD* with help of papal Rome, the Byzantine Empire had, in an institutional sense alienated our Lord Jesus Christ. Rather than henceforth fighting for preservation of a Christian Empire, the *second* and *third* crusades would be about recapture of the earthly Jerusalem. Attention had shifted from building a Christian Empire to rivalry with Islam over Jersalem and Palestine.

> Why are rivalries unspiritual, and for those who seek to live righteously by faith in Jesus Christ, not rational?

Spiritual Insight 24 *Whenever a person engages in a rivalry, his or her objectives no longer are guided by Father, Son, and Holy Spirit, but by actions of another human being.* IN CONTEXT OF A RIVALRY, THE GOAL IS ONE-UPPING OF ONE ANOTHER, *exactly what would transpire in relations between Christianity and Islam in context of wars for control of Jerusalem. We find then that engagement in a rivalry induces a person who believes in Jesus Christ to, rather subconsciously, become an idolater.*

Spiritual Insight 25 *It cannot be rational to confess Jesus as Lord, yet have objectives of life be induced by a fellow human being.*

Concerning rivalries, placing of trust in man, as opposed to The Father, and necessity of placing of trust in The Father, consider the following words in James 3:14-16; Galatians 5:19-21; and Jeremiah 17:5-6; 7-8.

> And if bitter zeal ye have, and RIVALRY in your heart, glory not, nor lie against the truth; this wisdom is not descending from above, but earthly, physical, demon-like, FOR WHERE ZEAL AND RIVALRY ARE, THERE IS INSURRECTION AND EVERY EVIL MATTER.

> And manifest also are the works of the flesh, which are: Adultery, whoredom, uncleanness, lasciviousness, idolatry, witchcraft, hatred, STRIFES, emulations, wraths, RIVALRIES, dissensions, sects, envyings, murders, drunkennesses, revellings, and such like, of which I tell you before, as I also said before, that those doing such things the reign of God shall not inherit.

> Thus says the Lord: "Cursed is the man who trusts in man and makes flesh his arm, whose heart turns away from the Lord (*who deviates to doing of evil for arrival at any sort of prosperity*). He is like a shrub in the desert, and shall not see any good come. He shall dwell in the parched places of the wilderness, in an uninhabited salt land."

> "Blessed is the man who trusts in the Lord, whose trust is the Lord (*who, whenever there are challenges in course of living of life, will not deviate to doing of evil, as such continues in doing of good while waiting and seeking for resolution of challenges*). He is like a tree planted by water, that sends out it's roots by the stream, and does not fear when heat comes, for it's leaves remain green, and is not anxious in the year of drought, for it does not cease to bear fruit."

Islam attempted to turn Christianity into a rival, and, rather than trusting in Jesus Christ and avoiding a rivalry, the Emperor of the Byzantine

Empire trusted in man, engaged in a rivalry. The Byzantine Empire never was an oppressor of Arabs, had done nothing to induce aggression of Islam towards the Byzantine Empire. Remember that with Constantinople established in 325 AD, and Islam formulated between 612 and 615 AD, Constantinople could not have been established in context of a defeat of Muslims.

Historical Spiritual Nugget 4 *At timing of establishment of Constantinople, and for close to 300 years subsequently, Islam did not exist.*

But the spirit of those times was '*take as much as you can*' not for peace or prosperity, but merely for self aggrandizement. While the Byzantine Empire had for the most part been righteous in it's own expansion decisions, it also had made mistakes in context of expansion for the sake of self aggrandizement. Note, however, that as already highlighted, the Byzantine Empire did not oppress people within it's enclaves. Relative to it's resources, however, it attempted to overexpand, resulting in exhaustion of it's military forces. The decision to extend the Empire in a self aggrandizing manner resulted in a departure from protection of land that was being farmed by the free small farmer, a protection, which ensured that the rich did not end up owning just about all of the available land. In this respect, consider a related historical narrative in *HWE*, pg. 168.

> "The trend toward privatization of land and military predominance had begun under the previous dynasty when the emperor had given out immense lands to local magnates in exchange for military support. These grants, known as *pronoia*, were at first not supposed to be hereditary possessions, but in time they became so and took on a nature similar to the fief in western European feudalism."

Consistent with the implication that the Byzantine Empire had begun to lose it's way in a spiritual sense at timing of request for assistance from papal Rome in 1095 AD, consider the following words about that time in *HWE*, pg. 168.

> "It was at this dark moment that the Empire was saved through the leadership of Alexius Commenus, a military figure who seized Constantinople and set himself up as Emperor in 1081 AD."

> "Alexius was a representative of the locally powerful military aristocracy that had recently begun to appear within the empire. His seizure of power marked the domination over the state by the new aristocracy and led to the gradual eclipse of the imperial bureaucracy and of the civil and military institutions by which

the Macedonian emperors had exerted centralized control. Under Alexius and his successors, the accumulation of lands and serfs, and the formation of private armies by local men of influence, went unchecked. WITH THE WEAKENING OF CENTRAL CONTROL AND THE GROWTH OF THE LOCAL MAGNATES, A SOCIETY THAT IN STRUCTURE RESEMBLED THE FEUDALISM OF EUROPE AND JAPAN AROSE."

Prophecy Insight 20 *We previously have established, in context of discussions that relative to the* CHURCH IN PERGAMUM, *that the* CHURCH IN THYATIRA *commenced no later than 1095 AD.*

Prophecy Insight 21 *Given the previous dynasty that induced departures from protections for the free farmer had commenced in 1056 AD, and given the Byzantine Empire's focus on self aggrandized expansion began to suffer setbacks in 1071 AD (HWE, pg. 168), the year 1056 AD is a safe choice for commencement of the time of the* CHURCH IN THYATIRA.

Prophecy Insight 22 *Applying* BIC, *the time of the Church in Pergamum ended about 1055 AD.*

For arrival at timing of the end of the time of the CHURCH IN THYATIRA, as already established, we apply BIC, as such, peruse the message of our Lord Jesus Christ to the *Church in Sardis*. In the message to the Church in Sardis, in addition to the seven stars (seven messengers), our Lord Jesus Christ also is having the seven spirits of God (Revelation 3:1). In the message to the Church in Sardis, the Lord Jesus Christ declares that whereas the Church has a name that it is alive, it in reality is dead. The Lord Jesus Christ provides the Church, however, with an opportunity to repent, else whatever seemed to remain alive also would die (Revelation 3:2-3). Given the Church in the Western Roman Empire, the papal Church already was considered to be dead, as such never was discussed, the Church in Sardis remains located in Asia. Two events enable establishment of timing of commencement of the Church in Sardis. First, consequent on overthrow of the Byzantine Empire by Ottoman Turks, The Church in Asia died in 1454 AD. We have then that the Church in Sardis did not reform, as such died. The warning event that preceded eventual death of the Church in Asia, the event that was supposed to sensitize the Church in Sardis to her true condition was sacking of Constantinople in 1204 AD by Crusaders, who, in context of a Fourth Crusade for Jerusalem, abandoned that objective, and rather sacked Constantinople itself. That Crusade commenced in 1203 AD. In presence of confluence of words of our Lord Jesus Christ, and the historical evidence, it is clear that, by 1204 AD, the time of the Church in Sardis already had commenced. Opportunity presented for reformation of the Church in Sardis is evident in the historical fact that Constantinople was recaptured by the

Greeks in 1261 AD. Given the Greeks were not part of papal Rome, practiced what is referred to as an Orthodox Christianity, the Church in Sardis had opportunity, once again to regain its' spiritual footing in Jesus Christ. The historical evidence indicates this opportunity did not materialize, this likely because the Greek Orthodox Church had, itself devolved into celebration of symbolisms, as opposed to celebration of Christ Himself.

Prophecy Insight 23 *The year 1202 AD is the latest possible date for timing of cessation of the time of the* CHURCH IN THYATIRA.

The weakness of 1202 AD as timing of cessation of the time of the CHURCH IN THYATIRA resides in absence of statement of any defining events. With respect to the timeline for the Churches in Ephesus and Smyrna, we had the 10-year persecution under Emperor Diocletian as marker for establishment of timelines. With respect to the timeline for the Churches in Smyrna and Pergamum, we had location of the Church in Asia for guidance. For arrival at a timeline for the Churches in Pergamum and Thyatira, we had the alliance between the Byzantine and papal Churches for guidance that enables establishment of the timeline. In absence of any specific events that transpire in context of timeline for the Church in Sardis, however, there does not exist any event for inferring of timing of commencement of the Church in Sardis, an event that naturally coincides with cessation of the Church in Thyatira.

For a stab at rigorous establishment of a timeline, with extension of the BIC principle to the sixth Church, the Church in Philadelphia, I check for presence of any defining event. Providentially, and as would be expected of a Lord and Savior who seeks for the prophecy to be understood, there exists a defining event that transpired in context of timeline for the Church in Philadelphia. In Revelation 3:10, our Lord Jesus Christ prophecies an hour of trial to come upon the world in context of the timeline for the Church in Philadelphia. Using the 'a day for a year' principle, an hour of prophetic time translates into 5 months of calendar time.

In 1203 AD, the fourth crusade massed for emancipation of Jerusalem from Islam. In January of 1204 AD, the crusade changed course, decided to attack Constantinople, the very city that had requested for help from the Crusaders, that is, from enclaves ruled over by Papal Rome. By May of 1204 AD, Constantinople had fallen and been subjected to looting by the crusaders.

Historical Spiritual Nugget 5 *From January to May of 1204 AD is exactly 5 months of calendar time.*

Why did the Crusade change course?

Historical Spiritual Nugget 6 *I am convinced in my spirit that papal Rome decided to sacrifice the Byzantine Empire for it's very own safety. By weakening the defenses of Constantinople, and showing how Constantinople could be overthrown, the Crusaders prepared the ground for eventual sacking of Constantinople by Ottoman Turks in 1453 AD. By ceding the Byzantine Empire to Ottoman Turks, who did not have any religion of their own (HWE, pgs. 178-179), but who increasingly were being assimilated into Islam, papal Rome increased it's chances for stemming onslaught of Islam into Western Europe. In this respect, prior to being beaten back, note that Islamic Jihad progressed as far as some regions of Spain (HWE, pg. 183).*

We have then that within 110 years of the request for help from papal Rome, militaries who owed allegiance to papal Rome had turned on the Byzantine Empire, would sack and pillage their Christian cousin, Constantinople. The warning given by The Father in Jeremiah 17:5-6 that it is not wise to place trust in man, in the sense of doing of things that are wrong - engaging in a rivalry with Islam, a rivalry that required partnership with a self acknowledged apostate cousin - had come to pass.

Spiritual Insight 26 *If you seek the help of our Lord Jesus Christ, do not do what you already know to be wrong in order to avert trouble. Trust in The Lord and Savior Jesus Christ.*

Given the Fourth Crusade commenced 1203 AD, and given the time of the Church in Philadelphia had to have commenced prior to 1203 AD, we have that the time of the Church in Sardis ended prior to 1203 AD. The latest date then for cessation of the time of the Church in Sardis is 1202 AD. By BIC, clearly, the timing of cessation of the Church in Thyatira, which must coincide with timing of commencement of the Church in Sardis precedes 1202 AD. The declaration that the Church in Sardis appears to be alive, but in actual fact is dead implies material prosperity that is not accompanied by spiritual prosperity. Given the material prosperity from success of the First Crusade lasted from 1099 AD through 1187 AD, which is timing of recapture of Jerusalem by Muslims, the year, 1100 AD can be deduced to be timing of commencement of the Church in Sardis. We have then that the time of the Church in Thyatira had to have ended with capture of Jerusalem from the Muslims in 1099 AD.

Prophecy Insight 24 *The timeline of the Church in Thyatira is 1056 to 1099 AD.*

Spiritual Insight 27 *It is a godly thing to ask for righteous help (help that consists of righteous actions from a helper) from someone you believe can be of help to you. But if the Holy Spirit resists your willingness to ask for help from a particular source, be wise enough to desist, be wise enough to wait for The Father to provide the help that you need.*

The Lesson for us today from the message to the Church in Thyatira?

What are the things that the Church in Thyatira got so right (Revelation 2:19), such that our Lord Jesus Christ would not judge the Church as a whole, would judge only those who adhered to idols or practiced sexual immorality directly (Revelation 2:21-23)? In this respect, consider the words of our Lord Jesus Christ to the faithful in Revelation 2:24-25.

> And to you I say (the messenger to the Church in Thyatira), and to the rest who are in Thyatira, as many as have not this teaching (*idolatry, whoredom, and the teachings of Jezebel*), and who did not know the depths of the Adversary (*who did not like Solomon seek to experience evil to the fullest extent possible*), as they say; I will not put upon you other burden; but that which ye have - hold ye, till I may come.

> What are these things the faithful were supposed to hold fast to until Jesus may come?

✠ Good works

✠ Love

✠ Ministrations to the saints and to the world in general in context of the preaching of the gospel

✠ Faith of Jesus

✠ Endurance

✠ Works that at the end are greater than at the first

In presence of the six attributes listed, our Lord Jesus Christ declares that He will not include the righteous in the judgment of those who are evil within Churches that purportedly bear His name and are supposed to bring Him glory. Note that those who are being judged, and those who are exonerated from judgement all belong to the same Church body, the CHURCH IN THYATIRA.

Prophecy Interpretation 8 *If you seek to be excluded from judgment of evil doers, if you seek to be judged on your own merit, as opposed to being lumped with evil doers, our Lord Jesus Christ has enumerated the sorts of qualities to which you need to attain.*

The promises from our Lord Jesus Christ, which, as is evident in Revelation 2:29, you will do well to note are addressed to all believers (all Churches)?

And he who is overcoming, and who is keeping unto the end my works, I will give to him authority over the nations, and he shall rule them with a rod of iron - as the vessels of the potter they shall be broken - as I also have received from my Father; and I will give to him the morning star. He who is having an ear - let him hear what the Spirit saith to the assemblies (Revelation 2:26-29).

The Message to the Church in Sardis

As already discussed, while the Church in Sardis seemed to be alive, meaning it was materially prosperous, it simultaneously was deficient in spiritual prosperity. So then, the Lord Jesus Christ commands the Church to reform, else whatever seemed to remain alive soon would die. In the preceding discussion, we established that the Church in Sardis remained from capture of Jerusalem from the Muslims in 1099 AD to recapture of Jerusalem by Muslims in 1187 AD.

Prophecy Principle 28 *The timeline of the Church in Sardis is 1100 to 1187 AD.*

When our Lord Jesus Christ made a cameo, appeared to Joshua, who was Commander of the hosts of Israel at timing of invasion of the promised land by God's people, Joshua asked,

ARE YOU FOR US OR FOR OUR ADVERSARIES?

to which our Lord Jesus Christ replies:

"No, but as Commander of the army of the Lord I have now come (Joshua 5:14)."

Prophecy Insight 25 *The Love agenda that was the Byzantine or Christian Empire demonstrated to the whole world that our Lord Jesus Christ does not engage in rivalries with other faiths. Since Christians lost some battles, and Muslims lost some battles, each at different points in time, neither could claim that it was fighting for God. After all, by definition, God would win every single time.*

Prophecy Insight 26 *The Father fights for glorification of good, and destruction of evil. Sometimes, He demands that His Generals, such as Apostles* PETER, PAUL, *and* JAMES *lay their lives down so as to provide blood seed for the fight. Sometimes He raises up a* CONSTANTINE THE GREAT *to destroy the evildoers. In the sense that The Father can demand a sacrifice from you in the fight for triumph of good over evil, The Father does not necessarily fight for any one person, entity, or country. But if, like Joshua you are on the side of righteousness, you can be sure that whatever The Father asks of you is what is good for you, is what He will accomplish in you, through you, and for you.*

Have you ever heard of an Overarching General or Commander who won a war without a single loss of life?

In His message to the Church in Sardis, our Lord Jesus Christ declares
that,

> And to the messenger of the assembly (Church) in Sardis write:
> These things saith He who is having the Seven Spirits of God,
> and the seven stars: I have known thy works, and that thou hast
> a name that thou dost live, and thou art dead; thou hast a few
> names in Sardis who did not defile their garments, and they shall
> walk with me in white, because they are worthy (Revelation 3:1,
> 4).

Prophecy Insight 27 *If, in midst of a decadent, dead Church you are faithful
to Christ, the Lord Jesus Christ declares that you will be judged on basis of
your faithfulness, on basis of your worthiness.*

The Lesson for us today?

Consider this, that our Lord Jesus Christ declares, you can be WORTHY
to walk with Him. He further declares in Revelation 3:5 that if you continue
to overcome, He will confess your name before His Father and before His
messengers. So then, if you will not allow yourself to be swayed by the
times, if you will not drift with the crowd, as such no longer pay attention to
the directives of your Lord and Savior, if you will stay the course with Jesus
Christ and not deny the faith, The Father and His messengers will know
your name, and you, much like the 144,000 of Revelation 7:1-10 will walk
with Christ. Apostle Paul frames this as follows in Galatians 4:9,

> "BUT NOW THAT YOU HAVE COME TO KNOW GOD, OR RATHER TO BE
> KNOWN BY GOD..."

An important condition to be fulfilled (*for an exposition of rationality of the
words by Jesus to follow*, check out CHAPTER 16 of my book, 'True Sanctification')?

> He who is loving father or mother above me, is not worthy of
> me, and he who is loving son or daughter above me is not worthy
> of me (Matthew 10:37).

Friend, it is a glorious thing to get to know God. Yet, it is even more
glorious to be known by God, and that by name.

The Message to the Church in Philadelphia

In the discussion of the message to the *Church in Sardis*, we arrived at the inference that the time of the CHURCH IN PHILADELPHIA commenced in 1188 AD, the year of commencement of the Fourth Christian Crusade for emancipation of Jerusalem, but which would turn about for focus on sacking of Constantinople. We further established that the five months spoken of by our Lord Jesus Christ pertain to the five months during which Constantinople was attacked then sacked by the crusaders, who consisted largely of French, German, Venetian, and Flemish forces (*HWE*, pg. 169).

> But if the five months pertain only to the Byzantine Empire, how it is that they represent a time of trial that is about to come upon all the world, a time 'to try' those dwelling upon the earth?

> The key here is the declaration that the time of trial comes 'to try' those dwelling upon the earth.

THE SCRIPTURE VERSE?

> Because thou didst keep the word of my endurance, I also will keep thee from the HOUR OF THE TRIAL that is about to come upon all the world, 'TO TRY' those dwelling upon the earth (Revelation 3:10)

Prophecy Principle 29 *The term 'to try' means to, on basis of their responses to an event, or events, induce a revelation of the state of people's hearts, that is, attitudes towards God, this so The Father can demonstrate justice of a grand judgment to be imposed on the people.*

Whenever The Father seeks to arrive at a grand judgment of people, one important avenue via which He produces evidence not for Himself, but for all of the spiritual realm so the justice of His character is evident, is to judge actions that are directed at a person or a group of people who, themselves are faithful to Jesus Christ. Since faithfulness to Jesus Christ implies walking in love towards all men, particularly fellow believers in Christ, in the direction of hatred towards such persons or groups by people who they have loved, The Father acquires evidence that shuts the mouths of those who seek to foster injustice in this world. I have rigorously developed and elaborated on this principle in *Chapter 2* of my book, 'True Sanctification'.

Necessity of Grand Judgments 5 *It is an established spiritual principle that The Father uses evil targeted at those who are faithful to Jesus Christ as evidence for what is in the heart of 'OTHER GROUPS' of people. These other groups of people can be either of 'Pretense Christians', or 'Non-Christians'. In* *the repayment of evil from such* OTHER GROUPS *for love that they received from those who have faith in Jesus Christ. The Father demonstrates evil inherent in the hearts of such* OTHER GROUPS.

Supporting Scriptural evidence?

"I the Lord search the mind and try the heart, to give every man according to his ways, according to the fruit of his doings (Jeremiah 17:10)."

And you shall remember all the way which the Lord your God has led you these forty years in the wilderness, that he might humble you, testing you to know what was in your heart, whether you would keep His commandments, or not (Deuteronomy 8:2).

Prophecy Insight 28 *In the demise of faith in Jesus Christ that transpired in Asia subsequent to 1453 AD, The Father demonstrated that Abraham's other biological children did not inherit with Isaac because He The Father knew they would not as a people embrace the gospel of Jesus Christ. By this declaration, if Jesus had conducted His three and a half years of ministry in Asia, He would not have found 12 men (with Apostle Paul as substitute for Judas Iscariot) that could change the world.*

Prophecy Insight 29 *Consider that Christians in Western Europe endured persecution from the papal Church from about 1500 AD through 1775 AD, yet the faith survived. We have fulfilled then the prophecy in Genesis 9:27 that, spiritually speaking, the descendants of Japheth (*THE FATHER OF WESTERN EUROPEANS*) will dwell in the tents (*THE FAITH ENTRUSTED BY THE FATHER*) to descendants of Shem (*FATHER OF THE JEWS*). Given descendants of Ham have been rescued from the curse in Genesis 9:27 that they will be servants to the descendants of Japheth, this by the sacrifice made by the only begotten Son of God (Galatians 3:13-14) - the same sacrifice that enables descendants of Japheth dwell in the tents of Shem - whoever seeks to act on that curse will lose every spiritual blessing and reality that accrues from all that Jesus has done for all of mankind.*

Historical Spiritual Nugget 7 *The then known civilized world consisted primarily of Western Europe and Asia. It is normatively and objectively true that as at 1203 AD, America had yet to be discovered. The contiguous land mass that is the United States of America was discovered in 1457 AD by John Cabot.*

We have then that the five months did not portend trouble for the whole world, rather would reveal the state of the hearts of men in all the world towards The Father and the Lord Jesus Christ. Since the events brought some hardship into the lives of people within the Byzantine Empire, the events served for trying of the hearts of people who lived outside of the Byzantine Empire. If people OUTSIDE OF THE BYZANTINE EMPIRE would rejoice on hearing what had transpired, their reaction would judge them, would reveal their hearts. If people's hearts were pained that such a travesty could occur, their reaction also would judge them, would reveal the state of their hearts towards The Father.

Prophecy Principle 30 *When the entire church (the Church in Philadelphia) has only a little power, yet is faithful to The Father (Revelation 3:8), it's love and actions already are laid bare before The Father, The Son, The Holy Spirit, The Father's messengers, and all of the spiritual hosts of the universe. In presence of the evidence, there is not any demand for a grand judgment of that Church. The Church is spared an event that tries the hearts of those who profess faith in the name of Jesus Christ (Revelation 3:10).*

Prophecy Principle 31 *When the church is not faithful to Christ (e.g. the Church in Sardis), there can be demand for a grand judgment (Revelation 3:3). So then, when the Church is not united in it's faithfulness to The Father, the Church is judged in context of grand judgments, but those already known to be faithful walk with Christ (Revelation 3:4).*

Events that transpired subsequent to the sacking of Constantinople by those who ought to be it's friends, suggests that the world outside of the Byzantine Empire did not fare very well in respect of whatever was revealed about the state of their hearts towards The Father. As you will discover in CHAPTER 9, whenever nations fail a grand judgment, meaning they choose hatred over love as rubric for life, The Father declares that they always will turn the hatred on one another. In this respect, consider the following quotes from *HWE*, the history text I have adopted as reference text. I note here that the year 1204 AD belongs to the thirteenth century.

> "At then end of the thirteenth century France and England were at war, and military costs rose sharply as the scale and scope of war increased (*HWE*, pg. 213)."

> "By 1300 AD, however, universal monarchy was an impossible dream. Papal success in reducing the empire had been all but complete, and national monarchies, long devoted to the consolidation of their power, had begun to grow strong and independent. With the assertion and expansion of royal authority came the concomitant needs for new sources of revenue and a wider tax base - NEEDS THAT INEVITABLY LED TO CONFLICT BETWEEN THE MONARCHIES AND THE PAPACY (*HWE*, pg. 213)."

"In 1295 AD the monarchs of both France and England demanded clerical subsidies to finance the war. Pope Boniface VIII resisted the levies, and in the following year promulgated the bull *Clericis Laicos*, decreeing excommunication to any who taxed the church or who paid such taxes (*HWE*, pg. 213)."

"Faced with the concerted opposition of the two most powerful monarchs of the west, Boniface was forced to retreat, seeking to placate the kings by permitting taxation of the clergy 'in times of great stress' and, incidentally, by canonizing King Louis IX in 1297 (*HWE*, pg. 213)."

"In 1302, where angry Flemish townsmen slew thousands of French nobles, that Philip's power was ebbing, Boniface issued the bull '*Unam Sanctam*'. Here the pope declared that it was necessary for the temporal authority to be subject to the spiritual authority and that every human being to be saved must be subject to the Roman Pontiff (*HWE*, pg. 214)."

"In 1307 the king ordered the arrest of all the Templars in France and charged them with acts against God and sordid sexual abuses. Imprisonment torture and the execution of several score of their number at the stake elicited confessions from the survivors (*HWE*, pg. 214)."

It is clear from the quotes that, subsequent to sacking of Constantinople, an event that was carried out primarily by French, German, Venetian, and Flemish forces who had implicit blessing of papal Rome, that trouble between kings of these countries, and between papal Rome and the kings, and between the kings, the papacy, and the soldiers who were agents for sacking of Constantinople became order of the day. With respect to the plights of the Templars, note that French Templars were instrumental to, played a key part in the sacking of Constantinople in 1204 AD (*HWE*, pg. 169). Now their own king, and papal Rome were punishing them for their sins. We see then that, consistent with The Father's declaration, whenever a group of people choose hatred against another group who is not doing to them any evil, they eventually begin to hate and fight one another.

Necessity of Grand Judgments 6 *Whenever The Father tests the nations for arrival at grand judgments, He does not ask whether they pray to Him;* RATHER HE ASKS WHETHER THEY REWARD LOVE WITH LOVE. *Whenever there is evidence that, on a grand scale, they reward love with hatred, they fail the test and eventually turn their hatreds on one another. Why is this guaranteed to occur? Because justice demands that The Father lifts His protections over such nations, such that they arrive under the influence of the devil.*

With the glory of the Byzantine Empire now eclipsed, divisions between papal Rome and kings became even more visible. In this respect, note that the foremost theologian of the day, *Thomas Aquinas* (*died*, 1274 AD) had emphasized importance of faith for knowledge of divine law, with outcome each man was responsible to God in context of his own faith, and in context of moral laws instituted by man that are in consonance with divine law. Faith, however, was to be derived from, and augmented with reasoning, with outcome every living soul ought to exercise faith only if he or she, on basis of reasonings, arrives at faith. While the church is a guardian of Christian faith, given each man is a 'living soul', the church could not declare that man ought to obey without faith. It is straightforward to see from bulls issued by papal Rome that the papal Church explicitly violated terms of Christian faith, attempted to assume the place of Christ and the Holy Spirit in lives of believers. Given only our Lord Jesus Christ is Head of the Church (Ephesians 5:23; Colossians 2:19), and given all who are in Christ are equal (Colossians 3:11), no believer - Apostle, Teacher, Prophet or otherwise, has the right to impose himself or herself on any other believer. For a more elaborate elucidation of absence of any hierarchy in context of the body of Christ, check out *Chapter 18* of my book, True Sanctification.

Historical Spiritual Nugget 8 *In presence of righteous teachings on part of Thomas Aquinas, who himself was a Monk in one of the orders of the papal Church, the papal Church continued on in it's apostasy from teachings of our Lord and Savior Jesus Christ, asserted that it had the right to impose doctrines on fellow believers.*

It is unequivocally clear in Christian Scriptures that both reasoning and faith are part of our life in Christ; that The Father expects believers to apply their reasoning to their interactions with Him.

> COME, I PRAY YOU, AND WE REASON, SAITH JEHOVAH, if your sins are as scarlet, as snow they shall be white, if they are red as crimson, as wool they shall be! If ye are willing, and have hearkened, the good of the land ye consume (Isaiah 1:18-19).

> And Jesus having known their reasonings, answering, said unto them, "WHAT REASON YE IN YOUR HEARTS (Luke 5:22)."

> And Paul having remained yet a good many days, having taken leave of the brethren, was sailing to Syria - and with him are Priscilla and Aquila - having shorn his head in Cenchera, for he had a vow, and he came down to Ephesus, and did leave them there, and HE HIMSELF HAVING ENTERED INTO THE SYNAGOGUE DID REASON WITH THE JEWS (Acts 18:18-19).

But sanctify the Lord God in your hearts, and ALWAYS BE READY TO GIVE A DEFENSE TO EVERYONE WHO ASKS YOU A REASON FOR THE HOPE THAT IS IN YOU, with meekness and fear (actually means, with meekness - absence of pride - towards another, and reverence for The Father) - 1Peter 3:15.

The goodness of reason and knowledge teach me, for in thy commands I have believed (Psalms 119:66).

Whatever does not proceed out of faith is sin (Romans 14:23).

And THE RIGHTEOUS (JUST) BY FAITH SHALL LIVE, and if he may draw back, my soul hath no pleasure in him, and we are not of those drawing back to destruction, but of those BELIEVING TO A PRESERVING OF SOUL (Hebrews 10:38-39).

And this is His command, that we may believe in the name of His Son Jesus Christ, and may love one another, even as He did give command to us (1John 3:23).

The spiritual man judges all things, but (*in matters that solely pertain to conduct of his or her life, not matters of morality*) is himself to be judged by no one. "For who has known the mind of the Lord so as to instruct him?" But we have the mind of Christ (1Corinthians 2:15-16).

"Brethren, if any man is overtaken in a trespass (*if any man is caught up in moral sin*), you who are spiritual should restore him in a spirit of gentleness...(Galatians 6:1)."

Spiritual Insight 28 *Any Church, which demands obedience by force from those who have faith in Jesus Christ is an apostate Church. Even to the unsaved, The Father declares, 'Whosoever is willing' (Revelation 22:17), or 'Whosoever believes' (John 3:16). This also is the standard in Church.* THE CHURCH IS TO TEACH, NOT COERCE, OR COMPEL.

Spiritual Insight 29 *There does not exist any church body whom our Lord Jesus Christ gives power to command allegiance that is not an outcome of faith in righteousness of edicts that are issued by such a church. An earthly church body - an earthly church organization - is not the body of Christ. It is believers within every church body who are true to Jesus Christ who constitute the body of Christ.*

Spiritual Insight 30 *Any church body that declares it can curse believers merely because they disagree on matters of faith attempts to curse Jesus Christ and surely will fall flat on it's face.*

Spiritual Insight 31 *Who is it who truly loves Jesus Christ, yet has capacity for cursing his brother or sister - whom he or she is supposed to love with the love of Christ - merely because both exercise faith for disagreement over matters that are not moral in character?*

Spiritual Insight 32 *In matters of morality, we are not called to judge one another,* WE ARE CALLED TO ATTEMPTS AT RESTORING ONE ANOTHER. *Believers who focus on restoring do not simultaneously focus on passing judgments. A restorer recognizes sin only so he or she can exhort, instruct, reprove, correct, or rebuke (1Timothy 5:1, 20; 2Timothy 4:2, 3:16) not so he or she can pass judgment.*

Spiritual Insight 33 *The command from our Lord Jesus Christ is "judge not, that you may not be judged (Matthew 7:1)."*

How then about the health and welfare of the people? Between *1315 and 1317*, crops failed all over Europe and people starved, with mortality rates as high as 10% of the population. The *Black Death* or *Bubonic Plague* of *1348-49 AD* would be worse, inducing mortality rates across both Asia and Europe as high as 30% of the population. The Black plague continued to recur at about 10-year intervals up until about 1500 AD (*HWE*, pg. 215). While the plagues induced some people to seek solace in religion and faith, it induced others to seek to live even more lustily than ever before, such that much as was the case with raising of Lazarus from the dead, an event representative of God's judgments induced some to believe, others to an increase in severity of bad behaviors (John 11:45-53).

The Timeline of the Church in Philadelphia

In His message to the Church in Philadelphia, our Lord Jesus Chris declares that,

> "I have known thy works; lo I have set before thee a door - opened, and no one is able to shut it, because thou hast a little power, and didst keep my word, and didst not deny my name...(Revelation 3:8)"

The words of our Lord Jesus Christ reveal that while the CHURCH IN SARDIS had become dead, with only a little power, the CHURCH IN PHILADEL-PHIA would remain true to our Lord Jesus Christ. So then, whereas the Church in Sardis is the Church that submitted to decadence of idolatry and whoredom introduced by Papal Rome into the Byzantine Empire, the Church in Philadelphia is the resurgent Church committed to purity of faith in the name of Jesus Christ. Given the Church in Philadelphia clearly was located in the Byzantine Empire, and given the Byzantine Empire ceased to exist in *1453 AD* when it was sacked by the Ottoman Turks, it would seem that the time of the Church in Philadelphia ended in *1453 AD*.

Prophecy Principle 32 *The timeline for the* CHURCH IN PHILADELPHIA *is 1188 to 1453 AD.*

The Lesson for us today?

In Revelation 3:11, our Lord Jesus Christ admonishes those who have faith in His name as follows.

> Lo, I come quickly, be holding fast that which thou hast, that no one may receive thy crown.

In the words above, our Lord Jesus Christ declares that every crown already created by The Father ultimately will be awarded to someone (James 1:12). If you refuse the works that The Father seeks to achieve in partnership with you (Ephesians 2:10), The Father will seek out another to whom that crown can be awarded (Revelation 3:11). Note that no one can compete with you for your crown (Hebrews 12:1-2). No one can say they became more faithful than you, as such deserve your crown. In fact, the Holy Spirit declares through the Apostle Paul as follows:

> For we do not make bold to rank or to compare ourselves with certain of those commending themselves, but they, among themselves measuring themselves, and comparing themselves with themselves, are not wise (2Corinthians 10:12).

If others are faithful, they achieve faithfulness in respect of other sets of works. But faithfulness in other sets of works cannot qualify them for your works, meaning a person cannot by being faithful in what is committed to him or her lay claim on your works, or your crown. But if you refuse the works, if you will not walk with Christ in context of whatever He asks of you, then you refuse the crown and The Father must seek out another, perhaps in a next generation who will fulfill the works you rejected.

Consider the children of Israel. The Father did His part. Having prophesied to Abraham that the iniquity of the Amorites and Hivites had yet to be full (Genesis 15:14-16), and having rescued the children of Israel from Egypt at the point in time when iniquity of the Canaanites had become full (Exodus 14), upon arriving at border of Canaan, the children of Israel rebelled, refused to enter the promised land (Numbers 13:26-33; 14:1-10). What then happened? With exception of Joshua and Caleb, the two persons who, apart from Moses, Aaron, and Aaron's righteous children did not rebel against God, over the course of 40 years that entire generation perished in the wilderness (Numbers 14:11-38; 1Corinthians 10:1-5).

But was the promise still fulfilled? Absolutely.

It was the children of the generation that perished in entirety that fulfilled the promise, that inherited the promised land. Joshua and Caleb, both of whom were faithful to the vision 38 years previously, went on to enter into the promised land.

Note, however, that entry of Joshua and Caleb into the promised land, both of whom were faithful to the vision, also was delayed by 38 years. The disobedience of the majority then can delay grand purposes that are set in motion by The Father Himself.

Spiritual Insight 34 *Man can, by disobedience, delay God's good purposes for welfare of a group of people. The Father's promises always will be fulfilled, however, with outcome there always will exist some group of people, in future who choose to fulfill The Father's good will.*

Spiritual Insight 35 *You cannot, by refusing to do the works committed to you by The Father, frustrate The Father's purposes on earth. The Father always will find a group of people in time who will partner with Him for fulfillment of His will.*

The promise from our Lord Jesus Christ to those who hold fast what is committed to them by The Father (Revelation 3:12)?

He who overcomes, I will make him a pillar (a stalwart) in the temple of My God, and he shall go out no more. I will write on him the name of My God and the name of the city of My God, the New Jerusalem, which comes down out of heaven from My God. And I will write on him My new name.

So Let It Be Lord Jesus, Amen.

The Message to the Church in Laodicea

In the words of our Lord Jesus Christ, the Church that emerges out of the Church in Philadelphia, the CHURCH IN LAODICEA is nothing short of pathetic. The Church in Laodicea is neither *cold* nor *hot*, meaning it does not give it's all to Jesus Christ. While the Church in Laodicea believes itself to be rich and in need of nothing, The Lord Jesus Christ declares that the Church is *wretched, miserable, poor, blind,* and *naked* (Revelation 3:17).

✠ Wretchedness implies unpleasantness. While the bride of Christ is beautiful (Revelation 21:1-2, 10-14), the Church in Laodicea is unpleasant in appearance.

✠ While the reign of our Lord Jesus Christ is "righteousness, peace, and joy in the Holy Spirit (Romans 14:17)," the Church in Laodicea is miserable, lacking in joy.

✠ While our Lord Jesus Christ became poor so you and I can be rich (2Corinthians 8:9), or better still wealthy, the Church in Laodicea is poor, that is, lacking in the life of God.

✠ While only those who are of the world are supposed to be blind (2Corinthians 4:4), the Church in Laodicea is blind, yet is unaware of it's blindness. A person who is blind, yet unaware of blindness is a danger to himself or herself, and to others.

✠ While the Church in Laodicea considers itself well adorned in raiment, our Lord Jesus Christ declares that she is in utmost nakedness (Isaiah 47:3; Ezekiel 16:36-37).

SO THEN, OUR LORD JESUS CHRIST COUNSELS THE CHURCH IN LAODICEA TO BUY FROM HIM:

✠ Gold fired by fire that the Church might be rich, or better still wealthy. 'Gold that is fired by fire' is allegory for faith that is *pure*, *sincere*, and *genuine* (1Peter 1:6-7).

✠ White garments that the Church may be arrayed, and the shame of it's nakedness not be manifest. Note the nakedness does not cease to be shameful, rather it merely is no longer visible to others. This is equivalent to a sinner repenting, then accepting the righteousness of Jesus Christ as covering for his or her self righteousness (Galatians 3:27) - self righteousness that is no more than filthy rags (Isaiah 64:6), that is wretched in appearance.

✠ Eye-salve that the Church might be able to see (Isaiah 42:6-7).

Friend, note that the faith that is bought is pure, sincere, and genuine, but is not yet mature. Note that the righteousness that is bought does not yet transform the sinner, merely prevents the shameful nakedness of the sinner from being seen. Lastly, note that the eye salve enables clarity of sight, enables the sinner see himself or herself as he or she really is, such that he or she recognizes whatever needs to be fixed.

What then is the price of gold that is fired in fire, the righteousness of Jesus Christ, and eyesalve that enables clarity of sight?

Willingness, Brother; Willingness, Sister.

All it takes is your willingness to reason with our Lord Jesus Christ, willingness to respond to the evidence and outcome of your reasonings with Christ, and willingness to act in faith consequent on outcome of your reasonings with Jesus. For more on importance of willingness, see Chs. 13 & 14 of my book, True Sanctification.

Prophecy Principle 33 *Willingness to reason, willingness to respond to evidence and outcome of reasonings with Christ, and willingness to act in faith on outcome of reasonings all require exertion of effort, as such imply willingness to incur a cost, willingness to buy from Jesus Christ.*

The Supporting Evidence? In Revelation 3:19-20, our Lord Jesus Christ declares:

As many as I love, I do convict and chasten; be zealous, then, and reform; lo, I have stood at the door, and I knock; if any one may hear my voice, and may open the door I will come in unto him, and will sup (*reason with*) him, and he with me.

Prophecy Principle 34 *If all you have to do in order to commence engagement in honest reasonings with Jesus Christ is, 'open the door of your heart', then it all begins with no more than your willingness.*

Consistent with Christian Scriptures, the time of the reformation begins right after wars, conflicts, famine and plagues already discussed, most of which had ended by about 1500 AD. In this matter, it is important to note that just about every reformer was born shortly subsequent to demise of the Christian Byzantine Empire, demise that as we already established, transpired in 1453 AD. We have then that some of the earliest reformers, such as *Desidirius Erasmus*, who published a new Greek Edition of the New Testament derived from older parchments was born in *1516 AD, John Colet* (1466-1519 AD) in *1466 AD, Martin Luther* (1483-1546 AD) in *1483 AD, Andrea von Bodenstein (Carlstadt)*, a contemporary of Martin Luther's, *Huldreich Zwingli* (1484-1531) in *1484 AD*, and *John Knox* (1513-72) in *1513 AD*. all lived within the same time frame. We find then that the judgments of The Father translated into new inspiration and light within Christendom.

Spiritual Insight 36 *Whenever the righteous lay to heart judgments by The Father, as such seek The Father with greater urgency and effort and wisdom, this always translates into new light, new revelations, new anointing from the Holy Spirit to the glory of Father and Son.*

With the reformation came persecution from Papal Rome. A couple of years ago (in 2016), Pope Francis apologized to all of Protestant Christianity for persecutions that occurred in course of the Reformation. Persecution that occurred in context of the reformation continued in guise of what essentially were forced relocations of Protestants from all over Europe to what then was the new world, what now is the United States of America. Given the USA remained a colony of Great Britain until independence in 1776, effectively persecution did not end until the United States attained to independence in 1776.

The Timeline of the Church in Laodicea

Friend, the gospel having been opened up to individuals, with Christ now living in our hearts by faith, there now no longer is any timeline for the Church of Christ, that is, the Church in Laodicea. Note that whereas the Church in Laodicea is neither hot nor cold, the Lord Jesus Christ issues an invitation that will lead to a regaining of 'hotness', and leaves the matter in entirety open to the response to His invitation. Our Lord Jesus Christ does not conclude the matter, leaves the state of the Church to decisions made by you and I. If you and I respond rightly, the Church in Laodicea becomes hot, becomes fervent for Christ. If you do not respond, and others do not respond, then the Church in Laodicea either stays lukewarm or becomes cold.

So then, the timeline of the Church in Laodicea?

Prophecy Principle 35 *Friend, the time of the Church in Laodicea commenced in 1454, but never will end, will be with us until if necessary, the coming of our Lord Jesus Christ a second time. If you choose to respond to Jesus, choose to buy of Him gold fired in fire, white raiment for your clothing, and eyesalve that you may see, and if you are willing to exert effort to know Jesus as Lord and Savior, then your time on earth will be filled with the joy that comes from fellowship with Father, Son, and Holy Spirit.*

Prophecy Principle 36 *Our Lord Jesus Christ has left the matter of what happens to the Church in Laodicea in entirety in your hands and mine. Will you not choose to honor and glorify the Savior and Lord who has done so much for you, who is the source of your life in God?*

The Presence of Christ and the Church in Laodicea

In all of the messages to the other Churches, our Lord Jesus Christ addresses believers in the third person, that is, within context of delivery of His message to the Church by the messenger of that Church. His appeals then are conveyed by the messengers of the Churches. It is unequivocally the case, however, that the PRESENCE OF CHRIST arrives in context of the CHURCH IN LAODICEA. This is evident in the fact that it only is in context of the message to the Church in Laodicea that our Lord Jesus Christ addresses individuals directly. Not only does the Lord Jesus address all of mankind directly, but also HE DECLARES HIS PRESENCE AT THE DOOR OF THEIR HEARTS. If any man, male or female would open the door of their hearts to Him, this willingly, He would come in to them, and fellowship with them. In the message to the Church in Laodicea, however, as already enunciated, but worthy of reiteration, our Lord Jesus Christ addresses as follows.

> As many as I love, I do convict and chasten; be zealous, then, and reform; lo, I have stood at the door, and I knock; if any one may hear my voice, and may open the door I will come in unto him, and will sup (*reason with*) him, and he with me (Revelation 3:20).

Several truths are critical here, and I enumerate as follows.

✠ First, "HOW MANY PEOPLE DOES JESUS LOVE?" Well, we already established that He loves all men, and died for all men (John 3:16; 12:32). In the declaration in Revelation 3:20 that He speaks to all those whom He loves, our Lord Jesus Christ declares that He now appeals to all hearts directly, such that either of AN EXISTING BELIEVER, or A NON-BELIEVER can, on basis of their responses to Him, be convicted of their sin, and reform.

✠ Second, in the words, 'ANY ONE', which is, reminiscent of 'WHOSOEVER' in John 3:16, or 'ALL MEN', in John 12:32, our Lord Jesus Christ reiterates that He speaks to all men, male or female, CURRENT BELIEVING, or YET TO BELIEVE.

✠ Third, Jesus is standing at the door of the heart, meaning His presence is with us. It is unequivocal then, that The PRESENCE OF CHRIST arrives on earth in context of the time of the CHURCH IN LAODICEA, in context of the Church that never ends.

✠ Fourth, either of a current believer, or a person who is yet to believe can hear the voice of Christ (John 10:16,27). BUT IS THERE SOME DESCRIPTION OF THOSE WHO CAN HEAR HIS VOICE? Well, first, all those whom The Father already gives to Him (John 6:37,39), and second, all those who, somehow, hear His voice (John 6:37,40). All those who believe in love as the truth about how man is supposed to live are born of God, are born of The Father, and hear the voice of Jesus (John 18:37; 1John 4:7; 5:1).

✠ Fifth, those who hear the words of Jesus Christ either believe in the way of love, but have yet to believe in Jesus Christ (1John 4:7), or already have believed (1John 5:1) and as such have chosen the way of love, but have yet to arrive at fellowship with Christ.

✠ Sixth, the goal of the PRESENCE OF CHRIST is that we might, in addition to fellowship of the Holy Spirit, arrive at fellowship with The Father and The Son (1John 1:1-4).

Prophecy Insight 30 *Friend, it is a person who loves that is accepted of The Father. Receiving Jesus as Lord and Savior enables you receive the Love of God, makes it easier for you to walk in Love, makes it easier for you to be accepted of The Father.* WHY GO IT ALONE, WHEN YOU CAN HAVE HELP FROM FATHER, SON, AND HOLY SPIRIT?

Prophecy Insight 31 *The Father desires more than just to accept you, seeks to have fellowship with you. But if you are to arrive at fellowship with The Father, you have to receive Jesus as Lord and Savior, then obey the Holy Spirit, such that you are able to hear and behold the Lord Jesus (John 6:40), as such enter into fellowship with Father, Son, and Holy Spirit.*

Prophecy Insight 32 *The process via which you qualify for fellowship with The Father and The Son, is the process of sanctification. I have written an entire book for your benefit, titled* TRUE SANCTIFICATION *that illuminates your path towards experience of the* PRESENCE OF CHRIST, *the path that facilitates arrival at fellowship, not just with the Holy Spirit, but with Father and Son.*

The promise from our Lord Jesus Christ to those who engage with Him in reasoning and go on to know Him, and go on to overcome?

> He who is overcoming - I will give to him to sit with me in my throne, as I also did overcome and did sit down with my Father in His throne (Revelation 3:21).

Spiritual Insight 37 *If you seek a God willing to reason with you, you seek fellowship with Jesus Christ, The Father of Jesus Christ, and the Spirit of Father and Son, the Holy Spirit.*

Spiritual Insight 38 *If you do not yet know reality of fellowship of Father, Son, and Holy Spirit, it is not the promise that fails, it is that you have yet to understand how the fellowship is activated, and what is required of you for activation of the fellowship.*

Spiritual Insight 39 *I, by the grace of our Lord Jesus Christ have experienced, and am experiencing what it means to have fellowship with Father, Son, and Holy Spirit. This is essence of my books titled, 'IN JESUS NAME', and 'TRUE SANCTIFICATION'. Do not consider the weight of money required to* *buy these books. Buy these books. More importantly, read these books and seek to practice the divine truths that are revealed to you through me, from Father, Son, and Holy Spirit for arrival at spiritual, cognitive, physiological, and material blessings.*

Spiritual Insight 40 *I ask of you to respond to what you read with your reasoning, and with your faith, and then to go on to do whatever the Holy Spirit inspires in you - in response to your faith and reasoning over what you learn - for arrival at fellowship with Father, Son, and Holy Spirit.*

Presence Equates to Reign

With respect to the REIGN OF OUR LORD JESUS CHRIST, we already read as follows in Luke 17:20-21.

> And having been questioned by the Pharisees, when the reign of God doth come, He answered them, and said, the Reign of God doth not come with observation (*does not come as a physical phenomenon that has a location*); nor shall they say, Lo, here; or lo, there; for lo, the REIGN OF GOD IS WITHIN YOU.

In respect of arrival of the PRESENCE OF CHRIST, and as we already have seen, our Lord Jesus Christ declares as follows:

> Lo, I have stood at the door (*of the hearts of men*), and I knock; if any one may hear my voice, and may open the door, I will come in unto him, and will sup with him, and he with me (Revelation 3:20).

Presence is Spiritual 19 *Friend, it is straightforward to see that the Reign of God, equivalently, the* REIGN OF CHRIST *corresponds with the* PRESENCE OF CHRIST.

Presence is Spiritual 20 *Since the time of the Church in Laodicea, since about 1454 AD, the* REIGN OF CHRIST *has been on this earth.*

Presence is Spiritual 21 SUPPORTING EVIDENCE? *It was in the 1450s, exactly at commencement of the time of the Church in Laodicea that the* GUTENBERG PRESS, *which made the Bible available en masse to ordinary Christians, was invented.* HALLELUJAH!!!

The Gutenberg Press, The Bible, and the Presence of Christ

IN ANCIENT TIMES, PEOPLE TOOK ON THE FAITH OF THEIR KINGS. This was the case in Christian regions as well. If the king of a *Germanic Tribe* converted to Christianity, all of his subjects also were expected to become Christians. In this respect, note that prior to the *1450s*, invention of the *Gutenberg Press*, and availability of the *Gutenberg Bible*, Christian Scriptures were copied by hand, were available only to Monks and Priests.

Historical Spiritual Nugget 9 *In ancient times, people took on the faith of their kings. Religion had a national character.*

Historical Spiritual Nugget 10 *It was this national character of religion of which the original 12 Apostles had been desirous.*

If people were to be able to fellowship with Christ directly, Christian Scriptures had to become available to the individual Christian. The reasoning is as follows. While the Bible is not Jesus Christ, the Bible is written to provide us with revelations of Jesus Christ. Absent mastery of the revelations already encapsulated in Christian Scriptures, a man cannot expect any new revelations from Jesus Christ. You see then that the Bible is like a litmus test of the extent to which a person truly has desire for knowledge of Christ. A person who truly has desire for knowledge of Christ '*studies to show himself or herself approved to God, a workman who needs not be ashamed of his knowledge*' (2Timothy 2:15). A person who lacks any real desire for knowledge of Christ makes excuses for why they do not have any regard for the content of their Bible. It is straightforward that mastery of the revelations of Jesus Christ already provided us in the Bible - mastery that is evident in obedience to Christ, is litmust test of those who have opportunity for actualization of the Presence of Christ.

You see then that arrival of the Presence of Christ at commencement of the time of the *Church in Laodicea* in *1454 AD*, and starting in the *1450s*, availability of the Gutenberg Bible to individual Christians is no coincidence. An English translation of the Bible would arrive in form of the King James Version of the Bible in the *1600s*. You further arrive at the realization that absent a *Medium*, such as the Bible, through which individuals could learn of Christ, domicile of the Gospel at level of the individual, with outcome Churches are the body of Christ only if, individual members are in the body of Christ (1Corinthians 12:27; Romans 12:5; 1Peter 2:4-5; 1Corinthians 3:16; Ephesians 2:19-22), implementation of a meritocracy in context of the Presence of Christ would not have been possible.

Prophetic Lessons 7 *The time from ascension of Christ about 27 AD to 1453 AD served to prove that all institutions of earth - kingdoms, churches, family structures etc. - inherently lack capacity for anchoring of the Grace of God.*

Prophetic Lessons 8 *So then, the Grace of God had to be anchored spiritually by Christ Himself, resulting in necessity of a medium via which people* *could get to know Christ for themselves. Using His foreknowledge, The Father began compilation of exactly such a Medium - The Bible - from the time of Moses. This is the reason every Book of the Old Testament says something about Christ or the New Covenant, and the reason all of the New Testament glorifies Christ.*

Prophetic Lessons 9 *If you aspire to become a Power for Christ, recognition you cannot accrue to yourself, that you become aware of, because The Holy Spirit points out the fruit of it, you must seek to master and obey the commands of our Lord Jesus Christ, which, as you already know can be summed up as: (i) have faith in my name; and (ii) love others and yourself with the Love of God.*

The Person of our Lord Jesus Christ

At commencement of each and every message to the seven churches, our Lord Jesus Christ provides a description of His person. We already have discussed the description at commencement of the message to the CHURCH IN EPHESUS, the depiction of Himself as holding the seven stars, and walking among the seven lampstands. At commencement of the message to the CHURCH IN SMYRNA, our Lord Jesus Christ has this to say in respect of Himself (Revelation 2:8).

> "And to the messenger of the assembly (Church) of the Smyrneans write: These things saith the First and the Last, who did become dead and did live."

OUR LORD JESUS CHRIST IS THE LAST BECAUSE HE IS THE LAST ADAM (1Corinthians 15:45-47). The Last iteration of a man who, like the very first Adam, is born directly of God. In the characterization of Adam as the first man, and characterization of Jesus as the last Adam, there is indication of feasibility of intermediate realizations of 'FIRST BORNS' (Hebrews 12:22-24), that is, men who like Adam are the first of their kind. Consistent with this feasibility, Hebrews 12:9; & 2:14 declare as follows.

> Then, indeed, fathers of our flesh we have had, chastising us, and we were reverencing them; shall we not much more rather be subject to THE FATHER OF THE SPIRITS, and live?

> Seeing, then, the children (*spirits, of which God is The Father*) have partaken of flesh and blood, He Himself also in like manner did take part of the same, that through death He might destroy him having the power of death - that is, the devil.

Prophecy Insight 33 ABRAHAM, *Father of Faith is a first of his type.* SAM-
SON, *the single-handed deliverer is a first of his type.* SAMUEL, *the first High
Priest who was not of the tribe of Levi was a first of his type. The prophet,* ELI-
JAH *was a first of his type. The indication from Scriptures is that The Father
provided spirits, who came to earth as these persons, opportunity for living on
earth. None turned out perfect. Abraham lied (Genesis 20:1-2). Samuel could
not produce children who, like him, reverenced The Father (1Samuel 8:1-3).
Elijah got discouraged, needed encouragement of The Father (1Kings 19:1-
18). Suffering from loneliness, Samson went in to a prostitute (Judges 16:1).
Only our Lord Jesus Christ, the last Adam, who is incarnation of the Word of
God, who Himself is God, lived a perfect life on earth.*

> Can you think of any other persons in the Bible who come across
> as first of their kind?

That our Lord Jesus Christ died, yet lived again is straightforward, alludes to the death and resurrection on the third day. There is slightly more
to this, however, which is, absent some cameos, until the resurrection of
our Lord Jesus Christ from the dead, THE WORD, who is God (John 1:1), as
such Spirit (John 4:24), who put on flesh in person of Jesus Christ (John
1:14) could not participate in affairs of this life. Given the WORD IS GOD,
and THE FATHER IS GOD, The Father also could not participate in affairs of
this life, with outcome all of the interactions with Israel were intermediated
by messengers whom The Father provided with authority to speak in His
name (Zechariah 12:8; Galatians 3:19-20; Hebrews 1:1-4). Only subsequent
to resurrection of our Lord Jesus Christ is The Word, through you and I, as
persons who are conformed to the image of Christ (Romans 8:29) - He who is
image of the Word, that is of the invisible God (Colossians 1:15), who Himself
(The Word) is in The Father, and The Father in Him (1John 5:7) - participant
in affairs of this life.

> THAT OUR LORD JESUS CHRIST IS 'THE FIRST' REITERATES THE
> FACT THAT HE IS THE FIRST BORN OF ALL CREATION (Colossians
> 1:15; Hebrews 1:6).

Is our Lord Jesus Christ then a created being?

The Father is Spirit (John 4:24). In order for The Father to create a
physical universe, He needed a physical image of Himself (Colossians 1:15).
Our Lord Jesus Christ is that physical image. The Father went on to create
us in the image of Himself, that is in the image of Jesus Christ (Genesis
1:26-27). So then, it is not that Christ is like us in form, it is that we are
created in His image. For ease of understanding, however, Jesus is described
as having the 'form of a man' in each of the Books of Ezekiel and Revelation.

All of God's creation is domiciled in Christ - He who is the same yesterday, today, and forever (Hebrews 13:8), with outcome all of God's creation remains the same forever. With God's creation domiciled in Christ, The Father ,who is Spirit, who exists independent of His physical image can interact with His physical image and take out whatever needs to be taken out of it (John 15:1-2), and bring into it whatever He deems to be good (James 1:17). So then, Jesus is the vine, and His Father the spiritual Husbandman.

I ask then, relative to us, is our Lord Jesus Christ created or is He God? Stated somewhat differently, suppose, hypothetically, that Jesus could die a permanent death. Since we all live in Him (*that we live in Him does not imply we abide in Him*), upon the death of Jesus Christ, we all immediately would cease to exist. All reality immediately would cease to subsist.

Spiritual Insight 41 *If we abstract away from all of the accompanying metaphysical considerations, for all practical purposes, hypothetically, in the event Jesus were, in an eternal sense, to die (meaning death of The Word of God), we would arrive at cessation of reality of life. Given Jesus only is physical manifestation of the Word of God, and given The Word, who is God remained alive in the heavens, this while Jesus lay dead for three days in the grave on earth, for all practical purposes, God remained alive. For all practical purposes then, The Word is God, and Jesus is physical manifestation of The Word of God.*

At the risk of sounding blasé, is the practical not equally as important as the metaphysical?

The Metaphysical?

That is, in Christ God was reconciling the world to Himself, not counting their trespasses against them, and entrusting to us the message of reconciliation (2Corinthians 5:19).

Jesus is God with a physical form. The physical form of God cannot be less than God.

Prophecy Principle 37 *Jesus is God in a physical form. Since The Father is Spirit and does not have any physical form, the only God you and I ever will see is Jesus Christ. So then, metaphysically, Jesus is God, but yet not The Father.*

At commencement of His message to the CHURCH IN PERGAMUM, our Lord Jesus Christ declares:

And to the messenger of the assembly (Church) in Pergamos write: These things saith He who is having the sharp two-edged sword (Revelation 2:12).

The sharp two-edged sword refers to the 'RECKONING' of God, which pierces asunder to the revealing of the thoughts of the heart (Hebrews 4:12). To 'RECKON' is to take account, to weigh, to judge. Our Lord Jesus Christ declares that His reckoning of your life discerns the secrets and intents of your heart. In these words, our Lord Jesus Christ declares that any attempts at hiding your motives, intents, and deliberate evil thoughts about others - as opposed to tempting evil thoughts, which you discard - are futile. Our Lord Jesus Christ declares that to Him, you are an open book, such that were you to hide in the deepest of the depths of the ocean, even there you would be an open book to His eyes (Psalm 139).

Prophecy Principle 38 *Our Lord Jesus Christ declares that you are an open book to Him, meaning you cannot deceive Him. He may tolerate your pretense for a season, but if you do not repent, eventually He will spew you out of His mouth (Revelation 3:16).*

At commencement of His message to the CHURCH IN THYATIRA, our Lord Jesus Christ declares:

> And to the messenger of the assembly of Thyatira write: These things saith the Son of God, who is having His eyes as a flame of fire, and His feet like to fine brass (Revelation 2:18).

Our Lord Jesus Christ declares that while He has the form of a man (Revelation 1:13), He is not a man, for there does not exist any man whose eyes are as a flame of fire, and feet like to fine brass.

Prophecy Principle 39 *While Jesus has the form of a man, this because man was made in His image, Jesus is not a man, so do not think of Jesus as a man, think of Jesus as Lord and Savior.*

At commencement of His message to the CHURCH IN SARDIS, our Lord Jesus Christ declares:

> "And to the messenger of the assembly in Sardis write: These things saith He who is having the Seven Spirits of God and the seven stars..."

Since our Lord Jesus Christ has the SEVEN SPIRITS OF GOD, the SEVEN SPIRITS OF GOD simultaneously are the Seven Spirits of our Lord and Savior Jesus Christ. In the declaration that He has the Seven Spirits of God, our Lord Jesus Christ declares that He is one in essence with The Father, as such is as fully God as The Father is God. The supporting evidence from other writings of Christian Scripture are inclusive of John 15:26; Acts 16:7; and Philippians 1:19. The symbolism of Jesus having the Spirits of His

Father reinforces the symbolism that He is the image of the invisible God, as such for all practical purposes, God.

In Revelation 2:1, our Lord Jesus Christ holds the seven stars in His right hand. In Revelation 3:1, our Lord Jesus Christ has the seven stars, but they are no longer in His hand. This is important. In Revelation 2:1, the seven stars are, for lack of a better symbolism, 'TOOLS' in the hands of Jesus for accomplishing purposes of The Father, which also are purposes of our Lord Jesus Christ. In Revelation 3:1, the messengers belong to our Lord Jesus Christ, are not merely tools in His hand. Consistent with the switch in symbolism, it is in relation to the Church in Sardis that rewards to faithfulness to Christ are specified as rewards of relationship. We have then that it is part of The Fathers plan that, ultimately, our obedience to Christ translates into fellowship with Christ. In this respect, our Lord Jesus Christ declares:

> Thou hast a few names even in Sardis who did not defile their garments, and they shall walk with me in white, because they are worthy (Revelation 3:4).

Prophecy Principle 40 *Is it not a beautiful thing to worship a God who, after you prove yourself faithful, admits you into fellowship with Himself? Can a God who listens, who seeks to teach, who seeks to empower you with knowledge, wisdom, and understanding, who seeks to admit you into His fellowship simultaneously not seek your welfare?*

Prophecy Principle 41 *If man runs away from God, it is not because 'God is not Love', rather it is because man is blinded by the god of this world, such that he perceives God not to be Love. Whenever the light of the knowledge of God shines in the world, all who merely are deceived, as opposed to indulging in evil, respond to the light of the knowledge of God in the face of our Lord Jesus Christ (2Corinthians 4:6).*

At commencement of His message to the CHURCH IN PHILADELPHIA, our Lord Jesus Christ declares:

> And to the messenger of the assembly (Church) in Philadelphia write: These things saith He who is *holy*, He who is *true*, He who is having the *key of David*, He who is *opening* and no one doth shut, and He *shutteth* and no one doth open!

In the words to the messenger of the Church in Philadelphia, our Lord Jesus Christ re-emphasizes importance of HOLINESS, and LOVE FOR TRUTH, qualities without which no one will have opportunity to behold Him face to face, for those who truly serve God worship Him in spirit and in truth

(John 4:24), and *pursue* each of PEACE and HOLINESS (Hebrews 12:14; 2Peter 3:11). In 2Thessalonians 2:9-12, all who refuse to love the truth are deceived by false prophets.

The *key of David* represents the right to open the door for letting people in, and the right to shut the door for keeping of people out. Jesus illustrated this right in the parable of the ten virgins (Matthew 25:1-13). Since all judgment has been committed to our Lord Jesus Christ by The Father, our Lord Jesus Christ is the one who lets in, and who keeps out. Since the judgments of our Lord Jesus Christ are righteous altogether, this because He is Savior, as such cannot go against Himself, cannot condemn a person for whom He died, a person who truly is repentant of sin, who exerts effort for righteousness. The wisdom that establishes our Lord and Savior to be one and the same person guarantees that every judgment pronounced by our Lord Jesus Christ is righteous altogether.

Concerning judgment and repentance:

> For The Father judges no one, but has committed all judgment to the Son,, that ALL SHOULD HONOR THE SON JUST AS THEY HONOR THE FATHER. He who does not honor the Son does not honor The Father who sent Him (John 5:22-23).

> All that The Father gives me will come to me, and him who comes to me I will not cast out (John 6:37).

> I say to you, that so joy shall be in heaven over one sinner reforming, rather than over ninety-nine righteous men, who have no need of reformation (Luke 15:7).

> And this I pray, that your love yet more and more may abound in full knowledge, and all judgment (*discernment*), for your proving the things that differ (*such that in presence of differences of opinion, there is capacity for arriving at the truth*), that ye may be pure and offenceless - to a day of Christ, being filled with the fruits of righteousness which come through Jesus Christ, to the glory and praise of God (Philippians 1:9-11).

Prophecy Principle 42 *If our Lord Jesus Christ is the one who has the key of David, no man on earth can declare you unfit for salvation, can declare you unfit for fellowship with Father, Son, and Holy Spirit. Our Lord Jesus Christ, He who paid the price for your sin is the only one can keep you out. And He will not keep out the fruit of His own sacrifice and resurrection (John 6:37; Hebrews 12:1-2). Hallelujah! The name of our Lord Jesus Christ be praised.*

Prophecy Principle 43 *If you are bold to enter, not because you are brash, but because of the promise that calls you, and if you are willing to pay the price, you can know The Father, Son, and Holy Spirit to the extent to which your spirit is able to acquire the glory of Jesus Christ (2Thessalonians 2:14).*

Prophecy Principle 44 *People who truly love one another are willing to submit their differences of understanding of the gospel to mutually respectful discussion for arrival at knowledge of the truth of the gospel. Divisions within Christendom are evidence for imperfections and sins of men, not evidence for working of the Holy Spirit.*

At commencement of His message to the CHURCH IN LAODICEA, our Lord Jesus Christ declares:

> And to the messenger of the assembly (Church) of the Laodiceans write: These things saith the Amen, the witness - the faithful and true - the Chief of the creation of God.

Jesus is the *Amen* because all of the promises by The Father find their 'Yes' and 'Amen' in Him (2Corinthians 1:20). Jesus is *Witness* because He was the only companion to The Father at creation, and His witness is faithful and true (Proverbs 8: 22-31; John 1:1-3). As already discussed, Jesus has pre-eminence (Colossians 1:18) - is Chief over all of God's creation - because in Him all of creation consists (Colossians 1:17).

Prophecy Principle 45 *We pray 'in Jesus Name' because all of the promises given to us by God, given to us by The Father of our Lord Jesus Christ, find their 'Yes' and 'Amen' in the name of our Lord Jesus Christ.*

Prophecy Principle 46 *The phrases,*'IN JESUS NAME', *or* 'IN THE NAME OF JESUS CHRIST OUR LORD AND SAVIOR' *are not mere aphorisms, are not mere words. If you are to pray with those phrases effectively, five truths must reside in your heart and be reflected in your actions, namely: (i) faith that Jesus is the Son of God, and that He lived a sinless life, this so His obedience can be credited to you, so you can be saved; (ii) faith that Jesus died on the Cross at Calvary, this, so your sins can be forgiven; (iii) faith that Jesus resurrected on the third day, this so you have power for overcoming sin, the devil, and the lusts that are in the world for arrival at a life of faith and love; (iv) faith that Jesus ascended back to heaven, this so you are able to receive the Holy Spirit; (v) faith that Jesus intercedes for you in heaven, this so His blood can be applied to your sanctification, edification, and glorification. If your utterance of* IN JESUS NAME *or* IN THE NAME OF JESUS CHRIST *does not embed any of these five truths, your prayers are just words, do not have power with The Father. For a thorough discussion of the five enumerated truths, pick up a copy of my book,* In Jesus Name. AMEN.

Summary

An important implication of the message from our Lord Jesus Christ to the seven churches?

> As an institution, papal Rome, which commenced 590 AD, and now is the Catholic Church, is not regarded by our Lord Jesus Christ as part of His Church, as part of His body.

This clearly is due to the fact that PAPAL ROME, and the inheritor of it's customs, the CATHOLIC CHURCH have substituted, and continue to substitute worship of idols for worship of The Father. Remember that Papal Rome did not emerge until *Constantine the Great* moved the seat of the Roman Emperor from Rome to Constantinople in *325 AD*. Up until that time, the Christian Church was one, there was not any real division within the Church. The COUNCIL OF NICAEA, the Council that transpired in Constantinople in *325 AD*, the Council that affirmed truth of a Triune God, did not have any Pope in attendance, involved the entire known Church, both East and West, was presided over by *Constantine the Great*. Given the WESTERN ROMAN EMPIRE did not give up idolatry, in order to gain acceptance, the Church in the Western Roman Empire, which did not have any Pope at timing of creation of the EASTERN ROMAN EMPIRE, fused worship of Christ with worship of idols for arrival at an idolatrous perversion of the faith of Jesus Christ. This fusion of worship of The Father with idolatry commenced about *590 AD*, that is, subsequent to demise of the Roman Empire in *476 AD*. In this respect, the first Pope for the papal Church, GREGORY I was instituted in 590 AD (*HWE*, pg. 194). As already intimated, insistence of papal Rome on worship of idols, and the demand that all Christians answer to the pope was essence of the schism that transpired between the Papal Church and the Byzantine Church in 867 AD.

> It is not impossible that the rise of Islam about 612 AD is predicated on the failure of the Church of the Western Roman Empire - the Church that allowed itself to be compromised, that transformed itself into papal Rome.

Prophecy Principle 47 *As is evident from our discussions of revelations of His Person by our Lord Jesus Christ, only He holds the key that admits or shuts anyone out of His reign. It is idolatry then for any person or human institution to arrogate to itself the power to admit into or shut anyone out of the reign of our Lord Jesus Christ.*

Prophecy Principle 48 *Our Lord Jesus Christ has declared that the gospel is to be received or shunned at the level of the individual person. "Lo, I have stood at the door, and I knock, if ANY ONE may hear my voice, and may open* *the door (receive me as Lord and Savior), I will come in unto him and will sup with him (reason and fellowship with him), and he with me" is declaration of our Lord Jesus Christ. Whoever declares otherwise, whoever attempts to institutionalize access to relationship with Christ is part constituent of the* MAN OF SIN *described in 2Thessalonians 2:1-12..*

But if Papal Rome, and hence the Catholic Church is not, institutionally, regarded by our Lord Jesus Christ as part of His body, how exactly can the Pope be revered as a leader of Christians? Is this not itself evidence for seeping of idolatry into all Protestant Church bodies?

While the papal Church was enemy of Christians during persecutions of the Middle Ages, persecutions that drove Christians to emigrate en masse to the United States of America, the papal Church claims this no longer is the case. Even if the papal Church still was enemy of Christians, given our Lord Jesus Christ expects you to love your enemy, you cannot justify hating either of Catholics or the pope. We have then that The Father and our Lord Jesus Christ expects you and I to love each of Catholics and the pope. In this respect, note that people born into the Catholic Church who do not know that the Church is apostate can, on basis of their willingness and effort for loving of others with the Love of Christ, be accepted of The Father. Equally importantly, it is not impossible that The Father can ask a righteous person who knows the Church is apostate to remain in that system, this because there are people whom he or she can impact righteously for Christ. Regardless, the requirement to love Catholics and their pope cannot equate to acceptance of the pope as a leader of Christians, not unless the term Christian now no longer means anything different from the term, Catholic.

In the timelines that we have established for the seven Churches, our Lord Jesus Christ demonstrates that evil does not triumph over good. In this respect, note that the timeline for the spiritually pure church that experienced persecution, the CHURCH IN SMYRNA, the *Perfect and Persecuted Church* is, at 40 years, the shortest of the seven timelines. This is followed by timelines for, respectively, the CHURCH IN THYATIRA, the *Church Characterized by Compromise* (44 years), and the CHURCH IN SARDIS, the *Church that is Dead* (88 years). With, for reasons that now are obvious, exclusion of the CHURCH IN LAODICEA, next, in order of lengths of time, are, respectively, the CHURCH IN EPHESUS, the *Good Church that Needed to Fix it's Love* (185 years); The CHURCH IN PHILADELPHIA, the *Church which achieves Faithfulness to Christ while Little in Strength* (266 years); and the CHURCH IN PERGAMUM, The *Good Church that is Troubled by Deviants* (731 years).

| Church | Timeline (AD) | | # of | Defining Characteristic |
	Starts	Ceased	Years	
Ephesus	100	284	185	The Church of the Church Fathers - not as perfect as Church of the Apostles
Smyrna	285	324	40	The Church of the Persecution; Shortest Timeline
Pergamum	325	1055	731	The Church Doing Things Right, But Deviants Not Heeding Correction
Thyatira	1056	1099	44	The Church of the Compromise; The Second Shortest Timeline
Sardis	1100	1187	88	The Church That Appears Alive, But is Dead. The Third Shortest Timeline
Philadelphia	1188	1453	266	The Church That is Weak in Earthly Terms, But Alive to Jesus Christ; the Third Longest Timeline
Laodicea	1454	No End	∞	The Church That Subsists While Timelines Are Suspended; The Gospel Belongs Now to Individuals, No longer is Subsumed in Institutions

Love of Truth 15 *Since Love can be extended to an enemy, Love is not dependent on friendship. While those who have faith in the name of Jesus Christ must love Catholics, in doing so, they must not abandon purity of their faith.*

Prophecy Interpretation 9 *Our Lord Jesus Christ declares that in His reign, times of prosperity are designed to far outnumber times of persecution.*

In conclusion, for us who live in these times, it is important to note that there really was only one church, the CHURCH IN EPHESUS, which evolved over time into the CHURCH IN SMYRNA, then into the CHURCH IN PERGAMUM, then into the CHURCH IN THYATIRA, then into the CHURCH IN SARDIS, then into the CHURCH IN PHILADELPHIA, then eventually into the Church not bound by any timeline, the CHURCH IN LAODICEA. Remember, worship of our Lord Jesus Christ now is fully spiritual, is no longer bound by any location whatsoever. In words that, again, emphasize dissociation of worship of God from congregations of people in a specific location by our Lord Jesus Christ, yet that emphasize the spiritual reality that you can be impacted by the grace that The Lord Jesus Christ has bestowed on a fellow believer, Apostle Paul declares spiritual nature of worship of God as follows in Romans 1:9-11.

> For God is my witness, WHOM I SERVE IN MY SPIRIT IN THE GOOD NEWS OF HIS SON, how unceasingly I make mention of you, always in my prayers beseeching, if by any means now at length I shall have a prosperous journey, by the will of God, to come to you, for I long to see you, THAT I MAY IMPART TO YOU SOME SPIRITUAL GIFT, that ye may be established.

Spiritual Insight 42 *While our Lord Jesus Christ can teach you Himself by revelation, He also has placed in the Church, APOSTLES, PROPHETS, SHEPHERDS & TEACHERS etc. who have gained insights into mysteries of the Gospel. These fellow believers are able to provide you with knowledge that makes it easier for you to arrive at the Presence of Christ. For more on the spiritual benefits of such giftings to the body of Christ, check out CH. 18 of my book, TRUE SANCTIFICATION.*

Prophecy Interpretation 10 *Only our Lord Jesus Christ can usher you into His presence, and only you, by yourself can qualify for arrival at His Presence. If anyone teaches otherwise, they attempt to lift themselves above Christ, as such are part constituent of the MAN OF SIN described in 2Thessalonians 2:1-12. If you do not insist on acquiring all of the understanding of how exactly to arrive at the PRESENCE OF CHRIST on your own, if you are truly humble enough to learn about the PATH, the PROCESS, and the PRINCIPLES from those who already have arrived at the PRESENCE OF CHRIST, you prove that you are wise.*

> The Church cannot say that because she did not preach to you, that it is impossible that you are saved.

Now that we find ourselves in a gospel that is individual and totally spiritual, both in it's reception, and in it's retention, we make the most of things by reaching for the deepest, fullest fellowship that is possible with our Lord and Savior Jesus Christ. Remember, we are able to arrive at the Presence of Christ, not because of our pursuit of it, but because we already are invited by The Father and our Lord Jesus Christ. Absent exertion of efforts for actualization of the Presence of Christ, however, we are unable to acquire this glory of our Lord Jesus Christ. Apostle Paul highlights importance of exercise of effort for arrival at the presence of Christ in the following words.

> Not that I have already obtained this or am already perfect; but I PRESS ON TO MAKE IT MY OWN, BECAUSE CHRIST JESUS HAS MADE ME HIS OWN (Philippians 3:12).

Spiritual Insight 43 *You are able to press on towards the* PRESENCE OF CHRIST *only because Christ already has invited you, already has made you His own. If you are to arrive at the* PRESENCE OF CHRIST, *however, and if you are to maintain that presence, you always must 'Press On'.*

> Therefore, since we are surrounded by so great a cloud of witnesses, let us lay aside every weight (weakness), and the sin which clings so closely, and LET US RUN WITH PERSEVERANCE the race that is set before us, LOOKING TO JESUS THE PIONEER AND PERFECTER OF OUR FAITH, who for the joy that was set before Him endured the cross, despising the shame, and is seated at the right hand of the throne of God (Hebrews 12:1-2).

Spiritual Insight 44 *If you are not willing to be sanctified, such that you are cleansed from your weaknesses and sins, if you are not willing to focus on Jesus and Jesus alone, who alone can perfect your faith, you are unable to arrive at the* PRESENCE OF CHRIST. *Only those who are willing to give up their old self (Matthew 16:24), who take up their cross (Matthew 10:38), who are willing to be sanctified (Romans 8:17), who will not be held back by friends, family, persecution, or cares of this life (Matthew 10:37; Luke 8:11-15) arrive at the* PRESENCE OF CHRIST.

Earthly Jerusalem Only Has Historical, Not Spiritual Significance

There perhaps is much to gain from walking the streets of the earthly Jerusalem, and envisaging the ministry of our Lord Jesus Christ while He was on earth. It is important to note, however, that if your faith resides in these experiences you find yourself in the same sort of idolatry as papal Rome.   In this respect, note the following words by our Lord Jesus Christ in John 20:29, and by Apostle Peter in 1Peter 1:8-9.

> Jesus said to him, "Have you believed because you have seen me? Blessed are those who have not seen and yet believe."

> WITHOUT HAVING SEEN HIM YOU LOVE HIM; THOUGH YOU DO NOT NOW SEE HIM, YOU BELIEVE IN HIM AND REJOICE WITH UNUTTERABLE AND EXALTED JOY. AS THE OUTCOME OF YOUR FAITH YOU OBTAIN THE SALVATION OF YOUR SOULS.

Remember, our Lord Jesus Christ declares that you can walk worthy of Him. What a glorious promise He holds out to us that, if we live to the praise of His glory, we can become worthy of His friendship. Whatever it is you lack, whether it be eyesalve for your eyes, or raiment for clothing, or gold that truly makes wealthy, our Lord Jesus Christ declares you can purchase from Him, not with money, but with RIGHTEOUS DESIRE, *righteous decisions*, RIGHTEOUS ACTIONS, and *righteous effort*. It is a glorious promise that is held out to you. I truly hope you will lay hold of it and hold fast till you go to be with our Lord and Savior Jesus Christ. He who has promised is able, and He will do it.

> Now to Him who is able to do exceedingly abundantly above all that we ask or think, according to the power that works in us, to Him be glory in the church by Christ Jesus to all generations, forever and ever. Amen (Ephesians 3:20-21).

> And to Him who is able to guard you not stumbling, and to set you in the presence of His glory unblemished, in gladness, to the only wise God our Savior, is glory and greatness, power and authority, both now and to all the ages! Amen (Jude 1:24-25).

CHAPTER 6

It is Symbolic, Not Sequential

Numerology IS THE SCIENCE OF MEANINGS OF NUMBERS. Whenever numbers are used intentionally, it can be possible that there exists some sort of hidden meaning waiting to be deciphered. Feasibility of hidden meanings is essence of 'codes' developed during war, which incorporate letters and numbers that ordinarily have different meanings. During the Second World War, an important contributor to defeat of Germany was, success at decoding of communication codes that were developed by the Germans. In order to ensure that the Germans did not infer that their code had been broken, Allied forces themselves developed a randomization code, a code that ensured they did not always act on information at their disposal, and that ensured a pattern could not be deduced from information on which they took action. Within context of *Numerology*, the code 2 3 4 5 could have interpretation as LIFE, with outcome, 2=L, 3=I, 4=F, and 5=E.

Prophecy Interpretation 11 *Numerology implies hidden meanings, or symbolisms. Hidden meanings or symbolisms cannot be assumed, must be rigorously deduced.*

While there exist seven churches in Revelation *Chs. 2* and *3*, the churches are not numbered. Given the churches are not numbered, we cannot attach any numbers to the churches. Remember, prophecy comes from The Father, Son, and Holy Spirit, and we never must impose our own understanding on interpretation of prophecy. Since our Lord Jesus Christ did not attach any numbers to the seven churches of Revelation *Chs. 2* and *3* - the seven churches whose spiritual meanings, and timelines are discussed in the preceding chapter - we cannot attach any numerology to interpretation of messages to those seven churches.

Sequel to Revelation *Ch. 5*, the numbers 1 through 7 are used extensively in the Book of Revelation. In this respect, with explicit numbering from FIRST to SEVENTH, in Revelation *Chs. 6 & 8*, there exist 7 Seals that are opened by our Lord Jesus Christ. During the time of the 7th seal (Revelation *chs. 8 & 9*), there exist 7 trumpets that are blown by messengers of Christ. In Revelation *ch. 10* there are 7 thunders speaking; in *chs. 16 & 17*, there are 7 vials of wrath. There are 2 witnesses, 2 olive trees, and 2 lampstands that stand before God, and there are 2 beasts that are agents of the devil.

Prophecy Principle 49 *In absence of any Numerology in Revelation Chs. 2 & 3, but, commencing with Revelation Ch. 6, introduction of numerology into prophecies that are entrusted to Apostle John by our Lord Jesus Christ, we have evidence that introduction of numerology is not coincidental, is intentional.*

Prophecy Principle 50 *A numerology that is developed and given to us by The Father and our Lord Jesus Christ belongs to The Father and our Lord Jesus Christ. We understand such numerology for our spiritual benefit, not so we can begin to act as if the numerology is our creation.*

If we are to understand the numerology that is introduced by our Lord Jesus Christ, we must commence in the very first chapter that presents such numerology, that is, Revelation *Ch. 6*. Commencing in Revelation *Ch. 6*, our Lord Jesus Christ successively opens 7 Seals. There is a temptation to think that merely because the 7 Seals are opened successively, that the SEALS, of necessity are deterministically sequential. This, however, need not be the case. As already demonstrated, numerology implies hidden meanings, that is, symbolisms, with outcome symbolism of the number 2 need not necessarily imply an event that precedes symbolism of number 3. In the illustration provided in the preceding, while the number 2 precedes the number 3 in context of the NUMBER LINE, the numerology generates L=2, and I=3. It is normatively true that, in context of THE ALPHABETS, the *Letter* I *precedes* the *Letter* L. Let Π denote the numerology that, using the preceding illustration, assigns letters to numbers, then $\Pi(2) = L$, and $\Pi(3) = I$. Clearly, and in context of the illustrative numerology, while 2 *precedes* 3 on the number line, in context of the alphabets, $\Pi(2) = L$ *does not precede* $\Pi(3) = I$; rather $\Pi(3)$ *precedes* $\Pi(2)$. We have then that it is straightforward that ordering of inputs into a numerology does not determine ordering of events that are symbolized by a numerology.

Prophecy Principle 51 *In the preceding illustration, the numbers, 2 3 4 5 are* ELEMENTS *of a numerology, and the alphabets,* L I F E *are* SYMBOLISMS *or* HIDDEN MEANINGS *that are embedded in a numerology. The symbol,* Π *denotes the* NUMEROLOGY *that maps* ELEMENTS *to* SYMBOLISMS *of a numerology, with outcome,* $\Pi(2) = L$; $\Pi(3) = I$; $\Pi(4) = F$; & $\Pi(5) = E$.

Prophecy Principle 52 *Ordering of elements of a numerology does not necessarily coincide with ordering of symbolisms that are hidden in elements of a numerology. Equivalently, symbolisms that are embedded in elements of a numerology need not have the same ordering as elements of a numerology.*

In context of the Seals that, commencing in Revelation *Ch. 6* are progressively opened by The Lord Jesus Christ, the numbers 1 through 7 are elements of the numerology, elements that incorporate hidden meanings or symbolisms. If hidden meanings or symbolisms that are embedded in the numbers 1 through 7 are credible, they must apply in every instance of application of said numerology in all of the Book of Revelation. We have then that any numerology deduced for the numbers 1 through 7 cannot be specific to the 7 Seals, must be deduced generically, as such must be shown to have application to interpretation of each of 7 SEALS, 7 TRUMPETS, or 7 VIALS of wrath, all of which are symbolic of events, times, or both.

Prophecy Principle 53 *If deduction of the* SYMBOLISM *that is hidden in* ELEMENTS *of the numerology (Π) for the numbers 1 through 7, as applied in the Book of Revelation is credible, the numerology must be shown to have application to interpretation of each of 7* SEALS, *7* TRUMPETS, *or 7* VIALS *of wrath, all of which are symbolic of events, times, or both.*

In the preceding chapter, we discussed how it is that a mathematical deduction, such as encapsulated in $\Pi\,(numbers) = Alphabets$ attains to greater credibility whenever assumptions that are applied to the deduction are obtained outside of the specific context that is under consideration. If we are to apply this mathematical rule, credibility of the numerology Π that we arrive at for the *elements* 1 through 7 must be deduced, not from within the Book of Revelation itself, but from other Books of the Bible. In presence of deduction of the numerology from other Books of the Bible, the numerology is shown to be generic, is shown to have application, not just to the 7 Seals, but to each of 7 TRUMPETS, or 7 VIALS of wrath.

To see importance of this, suppose we deduce the numerology for the numbers 1 through 7 from the 7 Seals. Then we already have formulated an interpretation of the 7 TRUMPETS, or 7 VIALS.

But if the 7 TRUMPETS, or 7 VIALS are equivalent to the 7 SEALS, the switch from SEALS to either of TRUMPETS, or VIALS is redundant.

If the elements 1 through 7 each, have different meanings in context of the 7 SEALS, 7 TRUMPETS, or 7 VIALS, their interpretation is determined, not by the *Numerology*, but by their specific labels, meaning the Numerology is redundant.

In presence of the foregoing, the most robust understanding of the 7 SEALS, 7 TRUMPETS, or 7 VIALS, incorporates differences of meanings of *Seals*, *Trumpets*, or *Vials*, and consistency of symbolism of the NUMEROLOGY.

It is straightforward then that if the numerology that is deduced is robust, it must be possible to dissociate symbolisms embedded in the numbers 1 through 7 from meanings of SEALS, TRUMPETS, or VIALS. Clearly then, symbolisms embedded in the numbers 1 through 7 must be deduced generically from outside of the Book of Revelation, that is, from the Books of Genesis through Jude.

Prophecy Principle 54 *The numerology (Π) that enables deduction of symbolisms that are embedded in the numbers (elements) 1 through 7 must be generically deduced from outside of the Book of Revelation, that is, from the Books of Genesis through Jude.*

Prophecy Principle 55 *If the numerology (Π) that is deduced from the Books of Genesis through Jude is credible, it must be possible to infer consistency of the symbolism that is embedded in the numbers (elements) 1 through 7.*

Prophecy Principle 56 *Let the letter e denote a specific element of the numbers 1 through 7, and let the letter S denote a specific symbolism embedded in a specific element e. Then the exercise to follow involves establishment of the relation,*

$$\Pi(e) = S$$

In what follows, for each element e, that is, for each of numbers 1 through 7, first I state the numerology $\Pi(e) = S$, then provide the evidence or proof for credibility of the numerology. This is a standard approach in Mathematics to providing evidence for validity of assertions. In Mathematical parlance, first, I state the ASSERTION (*Axiom*) in respect of Π and S, then provide the EVIDENCE (*proof*) for the assertion.

The Numerology for the Element 1

As already established, the number 1 is an element of the numerology that is embedded in the Book of Revelation. In what follows, I decipher a consistent symbolism for the ELEMENT 1. Let S denote a symbolism. Then we seek to decipher a consistent symbolism, S_1, satisfying,

$$\Pi(1) = S_1.$$

Numerology 1 *Let $e_1 = 1$. Then e_1 is symbolic of a new beginning, or equivalently, the beginning of something new. S_1 equates then to a New Beginning (NB), with outcome,*

$$\Pi(e_1) = \Pi(1) = S_1 = NB.$$

The Evidence

Before man became 2 - Adam and Eve, male and female - Man was 1 - Adam only (Genesis 2:18). So then, beginning of life of man on earth is associated with $e(1) = 1$. In this respect, Adam is explicitly referred to as the FIRST MAN. Our Lord Jesus Christ is the Beginning, equivalently, FIRSTBORN of God's creation. Concerning Adam, our Lord Jesus Christ, and additional evidence for association of $e(1) = 1$ with a NEW BEGINNING.

> So also it hath been written, The FIRST MAN Adam became a living creature, the last Adam is for a life-giving spirit (1Corinthians 15:45).

> And Himself (our Lord Jesus Christ) is the head of the body - the assembly - who IS A BEGINNING, A FIRST-BORN out of the dead, that He might become in all things - Himself, FIRST (Colossians 1:18).

> (*God speaking*) But he shall acknowledge the son of the unloved wife as THE FIRSTBORN by giving him a double portion of all that he has, for he is THE BEGINNING of his strength; the right of the firstborn is his (Deuteronomy 21:17).

> "Reuben, you are MY FIRSTBORN, my might and THE BEGINNING of my strength...(Genesis 49:3)"

Prophecy Principle 57 *The number 1 is symbolic of New Beginnings (NB).*

The Numerology for the Element 2

Numerology 2 *Let $e_2 = 2$. Then e_2 is symbolic of 'Companionship that is rooted in Pursuit of a Common Purpose (CP)'. S_2 equates then to CP, with outcome,*

$$\Pi(e_2) = \Pi(2) = S_2 = CP.$$

The Evidence

The case for association of CP with $e_2 = 2$ in context of man's existence already is made in Genesis 2:18, which declares,

> And the Lord God said, It is not good that man should be alone; I will make him a helper comparable to him (Genesis 2:18).

When The Father would destroy the earth with a flood in the days of Noah, what then were designated 'unclean animals' were brought into the Ark in TWOS - male and female (Genesis 6:19-20; 7:2). The unclean animals were to have companionship in context of capacity for maintenance of their species.

The evidence that two is associated with companionship in context of the animals brought into the ark?

You shall take with you seven of each of every clean animal, A MALE AND HIS FEMALE; two each of animals that are unclean, A MALE AND HIS FEMALE; also, of fowl of the heavens seven pairs, a male and a female, TO KEEP ALIVE SEED ON THE FACE OF ALL THE EARTH (Genesis 7:2-3).

Prophecy Principle 58 *Whether it be man or animals, Companionship that is Rooted in Pursuit of Purpose (CP) is explicitly linked with 2.*

Spiritual Insight 45 *Since both man, and carnivorous animals would, subsequent to the flood, begin to eat clean animals for food, given The Father knew He would grant this ahead of time, saving of 7 pairs of clean animals, and only 2 pairs of unclean animals ensured survival, non-extinction of clean animals.*

So then, is companionship always male and female?

Absolutely Not. Companionship only need be rooted in pursuit of purpose. This is evident in rooting of companionship of animals, which subsisted in context of the flood, with maintenance of each species of animals. This also is evident in rooting of Adam's companionship in finding of a helper for achievement of his purpose.

Prophetic Lessons 10 *In context of The Father's will, companionship is arrived at in context of two people working together for achievement of a purpose.*

While Eve was designated Adam's helper, Eve simultaneously would be a counterpart to Adam, that is, an equal of Adam. This is evident in the fact that God called both Adam and Eve 'MAN', with outcome Adam is MALE MAN, and Eve, FEMALE MAN (Genesis 1:27). We have then that Eve is not Adam's helper because she is inferior, that Eve is Adam's helper because one of the two had to be leader of the team. In God's infinite wisdom, the male man, *Adam* was better suited to lead than the female man, *Eve*.

Spiritual Insight 46 *It is a fact that no matter how talented any two people are, only one can be designated head of the unit. This always is the only recipe for order. The Father has designated the* MALE MAN *the leader in context of a* MARRIAGE OF EQUALS *between a male man and female man for arrival at order, not as an arrangement of subservience.*

Spiritual Insight 47 *Careful thought about Eve's sin reveals she sought to be leader, she sought to lead an agenda, hence her coveting of the fruit of knowledge of good and evil, and offer of the fruit to her husband. In the declaration that it was Eve who made him eat, Adam acknowledged acquiesce to an agenda brought forth by his wife. That desire for her own agenda, at expense of designated leadership of her husband, plunged man's existence into a futility, which only could be mediated by incarnation of God on earth for our salvation.*

Am I saying then that a woman cannot head a purpose? In an imperfect world, clearly this is not the case. *Aquila* and his wife, *Priscilla* were teachers in the body of Christ (Acts 18:26; Romans 16:3; 1Corinthians 16:19). We know that there were several women who worked with Paul (Philippians 4:2), and know all four unmarried daughters of Philip the Deacon prophesied (Acts 21:8-9). In Old Testament times, the Prophetess Deborah was a JUDGE - a spiritual leader - over the people of Israel (Judges 4:4).

Spiritual Insight 48 *Male man is leader in the home does not imply female man cannot be a leader in context of society at large. Apostle Paul celebrated a woman by name as a leader of a local church in which he was an apostle and teacher (Romans 16:1-2). The Prophetess Deborah did not partner with her husband for saving of Israel; rather, partnered with a man, by name, Barak, chosen for that purpose by God (Judges 4:4-7). But Deborah led the people spiritually and socially, allowed the man who partnered with her to lead the people politically and militarily. Deborah did not have hubris of hedonistic feminism, of declaring she did not need a man. The man partnered with her did not encroach on her leadership, respected Deborah's spiritual and social leadership (Judges 4:8).*

The spiritual principle is that if a woman is head of a particular purpose, and is married, in context of her marriage, The Father still expects her to be her husband's helper. If her husband does not want to be leader in the marriage, she is to encourage, and with words that are spoken in, and with love, challenge her husband to take up the mantle of spiritual leadership in their home. Part of the rationale for this, is the spiritual reality that a man, who himself is spiritually weak, is unlikely to raise male children who, themselves are spiritually sensitive to God. Given women tend to depend more on INTUITION than RATIONALIZATION for understanding of things, however, a female child from a home that is characterized by a spiritually weak father easily can arrive at spiritual sensitivity towards The Father.

Spiritual Insight 49 *The Father's admonition to women is that they are to encourage their husbands to be* CONCEIVERS, FORMULATORS, *and* IMPLEMENTERS *of love agenda for their families.*

Spiritual Insight 50 *Intuition can be catalyst for application of rational arguments to a particular matter that is under consideration. Intuition further enables refinements to rational courses of action, refinements that induce improvements to outcomes. Rationality of men, and intuition of women are designed to be complements, not substitutes. Whenever society denigrates either of rationality or intuition, it does so at it's very own peril.*

Spiritual Insight 51 *If society decides to rely only on female intuition, which in absence of well articulated reasonings may not take account of all parameters that are important, as such can be wrong, if society decides to denigrate rationality of men, as such refuses to consider rational arguments, all that will be left in future is disaster for entirety of society. Disaster is guaranteed because* INTUITION THAT IS BUILT ONLY ON INTUITION EVENTUALLY ONLY CAN DEVOLVE INTO SUPERSTITION.

With respect to additional evidence, in context of achievement of a purpose - preaching of imminent reign of God - *Jesus sent His disciples out in* TWOS (Mark 6:7; Luke 10:1). In this action, Jesus reinforces the preceding discussion, enunciates that 'Companionship implicit in 2' is derived in context of *pursuit of purpose*. Note that companionship here means friendship, not romantic love. While romantic love is a specific form of friendship, or is supposed to be a specific form of friendship, '*Companionship* of 2' is specific to friendship. The travesty in today's world is the reality that marriage is more likely to be associated with sexual desires, money, and cares of this life, than it is associated with development of a romantic friendship that embeds pursuit of purpose. The Father advises that marriage not be about sex, that it be about two people getting to know each other as fully as they possibly are able.

Spiritual Insight 52 *In Christ,* COMPANIONSHIP IS ROOTED IN EQUALITY OF FRIENDSHIP, *yet is compatible with designation of one or the other as leader. Whenever those who become leaders excel in love - the ideal of our Lord Jesus Christ, which, however, may not subsist in reality - human error apart, those who follow can trust that directives of leadership are rooted in love, are in entirety for their benefit.*

Prophecy Principle 59 *The* ELEMENT *2 is symbolic of* COMPANIONSHIP OF FRIENDSHIP *that is produced in context of* PURSUIT OF PURPOSE, *and that is rooted in* EQUALITY *of intrinsic worth of all men - male or female.*

The Numerology for the Element 3

Numerology 3 *Let $e_3 = 3$. Then e_3 is symbolic of 'Arrival at an Inner Circle of Friendship (CF)'. S_3 equates then to CF, with outcome,*

$$\Pi(e_3) = \Pi(3) = S_3 = CF.$$

The Evidence

The Father, Word, and Holy Spirit are the THREE (3) that bear witness in heaven (1John 5:7). On the earth, the THREE (3) that bear witness - the water, the blood, and the Spirit - all are fully domiciled in you and I as representatives of our Lord Jesus Christ (1John 5:8). This is evident in the fact that you and I are washed in water, equivalently, baptized in water as a sign that we have accepted the justification made available in Christ (1Peter 3:21); washed in the blood of our Lord Jesus Christ, that is, sanctified (1Peter 1:1-2); and filled with the Holy Spirit, that is, glorified (2Corinthians 3:18). Remember a representative, equivalently, emissary, or ambassador is not the same as the entity that is represented.

You and I are representatives of, we are not Jesus Christ.

ADDITIONAL SCRIPTURAL EVIDENCE THAT YOU AND I ARE WITNESSES FOR JESUS, ARE THE WITNESSES OF 1JOHN 5:8?

Thus it hath been written, and thus it was behoving the Christ to suffer, and to rise out of the dead the third day, and reformation and remission of sins to be proclaimed in His name to all the nations, beginning from Jerusalem: and YE - YE ARE WITNESSES OF THESE THINGS (Luke 24:46-48).

But ye shall receive power at the coming of the Holy Spirit upon you, and YE SHALL BE WITNESSES TO ME both in Jerusalem, and in all Judea, and Samaria, and UNTO THE END OF THE EARTH (Acts 1:8).

This Jesus did God raise up, of which we are all witnesses (Acts 2:32).

And I saw the woman drunken from the blood of the saints, and from THE BLOOD OF THE WITNESSES OF JESUS, and I did wonder - having seen her - with great wonder (Revelation 17:6).

In respect of the ELEMENT 3, note that there were THREE (3) disciples in the inner circle of our Lord Jesus Christ (Matthew 17:1; Mark 5:37; Mark 9:2; Mark 14:33). Peter, James, John completed the inner circle of friendship of our Lord Jesus Christ. Note also that our Lord Jesus Christ was in the grave for THREE (3) days - Friday, Saturday, and Sunday (Acts 10:39-41; 1Corinthians 15:3-4). The three days in the grave ensured that we would be complete in our Lord Jesus Christ (Colossians 2:9-10). Concerning COMPANIONSHIP of 2 and INNER CIRCLE of 3, consider the following words from Hosea 6:2.

> He doth revive us after TWO (2) days, in the THIRD (3) day He doth raise us up, and we live before Him.

Prophecy Principle 60 *The number 3 is symbolic of* ARRIVAL AT AN INNER CIRCLE OF FRIENDSHIP.

Prophecy Principle 61 *It is straightforward that it is better to be raised up than to be revived. So then* ARRIVAL AT AN INNER CIRCLE OF FRIENDSHIP, *which of necessity must revolve around purpose, and is symbolized by 3, is more desirable than* COMPANIONSHIP OF *2* THAT IS ROOTED IN PURPOSE.

Spiritual Insight 53 *In the symbolism of 3 as having meaning of Friendship, The Father declares that while marriage induces companionship,* COMPLETENESS OF FRIENDSHIP *between husband and wife arrives at timing of addition of a child to a marriage. This is the reason The Father allowed parents to redeem their first born child from Him (Numbers 18:15).*

The Numerology for the Element 4

Numerology 4 *Let* $e_4 = 4$. *Then* e_4 *is symbolic of 'Grand Judgments (GJ)'.* S_4 *equates then to GJ, with outcome,*

$$\Pi(e_4) = \Pi(4) = S_4 = GJ.$$

The Evidence

In our discussion of the message to the CHURCH IN PHILADELPHIA, we saw how The Father utilized treatment of the Byzantine Empire by Crusaders to arrive at a grand judgment of the then known world. First, the CHURCH IN PHILADELPHIA had to be seen to be righteous, and then her treatment had to be applied to arrival at a grand judgment of others. Simultaneity of DETERMINATION OF RIGHTEOUSNESS and ARRIVAL AT GRAND JUDGMENTS OF EVILDOERS is established by the words of our Lord Jesus Christ in the '*parable of the weeds*' in Matthew 13:24-30; 36-43. With focus on the most relevant excerpt, our Lord Jesus Christ declares as follows.

The Son of Man will shall send forth His messengers, and they shall gather up out of His kingdom (*reign*) all the stumbling-blocks, and those doing the unlawlessness, and shall cast them to the furnace of the fire; there shall be the weeping and the gnashing of the teeth (Matthew 13:41-42).

WITH RESPECT TO SYMBOLISM OF THE NUMBER 4, CONSIDER THE FOLLOWING.

Ho! ho! Flee from the land of the north, says the Lord; for I have spread you abroad as the FOUR WINDS of the heavens, says the Lord (Zechariah 2:6).

Thus says the Lord: "For three transgressions of Tyre, and FOR FOUR, I WILL NOT REVOKE THE PUNISHMENT; because they delivered up a whole people to Edom, and did not remember the covenant of brotherhood (Amos 1:9)."

Thus said Jehovah: "For three transgressions of Judah, and FOR FOUR, I WILL NOT REVOKE THE PUNISHMENT; because they have rejected the law of the Lord, and have not kept His statutes, but their lies have led them astray, after which their fathers walked (Amos 2:4)."

Jesus said to them, "My food is to do the will of Him who sent me, and to accomplish His work. Do you not say, 'THERE ARE YET FOUR MONTHS, THEN COMES THE HARVEST? I tell you, lift up your eyes, and see how the fields are already white for harvest (John 4:34-35)."

And after these things I saw FOUR MESSENGERS, standing upon the FOUR CORNERS of the land, holding the FOUR WINDS of the land, that the wind may not blow upon the land, nor upon the sea, nor upon any tree; and I saw another messenger going up from the rising of the sun, having a seal of the living God, and he did cry with a great voice to the FOUR *messengers*, to whom it was given to injure the land and the sea, saying, "Do NOT INJURE THE LAND, NOR THE SEA, NOR THE TREES, TILL WE MAY SEAL THE SERVANTS OF OUR GOD UPON THEIR FOREHEADS (Revelation 7:1-3)."

Matthew 13:36-43 and Revelation 7:1-3 make clear that IDENTIFICATION OF THE RIGHTEOUS and GRAND JUDGMENTS that are outcomes of revealing of the hearts of those who love evil occur simultaneously. Consistent with inferences arrived at in the preceding chapter, The Father assures us that the righteous will not be punished along with those who cling to evil, will not be punished along with those who are wicked.

Prophecy Principle 62 *The Scriptures are very clear; the* ELEMENT *4 is symbolic of Grand Judgments, equivalently, identification of the righteous.*

Prophecy Principle 63 *Symbolically, the* ELEMENT *4 provides reassurance that those who love righteousness never will be punished along with those who love evil, never will be punished along with those who love wickedness.*

| The Numerology for the Element 5 |

Numerology 5 *Let* $e_5 = 5$. *Then* e_5 *is symbolic of 'Maturity of Righteousness (MR)'.* S_5 *equates then to MR, with outcome,*

$$\Pi(e_5) = \Pi(5) = S_5 = MR.$$

The Evidence

CONSIDER THE FOLLOWING WORDS IN ISAIAH 17:6.

> It shall be as when the harvester gathers the grain, and reaps the heads with his arm; it shall be as he who gathers heads of grain in the valley of Rephaim. Yet gleaning grapes will be left in it, like the shaking of an olive tree, TWO OR THREE OLIVES AT THE TOP OF THE UPPERMOST BOUGH, four or five in it's most fruitful branches.

We already have established that the *elements* 2 or 3 can apply to either of the righteous or the wicked. We further have established that *identification of the righteous* enables GRAND JUDGMENTS of the wicked in context of symbolism of the *element* 4. For an understanding of symbolism of the *element* 5, I build on the parable of the weeds (Matthew 13:24-30; 36-43) that is instrumental to discussions of the *element* 4. For ease of understanding, I replicate the relevant passage and add the words in subsequent verses that enable arrival at an understanding of symbolism of the *element* 5.

> The Son of Man will shall send forth His messengers, and they shall gather up out of His kingdom (*reign*) all the stumbling-blocks, and those doing the unlawlessness, and shall cast them to the furnace of the fire; there shall be the weeping and the gnashing of the teeth. Then shall the righteous shine forth as the sun in the reign of their Father. He who is having ears to hear - let him hear (Matthew 13:41-43).

Note that while those who are stumbling-blocks, and those who are law-less are cast into the furnace of fire, the righteous are allowed to remain and flourish, and shine as the sun in the reign of their Father, our Father in heaven. We arrive then at the following logical progression to the sym-bolism. Remember, we already established, in *Chapter 3*, that the REIGN OF GOD, equivalently, the REIGN OF CHRIST occurs in the hearts, equivalently, spirits of those who have faith in Christ, as such transpires on earth.

✠ Element 1: NEW BEGINNINGS - man either starts off on a path of righteous-ness, or embarks on a path of evil.

✠ Element 2: COMPANIONSHIP - Companionship that is rooted in pursuit of Righteousness; or Companionship that is rooted in pursuit of Evil.

✠ Element 3: INNER CIRCLE OF FRIENDSHIP: Arrival at Inner Circle of Friendship that is rooted in pursuit of Righteousness; or Arrival at In-ner Circle of Friendship that is rooted in pursuit of Evil.

✠ Element 4: GRAND JUDGMENTS of the Wicked that require *Identification* of The Righteous.

✠ Element 5: MATURITY OF RIGHTEOUSNESS: The Righteous Flourish, and Shine as the Sun in the reign of their Father.

Parallel with the imagery in Isaiah 17:6?

✠ Element 1: Olive Tree is planted; signifies New Beginnings.

✠ Elements 2 & 3: Some boughs yield 2 OLIVES (Companionship of Friend-ship), some boughs yield 3 OLIVES (Arrival at Inner Circle of Friend-ship).

✠ Elements 4 & 5: The most fruitful boughs yield 4 or 5 OLIVES

  ॐ Since 3 transgressions are less than 4 transgressions, and since GJ is associated with ELEMENT 4, evil that is associated with 4 OLIVES is more fruitful than evil that is associated with 3 OLIVES. Remember, in context of the ELEMENT 4, the *Righteous* merely are identified.

  ॐ Since FLOURISHING OF THE RIGHTEOUS is more fruitful than AR-RIVAL AT INNER CIRCLE OF FRIENDSHIP, righteousness that is as-sociated with 5 OLIVES is more fruitful than righteousness that is associated with 3 OLIVES. Note that *flourishing* implies HAPPEN-INGS, meaning the ELEMENT 5 implies materialization of some fruit of righteousness in lives of the righteous.

Prophecy Principle 64 *Combined, the evidence for Elements 1, 2, 3, & 4, Matthew 13:24-30; 36-43, and Isaiah 17:6 agree that, for the wicked, the relevant elements are 1, 2, 3, & 4, and for the righteous, corresponding elements are 1, 2, 3, & 5.*

Prophecy Principle 65 *Consistent with necessity of separation of the wicked from the righteous (Matthew 13:49-50; 25:32–46; Hebrews 7:26), there exists some segmentation between symbolism for the wicked, and symbolism for the righteous.*

Additional Supporting Evidence?

In the parable of the talents, which comes to us in Matthew 25:14-30, our Lord Jesus Christ depicts a righteous Lord who delivered 1, 2, or 5 talents to each of three stewards of His resources. In the assertion that the talents were delivered to each *according to his or her ability*, the Lord Jesus Christ emphasizes that His reign functions as a MERITOCRACY. Our focus, first and foremost, is not on what the stewards did with the talents that were delivered to them, but on consistency of the numerology that is embedded in the parable with the Π-*numerology* that we are establishing in this chapter.

In the Π-*numerology* that we have established, 3 TALENTS do not qualify as start-up resources for stewards of the grace of God. This is the case because the ELEMENT 3 signifies *arrival at an inner circle of friendship*, an outcome that requires prior arrival at friendship. We find then that exclusion of 3 TALENTS is consistent with the Π-*numerology*. Consider then the ELEMENT 4 of the Π-*numerology*. In presence of a determination by their Lord that they were worthy of talents, there is not necessity of a *Grand Judgment*, hence, 4 TALENTS, which would signify *judgment*, ought not to be included. We find then that exclusion of 4 TALENTS is consistent with the Π-*numerology*. Given 1 signifies *New Beginnings*, which can be good, or evil; given 2 signifies *companionship of friendship*; and given 5 signifies *maturity of righteousness*, that is, persons that are deemed deserving of a reward, equivalently, a trust, a righteous Lord can confer each of 1, 2, or 5 talents on His stewards. In the consistency of conferment of 1, 2, or 5 TALENTS on His stewards, our Lord Jesus Christ provides a parable whose numerology is consistent with characterization of 5 as symbolic of MATURITY OF RIGHTEOUSNESS.

The outcome of the parable for the steward who received 1 TALENT conforms with the Π-*numerology*. Upon return of His Lord, the steward who received the 1 TALENT confessed dislike for His Lord, dislike that induced him not to embark on any attempt at multiplying the talent. We have then that the steward chose a path of evil, a path of evil that resulted in arrival at a *Grand Judgment*. Simultaneously, the other two stewards, who exercised efforts for multiplying of their talents were received into the joys of their Lord.

Prophecy Principle 66 *The parable of the talents provides corroboration for the Π-numerology, that generates the following nomenclature:*

$$\Pi(1) = NB$$
$$\Pi(2) = CP$$
$$\Pi(3) = CF$$
$$\Pi(4) = GJ$$
$$\Pi(5) = MR.$$

The Principle of Thanksgiving and Non-giving In to Jealousies

In the parable of the talents, while believers who receive either of 2 or 5 talents are associated with good attitudes, the believer who receives only 1 talent is associated with a bad attitude.

> Why was the believer who was entrusted with 1 talent evil minded about the whole exercise?

Well, in presence of conferment of 2 or 5 talents on the other believers, he or she felt that he or she was not appropriately appreciated. We find then evidence for ENVY, JEALOUSY, SINFUL PRIDE etc. But if a believer with 1 TALENT feels unappreciated, evidence for underappreciation is best demonstrated via multiplying of 1 TALENT into 3 TALENTS, for a 200% net return on investment. Given believers conferred with either of 2 or 5 talents each only generated a 100% return, it would be obvious to the Lord Jesus Christ that the believer with the 2 or 5 talents might not be deserving of greater trust. You see then that investing of the 1 talent could have created a new impression, a new beginning for the believer with the 1 TALENT; on the contrary the believer ended up being judged to be unworthy of the trust that was reposed in him or her.

THE KICKER?

The Lord Jesus Christ did not judge worthiness of the believers on basis of their initial endowments of talents, but on the faithfulness with which the talents were deployed. Qualitatively, the two believers with good attitudes, who each delivered a 100% return received exactly the same reward - an increase to their responsibilities, and participation in His joys (Matthew 25:21,23). You see then that if the evil minded believer had been faithful in deployment of the 1 TALENT, had produced 2 TALENTS, he or she would, in actual fact have arrived at exactly the same sort of reward as believers who started out with larger endowments of talents.

Scriptural evidence for, conditional on degree of faithfulness, equality of reward?

Who then is Paul, and who is Apollos, but ministers through whom you believed, as the Lord gave to each one? I planted, Apollos watered, but GOD GAVE THE INCREASE. *So then neither he who plants is anything, nor he who waters, but God who gives the increase.* Now he who plants and he who waters ARE ONE, and EACH ONE WILL RECEIVE HIS OWN REWARD ACCORDING TO HIS OWN LABOR (1Corinthians 3:5-8).

Spiritual Insight 54 *Our Lord Jesus Christ does not judge faithfulness on basis of your past preparation, rather judges faithfulness on basis of your current willingness and effort. If you will do the most that you are able, in power of the Holy Spirit, with whatever you already are blessed with, you earn exactly the same reward as he or she who, perhaps due to circumstances of birth, started out with better preparation than yourself.*

Spiritual Insight 55 *The key to making the most of life is to seek, always, in power of the Holy Spirit, to make the most of whatever resources already are at your disposal. Our Lord Jesus Christ was able to feed 5,000 men with 5 Loaves and 2 Fish, because He focused on making the most of resources that were at His disposal.*

Spiritual Insight 56 *When Apostle Paul declares, in Philippians 4:13 that "I* CAN DO ALL THINGS THROUGH CHRIST WHO STRENGTHENS ME," *he declares that he always is able to make the most of whatever resources are at his disposal.*

In respect of importance of a spirit of thanksgiving towards The Father, consider the following words from Scriptures.

I want you to know, brethren, that our fathers were all under the cloud, and all passed through the sea, and all were baptized into Moses in the cloud and in the sea, and all ate the same supernatural food and all drank the same supernatural drink. For they drank from the supernatural Rock which followed them, and the Rock was Christ. Nevertheless with most of them God was not pleased; for they were overthrown in the wilderness. NOW THESE THINGS ARE WARNINGS FOR US, NOT TO DESIRE EVIL AS THEY DID. NEITHER MURMUR YE, AS ALSO SOME OF THEM DID MURMUR, AND DID PERISH BY THE DESTROYER (1Corinthians 10:1-6,10).

Always rejoice you; continually pray ye; in every thing give thanks, for this is the will of God in Christ Jesus in regard to you (1Thessalonians 5:18).

Friend, brother in Christ, sister in Christ, or seeker after truth, if you seek to understand the principle of 'THANKSGIVING', if you seek to understand it's importance for your race towards Christ (Hebrews 12:1-2), it's importance for your growth in Christ, pick up a copy of my book, In Jesus Name, and read the chapter on 'Thanksgiving' (*Chapter 8*) at your earliest opportunity and convenience. If there is one principle that you cannot afford not to understand how to practice for building of yourself up in your most holy faith in Christ, it is the principle of thanksgiving.

Spiritual Insight 57 *Whenever The Father gives 1 talent, it is to test the heart, it is so believers can demonstrate the state of their hearts; can demonstrate whether their hearts are filled with thanksgiving or resentment towards The Father. Thanksgiving in the heart turns 1 talent into a* NEW BEGINNING. *Resentment in the heart turns 1 talent into new evidence that facilitates* GRAND JUDGMENTS.

Prophecy Principle 67 *The number 5 is symbolic of* MATURITY OF RIGHTEOUSNESS.

LET US THEN RETURN TO THE IMAGERY IN ISAIAH 17:6. The imagery turns out very clear. During harvest, uppermost boughs have two or three olives, but the most fruitful boughs have four or five. Consider then the imagery. Boughs (Branches) that are most interested in companionship and an inner circle of friendship grow the most, become the uppermost branches, generate two or three olives. Branches that focus on companionship, friendship, and fruitfulness, evident in progression to either of GRAND JUDGMENTS, or MATURITY OF RIGHTEOUSNESS produce four or five olives.

But the most fruitful branches are not the uppermost branches.

The Lesson?

First, if you want to be as fruitful as you need to be in this life, FRUITFULNESS OF THE PURPOSE committed to you by The Father must become more important than either of *comfort of friendship* (symbolism of the *element* 2) or *inner circle of friendship* (symbolism of the *element* 3).

If you are unable to find earthly friendship, or an inner circle of friendship in midst of righteous, loving, joyous pursuit of purpose, do not give up fruitfulness of purpose (symbolism of the *element* 5) for friendship. In this respect, consider that Moses could not really be said to have arrived at any friendships, could not even enjoy companionship of his wife and children, who, out of respect for the work committed to him, went back to Midian with their Uncle. For Moses, the job of leading Israel was an extremely 'lonely' job. While Caleb was a friend to Joshua, the two men spent most of their time fighting for settling of Israel in the promised land, did not have time for development of their friendship. If they instead, had focused on spending of time together, they each would have been less fruitful in pursuit of their God-given purpose. It is not impossible that The Father can desire that you be in some 'aloneness', such that in midst of your solitude and dependence on His spiritual presence for friendship, much like Moses and Paul (Galatians 1:15-20), you are ushered into the most wonderful truths, knowledge, and wisdom - truths, knowledge, and wisdom that you then share with the rest of the body of Christ, and with the world.

But is it possible to experience friendship with The Father and The Son?

The problem my friend is the spiritual reality that the world has changed the meaning of friendship. In today's world, people interpret friendship as someone who stands by you no matter what; someone with whom you spend time in banter and recreation, but perhaps never really get to know. This is not The Father's definition of friendship. The Father never stands by any one no matter what (Hebrews 12:14). If you devolve into love for evil (Galatians 5:18-21), or if you deny faith in Jesus Christ (2Timothy 2:12), The Father will not stand by you (2Corinthians 6:17-18). With The Father and The Son, friendship consists in knowledge and celebration of one another in context of pursuit of godly (loving) purposes and aspirations (Matthew 11:27; John 17:4; Philippians 2:9-11). In context of this definition of friendship, while they fellowship with you in Spirit, you are able to arrive at friendship, equivalently fellowship of The Father, and The Son (1John 1:1-3). In respect of friendship, consider the following Scripture.

You are my friends if you do what I command you. This I command you, to love one another (John 15:14).

No more do I call you servants, because the servant hath not known what his lord doth, and you I have called friends, because all things that I heard from my Father, I did make known to you (John 15:15).

Spiritual Insight 58 *While friendships are easy to pursue in times of peace, such as was the case in context of timing of earthly ministry of our Lord Jesus Christ, such that Jesus could transition from regarding His disciples as students, to regarding them as friends (John 15:15), this typically is not the case during times of transitions or warfare.*

Spiritual Insight 59 *The invitation from The Father and The Son is an invitation to fellowship, is an invitation to friendship. Only those who get to know The Son, however, gain access to friendship with The Father.*

Spiritual Insight 60 *Since our Lord Jesus Christ has called us friends (John 15:14-15), if we do not get to experience His friendship, it only is because we do not get as close to Him as we need to be.*

> If you sidestep the demands of love, this because you are in haste of pursuit of purpose, you might become the uppermost branch, yet not become the most fruitful branch.

Second, never deem yourself so much in haste in context of pursuit of purpose that you are unable to take time out to love a neighbor (remember the *Parable of the 'Good Samaritan'* - Luke 10:29-37). In midst of a famine that was allowed by The Father, The Father arranged affairs of Prophet Elijah, such that a widow and her son could be saved from death, then could be brought into knowledge of The Father (1Kings 17:8-24; Luke 4:24-26). The Father never gets so caught up in purpose that He loses sight of any one individual. With the Father, there never is any purpose so grand it justifies trampling of a single person into the ground, or neglect of demands of love for anyone. For additional discussion of imperative of love in context of pursuit of grand and lofty objectives, check out *Chs. 3 & 4* of my book, 'TRUE SANCTIFICATION'.

Spiritual Insight 61 *The race to bear fruit for The Father is not to the swift or the strong, but by the Spirit of the almighty God (Zechariah 4:6).*

> Is the imagery in Isaiah 17:6 appropriate to our relationship with our Lord Jesus Christ, and are the lessons scriptural?

ABSOLUTELY.

In John 15:5, 8, 16-17, Jesus declares as follows.

> I am the vine, you are the branches. He who abides in me, and I in him, he it is that bears much fruit, for apart from me you can do nothing. BY THIS MY FATHER IS GLORIFIED, THAT YOU BEAR MUCH FRUIT, AND SO PROVE TO BE MY DISCIPLES. You did not choose me, but I chose you and appointed you that you should go and bear fruit and that your fruit should abide; so that whatever you ask The Father in my name, He may give it to you. This I command you, to love one another.

The Father has called us to bear fruit, that is, to produce good works (Ephesians 2:10), such that He is glorified. We are able to produce good works only if we abide in Christ. But all good works must be bound up in love, for only a person who loves can please The Father. I discuss the following characterization of essence of The Father in detail in my book, 'True Sanctification', and in my Medium post of January 3, 2019 titled, 'God, Love, Essence, Time, and Choice'; here, I merely provide this glorious insightful delineation of who The Father has revealed Himself to be.

> The Father spends all of His time - each and every second, minute, hour, day, week, month, year, decade, century, millennium - CONCEIVING loving things to do in future; FORMULATING loving things to do in the present; and IMPLEMENTING loving things that He conceived in prior periods.

> 'GOD IS LOVE' is a statement of intentions and actions, not some mere metaphysical aphorism.

> God is Love because Love is what He does, and because Love is what He contemplates to do.

> All of The Father's projects or purposes are purposes of Love.

> The Father declares that you are defined by the sorts of projects or purposes that attract your energies.

Spiritual Insight 62 *If you seek to be all that Father, Son, and Holy Spirit desire you to be, purpose must not be sacrificed for comfort of friendship, and pursuit of purpose must not override overarching objective of love for others.*

The Numerolgy for the Element 6

Numerology 6 *Let $e_6 = 6$. Then e_6 is symbolic of 'Judgment of the Wicked (JW)'. S_6 equates then to JW, with outcome,*

$$\Pi\left(e_6\right) = \Pi\left(6\right) = S_6 = JW.$$

The Evidence

In Matthew 16:1-4, and John 6:30-31, the Jews asked for a sign from Jesus. In essence, they asked for yet another miracle in relation to multiplying of 5 loaves and 2 fish for feeding of a multitude. In response, Jesus told them to focus on the spiritual food, not the physical food, this because the spiritual food lasts for eternity, the physical food, but for a moment (John 6:25-58). At this point, and for the very first time in either gospel, Jesus prophesied His death and resurrection (Matthew 16:4, 21-23; John 7:32-34). In His emphasis on spiritual, as opposed to physical food, many who had followed Him became disenchanted with Him. In their minds, all they could appreciate was an earthly kingdom, not ushering in of a spiritual kingdom ruled over by our Lord Jesus Christ, He who is King of kings, and Lord of lords.

The aftermath (John 6:66-69)?

> After this many of His disciples drew back and no longer went about with Him. Jesus said to the twelve, "Do you also wish to go away?" Simon Peter answered Him, "Lord, to whom shall we go? You have the words of eternal life; and we have believed and have come to know, that you are the Holy One of God."

Clearly, Jesus was aware that the people had rejected His message of a spiritual kingdom, only were interested in a prophet who would usher in a physical earthly kingdom, the sort of earthly kingdom for which zealots, who are personified by Barabbas were fighting. It was the decision to focus on ushering in of an earthly kingdom that led to demand for release of Barabbas, as opposed to Jesus Christ at Passover (Matthew 27:16-26; Mark 15:11-15; Luke 23:18-19; John 18:39-40), a decision that eventually would lead to destruction of Jerusalem and it's temple by Roman General Titus in 70 AD. Note Barabbas was a murderer, a man who had killed fellow Jews who seemed to stand in way of his insurgency against the Roman occupation. Yet when faced with a choice between Jesus - a man who had *healed them*, who had *fed them*, who had *freed them* from demonic possession - and Barabbas, the Jews chose Barabbas.

Spiritual Insight 63 *Whenever people declare that they love liars, thieves, and murderers, this only so they can spite the righteous through whom they already have been blessed, they cast their souls resolutely on paths that only lead to destruction.*

So then what happened next (Matthew 17:1-3)?

> And AFTER SIX DAYS Jesus took with Him Peter and James and John his brother, and led them up a high mountain apart. And He was transfigured before them, and His face shone like the sun, and His garments became white as light. And behold, there appeared to them Moses and Elijah, talking with Him.

In the verses that follow, The Father declares, "THIS IS MY BELOVED SON, WITH WHOM I AM WELL PLEASED; LISTEN TO HIM." In the transfiguration, Jesus receives encouragement and reassurance via companionship of Moses and Elijah. The words from The Father were directed at Peter, James, and John to the extent that, no matter whether they fully understood or not, henceforth, they were to make even more sure to listen to Jesus. To listen here means to imbibe, practice, obey whatever they were taught by Jesus.

So then, from the timing of rejection of pursuit of spiritual realities for focus on earthly realities to transfiguration of Jesus, to affirmation of the fact that the course was fully set for death and resurrection of our Lord Jesus Christ was six days. In essence, The Father and our Lord Jesus Christ provided the Jewish nation with six days for reversal of their course of action. With their attitudes and decisions set, SIX DAYS later, at transfiguration of Jesus, Jesus received encouragement from Moses and Elijah, and Peter, James, and John were warned to make sure to listen to Jesus. The timing of the warning is important, for in Matthew 16:22-23, Peter had accosted Jesus on account of the prediction of His death and resurrection, and attempted to rebuke his teacher. In the warning from The Father, Peter especially was warned not to deviate from words of His teacher, from words of our Lord and Savior Jesus Christ. While Peter was not attentive to this warning, as such was desired by the devil (Luke 22:31), through intercession of our Lord and Savior Jesus Christ for his soul (Luke 22:32), Peter found genuine repentance from his stubbornness towards The Father (Luke 22:62; John 21:15-19).

Prophecy Principle 68 *With the characterization done by Father and Son, the element 6 stands for a time interval, which precedes activities that have to do with judgment of evil, and commencement of The Father's agenda for freeing of the righteous from those who are evil.*

Do we have any other corroborating evidence from the Scriptures?

Then he cried in my ears with a loud voice, saying, "Draw near, you executioners of the city, each with his destroying weapon in his hand. And lo, SIX MEN came from the direction of the upper gate, which faces north, EVERY MAN WITH HIS WEAPON FOR SLAUGHTER IN HIS HAND, and with them was a man clothed in linen, with a writing case at his side. AND THEY WENT IN AND STOOD BESIDE THE BRONZE ALTAR (Ezekiel 9:1-2)."

And the Lord said to him, "Go through the midst of the city, through the midst of Jerusalem, and put a mark on the foreheads of the men who sigh and cry over all the abominations that are done within it (Ezekiel 9:4)."

To the others He said in my hearing, "Go after him through the city and kill; do not let your eye spare, nor have any pity. Utterly slay old and young men, maidens and little children and women; but do not come near anyone on whom is the mark; and BEGIN AT MY SANCTUARY" So they began with the elders who were before the temple. Then He said to them, "Defile the temple, and fill the courts with the slain. Go out!" And they went out and killed in the city (Ezekiel 9:5-6).

AT THE END OF SIX YEARS each of you must set free the fellow Hebrew who has been sold to you and has served you six years; you must set him free from your service. But your fathers did not listen to me or incline their ears to me (Jeremiah 34:14).

"If your brother, a Hebrew man, or a Hebrew woman, is sold to you, he shall serve you SIX YEARS, and in the seventh year you shall let him go free from you. And when you let him go free from you, you shall not let him go empty-handed; you shall furnish him liberally out of your flock, out of your threshing floor, and out of your wine press; as the Lord your God has blessed you, you shall give to him (Deuteronomy 15:12-14)."

It is clear that Ezekiel 9:1-2 associates the *element 6* with The Father's judgment agenda. Consistent with inferences from the life and ministry of our Lord Jesus Christ, introduction of the *element 6* is associated with commencement of (Ezekiel 9:4), and execution of The Father's judgment agenda (Ezekiel 9:5-6). Consistent with the declaration by Apostle Peter in 1Peter 4:17, judgment commenced in the sanctuary, with those who were supposed to be leaders of God's people (Ezekiel 9:6-7).

Prophecy Principle 69 *The element 6 clearly is associated with commencement, and execution of The Father's Judgments on those who love evil.*

In Jeremiah 34:14 and Deuteronomy 15:12-14, the *element 6* is associated with freedoms for people who, somehow, had fallen into servitude of their fellow men. Freedom then is conditioned on arrival at the *element 6*. Given our Lord Jesus Christ appears a second time because evil men insist on not living at peace with those who love the name of Jesus, our Lord Jesus Christ appears a second time primarily for freeing of believers in His name from oppression of evil. The *element 6* is symbolic of '*freedom from oppression*' agenda that frees the righteous from persecutions of the wicked.

CONSISTENT WITH THE FOREGOING, DEUTERONOMY 15:16 AND REVELATION 14:1-3 STATE AS FOLLOWS.

You shall remember that you were a slave in the land of Egypt, and the Lord your God REDEEMED YOU; therefore I command you this (*to release your fellow Israelite after 6 years*) today.

Then I looked, and lo, on Mount Zion stood the Lamb, and with Him a hundred and forty-four thousand who had His name and His Father's name written on their foreheads. And I heard a voice from heaven like the sound of many waters and like the sound of loud thunder; the voice I heard was like the sound of harpers playing on their harps, and they sang a new song before the throne and before the four living creatures and before the elders. NO ONE COULD LEARN THAT SONG EXCEPT THE HUNDRED AND FORTY-FOUR THOUSAND WHO HAD BEEN REDEEMED FROM THE EARTH.

Prophecy Principle 70 *The element 6 is symbolic of the grace period that precedes judgment of the wicked, activities necessary for execution of judgment on the wicked, and execution of judgment of the wicked.*

Prophecy Principle 71 *Grand Judgments that transpire in context of symbolism of the element 4 are executed in context of symbolism of the element 6. Given symbolism of the element 5 does not pertain to the wicked, only pertains to the righteous, the transition from element 4 to element 6 of the Π-NUMEROLOGY is consistent with symbolism of a grace period for turning away from rejection of the Love of God.*

The Numerology for the Element 7

Numerology 7 *Let $e_7 = 7$. Then e_7 is symbolic of 'Completeness and Commencement of New Agenda (CC)'. S_7 equates then to CC, with outcome,*

$$\Pi\left(e_7\right) = \Pi\left(7\right) = S_7 = CC.$$

The Evidence

Symbolism of the *element* 7 perhaps is easiest to establish. The *element* 7 signifies completeness. While it is not exogenous evidence, that is, is not from outside of the Book of Revelation, The choice of 7 churches by our Lord Jesus Christ in Revelation Chapters 2 and 3 resides in the fact that the complete history of His Church is embodied in 7 churches. We have then that 7 CHURCHES signify completeness of history of the Church. The exogenous evidence is embedded in Genesis 2:1-2.

> And the heavens and the earth are completed, and all their host; and God COMPLETETH BY THE SEVENTH DAY HIS WORK WHICH HE HATH MADE, and ceaseth by the seventh day from all His work which He hath made.

But did The Father stop working?

But Jesus answered them, "MY FATHER IS WORKING STILL, and I am working (John 5:17)."

Clearly, the term, 'WORKING STILL' refers to the fact that The Father in reality never has ceased to work since completion of creation week. Concerning the fact that He has been working all the while since creation week, The Father Himself declares in Isaiah 43:19, 42:9.

> See, I AM DOING A NEW THING! Now it springs up; do you not perceive it? I am making a way in the desert and streams in the wasteland.
>
> Behold, the former things have come to pass, and NEW THINGS I NOW DECLARE; before they spring forth I tell you of them.

If The Father has continued working since Creation Week, we arrive at the inference that The Father rested from the work that had to do with Creation, commenced on other work, such as the work that has to do with the Redemption that is available to us in Christ, work to which The Father alludes in Genesis 3:15.

Spiritual Insight 64 *If your ceasing from work is like that of The Father, it means you rest by faith in completeness of a work that is done, take up new work that is in need of completion. This, as we already have seen is essence of Godliness, which is, continuation of CONCEPTION of loving things to do in future; FORMULATION of loving things to do in the present; and IMPLEMENTATION of loving things that were conceived in prior periods.*

Spiritual Insight 65 *Only people who are able to rest - to take their attention off - from work that they deem completed have capacity for producing things that are new. Sabbath rest once a week provides us with opportunity to rest from work that was completed in course of the previous week, this so we have capacity for producing of new things in the week to follow.*

Spiritual Insight 66 *Resting once a week from normal everyday work that produces a living is wisdom, not only for disciples of Jesus Christ, but for all of mankind. For more on weekly Sabbath rest, which is not compulsory, but yet an activity that brings blessings into the life of a believer in the name of Jesus Christ, see CH. 26 of my book, In Jesus Name.*

In addition to the evidence from Genesis 2:1-2, Israelites who were indentured servants were set free at commencement of the 7th year from the starting date of their indenture (Deuteronomy 15:12-14). The 7th year represented then, not only COMPLETENESS of their obligation, but with gifts from their prior employer, COMMENCEMENT of a new agenda. In the same vein, land was farmed for 6 years, then allowed to rest in course of the 7th year (Leviticus 25:3-5), resulting in combination of COMPLETENESS of one farming agenda, and opportunity for COMMENCEMENT of a new agenda.

Prophecy Principle 72 *The element 7 symbolizes COMPLETENESS OF A PRE-EXISTING AGENDA, and COMMENCEMENT OF NEW AGENDA.*

The Numerology for the Element 10

Numerology 8 *Let $e_{10} = 10$. Then e_{10} is symbolic of 'Grand Judgment of a Grand Purpose (JP)'. S_{10} equates then to JP, with outcome,*

$$\Pi\left(e_{10}\right) = \Pi\left(10\right) = S_{10} = JP.$$

The Evidence

Symbolism of the *element* 10 is evident in the fact that the 10 COMMAND-MENTS or MATTERS (*YLT*) were given to the children of Israel as an act of *Grand Judgment of a Grand Purpose (JP)*. That is, it had become evident to The Father, that absent specification of implications of '*loving of the neighbor*', that not even His chosen people could be expected to treat his or her neighbor right.

The Scriptural Evidence?

Why then the law? on account of transgressions it was added (it was added because sin was multiplying), till the seed (Jesus) might come to which the promise hath been made, having been set in order through messengers in the hand of a mediator (Galatians 3:19).

And he is there with Jehovah forty days and forty nights; bread he hath not eaten, and water he hath not drunk; and he writeth on the tables the matters of the covenant - the ten matters (Exodus 34:28).

With respect to additional evidence, when The Father would implement a *Grand Judgment of the Grand Purpose* that was the 12 tribes of the sons of Israel, He stripped away 10 tribes that, via His foreknowledge, He knew would not ever desire to have relationship with Him. In this respect, consider 1Kings 11:30-31, and 1Kings 12:22-24.

And Ahijah layeth hold on the new garment that is on him, and rendeth it - twelve pieces, and saith to Jeroboam, "Take to thee TEN PIECES, for thus said Jehovah, God of Israel, lo, I am rending the kingdom out of the hand of Solomon, and have given to thee ten tribes (1Kings 11:30-31)."

And the word of God is unto Shemaiah a man of God, saying, Speak unto Rehoboam son of Solomon, king of Judah, and unto all the house of Judah and Benjamin, and the rest of the people, saying, "Thus said Jehovah, ye do not go up nor fight with your brethren the sons of Israel; turn back each to his house, FOR FROM ME HATH THIS THING BEEN;" and they hear the word of Jehovah, and turn back to go according to the word of Jehovah (1Kings 12:22-24).

Consider then the Greatness of The Father. The two prophets whose ministries we know the most about - ELIJAH and ELISHA - were prophets to those 10 TRIBES. You see then the wisdom, righteousness, and justice of The Father, which is, while He, of necessity must act on His foreknowledge, else He is a God who does not plan ahead, everyone is judged on basis of their actions; and those whom He sees to be most at risk of rejecting truth, on them He lavishes more of His mercy and efforts.

> Is it not spiritual blindness, and giving of the heart to things that do not profit, which makes people run away from such a God?

Prophetic Lessons 11 *Elijah and Elisha could have had easier ministries in Judah, the kingdom, which tended to have righteous kings. But The Father had sent them to the lost sheep of the house of Israel - the 10 tribes. Those who are wise do not compare themselves with others, do not compare their comforts, houses, or cars with others, only ask themselves, "AM I DOING WHAT THE FATHER HAS REVEALED THAT HE EXPECTS OF ME?"*

Prophecy Principle 73 *The element 10 symbolizes* GRAND JUDGMENT OF A GRAND PURPOSE (JP) *that result in better convergence of evolution of life and affairs on earth towards achievement of a Grand Purpose.*

The Numerology for the Element 12

Numerology 9 *Let* $e_{12} = 12$. *Then* e_{12} *is symbolic of 'Completeness of a Grand Purpose (CG)'.* S_{10} *equates then to CG, with outcome,*

$$\Pi(e_{12}) = \Pi(12) = S_{12} = CG.$$

The Evidence

Symbolism of the *element* 12 is very straightforward, perhaps the easiest to establish. Our Lord Jesus Christ deliberately chose 12 disciples (Luke 6:13; Mark 3:14; Matthew 10:1-4). Upon His ascension back to the heavens, his disciples were so convinced about importance of 12, they cast lots for choice of *Matthias* as replacement for Judas Iscariot. It is straightforwardly true, however, that The Father having had to raise Apostle Paul for the ministry to the Gentiles, that it is not Matthias who receives that 12th crown, that rather, it is Apostle Paul. I believe Matthias being the great brother in Christ that he must have been simply will respond, "just and true are your ways Father, thou King of saints (Revelation 15:3)."

In the arrangement that Israel had 12 sons for arrival at 12 tribes, there is corroboration for symbolism of ELEMENT 12 as signifying Completeness of Grand Purpose. In the splitting of the sons of Israel into Judah (2 tribes) and Israel (10 tribes), The Father declared that the *Completeness of Grand Purpose* now would be directed through Judah, that is, through the seed to whom the promises belong - our Lord Jesus Christ (Galatians 3:16-17), who reconstituted the *Completeness of Grand Purpose* around 12 DISCIPLES who would go on to become APOSTLES. In this respect, Apostle Paul writes as follows.

> And to Abraham were the promises spoken, and to his seed; He doth not say, 'and to seeds', as of many, but as of one, and 'to thy seed', which is Christ; and this I say, a covenant confirmed before by God to Christ, the law, that came four hundred and thirty years after, doth not set aside, to make void the promise (Galatians 3:16-17).

It is important to note that Completeness does not imply Completion. In this respect, subsequent to choosing of the 12, our Lord Jesus Christ commands them as follows.

> Having gone, then, disciple all the nations, (baptizing them - to the name of The Father, and of the Son, and of the Holy Spirit, teaching them to observe all, whatever I did command you,) and lo, I am with you all the days - till the full end of the age (Matthew 28:19-20).

For concreteness, while a university's ranking can improve from 140 to 60, throughout all of that time, it's charter can remain exactly the same. While a boxer can improve from *4 wins, & 4 losses, 4-4,* to *12-4,* his *weight, reach, torso strength,* and *weight of biggest punch landed* can remain exactly the same. So then, we conclude he learnt something from those four losses.

Prophecy Principle 74 *The element 12 symbolizes* COMPLETENESS OF A GRAND PURPOSE (CG). *Note* COMPLETENESS DOES NOT IMPLY COMPLETION, *rather implies Presence of all of the* CORE RESOURCES *that are required for achievement of a Grand Purpose.*

Prophecy Principle 75 *Completeness is the state of things, the core that, regardless of progress with respect to achievement of Grand Purposes, does not change.*

Summary of The Father's Numerology

In the presence of our Lord Jesus Christ, I adjure you not to attempt to convert the Π-*numerology* that we have inferred, but which belongs to The Father and The Son into your own numerology. If you attempt to turn The Father's numerology into your very own numerology, you attempt to play god, meaning you run foul of The Father. Following is a summary of the NUMEROLOGY OF THE FATHER, as developed in context of the Π-*numerology* that we have inferred.

Numerology of The Father

✠ Element 1 (NB): NEW BEGINNINGS - man either starts off on a path of righteousness, or embarks on a path of evil.

✠ Element 2 (CP): COMPANIONSHIP OF PURPOSE - Companionship that is rooted in pursuit of Righteousness; or Companionship that is rooted in pursuit of Evil.

✠ Element 3 (CF): INNER CIRCLE OF FRIENDSHIP: Arrival at Inner Circle of Friendship that is rooted in pursuit of Righteousness; or Arrival at Inner Circle of Friendship that is rooted in pursuit of Evil.

✠ Element 4 (GJ): GRAND JUDGMENTS of the Wicked that require identification of The Righteous.

✠ Element 5 (MR): MATURITY OF RIGHTEOUSNESS: The Righteous Flourish, and Shine as the Sun in the reign of their Father.

✠ Element 6 (JW): COMMENCEMENT OF PERIOD OF JUDGMENT & EXECUTION OF JUDGMENT ON THE WICKED.

✠ Element 7 (CC): COMPLETENESS OF A PRE-EXISTING AGENDA & COMMENCEMENT OF A NEW AGENDA

✠ Element 10 (JG): GRAND JUDGMENT OF A GRAND PURPOSE

✠ Element 12 (CG): COMPLETENESS OF A GRAND PURPOSE

Using acronyms that are derived for symbolisms that are embedded in each of the elements (numbers) of The Father's Numerology, the ordering of the resulting symbolism is:

1. ELEMENT 7 (CC)

2. ELEMENT 3 (CF)

3. ELEMENT 12 (CG)

4. ELEMENT 2 (CP)

5. ELEMENT 4 (GJ)

6. ELEMENT 10 (JG)

7. ELEMENT 6 (JW)

8. ELEMENT 5 (MR)

9. ELEMENT 1 (NB)

It is straightforward to see that, with exception of ELEMENT 4, ordering of the elements of the Π-*numerology* does not line up with symbolisms that are embedded in the Π-*numerology*. In addition, and perhaps more importantly, we have that the Π-*numerology* can be segmented into two parts: A SEGMENT I for those who love evil, and a SEGMENT II for those who love righteousness. This segmentation, which is not characteristic of the numbers themselves reveals non-triviality of the Π-*numerology*. The two segments are, respectively:

✠ Segment I - THOSE WHO LOVE AND DO EVIL

     ॐ ELEMENT 1 (NB)

     ॐ ELEMENT 2 (CP)

     ॐ ELEMENT 3 (CF)

     ॐ ELEMENT 4 (GJ)

     ॐ ELEMENT 6 (JW)

✠ Segment II - THOSE WHO LOVE AND DO RIGHTEOUSNESS

     ॐ ELEMENT 1 (NB)

     ॐ ELEMENT 2 (CP)

     ॐ ELEMENT 3 (CF)

     ॐ ELEMENT 5 (MR)

     ॐ ELEMENT 7 (CC)

     ॐ ELEMENT 10 (JG)

     ॐ ELEMENT 12 (CG)

As already discussed, as outlined, the Π-*numerology* will be applied to interpretation of the 7 SEALS, 7 TRUMPETS, and 7 VIALS of the Book of Revelation. It further will be applied wherever the ELEMENTS 10 and 12 are encountered, and are deemed to be of importance. All other symbolisms that are required for interpretation of prophecies that are entrusted to Apostle John by our Lord Jesus Christ will be developed as we go along.

Outside of interpretation of prophecies that come to us in the Book of Revelation, these are the takeaways from THE FATHER'S NUMEROLOGY for everyday Christian living.

The Symbolism of the Element 1: Never despise NEW BEGINNINGS, for The Father specializes in bringing forth new things through those who love Him, through those who are called according to His purpose (Romans 8:28).

The Symbolism of the Element 2: It is a godly thing to seek companionship, either in course of marriage or friendship. Essence of companionship or friendship is receipt of love from another person, and development of capacity for loving another person. Since love requires demonstration, spending of time on conception, formulation, and implementation of purposes of love, and on actions that actualize purposes of love is essence of godly living.

The Symbolism of the Element 3: Either of companionship or friendship is not fruitful until it gives birth to something. If marriage or friendship is in entirety rooted in frivolity, it lacks capacity for giving birth to anything that is truly meaningful. Each of companionship and friendship are meant then to be rooted in pursuit of purposes, equivalently, aspirations. It is the desire of The Father that the companionships that you most cherish mature into an inner circle of friendship.

If your companionship or friendship does not seem to have any capacity for giving birth to something meaningful, Reassess, Recalibrate, Redirect.

The Symbolism of the Element 4: If you choose sin or evil, a day of GRAND JUDGMENT always will arrive; a day on which essence of who you are, which is evil, is formally established by The Father.

The Symbolism of the Element 5: If you choose righteousness, do not allow either of companionship or friendship prevent you from pursuit of, and arrival at fruitfulness, at maturity.

The Symbolism of the Element 6: A day for commencement of execution of judgment on sin or evil always will arrive. Naturally, only those deemed to be evil in context of Grand Judgments receive execution of judgment from The Father.

The Symbolism of the Element 7:   Only those who, like The Father, believe they are able to continue to do *New Things* truly have capacity for combining COMPLETENESS OF A PRE-EXISTING AGENDA, and COMMENCEMENT OF A NEW AGENDA.

The Symbolism of the Element 10:   Grand Judgments induce events that better converge the future towards achievement of purposes of The Father. If you seek to benefit from JG, choose righteousness, that is, the Love of Christ always.

The Symbolism of the Element 12:   If you are to arrive at the resiliency of The Father, the resiliency that pursues purposes for thousands of years, and sees them through, there must be core things about you that do not change, that from day to day, month to month, and year to year remain exactly the same. If you are a NEOPHYTE, *this core* ought to be always making effort by choice of the Love of God, to remain in the Presence of Christ. If you are a POWER FOR CHRIST, *this core* ought to be demonstrations of the Love of God, brotherly kindness, and a life, which revolves around *Conception*, *Formulation*, and *Implementation* of Love Projects. These things help maintain the spiritual reality of the Presence of Christ. In *Chapters 7 & 8*, we saw how having a core that does not change is a necessary condition for generation of new things.

CHAPTER 7

Invitation to See The Things That Are

Revelation *ch. 3* ends with discussion of the CHURCH IN LAODICEA, the Church which, as we have seen in Chapter 5, persists until the end of time. Our Lord Jesus Christ having won the right to have HIS PRESENCE here on earth, regardless of the state of the Church in Laodicea, the *Presence of Christ* is spiritual reality.

Prophetic Lessons 12 *Regardless of spiritual state of the Church, the PRESENCE OF CHRIST on earth is spiritual reality.*

Clearly, the Church in Laodicea is representative of the worldwide Church. This is evident in individualization of the Presence of Christ, such that the reality of the Presence of Christ is not conditioned on the state of the Church, but on responses of individuals to the grace of our Lord and Savior Jesus Christ. I have provided rigorous evidence for conditionality of reigning with Christ on fellowship with The Father, Son, and Holy Spirit in Chapters 3 and 5. In this respect, it is important to note, once again, that only those who, while in the Holy Spirit, are ushered into the Presence of Christ, who then introduces them to The Father, reign with Christ. In this sense, to reign with Christ is tantamount to actualization of the Presence of Christ. Note then the important difference.

Prophetic Lessons 13 *All, who, in their hearts (spirits) truly desire to walk in love towards each and every one of their neighbors are in the Presence of Christ. Only those, however, who are ushered into the Presence of Christ by The Holy Spirit actualize the Presence of Christ. Those who are ushered into the Presence of Christ, who, as such, actualize the Presence of Christ, are those who arrive at love for others that is totally unblemished. Only those who start off with the LOVE OF CHRIST can develop love that is totally unblemished.*

Prophetic Lessons 14 *While the Presence of Christ is spiritual reality,* THIS REALITY IS EVIDENT TO THE WORLD ONLY IF INDIVIDUALS WHO HAVE FAITH IN JESUS CHRIST ACTUALIZE THE PRESENCE OF CHRIST, *arrive at fellowship with The Father, and The Son. Since only those who already have fellowship with the Holy Spirit arrive at the Presence of Christ, individuals who arrive at the Presence of Christ have fellowship with Father, Son, and Holy Spirit.*

So then, our Lord Jesus Christ declares that the Church in Laodicea is wretched, miserable, poor, and blind, yet is unaware of her true state. The Church in Laodicea is asked to repent, is asked to buy of the Lord Jesus Christ, *gold fired by fire* (GENUINE FAITH), *white raiment* (RIGHTEOUSNESS OF JESUS CHRIST), and *eye-salve* (CAPACITY FOR PERCEIVING THE TRUE STATE OF THINGS). Our Lord Jesus Christ then leaves the outcome of the matter open. In the leaving open of the outcome of the matter, the state of the Church of Christ becomes an open matter that is determined at any given point in time.

Prophecy Insight 34 *In the 'leaving open' of the response of the Church in Laodicea to the pleas of our Lord Jesus Christ, the Church in Laodicea becomes representative of the state of the Church at any given point in time.*

Now then, we arrive at *ch. 4* of the *Book of Revelation.* In Revelation 4:1, Apostle John is invited to come and see 'WHAT IT BEHOVETH TO COME TO PASS AFTER THESE THINGS'. Since the Church of Laodicea is the Church that lasts for all of the rest of time, the phrase, '*what it behoveth to come to pass after these things*' implies things that come to pass in context of the time of the Church in Laodicea. As we shall see, for credibility of the spiritual principle for governance of affairs of earth that is elucidated to Apostle John in the visions, The Father provides a foretaste of the things to come in context of the first six Churches of Revelation Chapters 2 and 3. This is a principle of The Father's, which is, prior to arrival of a spiritual reality, provision of 'SHADOWS' or 'TYPES'. In this vein, we know that MOSES WAS A TYPE OF CHRIST (Deuteronomy 18:15; Hebrews 3:1-6; 2Corinthians 3:7-18); that MELCHIZEDEK WAS A TYPE OF CHRIST (Hebrews 5:6,10; 6:20; 7:11,17); and that OTHNIEL (Judges 3:9-10), SAMSON (Judges 13:25; 14:19; 15:14), GIDEON (Judges 6:34), DAVID (Psalms 51:11), and JEPHTHAH (Judges 11:29) all were types of Christ (Hebrews 11:32), that all were clothed with the Holy Spirit prior to the time of giving of the Holy Spirit to all men, a time that commenced only after ascension of our Lord Jesus Christ to heaven (John 16:7). We further know that the service of the sanctuary that was instituted in context of the Old Covenant foreshadowed the spiritual ministry of our Lord Jesus Christ as High Priest in the heavenly sanctuary (Hebrews 10:1-18).

Prophecy Interpretation 12 *While* 'THE THINGS THAT BEHOVETH TO COME TO PASS AFTER THESE THINGS' *pertain to visions of the spiritual system for governance of affairs on earth, a spiritual system that could come into play fully, only upon arrival of the* PRESENCE OF CHRIST, *as such came into full force with commencement of the Church in Laodicea, The Father provides a* SHADOW *(*TYPE, *or* FORETASTE*) of these things in context of events that transpired in course of timelines for the first 6 Churches of Revelation Chs. 2 and 3.*

Prophecy Principle 76 *Provision of shadows prior to full institution of spiritual realities is a principle of The Father's that is demonstrated in all of Christian Scriptures.*

So then, Apostle John is transported IN THE SPIRIT to the throne room of God, and sees our Lord Jesus Christ seated in the throne of His Father (Revelation 3:21-22; 4:2-3), surrounded by the 4 LIVING CREATURES, and the 24 ELDERS. Prior to commencement of the visions that relate to the things to come, first, Apostle John is introduced, in Revelation *chs. 4 & 5*, to things that are, that is, to things that always will be, this because they are in Christ.

The Things That Are 1 *Our Lord Jesus Christ is seated in the throne of His Father as God. This* A THING THAT IS, A THING THAT ALWAYS WILL BE, *but yet a thing that is source of all that ever really will be in future, for only what is done in Christ survives onslaught of waves of time.*

In the throne room, there is giving of glory to our Lord Jesus Christ by the 4 LIVING CREATURES, and by the 24 ELDERS, all of whom have crowns of gold on their heads (Revelation 4:4), meaning they reign with our Lord Jesus Christ. Whenever the 4 LIVING CREATURES give glory, honor, and thanks to Jesus, He who is living to the ages of the ages (Revelation 4:9), with their crowns cast before the throne, the 24 ELDERS bow to our Lord Jesus Christ saying:

> Worthy art Thou, O Lord, to receive the glory, and the honor, and the power, because thou - thou didst create the all things, and because of thy will are they, and they were created (Revelation 4:11).

The Things That Are 2 *The truth that our Lord Jesus Christ is Creator, and that all things subsist in Him, and by His will, is a thing that is, that always will be.*

The conventional teaching about crowns that accrue to those who have faith in Christ is, they are received only at timing of death. Well, is this characterization of timing of receipt of crowns from our Lord Jesus Christ true?

And I saw, and lo, a white horse, and he who is sitting upon it is having a bow, and there was given to him a crown, and he went forth overcoming, and that he may overcome (Revelation 6:2).

Happy the man who doth endure temptation, because, becoming approved, he shall receive the crown of the life, which the Lord did promise to those loving Him (James 1:12).

And at the manifestation of the chief Shepherd, ye shall receive the unfading crown of glory (1Peter 5:4).

It is straightforward that only man that remains alive on earth has need of overcoming, and '*that he may overcome*'. This is evident in closing admonitions from our Lord Jesus Christ to each of the seven churches in Revelation *chs. 2 & 3*. On basis of *Revelation 6:2*, and closing admonitions referred to in Revelation *chs. 2 & 3*, it is unequivocal that crowns are expected to be received by believers while they remain alive on earth. Apostles James delineates that only those who are approved in context of challenges to their faith, that is, those who allow the LOVE OF CHRIST to be perfected in them, in context of challenges of life receive the crown of life, that is, life that is, age-during (John 17:3), commonly and somewhat inaccurately referred to as *eternal life* in the interpretive translations. Since life that is age-during is arrived at via knowledge of The Father and The Son, our Lord Jesus Christ affirms that the crown of life is received in this life. Apostle Peter adds the inference that crowns are received at the manifestation of our Lord and Savior Jesus Christ. Given our Lord Jesus Christ lives in the heavens, meaning it is only on earth that He manifests spiritually, all of the Scriptures agree that crowns are received on earth by believers who are alive, who, on basis of a meritocracy qualify for receipt of the crown of life.

The Things That Are 3 *Crowns are received on earth, at timing of a manifestation of our Lord Jesus Christ by believers who are alive, who, on basis of maintenance of their love in context of challenges to their faith, allow the Love of Christ in them to be perfected.*

The Things That Are 4 *Only the 24* ELDERS *have crowns; the 4* LIVING CREATURES *do not have crowns. We arrive then at an insight, which is, only the 24* ELDERS *already had arrived at approval of Christ.*

The dichotomy between 'eternal life', an outcome, and 'being in Christ', the source of life that subsists for all time?

The Things That Are 5 *The term,* 'ETERNAL LIFE' *presumes that a believer becomes a source of life to himself or herself. The more accurate rendition as,* 'LIFE THAT IS AGE-DURING' *means a believer receives life that lasts for all* *of the ages that already are created, that already are planned by our Lord Jesus Christ. Since Jesus lives forever, and desires that life remain on earth forever, the spiritual reality that the spirit of such a person, which is in Christ, participates in affairs of life forever is an outcome, not a cause.*

Prophecy Insight 35 *I discern only* TWO AGES *that have been created by our Lord Jesus Christ -* THE AGE OF THE MESSENGERS, *an age that is inclusive of ministries of our Lord Jesus Christ, and ministries of the apostles, and the age of* THE PRESENCE OF CHRIST.

Prophecy Insight 36 *In Chapter 4, I provided evidence from Malachi 3:1 that our Lord Jesus Christ is designated, the '*MESSENGER OF THE COVENANT*'. Consistent with designation of our Lord Jesus Christ as a messenger, our Lord Jesus Christ referred to Himself as, 'sent by The Father' (John 7:28). The apostles referred to themselves as messengers (Galatians 4:14).*

Who then are the 4 living creatures, and the 24 Elders?

And when he took the scroll, the four living creatures and the twenty-four elders fell before the Lamb, having each one harps and golden vials full of perfumes, which are the prayers of the saints, and they sing a new song, saying, Worthy art thou to take the scroll, and to open the seals of it, because thou wast slain, and didst redeem us to God in thy blood, out of every tribe, and tongue, and people, and nation, and didst make us to our God kings and priests, and we shall reign upon the earth.

SEVERAL FACTS STAND OUT IN REVELATION 5:8-10, NAMELY, THE 4 LIVING CREATURES AND THE 24 ELDERS:

✠ Are former sinners, who have received Jesus as Lord and Savior, who have allowed themselves to be washed in the cleansing blood of Jesus Christ.

✠ Have come out of every tribe, and tongue, and people, and nation, as such are men, male or female, but then, in Christ, spiritually speaking, there is neither male nor female; that is, all are equal in intrinsic worth.

✠ Now are kings and priests to God in Jesus Christ.

✠ Will Reign upon the earth.

✠ Offer up the prayers of the saints as perfumes unto The Father and The Son.

The Things That Are 6 *In Revelation ch. 5, the 4 living creatures, and 24 Elders are believers in the name of Jesus Christ who are on earth, who as yet are anticipating the Reign of Christ. In Revelation ch. 11, the 24* ELDERS *announce commencement of the* REIGN OF CHRIST.

The Things That Are 7 *While the 24* ELDERS *already are 'approved' in Christ (they only have crowns), the 4* LIVING CREATURES *are sincere believers in the name of Christ who are obedient to Christ, but who, at timing of a manifestation of Christ, have yet to attain to approval in Christ.*

The Things That Are 8 *In the depiction of the throne room, our Lord Jesus Christ affirms a thing that always is, a thing that always will be, which is, always the body of Christ will consist of believers who are perfected and already approved, and believers who yet are on the path towards acquiring approval of Christ.*

In Chapter 18 of my book, TRUE SANCTIFICATION, using terminologies of *'spiritual maturity'*, equivalently, *'a perfect man'* (Hebrews 5:14; Ephesians 4:13), or *attainment to 'a measure of the stature of the fullness of Christ'*, I discuss how it is that believers who are described as 'Powers' (*YLT*) are those who have attained to spiritual maturity in Christ. Given we already are in the time of the Presence of Christ, these are the believers who, simultaneously, have attained to, that is, have merited the Presence of Christ. It is out of this population of believers that The Father calls to Himself, Apostles, Prophets, and Teachers.

The Things That Are 9 *The* PRESENCE OF CHRIST *already has arrived at commencement of the time of the Church in Laodicea. Only those who respond to the invitation from Christ (Revelation 3:20), who then go on to arrive at fellowship with Him (Revelation 3:20), which, as we already established, occurs in the Holy Spirit (Ephesians 2:18), realize, attain to, or actualize the Presence of Christ.*

The Things That Are 10 POWERS, *out of whose population, The Father calls to Himself, Apostles, Prophets, and combo of Shepherds & Teachers, are believers in the name of Jesus Christ who have attained to spiritual maturity in Christ. In the time of the Presence of Christ, it is those who are perfected, who attain to spiritual maturity who actualize, that is, attain to the Presence of Christ.*

In the declaration that the 4 creatures and 24 Elders offer up prayers of the saints to The Father, our Lord Jesus Christ declares that prayers of the saints are more effective in presence of *Powers* within populations of believers. First, since POWERS are more in tune with the will of The Father, their prayers, which are more in line with those of the Holy Spirit, empower prayers of all of the saints of God.

How is this, and why is this important?

This offering up of the prayers of the saints is not about an asking for cars, houses, jobs etc., that is, things of this life, which The Father loves to provide for those who love Him, loves to provide to those who ask not for their pleasures, but so His name is glorified. Rather, this offering up of prayers relates to the perfection of The Father's spiritual agenda on earth. When there do not exist any Powers who are able to discern the Heart of The Father, that is, His perfect will for the earth, the saints do not pray as they ought, and intercession of the Holy Spirit for the saints becomes a necessity. When there exist Powers who discern the will of The Father, however, their prayers become vials that transform prayers of the saints into perfumes to the glory of The Father. This transformation occurs because, with Powers guiding other believers, believers - SAINTS - are guided into the perfect spiritual will of The Father, spiritual will that is evident in righteous, loving agenda.

The Things That Are 11 *The Father is pleased whenever there is discernment of His will in the earth that is evident in marshalling of (i) believers, (ii) non-believers who seek to participate in agenda that are rooted in demonstrations of love, and (iii) resources towards actualization of His will. Whenever there exists such agenda of love (such good works) that are spearheaded by Powers, the prayers of the saints are more pleasing to The Father.*

Second, given the reality of the Presence of Christ is not evident to the world whenever the earth is lacking in Powers, prayers of the saints are empowered by presence of Powers, that is, by existence of living testimony to the reality of the (Spiritual) Presence of Christ on earth. In this respect, our Lord Jesus Christ declares as follows.

When I am in the world, I am a light of the world (John 9:5).

Ye are the light of the world, a city set upon a mount is not able to be hid; nor do they light a lamp, and put it under the measure, but on the lamp-stand, and it shineth to all those in the house; SO LET YOUR LIGHT SHINE BEFORE MEN, THAT THEY MAY SEE YOUR GOOD WORKS, and may glorify your Father who is in the heavens (Matthew 5:14-16).

Some Corroborating Scriptural Evidence?

And this is the boldness that we have toward Him, that IF ANYTHING WE MAY ASK ACCORDING TO HIS WILL, HE DOTH HEAR US, and if we have known that He doth hear us, whatever we may ask, we have known that we have the requests that we have requested from Him (1John 5:14-15).

And, in like manner also, the Spirit doth help our weaknesses; for, what we may pray for, as it behoveth us, we have not known, but the Spirit Himself doth make intercession for us with groanings unutterable, and He who is searching the hearts hath known what is the mind of the Spirit, BECAUSE ACCORDING TO GOD HE (THE SPIRIT) DOTH INTERCEDE FOR THE SAINTS (Romans 8:26-27).

Thy reign come: THY WILL COME TO PASS, as in heaven also on the earth (Matthew 6:10).

Ye did not choose out me, but I chose out you, and did appoint you, that ye might go away, and might bear fruit, and your fruit might remain, THAT WHATEVER YE MAY ASK OF THE FATHER IN MY NAME, HE MAY GIVE YOU (John 15:16).

But seek ye first the reign of God and His righteousness, and all these (*the things of this life*) shall be yours as well (Matthew 6:33).

Prophetic Lessons 15 *If none of believers in Christ discern the Heart of The Father, how exactly is The Father to actualize His will - His Love for man - on the earth? When the Holy Spirit prays for the saints according to the will of The Father, this translates into specific demonstrations of the Love of The Father on earth only if one believer, at the very least, arrives at discernment of the will of The Father.*

Prophetic Lessons 16 *If you were The Father, and none of your children discern your heart as to objectives you seek to accomplish on earth, would you be pleased with your children?*

The Things That Are 12 *A Church that is lacking in Powers is lacking in believers who have crowns, as such deviates from the things that are, from the things that are supposed always to be. If the Church is, in reality, the body of Christ, it always will have Powers, out of whose populations our Lord Jesus Christ calls forth Apostles, Prophets, and combo of Shepherds & Teachers.*

Consistent with characterization of the Elders as Powers, the 24 ELDERS are clothed in white garments - the righteousness of Christ (Revelation 3:4; Galatians 3:27), and have golden crowns on their heads (2Timothy 4:8; James 1:12; 1Peter 5:4; Revelation 2:10; 3:11).

Alright then, but how exactly is it possible for the 4 LIVING CREATURES, and the 24 ELDERS to continuously, and without ceasing *give glory to God* (Revelation 4:8-11)?

In order to arrive at an answer to this question, we need arrive at a spiritual characterization for the 'glory of God'.

So then, what exactly is the glory of God?

And Jesus having heard, said, "*This ailment is not unto death, but for the glory of God, that the Son of God may be glorified through it* (John 11:4)."

Jesus saith to her, Said I not to thee, that if thou mayest believe, THOU SHALT SEE THE GLORY OF GOD (John 11:40)?

FOR ALL DID SIN, AND ARE COME SHORT OF THE GLORY OF GOD (Romans 3:23).

And we - we ought to give thanks to God always for you, brethren, beloved by the Lord, that God did choose you from the beginning to salvation, in sanctification of the Spirit, and belief of the truth, to which He did call you through our good news, TO THE ACQUIRING OF THE GLORY OF OUR LORD JESUS CHRIST (2Thessalonians 2:13-14).

Whether, then, ye eat, or drink, or do anything, DO ALL TO THE GLORY OF GOD (1Corinthianss 31:10).

That in the name of Jesus every knee may bow - of heavenlies, and earthlies, and what are under the earth - and every tongue may confess that Jesus Christ is Lord, TO THE GLORY OF GOD THE FATHER (Philippians 2:10-11).

THE HEAVENS DECLARE THE GLORY OF GOD; and the firmament shows His handiwork. Day unto day utters speech, and night unto night reveals knowledge. There is no speech nor language where their voice is not heard (Psalms 119:1-3).

Prophecy Interpretation 13 *All of Scriptures unequivocally declares that the Glory of God is seen on earth, meaning the 4* LIVING CREATURES, *and 24* ELDERS *give glory to God on earth. Given all that we do is supposed to glorify God, and given there always are people who are in daylight, that is, working on earth, glory accrues to God unceasingly from His saints on earth.*

The Things That Are 13 *Combined, the Scriptures declare that the Glory of God is either of* THE CHARACTER AND ESSENCE OF GOD, *or* WORKS (ACTIONS) THAT DIRECT PEOPLE'S ATTENTION TO THE CHARACTER AND ESSENCE OF GOD, *which is Love (1John 4:8). In this sense, nature consists of works - created things - that direct people's attention to the character and essence of God.*

What then is the distinction between the 4 LIVING CREATURES, and 24 ELDERS?

While the 4 LIVING CREATURES, and 24 ELDERS all are redeemed from the earth, only the 24 ELDERS have attained to the righteousness of Christ. By this, our Lord Jesus Christ symbolizes that whereas the 24 ELDERS are conformed to the image of Christ, as such have become sons of God, the 4 LIVING CREATURES have yet to attain to sonship in Christ. In this respect, note that a child of God is not equivalent to a son of God. A child of God is a person who is born of God, but who has yet to arrive at spiritual maturity.

The evidence that while all who believe in Jesus Christ are born of God, as such children of God, that not all are sons of God?

But as many as did receive Him to them HE GAVE AUTHORITY TO BECOME SONS OF GOD - to those believing in His name - who - not of blood nor of a will of flesh, nor of a will of man but - of God were begotten (John 1:12-13).

Because whom He did foreknow, He also did FOREAPPOINT, CONFORMED TO THE IMAGE OF HIS SON, that he might be first-born among many brethren (Romans 8:29).

For Him who did not know sin, in our behalf He did make sin, that WE MAY BECOME THE RIGHTEOUSNESS OF GOD in Him (2Corinthians 5:21).

If you receive authority to become a son, you are yet to arrive at sonship. If you are appointed to become conformed to the image of Jesus Christ, only upon acknowledgement of Jesus as Lord and Savior are you able to commence on such an adventure. If Jesus was made sin so you are able to become the righteousness of God, at timing of your confession of faith in Christ, you became a child of God, earn the opportunity, authority, or right to begin the journey that enables you become the righteousness of God. In ancient writings, until a male child became of age, he was not considered a son. Our Father relates to us in exactly the same manner, namely, while upon your receiving of Jesus as Lord and Savior, He acknowledges you as His child, until you become like Christ, you do not attain to stature of a son. We have then that a son of God is a Power, a believer in Christ who has attained to spiritual maturity, a believer who has attained to a measure of the stature of the fullness of Christ.

The Things That Are 14 *The 4* LIVING CREATURES *are children of God who have yet to attain to sonship in Christ, as such, have yet to acquire character and essence of Christ.*

Who then are the 4 living creatures?

THE LIKENESS OF A CALF: The first living creature has the form of a calf. Calves feed on milk, and follow their mother wherever she goes, do not as yet have their own sense of direction. By the same token, immature believers are characterized as feeding on, or only desiring milk, as opposed to meaty food (1Corinthians 3:1-4; Hebrews 5:11-14). Since a son of God is guided by The Holy Spirit only (Romans 8:14), and feeds on meat, not milk (Hebrews 5:11-14), a calf is representative of believers in Christ who, as yet, are spiritually immature.

Prophecy Insight 37 *It is not so much that the likeness of a calf does not want to love, rather, it is the case that he or she has yet to receive the Holy Spirit, He who brings to the calf, the Love of Christ.*

THE LIKENESS OF A LION: The likeness of a lion typifies immature believers in Christ who, as yet, continue to think that it is via demonstrations of strength that unbelievers will be drawn to our Lord Jesus Christ. Rather than believe their Lord and Savior that the way that works best for wooing of people to Christ is the way of Love, they think they know better than their Lord and Savior, desire to demonstrate, via miracles and supernatural events, that there is not any god greater than their God. Until he arrived at the realization that The Father's way of love was best, Elijah was such an immature child (*1Kings 17:1; 18:16-46; 19:1-18*). Yet, because his heart was pure, and he eventually accepted correction, The Father was pleased with Him. While still disciples of Christ, Apostles James and John demonstrated the spirit of a lion, until forbidden by Jesus, sought to destroy a village that refused to receive Jesus with fire (Luke 9:51-56). The Father's admonition to believers in Christ who, in spite of teachings of their Lord and Savior continue to focus on demonstrations of strength, as opposed to demonstrations of love?

"Not by a force, nor by power, but - by my Spirit, said Jehovah of Hosts (Zechariah 4:6)."

And hope does not disappoint us, because GOD'S LOVE HAS BEEN POURED INTO OUR HEARTS THROUGH THE HOLY SPIRIT which has been given to us (Romans 5:5).

Prophecy Insight 38 *The believer typified by a calf does not as yet have any personal spiritual compass, is impressioned by it's mother. The believer typified by a lion has arrived at a personal compass that is contrary to the admonition of his or her Lord and Savior - demonstrations of strength, as opposed to demonstrations of love.*

Prophecy Insight 39 *It is not that the likeness of a lion does not believe in the Love of God, rather, it is the case that much like before his conversion (Luke 22:31-32), like Apostle Peter, he or she seeks to be convinced that the Love of God is better than demonstrations of strength.*

THE LIKENESS OF AN EAGLE: Eagles love to soar, have learnt to apply currents of air and their large strong wings to soaring way up into the sky. Eagles' talons are strong, while in flight, can be applied to catching of prey from off the ground. Eagles are bundles of natural talent. The likeness of an eagle typifies believers who still live by their natural, as opposed to spiritual abilities. Believers who have naturally strong voices that are good for oration, or for singing, but whose natural ability is not infused with the Holy Spirit have form of eagles. Talent is not anointing of The Holy Spirit; there are lots of persons who do not believe in Christ who are very talented at whatever it is that they do. Believers who have a strong will, who are able to decipher a good thing to do, and have the will to do it, but who do not yet understand the difference between what is good to do, and what is right to do have form of eagles. In this respect, while it was good for Jesus to hasten to Bethany to heal Lazarus, this prior to his dying, Jesus discerned that this was not the right thing to do, discerned that a wait of four days, this so He would have to raise Lazarus from the dead was the right thing to do (*John ch. 11*). Healing, Jesus already had done many times over. Raising of a man who had been dead for four days, whose body already had the stink of death, The Father declared was necessary for raising the bar, for ensuring that the decision to put Jesus to death would be seen for what it really was, hatred of righteousness. Believers in Christ are not born of the will, are born of God (John 1:13). Concerning importance of not seeing each other in likeness of eagles, through Apostle Paul, The Holy Spirit admonishes as follows.

> "Therefore, from now on, WE REGARD NO ONE ACCORDING TO THE FLESH. Even though we have known Christ according to the flesh, yet now we know Him thus no longer. Therefore, if anyone is in Christ, he is a new creation; old things have passed away; BEHOLD, ALL THINGS HAVE BECOME NEW. NOW ALL THINGS ARE OF GOD...(2Corinthians 5:16-18)"

Prophecy Insight 40 *When Jesus declares in the Beatitudes that "Happy the poor in spirit because theirs is the reign of the heavens (Matthew 5:3)", he declares that only those who do not feel self sufficient (Philippians 3:3), who arrive at the recognition that He, Jesus is their sufficiency (2Corinthians 3:5), mature into sons of God.*

Prophecy Insight 41 *It is not that the likeness of an Eagle does not believe in the Love of God, rather, it is the case that his or her understanding of the*

Love of God still is discolored by the lusts of the world. When a woman uses sex as a weapon in her marriage, this is only because her understanding of the Love of God still is discolored by the lusts of the world. If a woman truly understands the Love of God, she will not want her husband burning with passion of unfulfilled legal desire for sex out in the world.

THE LIKENESS OF MAN: Every believer who still is caught up in the lusts of the flesh - *fornication, adultery* etc.; the lusts of the eyes - *covetousness*, and *evil desires* in respect of others, this only because they seem to be doing well; and the pride of life - *feelings of intrinsic superiority* that derive from origins, status, power, or wealth has the form of a man. In this respect, consider the following Scriptures.

> For yet ye are fleshly, for where there is among you envying, and strife, and divisions, are ye not fleshly, and in the manner of men do walk (1Corinthians 3:3)?

> Do not love the world or the things in the world. If anyone loves the world, the love of The Father is not in him. For all that is in the world - the lust of the flesh, the lust of the eyes, and the pride of life - is not of The Father but is of the world. And the world is passing away, and the lust of it; but he who does the will of God abides forever (1John 2:16-17).

> For as many as are led (*guided, taught, transformed*) by the Spirit of God, these are sons of God (Romans 8:14).

The Things That Are 15 *The goal of faith in Christ is transformation of a man - male or female - into the image of Jesus Christ. Until some minimum threshold of transformation is attained, a person who has faith in Jesus Christ still is no more than a man, has yet to become a son of God.*

The Things That Are 16 *Guidance of the Holy Spirit that is characteristic of sons of God is arrived at in context of reasonings with, and fellowship of Father, Son, and Holy Spirit, all of which occurs in the spirit; those who worship The Father worship Him in spirit and in truth (John 4:24).*

The Things That Are 17 *It is not that the likeness of a man does not believe in the Love of God; rather, it is the case that he or she still confuses the will and desires of man with the Love of God, that is, with the will of God.*

> And do not be conformed to this world, but be transformed by the renewing of your mind, that you may prove what is that good and acceptable and perfect will of God (Romans 12:2).

If you have attained, you must acknowledge to yourself

If you have attained to SONSHIP IN CHRIST, you have to acknowledge what it is to which you have attained, else you do not walk by faith, do not love yourself, do not accept evidence that is provided you by Father, Son, and Holy Spirit. If you do not accept evidence presented to you by The Holy Spirit in respect of the spirituality to which you have attained, at point of manifestation of the righteousness that is promised to those who have faith - the righteousness that you believed is attainable - you adopt false humility, refuse to glorify Christ for what He has wrought in you. Well, if you refuse to glorify Christ for what He has wrought in you, how exactly do you think you will be able to maintain the attainment? If you will not love yourself, this because you refuse to accept a truth about yourself, how exactly are you to remain in the truth of Christ? We are not talking here of bragging to others; we are talking about you, rejoicing in the presence of Christ in respect of the promise that He made, the promise that He has actualized in you. Each time that I have arrived at the recognition that The Father, Son, and Holy Spirit have elevated my spirituality, while I did not know exactly what time the elevation transpired, I acknowledged the elevation, rejoiced in the evidence that was present in my spirit and in my capacity for love as to the work that had been accomplished in me. Friend, do you expect to know at exactly what time, the perfection of your righteousness arrives in your spirit? Well then, listen to the words of our Lord Jesus Christ Himself in John 3:8.

> The Spirit where He willeth doth blow, and His voice thou dost hear, but thou hast not known whence He cometh, and whither He goeth; thus is every one who hath been born of The Spirit (John 3:8).

Prophecy Insight 42 *If, as we already have discussed, your growth is of God, how exactly are you to know the exact time at which the growth is perfected in you by Father, Son, and Holy Spirit? If you are fully aware, is the growth not then your work, as opposed to that of The Father, Son, and Holy Spirit?*

When Jesus declared in *John 14:6* that: "I AM THE WAY, THE TRUTH, AND THE LIFE," He was not devolving into sinful pride, He was walking by the faith that works by love, by the faith that must believe in, and act on the truth about Himself or Herself. My book, 'True Sanctification' deals, in entirety, with helping you understood, and actualize the process that transforms you from a *child of God* into a SON OF GOD.

The evidence that you have attained to sonhood in Christ?

♣ Sin has lost it's appeal. It is not that you resist sin; rather, it is the case that sin has lost it's appeal.

♣ It is not that you do not hate; hatred has lost it's appeal.

♣ There is not any desire to make money via means that are under-handed, illegal, or unethical.

♣ You are filled with the Love of God.

♣ You do not attempt to justify weaknesses; you do not get obsessed with weaknesses; you submit weaknesses to the blood of Christ, and overcome in the power of the Holy Spirit.

♣ You are bearing fruit for Christ. You are kind, patient, gentle, sincere, characterized by good motives, knowledgeable, persevering, godly etc.

♣ People are able to see in you the righteousness, peace, and joy that come from believing in Jesus Christ. This is evident in your decisions, and the way you treat people; and in your response to challenges of life.

♣ You attain to Godliness. Every day is spent CONCEIVING loving things (*Love Projects*) to do in future; FORMULATING loving things to do in present; and IMPLEMENTING loving things that were conceived in prior periods.[1]

THE EVIDENCE THAT ONLY IS AVAILABLE TO YOU, THAT NO ONE ELSE EXPERIENCES?

The Things That Are 18 *You arrive at reality of fellowship with Father, Son, and Holy Spirit. This reality is, in entirety, spiritual. You are filled with Love for Life. You look forward to the next day, because the next day provides yet another opportunity for pursuit of* LOVE *and* GODLINESS.

The Things That Are 19 *If you have attained, but do not acknowledge to yourself, you cannot remain in the standing to which you attain in Christ.* BUT HOW DO YOU ACKNOWLEDGE? *By glorifying Father, Son, and Holy Spirit for what they have, through the* GRACE *of Christ,* LOVE *of The Father, and* FELLOWSHIP *of the Spirit, produced in you, which is, a unique realization of the image of Christ.*

The Things That Are 20 *When the Elders declare, "And didst make us to our God kings and priests, and we shall reign on the earth (Revelation 5:10)," simultaneously, they acknowledge what they have become, yet ensure that the focus is on what God has done, as opposed to what they have become. If you seek to maintain sonship in Christ, you must be like the 24* ELDERS.

---

[1]For a blog post on *Godliness*, check out my blog post of April 21, 2019 titled, 'GOD, LOVE, ESSENCE, AND TIME' on the *Medium* Social Media Platform.

Now, you have need of true humility and meekness

Having passed the test of the evidence, now you arrive at the realization that only TRUE HUMILITY and MEEKNESS can keep you in sonship of The Father. Since The Father resists the proud (James 4:6; 1Peter 5:5), the moment you allow arrival at sonship *get in your head*, is the moment you begin to lose your standing in Christ. To see this, consider the words of our Lord Jesus Christ to His disciples in Luke 10:19-20, this after they returned from their evangelical travels.[2]

> Lo, I give to you authority to tread upon serpents and scorpions, and on all the power of the enemy, and nothing by any means shall hurt you; but, in this rejoice not, that the spirits are subjected to you, but rejoice that your names were written in the heavens.

If you focus on the work that Jesus does through you, it is inevitable that pride will set in, that you will begin to make more of yourself than you are in reality. This perhaps is exactly how sin found it's way into the heart of Lucifer, via a focus on how important he had become to God. If you rather focus on how it is that absent the grace of God you would not have opportunity to become like Christ, your eyes are focused on the grace of God and you give glory for the opportunity afforded you to partner with the almighty God. The Apostle Paul places the demand for true humility in this perspective in 1Corinthians 4:7.

> For who makes you differ from another? And what do you have that you did not receive? Now if you did indeed receive it, why do you boast as if you had not received it?

Providing support for the demand for true humility or meekness, Apostle James adds as follows in James 3:13.

> Who is wise and understanding among you? Let him show by good conduct that his works are done in the meekness of wisdom.

Prophecy Insight 43 *Wisdom is characterized by meekness. Only those who are MEEK or TRULY HUMBLE have the capacity for continuance in works that are new, and that glorify Father, Son, and Holy Spirit.*

The promise from our Lord Jesus Christ is, "Blessed are the meek for they shall inherit the earth (Matthew 5:5)."

---

[2]For a blog post on *True Humility*, check out my blog post of August 12, 2017 titled, 'THE HUMBLE DIE' on the *Medium* social media website.

What then are 'meekness' and 'true humility'?

Spiritual Insight 67 *Meekness only can be demonstrated alongside wisdom. If you are meek, when you relate with people, all they remember is the wisdom of your words, not the air with which the words are spoken.*

A MEEK person is so confident in the wisdom he or she has, wisdom that ultimately comes from The Father, that he or she no longer has any need for validation from men. Remember, absent arrival at some agreement, no one is able to influence others. A meek person seeks to have his or her words considered, as such, frames words in a manner that others can understand and consider for discussion or agreement. If the words are accepted, meekness only considers that other wise men have perceived wisdom of his or her words, does not consider itself to have been wiser than all others. If the words are rejected, meekness continues to recognize wisdom of the words that were spoken, entrusts response to the words to The Father, trusts in The Father, does not engage in any rivalry in respect of words that are spoken. When you become so confident of access to the wisdom of God, that you no longer seek validation for your words, with outcome you are able to take rejection of your words with the same equanimity with which you respond to acceptance of your words, you are practicing meekness of wisdom.

Spiritual Insight 68 *True humility recognizes that there always is room for improvement, as such does not keep the gaze on past attainments, always is looking forward to becoming better (Philippians 3:12-16). In presence of such an attitude, true humility does not focus on comparisons with others, sees itself as the only yardstick that is of consequence (2Corinthians 10:12). The Scriptures declare that the humility that is about maintenance of* A DROOPY, NON-CONFIDENT POSTURE, *that is about* DRESSING DOWN, *that is about words that seem to* SELF ABNEGATE *in some derogatory sense is a false humility, is not a humility that is of Christ (Colossians 2:18-23).*

The 7 Spirits of God

In Revelation 4:5, there are 7 Spirits of God. We already have seen in the preceding chapter that the number 7 symbolizes completeness, and commencement. We have then that our Lord Jesus Christ declares that His Spirit is a Spirit that completes one agenda, then commences on a new agenda. This, of course is a characteristic of The Father. Given Father, Word, and Holy Spirit are one, we must expect that, like The Father, the Holy Spirit seeks to complete existing agenda, then commence new agenda. You see then that the Holy Spirit, who, by virtue of oneness with The Father also is God, spends the time CONCEIVING of new loving things to commence in future; COMMENCING new loving things for the present; and COMPLETING new loving things that were conceived in prior periods.

The Things That Are

THE THINGS THAT ARE do not change, always remain the same. Why are they able to remain the same? Because they are in Christ, and our Lord Jesus Christ is 'THE SAME YESTERDAY, AND TODAY, AND FOREVER (HEBREWS 13:8)'. Powers are attained to in Christ; the thrones on which the 24 ELDERS are seated subsist only in Christ; since The Father is in Christ, and Christ is in The Father (John 14:11; 1John 5:7), the throne of The Father is in Christ. If you seek to be part of The Things That Are, you seek to remain in Christ.

Who is it that remains in Christ?

And the world doth pass away, and the desire of it, and he who is doing the will of God, he doth remain - to the age (1John 2:17).

The Things That Are 21 *If you seek to be part of The Things That Are, you seek to do the will of The Father. The will of The Father is that you believe in the name of Jesus Christ, and, no matter the extent to which he or she differs from you, that you love your neighbor (1John 3:23).*

CHAPTER 8

What Are, & What Comes Next

The work of salvation was finished from the foundation of the world, then, for our sakes, manifested in these end times. Just about all of the prophets of old whose words are recorded in the Old Testament prophesied about manifestation of the work of salvation in PERSON and MINISTRY of our Lord and Savior Jesus Christ. For an introduction to some of these prophecies, check out *Ch. 9* of my book, TRUE SANCTIFICATION. In respect of revolving of all of history around the Person of our Lord Jesus Christ, Apostles Peter and Paul each declare as follows.

> Of this salvation the prophets have inquired and searched carefully, *who prophesied of the grace that would come to you,* searching what, or what manner of time, the Spirit of Christ who was in them was indicating when He testified beforehand the sufferings of Christ and the glories that would follow. To them it was revealed that, not to themselves, but to us they were ministering the things which now have been reported to you through those who have preached the gospel to you by the Holy Spirit sent from heaven - things into which *messengers* (as already discussed, I here substitute the accurate interpretation of the word rendered 'Angel' by the *NKJV*) desire to look into (1Peter 1:10-12).

> In many parts, and many ways, God of old having spoken to the fathers in the prophets, in these last days did speak to us in a Son, whom He appointed heir of all things, through whom also He did make the ages (Hebrews 1:1-2).

Consistent with my assertion in the preceding chapter, Hebrews 1:1-2 states very clearly that our Lord Jesus Christ created the ages, meaning

159

there exist, at the very least two ages. I have asserted in the preceding chapter that I believe there to be only two ages - the age of the messengers, and the age of the Presence of Christ. Consistent with likelihood of a restriction to only two ages, our Lord Jesus Christ and Apostle Paul declare as follows in Luke 18:29, and Hebrews 6:5.

> "And He said to them, verily I say to you, that there is not one who left house, or parents, or brothers, or wife, or children, for the sake of the reign of God, who may not receive back manifold more in this time, AND IN THE COMING AGE, LIFE AGE-DURING."

> And did taste the good saying of God, the powers also OF THE COMING AGE (Hebrews 6:5).

Prophecy Insight 44 *The 'coming age' is not tantamount to the coming ages, signifies one additional age, does not signify more than one additional age.*

Someone might argue that Ephesians 2:7 is contradictory, suggests that, subsequent to the age of the messengers, there are more than one age yet to come. This my friend may well be possible. Compare, however, renditions of the passage, with the preceding two Scriptures, then let us apply principles of interpretation of the English language. Ephesians 2:7 states as follows.

> That He (The Father) MIGHT SHOW, IN THE AGES THAT ARE COMING, the exceeding riches of His grace in kindness toward us in Christ Jesus.

Prophecy Insight 45 *It is unequivocal that the word MIGHT implies uncertainty, does not imply certainty. In Luke 18:29, and Hebrews 6:5, the assertion of 'AN AGE TO COME' is emphatic, unequivocal. So then, maybe there will be more than two ages. Apostle Paul makes clear, however, that his reference to feasibility of more than one age to come is a 'MIGHT SITUATION', not a certainty.*

With the work of salvation finished from the foundation of the world, the names of all who will be saved ALREADY ARE written upon the scroll of life from the foundation of the world (Matthew 25:34; Hebrews 4:3; Revelation 17:8). Given, absent shedding of blood, we could not have been saved - for without the shedding of blood there is not any remission of sin (Hebrews 9:22), the price of sin had to be paid from the foundation of the world. So then, there is a Lamb slain from the foundation of the world for the remission of our sins (Revelation 13:8; 17:8), this so we can be saved.

The Things That Are 22 *If the wages of sin is death (Genesis 2:15-17; Genesis 3:1-5), and yet Adam and Eve did not die at timing of their sin, without recourse to Scriptures, it necessarily must be the case that a remedy was introduced either at timing of commitment of the sin, or prior to commitment of the sin.*

The Things That Are 23 *Scriptures declare that The Father and The Son had a remedy in place prior to commitment of sin by Adam and Eve. This remedy is "The Lamb that was slain from the foundation of the world for remission of our sins."*

Revelation 5:1 introduces a Scroll in the right hand of Him who was seated on the throne, a Scroll written within and on the back, sealed with 7 SEALS. As we soon will embark upon discovery of it's contents (in the very next chapter), this Scroll revealed the things that are to come, which are two sets of things:

✠ The Spiritual System for Governance of Life & Affairs on Earth (SSGLAE). An SSGLAE:

  ৺ that will operate in perpetuity;

  ৺ whose evolution over time is conditioned on responses of individuals, the Church, and the Nations (Civil Governments) to The Father;

  ৺ which pre-specifies consequences of right actions, and wrong actions for each of individuals, the Church, and the Nations;

  ৺ which, for ensuring that evil persons, Churches, or Nations who understand it are not able to subvert it, incorporates The Father's right to introduce an unanticipated perturbation for benefit of those who love the name of Jesus Christ.

Whenever responses to actions are just, consequences of actions - both right and wrong - are pre-specified ahead of time. Whenever justice is made up as people go along, this is evidence for *mob mentality, collusion,* and *injustice,* characteristics of societies that end up destroyed by The Father. The Father did not declare destruction of *Nineveh* because *Assyrians* would not pray to Him. The Father declared destruction of *Nineveh* because *Ninevites* mistreated one another, and because Assyrians dwelling in Nineveh mistreated Assyrians dwelling in Babylon. It was the very same Babylon, which had been mistreated for upwards of *500* years, that The Father raised up for razing of Nineveh to the ground, and destruction of all of it's substance about *612* BC.

The Things That Are 24 *The Father never has destroyed any society or city because they will not pray to Him. Every society or city that has been destroyed by decree of The Father (Sodom & Gomorrah; Jerusalem; Nineveh; Tyre & Sidon) ended up in such a plight because the rich and the strong oppress each of the not-so-rich, and those who, by virtue of a lacking in political influence or power, are deemed to be weak.*

The Things That Are 25 *Any just system is characterized by pre-specification of consequences for each of right or wrong actions. In the pre-specification of consequences for each of right or wrong actions, The Father declares that He does not delight in infliction of pain on mankind, that His delight is in* RIGHTEOUSNESS *(right actions),* JUSTICE, *and* LOVE.

Who then constitute THE NATIONS? The key resides in the words of the 4 LIVING CREATURES, and 24 ELDERS, and in other passages of Scripture outside of the Book of Revelation. In the words of the 4 LIVING CREATURES, and 24 ELDERS recorded in Revelation 5:9, that they are redeemed out of every *tribe, tongue, people,* and *nation.* In presence of this inference, believers in the name of Jesus Christ are not constituted to be part of the nations. We have then that THE CHURCH - the spiritual entity, not denomination - an entity, which consists of all those who believe in Jesus Christ is, in entirety, distinct and dichotomous from THE NATIONS. So then, in so far as Father, Son, and Holy Spirit are concerned, everyone who does not, as yet, profess faith in Christ is subject only to civil government, as such part of the Nations.

The Evidence from Scripture outside of the Book of Revelation?

But you are a chosen race, a royal priesthood (*royal* means *kingly*, so then, *kings and priests*), a holy nation (*a new nation called* THE CHURCH), God's own people, that you may declare the wonderful deeds of Him who called you out of darkness into His marvelous light (1Peter 2:9).

Wherefore, remember, that YE WERE ONCE THE NATIONS in the flesh, who are called Uncircumcision by that called Circumcision in the flesh made by hands, that YE WERE AT THAT TIME APART FROM CHRIST, having been alienated from the Commonwealth of Israel, and strangers to the covenants of the promise, having no hope, and without God, in the world; and NOW, IN CHRIST JESUS, YE BEING ONCE AFAR OFF BECAME NIGH IN THE BLOOD OF THE CHRIST (Ephesians 2:11-13).

FORBIDDING US TO SPEAK TO THE NATIONS THAT THEY MIGHT BE SAVED, to fill up their sin always, but the anger did come upon them - to the end (1Thessalonians 2:16).

Beloved, I call upon you, as strangers and sojourners (The Church), to keep from the fleshly desires, that war against your soul, HAVING YOUR BEHAVIOR AMONG THE NATIONS RIGHT, that in that which they speak against you as evil-doers, of the good works having beheld, they may glorify God in a day of inspection (1Peter 2:11-12).

The Things That Are 26 *Scriptures are very clear,* THE NATIONS *are 'THEY' who have yet to profess faith in Jesus Christ. Correspondingly, the Church consists only of those who have professed faith in Jesus Christ.*

The Things That Are 27 *Spiritually speaking, every individual either is a member or citizen of The Church, or a citizen of The Nations.*

Does this then mean that only those in The Church can be saved?

ABSOLUTELY NOT! As we already have established in Chapter 3, there exist two classes of persons who are accepted of God, namely:

♣ Group I: Suppose, regardless of absence of faith in Christ, but not rejection of the personal realization that Jesus is the Son of God, there exist citizens of the nations who choose the LOVE OF GOD as *Way of Life*. Refer to these people as, LOVING CITIZENS OF THE NATIONS. In presence of this dichotomy, the Nations comprise of LOVING CITIZENS OF THE NATIONS (LCN), and HATEFUL CITIZENS OF THE NATIONS (HCN). If all citizens of the nations, adopt the Love of God as way of life, then all are classified as LCN. A person who has received revelation of truthfulness of characterization of the PERSON OF CHRIST, but who rejects such appeal from his or her own heart, is not part of the LCN, is part of the HCN, for he or she has chosen hatefulness of Christ.

♣ Group II: Suppose, consistent with the directive of our Lord and Savior, those who profess faith in Jesus Christ adopt the LOVE OF GOD as *Way of Life*. Refer to these people as, CITIZENS, OR MEMBERS OF THE CHURCH (MTC). Denote by PMTC, MEMBERS OF THE CHURCH who, by virtue of their faithfulness to the name of Christ, have become Powers to the glory of The Father. Let MTC who have yet to be recognized by The Father as Powers be termed Neophytes. With 'PRETENSE' evident in unwillingness to adopt the Love of Christ as way of life, let persons who pretend to have faith in Jesus Christ be denoted PRETENSE BELIEVERS IN CHRIST (PBC), or Charlatans.

The Things That Are 28 *The Nations comprise of* LCN *and* HCN. *The Church comprises of* NEOPHYTES, POWERS, *and* CHARLATANS.

The Things That Are 29 *In The Father's mercy, while LCN do not have ca-pacity for arrival at the Presence of Christ, as such do not reign with Christ, they, alongside* NEOPHYTES *and* POWERS *arrive at salvation that is promised to faith in Jesus Christ. It is only those who are* POWERS, *however, who earn the opportunity to* REIGN WITH CHRIST.

The Justice of The Father is evident in salvation of each of LCN and NEO-PHYTES. Persons who are NEOPHTYES profess faith in Jesus Christ, and are expected to adopt love as way of life. Since these persons are, by assump-tion, genuine believers, because they adopt attitudes of either of the *calf*, eagle, *lion*, or man, they do not progress from NEOPHYTES to POWERS. We have then that their commitment to the Love of God as Way of Life is not es-tablished beyond any doubt. Regardless then of faith in Christ, and access to the Holy Spirit, The Father and The Son cannot, on basis of the evidence, DEMONSTRATE faithfulness of their commitment to the Love of God.

Consider then, the LCN. Persons who are LCN either have not heard about Christ, or due to imperfections that are inherent in physical entities that are supposed to represent Christ are, in Sovereignty of The Father, not induced to arrive at faith in Jesus Christ. Within the latter scenario, while physically they are in proximity to Churches, as such are aware of belief in Christ, The Father, Son, and Holy Spirit do not provide such per-sons with a personal conviction, equivalently, personal revelation of Jesus Christ. These persons attempt to walk in the Love of God in their own power and strength. Given they do not reject Christ, rather anonymously, help is provided through ministration of the Holy Spirit. Given they do not have relationship with Christ, however, they are unable to arrival at either of fel-lowship of the Holy Spirit, or the PRESENCE OF CHRIST. Since they do their best with their resolve, however, in reality, and with focus on outcomes, they are not much different from NEOPHYTES.

The Things That Are 30 *In terms of judgment of character, that is, ascer-tainment of faithfulness to the Love of God as Way of Life,* NEOPHYTES - *per-sons who have faith in Christ, but whose faithfulness could not be credibly determined, do not differ significantly from* LCN - *persons who attempted, in their own power, yet unbeknownst to them with help of the Holy Spirit, to op-erate in the Love of God. The Father has decided that His Mercy will cover shortcomings of* NEOPHYTES *and* LCN, *such that they are saved, that is, are able to enter into the New Jerusalem, but do not reign with The Lord Jesus Christ.*

The Scriptural Evidence?

HAPPY ARE THOSE DOING HIS COMMANDS THAT THE AUTHORITY
SHALL BE THEIRS UNTO THE TREE OF LIFE, AND BY THE GATES THEY

MAY ENTER INTO THE CITY. But without (outside the gates of the City of God, the New Jerusalem) are the dogs (*those who believe in, and practice sexual immorality*), and the sorcerers (*those who abandon reasoning for superstition, this so they can justify oppression of others*), and the whoremongers, and the murderers, and the idolaters, and every one who is loving and is doing a lie (Revelation 22:14).

The Things That Are 31 *Our Lord Jesus Christ is very clear that Pretense Believers in Christ (CHARLATANS) will not gain access to the New Jerusalem. So then, the New Jerusalem is a spiritual entity comprising only of those who genuinely are disciples of Christ.*

The Things That Are 32 *The Scriptures are very clear, while there exist people outside of the New Jerusalem who, by doing of commands of our Lord Jesus Christ, are able to join up with those who, having genuine faith in the Lord Jesus Christ (NEOPHYTES or POWERS), already are citizens of the New Jerusalem (Philippians 3:20; Hebrews 12:), there simultaneously exist persons outside of the New Jerusalem who, by virtue of their choices, are not able to gain entrance into the New Jerusalem.*

What are the commands of our Lord Jesus Christ?

A new commandment I give to you, that ye love one another; according as I did love you, that ye also love one another; IN THIS SHALL ALL KNOW THAT YE ARE MY DISCIPLES, IF YE MAY HAVE LOVE ONE TO ANOTHER (John 13:34-35).

Not every one who is saying to me 'Lord, lord', shall come into the reign of the heavens; but he who is doing the will of my Father who is in the heavens. Many will say to me in that day, Lord, lord, have we not in thy name prophesied? and in thy name cast out demons? and in thy name done many mighty things? and then I WILL ACKNOWLEDGE TO THEM, THAT - I NEVER KNEW YOU; DEPART FROM ME, YOU WHO PRACTICE LAWLESSNESS! (MATTHEW 7:21-23).

The Things That Are 33 *Friend, note that it is those who do His commands that gain access into the New Jerusalem, meaning, prior to qualification for entrance into the New Jerusalem, those who gain entrance ALREADY ARE OBEDIENT TO CHRIST. It is unequivocal then, that those who choose to love their fellow man in context of the Love of Christ -LCN - have opportunity for gaining entrance into the New Jerusalem.*

The Things That Are 34 *Friend, Jesus declares to you that, in so far as ascertainment of discipleship is concerned, that PROFESSION OF HIS NAME IS*

IRRELEVANT, *declares only doing of His will, which is, adoption of the Love of God as Way of Life is what counts. So then, each of LCN, NEOPHYTES, and POWERS are judged to be disciples of Jesus Christ.*

The Things That Are 35 *Just because an LCN has been witnessed to about Christ, but has yet to receive Jesus as Lord and Savior does not imply that he or she has rejected Christ. All the while that Apostle Paul was persecuting Christians, he knew of Christ (he was a contemporary of Christ), had definitely been witnessed to by Stephen (Acts 6:8 through 8:1), but had not yet received a manifestation of Christ, that is, had yet to be compelled by the Holy Spirit, on basis of reasonings and evidence, to arrive at a decision for, or against Christ. So then, Apostle Paul confesses that he persecuted the Church out of spiritual ignorance of reality of Christ, as opposed to rejection of Christ (Galatians 1:13-17; 1Corinthians 15:9-11). When eventually he received a manifestation of Christ, he repented and was saved.*

The Things That Are 36 *If LCN receive manifestations (knowledge or evidence) of the PERSON OF CHRIST, but reject witness of their own hearts and spirits as to truthfulness of the manifestation, they cease to be disciples of Jesus Christ, become part of the HCN.*

The Things That Are 37 *Adoption of HATRED AS WAY OF LIFE is sufficient for characterization of a person as alienated from Christ and the New Jerusalem (1John 2:9-11; 3:10, 14-15). All it takes for a person to be HCN is hatred for any one person.*

WHY IS HATRED, OF AS MUCH AS ONE PERSON, DISTASTEFUL TO THE FATHER?

First, Would you love a God who overlooks hatred merely because you are the only one who is hated?

Second, Hatred implies a desire to hurt another, a desire that is dichotomized from character of another.

Spiritual Insight 69 *It is normative that HATRED DOES NOT EQUATE TO JUSTICE. Justice always implies a one-time fair trial in the public space (absence of double jeopardy), pre-specification of consequences and/or penalties, and a terminal date for consequences and/or penalties.*

Evidence for Two Groups of Believers in Christ

In the foregoing, I have provided some initial evidence for presence of two groups of believers in Christ, namely NEOPHYTES, and POWERS FOR CHRIST.

As I already have enunciated, POWERS are, on basis of attainment to certain spiritual realities, recognized by The Father as co-regents of the heavens with Christ. Since there is not any partiality with The Father (Romans 2:11; Colossians 3:25; 1Peter 1:17), if you attain to these spiritual realities, He will not recognize another, yet refuse to recognize you. Just as grades issued by a Professor are credible only if every student has equal opportunity for earning the highest grade, that is, an 'A', so also while everyone has equal opportunity with The Father, only those who actually attain to His preset and advertised standards are recognized by Him as POWERS FOR CHRIST.

Love of Truth 16 *Whenever standards are advertised, and there is not any partiality in the advertiser, there is both equality of opportunity, and meritocracy.*

The supporting evidence from Scripture for two groups of believers in Christ?

> Jesus said to her, I am the rising again, and the life; he who is believing in me, even if he may die (spiritually), shall live (spiritually); and every one who is living (spiritually) and believing in me shall not die - to the age (John 11:25-26).

The key to knowing that our Lord Jesus Christ speaks spiritually? He declares that He who is living and believing in Him will not die. If Jesus refers to physical life, all who believe in Him at any point in time are living, none can be dead. The only way some can be living and believing, and others ONLY BELIEVING is if some already have attained to eternal life, and others believe, but have yet to arrive at eternal life. In this respect, note the careful choice of words, which is, a contrasting of those who are '*believing in Him*', with those who are '*living and believing in Him*'. Since those who merely believe are alive, else they cannot then die, clearly the distinction between '*believing in Him*', and '*living and believing in Him*' is spiritual.

In this respect, consider the following Scriptures.

> But as many as did receive Him to them HE GAVE AUTHORITY TO BECOME SONS OF GOD - to those believing in His name (John 1:12).

> Then Jesus said to those Jews who believed in Him, If you abide in My word, you are my disciples indeed. And you shall know the truth, and the truth shall make you free (John 8:31-32).

> And this is life age-during, that they may know thee, the only true God, and Him whom thou didst send - Jesus Christ (John 17:3).

> My little children, of whom again I travail in birth, TILL CHRIST MAY BE FORMED IN YOU (Galatians 4:19).

Clearly, the difference between a person *'who still is on the way to becoming a son of God'*, and a person *'who already has actualized sonship in God'* is knowledge of The Father and The Son. Since only those who know Father and Son actually arrive at eternal life here on earth, at any point in time, there exist two groups of Christians: those who are on the way to becoming sons of God - those who can still die spiritually because they have yet to arrive at life that is age-during; and those who have become sons of God - those who are living and believing in Jesus Christ. Those who already have gotten to know Father and Son already have Christ formed in them, have become the righteousness of God. Those who yet are on the way to arrival at *'Christ formed in them'* have yet to attain to the righteousness of God, still yet can die (spiritually), but will be raised to life that is age-during by our Lord Jesus Christ.

John 8:31-32 provides rich insight on the matter. If a person is to become a disciple of Jesus, he or she practices the commands of Jesus Christ. Only as he or she practices the commands is he or she able to arrive at knowledge of the truth, knowledge that makes a person arrive at freedom in his or her spirit. Let us denote a disciple who has arrived at knowledge of the truth, a POWER FOR CHRIST. Then this believer is a disciple of Christ who has arrived at knowledge of the truth, with outcome there exist some believers, NEOPHYTES who still are on the way to arrival at knowledge of the truth. Since knowledge of the truth implies arrival at freedom in the spirit, this evident in the declaration by our Lord Jesus Christ that His reign occurs in our hearts, that is, in our spirits (Luke 17:21), we arrive at the inference that POWERS FOR CHRIST have arrived at experience of the REIGN OF CHRIST, as such have become SONS OF GOD, have Christ formed in them. So then, NEOPHYTES are disciples who have yet to actualize the REIGN OF CHRIST in their spirits, disciples who still are on the path to maturity in Christ.

The Things That Are 38 *It is unequivocal in Scriptures, believers in Christ, equivalently, disciples of Christ, equivalently, those who have faith in the name of Jesus Christ, consist of two groups, Neophytes - genuine believers who still are on the path towards actualization of the* PRESENCE OF CHRIST *in their spirits, and Powers for Christ - genuine believers who have arrived at actualization of the* PRESENCE OF CHRIST *in their spirits.*

The Things That Are 39 *Disciples of Christ who are recognized by The Father as Powers for Christ arrive at* LIFE THAT IS AGE-DURING *here on earth. It is subsequent to their death that Neophytes are bestowed with* LIFE THAT IS AGE-DURING. LIFE THAT IS AGE-DURING, *first and foremost, is spiritual, not physical. Attainment to* LIFE THAT IS AGE-DURING *implies the spirit of a disciple of Christ has become bound up in The Father and The Son, both of whom are Spirits, but yet are one in essence (1John 5:7), with outcome he or she experiences the Life of Father and Son.*

The Things That Are 40 *And this is the testimony, that* LIFE AGE-DURING *did God give to us, and this - the life - is in His Son; he who is having the Son (he in whom Christ is formed,* HE WHO HAS ARRIVED AT KNOWLEDGE OF THE TRUTH, *he who has become a son of God) hath the life; he who is not having the Son of God - the life he hath not (1John 5:11-12).*

An Important Validating Scripture for Existence of Neophytes

The teachings of Scriptures are as follows. The goal of faith in Christ is acquiring of the glory of Christ, that is acquiring of the nature of Christ (2Thessalonians 2:14). When a believer acquires the nature of Christ, he or she becomes the new creation that he or she already is declared to be by virtue of the righteousness of Christ (2Corinthians 5:17; Galatians 6:15; 5:6). If the believer feeds the nature of Christ in himself or herself, he or she grows with growth made possible by Father, Son, and Holy Spirit until he or she is perfected in the nature of Christ. So then, a person who has arrived at perfection of the nature of Christ, who has become a son of God is no longer just a man, has become a member of a new race, a race marked out as SONS OF GOD (1Peter 2:9). While a believer in Christ remains on the path to becoming a son of God, he or she either acts maturely as A SON OF GOD TO BE, or acts immaturely, as the 'SENSUAL MAN' he or she is supposed to transcend via actualization of the nature of Christ.

In Galatians 6:7-8, with the recognition that those who become sons of God are POWERS FOR CHRIST, and that those who are NEOPHYTES either are progressing towards sonship, or regressing towards earthy, sensual nature of man, Apostle Paul writes as follows.

> Be not led astray; God is not mocked; for what a man may sow - that also he shall reap, because he who is sowing to his own flesh, of the flesh shall reap corruption; and HE WHO IS SOWING TO THE SPIRIT, of the Spirit SHALL REAP LIFE AGE-DURING (Galatians 6:7-8).

Prophetic Lessons 17 *Friend, there is not any shame in being a* NEOPHYTE, *for all who become* POWERS FOR CHRIST *start out as* NEOPHYTES. *All that The Father asks, is that you be a* NEOPHYTE *that is not sowing to the fleshly nature, that rather, is sowing to the Spirit, as such progressing towards acquiring of the glory (nature, and character) of Christ.*

Prophetic Lessons 18 *The Scriptures are very clear,* NEOPHYTES, *those who still require spiritual milk, as opposed to spiritual meat for their spiritual build up, either are progressing towards the nature of Christ, as such progressing towards maturation into* POWERS, *or are regressing towards sensual, sinful nature of man. Those who already are spiritual, however, who already feed on spiritual meat, that is,* POWERS, *have been perfected in the nature of Christ.*

You are saved by your obedience, not by how much growth you attain

It is important to reiterate at this point that you are not to fret over whether or not you have attained to eternal life on earth. You are not to fret because, as already discussed, the responsibility for your spiritual growth resides in The Father. One way to think about this is as follows.

At timing of confession of faith in Jesus Christ, you receive the nature of Christ. Friend, only The Father, Son, and Holy Spirit can grow this nature that is given to you as a gift. Your part? Total commitment to walking in the Love of Christ. So long, as you maintain total commitment to walking in the Love of Christ, do not excuse any hatred whatsoever, it is not your growth that saves you, rather it is the same grace that provided you with the nature of Christ that saves you. Hallelujah!!!

Prophecy Principle 77 *You are not saved by your growth in Christ, you are, via your obedience to Christ, by your willingness and effort to become like Christ, saved by the same grace that, as a gift, provided you with the nature of Christ.*

The Evidence that your growth does not reside in entirety under your control, is linked to that of the rest of the Church?

Rather, speaking the truth in love, we are to GROW UP in every way into Him who is the head, INTO CHRIST, FROM WHOM THE WHOLE BODY, joined and knit together by every joint with which it is supplied, when each part is working properly, MAKES BODILY GROWTH and upbuilds itself in love (Ephesians 4:15-16).

Let no one disqualify you, insisting on self-abasement and worship of angels, taking his stand on visions, puffed up without reason by his sensuous mind, and not holding fast to the Head (Christ), FROM WHOM THE WHOLE BODY, nourished and knit together through it's joints and ligaments, GROWS WITH A GROWTH THAT IS FROM GOD (Colossians 2:18-19).

And that Christ may dwell in your hearts through faith; THAT YOU, being rooted and grounded in love, MAY HAVE POWER TO COMPREHEND WITH ALL THE SAINTS what is the breadth and length and height and depth, and to know the LOVE OF CHRIST which surpasses knowledge, THAT YOU MAY BE FILLED with all the fullness of God (Ephesians 3:17-19).

Friend, your growth is aligned with that of the body of Christ. Note your growth is not aligned with that of the Church, which can be apostate to Christ. Rather, your growth is aligned with that of every other believer that is in the body of Christ. Given The Father, Son, and Holy Spirit seek that your growth benefit others, and that others' growth benefit you, there are constraints on your growth about which you can do nothing.

I illustrate.

Many righteous persons prayed for arrival of John the Baptist and the Messiah, that is, our Lord Jesus Christ. Yet, many died before the promise of arrival of these two persons who would usher the world into a higher realm of spirituality could be fulfilled. Luke 2:22-38 provides record of only two very old persons whose wish to be alive to witness the birth of the Messiah was granted by The Father, namely, Simeon and Anna the prophetess. It did not matter how righteous those who died before materialization of the promise were, they could not attain to the level of spiritual maturity signified by arrival of John the Baptist and our Lord Jesus Christ. This limit on their spiritual growth was imposed by God. If they prayed and fasted on end, it would not have changed the fact that they would die before the time appointed of The Father for manifestation of John the Baptist and our Lord Jesus Christ to the world. So then, John the Baptist is the greatest man born of woman (Matthew 11:11), for only he of all who came before him tasted each of the old and the new covenants, for he was taught directly of God, else he could not have been baptizing beyond the Jordan. PRIOR TO JOHN THE BAPTIST, NO ONE EVER HAD BAPTIZED PEOPLE UNTO REPENTANCE. Yet, every one who participates in the good news of our Lord Jesus Christ is greater than John the Baptist (Matthew 11:11), not because they are greater in stature or achievement, but because the glory in which we participate is greater than the glory that John the Baptist helped usher out of the way, glory of which he did not fully participate (2Corinthians Chapter 3).

So then friend, all The Father, Son, and Holy Spirit expect of you is that you make the most of the spiritual opportunities that they make available to you in Christ. So long as you are not disobedient to Christ and the Holy Spirit, whatever growth to which you attain here on earth will be sufficient for your salvation, and for your arrival at peace and joy in the Holy Spirit. The primary things then are your willingness, effort, and obedience.

Prophecy Principle 78 *The glory that currently is available in God, glory that is determined by purposes of God that already are actualized in the earth, is a determinant of everyone's growth in Christ. Just obey Father, Son, and Holy Spirit and leave the matter of exactly how much glory already is available to God.*

The Dichotomy Between the Body of Christ and the Church

With respect to the relationship between Christ, His body, and the Church, consider the following words from Ephesians 5:25-27.

> Husbands, love your wives, as Christ loved the church and gave Himself up for her, that He might sanctify her, having cleansed her by the washing of water with the word, that He might present the church to Himself in splendor, without spot or wrinkle or any such thing, that she might be holy and without blemish.

It is clear from Ephesians 5:25-27 that the church is redeemed by Christ so it can be perfected. Given the church is not perfected at time of her redemption (*while we were yet sinners, Christ died for us*), the church is perfected only if it submits to the cleansing work of the Father, Son, and Holy Spirit. If the church does not submit to the cleansing work, our Lord Jesus Christ is unable to present the church to Himself in splendor, without spot or wrinkle or any such thing. When the church submits to Christ, the Church is His body. When only some individual believers within the Church submit to Christ, the body of Christ, which consists only of genuine believers, is not equivalent to the Church. The Church then consists of all who are called to Christ. Consider then the words of our Lord Jesus Christ in respect to those whom He calls in Matthew 22:14.

> For many are called, and few are chosen.

Prophecy Insight 46 *Many are called, and few are chosen, not because The Father is partial or picks at random. Many are called, and few are chosen because not all are willing to be cleansed of their sins and weaknesses. When all who are called do not submit to cleansing, the entirety of those who are called (the Church) does not coincide with those who actually participate in the body of Christ (those who are called, and are chosen).*

Prophecy Insight 47 *Dichotomy between the Church and the body of Christ is essence of the Church in Laodicea. The Church in Laodicea is Lukewarm, as such can be spit out (Revelation 3:14-16), yet whoever would buy eyesalve to see, raiment to wear, and gold that is tried in the fire for true wealth from our Lord Jesus Christ enters into fellowship with Him (Revelation 3:18-22). Spiritually then, the Church can be dichotomized from the body of Christ.*

> For more on how to ensure you are not only called, but chosen, check out my books, 'True Sanctification' (Amazon.com), and 'Divine Meritocracy' *(soon to arrive at a store near you).*

The Lamb Slain from the Foundation of the World

So then, no one was found in heaven, on earth, or under the earth to open the Scroll, which was sealed with 7 SEALS (Revelation 5:2-4). Note that with the Scroll written upon within and on the back, opening of the Scroll has nothing to do with reading of the Scroll, rather has to do with interpretation or revelation of what is written on the Scroll. This is evident in the fact that were the problem to be access to, or language of the Scroll, with writings on the outside, some of the writings easily could have been deciphered.

Prophecy Insight 48 *Inability of all who are in heaven, on earth, or under the earth at opening of the Scroll has nothing to do with access, or language, has to do with understanding of contents of the Scroll.*

While Apostle John was weeping that no one was found to open the Scroll, one of the 24 ELDERS mentions to him that our Lord Jesus Christ overcame, as such is able to loose the 7 SEALS of the Scroll. While the Elder yet was speaking, a Lamb, which had appearance that it had been slain, appeared in midst of the throne. This Lamb has 7 HORNS and 7 EYES symbolizing the 7 SPIRITS of God that are sent to all the earth. As we already know, the number 7 represents COMPLETENESS of Pre-existing Agenda, and COMMENCEMENT of New Agenda. In the integration of the 7 SPIRITS into the body of the Lamb, we know that The Lamb is a manifestation of God, that is, a manifestation of The Word of God. Since The Word of God is Spirit (John 1:1-2), The Word always had been in the throne room of God, but now was manifesting in a pre-incarnate form as the Lamb slain from the foundation of the world. So then, the Lamb takes the Scroll from the hand that comes out of The Father - who is a Spirit, as such invisible, but whose image is Jesus Christ, and whose presence is in midst of the throne. In the designation of The Lamb as 'He' in Revelation 5:7, we know that characterization of The Word of God as the Lamb is figurative, not literal. From the taking of the Scroll by The Lamb to the end of Revelation Ch. 5, all that is done in the throne room of God is giving of praise to The Lamb and to The Father.

The Things That Are 41 *The* WORD OF GOD *is the Lamb that was slain from the foundation of the world; the same* WORD OF GOD *who tabernacled among us in the flesh in person of our Lord and Savior Jesus Christ.*

As already discussed, consider that a manifestation of the WORD OF GOD having been slain at the foundation of the world, that it would have been cheating on part of The Father for the same WORD to have continued to manifest among men. Given The Father Himself would manifest to the world only through His image, JESUS CHRIST, who would not come to the world until the end of times, in order not to be seen to be cheating, The Father also could not, in context of Old Testament times, manifest directly in physical form to man. So then, during the Old Testament, The Father would participate in affairs of life only through messengers who had authority to act in His name. In this respect, note that when The Father spoke to Moses in the mount, it was a messenger who appeared to Moses, not The Father or His only begotten Son (Acts 7:30-34). Consider also the following words in Galatians 3:19-20.

Why then the law? on account of the transgressions it was added, till the seed might come to which the promise hath been made, HAVING BEEN SET IN ORDER THROUGH MESSENGERS in the hand of a mediator - and the mediator is not of one (*the mediator was not always the same entity*), and God is one (*if the mediator had the same essence as God, then the mediator would be of one, for God is one*).

Prophecy Insight 49 *The cost to The Father of the Lamb slain from the foundation of the world resides in the fact that up until the advent of Christ, all physical manifestations of The Father on earth consisted of messengers. The Father could not manifest Himself via His only begotten Son, Jesus Christ.*

Prophecy Insight 50 *Given only our Lord Jesus Christ is the express image of God, physically speaking, The Father could not Himself interact directly with man. So then The Father would speak to man, but manifest physically only in context of messengers.*

The Lamb is Worthy Because He Overcame

If man was to be saved from sin, someone had to validate, in time and space, that is, in the flesh, the spiritual sacrifice represented by the Lamb that was slain from the foundation of the world. If man was to be saved from clutches of sin and the devil, someone had to come into this world and defeat *self (selfishness)*, the *devil*, sin, and lusts of the flesh, *lusts of the eyes*, and the *pride of life*. Our Lord Jesus Christ, He who is seated in the throne of the Father, is the one who won that victory for all of mankind. You see then that The Father operates a spiritual meritocracy.

The Things That Are 42 *The Father of our Lord Jesus Christ operates a spiritual meritocracy.*

Everyone who preceded Christ, who could be deemed a first of his type, FAILED TO OVERCOME. Enoch FAILED to win the victory - he could not translate his love for God into a purposeful agenda of love for other men. So God took him to heaven because he sought only to walk with God (Genesis 5:22-24). Moses FAILED because at the first he was too impatient (Exodus 2:11-12), and right at the end a little pride got the best of him (Numbers 20:9-12). Joshua FAILED because, prior to an important decision, he did not remember to pray; this resulted in a disobedience to The Father (Joshua Chapter 9). Elijah admitted to The Father that he had FAILED, that fire, brimstone, absence of rain, and famine, which he thought were bound to be successful, had failed to bring Israel to repentance (1Kings 19:4). All of the prophets sent to Israel FAILED to turn people to God. All of the righteous kings over Israel FAILED at turning of the people's hearts wholly towards God.

Adam FAILED, this because he loved his wife, Eve more than he loved God (Genesis 3:12). David committed adultery and murder (2Samuel 12:7-14), as such FAILED. Though he later repented, in the decision by Solomon to taste evil for himself (Ecclesiastes 1:16-17), Solomon FAILED the test of Love for Righteousness. Noah found grace in the eyes of God (Genesis 6:8) means yes, he was good, but only by standards of that time, not by God's eternal standards of righteousness; in presence of The Father's perfect standard, Noah FAILED. The only person who succeeded perfectly, who combined love for every single person with a righteous purpose rooted in the LOVE OF GOD is our Lord and Savior Jesus Christ.

The Things That Are 43 *We needed the incarnate Christ because absent actualization of the sacrifice made from the foundation of the world in affairs of this life, in space and in time, the benefits of that sacrifice could not become full reality. Post advent of our Lord Jesus Christ, we are called to acquiring of the glory of Christ (2Thessalonians 2:14), that is, to arrival at reality of The Presence of Christ.*

The Lamb's Book of Life

Revelation 13:8, & 17:8 establishes existence of a BOOK OF LIFE of the Lamb slain from the foundation of the world. Not only is this BOOK OF LIFE that of the Lamb, however, it also has been filled with names of the saved from the foundation of the world. Some people have interpreted this as predestination, as implying God determines who gets saved, and who is lost to His grace. If this is true, clearly The Father does not operate a spiritual meritocracy, rather operates some of paternalistic system within which His favor is bestowed purely on random.

> So then, does The Father predestinate to salvation in sense of a pre-determination of persons who must be unable to respond to His grace?

ABSOLUTELY NOT! That God knows the choices you will make cannot be interpreted to imply He imposed the choices on your person. Dichotomy of FORESIGHT, equivalently, FOREKNOWLEDGE of The Father from imposition of any outcome on people is evident in the following words of Scripture in Romans 8:28-30.

> For those whom He (The Father) FOREKNEW He also predestined to be conformed to the image of His Son, in order that He might be the first-born among many brethren. And those whom He predestined he also called; and those whom He called he also justified; and those whom He justified He also glorified.

Since The Father dwells in eternity, He already has come into contact with (*has arrived at foreknowledge of*) every spirit that will respond positively to His Essence and Character, both of which are rooted in the spiritual reality that He is Love. Since we are spirit, soul, and body, and since every spirit is created by God, who Himself is The Father of spirits, ever before He provides us with a body for coming into the world, we come into contact with The Father. The only difference between how we come into the world, and incarnation of our Lord Jesus Christ is, for us, the requirement of sex between a mother and father, but for Jesus, only the requirement of the Holy Spirit. Note Mary, the mother of Jesus only was carrier of Jesus Christ, that her eggs could not have participated in gestation of our Lord Jesus Christ. In this respect, we know, in today's world, that a fertilized egg obtained from one woman can be inserted into the womb of a totally different woman for arrival at a new born baby.

IF YOU THEN ASK,

"where did the fertilized egg that was implanted into Mary come from?"

then I rejoin with,

"where did the original life given to Adam come from?"

"Was Adam produced from a fertilized egg obtained from a woman?"

and

"Is it ever possible for the first couple on earth to have been produced from a fertilized egg obtained from a woman?"

If there exists a fertilized egg for creation of Adam, an egg, which then must be implanted in a womb, implying existence of a woman, Adam is not the first human created by God, and we arrive at a contradiction. Since Adam was not a woman, as such did not have a womb, Eve could not have been created from a fertilized egg. We have then that neither of Adam nor Eve could have been produced from a fertilized egg, either in a woman's womb, or obtained from a woman.

"Does science have an answer to the 'origin of life' question?"

Science throws it's hands up in the air and exclaims that somehow a cell obtained consciousness and morphed into life.

Yet scientists expect that any cells they find in a petri dish in a laboratory were placed there by someone.

Spiritual Insight 70 *Friend, do you consider science's 'HANDS UP IN THE AIR' explanation more credible than intentional creation by an almighty, yet loving God who describes Himself as Love?*

Spiritual Insight 71 *Friend, evolution is a theory, a competing philosophical rationale for life, is not fact, is interpretation of scientific evidence.*

Spiritual Insight 72 *A priori, Creationism is a more plausible rationale for life than evolution.*

In order to incorporate responsive spirits whom He encounters within Himself into His agenda, The Father declares their salvation at the foundation of the world, orchestrates their birth in time and space, then calls, justifies, and glorifies them. Predestination then consists in the spiritual reality that The Father does not leave arrival at the PRESENCE OF CHRIST by those whom He foreknows to chance. Rather, The Father prepares, ahead of time, opportunities and challenges that are designed to enable those whom He foreknew arrive at faith in, knowledge of, and love for Christ. This is essence of predestination.

The Things That Are 44 *Predestination means The Father does not leave arrival at the* PRESENCE OF CHRIST, *by those whom He foreknows to chance. Rather, The Father prepares, ahead of time, opportunities and challenges that are designed to enable those whom He foreknew arrive at faith in, knowledge of, and love for Christ.*

Given those whom He foreknew have to respond appropriately to opportunities and challenges that are placed in their path, the Presence of Christ is not given as a gift, is earned in context of a meritocracy, in context of, much the same as Christ, overcoming of self, sin, lusts, and the devil. The key here is the fact that the foreknowledge of God precedes His predestination, meaning the predestination is an acknowledgement of responses to Himself, not a random assignment of salvation. If salvation were available only by random assignment, The Father would be a hypocrite, for Love does not declare that another's actions are irrelevant to their outcomes. A God who Himself delights in Justice (Jeremiah 9:23-24) cannot assign salvation randomly, yet remain Just.

Just as a firm assesses several candidates as future candidates for CEO, then decides on a particular candidate, and grooms the candidate into a CEO, so also is The Father's predestination. Ideally, the candidate chosen to be groomed into a future CEO by a firm is not randomly selected, is picked for his or her qualities and ability. So it is exactly with The Father. The Father identifies, in eternity, spirits willing to work with Him in His plan of salvation, sanctification, edification, and glorification of man, and plans their birth and life into His agenda. This is not whimsical, capricious pre-destination, merely affirmation of choices already encountered in eternity. But while The Father knows who will, or will not respond to Him, no human being has the right to claim access to such knowledge.

Spiritual Insight 73 *Predestination recognizes and affirms choices The Father already has encountered in eternity, is not an arbitrarily random selection of persons for salvation.*

Spiritual Insight 74 *While The Father knows who will, and who will not respond to Him, no human being, no man ought ever dare to claim knowledge of what The Father knows, for only The Father dwells in eternity.*

> "...To Him who is sitting upon the throne, and to the Lamb, is the blessing, and the honor, and the glory, and the might - to the ages of the ages! and the four living creatures said, Amen! and the 24 Elders fell down and they bow before Him who is living to the ages of the ages."

> And, confessedly, great is the secret of piety - God was manifested in flesh, declared righteous in spirit, seen by messengers, preached among nations, believed on in the world, taken up in glory! (1Timothy 3:16).

> So then, the things to come? Well for that we have to proceed to Revelation *Ch. 9*, and opening of the 7 SEALS by our Lord and Savior Jesus Christ, equivalently, by the WORD OF GOD, the Lamb slain from the foundation of the world. To this, we turn our energies in the very next chapter.

CHAPTER 9

The Seven Seals: Introducing the SSGLAE

In the preceding chapter, we discussed the scene, in the throne room of The Father, in context of which THE WORD, who alone is worthy to open the Scroll that is sealed with 7 SEALS, takes the Scroll from the hand of His physical representation, who, in person of our Lord Jesus Christ has a separate existence. At this point then, we have covered, in entirety, Revelation *chs. 1 through 5.* In Revelation *ch. 6,* The Word sequentially opens the Seals on the scroll. Given the Seals are explicitly numbered as 1st, 2nd, 3rd, 4th, 5th, 6th, & 7th, the NUMEROLOGY OF THE FATHER that we established in *Chapter 6* applies to interpretation of each and every Seal. This of course implies THE SEALS ARE SYMBOLIC, as such must be interpreted in context of symbolisms that we established in *Chapter 6.* In *Chapter 6, using evidence from outside of the Book of Revelation,* and in so far as it relates to the EL-EMENTS 1 through 7, we established NUMEROLOGY that is incorporated into revelations that are entrusted to Apostle John. For ease of remembrance, I reproduce here summary of the Numerology.

Numerology of The Father

✠ ELEMENT 1 (NB): NEW BEGINNINGS - man either starts off on a path of righteousness, or embarks on a path of evil.

✠ ELEMENT 2 (CP): COMPANIONSHIP OF PURPOSE - Companionship that is rooted in pursuit of Righteousness; or Companionship that is rooted in pursuit of Evil.

✠ ELEMENT 3 (CF): INNER CIRCLE OF FRIENDSHIP: Arrival at Inner Circle of Friendship that is rooted in pursuit of Righteousness; or Arrival at Inner Circle of Friendship that is rooted in pursuit of Evil.

✠ ELEMENT 4 (GJ): GRAND JUDGMENTS of the Wicked that require identification of The Righteous.

✠ ELEMENT 5 (MR): MATURITY OF RIGHTEOUSNESS: The Righteous Flourish, and Shine as the Sun in the reign of their Father.

✠ ELEMENT 6 (JW): COMMENCEMENT & EXECUTION OF JUDGMENT ON THE WICKED.

✠ ELEMENT 7 (CC): COMPLETENESS OF A PRE-EXISTING AGENDA & COMMENCEMENT OF A NEW AGENDA

Given the ELEMENT 1 symbolizes New Beginnings, and the ELEMENT 7, simultaneity of Completeness of a pre-existing agenda, and Commencement of a new agenda, the 7 SEALS symbolize evolution of life on earth that purposely is designed never to end. This is evident in the symbolism that arrival at a 7ᵗʰ SEAL, which induces COMMENCEMENT OF A NEW AGENDA implies a NEW BEGINNING, that is, a new 1ˢᵗ SEAL. Since a NEW BEGINNING that is not completed does not make any sense, arrival at a new 1ˢᵗ SEAL implies a transversing of SEALS 1 through 7, and on and on it goes in a never ending cycle. By now, you probably are realizing the wonder of it all, realizing the reason why the Book of Revelation is silent on the Second Coming of Christ, which is, The Father's design is for life to persist on earth in perpetuity, that is, forever. More specifically, if a new 1ˢᵗ SEAL coincides with Commencement of a New Agenda in context of a 7ᵗʰ SEAL that is ending, there must exist some things that are, some things that do not change, some things that connect an *ending* 7ᵗʰ SEAL with a *new* 1ˢᵗ SEAL.

AS YOU SHALL SEE, NEW HEAVENS, NEW EARTH, AND THE NEW JERUSALEM, ALWAYS ARE.

Prophecy Principle 79 *With the 1ˢᵗ, 2ⁿᵈ, 3ʳᵈ, 4ᵗʰ, 5ᵗʰ, 6ᵗʰ, & 7ᵗʰ Seals all connected by the spiritual reality that individual believers in Christ all are, through all of the 7* SEALS, *in New Heavens, New Earth, and the New Jerusalem, the 7* SEALS *embed what is referred to in Mathematics as a* 'CONNECTED SET', *that is, a* MATHEMATICAL SPACE. *In a Mathematical Space, all operations that feasibly can subsist are expected to be rational.*

Prophecy Principle 80 NEW HEAVENS, NEW EARTH, & THE NEW JERUSALEM *become spiritual reality for the Church, as an entity, and for the Nations, as an entity if they respond positively to Powers that are members of the Body of Christ, who are commissioned by The Lord Jesus Christ to overcome in context of a* NEW BEGINNING, *that is, in context of a 1ˢᵗ SEAL.*

Prophecy Principle 81 *The 7* SEALS *embody the 'Spiritual System for Governance of Life & Affairs on Earth' (*THE SSGLAE*).*

From 1st SEAL through 7th SEAL, for individual believers in Christ, New Heavens, New Earth, and the New Jerusalem subsist, always are spiritual reality. If the Church honors her Lord Jesus Christ in context of a 1st SEAL, AS AN ENTITY, New Heavens, New Earth, and the New Jerusalem portend spiritual realities for the Church. If the Nations predicate civil laws, and societal interactions on the Love of Christ in context of a 1st SEAL, AS AN ENTITY, New Heavens, New Earth, and the New Jerusalem portend spiritual realities for the Nations. Let us state then three important truths.

Prophecy Principle 82 *The* BODY OF CHRIST *consists of* INDIVIDUAL BE-LIEVERS *in the name of Jesus Christ who each are in the* PRESENCE OF CHRIST. *Some of these believers are* NEOPHYTES, *and some are* POWERS FOR CHRIST. *If there is to be initiation of a 1st SEAL, the Body of Christ must consist of some Powers for Christ, that is, must consist of some believers who have attained to a measure of the stature of the fullness of Christ.*

Prophecy Principle 83 *The* BODY OF CHRIST *is not a physical organization on earth. The Father relates with physical denominations, such as Baptists, SDAs, Episcopals etc. only to the extent that leadership of such denominations are in the* PRESENCE OF CHRIST, *that is, are either of* NEOPHYTES, *or* POWERS FOR CHRIST, *but certainly, not* CHARLATANS.

Prophecy Interpretation 14 *The SSGLAE is, through Apostle John, conveyed to us by our Lord Jesus Christ so we are aware of* CONSEQUENCES *and* PUN-ISHMENTS *that subsist whenever either of the Church, or the Nations, or both* CHOOSE NOT TO DO WHAT IS RIGHT *in context of a 1st SEAL, that is, in context of opportunity for a* NEW BEGINNING *(remember the parable of the steward with the 1 talent?). Simultaneously, the SSGLAE creates awareness of* RE-WARDS *that accrue to the Church, or the Nations, or both if they* CHOOSE TO DO WHAT IS RIGHT *in context of a 1st SEAL. Given individuals belong to either of the Church or the Nations, the SSGLAE portends implications for every single individual, Christian, or non-Christian.*

The Connection with the Seven Churches in Asia?

As discussed in *Chapter 5*, THE TIME OF THE SEVEN CHURCHES in Asia served for achievement of the following.

♣ Disqualification of Nations of Western Europe as potential partners for the Gospel.

♣ Opportunity for Asia to become *Ground Zero* for spreading of the Gospel. As already established, Asia, that is, other descendants of Abraham did not seize the opportunity that presented itself.

♣ Time necessary for The Father and The Lord Jesus Christ to demonstrate to those who considered themselves favored - Jews, Western Europeans, and Asians, that none are able to anchor the GRACE OF GOD, that the Grace of God only can be anchored by Spiritual Presence of Christ on Earth, presence that arrived at commencement of the time of the Church in Laodicea - the Church whose time never ends; the Church that transforms into a worldwide Church.

Simultaneous with listed Agenda, THE TIME OF THE SEVEN CHURCHES provided our Lord Jesus Christ with opportunity to:

♣ Provide those of us who live in these times with events that are framed in time, events that provide evidence in history for workings of the SSGLAE in affairs of life on earth. You see then, that the SSGLAE is a thing that is; in this chapter, and the chapters to follow, you will find out that the SSGLAE always has been, that while bounded by time - this because our Lord Jesus Christ had to advent as a baby in time - that it was in effect in the time of the Old Covenant. Since our Lord Jesus Christ lives forever, and has earned the right to reign over life and affairs that transpire on earth, under the earth, and in the heavens, there no longer is any demand for interaction of time with the SSGLAE.

♣ Upon commencement of the time of the Church in Laodicea, that is, upon arrival of the Presence of Christ on earth, the SSGLAE ceased to be bound by time; like principles of Physics and Mathematics, only would respond to man's actions, and Sovereign interventions on part of The Father.

Spiritual Insight 75 *The Father is the consummate 'MAKE THE MOST OF THE TIME' person. The time of the seven churches served primarily for disqualification of all claimants, other than the spiritual presence of our Lord Jesus Christ. This was tantamount to engaging in a court case for proving that only the Presence of Christ could get the job done. While the court case was ongoing, thoughtfully, out of love for us, The Father worked evidence for spiritual reality of the SSGLAE into the time to be taken up by the court case. You see then, that The Father believes always in having some ongoing love project agenda.*

The Evidence For God's Desire for a Never Ending Cycle of Life on Earth?

For thus said Jehovah, Creator of earth, and it's Maker, He established it - not empty He prepared it, FOR INHABITING HE FORMED IT; I am Jehovah, and there is none else (Isaiah 45:18).

I HAVE MADE THE EARTH, AND CREATED MAN ON IT. I - My hands - stretched out the heavens, and all their host I have commanded (Isaiah 45:12).

The Things That Are 45 *The unending rotation of the earth around it's own axis, and around the sun is symbolic, is symbolic of the intent of The Father that life persists on earth in perpetuity.*

The Things That Are 46 *It was while the earth kept on rotating around the sun in exactly the same manner that it had done for thousands of years that, at different times,* ISAAC NEWTON *discovered the law of gravity;* MARIE CURIE *arrived at breakthroughs in Chemistry and Physics;* ROBERT BOYLE *developed an entire new line of knowledge now known as Chemistry; and* COPERNICUS, KEPLER, *and* GALILEO GALILEI *arrived at the inference that the earth rotated around the sun, and not vice versa.*

The Things That Are 47 *It is in the acknowledgement of the things that are, of the things that are immutable, of the things that do not change, that we arrive at insights, which produce things that are new.*

The Scriptural Evidence?

Call unto Me, and I do answer thee, yea, I declare to thee great and fenced things - thou hast not known them (Jeremiah 33:3).

Daniel answered and said: "Blessed be the name of God forever and ever, for wisdom and might are His. And He changes the times and the seasons; He removes kings and raises up kings; HE GIVES WISDOM TO THE WISE (*the acknowledgement of existence and rights of God is the beginning of wisdom - Proverbs 9:10*), and knowledge to those who have understanding (*it is those who have understanding of importance of acknowledgment of God who arrive at knowledge that is deep*). HE REVEALS DEEP AND SECRET THINGS; He knows what is in the darkness, and light dwells with Him (Daniel 2:20-22)."

For the Lord Jehovah doth nothing, except He hath revealed His counsel unto His servants (equivalently, *emissaries, or ambassadors*) the prophets (Amos 3:7).

The Things That Are 48 *If you seek to discover new things; if you seek continuity of arrival at newness in your life; it all commences with that most important of immutables, which is, reverence for, acknowledgment of, desire for revelations of, and a seeking after of the only true and wise God, Creator of Heaven and Earth, Father of our Lord and Savior Jesus Christ.*

Prophecy Principle 84 *The 7* SEALS *are symbolic of The Father's desire for perpetuity of life, newness, and righteous activity on earth.*

Prophecy Principle 85 *Since The Father always is* COMPLETING, *and* COM-MENCING, *The 7* SEALS *simultaneously are part of the things that are, and the things that are to come.*

The 7 Seals: A Summary

- ✠ 1ˢᵗ Seal: New Beginnings for the Gospel. The Father commissions the BODY OF CHRIST to overcome *sin*, self, the *world*, and the devil. The *Body of Christ*, which may not coincide with physical entities (Christian Denominations) that label themselves as Churches, *but which yet starts off as a subset of those physical entities*, becomes an agent of change in context of interactions with the Nations. Only THE BODY OF CHRIST is an AGENT OF CHANGE in context of the 1ˢᵗ Seal. CHURCH DE-NOMINATIONS, and THE NATIONS respond either negatively or positively to demonstrations of the Love of God that are produced by the Body of Christ, which is led by POWERS FOR CHRIST. If Church Denominations respond positively to the evidence for victory over sin, self, the world, and the devil, as such are willing to be perfected in the Love of Christ, they please their Lord and Savior Jesus Christ. IF THE NATIONS RE-SPOND POSITIVELY, they base civil laws, and principles that undergird interactions within society on the Love of God. While The Father would rather that The Nations go on to believe in Jesus Christ, in His mercy, love, and wisdom, so long as people love one another, so long as civil laws promote love for one another, and so long as personal revelations of Christ of which people are convicted are not rejected, The Father has chosen not to demand faith in Jesus Christ for acceptance into His Grace. If Church Denominations respond negatively, they refuse to ac-knowledge that the work that they *see*, *hear about*, and *encounter* is of The Holy Spirit, as such refuse to submit themselves to their Lord and Savior, Jesus Christ. If THE NATIONS RESPOND NEGATIVELY, they reject the Love of God as basis for civil laws and societal interactions, as such choose HATRED, and LOVE OF MONEY as basis for civil laws. If THE NATIONS and CHURCH DENOMINATIONS respond positively, there is transition, not to the 2ⁿᵈ Seal, but to the 7ᵗʰ TRUMPET of the 7ᵗʰ SEAL. If the nations respond negatively, there is transition to the 2ⁿᵈ Seal. The 2ⁿᵈ Seal ushers in NATURAL CONSEQUENCES of the choice of *hatreds* and *love of money* as basis for civil laws, and societal interactions. If the Nations respond negatively, whether Church Denominations respond negatively or positively, everyone ends up with the nations in the 2ⁿᵈ Seal.

- ✠ 2ⁿᵈ Seal: Arrival at a 2ⁿᵈ SEAL implies that while there exist individuals within nations who have rejoiced in the good news of Christ, as such have become part of THE BODY OF CHRIST, or adopted the LOVE OF

GOD as rubric for life, like the Jewish Nation, nations and their leaders have, as entities, rejected the GOOD NEWS OF CHRIST. This is evident in civil laws that do not reflect the Love of God, and civil laws, which enable the rich continue to take advantage of the not-so-rich. We have then that *The Nations* seek each others' COMPANIONSHIP in context of maintenance and pursuit of evil, and THE BODY OF CHRIST finds companionship of righteousness within herself. If Church Denominations chose to be perfected in context of the 1st SEAL, the Body of Christ coalesces into Church Denominations. If Church Denominations refused to be perfected in context of the 1st SEAL, Church Denominations devolve into evil associations, hatreds, and fightings. Since HATRED and LOVE OF MONEY must, eventually produce frictions and fighting within any companionship of evil, nations fight each other, kill each other, resulting in *wars*, and *rumors of wars*, yet the end is not. The exact words of our Lord Jesus Christ? "*And you will hear of wars and rumors of wars.* SEE THAT YOU ARE NOT TROUBLED; *for all these things must come to pass,* BUT THE END IS NOT YET. For nation will rise against nation, and kingdom against kingdom. And there will be famines, pestilences, and earthquakes in various places. ALL THESE ARE BEGINNING OF SORROWS *(Matthew 24:6-8)*." You see then that *wars* and *rumors of wars* are not predictors of the Second Coming of Christ, rather are evidence for choice of evil at a societal scale, and predictors of impending judgment of nations in context of a 4th SEAL.

✠ 3rd Seal: THE NATIONS, AND THE BODY OF CHRIST, arrive at their inner circles of friendship (CF). If the Body of Christ has coalesced into Church Denominations, CFs that subsist within the Body of Christ, which then is identical to the Church are rooted in the Love of Christ. WITHIN THIS CONTEXT, THE CHURCH is not characterized by divisions and strife (1Corinthians 1:10; 3:1-4; Ephesians 4:3; Romans 15:5-6; Philippians 1:27-28), rather is prepared for perfection, that is, maturity of righteousness, as such is able to skip the 4th Seal, arrive at the 5th Seal. Philippians 1:27-28 makes this very clear. If The Church is united, only destruction of the wicked transpires next, The Church is not persecuted, arrives at the 5th Seal. So then, there is not any meaningful persecution of the Body of Christ. IF THE CHURCH ARRIVES AT AN INNER CIRCLE OF FRIENDSHIP THAT IS EVIL, love of money and self trump love for Jesus Christ, with outcome the Church is splintered and weak, such that, while the nations are punished in context of the 4th Seal, for avoidance of persecution, The Church becomes a TURNCOAT, points out those who are faithful to Christ so they can be persecuted. Within this context, they morph into *Babylon the Great* which persecutes the Body of Christ in context of the 4th SEAL. Whether The Church chooses to be perfected, or not, *those who are faithful to Christ, that is, the Body of*

Christ are sealed with the Holy Spirit, that is, are identified. Once they are sealed, in sense of possibility of a devolution to unrighteousness, The Father will not allow any one have power over them. So then, '*he who is righteous remains righteous still, and he who is unrighteous remains unrighteous still (Revelation 22:11).*' The sealing (identification) of the righteous prepares the ground for judgment of the nations that subsists in context of the 4th SEAL.

✠ 4th Seal: The Father's GRAND JUDGMENTS of rejection of the Love of God as foundation for civil laws and societal interactions, rejection that was hurtful to both Christians and non-Christians, and which transpired in context of the 1st SEAL arrive. Why this long (two intervening Seals)? Because The Father judges people by their actions, and prior to arrival at Grand Judgments, actions must unambiguously reveal a heart that is rebellious or non-submissive to The Father. BABYLON, THE GREAT WHORE, equivalently, the apostate Church, who worked against the perfection of The Church in context of the 1st Seal is judged by The Father in context of the 4th Seal. Some of this judgment is executed by the very same nations with which Babylon committed harlotry in context of the 1st Seal (Revelation 17:15-18). The command to those who are faithful to Christ, to '*come out of Babylon*' (Revelation 18:4-5), so as not to partake of her judgment (Revelation 18:8, 20-24) go forth in context of the 3rd SEAL, coincide with sealing of those who are faithful to the name of Jesus Christ. Since the nations persecute the faithful in context of the 4th Seal, the command not to buy or sell, except a person has the mark of the beast (Revelation 13:17-18) goes forth under the 4th Seal, represents economic persecution of those who are faithful to the name of Jesus Christ. The decision to persecute the righteous provides unambiguous evidence that THE NATIONS choose evil over righteousness.

✠ 5th Seal: Maturity of Righteousness. Clearly, if the Church does not arrive at an inner circle of friendship in context of the 3rd SEAL, it simultaneously cannot SHINE AS THE SUN in context of Maturity of Righteousness. SUPPOSE THEN THAT THE CHURCH DID NOT ARRIVE AT AN INNER CIRCLE OF FRIENDSHIP IN CONTEXT OF THE 3rd SEAL, WITH OUTCOME, IT PASSED THROUGH A 4th SEAL. Within context of a passing through the 4th SEAL by The Church, those who are righteous, those who are killed for their faith in Jesus Christ in context of persecutions that subsisted during the 4th SEAL are shown under the altar, petitioning The Father for justice in course of the 5th SEAL (Revelation 6:9). IF THE CHURCH ARRIVED AT AN INNER CIRCLE OF FRIENDSHIP IN CONTEXT OF THE 3rd SEAL, it arrives at Maturity of Righteousness in context of the 5th SEAL Seal. This Maturity of Righteousness *triggers* a 7th SEAL, which devolves into

a new 1ˢᵗ Seal for The Church; a new 1ˢᵗ Seal that coincides with a 7ᵗʰ
SEAL for The Nations.

✠ 7ᵗʰ Seal (Trumpets 1 through 6 : 'GP7' Path of SSGLAE only): THE NATIONS
are punished for all of their sins, particularly persecution of the saints
during the time of the 4ᵗʰ SEAL, in context of Trumpets 1 through 6
of the 7ᵗʰ Seal. Those who are sealed by The Father in context of the
3ʳᵈ SEAL are not hurt by any of these punishments. While the punishments are ongoing, those who are sealed by The Father become seed
for the new 1ˢᵗ Seal that arrives for THE BODY OF CHRIST. You see then
that Activities designed for COMPLETENESS of an existing SSGLAE are
simultaneous with COMMENCEMENT of a New SSGLAE.

✠ 6ᵗʰ Seal & 7ᵗʰ Trumpet of 7ᵗʰ Seal:

ॐ Progression from 1ˢᵗ Seal to 7ᵗʰ Trumpet of the 7ᵗʰ Seal (The 'BP7'
Path): The nations having responded positively to the Love of God,
having based civil laws on the Love of God, are admitted into the
New Jerusalem in context of the 7ᵗʰ Trumpet of the 7ᵗʰ Seal (Revelation
22:14,17) The Church having been perfected, there is actualization
of the Presence of Christ for entirety of the Church (Revelation 22:1-
5) and the heavens and earth are, on that basis, transformed into
new heavens and new earth in which righteousness dwells (2Pe-
ter 3:13). The Church dwells (*spiritually*) in the New Jerusalem,
and The Nations come into the New Jerusalem to partner with The
Church for producing NEW THINGS on earth (Revelation 22:12).
The minority of people who choose evil remain in the new heavens and new earth, are able to hurt one another only, and do not
gain access to spiritual realities of the New Jerusalem (Revelation
22:15). We have then that The Father's objective of perfection of
The Church is completed, ushering in commencement of a new 1ˢᵗ
SEAL. The New 1ˢᵗ SEAL that commences no longer is about THE
CHURCH witnessing to THE NATIONS, but about partnerships between The Church and The Nations that produce new things on
earth. The BP7 PATH resolves into the UTOPIA that is depicted in
Revelation ch. 22.

ॐ Progression of The Church through the 5ᵗʰ Seal (avoidance of the
4ᵗʰ Seal) - The 'GP7' Path: A 6ᵗʰ SEAL for THE NATIONS coincides
with the 7ᵗʰ Trumpet of the 7ᵗʰ Seal for The Church. Judgment is
executed on The Nations in context of the 6ᵗʰ SEAL. The Church
having matured in context of the 5ᵗʰ SEAL, goes on to be perfected
in context of the 7ᵗʰ Trumpet of the 7ᵗʰ Seal, as such, attracts the
Presence of Christ for descent of the New Jerusalem. All those who

among the nations who chose the Love of God as basis for interactions with others are admitted into the New Jerusalem in context of the 7th Trumpet of the 7th Seal. The Nations having not adopted the Love of God as basis for civil laws, they are consigned to OLD HEAVENS AND EARTH that are not located in the Presence of Christ. For the Church, the GP7 path resolves into the UTOPIA that is depicted in *Revelation ch. 22*.

ↄ Progression of The Church through the 4th Seal - The 'RP7' Path: A 6th SEAL for THE NATIONS coincides with the 7th VIAL of the 7th Seal for The Body of Christ. Judgment is executed on The Nations, the devil, and the two beasts in context of the 6th SEAL. Upon arrival of the righteous who were sealed in context of the 3rd SEAL at the 7th Seal, spiritually, they are reconstituted into The Church, and are perfected. This implies coincidence of the 7th Seal with a New 1st SEAL. Having arrived at perfection in context of the New 1st SEAL that *redefines* them as The Church (The New Church), The New Church attracts the Presence of Christ for descent of the New Jerusalem, and arrival at NEW HEAVENS AND A NEW EARTH. All those who among the nations chose the Love of God as basis for interactions with others are admitted into the New Jerusalem in context of the 7th VIAL of the 7th Seal. The Nations having not adopted the Love of God as basis for civil laws, find themselves consigned to OLD HEAVENS AND EARTH, that is, find themselves removed from the Presence of Christ. The RP7 PATH resolves into the spiritual resolution that is depicted in *Revelation ch. 21*, but yet immediately, based on right choices can transition itself to the more more glorious spiritual resolution (UTOPIA) that is depicted in *Revelation ch. 22*.

Prophecy Insight 51 *Whenever incentives for doing what is right are designed, such that they are effective, they satisfy what is referred to as an* INCENTIVE COMPATIBILITY CRITERION *(ICC). The three feasible paths outlined for the SSGLAE satisfy an ICC. When The Church and The Nations oblige The Father, only 2* SEALS *are activated -* SEALS *1 & 7, there is not any pain or sorrow for anyone in society, and only ONE SSGLAE is required for arrival at the* UTOPIA *that is depicted in Revelation ch. 22. When The Church fully obliges The Father (passes through the 5th* SEAL*), but the Nations do not, there is pain for The Nations, and only the Seal that represents pain for The Church is skipped, this for arrival at activation of 6 out of 7* SEALS*; The Church arrives at the* UTOPIA *that is depicted in Revelation ch. 22. When neither The Church nor The Nations oblige The Father, all 7* SEALS *are activated, there is pain for The Church and The Nations, and THREE SSGLAEs are required for arrival at the* UTOPIA *that is depicted in Revelation ch. 22.*

What Sorts of Civil Laws are implied by the Love of God?

♣ Laws of Morality, which can be boiled down to:

     ༄ Honor to whom honor is due

     ༄ Thou shalt not steal

     ༄ Thou shalt not commit adultery

     ༄ Thou shalt not commit murder

     ༄ Thou shalt not bear false witness against thy neighbor

     ༄ Thou shalt not covet your neighbor's spouse or property

♣ In terms of some specifics that have come to light as important:

     ༄ Laws that Mitigate Oppression

     ༄ Laws that do not Embed Discrimination, that is, conditional on qualifications, civil laws that ensure equality of access to opportunities for employment

     ༄ Laws that Ensure Everyone Willing and Able to Work Full Time Has Sufficient Income for Maintenance of Dignified Living.

     ༄ Absence of Dichotomy Between Laws on the Books and Systems in Place: while Civil Laws proclaim everyone is equal in the sight of God, systems can be put in place for arrival at a Class Based system, an oppressive system that is contrary to the Love of God. The Father expects that Systems instituted for facilitation of Laws on the Books which pertain to equality of all agents are designed to be effective.

     ༄ Structures for Implementation of Civil Laws that Work as they Ought

     ༄ Civil Laws which Enable Markets that Encourage and Facilitate New Innovations

     ༄ Protection for Innovations, such that the Already Rich are not Able to Steal from Innovators who still are in process of building wealth

     ༄ Laws, which ensure, in absence of any unexplained gaps in people's work history, that there does not exist any merit to checks for criminal history.

     ༄ Laws, which ensure checks for criminal histories are conditioned, in entirety, on an offer of employment.

ℑ Laws, which ensure encounters with the law that transpire, in entirety, within people's personal lives, and that are not directly relevant to job requirements are not available for consumption of either of the general public, or recruiters within organizations.

ℑ Laws that penalize recruiters for non-shortlisting of job candidates on basis of non-job relevant encounters with the Law.

ℑ Laws that do not prevent those who have paid their dues for past mistakes from being integrated back into the work force.

Prophetic Lessons 19 *Friend, the sorts of civil laws demanded by our Lord Jesus Christ are no more than many reasonable men all over the world advocate for proper and equitable functioning of society.*

Balancing of Remediation and Punishment

If there do not exist any penalties for wrong behaviors, people do not have any incentive for eschewing of wrong behaviors. While penalties must exist for wrong behaviors, civil laws that are founded on the LOVE OF GOD stipulate penalties that are cognizant of weightiness of wrong behaviors, and conditional on such weightiness allow for remediation of wrongdoers. What perhaps is the best illustration of such balance is the approach stipulated by The Father for dealing with stealing. In ancient Israel, if a man was caught stealing, he was required to repay, in money, what was stolen (Exodus 22:1, 8-9). If it turned out that such a person did not have a job, hence the decision to steal, society was sensitized to plight of such a man, as such had to provide a job that would facilitate repayment of whatever it was that had been stolen. In ancient times, this meant an indentured service (Exodus 22:3), from which after 6 years he was freed with blessings from his former master (Deuteronomy 15:12-15). You see then that the law focused, not only on imposition of a penalty, but also on addressing of the source of the wrong behavior, which is, lack of a job, equivalently, absence of income. In the United States of America, prison time for wrong behavior has, in of itself, become a social ill that requires attention of the society for arrival at improvements to civil laws. In this respect, note that The Father did not allow for incorporation of prisons into the civil code that was instituted for ancient Israel. There is a lesson in this for all of modern society.

Prophetic Lessons 20 PUNISHMENTS ARE NOT EQUIVALENT TO PENALTIES. *Punishments seek to prove that people in charge of law enforcement have power to deal with others within society, particularly, weaker segments of society. Punishments are characteristic of societies within which civil laws are not premised on the Love of The Father. Penalties seek to deter future recurrence of wrongdoing or criminal behavior. Penalties are characteristic of societies within which civil laws are premised on the Love of The Father.*

Focus on Prevention of Crime, as Opposed to Policing of Crime

Whenever societies focus on policing of crime, law enforcement is not rewarded on basis of absence of either of crime, or wrongdoing, rather are rewarded on basis of evidence for successful policing. Within context of successful policing, evil elements in society can target weaker elements who, in presence of challenges of life, might have propensity for seeking of shortcuts for arrival at remediation of their circumstances. So then, young black kids seeking decent jobs may find it difficult to do so, this such that they are pushed into the drug trade where eventually they either end up *dead* or '*in jail*'. Given either of *dead* or *in jail* bolsters statistics for success of policing, the law does not have any incentive for active and effective dissuasion of padding of statistics on policing of crime via pushing of bottom strata of society into '*desperate*' situations. Suppose, however, that law enforcement is rewarded primarily on basis of absence of crime, or wrongdoing. Within this context, 200 armed robberies that are successfully resolved for a 100% success rate do not paint quite as good a picture as a 75% success rate at resolution of 20 armed robberies. Whenever law enforcement is rewarded on basis of crime prevention, policemen, prosecutors, and Judges DO NOT HAVE ANY INCENTIVE for padding of *arrest records*, *aggregate numbers of convictions*, and *aggregate numbers of successfully resolved prosecutions*. It becomes more difficult then for law enforcement to be cajoled into schemes that impoverish society, into schemes that induce more and more people to get into trouble with the law. Whenever higher numbers for *arrest records*, *aggregate numbers of convictions*, and *aggregate numbers of successfully resolved prosecutions* are metrics for policing success, law enforcement always can make a case for an even larger workforce, an outcome that deepens the problem.

Prophetic Lessons 21 *Societies that focus more on punishment, than on balancing of penalties, and, conditional on specific wrongs or crimes, feasibility of remediation, do not conform with societies within which civil laws are premised on the Love of The Father.*

Prophetic Lessons 22 *Societies that focus more on policing, than on prevention of either of crimes or wrongdoing, do not conform with societies within which civil laws are premised on the Love of The Father.*

Illustration of Civil Laws that are premised on the Love of God: Abortion

When it comes to abortion, *role play* that is evident in people's characterization of themselves as PRO-LIFE, or PRO-CHOICE, characterizations I have proved are, in essence, identical (in my *Medium* blog post titled, '*Political 'Yay' and 'Nay' Grounded in Normative Gray*', published, September 3, 2018) merely politicizes the abortion question.

'Pro-Life' and 'Pro-Choice' are no more than political slogans.
The problem? Some people take the slogans too seriously, take
themselves too seriously.

In the blog post to which I allude, I demonstrate that so long as there is
attempt at balancing of the two political extremes, that the PRO-LIFE *vis-a-vis* PRO-CHOICE debate merely creates jobs, and does not hurt anyone, as
such produces a desirable outcome - JOB CREATION, and SEMBLANCE OF A
POLITICAL DIVIDE - within any society.

Spiritual Insight 76 *Activities that create* SEMBLANCE OF A POLITICAL DIVIDE
*are beneficial for society; transform political divide into no more than role play.
Introduction of* REAL POLITICAL DIVIDE *into any political landscape always is
costly. Just ask the United States of America.*

In my post, so long as a woman is willing to take educational classes,
classes which relate to importance of consideration of real emotional and/or
spiritual implications of the decision to undertake an abortion, and so long
as the abortion is restricted to no more than the first trimester of a pregnancy, if a woman were to insist on an abortion, the State ought to allow
access to resources that enable her desire.

How is this in accordance with teachings of Jesus Christ?

Which is worse, to, subsequent to provision of educational insights, grant
a woman an abortion that she desires, with outcome she is responsible for
her emotional, guilt, or satisfaction outcomes, or to subject a child to a life
that is devoid of love, to insist that a child be raised by a woman who does
not have any affection for the child?

If society insists that the woman have the child, while the child may end
up with some guilt, there is not any guilt that can be imposed on the woman.
If the woman is unable to love the child, she already was honest enough to
own up to such a predicament. The child, however, remains responsible to
God for dealing with the loveless situation into which he or she has been
domiciled by society. So then, society plays *god*, perhaps seeks to multiply
'*problem children*' who make their own children, who lack capacity for love,
look like saints.

If you were a child, and you had a choice as to being raised
by a woman who already has confessed that she lacks the emotional and spiritual maturity for being a mother, would you choose
to come into the world?

Love of Truth 17 *Justice demands that, in a world, which already is significantly messed up with sin, evil, and suffering, that we do not compound the
problem, that we do not insist on bringing children into loveless situations.*

Suppose, however, that we believe in eliminating opportunities for abortion, and that both the Church and the Nations agree this is a worthwhile objective. Well then, if the Church and The Nations are to demonstrate righteousness, mercy, justice, and truth, a banning of abortion must be preceded by:

- ♣ BANNING OF CONTRACEPTIVES. It is hypocritical for society to license contraceptives, yet complain that women arrive at pregnancies that they do not want.

- ♣ MOVIES & SEX SCENES: Regardless of their ratings, banning of sex scenes in all movies.

- ♣ MUSIC: Banning of music that glorifies non-marital sex.

- ♣ BOOKS: Banning of books that glorify sex between persons who are not responsible enough to get married. Books with sex scenes to be rated for adults only.

- ♣ ADOLESCENT DATING: Parents making it clear to adolescents that they only can date in groups, that a boy and a girl cannot hole themselves up in their room, or go alone on a date. Is there any adult out there who really thinks adolescent boys and girls hole up in their bedrooms because doing of homework is so much more pleasurable when it is undertaken in bedrooms?

- ♣ ROLE MODELING 1: Women no longer declaring that they can have as much sex as they want, and with as many men as they deem fit. If women make such declarations, how exactly are teenagers to be dissuaded from premature sex, and unwanted pregnancies?

- ♣ ROLE MODELLING 2: Men not talking about women as if they are no more than sexual escapades, with outcome adolescent boys increasingly do not see adolescent girls merely as *booty calls*, or *tallies of conquests.*

- ♣ CP & CF: More of activities that enable men and women arrive at true *companionship* and *friendship* that are rooted in purposeful activities (CP & CF) which involve populations of males or females.

- ♣ MARRIAGE: With the wife female, and husband, male, glorification of marriage as friendship between husband and wife. Society can define marriage otherwise, the Church can do none else.

Prophecy Interpretation 15 *Any Nation, which willingly, and with cooperation of it's citizenry embarks on outlined preceding initiatives can declare that the decision to impose an outright ban on abortion is predicated on the Love of God.*

The SSGLAE: Demonstration of Reality of Person of Christ

As I already have articulated, and as already is evident in the preceding Summary, the purpose of the SSGLAE is establishment of paths for life and affairs on earth, paths that are outcomes of choices by individuals, The Church, and The Nations, and Sovereign interventions of The Father. In the statements of consequences and penalties, or rewards for each of choice of evil or righteous paths, The Father demonstrates His love for justice, His willingness to pre-specify rewards for what is good, and penalties for what is evil. The dichotomization works as follows. If, much like the Jewish Nation, Church leadership chooses to resist their Lord and Savior, much like the disciples of Jesus Christ, individuals who respond are not penalized for sins of the leadership who, typically will be aligned with majority of those who profess faith in Jesus Christ. If, much like the Roman nation, The Nations reject the Love of God as basis for civil laws and interactions within society, individuals who, regardless, choose to love their fellow man are not condemned along with the leadership of The Nations, and the larger body polity. How do we know that rejection of the Love of God by leadership of The Nations implies rejection by the larger body polity? Leaders are able to reject the Love of God as basis of civil laws only because the majority of the people do not have any desire for living by the Love of God. In the FULFILLMENT of rewards for what is good, or consequences and penalties for what is evil, we arrive at CONCRETE EVIDENCE for reality of Father, Son, and Holy Spirit.

The Things That Are 49 *In the dichotomization of Individual believers in Christ from The Church, dichotomization of The Church from The Nations, and stipulation of standards that are customized to individual believers in Christ, the Church, or the Nations, The Father demonstrates His delight in Mercy, Righteousness, and Justice (Jeremiah 9:23-24).*

The Things That Are 50 *The Father believes in reasonings that revolve around evidence (Isaiah 1:18). In the fulfillment of consequences or rewards that are promised in context of the SSGLAE, The Father provides the entire world - Christian or non-Christian - with evidence for reality of Himself, The Word, and the Holy Spirit.*

While this evidence is important, and while we shall see that there has been fulfillment of paths embedded in the SSGLAE - a spiritual system that will govern life and affairs on earth for as long as there is life on this earth - the most important evidence, the evidence that is perfectly incontrovertible is evidence for the PRESENCE OF CHRIST in lives of those who have faith in Jesus Christ.

The Things That Are 51 *When Jesus declares, "In this shall all know that ye are my disciples,* IF YE MAY HAVE LOVE ONE TO ANOTHER *(John 13:35)," He really means what He says.*

The Things That Are 52 *The manifestation of the* PRESENCE OF CHRIST, *which is attained to by* POWERS, *and consists in manifestation of* GODLINESS, BROTHERLY KINDNESS, *and* LOVE FOR ALL MEN *is the most incontrovertible evidence for reality of Father, Word, and Holy Spirit, is overarching purpose of the SSGLAE.*

FOR REITERATION:

✠ Godliness consists in spending of the time always in CONCEPTION of Love Projects for the future; FORMULATION of Love Projects for the Present; and IMPLEMENTATION of Love Projects that were conceived during prior periods. Love Projects are rooted in the Love of God, are projects that serve to bless mankind. For more on Godliness and it's interactions with the demand to love every single person, check out *Chapter 4* of my book, True Sanctification.

✠ Brotherly Kindness relates to the demand for demonstrations of Love within The Church. Our Lord Jesus Christ declares that a person who is godly, as such has capacity for *conception, formulation,* and *implementation* of LOVE PROJECTS demonstrates his or her love for God in the capacity for relating with love with those who have yet to attain to Godliness. Since those who attain to Godliness are expected to exhibit *brotherly kindness* towards those who have yet to attain, clearly, *a judgmental spirit is not evidence for Godliness.* On the contrary, it is MERCY, KINDNESS, COMPASSION, and EMPATHY that are demonstrations of Godliness between persons who profess faith in the name of Jesus Christ. For more on the demand for brotherly kindness from those who have faith in Jesus Christ, check out, *Chapter 3* of my book, True Sanctification.

✠ Love for All Men demonstrates that those who believe in Jesus Christ have capacity for loving those who are strangers (Luke 10:25-37; Titus 1:8; 1Timothy 3:2; 5:10), and for loving those who disagree with them with respect to how exactly to worship God (1Thessalonians 5:15). Since The Father judges persons based on their rubric for life - LOVE OF GOD *vis-a-vis* HATRED & LOVE OF MONEY - The Father has called Christians to witness to reality of Jesus Christ, but yet has not called us to any rivalry with other systems of faith. In this respect, it is important to note that attempts at demonstration of philosophical superiority of faith in Jesus Christ, to alternate systems of faith, attempts that are directed only at those who are willing to listen - with purchase of a book or literature, or reading of an article (or blog post) on such subjects, constituting willingness to listen - do not constitute rivalry. When a person buys a *koran* and reads that '*all non-Muslims are considered by Muslims to be condemned by God*', if he or she gets angry at such a declaration *in a book on Islam*, he or she proves himself or herself AN IDIOT AND A FOOL. The same goes for Christian literature. A person who purchases Christian literature, then gets angry that the literature makes arguments as to why faith in Jesus Christ is superior to Islam, IS AN IDIOT AND A FOOL. Rivalry always requires attempts at harming of another. Articulation of Christian philosophy, and demonstration of weaknesses of alternate philosophies do not qualify as rivalry. As I already have articulated, THE CHRISTIAN CRUSADES constituted engagement in rivalry with Muslims, rivalry of which The Father does not approve, rivalry that led in part to demise of the *Christian Byzantine Empire*.

Spiritual Insight 77 *A society, which declares that philosophical considerations, or comparisons of rationality of faith are exhibitions in rivalry seeks to enslave it's people. If the people seek to be enslaved, they do well to bow to such intellectual tyranny.*

Spiritual Insight 78 *If a philosophy of spirituality cannot explain to it's adherents rationales as to why it's system of spirituality is superior to competing systems of spirituality, why exactly should any rational person subscribe to such a philosophy?*

> The Scriptural Evidence for Importance of Demonstrations of the Presence of Christ on Earth by Powers.

First, consider Ephesians 4:7-9, 11-13, and 1Corinthians 13:8-10, which read as follows:

> And to each one of you was given the grace, according to the measure of the gift of Christ, wherefore, he saith, Having gone up on high He led captive captivity, and gave gifts to men, and that He went up, what is it except that He also went down first to the lower parts of the earth?

> He who went down is the same also who went up far above all the heavens, that He may fill all things - and He gave some as *apostles*, and some as *prophets*, and some as proclaimers of good news (*evangelists*), and some as shepherds & teachers, unto the perfecting of the saints, for a work of ministration, for a building up of the body of Christ, till we may all come to the unity of the

faith and of the recognition of the Son of God, to a perfect man, to a measure of stature of the fullness of the Christ.

> THE LOVE DOTH NEVER FAIL; and whether there be prophecies, they shall become useless; whether tongues, they shall cease; whether knowledge, it shall become useless; for in part we know, and in part we prophecy; and when that which is perfect may come, then that which is in part shall become useless.

Combined, the immediately preceding two passages demonstrate that arrival at a 'PERFECT MAN', that is, at A MEASURE OF THE STATURE OF THE FULLNESS OF CHRIST, equivalently, at the PRESENCE OF CHRIST is an important and immutable objective of our Lord and Savior Jesus Christ. For arrival at an enhanced appreciation of importance of arrival at the PRESENCE OF CHRIST, note that the descent of our Lord Jesus Christ into death and the grave was so He could resurrect, and rise above the heavens for filling all things, as such be able to perfect His body, that is, The Church.

The Things That Are 53 *The gifts of* APOSTLESHIP, PROPHECY, EVANGELISM, *and* SHEPHERDING & TEACHING *are given so the Church, the body of Christ can arrive at a measure of the stature of the fullness of our Lord Jesus Christ. This measure of the stature of the fullness of Christ is rooted in knowledge, is evident in unity of the faith (unity of believers), and transforms believers into a 'perfect man'.*

Do you still doubt that perfecting of the Church is the one overriding non-compromisable objective of Father, Son, and Holy Spirit? Consider then the words of our Lord Jesus Christ in John 17:20-23; and the words of Apostle Paul in Philippians 2:9-11.

> And not in regard to these alone do I ask, but also in regard to those who shall be believing, through their word, in me; that they all may be one, as Thou Father art in me, and I in Thee; THAT THEY ALSO IN US MAY BE ONE, THAT THE WORLD MAY BELIEVE THAT THOU DIDST SEND ME. And I, the glory that thou has given to me, have given to them, that they may be one as we are one; I IN THEM, AND THOU IN ME, THAT THEY MAY BE PERFECTED INTO ONE, AND THAT THE WORLD MAY KNOW THAT THOU DIDST SEND ME, and didst love them as Thou didst love me.

> Wherefore, also, God did highly exalt Him, and gave to Him a name that is above every name, that in the name of Jesus every knee may bow - of heavenlies, and earthlies, and what are under the earth - and EVERY TONGUE MAY CONFESS THAT JESUS CHRIST IS LORD, TO THE GLORY OF GOD THE FATHER.

For a thorough and detailed discussion of The Father's one overriding purpose - arrival of believers in Christ at a measure of the stature of Christ - pick up a copy of my book titled, 'True Sanctification'. In what follows, however, I go into a little more detail on what exactly the Holy Spirit implies by the term, 'RECOGNITION OF CHRIST'.

The 'Recognition' of Christ

In Ephesians 4:7-13, the gifts given by our Lord Jesus Christ are for building up of His body, the Body of Christ for arrival at:

♣ The Unity of the Faith

♣ Recognition of the Son of God

♣ Perfect Man

♣ A Measure of the Stature of the Fullness of Christ

All of the four expressions above mean exactly the same thing. Identicity of their meanings commences with a right spiritual understanding of the expression, 'RECOGNITION OF THE SON OF GOD'. For ease of understanding of what is to follow, I commence with two summarizing assertions, which are:

Prophecy Interpretation 16 *If all of Christianity had exactly the same* RECOGNITION OF THE SON OF GOD, *there would not exist any 'spiritual denominational walls' between those who profess faith in the name of Jesus Christ.*

Prophecy Interpretation 17 *Existence of Denominations does not, in of itself, imply existence, between Denominations, of spiritual denominational walls (SDW).*

Concerning importance of arrival at a *right recognition of the Son of God*, Apostle Paul prays as follows in Ephesians 1:17.

> That the God of our Lord Jesus Christ, The Father of glory, may give to you a spirit of wisdom and revelation in the recognition of Him (recognition of Christ).

Friend, if you seek to arrive at a right recognition of the Son of God, at a right recognition of Christ, you require a spirit of WISDOM and REVELATION. Note it is not your mind that somehow becomes wise; rather, it rather is the case that you receive from Jesus a spirit of wisdom and revelation that enables you arrive at a right recognition of His Person. I already have put the Scripture up previously, but here again, in presence of *importance of the Scripture*, importance of ACQUISITION OF A SPIRIT OF WISDOM AND REVELATION, and importance of *arrival at a right recognition of Christ*, I again proffer the Scripture in Matthew 11:27, and John 14:21.

All things were delivered to me by my Father, and none doth know The Son, except The Father, nor doth any know The Father, except The Son, and he to whom The Son may wish to reveal Him.

He who is having my commands, and is keeping them, that one it is who is loving me, and he who is loving me shall be loved by my Father, and I will love him, and will manifest myself to Him.

Friend, here again I reiterate an important truth, which is, only those who already have adopted the Love of God as rubric for life, only those who already are obeying Jesus Christ, are able to arrive at a revelation of His Person. You see then that the mere fact that you have professed faith in Jesus Christ does not qualify you for a revelation of Christ, that ONLY ADOPTION OF THE LOVE OF GOD AS RUBRIC FOR LIFE QUALIFIES YOU FOR A REVELATION OF CHRIST. If we are to collapse profession of faith in Jesus Christ, and adoption of the Love of God as way of life into one rubric, we arrive at the following immutable truth.

The Things That Are 54 *To declare faith in the name of Jesus Christ is to acknowledge Jesus to be the only begotten Son of God, Savior of the world, and to adopt the Love of God as rubric for life. But friend, this exactly is the declaration of the Holy Spirit in 1John 3:23, which declares: "And this is His command, that we may believe in the name of His Son Jesus Christ, and may love one another, even as He did command to us."*

Upon acquisition of a spirit of wisdom and revelation, you are able to answer two important questions, which are:

1. QUESTION #1: Who Exactly is Jesus Christ, &

2. QUESTION #2: Who is Jesus Christ to you.

Suppose we assume that your answer to QUESTION #1 is right, is appropriate, is an objective and true statement of, independent of your needs, who Jesus is. Suppose then that your answer to QUESTION #2 differs from your answer to QUESTION #1. Well, there and then, we arrive at the spiritual source of *spiritual denominational walls*, for in truth, your answers to QUESTIONS 1 & 2 ought in reality to be identical.

The Things That Are 55 *Who Jesus is objectively in reality, is exactly who He is supposed to be to you.*

℘ To THE CATHOLICS, Jesus is the Son of God who will not abandon traditions of men for embracing of new revelations of the truth of God. Consider that by this recognition, the Jews were right and wise to have rejected Jesus as the Messiah (Mark 7:8). We know then for a fact that the Catholic Recognition of The Son of God is partly true, yet partly false (Mark 7:7).

☙ To THE BAPTISTS, Jesus is the Son of God who will not accept any Christian who is not baptized via immersion in water. We know for a fact that, absent rejection of conviction of this truth, that this is not true. The thief who was on the cross next to Jesus, the thief who got saved, did not experience baptism by immersion, did not experience any baptism whatsoever - either by water or the Holy Spirit (Luke 23:32-33, 39-43). We see then that the Baptist Recognition of the Son of God is partly true, yet partly false.

☙ To the SEVENTH-DAY ADVENTISTS (SDA), Jesus is the Son of God who, if believers congregate on Sunday to praise His name, and to encourage one another in love, punishes those who believe in Him. We know for a fact that this SDA Recognition of the Son of God is partly true (*Jesus is The Son of God, and there is nothing wrong with congregating together on Saturday*), yet partly false, for we are not to judge others for esteeming every day alike, or judge others for esteeming one day above another (Romans 14:5-6). In this respect, even under the Old Covenant, there were holy convocations (*feast days*) that fell on Sunday, and that were celebrated on Sunday. Under the Old Covenant, the FEAST OF FIRST FRUITS, and the FEAST OF NEW GRAIN both *always* were celebrated via a holy convocation on Sundays. Given the two feasts relate to agricultural activity, celebration of the feasts right after the seventh-day Sabbath ensured the community could focus on work the rest of the week. For more on ceremonial feasts that were observed by the Jews, see the chapter titled, *'Importance of 'Time' Prior to Institution of the SSGLAE'*.

☙ To ORTHODOX CHRISTIANS, Jesus is the Son of God who relates more to us via symbols of our faith in Him, via liturgies, via sacraments, than through the Holy Spirit, a recognition we know very well to be false, for only those who are guided by the Holy Spirit are sons of God (Romans 8:14). We see then that the Orthodox Recognition of the Son of God is partly true, yet partly false.

I could go on and on, but I believe import of my words already is clear, that you arrive at the realization that *spiritual denominational walls* exist only because Christians arrive at, or adopt different recognitions of the Son of God.

Love of Truth 18 *All Spiritual Denominational Walls exist because different Denominations have arrived at* DIFFERENT RECOGNITIONS OF THE SON OF GOD.

Love of Truth 19 *If all Denominations are able to agree on the Central, equivalently,* CORE RECOGNITIONS OF CHRIST, *such that they are able to fellowship and cooperate around these Core Recognitions, there exists feasibility of*

Unity of the Faith, *AND agreement as to what exactly constitutes* a measure of the stature of the fullness of Christ, *as such agreement on what exactly constitutes a* 'Perfect Man'.

A Perfect Man

I have explored the notion of a 'Perfect Man' in more detail in *Chapter 21* of my book, In Jesus Name. Here, succinctly, it is important to note that a *Perfect Man* is not a man who is absolutely perfect, is not a man who does not make mistakes. On the contrary, and in so far as it relates to faith in Jesus Christ, a *Perfect Man* is a man who, inclusive of those who declare hatred for him or her, has arrived at capacity for loving all men. A *Perfect Man* can love a stranger in the same way he or she loves his or her own child, can love those who declare hatred, in much the same way as those who declare friendship. When he or she relates to others, a *Perfect Man* does not see *skin color, height, beauty,* weight, *intelligence,* or money, all he or she sees is another person, another human being created in the image of God, another person who may or may not yet have arrived at a realization of the glory conferred on him or her by his or her Creator. The declaration of Scriptures is that, absent arrival at faith in Jesus Christ, and transformation into *a measure of the stature of the fullness of Jesus Christ,* that attainment to a Perfect Man must be considered an exception, as opposed to the norm. If you consider the evidence in the world today for preponderance of hatred in the world, would you not declare that the Scriptures are righteous altogether?

Supporting Scripture for characterization of a Perfect Man?

But I say to you, Love your enemies and pray for those who persecute you, so that you may be sons of your Father who is in heaven; for He makes His sun rise on the evil and on the good, and sends rain on the just and on the unjust. You, therefore, must be perfect (*regardless of their love or hatred for you, you also must love all men*), as your heavenly Father is perfect (Matthew 5:44-45, 48).

And that Christ may dwell in your hearts through faith; that *you, being rooted and grounded in love, may have power to comprehend* with all the saints what is the breadth and length and height and depth, *and to know the love of Christ* which surpasses knowledge, *that you may be filled with all the fullness of God* (Ephesians 3:17-19).

We already have established, in presence of *identical recognitions of Christ,* that the fullness of God, that is, the *fullness of Christ,* is identical to a Perfect Man, is identical to *arrival at the Presence of Christ.*

So then, what is required for arrival at fullness of Christ?

1. *A rooting and grounding in love*, that is, a person who is filled with the Holy Spirit, and who is obeying Christ in respect of the command to love all men.

2. In presence of a rooting and grounding, receipt of power for comprehension, that is, receipt of *a spirit of wisdom and revelation* in the knowledge of Christ.

3. The End Outcome? Arrival at knowledge of the Love of Christ, which is tantamount to arrival at infilling of the FULLNESS OF GOD. Note that, as already discussed, INFILLING as outcome implies the lifting up to perfection is not of your works, rather, in response to your obedience to Christ, is the work of Father, Son, and Holy Spirit.

The Things That Are 56 *The Scriptures are very clear. In order to become a Perfect Man, you have faith in Christ, and are filled with the Holy Spirit, as such are rooted and grounded in love. While you obey the command to love all men, your understanding of the* LOVE OF GOD *starts out highly imperfect and deficient. Having taken the step to obey the commandment to love, you receive spiritual power from Christ that enables you comprehend largeness of the Love of God, comprehension that you share with other believers, with outcome you arrive at knowledge and infilling of the Love of God.*

The Things That Are 57 *A Perfect Man, a man who has become* A POWER FOR CHRIST, *who has arrived at* A TRUE RECOGNITION OF CHRIST, *who has* ACTUALIZED THE PRESENCE OF CHRIST, *who has arrived at a* MEASURE OF THE STATURE OF THE FULLNESS OF CHRIST, *is a man who has arrived at capacity for loving all men.*

The Things That Are 58 *If you entertain, as in consciously seek to retain any* RACIST, TRIBAL, NARCISSISTIC, *or* ETHNIC *biases, if you are not willing to relinquish any feelings of intrinsic superiority in relation to other persons, you* CANNOT *become a* POWER FOR CHRIST, *for you are unable to actualize the* PRESENCE OF CHRIST.

Core Recognitions of the Son of God

♣ Our LORD JESUS CHRIST is The Word of God, who, for as long as it is relevant to us, always has coexisted with The Father and The Holy Spirit as one, that is, as God (John 1:1-3; 1John 5:7).

⛭ Whether they be spiritual, or physical, all that exists was created by The Father for His physical representation, our Lord Jesus Christ, as such all things were created through Christ, and all things subsist in Him, with outcome all have essence of Christ, that is, are spirits having physical forms (Colossians 1:15-17). You see then that The Father has, in human parlance, and for lack of better typology, MESTASIZED INTO FATHER AND WORD all because He chose to engage in a Creation Agenda. A Wise Father made every effort to ensure that while His Creation would subsist in Him (in Christ, as such in The Word - Colossians 1:17, John 15:1), He Himself would be separate from that Creation, as such can introduce new things into it, and take things out of it (*John ch. 15*). In light of emergence of sin in The Father's Creation, we infer wisdom of The Father.

✠ The Father has given us Life, and this Life is domiciled in His Son, our Lord and Savior Jesus Christ (1John 5:11-12). It is not the case that The Father hates anyone who will not receive His Son, rather, it is the case that only those who receive His Son receive His Life. The Father has a right to stipulate how exactly man can arrive at friendship with Him. So long as a person loves his or her neighbor, The Father rewards such a person for their goodness. Such goodness, however, cannot be substituted for faith in Jesus Christ.

✠ Jesus is the Head of His Body (Ephesians 5:23) The Body of Christ consists of all believers (Ephesians 4:25; Romans 12:4-8). All believers are equal (Colossians 3:11), as such yield to one another on matters of faith by *conviction of reasoning, spiritual revelation, respect for a higher gift* (1Corinthians 2:6-16; 1Thessalonians 5:21), and ascertainment that the person proffering interpretation of faith can be regarded to have arrived at characterization as a POWER FOR GOD ('By their fruits - Galatians 5:22-26, you shall know them' is declaration of our Lord and Savior Jesus Christ in Matthew 7:15-23). In this sense, The Church attempts to recognize those given to her as APOSTLES, PROPHETS, and combo of SHEPHERDS & TEACHERS.

✠ All who do not obey the command to love come under judgment of The Son (John 5:22). The Father has given man choice, but as rationality would demand, has stipulated, ahead of time, rewards and penalties that accrue, respectively to righteous and evil behaviors.

♣ Our LORD JESUS CHRIST is The Word of God who became flesh, such that:

✠ HIS RIGHTEOUS LIFE could be credited to our benefit, this so we can be justified by The Father (Romans 3:24, 28; 5:1; 10:10).

✠ HIS DEATH could be credited to our benefit (Romans 8:1; Colossians 1:21-23; Hebrews 2:9), ensuring the price of sin is paid (Romans 6:23), ensuring the devil cannot declare that The Father is unjust to save those who, through their ancestors, Adam and Eve sold their birthright to him. Jesus now having won back our birthright (Colossians 2:13-15), the devil stands condemned by The Father (John 12:31; 16:11).

✠ HIS RESURRECTION could be credited to our benefit, this so we are able to become a new creation (Romans *Ch. 6*; Galatians 6:15; 2Corinthians 5:17), are able to overcome sin, the world, and the devil, are able to live righteously (1John 2:12-14; 5:4-5).

✠ HIS ASCENSION could bring to us the power of the Holy Spirit (John 16:7), the Spirit of God who only can bring us into fellowship with The Father and The Word (1Corinthians 1:9; 2Corinthians 13:14). The goal of the Holy Spirit is to bring you into fellowship with The Father and The Word (1John 1:1-4).

✠ His High Priestly Ministry brings to us the power of His blood for our cleansing from sin (1John 1:7; 3:3). It is in the sprinkling of His blood in our behalf that we are able to acquire power for overcoming of sins and weaknesses in power of the Holy Spirit (Hebrews 9:14). IT IS THE HIGH PRIESTLY MINISTRY OF OUR LORD AND SAVIOR JESUS CHRIST THAT PROGRESSES US FROM JUSTIFICATION, TO SANCTIFICATION, THEN ON TO GLORIFICATION.

♣ Our LORD JESUS CHRIST is The Word of God who commands us to:

✠ Believe in His Name, to believe that He is the only begotten Son of God, Savior and Lord of the world (Romans 10:9-11), King of kings, and Lord of lords (Revelation 19:16).

✠ Be filled with The Holy Spirit (Galatians 3:13-14), because this is the only path to receiving of the Love of God into our hearts (Romans 5:5), this so we can live by the faith that is premised on a receiving of the love of God (Galatians 5:6), as such be able to love as we have been loved by The Father (1John 4:7-8).

✠ Adopt the Love of God as way of life (1John 3:23; 4:7-14). Naturally, this implies absence of capacity for arrival at hatred merely because there exist some disagreements as to interpretation of Scripture.

✠ Live by the faith that works by love (Galatians 5:6), and to focus on acquiring the glory of Christ (2Thessalonians 2:14; Romans 12:2; 2Corinthians 3:18).

✠ Aspire to arrival at designation as a Power (Acts 1:8, Romans 8:38; 1Corinthians 12:28-29, YLT), as a believer in Christ who has arrived at a PERFECT MAN, at the PRESENCE OF CHRIST.

✠ Be His image to the world (Romans 8:29; 1Corinthians 15:47-49). In this declaration, our Lord Jesus Christ declares that worship of any imagery of His person is idolatry, is degradation of ourselves, for then we declare that we are not the image of Christ.

✠ Treat The Bible as the Word of Truth (2Timothy 3:15-17), that is, the CORE OF REVELATIONS which introduce us to the TRUTH OF GOD that is personified in character and essence of our Lord Jesus Christ (John 14:6), and which demonstrate to us that The Father reveals Himself to men and women who are imperfect, but who yet are desirous of living in the Truth of God (John 4:24; 2Thessalonians 2:9-10). When we learn from lives of imperfect men who had opportunity to acquaint themselves with God, we are wiser to avoid the same pitfalls that were outcomes of their imperfections (1Corinthians 10:6).

✠ Whenever possible, and so long as the fellowship is rooted in the Love of God, to gather with other persons who have faith in Jesus Christ for fellowship, for encouragement of, and loving of each other (Hebrews 10:24-25).

✠ Whenever possible, to seek to be baptized in water (Matthew 28:19), and with the bread and wine symbolic of the body and blood of Jesus Christ (1Corinthians 11:17-34), both of whom we are in fellowship with in the heavens (Hebrews 12:22-24), to participate in the Lord's Supper. So then, it is not that the bread and wine are transformed miraculously into the body and blood of Christ; rather, it is the case that we celebrate the fact that, spiritually, we are in the presence of Christ, as such are in fellowship with Jesus (His body) and His blood. Remember, TO BE IN THE PRESENCE OF CHRIST *is not the same as* to arrive at The Presence of Christ. The first - BEING IN THE PRESENCE OF CHRIST - must subsist if ever you are to become a Power for Christ, the second - ARRIVAL AT, *or* ACTUALIZATION OF THE PRESENCE OF CHRIST - is outcome of your success at being in the Presence of Christ.

Love of Truth 20 *None of the Core Recognitions of the Son of God that I have articulated can be characterized as intellectual doctrines, rather,* ALL RELATE TO HOW TO KNOW CHRIST, AND HOW TO LIVE TO CHRIST. *Our calling as disciples of Jesus Christ is to arrive at knowledge of Christ, and to live to the glory of Christ. It is those who arrive at* POWERS, *who arrive at the* PRESENCE OF CHRIST, *at a* 'PERFECT MAN', *at* A MEASURE OF THE STATURE OF THE FULLNESS OF CHRIST *who have maximized their capacity for living to the glory of Christ.*

But is it not important to have doctrines?

The problem with DOCTRINES is the fact that they take on a life of their own, become an end in of themselves, detract those who have faith in Jesus Christ from Jesus Himself, set themselves at the center of Christian experience. Any teaching in Christianity, which ultimately cannot be linked to Jesus Christ, His relationship with us, and it's implication for our relationships in this world, is an exercise in formulation of human precepts. More importantly, in the verse that is advanced as rationale for doctrines, the word translated 'doctrine' actually means 'teaching'. Using the *YLT*, 2Timothy 3:16-17 actually reads as follows.

> Every Writing is God-breathed, and profitable for TEACHING, for CONVICTION (of *sin, righteousness, truth, or judgment*), for SETTING ARIGHT (*correction*), for INSTRUCTION that is in righteousness (*content knowledge that is profitable for righteousness*), that the man of God may be fitted - for every good work having been completed.

It is the truth then that Apostle Paul does not recommend some rigid formulation of doctrine, rather recommends Scriptures as basis for teaching of believers about the good news of Jesus Christ.

Love of Truth 21 *Teachings that revolve, in entirety around your relationship with The Father, Son, and Holy Spirit, and how exactly this ought to affect your relationships,* AMONG EQUALS, *in Church, or in Society (the Nations) are formulated for your benefit, not for benefit of any Church or Christian organization.*

Short Illustrations of Spiritual Meaninglessness of Some Doctrines

Consider Doctrine of Purgatory. This doctrine instills fear, not love for God. But if you live a life of Love towards others, and a life that glorifies Jesus Christ via revealing of your faith in Christ in good works, The Father declares this is enough for your salvation. If you seek to be faithful to Christ then, ideally no one ought to recommend to you a *Doctrine of Purgatory*. Only a person looking for excuses as to why God's declarations about you are to be resisted - that is, a person seeking excuses for an accusation against the righteousness of faith that you have accepted from Christ - comes up with a doctrine designed to instill fear on those who already are seeking God. If at all anyone ought to be scared of God, ought it not to be those who live in stubborn rejection of His Love as basis for civil laws, and interactions within society? But the DOCTRINE OF PURGATORY is not designed for these, is designed for those who already are seeking after The Father. You see then that THE DOCTRINE OF PURGATORY DOES NOT GLORIFY CHRIST, only serves to declare to you the belief in another that he or she can resist your salvation. You would do well to stay away from such doctrines.

Consider Doctrine of State of the Dead: The Scriptures are clear that, if you are faithful to Christ until death, when you die, your spirit remains alive in Christ. The reasoning is very simple. Since you have taken on the life of Christ by faith (Galatians 2:20), and since your life is hid with Christ in God (Colossians 3:1-3), and since Christ cannot die (Revelation 1:17-18), it is unequivocally true that subsequent to your death, your life, your spirit persists in Christ (John 17:3; 1John 3:14; 5:12). If your spirit is perfected while you are on earth, or if you become a firstborn - the first to do something for God (Hebrews 12:22-24), every believer who comes after you has opportunity, where necessary, to be aided by your spirit. In this respect, using your spirit, which has been perfected with respect to exactly what it is that believer is in need of perfection, the believer receives help from the Lord Jesus Christ towards his or her perfection. Your spirit can remain with such a believer until his own spirit acquires essence of the victory that is represented by your spirit, with outcome your spirit receives a redeployment from The Lord Jesus Christ.

Hallelujah!!!

Spiritual Insight 79 *Do you not serve a wise, thoughtful, loving, and benevolent Lord and Savior?*

> Why your perfected spirit, and not the Holy Spirit?
>
> Well, would you rather your spirit were idle in eternity?

So then, your spirit, which does not have any body, which is in entirety spirit, continues to participate in affairs of life, but only in Christ, and only as deployed by Christ.

> ARE PEOPLE WHO DIE AWARE OF THIS?
>
> Well, what do you care. No one who dies comes back to tell us, and when you die, you will find out for yourself.
>
> The only way you will be able to find out is if you keep on worshipping The Father in truth and in your spirit.

The speculation about awareness or non-awareness subsequent to death creates opportunity for sorcerers and demons to attempt to manufacture evidence for either of bodily awareness, or spiritual awareness. In the command from The Father not to seek to communicate with the dead (Deuteronomy 18:9-14), we learn an important wisdom, which is, a doctrine that does not make any difference to how you live prior to a going away to be with the Lord does not have any relevance for your life Christ.

Love of Truth 22 *If a doctrine or teaching does not have any relevance for* KNOWLEDGE OF CHRIST, *or for* HOW TO LIVE TO THE PRAISE OF THE GLORY OF CHRIST *in course of your sojourn here on earth, it is nothing but intellectual speculation by men. Avoid getting caught up in such controversies.*

Love of Truth 23 *Nowhere in Christian Scriptures are Christians encouraged, advised, or mandated to come up with* DOCTRINAL STATEMENTS. *Teachings are principles, such as I have outlined, that Christians apply in their relationship with Christ, and in their relationship with one another, not* DOCTRINAL STATEMENTS *that adhere Christians to Church organizations. Doctrinal Statements (DS) are manufactures of men. While formulation of doctrinal statements is not necessarily wrong, it can be. Further, given DS direct attention towards a Church organization, as opposed to towards Christ, they tend to take on a life of their own, tend to be transformed into* IDOLS *that take attention of believers away from their Lord and Savior Jesus Christ.*

The 7 Seals

In presence of 7 SEALS, clearly, and as already evident in the *Summary* that I have provided, the end-game is the 7th Trumpet of the 7th Seal. In presence of this characterization of the end-game, the BEST POSSIBLE PATH is the path that minimizes effort, time, and pain, equivalently, that maximizes joy of individuals, The Church, and The Nations. In what follows, I apply this principle to ranking of all of the feasible paths that can be taken from the 1st SEAL to the 7th TRUMPET of the 7th Seal. In this respect, note that the RP7 PATH - the path that passes through VIALS, as opposed to TRUMPETS - is not an ideal path. For practical purposes, however, conditional on embarkment on the RP7 PATH, the resolving event is the 7th VIAL of the 7th Seal.

Prophecy Principle 86 *The* BEST PATH, *equivalently, the best equilibrium is the path that minimizes effort, time, and pain required for arrival at the 7th Trumpet of the 7th Seal. Simultaneously, the best path is the path that maximizes joy, equivalently, welfare of individuals, The Church, and The Nations.*

| The First Seal |

Under the 1st SEAL, the gospel goes forth conquering and to conquer (Revelation 6:1). Clearly, as already established in context of The Numerology of The Father, this is representative of New Beginnings for man. The *Crown* on the head of the rider of the horse signifies a believer who has arrived at, equivalently, actualized the PRESENCE OF CHRIST, a believer who has attained to a PERFECT MAN. WHITENESS of the horse represents pursuit of agenda that are righteous, that is, pursuit of LOVE PROJECTS. Given the rider of the horse conquers, and goes forth to conquer, there is guarantee, from The Father of a winning over of some fellow believers in Christ, as such guarantee of arrival at some Companionship of Purpose. If the Church and the Nations respond positively, Companionship of Purpose, *Inner Circle of Friendship*, and *Maturity of Righteousness* all are arrived at in context of the 7th TRUMPET of the 7th Seal. If either of the Church, or the Nations do not respond positively, Companionship of Purpose is arrived at in context of the 2nd SEAL.

If the nations refuse to premise civil laws and societal interactions on the Love of Christ, the 2nd SEAL is explicitly activated, with outcome each of The Church, and The Nations end up progressing to the 2nd SEAL.

Symbolism of the Trumpets 1 *If The Nations choose not to base civil laws and interactions within society on the Love of God, there is progression from the 1st SEAL to the 2nd SEAL.*

If not only individuals, but also nations respond to the gospel, allow Jesus reign in their affairs via adoption of His principles for ordering of civil society, *the kingdoms of this world become the Kingdom of our God and of His Christ.* Within context of this outcome, all of Seals 2 through the 6th TRUMPET of the 7th Seal are deactivated, and there is transition to the 7th TRUMPET of the 7th Seal. Within this context, all of Seals 2 through 7 are actualized in context of the 7th SEAL. Note, however, that within this context, only seals that pertain to righteousness, which as enumerated in *Chapter 6* are: the 1st, 2nd, 3rd, 5th, and 7th TRUMPET of the 7th Seal are fulfilled. Given the 7th SEAL symbolizes, in part, Completeness of a Pre-existing Agenda, fast tracking of events to context of the 7th Trumpet of the 7th Seal does not embed any contradiction.

Symbolism of the Trumpets 2 *If The Nations choose to premise civil laws and societal interactions on the LOVE OF GOD, there is progression directly from the 1st SEAL to the 7th TRUMPET of the 7th Seal. We have then that the 7th TRUMPET of the 7th Seal subsumes the 2nd, 3rd, and 5th Seals.*

Prophecy Insight 52 *The Best Good Path to the 7th TRUMPET of the 7th Seal (BP7): If nations acquiesce civil laws to the Love of God, CP, CF, MR, & CC all are arrived at in context of the 7th TRUMPET of the 7th Seal. Given this is the shortest possible path to the end-game, this path is the BEST GOOD PATH (BGP7) to the 7th TRUMPET of the 7th Seal.*

The Scriptural evidence for embedding of 2nd, 3rd, and 5th Seals in the 7th TRUMPET of the 7th Seal in context of the BP7 PATH?

> For we are His workmanship, CREATED IN CHRIST JESUS FOR GOOD WORKS, WHICH GOD PREPARED BEFOREHAND that we should walk in them (Ephesians 2:10).

> And lo, I come quickly, and my reward is with me, to render to each as his work shall be (Revelation 22:12, *YLT*).

It is normative, and unequivocal that WORK REFERS TO PURPOSE. If then, it is upon arrival at the UTOPIA described in *Revelation ch. 22* that purpose is assigned, clearly, Companionship of Purpose (CP) only can be accomplished in context of the *Utopia*, that is, in context of the 7th TRUMPET of the 7th Seal. Given CP must precede *Inner Circle of Friendship (CF)*, which then must precede *Maturity of Righteousness (MR)*, it is straightforward that, on the BP7 PATH, the 2nd, 3rd, and 5th Seals are fulfilled in context of the 7th TRUMPET of the 7th Seal. Given we exogenously (from other books of the Bible) derived symbolism of ELEMENT 7 to consist, in part, of *Completeness of a Pre-existing Agenda*, embedding of the 2nd, 3rd, and 5th Seals in the 7th TRUMPET of the 7th Seal cannot be deemed to embed any contradiction.

Prophecy Interpretation 18 *Our Lord Jesus Christ Himself confirms that, on the BP7* PATH, *the 7th* TRUMPET *of the 7th Seal subsumes the 2nd, 3rd, and 5th Seals.*

The Second Seal

Under the 2nd Seal, nations slay one another (Revelation 6:3-4). Signifying blood, the horse is red. With the rider of the horse not having a Crown, the rider is a spirit of hatred sent to amplify hatreds chosen within nations, this for arrival at *conflicts*, strife, fightings, *wars*, and *bloodshed*. Immediately, you see that in presence of a positive response to the gospel, that is, a premising of civil laws and societal interactions on the Love of God, that there cannot be explicit progression to the 2nd Seal. Clearly, killing of each other by The Nations is natural progression of rejection of the appeal from The Father that civil laws, and societal interactions be rooted in the Love of God. In the choice to reject the Love of God as foundation for civil laws, love is rejected as basis for running of affairs within nations, and for management of interactions between nations, with outcome interactions within and between nations devolve into hatreds. We arrive then at conflicts, wars, and slayings of one another, this both within, and between nations. Note it is not God who slays, it is nations slaying one another. The 2nd Seal then is natural outcome of rejection of the COMMON SENSE appeal from The Father that civil laws and interactions within, and between nations be rooted in demonstrations of the LOVE OF CHRIST FOR THE FELLOW MAN.

As discussed in Chapter 5, when the Emperor of the Byzantine Empire stopped caring about the welfare of the *free small farmers* who live within his kingdom, when he placed expansion of the kingdom ahead of welfare of his subjects, he began to suffer defeats on the battlefield. These defeats went on to weaken the empire, and resulted eventually in cessation of the Christian Civilization that was the Byzantine Empire.

Historical Spiritual Nugget 11 *For the Byzantine Empire, abandonment of the Love of God for decision making led to wars, conflicts, and at end of it all,* *cessation of the empire. Given the time of the Byzantine Empire (325 through 1453 AD) precedes the time of the Church in Laodicea (1454 AD to ∞), prior to it's full institution, The Father provides us with a shadow of governance of the SSGLAE in lives of men, and affairs of earth.*

Historical Spiritual Nugget 12 *The Father is not a respecter of persons, does not protect people who claim allegiance to Christ, but whose actions run contrary to such pronouncements.*

> Do you know of any other religion whose teachings, and credible historical evidence, reflect the justice that praying to the deity does not take precedence over treatments of fellow men?

Prior to timeless essence of the Church in Laodicea, events on earth were rooted in time, with outcome there were three, as opposed to two forces at work, namely, (i) as encapsulated in the SSGLAE, actions, and consequences; (ii) time specified for consequences; and (iii) righteous Sovereign interventions by The Father. In these times, timeless essence of the Church in Laodicea has reduced the forces at work to two, namely, (i) the SSGLAE, and (ii) righteous Sovereign interventions by The Father. For more on time as a spiritual governance mechanism in context of the Old Covenant, check out the chapter titled, *'Importance of 'Time' Prior to Institution of the SSGLAE.'*

The Things That Are 59 *In this time - the time of the Church in Laodicea, the time that never ends, absent arrival of Sovereign interventions on part of The Father, consequences of wrong behaviors last as long as it takes for people to arrive at repentance. By the same token, consequences of righteous behaviors last as long as people remain righteous.*

The aftermath of the FIRST WORLD WAR provides yet another illustration of how abandonment of the principle of the Love of God induced nations into slayings of one another. Upon the surrender of Germany for ending of the First World War, the Allies imposed draconian penalties on Germany, penalties the Germans clearly were unable to bear. Under the weight of those penalties, Hitler, and others like him, would, out of angst generated by seeming insurmountability of the weight, forment an even costlier SECOND WORLD WAR. At the end of the Second World War, with full recognition of the fact that they had contributed to emergence of yet another costly WORLD WAR, the Allies rightly implemented workouts that reflected principles of the Love of God.

RATHER THAN DEMAND, AS WAS THE CASE AFTER THE FIRST WORLD WAR, THAT GERMANY RECOMPENSE THEM FOR THEIR COSTS, THE ALLIES RATHER CONTRIBUTED TOWARDS THE REBUILDING OF GERMANY.

Today, Germany is friendly with all of those countries - the USA, Britain, and Russia - that fought to defeat it in course of the Second World War. Subsequent to the First World War, however, Germany and the Allies regarded themselves as adversaries.

Prophecy Principle 87 *The principle of the Love of God works in reality, is not mere philosophy. Whenever nations refuse to root civil laws in the Love of God, they set in motion wheels that lead, rather inevitably, to wars and slayings of one another.*

The Third Seal

During the time of the 3rd SEAL (Revelation 6:5-6), there is weighing of people's actions in a balance by a rider on a black horse, clearly an indication of a Grand Judgment. Note that there are not any actions undertaken in context of the 3rd SEAL that are acts of judgment, rather, there merely is introduction of impending judgment. Remember, in *Chapter 6*, we established that GRAND JUDGMENTS, that is, 4th SEALS always are preceded by IDENTIFICATION OF THE RIGHTEOUS. Remember also that we did not take this symbolism from the Book of Revelation, derived the symbolism, in entirety, without recourse to the Book of Revelation. Well, does the description of the 3rd SEAL accord with the symbolism, that is, with identification of the righteous.

Simultaneously, there is a command '*that the oil and the wine not be injured*' (Revelation 6:6). In Christian Scriptures, 'OIL' signifies the Holy Spirit, and 'WINE' signifies the blood of our Lord Jesus Christ. We have then the command that those who are *washed in the blood of Jesus Christ*, and are *filled with the Holy Spirit* are not be hurt in context of derivation of the Grand Judgment.

The Scriptural Evidence for the Typology?

In like manner, also the cup after the supping, saying, *This cup is the new covenant in my blood*, that for you is being poured forth. For I say to you that I may not drink of the produce of the vine (WINE) till the reign of God may come (Luke 22:20,18).

The cup of the blessing that we bless - is it not *the fellowship of the blood of the Christ*? the bread that we break - is it not the fellowship of the body of the Christ (1Corinthians 10:16).

And Moses taketh the anointing oil, and anointeth the tabernacle, and all that is in it, AND SANCTIFIETH THEM; and he poureth of the anointing oil on the head of Aaron, AND ANOINTETH HIM TO SANCTIFY HIM (Leviticus 8:10,12).

Concerning His Son, (who is come of the seed of David according to the flesh, who is marked out Son of God in power, according to THE SPIRIT OF SANCTIFICATION, by the rising again from the dead), Jesus Christ our Lord (Romans 1:4).

And we - we ought to give thanks to God always for you, brethren, beloved by the Lord, that God did choose you from the beginning to salvation IN SANCTIFICATION OF THE SPIRIT, and belief of the truth (2Thessalonians 2:13).

Those who are *washed in the blood of Jesus Christ*, and are *filled with the Holy Spirit* are believers in the name of Christ who have participated fully in the process of Sanctification. It is straightforward then that they are righteous. If these believers are not to be hurt, clearly, they first must be identified.

You see then, that we arrive at preceding of GRAND JUDGMENT by IDENTIFICATION OF THE RIGHTEOUS.

Given believers in question are sanctified, that is, have chosen friendship with Jesus over self, sin, the world, and the devil, they have arrived at an INNER CIRCLE OF FRIENDSHIP with our Lord and Savior Jesus Christ. Is there any evidence for satisfaction of this symbolism, which again, we derived, in entirety, outside of the Book of Revelation?

The link between the sealing of those not to be hurt, the blood of the Lamb, the Holy Spirit, and Inner Circle of Friendship with Christ?

In whom ye also, having heard the word of the truth - the good news of your salvation - in whom also having believed, YE WERE SEALED WITH THE HOLY SPIRIT of the promise (Ephesians 1:13).

And make not sorrowful the Holy Spirit of God, in which ye were sealed to a day of redemption (Ephesians 4:30).

And I saw another messenger going up from the rising of the sun, having a seal of the living God, and he did cry with a great voice to the four messengers, to whom it was given to injure the land and the sea, saying, "Do not injure the land, nor the sea, nor the trees, till we may seal the servants of our God upon their foreheads." And I heard the number of those sealed, (144 thousands were sealed out of all the tribes of the sons of Israel) - Revelation 7:2-4.

And I saw, and lo, a Lamb having stood upon the Mount Sion, and with Him an hundred forty-four thousands, HAVING THE NAME

OF HIS FATHER WRITTEN UPON THEIR FOREHEADS; these are they who with women are not defiled, for they are virgin; THESE ARE THEY WHO ARE FOLLOWING THE LAMB WHITHERSOEVER HE MAY GO; these were bought from among men - a first-fruit to God and to the Lamb (Revelation 14:1,4).

Numerology 10 *The* 144,000 *are sealed in context of the 3ʳᵈ* SEAL. *Given the righteous must be identified prior to institution of The Father's Grand Judgments, sealing of the* 144,000 *in context of the 3ʳᵈ* SEAL *fits perfectly into the Numerology of The Father.*

Numerology 11 *It is unequivocal that the 144,000 are* POWERS FOR CHRIST, *that is, constitute the* INNER CIRCLE OF FRIENDSHIP *for our Lord Jesus Christ. We arrive then at validation of the Numerology of The Father.*

Prophecy Interpretation 19 *The 3ʳᵈ* SEAL *relates, in entirety, to sealing of the* 144,000 *that is described in Revelation 7:1-8. The 144,000 are those who are not to be hurt in context of Grand Judgments to follow during the time of the 4ᵗʰ* SEAL.

The Wheat and the Barley

WHEAT and BARLEY are the main ingredients for making of bread. BREAD signifies the body of Christ (1Corinthians 10:16, see preceding). In the declaration that *Wheat* and *Barley* become expensive in context of the 3ʳᵈ SEAL, our Lord Jesus Christ declares difficulty of conversion of those who refused to choose Christ or the Love of God in context of either of the 1ˢᵗ or 2ⁿᵈ Seals. Given sealing of those who have faith in the name of our Lord and Savior Jesus Christ commences in context of the 3ʳᵈ SEAL, the Lord Jesus Christ declares that while the door into His salvation remains slightly ajar during the time of the 3ʳᵈ SEAL, entrance has become difficult. Entrance has become difficult, because while people have steeped themselves in evil for some time, as such are more difficult to convict of sin, simultaneously upon sealing of those who are faithful to Him, arrival of a spirit of judgment implies some '*standing back*' on part of The Holy Spirit.

The Scriptural Evidence?

Another simile He set before them, saying: The reign of the heavens was likened to a man sowing good seed in His field, and, while men are sleeping, His enemy came and sowed darnel IN THE MIDST OF THE WHEAT, and went away. And He answering said to them, He who is sowing the good seed is the Son of Man (JESUS), and the field is the world, and the good seed (*the* WHEAT), these are the sons of the reign (*the* BODY OF CHRIST), and the darnel are the sons of the evil one (Matthew 13:24-25, 37-38).

Verily, verily, I say to you, if THE GRAIN OF THE WHEAT, having fallen to the earth, may not die, itself remaineth alone; and if it may die, it doth bear much fruit; he who is loving his life shall lose it, and he who is hating his life in this world - to life age-during shall keep it (John 12:24-25).

For Jehovah thy God is bringing thee in unto a good land, a land of brooks of waters, of fountains, and of depths coming out in valley and in mountain: A LAND OF WHEAT, AND BARLEY, and vine, and fig, and pomegranate; a land of oil olive and honey; a land in which WITHOUT SCARCITY THOU DOST EAT BREAD, thou dost not lack anything in it; a land whose stones are iron, and out of its mountains thou dost dig brass (Deuteronomy 8:7-9).

Prophecy Principle 88 *The* WHEAT *and the* BARLEY *signify salvation, signify people who are saved, as such have become the body of Christ.*

We arrive then at an important qualification of teachings of Jesus Christ. Within context of the ministry of Jesus Christ, the ministry of John the Baptist represented a 1st SEAL period (Matthew 3:11-12). While the Pharisees and Sadducees did not allow themselves to be baptized by John, they were aware that the people considered JOHN THE BAPTIST to be a prophet from God (Matthew 21:25-27). Given the people submitted to the baptism of John (Luke 7:29-30), they had opportunity to become part of the REIGN OF GOD to be ushered in by our Lord Jesus Christ. In this respect, note that *Peter, James, John, Andrew, Philip,* and *Nathaniel* all were, to different degrees, disciples of John the Baptist.

Historical Spiritual Nugget 13 *Submission of the people to baptism of John the Baptist reveals conquering nature of a 1st SEAL period. Rejection of the baptism by the Pharisees and Sadducees set them on a collision course with our Lord Jesus Christ.*

Up until the crowds dispersed from Jesus (John 6:66), the Jews were in a 2nd SEAL period. Subsequent to this, the Jews entered into a 3rd SEAL period.

The Evidence?

From this time many of His disciples went away backward, and were no more walking with Him, Jesus, therefore, said to the twelve, "DO YE ALSO WISH TO GO AWAY?" Simon Peter, therefore, answered Him, "Sir, unto whom shall we go? thou hast sayings of life age-during; and we have believed, and have known, that thou art the Christ, the son of the living God (John 6:66-69)."

At rejection and crucifixion of Jesus Christ, the death of Jesus Christ being necessary, the Jews could not be punished for the action, hence they remained in a 3rd SEAL period (Luke 23:34; Acts 3:17-21). At timing of opposition of preaching of the gospel by Apostle Paul, the Jews having chosen to oppose the good news of Jesus Christ entered into a 4th SEAL period. It was during the time of the 4th SEAL that Jews were expelled from Rome (Acts 18:2, 5-6). Claudius ruled the Roman Empire from *41 to 54 AD*. Expulsion of the Jews from Rome is dated about *49 AD*. The pains of the Jewish nation, pains that commenced in *66 AD* with the invasion by Roman General Titus represent *Trumpets 1 through 6* of the 7th SEAL period. In *68 AD*, rather surprisingly, yet for protection of his, and his father's fortunes in presence of contention for assumption of Emperorship of Rome, a contest won by his father, General Titus withdrew from his encirclement of Jerusalem. With the words of The Lord Jesus Christ in their remembrance, The Church seized the opportunity to flee from Jerusalem, with outcome we infer arrival at salvation, equivalently, perfection of the Church. The zealots, who, via Barabbas had become co-rulers of the Jews with the Pharisees and the Sadducees, on the other hand, interpreted the withdrawal as a token of their eventual victory over the Romans. In *70 AD*, Roman General Titus returned for destruction of Jerusalem, and it's Temple, with outcome salvation of the Church (IDENTIFICATON OF RIGHTEOUS CHRISTIANS who were Jews) is simultaneous with execution of GRAND JUDGMENT on Jews who chose hatreds and love of money over the Love of Christ. We have then that the period, *68-70 AD* represented a 7th Trumpet of the 7th Seal period.

Historical Spiritual Nugget 14 *From the birth of John the Baptist about 4 AD through to 70 AD is representative of a full cycle of the SSGLAE that is specific to the Jewish Nation.*

The Things That Are 60 *The SSGLAE is an eternal principle that always has been, but had in past been implemented in context of constraints of time. The time element now having been removed, The Father brings the system to your awareness, this so the righteous can rejoice, and so those who love evil can reconsider their ways.*

I already have demonstrated that scarcity of *Wheat* and *Barley* depicted in context of the 3rd SEAL does not refer to incidence of physical famine. Regardless, however, there exists evidence in history that famines tend to be outcome of wars between nations. Given wars occur in context of 2nd SEAL periods, clearly, there exists some correlation, which is, whenever nations slay one another, this inevitably leads to famine.

Historical Spiritual Nugget 15 *While scarcity of Wheat and Barley that occurs in context of the 3rd SEAL is spiritual, not physical, as such relates to* *scarcity of feasibility of salvation, it is true that typically, famines are outcome of wars.*

As already is somewhat highlighted in *Chapter 5*, subsequent to sacking of Constantinople in *1204 AD*, France and England were at war. Subsequent to the war, particularly between *1315-17 AD*, there was famine all over Europe. This cycle of war and famine is replicated in history, over and over. Dearth of enough or affordable food was one of the pressures created in Germany in aftermath of the First World War, a pressure that eventually would induce a Second World War.

Regardless of incidence of famine in Europe in course of the 14*th century*, the reformation that would result in a sealing of those who truly love God still would commence in course of the 15*th century*. So then, consistent with the command 'not to hurt the oil (carriers of the Holy Spirit) and the wine (those sanctified by the blood of Jesus)', capacity for a resurgence of the gospel was not compromised by famines of the 14*th century*. In fact, the travails of the 14*th century* would drive some of the people to seek God more fervently, setting the stage for the reformation that would begin in the 15*th century*. We have then that the RIGHTEOUS SHINE AS THE SUN during the 15*th century*, that is, in context of a 5th SEAL period characterized by Maturity of Righteousness.

As I already have articulated, a 5th SEAL period devolves into a 7th SEAL period that, conditional on maturity of The Church can, simultaneously transform into a 1st SEAL period for the Church. We discussed this in context of the Summary of the 7 SEALS. The *Church of the Reformation*, the Church that kicks off the time of the CHURCH IN LAODICEA, represents a 5th SEAL period that matured into a 7th SEAL period, but which then transformed into a 1st SEAL period for the Church. Due to the fact that the *papal*, *Orthodox*, and *Anglican* Churches would not embrace The Reformation, the Church again was not perfected, with outcome Christians in Western Europe were subjected to significant persecutions. Eventually, the reformation resulted in relocation of most of those who truly loved Christ from Europe to the United States of America. But the believers still were not mature enough to produce a mature Church that could be perfected, with outcome the United States itself eventually would be embroiled in war and shortages of food, meaning sometime after arrival in the United States, there again was a reset to a 1st Seal period. While there was a reset to yet another first seal period, because the government of the United States would not root civil laws in the Love of God, 2nd and 3rd Seal periods followed to their logical conclusions. The treatment of American Indians perhaps is not the most important fault here, for American Indians had mistreated one another long before arrival of the White man. Rather, in the enablement of exploitation of Christian brothers and sisters by businesses, with banks giving loans, then yanking the demand for the produce away, then foreclosing on the land, which then was sold at a much higher value to railroad companies, the government showed it cared for the rich much more than faithful Christians seeking to build new lives in the new world.

Historical Spiritual Nugget 16 *Christians then, make the same mistake as Christians now, act as if governance is meant for those who are worldly, for those who lack restraint of GODLINESS and LOVE. It is time that Christians recognize that if they have the ability and resources, that they ought to demonstrate interest in governance for arrival at civil laws that are not just laws on the books, at civil laws that are enforced, that are appropriately supported institutionally, and that are secular in nature, but yet are founded on the Love of God.*

Prophecy Insight 53 *Now that you know, now that all of Christendom arrives at the realization that our Lord Jesus Christ actually seeks success of life on earth, with outcome His Second Coming is failure of mankind, failure of either of the Church, or the Nations, if we are to ensure that life on earth fails, not because of the Church, but because Nations reject the Love of God as basis for civil laws and societal interactions, it is time for Christians to take active interest in governance that introduces Godliness and Love into civil laws that are designed to be non-religious, into civil laws that maintain secular nature of society.*

I have provided examples of civil laws that are premised on the Love of God, that is, on Godliness and Love in the preceding.

Prophecy Insight 54 *Christians are not called to demand Christianity from their fellow citizens, rather are called to maintain dichotomy of Church and Nation. Christian principles are to be reflected in civil laws that are secular in nature. Christians who participate in governance are to participate as individuals, not as champions of any Church.*

Prophecy Insight 55 *Christians are not called to establishment of perfect societies. Consistent with prior discussion on abortion, attempts at arrival at perfect solutions are inconsistent with imperfections of human existence. In this respect, consider that, in The Father's best Utopia (Revelation ch. 22), He recognizes that there remain some deviants who, on basis of their choice of bad behaviors, refuse to enter into the New Jerusalem (Revelation 22:15).*

Prophecy Insight 56 *Civil laws are to reflect the best balance between demonstrations of the Love of God for individuals, and well being of society. It is straightforward, in context of such a rubric, that domiciling of a child in the arms of a mother who lacks capacity for loving of the child creates problems for mother, child, and society. We arrive then at the discernment that, conditional on seeking of an abortion within the first 6 to 8 weeks of a pregnancy,* *and conditional on willingness to consume information on potential hazards of the decision to abort a child, that it cannot be right in sight of our Lord Jesus Christ that a woman be forced to have a baby she does not think she can love.*

> With respect to abortion, why the restriction to the first 6 to 8 weeks?

If a woman seeks an abortion after *8 weeks* of pregnancy, it likely is the case that she is under some sort of emotional stress that makes her feel inadequate at carrying a baby to term. What such women need is encouragement, companionship, and friendship that helps them through the pregnancy. When a woman in such a situation receives such help, eventually she arrives at maturity of righteousness in respect of the pregnancy, and raising of the child. If society allows women who are more than 8 weeks pregnant to, under some fleeting feelings or emotions, access abortions, more likely than not, such an allowance leads to abuse, and regrets.

Spiritual Insight 80 *Rather than condemn women who seek late term abortions of pregnancies, abortion clinics, and ministries that focus on women within Churches ought to be empowered with counselors who are able to provide one-on-one help that is personalized, and that is able to devote appropriate amounts of time to such pregnant women. In an increasingly fragile world, a world in which women can have doubts about rightness of having a child, what we need more of is* COMPASSION, KINDNESS, COMPANIONSHIP, *and* FRIENDSHIP *that enables such women arrive at* MATURITY OF RIGHTEOUSNESS.

The SSGLAE in History: Some Evidences

The United States, which consisted of pilgrims, who themselves ran away from persecution, eventually would descend so low as to permit slavery, resulting eventually in slaying of one another in course of the civil war of 1861 to 1865, and a dealing with food shortages in aftermath of the war. We find then evidence that there was a reset to a 1st Seal, which then led to realization of the 2nd and 3rd Seals in the United States of America, and then onwards to their logical conclusions. It is possible that the civil rights movement of the late 1960s was yet another reset to a 1st Seal period, but which was not embraced by the larger body polity. The fact that war and meaningless loss of lives would follow shortly thereafter in context of the Vietnam war is consistent with the notion that the government of the United States did not embrace the spirit of the civil rights movement for arrival at civil laws that provided a better reflection of the Love of God. It is somewhat clear that the late 1990s, which somewhat coincided with the 'BAPTISM OF THE HOLY SPIRIT' movement represented yet another reset to a 1st Seal period. The attack on September 11, 2001 and the wrong subterfuge that induced the United States into war in the Middle East (Iraq) represent slayings that are outcome of rejection of the Love of God as foundation for civil laws of society. Note that in it's decision to invade Iraq, the United States deliberately wasted all of the goodwill that accompanied the war in Afghanistan, a war that at inception induced full support from all of the United Nations, resulting in a multilateral force invasion of Afghanistan that was led by the United States. In wake of the invasion of Iraq, that multilateral force would be whittled down to mostly two countries, the United States and Great Britain. War in the Middle East was followed by a recession, that is, shortages of resources, with outcome we have evidence for a 1st Seal devolving into 2nd and 3rd Seals, then onwards to their logical conclusions.

Prophecy Principle 89 *Even now, the government of the United States of America has yet to demonstrate any real commitment to civil laws that are rooted in the Love of God, to civil laws that truly are designed for protection of the weak within society. There is lots of lip service given to such protections, yet there exists little of such protections in reality. Incarceration laws, intrusion of the state into marital relations and upbringing of children, and employment discrimination laws all are contexts within which the government of the United States has yet to demonstrate a real commitment to protection of the weak in society.*

Prophecy Principle 90 *This book is The Father setting in motion yet another 1st Seal. The Father has supported this new SSGLAE with at the very least four additional repositories of knowledge and anointing of the Holy Spirit, repositories provided through me for aiding of the Church in arrival at maturity, namely:* 'TRUTHS THAT CREATE OR ENHANCE LOVING RELATIONSHIPS: THE CHRISTIAN PERSPECTIVE'; 'IN JESUS NAME'; 'TRUE SANCTIFICATION'; *and* 'DIVINE MERITOCRACY'.

Prophecy Principle 91 *The Father aims to root this reset to a 1st Seal in as much spiritual knowledge as possible.* BUT WILL THE CHURCH BUY OF THESE REVELATIONS OF OUR JESUS CHRIST, OR WILL THE CHURCH DECLARE THAT 'IT IS RICH AND IN NEED OF NOTHING'?

For illustration, consider Egypt. In wake of a popular uprising, and refusal to order shootings of demonstrators, then President of Egypt, *Hosni Mubarak* voluntarily stepped down from office, that is, offered an olive branch of love to his people. The government that took over subsequently, the *Muslim Brotherhood*, responded by putting Hosni Mubarak in jail on charges of corruption. Shortly thereafter, the Muslim Brotherhood was booted from office by a military General who continues in office till today, General Abdel Fattah el-Sisi. Since the decision to repay the olive branch of love offered by

Mubarak with hatred of incarceration, Egypt has not been the same, has been rocked by violence, fear, and loss of economic opportunities. With a 1st Seal period that is rooted in the LOVE OF GOD within reach, the people of Egypt chose hatred.

Historical Spiritual Nugget 17 *The real (spiritual) agents of the peaceful demand for change that transpired in Egypt, and of the peaceful response from the sitting President, Hosni Mubarak, could have been Powers for Christ, believers in Christ who, by very nature of their attainments, do not seek any fame from society. All we see, however, is the response of the society, the response of the nation to an opportunity for choosing of the Love of God.*

For illustration, consider Russia. In wake of toppling of the Czars, rather than punish the rich who had oppressed either of the poor, or those not as well off as themselves, with exception of fellow Bolsheviks, the Bolsheviks punished every land owning Russian and Ukrainian. No matter how well non-Bolsheviks had treated others in past, they were treated as enemies of the people, as enemies of the state. You see then that Bolsheviks commenced their communist rule with hatreds, that is, with an attachment to injustice. In presence of an opportunity for New Beginnings that produce justice and equity in civil society, Bolsheviks chose hatred and oppression. Lacking in enough food for feeding of the entire country, Ukrainians - the people who produced most of the food consumed in the country - were starved of food. Inclusive of intellectuals, any whim or caprice induced whisking of Russians off to Siberia. By the end of it all, it is estimated that over *3 million* Ukrainians died at the hands of those who supposedly had liberated them from tyranny of the Czars. The rule of the Czars left much to be desired, but the Bolsheviks outdid the Czars at oppression of their own people. Enter then the *Perestroika* period ushered in by the Premier who enabled dissolution of Communism, *Mikhail Gorbachev*. Rather than utilize Perestroika as an opportunity for *new beginnings*, insiders of the Communist party and the intelligence establishment kept most of the country's valuable assets to themselves. Yes, it is true they paid for the assets, but the average Russian did not arrive at opportunity for participation in the economic liberation of his or her country. Communism had been plagued with 'HAVES' and 'HAVE NOTS', Perestroika maintained the distinctions, merely introduced some redistribution within populations of 'RUSSIAN HAVES'. In presence of opportunity for *new beginnings*, Russia and just about all of the other regions that had made up the *USSR* chose hatreds, oppressions, and an 'I ONLY MATTER' character for running of their countries.

THE REASON RUSSIANS LOVE VLADIMIR PUTIN SO MUCH?

Putin at least seems to have Russian pride; if someone else were to take over running of the country, who knows, things perhaps could get worse. After all, there is an American President suspected of having leanings towards Russia, suspected of being a Russian mole.

Historical Spiritual Nugget 18 *The Czars were 'Orthodox Christians'. In the decision of the Bolsheviks to attack faith in God, as opposed to institution of good leadership that improved on performance of the Czars, the Bolsheviks wasted an opportunity for Russia's civil polity to be reformed in context of the Love of God. The spiritual movement that led to the dethronement of the Czars could have been propelled by Powers for Christ.*

For illustration, consider Ukraine. In wake of toppling of a regime that was considered a stooge for Russia via popular uprising, *Eastern Ukraine* refused to provide the new regime with opportunity for demonstration of genuine interest in the welfare of the people, insisted on secession from the Republic. I personally was appalled when the separatists would not respond to 'GOODWILL GESTURES' from the President of the Ukraine, goodwill evident in refusal to authorize shootings of protesters in Eastern Ukraine. Rather than engender any softening of their stance, the goodwill gesture engendered more of attacks on policemen who were being restrained by the government for benefit of the people. Supported purportedly by Russia, and without any instigating action from the new government, Eastern Ukraine decided to not leave any room for arrival at the Love of God. I understand that Russia was afraid that *NATO* was about to gain entry into Ukraine, as such sought Eastern Ukraine as a *buffer* between itself and any incursions by NATO into Ukraine. *But whenever people who used to be together are unwilling to negotiate their future, choice of war is predicated on outright rejection of grounding of relationships, decision making, and actions in Love.* The new regime in the Ukraine was willing to negotiate, offered to negotiate, yet Eastern Ukraine refused to consider any negotiations. In presence of negotiations, Russia could influence the discussion, ensure Eastern Ukraine received some autonomy, autonomy rooted in an agreement that were Ukraine to become part of *NATO*, NATO forces would not be present in Eastern Ukraine - the exact objective of Russia for instigation of conflict.

Reasonability of such an agreement?

A reasonable *NATO* and Ukraine Government has to recognize that, with *NATO* considered a threat by Russia, and this rightly so, location of *NATO* forces in Eastern Ukraine reasonably could be regarded by Russia as an act of aggression. The war in Eastern Ukraine, and subsequent difficulties with resources, such as food and water, is outcome of rejection of the Love of God as rubric for relationships, decision making, and actions.

Historical Spiritual Nugget 19 *The Love of God embeds willingness to consider needs of others, embeds willingness to negotiate outcomes, embeds rejection of a 'WINNER TAKES ALL' mentality. Four disciples of Jesus became* *pillars of the Christian Church - Apostles* PETER, JAMES, JOHN, *and* PAUL. *Regardless, tradition has it that all 12 of the Apostles had meaningful, successful 'careers' in different parts of the world, with outcome all, except Apostle John - who was deliberately preserved by will of The Father, this so Rome could realize it was The Father who allowed all others to be killed - paid the ultimate price for their faith in Jesus Christ.*

Spiritual Insight 81 *In Christ,* MERITOCRACY *serves only for a ranking of worth, does not induce a winner take all outcome. In Christ, all who are willing and qualified for work, arrive at opportunity for engagement in work that is meaningful and fulfilling.*

For illustration, consider Western Europe. In wake of forced relocations of those who disagreed with theology of any of Papal Rome, the Orthodox Church, or the Anglican Church from all over Western Europe by their kings, by 1793, non-Protestants retained by the kings of France in their domain had killed their royal family, and in total about 40,000 of their own people. In 1794, the person appointed Guardian of the new French Republic, *Robespierre* and his closest associates had been executed by the people. Given Robespierre, and his associates had, themselves ruled over a reign of terror that resulted in killing of about 40,000 of their own people, clearly, they reaped exactly what it was that they had sown. *How exactly was this anarchy of killing and tyranny different from tyranny of the kings of France?* Consider then the following quote from my adopted historical reference text, HWE.

> "In fact, the government, now called the Directory, restricted political power to men of substantial wealth even fewer in number than those who held power under the constitution of 1791 (*HWE*, pg. 364)."

Given the revolution did not solve the country's problems, by 1799, France ended up with yet another Emperor, a secularly anointed, *Napoleon Bonaparte*. Within no more than *6 years*, the much acclaimed French revolution had devolved into yet another autocratic form of government. To escape his insatiable desire for war, the French would, in 1814, agree to consignment of their Emperor to an Island, Elba.

Celebration of the French Revolution as a watershed moment in history of democracy is an exercise in intellectual and moral fraud.

Historical Spiritual Nugget 20 *In the decision to throw out* FAITH IN GOD *alongside dethronement of kings who seemed not to care about welfare of the people; in the decision to embrace* MURDEROUS RAGE *in implementation of* *the revolution, the French Revolution departed from the Love of God. Within 6* YEARS, *the revolution had produced the* STATUS QUO *that had necessitated the revolution:* AUTOCRATIC RULE SUPPORTED BY AN EVEN SMALLER SELECTION OF THE RICH IN SOCIETY.

In Britain, the industrial revolution was accompanied by continuity of clashes between '*the haves*' and '*have nots*'. By 1805, Western Europe was fully engulfed in war. War would continue intermittently, resulting in the two great wars, the FIRST and SECOND WORLD WARS. Absent interventions by descendants of the people forced away to the new world during each of the First and Second World Wars, it perhaps is the case that Western Europe is, today, in a very sorry state. We see then that subsequent to the strategy that marched faith in Jesus Christ out of Western Europe, all that Western Europe received in exchange was PAIN, PAIN, AND YET MORE PAIN.

Prophecy Principle 92 *Any Church, which refuses to allow those who treat others right opportunity for participation in life, this on basis of doctrinal disagreements, is an apostate Church in which The Father, Son, and Holy Spirit no longer have a part.*

Prophecy Principle 93 *Whenever Nations reject the Love of God as basis for civil laws and societal interactions, all that this creates is hatreds, and pain, pain, and yet more pain.*

Historical Spiritual Nugget 21 THE REFORMATION *was premised on* EQUALITY OF ALL BELIEVERS *before The Father, an assertion that is true. Equality of all believers, and of all men is essence of the* LOVE OF GOD. *Rejection of the* LOVE OF GOD *evident in persecution of reformers, and those who believed in the truths that they taught, produced pain, pain, and yet more pain in all of Western Europe.*

Prophecy Insight 57 *If you peruse the history of your country, do you observe events that herald adoption or rejection of the Love of God as basis for civil laws, societal interactions?*

The 4th Seal

Under the 4th Seal, Death is followed by Hades (the grave) and there was given to them authority to kill (over the fourth part of the land) with sword, and with hunger, and with death, and by the beasts of the land (Revelation 6:7-8). Under the 2nd Seal, the nations kill each other, meaning engage in wars with one another. Under the 4th Seal, Death and Hades are given power of the fourth part of the land for producing of death either via sword, or with hunger, or natural death, or by the beasts of the land. .

Prophecy Interpretation 20 *The 2ⁿᵈ* SEAL *embeds natural, equivalently, spiritual* CONSEQUENCES *of choice of hatreds, and love of money by The Nations. The 4ᵗʰ* SEAL *embeds* PENALTIES *from The Father for evil committed in context of the 1ˢᵗ and 2ⁿᵈ Seals.*

Prophecy Principle 94 *If The Nations reject the* LOVE OF GOD *in context of a 1ˢᵗ* SEAL, *it normatively must be true that they implement acts of hatred against those who abide in the Love of God.*

Since the 3ʳᵈ SEAL only pertains to the righteous, and the 4ᵗʰ SEAL only to those who love evil, the 3ʳᵈ and 4ᵗʰ Seals cannot be deemed to be sequential. This is evident in the fact that, while the righteous are being sealed with the Holy Spirit in context of the 3ʳᵈ SEAL, it simultaneously cannot be the case that there exists a void in lives of those who love evil. We arrive then at an important internal consistency with symbolism of the ELEMENTS 1 through 7, namely, that the 3ʳᵈ and 4ᵗʰ Seals are simultaneous, not sequential.

Prophecy Principle 95 THE *3ʳᵈ* & *4ᵗʰ* SEALS ARE NOT SEQUENTIAL, ARE SIMULTANEOUS.

Prophecy Interpretation 21 *Whenever The Church arrives at an* INNER CIRCLE OF FRIENDSHIP *(CF) in context of the 3ʳᵈ* SEAL, *it is not adversely affected by punishment of those who love evil. Whenever The Church refuses to submit to perfection, as such does not arrive at CF, The Church is weak, and herself points out those who are faithful to Christ to The Nations. We have then that persecutions of the righteous occur in context of the 4ᵗʰ* SEAL, *this because The Nations are upset at penalties meted out to them by The Father. The* MARK OF THE BEAST *transpires then in context of the 4ᵗʰ* SEAL.

Prophecy Interpretation 22 BABYLON THE GREAT, *Babylon the whore, is the apostate church that, in context of the 4ᵗʰ* SEAL *persecutes the saints. We have then that whenever The Church does not submit to The Father's perfection agenda, that the saints can have to die for their faith. Since Babylon can, as was the case with our Lord Jesus Christ, implement it's persecutions through the nations with whom she trades, killing of the saints can, in actuality be implemented by The Nations.*

Given the saints are sealed with the Holy Spirit, Death and Hades do not have power over those who are faithful to our Lord Jesus Christ. We further find that war, famines or shortages of food, and death are tools in the hands of The Father against those who choose love for evil over love for what is good. Since our Lord Jesus Christ now has the keys to death and the hades (Revelation 1:18), death and hades can be tools in the hands of The Father for punishment of evil. It is important to note here there is not any contradiction implied in simultaneity of the 3rd and 4th Seals. In *Ezekiel ch. 9*, right at the same time, sealing, equivalently, identification of the righteous produced slaughter of the wicked, with outcome the sealing and the slaughter were progressive, progressed from one part of the city to another.

Prophecy Insight 58 *Since our Lord Jesus Christ holds the keys to death and hades, you need not have any fear of death, for only He can allow your death. Since your death must induce your passing on to glory, for you already have passed from death to life (1John 3:14), there is not any reason for fear of death. So then, our Lord Jesus Christ has freed us from fear of death (Hebrews 2:15).*

The word '*Beasts*' refers to enemies of the gospel of Christ, who, perhaps are demonic in their constitution. In respect of encounters with such persons or entities, or characteristics of beasts Apostles Paul and Peter declare as follows.

> If after the manner of a man with wild beasts I fought in Ephesus, what the advantage to me if the dead do not rise? Let us eat and drink, for tomorrow we die (1Corinthians 15:32)!

> The Lord hath known to rescue pious ones out of temptation, and unrighteous ones to a day of judgment, being punished, to keep, and chiefly those going behind the flesh in DESIRE OF UNCLEANNESS (*do not want to relate face to face, seek to relate to others from behind*), and LORDSHIP DESPISING (*stubbornly refuse to recognize God as having lordship over the right way to live*); PRESUMPTOUS, SELF COMPLACENT (*reject feasibility of new knowledge*), dignities they are not afraid to speak evil of, and these, as IRRATIONAL NATURAL BEASTS, made to be caught and destroyed - in what things they are ignorant of, speaking evil - in their destruction shall be destroyed, about to receive a reward of unrighteousness, pleasures counting the luxury in the day (*find pleasure in idleness*), spots and blemishes, luxuriating in their DECEITS (*revel in capacity for, and implementation of deceit*), feasting with you, having eyes full of ADULTERY (*love to chase after married men or women*), and unable to cease from sin (*refuse help from God for their lack of capacity for cessation from sin*), enticing UNSTABLE souls (*develop falsehoods that are attractive to people who are unstable*), having an heart exercised in COVETOUSNESS, children of a curse (2Peter 2:9-14).

If you relate to another from behind, it is impossible to get to know that other person. It is normative then that people who seek to know others from behind only care about their own selves, care nothing for the person to whom they relate to from behind. We have then that no matter how much it may sound bitter, that homosexuality is declared to be beastly behavior by the Holy Spirit; this because it does not leave any room for one to get to know another. A homosexual may counter that he relates at other times with a partner face to face. But consider that at the time when sex is supposed to contribute to the knowing of each other, arrival at 'knowing' is impossible, for while engaged in sex, not kissing, the two lovers never can be 'face to face'. If heterosexual couples never engage in what derogatively is referred to as 'missionary position' sex, regardless of engagement in heterosexual sex, sex does not generate any capacity for knowing of each other. While masturbation, and all of the various forms of oral sex cannot be unambiguously characterized to be sin, I am convinced of the Holy Spirit that they constitute perversions, which those who believe in Jesus Christ do well to avoid. Perversion is evident in the fact that the mouth could not have been created for participation in oral sex. WE ALL KNOW WHAT THE MOUTH, IN REALITY IS TO THE BODY. If you feel differently, I admonish you to ask the Holy Spirit to reveal to you the heart of our Lord and Savior Jesus Christ on the matter.

> If someone mentions to you that I also have, in past, masturbated, or in context of marriage dabbled into oral sex, I respond, guilty as charged.

BUT THE TIMES OF IGNORANCE GOD ALWAYS OVERLOOKS, then when we arrive at revelational knowledge, He commands us to repent (Acts 17:30). MORE IMPORTANTLY, I FIND MYSELF IN GREAT COMPANY OF OTHER WITNESSES, for Apostle Paul declares as follows concerning believers in 1Corinthians 6:9-11.

> Do you not know that the unrighteous will not inherit the kingdom (*reign*) of God? Do not be deceived. Neither fornicators, nor idolaters, nor adulterers, nor homosexuals, nor sodomites, nor thieves, nor covetous, nor drunkards, nor revilers, nor extortioners will inherit the kingdom (*reign*) of God.

> And such were some of you (HALLELUJAH!!!). But you were washed (*I was washed*), but you were sanctified (*I was sanctified*), but you were justified (*I was justified*) in the name of the Lord Jesus and by the Spirit of our God.

> Hallelujah!!!

Life Nugget 1 *The Father seeks to cleanse you from sins and weaknesses (Hebrews 12:1-2).*

Life Nugget 2 *There does not exist any 7-STEP PROGRAM for enablement of your cleansing from sins and weaknesses.*

Life Nugget 3 *If you seek to be cleansed from sins and weaknesses, all you have to do is practice the faith, love, and hope embedded in (i) the name of Jesus Christ; (ii) the cleansing power in the blood of Jesus Christ (1John 1:7); and (iii) overcoming power of the Holy Spirit.*

Life Nugget 4 *My books, In Jesus Name, and True Sanctification detail how to practice the faith, love, and hope, which all are rooted in Jesus Christ, that enable you arrive at cleansing from sins and weaknesses.*

The Father and Suffering on Earth

The ungodly, and some who are moral, but who seek to not acknowledge existence of God, are wont to rail at presence of suffering in the world as evidence for either of non-existence, or irrelevance of God. Why the general polity somehow are blinded to RIDICULOUSNESS of such assertions, somewhat is baffling.

> Is it possible that there exists anyone who does not see that most of human suffering is man made?

In response, The Father declares that suffering, which subsists in context of the 2nd Seal is, in entirety, induced by celebration of selfishness and hatred over principles of the Love of God.

> HOW EXACTLY IS THE FATHER TO BLAME FOR THIS SORT OF SUFFERING?

Under the 4th Seal, arrival at the 4th Seal implies maturity of choices of evil, and maturity of evil associations. Given choice of evil in context of the 1st SEAL, or the 4th Seal implies doing of evil to those who are good, to those who love the name of Jesus Christ, punishment that arrives from The Father in context of the 4th Seal is a response from The Father to evil choices on part of The Nations. We have then again that suffering, which transpires in context of the 4th Seal is induced by choices of nations, is not a direct imposition from God. In aggregate, whether it be in context of the 2nd or 4th Seal, suffering is, in entirety, created by man's choice of evil over that which is good.

Prophecy Interpretation 23 *I discuss persecutions of the saints that are implemented by The Nations (The MARK OF THE BEAST), or Babylon (killing of the saints) in detail in* CHAPTER 11

Prophecy Interpretation 24 *The* VIALS OF THE WRATH OF GOD *that are enumerated in Revelation Ch. 16 are poured out as judgments in context of the 7* VIALS *of the 7th Seal. I discuss these vials in* CHAPTER 11.

The Fifth Seal

The 5th Seal symbolizes the Maturity of Righteousness. In context of the 5th SEAL, The Righteous Shine as the Sun in the reign of God (Matthew 13:43). MATURITY OF RIGHTEOUSNESS is attested to either by death, or by life. This is evident as follows in the following Scripture.

> For whoever may will to save his life, shall lose it, and whoever may lose his life for my sake shall find it (Matthew 16:25).

> Jesus said to her, I am the rising again, and the life; He who is believing in me, even if he may die, shall live; and every one who is living and believing in me shall not die - to the age (John 11:25-26).

In *Chapters 3, 7, & 8*, we identified two sets of persons who have sincere faith in Jesus Christ, NEOPHYTES - whose spirits are perfected post death, and POWERS, whose spirits already are perfected on earth. In presence of this dichotomy, while Neophyte believers receive MATURITY OF RIGHTEOUSNESS as a gift post death, it is during their time on earth that Powers attain to Maturity of Righteousness (MR). In John 11:25-26, while Neophytes can die spiritually, this because they have yet to attain to life that is age-during, at timing of physical death, Powers do not die spiritually, continue to experience the reality of Christ in some spiritual sense. In light of highlighted dichotomy, if spirits of those who are killed for Jesus Christ, who then desire justice are shown under the altar, it must be the case that they are spirits of NEOPHYTES, that is, spirits of believers whose spirits were not perfected prior to their giving of their lives for Christ. We have then that whereas either of NEOPHYTES, or POWERS can be martyred for sake of the name of our Lord Jesus Christ, only spirits of NEOPHYTES can be expected to be seen under the altar in context of a 5th SEAL.

LET US THEN CONSIDER THE SCRIPTURES.

During the time of the 5th Seal, in Revelation 6:9-11, the souls of those slain because of the word of God and because they bore testimony to reality of faith in the name of Jesus Christ cry out to God with a great voice, saying:

> "Till when, O Master, the Holy and True, does thou not judge and take vengeance of our blood from those dwelling upon the land (Revelation 6:9-10?"

> And there was given to each one white robes, and it was said to them that they may rest themselves yet a little time, till may

be fulfilled also their fellow-servants and their brethren, who are about to be killed - even as they (Revelation 6:11).

And there was given to her that she may be arrayed with fine linen, pure and shining, for the fine linen is the righteous acts of the saints (Revelation 19:8).

And the armies in the heaven were following Him upon white horses, clothed in fine linen - white and pure (Revelation 19:14).

In response, each is given a white robe, which signifies the righteousness of our Lord Jesus Christ (Isaiah 1:18; Revelation 3:18). In the acquisition of righteousness of Jesus Christ post death, we have confirmation of believers whose spirits were not perfected on earth.

THE SUPPORTING SCRIPTURAL EVIDENCE?

And there was given to her that she may be arrayed with fine linen, pure and shining, for the fine linen is the righteous acts of the saints (Revelation 19:8).

Prophecy Principle 96 *Believers that are depicted in Revelation 6:9-11 are believers who do not, of their own virtue, arrive at* MATURITY OF RIGHTEOUS-NESS *on earth, as such have their spirits perfected by the grace of Christ. We have then evidence for* NEOPHYTE *Believers. It is straightforward that these believers, who experience persecution and are killed for the sake of Christ, are representative of the RP7* PATH.

In the declarations of our Lord Jesus Christ, we arrive at insight into failure of the Reformation at generation of a truly vibrant Christian faith, which is, inability, or unwillingness of the reformers to arrive at characterization of a common faith, at a UNIFYING RECOGNITION OF OUR LORD AND SAVIOR JESUS CHRIST. In the proliferation of denominations, the Church arrived at a splinter, as such could not be perfected. This splinter has continued, and has become more severe. If the Church is to have any opportunity for being perfected, if she is to rise up from her ashes and become a force for good in this world, the Church must arrive at a UNIFYING RECOGNITION OF OUR LORD AND SAVIOR JESUS CHRIST.

Prophecy Interpretation 25 *Revelation 6:9-11 provides validating evidence for requirement of, at the very least,* THREE *SSGLAEs on the RP7 Path for arrival at the 7th* VIAL *of The 7th Seal.*

Prophecy Insight 59 *If* THE CHURCH *thinks it ever will gain strength against other philosophies that strive for the mind of man in context of continuation of denominational strife, The Church deceives herself, for Powers must be characterized by* BROTHERLY KINDNESS *and* LOVE *(2Peter 1:7), as such, across denominations, cannot be in strife in relation to one another.*

Prophecy Insight 60 *Absent arrival at a* UNIFYING RECOGNITION OF OUR LORD AND SAVIOR JESUS CHRIST, *The Church continues to resist efforts of her Lord and Savior for her perfection.*

Prophecy Insight 61 *The* RECOGNITIONS OF OUR LORD AND SAVIOR JESUS CHRIST *that I proffer in this book revolve, in entirety, around Person of our Lord and Savior Jesus Christ, serve as grounds for arrival, once again, at a common (similar, unifying)* FAITH *(Titus 1:4, Jude 1:3, 2Peter 1:1) in Jesus Christ.*

Additional Evidence for Characterization of Neophyte Believers

Friend, first, if the saints are perfected on earth, while on earth, they already are perfected on earth, are unblemished, as such do not need any robes for covering, as they are not characterized by any nakedness or blemish. In this respect, concerning the 144,000, Jude 1:24-25, and Revelation 14:5 declares as follows.

> And to Him who is able to guard you, not stumbling, and TO SET YOU IN THE PRESENCE OF HIS GLORY UNBLEMISHED, in gladness, to the only wise God our Savior, is glory and greatness, power and authority, both now and to all the ages! Amen.

> And in their mouth there was not found guile (falsehood or deceit), FOR UNBLEMISHED ARE THEY BEFORE THE THRONE OF GOD.

So then, when they die, having being in the Presence of Christ all the while, and more importantly, having actualized the PRESENCE OF CHRIST, consistent with the words of our Lord Jesus Christ in John 11:25-26, which we already have discussed, they become part of the assembly on Mount Zion, that is, the New Jerusalem.

The Fifth Seal Generated by a Willing Church

In Chapter 7, we arrived at the following characterization of the GLORY OF GOD.

> Combined, the Scriptures declare that the Glory of God is either of THE CHARACTER AND ESSENCE OF GOD, or WORKS (ACTIONS) THAT DIRECT PEOPLE'S ATTENTION TO THE CHARACTER AND ESSENCE OF GOD, which is Love (1John 4:8).

Consider now the following description of the New Jerusalem in Revelation 21:22-24.

And a sanctuary I did not see in it, for the Lord God, The Almighty, is it's sanctuary, and The Lamb, and the city hath no need of the sun, nor of the moon, that they may shine in it; FOR THE GLORY OF GOD DID LIGHTEN IT, and the lamp of it is the Lamb; AND THE NATIONS OF THE SAVED IN IT'S LIGHT SHALL WALK, and the kings of the earth do bring their glory and honor into it.

Combined, we arrive at the following prophetic inference, namely:

Prophecy Interpretation 26 THE LIGHT OF THE NEW JERUSALEM IS THE RIGHTEOUS WORKS OF THE SAINTS, *works that lighten the city, and it is in this light that the nations walk. In presence of the light, the nations bring their glory and honor into the New Jerusalem, with outcome there exist partnerships that are rooted in good works between The Church and The Nations.*

Throughout the Book of Revelation, and in Epistles of Paul, each of individual believers and the Church are referred to as the Bride of Christ, or the Wife of Christ (Ephesians 5:25-33).

What exactly does it mean to be a bride or wife of Christ?

Well, let us turn our attention to the original intent for Eve. When Adam was created, The Father saw that he was alone, sought to provide him with a help mate who simultaneously would be a 'counterpart' (Genesis 2:18). A 'HELP MATE' is someone who supports another with respect to actualization of purpose, not a person with whom a person has sex. When a help mate further is a counterpart, the help mate is someone who is capable of entering into a friendship with the person to whom they are a help. So then, Eve was created as help mate and counterpart for Adam, not as a person with whom Adam has sex. Sex is part of the relationship between Adam and Eve only due to demand for procreation - only because Adam and Eve simultaneously are entrusted with responsibility of filling the earth with offspring, as such have to '*know each other*' in an intimate sexual sense. Naturally, given The Father has given us richly all things to enjoy (1Timothy 6:17), conditional on the definition of '*enjoyment of sex*' between a couple, and consistency of such definition with the Love of God, sex ought to be enjoyed. In presence of marriage, Apostle Paul clearly asserts that sex is not only for procreation; that, given demonstrations of love for one another evoke natural and godly emotions in believers, that within context of marriage, sex also must be engaged in for release of natural and godly emotions that are outcome of demonstrations of love between husband and wife (1Corinthians 7:1-7). Relative to conception, the spirits subsisting in the man and the woman matter. While Eve remained desirous of knowledge of *good and evil*, she gave birth to *Cain and Abel*. You see then that she got her wish. When, subsequent to a witnessing of effects of evil she desired righteous seed, she had Seth. It was after Seth begot a son of his own that Seth and his descendants began to preach in the name of Jehovah (Genesis 4:25-26).

Spiritual Insight 82 *Sex that produces righteous seed is supposed to be rooted in a loving desire for intimate knowing of each other on part of husband (male man) and wife (female man). The passionate, lustful sex that is being sold in movies never should become typology for sex that subsists between disciples of Christ who are married to each other.*

Spiritual Insight 83 *The spirit at work in a married couple matter for the seed that they seek to conceive. It is best that the spirits be one, and that the couple desire production of righteous seed.*

Whenever Christian Scriptures refer to believers, or the Church as the BRIDE OF CHRIST, it is because we are *help mates* for Christ, and at the same time, in the sense that our Lord Jesus Christ has called us friends, *counterparts* to Christ (John 15:15). We know that it is possible for an earthly king to have a bosom friend among those who pay obeisance to him as king. History is replete with such relationships (2Samuel 15:37; 1Kings 4:5). So then, we are help mates to our Lord Jesus Christ, who is King of kings, and Lord of lords, and yet because He has made us kings and priests unto Himself (1Peter 2:9; Revelation 1:6; 5:10), we have opportunity to be His friend, to know secrets He only can or will reveal to friends. Because we are able to become His friends, our Lord Jesus Christ promises that if we overcome, we get to sit with Him in His throne, just as He has sat down in His Father's throne (Revelation 3:21). So if you a male man, do not be abashed that you are referred to as a bride of Christ for this does not signify that you develop female attributes, it merely indicates you are a help mate and friend to Christ.

Prophecy Principle 97 *You are described as the 'BRIDE OF CHRIST' only because a bride is typology for a* HELP MATE *who simultaneously is a* COUNTER-PART *to another. So then, do not feel abashed to be described as part of the Church, as a 'bride of Christ'.*

In what sense are you a help mate to Christ?

For God it is who is working in you both to will and to work for His good pleasure (Philippians 2:13).

That there might be made known now to the principalities and the authorities in the heavenly places through the assembly (*through the Church, that is, through you and I*), the manifold wisdom of

God, according to a purpose of the ages, which He made in Christ Jesus our Lord (Ephesians 3:10-11).

And we have known that to those loving God all things do work together for good, TO THOSE WHO ARE CALLED ACCORDING TO PUR- POSE; because whom He did foreknow He also did fore-appoint, CONFORMED TO THE IMAGE OF HIS SON, that He might be first- born among many brethren; and whom He did fore-appoint, these also He did call; and whom He did call, these also He declared righteous; and whom He declared righteous, these also He did glorify (Romans 8:28-30).

Spiritual Insight 84 *The Father has designed that you be conformed to the image of Christ in context of purposes to which He calls you, this because you love Him. It is a glorious thing to have opportunity to be conformed to the image of the only begotten Son of God, to the image of our Lord and Savior Jesus Christ. Amen.*

INTERLUDE

Alright then, a Recap.

First, note that the relationship between a 7th Seal and a 1st Seal is as follows: A 7th Seal always devolves into a new 1st Seal, such that at beginning, it is a 7th Seal, and at ending of the same 7th Seal, there is commencement and recharacterization of the 7th Seal as a new 1st Seal.

In summary, the following are the two other feasible paths to spiri- tual resolutions for the SSGLAE, one through the 7th TRUMPET of the 7th Seal (the GP7 PATH); the other through the 7th VIAL of the 7th Seal (the RP7 PATH).

Prophecy Insight 62 *The Good Path to the 7th TRUMPET of the 7th Seal (GP7): A transition from 1st to 2nd to 3rd to maturity (figuratively under the 5th SEAL, but no corresponding event), and arrival at the 1st Trumpet of the 7th Seal, and traversing of TRUMPETS 1 through 6 of the 7th Seal, then simultaneity of the 6th Seal, and the 7th TRUMPET of the 7th Seal. The Church arrives at the UTOPIA depicted in Revelation Ch. 22.*

OR

Prophecy Insight 63 *The 'Reset' Path to the 7th VIAL of the 7th Seal (RP7): A transition from 1st to 2nd to 3rd to non-arrival at maturity, with outcome the Church experiences persecution in context of the 4th SEAL, and there is a cry for vengeance in context of the 5th SEAL from the saints who are persecuted. Using those individuals who remain faithful to Christ as new nucleus for the Church, while the nations experience VIALS 1 through 6 of the 7th SEAL, there is a reset to a 1st SEAL period for the Church. For The Church (C) then, we arrive at COMMENCEMENT of SSGLAE #C2, that is, transversal of the 7 VIALS of the 7th Seal. The 7th VIAL of the 7th Seal ushers in the SPIRITUAL RESOLUTION depicted in Revelation ch. 21. For arrival at UTOPIA depicted in Revelation Ch. 22, during the follow-up SSGLAE for The Church, 'SSGLAE #C3, 1st SEAL', which of course is simultaneous with the 7th VIAL of the 7th Seal that transpires in context of SSGLAE #C2, the nations acquiesce to premising of civil laws and societal interactions on the LOVE OF GOD.*

Prophecy Insight 64 *The path that best serves the Church - the BP7 path of the SSGLAE, simultaneously is the path that best serves those who choose not to believe in Jesus Christ. The worst path for the Church (RP7) is the worst path for those who choose not to believe in Christ. The second best path for the Church (GP7) is the second best path for those who choose not to believe in Christ.*

Prophecy Insight 65 *Regardless of faith in, or absence of faith in Christ, the 'Spiritual Governance of Life and Affairs on Earth' embedded in the SSGLAE represents a GENERAL EQUILIBRIUM Solution to back dropping of time to canvas of life, with outcome everyone can focus on determination of their actions, with outcome everyone can focus on living of life to the fullest.*

Trumpets 1 through 6 of the 7th Seal

If The Nations do not acquiesce to premising of civil laws and societal interactions on the Love of God, either of the GP7 or RP7 SSGLAE PATHS are activated. Each of these paths requires transversing of TRUMPETS 1 through 7 (THE GP7 PATH), or Vials 1 through 7 (THE RP7 PATH) of the 7th SEAL. The TRUMPETS or VIALS are constituted as penalties that are imposed on The Nations for sins committed in context of the 4th SEAL, that is, in context of persecution of The Church. Note that while The Church is not persecuted in context of the GP7 PATH, this is due to unity and strength of The Church, not for lack of trying on part of The Nations. Since penalties for evil are predicated on intent and actions, as opposed to success of intent and actions, regardless of incidence of the GP7 or RP7 PATHS, The Nations transverse the TRUMPETS or VIALS of the 7th SEAL.

Prophecy Interpretation 27 TRUMPETS *1 through 7 of the 7*th SEAL, *and Vials 1 through 7 of the 7*th SEAL *are alternates, pertain, respectively to either of the GP7 or RP7 paths of the SSGLAE. I discuss the 7 VIALS and the RP7 PATH in chapter 11.*

It is very clear that the saints still are on earth during the time of the 7th SEAL, hence their sealing in context of the 3rd SEAL, prior to arrival at the 7th Seal. In respect of the fact that the saints still are on the earth, consider Revelation 6:6; 7:3; 9:4.

> And I heard a voice in the midst of the four living creatures saying, "A measure of wheat for a denary, and three measures of barley for a denary, and the oil and the wine thou mayest not injure."

> "Do not injure the land, nor the sea, nor the trees, till we may seal the servants of our God upon their foreheads."

> And it was said to them that they may not injure the grass of the earth, nor any green thing, nor any tree, but - the men only who have not the seal of God upon their foreheads.

The words in Revelation 9:4 are spoken in context of the 5th TRUMPET of the 7th Seal. Prior to blowing of the 5th TRUMPET, the third of the trees and the green grass had been burnt up under the 1st Trumpet. Grass symbolizes men, good or bad. A tree symbolizes a believer, who either may be genuine or a charlatan. With respect to characterization of grass, consider Isaiah 51:12-13; 1Peter 1:24-25; Isaiah 44:3-4.

> I, I am He that comforts you; who are you that you are afraid of man who dies, of THE SON OF MAN WHO IS MADE LIKE GRASS, and have forgotten the Lord, your Maker, who stretched out the heavens and laid the foundations of the earth, and fear continually all the day because of the fury of the oppressor, when He sets himself to destroy? And where is the fury of the oppressor?

> For "*All flesh is like grass and all it's glory like the flower of grass. The grass withers, and the flower falls, but the word of the Lord abides forever.*" That word is the good news which was preached to you.

> For I will pour water on the thirsty land, and streams on the dry ground; I will pour my Spirit upon your descendants, and my blessing on your offspring. THEY SHALL SPRING UP LIKE GRASS amid waters like willows (trees) by flowing streams.

Prophecy Insight 66 *In Scripture, grass is representative of all men - believers or unbelievers.*

Prophecy Principle 98 *The Father admonishes you not to be afraid of man, to, if need be, that is, if so guided by the Holy Spirit, be willing to lay your life down for truth, love, righteousness, and justice, for your Lord and Savior Jesus Christ. Do not be afraid of man who, after he or she has killed you, himself or herself inevitably dies.*

In Christian Scriptures, only believers - charlatan or genuine - have characterization as trees. In this respect, consider Jeremiah 17:7-8; John 15:6; Matthew 3:10; Galatians 5:22-23; and 1Peter 4:17-18.

> Blessed is the man who trusts in the Lord, whose trust is the Lord. HE IS LIKE A TREE PLANTED BY WATER, that sends out it's roots by the stream, and does not fear when heat comes, for it's leaves remain green, and is not anxious in the year of drought, for it does not cease to bear fruit.

> You did not choose me, but I chose you and appointed you that you should go and BEAR FRUIT (*only trees bear fruit*) and that your fruit should abide; so that whatever you ask the Father in my name, He may give it to you.

> Even now the axe is laid to the root of the trees; EVERY TREE THEREFORE THAT DOES NOT BEAR GOOD FRUIT (every believer who turns out to be a charlatan, a pretender, a hypocrite) is cut down and thrown into the fire.

> But *the fruit of the Spirit* is love, joy, peace, patience, kindness, goodness, faithfulness, gentleness, self control; against such there is no law.

> For the time has come for judgment to begin with the household of God; and if it begins with us, what will be the end of those who do not obey the gospel of God? And if the righteous man is scarcely saved, where will the impious and sinner appear?

Symbolism of the Trumpets 3 *Symbolically, Believers are* TREES, *the planting of the Lord. False Believers are cut down in course of judgment that begins within the household of God, are the first to be cut down under the 7th Seal. You see then that the Numerology of The Father remains validated, that the 1st* TRUMPET *symbolizes New Beginnings.*

Symbolism of the Trumpets 4 *Charlatan believers are destroyed in context of the 1ˢᵗ* TRUMPET *of the 7ᵗʰ* Seal. *This prepares The Church for perfection in context of the 7ᵗʰ* TRUMPET *of the 7ᵗʰ* Seal, *an event that triggers a new SSGLAE (SSGLAE #2) for both The Church and The Nations.*

Prophecy Interpretation 28 *By the 5ᵗʰ* TRUMPET *of the 7ᵗʰ* SEAL, *only two kinds of people are left on the earth,* THE TRULY RIGHTEOUS, *who are symbolized by '*TREES*', the planting of the Lord, as such cannot be hurt, and* EVIL MEN *(symbolized by '*GRASS*') who are not sealed with the promised Holy Spirit.*

Symbolism of the Trumpets 5 *Evil men are tortured - punished - but not killed in context of the 5ᵗʰ* TRUMPET. *The Father tortures them, because they chose deliberately to torture His saints. The length of time covered by the 5ᵗʰ* TRUMPET *is (a day for a year) 150 years. This appendage of time applies solely to the time of the Christian Byzantine Empire. More on this, in chapter 11.*

In course of the 2ⁿᵈ TRUMPET, something that looks like a mountain which is on fire is cast into the sea, resulting in the death of a third of living creatures in the sea, and loss of a third of ships. In Scripture, the 'sea' represents *'trouble'* that is foamed either by righteousness, or by the devil, and ships represent *'commerce'*. Given the TRUMPETS are instruments of The Father for judgment, *the sea represents trouble against the righteous that is quelled by The Father.* As part of the quelling of the trouble against the righteous, the world's capacity for commerce is injured via (figuratively) destruction of a third of the ships. In respect of characterization of the SEA and SHIPS, consider Isaiah 48:18; 51:15; Jeremiah 31:35; Jeremiah 51:42; Ezekiel 26:3; 27:9.

> O that thou hadst attended to my commands, then as a river is thy peace, and *thy righteousness as billows of the sea.*

> And I am Jehovah thy God, *quieting the sea, when it's billows roar,* Jehovah of Hosts is His name.

> Thus said Jehovah, Who is giving the sun for a light by day, the statutes of moon and stars for a light by night, *quieting the sea when it's billows roar,* Jehovah of Hosts is His name.

> COME UP AGAINST BABYLON HATH THE SEA, WITH A MULTITUDE OF IT'S BILLOWS IT HATH BEEN COVERED.

> Therefore, thus said the Lord Jehovah: Lo, I am against thee, O Tyre, and have caused to come up against thee many nations, as *the sea causeth it's billows to come up.*

> Elders of Gebal and it's wise men have been in thee, strengthening thy breach; all ships of the sea and their mariners, have been in thee, to trade with thy merchandise.

Symbolism of the Trumpets 6 Billows of the Sea *are representative of* Trouble. *Whenever The Righteous shine as the sun in the reign of our Lord Jesus Christ, the evidence that man can live righteously is regarded as* 'Trouble' *by those who have given their hearts over to evil.*

Spiritual Insight 85 *Persecution of the Righteous always is outcome of condemnation felt in hearts of those who love evil, condemnation that derives from provision of evidence that man can overcome sin, the devil, and the world. Hallelujah!!!*

Symbolism of the Trumpets 7 *Trouble roused against the righteous, against those who are sealed with the Holy Spirit is quelled in course of the 2nd* Trumpet. *Consistent with* Numerology of The Father, *the 2nd Trumpet reveals friendship of The Father with The Church.*

With respect to events that transpire in context of the 3rd Trumpet, '*waters*' represent people; '*rivers*' represent peace, righteousness, or life; and '*fountains*' represent life or cleansing from sin and unrighteousness. In this respect consider Revelation 17:15; John 7:38; Isaiah 66:12; Zechariah 13:1-2; Jeremiah 2:13.

> And he saith to me, "The waters that thou didst see, where the whore doth sit, are peoples, and multitudes, and nations, and tongues."

> He who is believing in me, according as the Writing said, "Rivers out of his belly shall flow of living water."

> "For thus said Jehovah: Lo, I am stretching out to her peace as a river..."

> In that day *there is a fountain opened to the house of David and to the inhabitants of Jerusalem, for sin and for impurity.* And it hath come to pass, in that day, an affirmation of Jehovah of Hosts, I cut off the names of the idols from the land, and they are not remembered any more, and also the prophets and the spirit of uncleanness I cause to pass away from the land.

> For two evils hath my people done, Me they have forsaken, a fountain of living waters, to hew out for themselves wells - broken wells, that contain not the waters.

Symbolism of the Trumpets 8 *During the blowing of the 3rd* Trumpet, peace of mind *and* love for life *are taken away from the unrighteous. Relatedly,* opportunity for cleansing from sin also is taken away. *This is done* *because, the judgment of The Father having observed, they are desirous of repentance merely for avoidance of further judgment. Because of this, the un-righteous become bitter against the righteous, and die from their bitterness, meaning bitterness produces diseases that are deadly.*

Symbolism of the Trumpets 9 *Consistent with Numerology of The Father, the 3rd TRUMPET reveals an INNER CIRCLE OF FRIENDSHIP between The Father and The Church, an INNER CIRCLE into which those who refused to repent in context of the 1st and 2nd TRUMPETS now are unable to gain access.*

Prophecy Principle 99 *The Father seeks to be worshipped in spirit and in truth, does not seek numbers primarily, seeks primarily sincerity, genuine-ness of relationship, seeks an INNER CIRCLE OF FRIENDSHIP. If people declare that they will not repent until they observe His judgments, that is, that they will seek Him only by sight, not by faith, by the time His judgments arrive, repentance will be too late, no longer will be available.*

We arrive then at consideration of the 4th Trumpet (Revelation 8:12-13). Revelation 8:12 and Genesis 1:16-17 read as follows.

> And the fourth messenger did sound, and smitten was the third of the sun, and the third of the moon, and the third of the stars, that darkened may be the third of them, and that the day may not shine - the third of it, and the night in like manner.

> And God maketh the two great luminaries, the great luminary for the rule of the day, and the small luminary - and the stars - for the rule of the night; and God giveth them in the expanse of the heavens to give light upon the earth.

The sun, moon, and stars are lights. Lights enable us to see. Consider, however, phraseology of Revelation 8:12. In standard interpretation of Eng-lish vocabulary, the emphasis is not on the sun, or moon, or stars, but on the smiting of a 3rd of the sun, or a 3rd of the moon, or a 3rd of the stars. Right-ness of this interpretation is evident in the assertion, to wit, '*that darkened may be the third of them,*' such that the day may not shine. If striking of a 3rd prevents the day from shining, clearly striking of a 3rd of the sun totally de-stroys the sun, meaning the sun itself is not focus of the symbolism. Given each of the sun, moon, and stars are created to provide light, the nouns that are qualified by 'a 3rd' are, in entirety, identical in their symbolism. So then, it is the 'smiting', and the element 3rd that are of importance.

The smiting of the 3rd of the sun, and the 3rd of the moon, and the 3rd of the stars, such that the day may not shine symbolizes introduction of incapacity for arrival at inner circles of friendship. You see then that the symbolism of 'a

3ʳᵈʾ and 'smiting' ties in perfectly with NUMEROLOGY OF THE FATHER. Given the INNER CIRCLE OF FRIENDSHIP with The Father is established in context of the 3ʳᵈ Trumpet, The Father declares that, in context of the 4ᵗʰ TRUMPET, He destroys any capacity of the nations for arrival at an inner circle of friendship that is formed around evil. You see then, that as already discussed, it is the judgments of The Father, and demonstrations of His Sovereign power that, in context of the GP7 PATH, protect the righteous from persecution. So then, those who love evil grope around in darkness, but yet are unable to form any alliances in context of their darkness.

> What sorts of activities are characteristic of those who walk in darkness?

> And have no fellowship with the unfruitful works of the darkness and rather even convict (*of sin*) - Ephesians 5:11.

> The night did advance, and the day came nigh; LET US LAY ASIDE, THEREFORE, THE WORKS OF DARKNESS, and let us put on the armor of the light; as in day-time, let us walk becomingly; not in revelings and drunkennesses, not in chamberings and lasciviousness, not in strife and emulation; but put ye on the Lord Jesus Christ, and for the flesh take no forethought - for desires (Romans 13:12-14).

Symbolism of the Trumpets 10 *The 4ᵗʰ Trumpet ushers in darkness, that is confusion and ignorance that mitigates formation of any Inner Circles of Friendship around evil.*

Symbolism of the Trumpets 11 *Consistent with* NUMEROLOGY OF THE FATHER, *the 4ᵗʰ Trumpet is associated with* GRAND JUDGMENTS, *and builds on the symbolism for the* ELEMENT *3.*

We already have arrived at understanding of events that transpire in context of the 5ᵗʰ Trumpet. Matthew 13:36-43 establishes the link with Maturity of Righteousness. I reiterate here Matthew 13:43.

> Then (*subsequent to torture of those who love evil*) shall the righteous shine forth as the sun in the reign of their Father. He who is having ears to hear - let him hear.

Symbolism of the Trumpets 12 *Torture of those who love evil in course of the 5ᵗʰ* TRUMPET *of the 7ᵗʰ Seal creates room for the saints, such that they are able to 'shine as the sun in the reign of our Lord Jesus Christ'. You see then that the 5ᵗʰ* TRUMPET *satisfies symbolism of the* ELEMENT *5 as Maturity of Righteousness in the Numerology of The Father.*

In course of the blowing of the 6th Trumpet, the four messengers who are bound at the great river Euphrates are loosed and given authority to kill a third of men over a period spanning in total, an *hour*, a *day*, a *month*, and a *year* for arrival at a total of $391\frac{1}{24}$ years *(a day for a year)*. Added to the 150 years of torture in context of the 5th Seal, we arrive at a total of $541\frac{1}{24}$ years of trouble for those who reject the Love of God as basis for interactions between men. Consistent with a taking away of opportunity for cleansing from sin in context of the 3rd Trumpet, Revelation 9:20-21 declares:

> And the rest of the men, who were not killed in these plagues, neither did reform from the works of their hands, that they may not bow before the demons, and idols, those of gold, and those of silver, and those of brass, and those of stone, and those of wood, that are neither able to see, nor to hear, nor to walk, yea they did not reform from their murders, nor from their sorceries, nor from their whoredoms, nor from their thefts.

In aggregate, it is evident that all of the Trumpets that are blown in context of the 7th Seal either enhance perfection of the Church - via elimination of false believers - or bring judgments of The Father on those who are evil and wicked.

Symbolism of the Trumpets 13 *The blowing of the 6th* TRUMPET *ushers in destruction of some of the evil men who remain. The Father having removed His Spirit from remonstration with the evil and wicked, evil or wicked men who remain alive are unable to arrive at repentance. The Father demonstrates that it is His Spirit that draws men to repentance and righteousness.*

Within context of TRUMPETS 1 through 7 of the 7th SEAL, we arrive at Grand Satisfaction of the Numerology of The Father.

Symbolism of the Trumpets 14 *A* SEAL *symbolizes* EVENTS *that transpire on earth. A* TRUMPET *symbolizes* JUDGMENTS & REWARDS *of The Father. Regardless, the* ELEMENTS *1 through 7 have exactly the same symbolism.* HALLELUJAH!!!

Symbolism of the Trumpets 15 TRUMPET *1 Commences perfection of The Church, a work that is evident in cleansing of false believers out of the Church.* TRUMPET *7 Completes perfection of The Church. Simultaneously,* TRUMPET *1 Commences extinguishment of capacity of evil doers for doing of evil. This work is Completed in context of the 7th* TRUMPET.

The 7th Trumpet of the 7th Seal

In respect of the time of the 7th Trumpet that is blown under the 7th Seal, we have the following proclamation in Revelation 10:5-7.

And the messenger whom I saw standing upon the sea, and upon the land, did lift up his hand to the heaven, and did swear in Him who doth live to the ages of the ages, who did create the heaven and the things in it, and the land and the things in it, and the sea and the things in it - that time shall not be yet, but in the days of the voice of the seventh messenger, when he may be about to sound, and the secret of God may be finished, as He did declare to His own servants, to the prophets.

And what is the secret of God?

In regard to which ye are able, reading it, to understand my knowledge in the secret of the Christ, which in other generations was not made known to the sons of men, as it was now revealed to His holy apostles and prophets in the Spirit - that the nations be fellow-heirs, and of the same body, and partakers of the promise in the Christ, through the good news (Ephesians 3:5-6).

Of which I - I did become a ministrant according to the dispensation of God, that was given to me for you, to fulfil the word of God, the secret that hath been hid from the ages and from the generations, but now was manifested to his saints, to whom God did will to make known what is the riches of the glory of this secret among the nations - which is Christ in you, the hope of glory, whom we proclaim, warning every man, and teaching every man, in all wisdom, that we may present every man perfect in Christ Jesus (Colossians 1:25-28).

In the two sets of immediately preceding Scriptures, we find validation for the premise that The Father's unyielding objective is *perfecting of His Church*, an objective that is attained to in context of the 7th TRUMPET of the 7th Seal. Importantly, we have additional confirmation that the secret relates to how exactly the nations have been incorporated into the good news of salvation in our Lord Jesus Christ. Prophecies provided Apostle John provide significant insights into how exactly the nations are incorporated into the salvation made possible in the name of our Lord and Savior, Jesus Christ.

Events that transpire in Context of the 7th TRUMPET of the 7th Seal

And the 7th messenger did sound, and there came great voices in the heaven, saying, "The kingdoms of the world did become those of our Lord and of His Christ, and He shall reign to the ages of the ages (Revelation 11:15)!"

In the words in Revelation 11:15, we find corroboration that the time of the 7th TRUMPET of the 7th Seal relates to coronation of our Lord Jesus Christ as King of kings and Lord of lords over the nations of the earth. This coronation, of course, is spiritual, is, in entirety, a spiritual event.

Prophecy Interpretation 29 *When Revelation Chs. 21 and 22 declare that the nations bring their glory into the New Jerusalem, they declare that, having acquiesced to premising of civil laws, and societal interactions on the Love of God, that the nations have acknowledged Jesus as* KING OF KINGS, *and* LORD OF LORDS.

Love of Truth 24 *What did the nations have to do in order to acknowledge Jesus as King of kings, and Lord of lords? Well, they had to treat one another right. Can it ever be rational that a society feels it is humiliating to acknowledge someone as king merely by treating one another right? Is maintenance of good behavior among subjects not the mark of a good king? Do people not do some form of obeisance to their earthly presidents and kings?*

Sin Problem 1 *Societies that are willing to honor their presidents or kings, people who are just like them, who perhaps went to school with them, who then are appointed or elected by them for their welfare, but who consider it humiliating to acknowledge Jesus via premising of civil laws and societal interactions on the Love of God are starkly irrational, non-cognitive.*

The victory of our Lord and Savior Jesus Christ having been won in context of resistance of the nations (the GP7 path), there is demand for judgment of the wicked, and reward for the righteous. With respect to evidence that judgment of those within nations who persist in evil comes afterwards, consider Revelation 11:16-19.

> And the twenty and four elders, who before God are sitting upon their thrones, did fall upon their faces, and did bow before God, saying, "We give thanks to Thee, O Lord God, the Almighty, who art, and who wast, and who art coming, because thou hast taken thy great power and didst reign; and the nations were angry, and Thine anger did come, and the time of the dead, to be judged, and to give the reward to Thy servants, to the prophets, and to the saints, and to those fearing Thy name, to the small and to the great, and to destroy those who are destroying the land. And opened was the sanctuary of God in the heaven, and there was seen the ark of His covenant in His sanctuary, and there did come lightnings, and voices, and thunders, and an earthquake, and great hail."

Note how Revelation 11:18 declares that *"Thine anger did come"*, and how Revelation 11:19 declares *"there did come lightnings, and voices, and thunders, and an earthquake, and great hail"*. A juxtaposition of these descriptions with Revelation 6:12-17, which provides a description of events that transpire under the 6th Seal provides confirmation that events which transpire under the 6th Seal occur in simultaneity with the 7th Trumpet of the 7th Seal. In this respect, Revelation 6:16 highlights the *'anger of the Lamb'*, and Revelation 6:12-13 highlight the *earthquake and the hail*. With respect to all of the other seals (1 through 6), only in context of the 6th Seal do we have *'anger of the Lamb'*, and *'a great earthquake'*.

It is straightforward and clear from the preceding that the mystery having been finished in context of the 7th Trumpet of the 7th Seal, all that is left is giving of rewards to the righteous, and judgment of the wicked. Rewards for the righteous, and execution of judgment on the wicked occur in context of the 6th Seal, and in simultaneity with the 7th Trumpet of the 7th Seal.

Prophecy Principle 100 *We arrive at confirmation of simultaneity of the 6th* Seal, *and the 7th Trumpet of the 7th Seal.*

The Sixth Seal

Consistent with all of the foregoing, the cry from men at onset of the 6th Seal is as follows:

> And the kings of the earth, and the great men, and the rich, and the chiefs of thousands, and the mighty, and every servant, and every freeman, hid themselves in the dens, and in the rocks of the mountains, and they say to the mountains and to the rocks, Fall upon us, and hide us from the face of Him who is sitting upon the throne, and from the anger of the Lamb, because come did the great day of His anger, and who is able to stand?

Clearly, the 6th Seal ushers in the final judgments of our Lord Jesus Christ. What is of importance is the fact that the judgments of The Father are executed, and because the capacity for repentance already is removed from those who love evil, they lack capacity for repentance (Revelation 16:11, 21).

The SSGLAE: A Wrap Up

As the Holy Spirit has made abundantly clear in this chapter, the Seal System for Governing of Life and Affairs on Earth (SSGLAE) revolves around several integrated agenda. The overarching agenda that NEVER will be compromised, that must be achieved is perfection of the body of Christ, is arrival of the Church at a *'perfect man'*, at *'a measure of the stature of the fullness of our Lord Jesus Christ'*. The Father has designed that this objective be achieved in context of existence of Nations. Given our Lord Jesus Christ already has won authority over the earth from the devil, any resistance to premising of civil laws, and societal interactions on the LOVE OF CHRIST ultimately is futile, for our Lord Jesus must actualize the victory that already is won. We have then progression through all of the 7 Seals that make up the SSGLAE for arrival at the victory of our Lord and Savior Jesus Christ.

Hallelujah!!!

Symbolism of the Trumpets 16 *If the nations will put selfishness, greed, avarice aside, they recognize that the best choice for the whole earth is choice of the BP7 equilibrium.*

Whenever governments intervene in private sectors with monies or capital, this because otherwise society crumbles, for preservation of objectivity or neutrality, the government does not accept VOTING SHARES in private concerns, rather obtains what can be referred to as a GOLDEN CLAUSE. The GOLDEN CLAUSE provides governments with the right, under certain pre-specified conditions, to determine the course of affairs within private concerns in which, for ultimate good of society, it has invested some capital.

Prophecy Principle 101 *With The Father having the* GOLDEN CLAUSE, *the SSGLAE is prime evidence that The Father indeed has given man choice, and that while He holds the* GOLDEN CLAUSE *(trump card) for intervention in affairs that transpire on earth, evolution of history on earth primarily is consequence of man's choices.*

Prophecy Principle 102 *The die is cast. Our Lord Jesus Christ either will reign over the earth as King of kings, and Lord of lords, or eventually life will cease on earth. The Book of Revelation is not about timing of cessation of life on earth, rather is about rewards of choosing to live by the Love of Christ, and consequences and punishments of the deliberate decision to refuse to live by the Love of Christ.*

Prophecy Principle 103 *If life will end on earth, this because The Father perceives neither of the Church nor the Nations ever will conform with His will, the ending will be sudden, unanticipated, and naturally, fatal.*

The Things That Are 61 *The SSGLAE is wisdom, love, mercy, and righteousness of a Good, Good, Father.*

CHAPTER 10

Why the Revelations?

From credible traditions of the Christian Church, we know that Apostle John was the last of the original 12 Apostles to go on to be with the Lord. Polycarp (*69-155 AD*), a 2nd generation Apostle, writes about Apostle John. It is believed that it was Apostles *John* and *Polycarp* who compiled the Books of the Old and New Testament as core canon for guidance of future generations in transversing of their faith in Jesus Christ. With all of the other of the original apostles dead, and The Church not having, contrary to initial beliefs of the original 12 Apostles, taken over the world, prior to his visions, it is not inconceivable that Apostle John was dealing with some perplexing thoughts.

Love of Truth 25 *Perplexing thoughts are not doubts. Whenever outcomes seem not to coincide with expectations, perplexing thoughts are characteristic of people whose faith are rooted in the expectation that while faith is metaphysical, it simultaneously must, in context of it's metaphysics, be rational.*

So then, enter our Lord Jesus Christ with words of encouragement, first and foremost for Apostle John himself, then for his contemporaries, and then for us, who through him would obtain encouragement of our faith from the Scriptures. In my book, TRUE SANCTIFICATION, I demonstrate that the purpose of PROPHECY, hence the purpose of PROPHETS, is provision of Encouragement to the saints, to fellow believers in the name of Jesus Christ.

Prophecy Principle 104 *The overarching purpose of the revelations provided Apostle John by our Lord Jesus Christ is encouragement and knowledge for his faith, for faith of his contemporaries, and faith of future generations of those who repose faith in the name of Jesus Christ.*

Prophecy Principle 105 *In what follows,* Apostle John *is a 'shadow' of you and I, a shadow for every person who has faith in the name of Jesus Christ.*

First, In *Revelation ch. 1,* our Lord Jesus Christ reminds Apostle John, and every believer in the name of Jesus Christ that we are not to think of Him as a man, that we are to realize He is a spiritual being, that He neither is White, nor Black, that He is the risen Lord. It was in context of the revelations that Apostle John arrived at the insight that Jesus is The Word of God (Revelation 19:13) who put on likeness of man for purpose of our salvation from sin, for purpose of our reconciliation with both Himself, and His Father (2Corinthians 5:19). The imagery of Jesus as having the 7 Spirits of God (Revelation 3:1; 5:6), and *seated in His Father's throne* (Revelation 3:21; 21:5-7), reinforce to Apostle John spiritual equality of Jesus with His Father.

Love of Truth 26 *Jesus lived as a man for only three and a half years, this, while He was on earth in likeness of a man. If you think of Jesus as a man, you do not relate with Him in eternity, you relate with Him in context of His sojourn on earth. But His sojourn on earth was so you could relate with Him in eternity (John 3:16; 17:3), meaning when you attempt to relate to Him as a man, you live in error, are unable to arrive at relationship with Him. So then, Apostle Paul reiterates that Jesus is not a man, that He is a* Life Giving Spirit *(1Corinthians 15:45) and that if you seek to know Christ, you no longer consider Him a man (2Corinthians 5:16).*

Love of Truth 27 *Jesus cannot be 'the one who was, who is, and who is to come' (Revelation 1:4,8; 4:8), yet be a man.*

Regardless of His spiritual equality with The Father (John 10:30; 1John 5:7; Hebrews 1:8; Philippians 2:6), our Lord Jesus Christ reveals to Apostle John that, The Father having *'giving birth to Him'*, not via His incarnation on earth, but in eternity as The Word of God, that, in terms of spiritual authority, He receives everything from The Father (Revelation 1:1-2). While this *giving birth* is an attempt, at describing in human language an event that is beyond our imagination, well before the concept of *cell division* was identified by science in *1879* by Walther Flemming, a 2nd generation Apostle, Tertullian (*155-240 AD*) described this giving birth (*I paraphrase*) as:

> 'The Father mestasizing Himself for production of a Son, for re-production of Himself as The 'Word of God".

Love of Truth 28 *A God who can create the cell, a biological entity that mestasizes, such that it perfectly reproduces itself, must Himself have capacity for self mestasization.*

Love of Truth 29 *Long before science discovered cell division, The Father already alluded to us that He has capacity for mestasizing Himself.*

In *Revelation ch. 1*, The Lord Jesus Christ goes on to introduce the revelations to come as consisting of three parts: THE MESSAGES TO THE SEVEN CHURCHES; THE THINGS THAT ARE; and THE THINGS TO COME.

Prophetic Encouragement 1 *In the declaration to Apostle John that there are* THINGS TO COME, *there is clear affirmation that everything was going according to plan, that The promise of The Father had not failed. So now, Apostle John is able to perk up, is encouraged, knows there is a reason for what otherwise might seem a disappointment. As he would find out, any sense of having arrived at a disappointment was rooted, in entirety, in ignorance.*

> Prophetic Encouragement of the Messages to the 7 Churches

The messages to the Seven Churches are domiciled in *Revelation chs. 2 and 3*. In the messages, Apostle John arrives at the realization that the *Second Coming* of Christ is not quite as imminent as the Apostles hitherto had assumed. First, the Lord Jesus Christ makes him realize that the Church of that time, the Church in Ephesus had lost her first love, and that there would be six more churches to come thereafter. So then, Apostle John arrives at the realization that the promise of the Lord Jesus Christ while He was on earth has not failed, and that The Father has a plan for The Church, a plan that reunites Heaven and earth in Christ (Ephesians 1:9-10; Revelation chs. 21 & 22).

In addition to the realization that there was time yet to come, and events yet to transpire in context of history of The Church, in the declaration of arrival of His Presence on earth in context of the last Church (the *Church in Laodicea*), The Church that does not end, Apostle John arrives at an important realization, that the promise of The PRESENCE OF CHRIST still yet was in the future. In the declaration to him in Revelation 22:20 that His Second Coming still yet was in the future, as such not the same as arrival of His Presence, our Lord Jesus Christ made Apostle John realize that His reign on earth is designed, first and foremost to be spiritual, and that His Second Coming is a conditional event, is conditioned on failure of the Church, or the Nations.

Prophetic Encouragement 2 *Apostle John realizes that the reign of Jesus Christ is, first and foremost spiritual, and that our Lord Jesus Christ seeks that we make the most of our time on earth, that we live life, and live it abundantly (John 10:10).*

Love of Truth 30 *The reign of our Lord Jesus Christ is designed to be spiritual, because God has given the earth to men (Psalms 115:16), not to Himself.*

As Creator, however, He retains RIGHT OF JUDGMENT, RIGHT *that now is entrusted to our Lord Jesus Christ (John 5:22).*

Prophetic Encouragement 3 *Apostle John arrives at the realization that the Second Coming of Christ will be outcome of failure of man at arriving at rationality, for the* LOVE OF GOD *is the only rubric for each of civil laws, and societal interactions that is fully, and in entirety, rational. He is not excited at possibility of failure of man, but yet rejoices in the spiritual reality that were The Nations to refuse to live at peace with The Church, that The Church will be rescued, that The Church will not be subjected to futility.*

Prophetic Encouragement of The Things That Are

WE HAVE ESTABLISHED THAT 'The Things That Are' ARE INCLUSIVE OF:

✠ Reality of our presence in the throne room of The Father, that is, in the presence of The Father and The Word.

✠ The spiritual reality that it is our good works that bring glory to The Father in every moment of time.

✠ That there exist two classes of humans in presence of The Father, NEOPHYTES who are in presence of Christ, but who have yet to actualize that spiritual reality in their own lives, as such have yet to arrive at The Presence of Christ; and POWERS, believers in Christ who have arrived at actualization of reality of The Presence of Christ.

✠ That The Spiritual System for Governance of Life and Affairs on Earth (SSGLAE) is 'A THING THAT IS' in perpetuity.

Prophetic Encouragement 4 *In the delineation to Apostle John of 'The Things That Are', Apostle John arrives at reiteration from The Lord Jesus Christ that His reign on earth first, and foremost is spiritual, and that there is a plan for governance of welfare of The Church, a plan, which ensures The Church does not become prey to evil on earth. Perhaps even more importantly, whenever The Church and The Nations are spiritually rational, the plan incorporates partnerships between The Church and The Nations. Hallelujah!!!*

Prophetic Encouragement 5 *In the delineation of 'The Things That Are', our Lord Jesus Christ enables Apostle John arrive at an important inference, which is, success of the Good News of Jesus Christ is not predicated on conversion of all men to faith in Jesus Christ, and is not predicated on, in fact, eschews coincidence of Church and State.*

In the delineation of 'The Things That Are', our Lord Jesus Christ reiterates to Apostle John the truth that he teaches so well in his epistle titled, THE EPISTLE OF 1JOHN, which is, in His mercy, The Father has declared that all who choose Love as Way of Life qualify for revelations of Christ. Simultaneously, LOVE AS WAY OF LIFE is evidence that a person truly has arrived at acknowledgement of revelations of Christ. So then, until a person rejects LOVE AS WAY OF LIFE, he or she has opportunity to enter into the New Jerusalem. If a person gains entry into the New Jerusalem via profession of Love as Way of Life, he or she has opportunity for fellowship of the Holy Spirit, but does not gain immediate access to Father and Son. When he or she proves that he or she can obey the Holy Spirit, then he or she gains access to The Son, and to The Father. A person who gains access to fellowship of the Holy Spirit, but goes on to repugn Love as Way of Life is expelled from the New Jerusalem, and per inspiration of the Holy Spirit (Hebrews 6:4-8), and declaration of our Lord Jesus Christ (Matthew 12:32; Mark 3:29; Luke 12:10) is impossible to restore.

Prophetic Word 3 *Let us be careful not to grieve the Holy Spirit, not to insist on validity of any hatreds whatsoever. Our Lord Jesus Christ is very clear; in presence of as little as one cherished hatred (1John 3:15; 4:7), you are unable to gain access into the New Jerusalem.*

Prophetic Word 4 *It is evident that there is not any person who desires to maintain* RACISM, NEPOTISM, TRIBALISM, *or* ETHNIC SUPERIORITY *in either of civil laws, or societal interactions that will gain access into the New Jerusalem. The person who realizes error of such feelings, however, but who has been prepared by his or her upbringing or environment to entertain such feelings, who then proceeds into the New Jerusalem via* DESIRE FOR LOVE AS WAY OF LIFE, *will find there is healing for all such feelings in Christ.*

Prophetic Word 5 *The SSGLAE, 'a thing that is', reveals* RIGHTEOUSNESS, WISDOM, JUSTICE, *and* LOVE *of The Father and The Son. The path (choice) - the Love of God as basis for interactions between believers - that best benefits The Church, also is the path (choice) - the Love of God as basis for civil laws, and societal interactions - that best benefits The Nations.*

Additional Evidence for Eternal Essence of the SSGLAE

In what follows, I show that the SSGLAE was demonstrated in the ministry of Christ. The ministry of Christ represented a NEW BEGINNING (NB), for Jesus was the Lamb, the first Lamb sent for salvation of the world from sin (John 1:29,36). The 12 disciples of our Lord Jesus Christ represented His COMPANIONSHIP OF PURPOSE (CP). His INNER CIRCLE OF FRIENDSHIP (CF) consisted of *Peter, James,* and *John.* The disciples having not been perfected prior to His crucifixion, Maturity of Righteousness (MR) was not attained, with outcome the disciples could not pray with Christ (Mark 14:37), with outcome our Lord Jesus Christ, who alone was perfected (Hebrews 7:28; 4:15), experienced persecution in context of a Grand Judgment (GJ) of the Jews. In this respect, subsequent to his denial of Christ (Luke 22:61), Apostle Peter found repentance (Luke 22:62), was restored (John 21:15-17), and was commanded to tend to affairs of his Lord Jesus Christ (John 21:19). Upon resurrection of our Lord Jesus Christ, since our Lord Jesus Christ had become the firstborn from the dead, the pre-eminent one among many brethren (Colossians 1:18; Revelation 1:5), another New Beginning was instituted, with outcome we arrive at Commencement of SSGLAE #C2. With their faith in Christ now restored, the Apostles could be perfected, and their attainments to CP and CF, arrived at in context of SSGLAE #C1, carried over to SSGLAE #C2. Having, however, not arrived at MR in context of SSGLAE #C1, obedience to Christ to remain in Jerusalem until the infilling of the Holy Spirit became test of Maturity of Righteousness. The disciples having passed the test, arrived at MR, as such, received the baptism of the Holy Spirit, with outcome MR was achieved. Given man was not to be penalized for crucifixion of Christ, and given no other nation apart from the Jewish Nation had opportunity for acquiescing to the Love of God, Pentecost became a rallying point for a New Beginning. We arrive then at Commencement of SSGLAE #C3. Given The Nations did not acquiesce to the Love of God in context of preaching of the Good News of Christ, there was progression to a 2nd Seal period. In what follows, I focus exclusively on progression of SSGLAE #C3 in context of The Church. So then, The Church could be said to arrive at CP in identification of Deacons (Acts 6:1-7), and in the decision to hold all things in common, such that none had too much, and none too little (Acts 4:32-37). An Inner Circle of Friendship would arrive in context of admission of Apostle Paul, and deserving believing Gentiles into ranks of Apostles. In presence of non-acquiesce of The Nations to the Love of God, but yet arrival at MR by the Church - an inference evident in the words of our Lord Jesus Christ, which declare that the Church that preceded the Church in Ephesus, The Church of the original 12 Apostles was perfected (Revelation 2:4), there was not a grand persecution of The Church, rather, the blood of the Apostles served as seed for growth of the Good News of Jesus Christ. In the Epistles to the *Ephesians*, *Colossians*, and *1Thessalonians* from Apostle Paul, we find additional evidence that the Church arrived at MR, as such went on to be perfected.

Love of Truth 31 *The SSGLAE is* 'a thing that is', 'a thing that always has been', *but now is revealed to those who have faith in Jesus Christ, and to The Nations, this so importance of choices that relate to adoption or rejection of the Love of God as basis for interactions in Church, as basis for civil laws, and basis for societal interactions for future outcomes - consequences, and* *either of punishments or rewards - is known to all, so none can declare they are unaware of consequences of their choices.*

The SSGLAE existed in context of the Old Covenant with Israel. For illustration, and with David as the first king chosen by The Father Himself, I provide evidence for governance of the SSGLAE in life and affairs of descendants of Jacob.

With institution of David as the first king chosen by The Father, we arrive at an NB (1Samuel 13:13-14; 15:28). At recognition of David by Judah as king (2Samuel 2:1-4), we arrive at CP. Recognition of David as king by the rest of the 10 tribes of Israel, a matter that took 7 years (2Samuel 5:1-5), enabled arrival at CF. So then, now opportunity for arrival at MR. But then, crucially, David goes on to disobey God in two major instances, that is, the numbering of men of fighting age (*2Samuel ch. 24*), and the murder of Uriah (*2 Samuel chs. 11 & 12*). So then, David was unable to usher the 12 tribes of Israel into MATURITY OF RIGHTEOUSNESS. In respect of the damage that David did to the objective of arrival at MR, David remonstrates with himself in presence of God in 2Samuel 24:10, and The Father, through Prophet Nathan declares as follows in 2Samuel 12:9,13-14.

> And David's heart condemned him after he had numbered the people. So David said to the Lord, "I have sinned greatly in what I have done; but now, I pray, O Lord, take away the iniquity of your servant, for I have done very foolishly."

> WHY HAVE YOU DESPISED THE COMMANDMENT OF THE LORD, TO DO EVIL IN HIS SIGHT? You have killed Uriah the Hittite with the sword; you have taken his wife to be your wife, and have killed him with the sword of the people of Ammon. So David said to Nathan, "I have sinned against the Lord." And Nathan said to David, "The Lord also has put away your sin; you shall not die." However, BECAUSE BY THIS DEED YOU HAVE GIVEN GREAT OCCASION FOR THE ENEMIES OF THE LORD TO BLASPHEME, the child also who is born to you shall surely die.

Historical Spiritual Nugget 22 *David's sin against Uriah was a personal sin, a deliberate choice that attempted to assert that a king can do whatever he or she wants. The Father demonstrated to David that, in His Reign, there is not any such thing as a king who can do whatever he or she wants. In The Reign of Christ, only those who are perfected with respect to the LOVE OF GOD are advanced to kingship.*

Historical Spiritual Nugget 23 *The Holy Spirit makes clear that the decision to number the fighting men of Israel, a decision contrary to explicit commands* *from The Father, was outcome of the fact that Israel was refusing to practice the* LOVE OF GOD *towards one another, so then, The Father removed His spiritual protection from the people, with outcome a spirit from their adversary, the devil, was able to gain influence over their king, as such move their king to act against welfare of the people (2Samuel 24:1). It was the mercy of Jehovah that limited deaths among the people to no more than 70,000 men.*

The Church, as represented by the 12 tribes, not having arrived at MR, and the nations around them not having been at fault, there was a reset to a 1ˢᵗ SEAL period, with outcome there was arrival at an NB in context of SSGLAE #C2. Enter then Solomon. Solomon starts off well, chooses wisdom as companion for arrival at CP consisting of himself, wisdom, and the people (*1Kings 3:5-15*). In the partnership with Hiram, king of Tyre for building of the temple, Solomon arrived at CF that was rooted in wisdom and good purpose (*1Kings 5:1-18;7:13,40,45; 9:11-27; 10:11,22*). So then, now time for arrival at MR. But then, Solomon begins to worship idols (*1Kings 11:1-8*), with outcome there is not arrival at MR. So then, there is reset to an NB in context of SSGLAE #C3, an SSGLAE rooted in break up of the 12 tribes into THE NATION OF JUDAH, consisting of two tribes, *Judah* and *Simeon*; and THE NATION OF ISRAEL, consisting of the remainder 10 tribes (1Kings 11:11-13). Note that due to the fact that the *tribe of Simeon* was small, and lived in midst of the tribe of Judah, that is, was, by design of The Father, surrounded by the *tribe of Judah*, eventually the tribe of Simeon lost it's identity, with outcome both tribes simply came to be known as JUDAH. I could go on, and on, but it already is unambiguously clear that The SSGLAE always has been, is, and will remain for as long as life remains on earth.

> Did this cycle of SSGLAE ever terminate, ever arrive at a terminal conclusion, ever arrive at a final SSGLAE?

THE ANSWER OF COURSE IS A RESOUNDING YES!!!

Eventually, the entire NATION OF ISRAEL was taken captive to Assyria, where they all likely died during destruction of Nineveh in 612 BC. In this respect, and for avoidance of doubt, the Scriptures state as follows.

> Now the king of Assyria went throughout all the land, and went up to Samaria (capital of Israel) and besieged it for three years. In the ninth year of Hoshea, the king of Assyria took Samaria and carried Israel (the entire nation) away to Assyria, and placed them in Halah and by the Habor, the River of Gozan, and in the cities of the Medes (2Kings 17:5-6).

> THEREFORE THE LORD WAS VERY ANGRY WITH ISRAEL, AND RE-MOVED THEM FROM HIS SIGHT; THERE WAS NONE LEFT BUT THE TRIBE OF JUDAH ALONE (2Kings 17:18).

With respect to the NATION OF JUDAH, the rending of the veil between the *Holy Place* and *Most Holy Place* of the Jewish Sanctuary at timing of death of Jesus Christ signified an end to characterization of the JEWISH NATION as God's people, as God's family. Jews could still be part of God's people, but only via profession of faith in the name of Jesus Christ. In this respect, the Scriptures declare as follows.

> For whoever does the will of My (*Jesus speaking*) Father in heaven is My brother, sister, and mother (Matthew 12:50).

> And Jesus having uttered a loud cry, yielded the spirit, and THE VEIL OF THE SANCTUARY WAS RENT IN TWO, from top to bottom (Mark 15:37-38).

> But even to this day, when Moses is read, a veil lies on their heart. NEVERTHELESS WHEN ONE TURNS TO THE LORD, THE VEIL IS TAKEN AWAY. Now the Lord is the Spirit; and where the Spirit of the Lord is, there is liberty. But we all, with unveiled face, beholding as in a mirror the glory of the Lord, are being transformed into the same image from glory to glory, just as by the Spirit of the Lord (2Corinthians 3:15-18).

> But you (believers in Christ) are a chosen race, a royal priesthood, a holy nation, God's own people, that you may declare the wonderful deeds of Him who called you out of darkness into His marvelous light. ONCE YOU WERE NO PEOPLE BUT NOW YOU ARE GOD'S PEOPLE; once you had not received mercy but now you have received mercy (1Peter 2:9-10).

You see then that there arrived, in eventuality a terminal SSGLAE for each of the NATION OF ISRAEL, and NATION OF JUDAH. The terminal SSGLAE for Judah (the Jews) ushered in the first SSGLAE for The Church, the SSGLAE that commenced with baptism of the Holy Spirit at Pentecost. Note that the SSGLAE that commenced with ministry of our Lord Jesus Christ, that is, with ministry of John the Baptist was for Jesus, not for The Church. This the reason that, inclusive of His disciples, and the Jewish Nation, ALL OF WHOM FAILED, all were forgiven, all were covered by the perfect life and sacrifice of Christ. In the evidence for existence of terminal SSGLAEs in prior history, there is assurance that The Father will not allow an indefinite number of SSGLAE, that if either of The Church or The Nations stubbornly refuse to cooperate with The Father, that there will be an end to life on earth.

> The only difference between operation of the SSGLAE prior to, and in context of the Church in Laodicea?

Prophecy Insight 67 *While prior to the time of the* CHURCH IN LAODICEA, *the SSGLAE functioned in context of time, that is was bounded by specifications of time, in these days, in the days of the* CHURCH IN LAODICEA, *the SSGLAE is no longer bounded by time, functions only on basis of consequences of man's choices, and righteous interventions of The Father.*

Prophecy Insight 68 *Prior to advent of our Lord Jesus Christ, the SSGLAE was bounded by time because our Lord Jesus Christ had to be born on earth in fullness of time (Galatians 4:4-5). Prior to the time of the* CHURCH IN LAODICEA, *the SSGLAE was bounded by time, because arrival of the* PRESENCE OF CHRIST *had to emerge in fullness of time (Revelation 3:20). These two events having already occurred in time, there do not exist any longer any boundaries of time in governance of the SSGLAE.*

Prophetic Encouragement of The Things That Are To Come

The 'things that are to come' must be interpreted in relation to location of Apostle John at about *100 AD*, and the fact that all of the evidences for the SSGLAE that transpired in context of the time of the CHURCH IN EPHESUS and the CHURCH IN SMYRNA (*100-324 AD*); the time of the CHRISTIAN BYZANTINE EMPIRE (*325-1453 AD*); and the time of the CHURCH IN LAODICEA (*1454 AD* to ∞) all still were in the future.

Prophetic Encouragement 6 *All timed events that are alluded to in the Book of Revelation relate, relative to the time of Apostle John, to* 'THE THINGS THAT ARE TO COME'. *These timed events are introduced primarily for benefit of those of us who live in these times, those of us who now can look back and find evidence that the SSGLAE has worked exactly as instituted by The Father.*

Concluding Words

In the next chapter, I turn attention to a discussion of some of the timed events that are introduced in context of the SSGLAE. Given all timed events, that is, all of the 'THINGS THAT ARE TO COME', subsist in context of the SSGLAE, that is, 'THE THINGS THAT ARE', they all are no more than specific examples, equivalently, instances of governance of the SSGLAE.

> For whatever was written in former days was written for our instruction, that by steadfastness and by the encouragement of the Scriptures we might have hope (Romans 15:4).

We have need of hope because, thus far The Nations have not shown any sign that they are willing to premise civil laws and societal instructions on the Love of God. The assurance from The Father is that the choice of hatred shall be more painful for them, than it is for those who love the name of

Jesus Christ. In the final analysis, given triggering of the Second Coming of Christ produces salvation for the righteous, and destruction for those who choose evil, in terms of final outcomes, it continues to be wise to hate evil, and to love righteousness.

And to Him who is able to guard you not stumbling, and to set you in the presence of His glory unblemished, in gladness, to the only wise God our Savior, is glory and greatness, power and authority, both now and to all the ages! Amen (Jude 1:25).

Even so, Yes, come Lord Jesus.

CHAPTER 11

Fitting in Some of the Details

In terms of chapters (*chs.*) of the Book of Revelation, we have covered, in entirety, *chs.* 1 through 6, *chs.* 8 through 9, and the sealing of the 144,000 in Revelation 7:1-8 (a little bit more to say about this in the next chapter). While we have touched on some matters in Revelation *chs.* 21 & 22, we have yet to embark on an exhaustive and detailed exposition of the two chapters. All of the spiritual insights that are domiciled in *Chapters 1 through 9* of this book have some measure of spiritual significance. Most importantly, however, all of the discussions enable establishment of a 'BIG PICTURE' understanding of essence of the Revelations that are entrusted to Apostle John by our Lord Jesus Christ.

Prophetic Lessons 23 *All of the discussions in Chapters 1 through 9 of this book are sufficient for establishment of a* BIG PICTURE *for all of the revelations that are entrusted to Apostle John by our Lord and Savior Jesus Christ.*

Whenever an ARTIST attempts to create something new, he or she commences with an *outline*, that is, a BIG PICTURE, then begins to fill in the details. If the painting consists of the head of a woman, he or she first outlines the head, then fills in the eyes and everything else. Prior to commencement of a work of sculpture, a SCULPTOR first determines exactly how large a block of stone or iron is required for completion of the job, that is, commences with a BIG PICTURE. Whenever a MATHEMATICIAN seeks to build a new theoretical model, *absent building of a* BIG PICTURE, the model inherently lacks any structure, as such is unable to generate any details.

Love of Truth 32 *If there were not any science to works of art, or sculptures, we would not be able to identify great artists and sculptors. It is precisely* *because he introduced* A NEW SCIENCE *in formulation of his paintings that* MICHELANGELO *is considered one of the greatest artists of all time.*

What I have done in this book, which is, develop a BIG PICTURE of essence of the revelations that were entrusted to Apostle John, is a normatively desirable feature of innovative scientific work that is well done, of innovative work, which conforms with principles of science. Introduction of principles of science is evident in development of the Numerology of The Father, and imposition of the scientific principle that while spiritual revelations are *metaphysical* in nature, it is desirable that the *metaphysics* satisfy an important principle of rationality, that the metaphysics be INTERNALLY CONSISTENT.

Love of Truth 33 *Ask yourself, do you know of any interpretations of the Book of Revelation that harmonize interpretation of the* MESSAGES TO THE SEVEN CHURCHES *with the 7* SEALS OF REVELATION CHS. 6 & 7, *then with the 7* TRUMPETS OF THE 7th SEAL? *This book provides you with such a harmonization. This is one important illustration of uniquely realized internal consistency of the exposition of the Book of Revelation that you find in this Book.*

Love of Truth 34 *Remember, any interpretation of the Book of Revelation, which asserts that the revelations relate to the* SECOND COMING OF JESUS CHRIST *does not pass the scientific test of* INTERNAL CONSISTENCY *that is required for arrival at a credible exposition of revelations entrusted to Apostle John by The Lord Jesus Christ.*

I assure you that you are reading the *first and only* exposition of the Book of Revelation that is characterized by internal consistency, which is validated by all other 65 Books of the Bible. Note that, as I already have well demonstrated, internal consistency does not derive merely from consistency of interpretation of the visions, but from imposition of principles of interpretation that are derived, in entirety, from other 65 Books of the Bible.

Love of Truth 35 *The Big Picture that I have introduced in chapters 1 through 9 of this book provides a credible foundation for interpretation of* PROPHETIC EVENTS *that are illustrations of the SSGLAE, and/or* DETAILS OF PROPHECIES *that are provided in revelations entrusted to Apostle John by our Lord and Savior Jesus Christ. In absence of such a Big Picture, credibility of any interpretations of the Book of Revelation are difficult to discern, are difficult to ascertain.*

What then is this BIG PICTURE at which we have arrived?

✠ THE MESSAGES TO THE SEVEN CHURCHES signify a time period during which The Father, Son, and Holy Spirit apply their time to demonstration of necessity of rooting access to the grace of God in Jesus and Jesus alone, and necessity of stipulation of the grace of God as operating at level of individuals. So then, the PRESENCE OF CHRIST arrives on earth at commencement of the time of the Church in Laodicea; that is, about *1454 AD*, at timing of availability of the Bible to individuals, this made possible by wisdom from The Father that induced invention of the Gutenberg Press. The Church then is a composite of individuals who each have a faith-love relationship with Jesus Christ. Note this is not a reversible process. The Church cannot bring together *300* people who lack relationship with Christ, then declare that merely because they showed up at a congregational meeting, that they now are members of the body of Christ. For our sakes, The Father has provided some time based events that transpired in course of the time of the seven churches as empirical evidence for veracity of governance of the SSGLAE.

✠ The Spiritual System for Governance of Life & Affairs on Earth (SSGLAE) is, since the time of the Church in Laodicea, and with exception of Sovereign interventions on part of The Father, the only arbiter of evolution of life and events on face of the earth. So then, while there was a god of the age that ended with the Church in Philadelphia, the devil (2Corinthians 4:4), he having been defeated squarely and fairly on his own ground by our Lord Jesus Christ, has had authority over life and affairs of earth wrested out of his control. If man continues to submit to gods that have been dethroned, who to those of us who believe in Christ are no gods (Galatians 4:8), for to us there only is one God, Father of us all, Creator of Heaven and Earth (1Corinthians 8:4-6), the SSGLAE still will rule over life and affairs on earth. If man submits to The Father, chooses love as way of life (the Nations), or willingly chooses to be perfected in love (the Church), the SSGLAE still will rule over life and affairs on earth. THIS OUGHT TO BE A RATHER SOBERING REALIZATION. In presence of empirical evidence for veracity of the SSGLAE, in respect of which I already have provided plenty, and still yet will provide more, do we not arrive at what we refer to as a *no-brainer* decision? WHY SUBMIT TO THE DEVIL IF HE CAN'T PROTECT YOU FROM JUDGMENTS OF THE FATHER?

✠ While *Seals* symbolize EVENTS on earth, and *Trumpets*, JUDGMENTS & REWARDS of The Father, the ELEMENTS 1 through 7 have exactly the same interpretation in context of either of Seals, or Trumpets. We arrive then at validation of the NUMEROLOGY OF THE FATHER, which as you well know, we derived, in entirety, from outside of the Book of

Revelation, that is, from rest *65 Books* of the Bible. As you soon shall see, this consistency extends to the 7 VIALS of the 7th Seal.

Prophetic Lessons 24 *The Gospel operates at level of individuals, not at level of Church Organizations. This is an immutable spiritual principle, a principle whose actualization took more than a Millenium of work from The Father, Son, and Holy Spirit. Whoever attempts to specify that his or her church organization is identifier of people who know Christ is a 'MAN OF SIN' (2Thessalonians 2:1-12), a man who seeks to exalt his or her throne above that of God Himself.*

Prophetic Lessons 25 *That all believers in Christ are in the* PRESENCE OF CHRIST *is reality of our Lord Jesus Christ and spiritual benefit for all who choose to have faith in the name of Jesus Christ. Being in the Presence of Christ becomes spiritual reality of an individual believer whenever he or she actualizes, equivalently, acquires the reality of the Presence of Christ.*

Prophetic Lessons 26 *The threshold to be met, and the timing of the* SPIRITUAL REVELATION OF CHRIST *that triggers actualization of the Presence of Christ are, in entirety, secrets of Father, Son, and Holy Spirit. One thing, however, is sure. If you will unflinchingly commit yourself to the way of love, and not excuse any incapacity at love; if you always will submit any incapacity at love for cleansing in the blood of Jesus Christ, such that there is not in you any room for hatred, malice, spite, envy, jealousy, sinful pride, air of superiority etc., the timing of actualization of the Presence of Christ in your life surely will arrive.*

Prophetic Lessons 27 *The SSGLAE is instituted for your spiritual welfare and mine.*

Prophetic Lessons 28 *For* POWERS FOR CHRIST, *New Heavens, New Earth, and the New Jerusalem, equivalently, the Presence of Christ, always are spiritual reality. It is this spiritual reality that* CONNECTS *all 7* SEALS *of the SSGLAE.*

Prophetic Lessons 29 *Whether* NEW HEAVENS, NEW EARTH, *and the* NEW JERUSALEM *become spiritual reality for the Church, and the Nations is function of their institutional responses to The Father.*

Having established the Big Picture, and INTERNAL CONSISTENCY of the Big Picture, we arrive at an important question namely:

> Can all of the rest of the Book of Revelation be jointed together, such that they produce a *harmonious mosaic*, which fits *asymptotically perfectly* into the Big Picture already established in *chapters 1 through 9*?

This chapter goes about providing an answer to this question, an answer whose credibility you will be able to infer for yourself. Fitting of these specific events in context of the SSGLAE builds confidence, provides additional corroboration for veracity of the SSGLAE, as won for us by our Lord Jesus Christ, and instituted by The Father for our benefit.

What then is left to explain of the Book of Revelation?

In what follows, I fit events in Revelation 10; the *Two Witnesses* of Revelation 11; the *Woman* of Revelation 12; Revelation 14:14-20 (encapsulates a more detailed discussion of Revelation *ch.* 7); the *Two Beasts* of Revelation 13; the *Three Angels* of Revelation 14; the *great prostitute* and the *beast* of Revelation 17; the *destruction of Babylon* in Revelation 18; events depicted in Revelation 19; The *7 Vials* of Revelation 15 & 16; and events that have to do with *binding and loosing of the devil* in Revelation 20:1-15 into the SSGLAE. I defer the detailed and rigorous exposition of Revelation *chs. 21 & 22* until *Chapters 16 and 17*.

11.1   Events of Revelation 10

In *Revelation 10:1-4*, 7 THUNDERS speak, at which point Apostle John seeks to write words that had been spoken. But the STRONG MESSENGER who had his right foot on the sea, and his left foot on the land forbade writing of words spoken by the 7 THUNDERS. The reason for the forbidding is straight-forward. In order for The Father to checkmate evil people who, on basis of an understanding of prophecies in Book of Revelation, attempt to con both God and the Church, some knowledge has to be preserved unknown to man, has to be known only to Father, Son, Holy Spirit, and messengers who have been allowed into such secrets. Whenever evil people attempt to game God and the Church, this because they think they know what comes next, there always will be a surprise from The Father that catches them unawares. This is the reason the Scriptures declare that:

> Who can search out our crimes? We have thought out a cunningly conceived plot. For the inward mind and heart of a man are deep. But God will shoot His arrow at them; they will be wounded suddenly. Because of their tongue He will bring them to ruin; all who see them will wag their heads. Then all men will fear; they will tell what God has wrought, and ponder what He has done. Let the righteous rejoice in the Lord, and take refuge in Him! Let all the upright in heart glory (Psalm 64:6-10)!

> He (*God*) frustrates the devices of the crafty, so that their hands cannot carry out their plans. He catches the wise in their own

craftiness, and the counsel of the cunning comes quickly upon them. They meet with darkness in the daytime, and grope at noon-time as in the night. But He saves the needy from the sword, from the mouth of the mighty, and from their hand. So the poor have hope, and injustice shuts her mouth (Job 5:12-16).

When people say, "There is peace and security," then sudden destruction will come upon them as travail comes upon a woman with child, and there will be no escape. But you are not in dark-ness, brethren, for that day to surprise you like a thief. For you are all sons of light and sons of the day; we are not of the night or of darkness (1Thessalonians 5:3-5).

Prophecy Principle 106 *If evil men think that an understanding of prophecy will enable them con The Father and the body of Christ, they are in for an extremely rude shock.*

Prophecy Principle 107 *If you and I trust in the Lord Jesus Christ, and walk in the light as He is in the light, injustice shuts her mouth, and we triumph in Christ over all schemes of evil men, in Jesus Name. Amen.*

In *Revelation 10:5-7*, the messenger declares that the mystery of God - how it is the nations are part of Christ, and the perfecting of the saints - will be fulfilled in context of the 7th Trumpet of the 7th Seal. Apostle John was told to eat the LITTLE SCROLL in the hands of the messenger (not the Scroll of Revelation *ch.* 5, whose 7 SEALS are opened by our Lord Jesus Christ), which would be sweet in his mouth, but bitter in his stomach. He then was told that he must again prophesy about many peoples, and nations, and tongues, and kings.

Prophecy Interpretation 30 *The* LITTLE SCROLL *is a miniature of the Scroll whose 7* SEALS *are opened by our Lord Jesus Christ. The* LITTLE SCROLL *can, for lack of better terminology, be referred to as the 'experiment' of convergence of Church and State that was essence of the Christian Byzantine Empire.*

Prophecy Interpretation 31 *Since the* SCROLL *of Revelation ch. 5 commences with a 1st* SEAL, *any miniaturization of the Scroll for arrival at a* LITTLE SCROLL *must embed clear evidence for Incidence of a 1st* SEAL, *that is, evidence of a Power for Christ who goes forth conquering, and to conquer.*

A Word on Experiments

History is full of experiments that originated directly from The Father. History further is full of experiments that are proposed by men, and adopted by The Father. The Father's decision to make a nation for Himself through descendants of Abraham can be referred to as an experiment. Consider, however, the outcome of the experiment, which is, a people - Jews - known all over the world for intelligence and wealth.

Prophetic Lessons 30 *Would you hate to be part of an experiment in which, if you exhibited good character, you would become known for* INTELLIGENCE *and* WEALTH?

Prophetic Lessons 31 *Would you hate to be part of an experiment in which, the originator of the experiment does not consider you an input into His experiment, rather formulates the experiment for your benefit, such that you are both participant in, and beneficiary of the good that is outcome of the experiment?*

Prophetic Lessons 32 *The only reason that The Father can be characterized as running* 'EXPERIMENTS' *is, because He designs* GOOD PURPOSES *for each and every person who responds to His Love. Only in the sense that He, of necessity, has to* CHART THE PATHS *that enable achievement of such purpose, can The Father be deemed to be running* EXPERIMENTS. EVERY PURPOSE (EXPERIMENT) THAT IS CHARTED BY THE FATHER IS A GOOD PURPOSE.

It is important to discuss the word 'EXPERIMENT' because, in a spiritual sense, the word now is abused in society. You may not be aware, but there are experiments going on all around you. In fact, it has gotten to the point that if *firms, countries,* or *factions* within societies are not running some experiment, that they are in danger of being deemed irrelevant. In this respect, increasingly, people refer to the United States of America as an experiment. This has included the current Chief Justice of the United States of America, *Justice Roberts.* If you doubt, listen to his acceptance speech at his inauguration as Chief Justice of the Supreme Court of the United States of America. The Chief Justice MIGHT BE IGNORANT OF SPIRITUAL IMPORT OF HIS WORDS; it is normative, however, that to characterize a country, which already exists, as an 'EXPERIMENT' is a declaration of evil.

Love of Truth 36 *An experiment is an experiment (a statement of a 'truism') only if the objective to be achieved does not as yet exist. In presence of stated normative, a country that already exists cannot itself be characterized as an experiment. Only objectives that are pursued within a country that already exists can have characterization as experiments.*

Love of Truth 37 *If a country, which already exists, has characterization as* AN EXPERIMENT, *rather unwisely there is a declaration that success of the country, equivalently continuity of* EXISTENCE, PROGRESS, WELFARE, *and* ECONOMIC DEVELOPMENT *of the country is in doubt. This is a declaration of faithlessness, and a declaration of faithlessness is evil (Romans 14:23).*

Whatever does not proceed out of faith is sin (Romans 14:23).

For He who would love life and see good days, let him refrain his tongue from evil, and his lips from speaking deceit. Let him turn away from evil and do good; let him seek peace and pursue it (1Peter 3:10-11).

If you are not aware of it, be aware now that you are surrounded by EXPERIMENTS, that the desire to run EXPERIMENTS has become ubiquitous in those who have either of money or power in society. The problem with this status quo resides in the spiritual reality that, in a world which seeks to assert that there does not exist any objective truth, some, or many of the experiments are lacking in either of moral or spiritual boundaries. Some of the experiments are, in fact, seeds of evil, equivalently, seeds of the devil.

When a society or country chooses to conduct an experiment that is designed for impoverishing those in the bottom cadres of income in society, this is evil masquerading as an experiment.

When an experiment is designed for expropriation of some individual, or segment of society, this is evil masquerading as an experiment.

Love of Truth 38 *An experiment whose objective is evil does not qualify for characterization as an experiment, has characterization only as an exercise in evil.*

Experiments in False Humility

An experiment, of which I have become acutely aware in the United States of America, and other parts of the world, is an experiment in FALSE HUMILITY. In context of the experiment, people with money or power, and those in lower income strata of incomes in society, conspire against a person with a professional profile, a person who either does his or her professional job well, or who actually is brilliant at his or her professional job. The demand for false humility asserts that if such a person is humble, that he or she will be willing to do any sort of job that is available for maintenance of life and maintenance of his or her family.

Love of Truth 39 *This is not an experiment in humility, this is an exercise in evil.*

Love of Truth 40 *It never can be righteous for a person who has not violated any of the ethics of his or her profession to lose his or her opportunity for earning income in context of the profession.*

If a person has, post High School, spent 11 years studying to become a Medical Doctor, if such a person has not violated any of the ethics of the profession, how exactly is it humility for such a person to act as if he or she is not qualified to be a Medical Doctor? If a person has spent 11 years studying to become a highly specialized Engineer, if such a person is not guilty of any professional misconduct, how exactly is it humility for such a person to act as if he or she is not qualified to be a highly specialized Engineer?

Love of Truth 41 *Christian Scriptures are very clear, the demand that people act as if they are* NOT CONFIDENT, *the demand that they* DRESS DOWDY, *that they* LOOK UNKEPT, *the demand that they* DROOP THEIR SHOULDERS *and* APPEAR NOT TO HAVE SELF ESTEEM *all are rooted in evil, in demand for false humility, in the demand that people act as if they are less than others.*

Love of Truth 42 *Any society, which demands that some segments of the society act as if they are less than others rejects the Love of God, the Love of Christ, as basis for civil laws, and societal interactions.*

> Let no one cheat you of your reward, taking delight in false humility and worship of angels (messengers), intruding into the things he hath not seen, being vainly puffed up by the mind of his flesh. These things indeed have an appearance of wisdom in SELF-IMPOSED RELIGION, FALSE HUMILITY, and NEGLECT OF THE BODY, but are of no value against the indulgence of the flesh (Colossians 2:18,23).

> Righteousness exalts a nation, but sin is a reproach to any people (Proverbs 14:34).

The Things That Are 62 *The Father's declaration is, rejection of equality of fellow men* ALWAYS *will be a recipe for reproach in each and every nation. The Father has set in spiritual law the principle that, no matter what a country does, if it rejects equality of fellow men, it cannot achieve any exaltation, only will be characterized by reproach.*

The Things That Are 63 *Only countries, which practice righteousness - equality of all men - experience exaltation.*

Look all around you, all around the world, do you see any country, which does not practice equality of all men achieving exaltation? The USA used to be such a country, now all it suffers is reproach. The USA cannot produce well rounded leaders, has not been able to do so for upwards of 19 years. Currently, the USA spends time talking about how it's elections are being subverted by foreign countries. A country, which is supposed to be a technological leader of the world spends odes of time lamenting on the world stage about how it's elections are being subverted by other countries?

Is this not a paradox of reproach?

Historical Spiritual Nugget 24 *In the elections that led to choice of* GEORGE W. BUSH *as President of the USA, George Bush was known only for being Evangelical, Al Gore was known only for being a Technocrat. Neither was well rounded. Neither had the well roundedness of a George Bush, Snr., or a Bill Clinton. Barack Obama became President of the USA not on basis of well roundedness, but on basis of hope that something different and fresh (Black, Intellectual, and Soft Spoken) could make a difference. It is matter of fact that hope did not quite pan out. His competition, John McCain did not become well rounded until the elections already were over. One must celebrate, however, arrival of John McCain at the compassion that, were it to have been in his possession much earlier, perhaps could have made him a President of the USA.*

When it comes to economic prosperity, the USA has been heading in an adverse direction for many years. We hear stories, and see pictures of people living on the streets all over the USA, but particularly in California, yet nothing concrete seems to happen in response to evidence that people willing and able to work, that people who in fact have jobs only are able to afford to live in tents on the streets.

All we hear about the USA today is reproach.

CONSIDER RUSSIA. Because the country went from a Communism that never generated any real equality, to a Socialist Capitalism that did not generate any improvements to equality, Russia to a large extent has become irrelevant, that is, sidelined, in context of stature of countries in the world. While it was the right thing to do, via it's intervention in Syria, Russia sought to reinject itself onto the world stage, sought to generate it's own relevance. The action was right, and has been somewhat successful. The simultaneous objective of reinjection of relevance among comity of nations has, however, failed.

The other candidates for possibility of evidence for exaltation?

Britain has lost relevance. If it is indeed true that it was immigration issues that largely determined the BREXIT DECISION, as opposed to anger that all of the wealth generated by the country's notoriety for financial services was not dissipating into the rest of the country, Britain just might have shot itself in the proverbial foot and mouth. NONE OF THE COUNTRIES OF WESTERN EUROPE HAVE ANY STATURE ON THE WORLD STAGE. It seemed for a while that Germany would seize the world stage, but then a couple of knife attacks stifled the heart of the country.

WHY DID THE KNIFE ATTACKS WORK TO INDUCE GERMANY OFF THE WORLD STAGE?

It is not the Love of God to welcome people into your country, then absent doing of anything wrong or illegal, refuse to allow them opportunity to stay. While violence against society for wrong actions of governments never are righteous, when a person treks his or her way all the way from Syria to Germany, is welcomed with open arms into the country, then is told that he or she does not qualify to stay, there can be despair that can run such a person momentarily insane.

Historical Spiritual Nugget 25 *If you do not want all to enter, regulate entry. If you open your arms wide, do not close them in anticipation that a person will choose to harm society. The Father never ever practices anticipation in judgment. People are judged only by the course of their life, and their current actions, not by whatever it seems they may be capable of in future.*

When a country cannot see itself justified in context of actions that lead to internal turmoil, it is best to step off the world stage.

The Things That Are 64 *For ensuring that it was not He who induced them to evil, prior to choice of evil, The Father ensures anyone who seems to have tendency towards evil is loved just as much as those who show tendency towards what is good. This is exactly the reason The Father allowed Israel to be ruled first by Saul, then by David. Irrespective of access to the Holy Spirit by both men (1Samuel 10:10; 1Samuel 16:13), Saul chose evil, David chose righteousness.*

The Things That Are 65 *It is evil to not love, then to declare that he or she who was not loved, turned out to be evil.*

The Things That Are 66 *If you see yourself as having tendency towards evil, but in presence of blessings from God begin to think it is the case that you deceive God, know that the blessings you received, irrespective of which you went on to do evil to others, are the instruments of judgment in the hands of The Father, the instruments, which declare to all in the spiritual realm that you are a lover of evil.*

What then about China? China, the communist country that is attempting to lift it's people out of poverty, which is attempting to provide farmers in villages with decent standards of living, is the only country, other than the USA, which seems to be straddling the world stage. The USA continues to straddle only on basis of past glory. At the current time, in presence of some evidence that China is not committed in entirety to the Love of God, to equality of all men, China it would seem has begun to lose ground on the world stage.

The Things That Are 67 *The Father of our Lord Jesus Christ is not a respecter of persons. If a communist regime demonstrates love for it's people, treats it's people as equals, it will experience exaltation.*

The Things That Are 68 *The Father is not a politician, as such does not care about any label that is imposed on a government or country. The Father only cares about character of a government or country, about the extent to which a country bases civil laws, and societal interactions on equality of all men, on demonstrations of the Love of God.*

In actual fact, experiments that demand false humility are rooted in evil of covetousness from those in lower income strata of society, and desire for control of those in lower income strata of society by the already rich and powerful. If those in lower income strata of society clamor for those in the professions to be laid low, it is guaranteed that they in the lower strata cannot simultaneously seek to be lifted up in society.

The Things That Are 69 *In a society, it either is the case that the society attempts to uplift everyone, or it seeks to humiliate all. This is true because whenever a society attempts to humiliate any segment of itself, The Father ensures that those who seek to humiliate are, themselves, humiliated.*

In presence of attempts at humbling those in the professions via collusions that strip them of opportunity for making a living, welfare of those in lower strata of income in society only gets worse. You see then that whenever those in lower income strata of society clamor for humiliation of those in the professions, the rich and powerful accede only because this makes it possible for them to destroy the middle class, as such destroy the Upper Middle Class. So then, those in lower income strata lose opportunity to progress to MIDDLE CLASS, or UPPER MIDDLE CLASS, in essence shoot themselves in the proverbial foot and mouth.

Love of Truth 43 *If you are in a lower income strata of society, but desire to be in the professions, the only righteous path is acquisition of necessary qualifications for enhancement of your welfare. Covetousness of achievements or attainments of others is a sin, a sin that eats out the heart and soul of a nation.*

Love of Truth 44 *The assumption that those in the* MIDDLE CLASS, *or* UPPER MIDDLE CLASS *all are frauds is an exercise in covetousness, is an exercise in evil. If a person in the* MIDDLE CLASS, *or* UPPER MIDDLE CLASS *is guilty of any evil, the appropriate domicile for resolution is* COURTS OF LAW.

Love of Truth 45 *Any justice that is not pursued in the open, with clear statements of wrongdoing, and with opportunity for the accused to defend themselves out in the open, are exercises in evil. Societies that allow such exercises in evil to occur will, alongside perpetrators of such evil, be punished by The Lord Jesus Christ.*

✠ What makes for a Righteous Experiment?

♣ An objective that is RIGHTEOUS, that is, an objective which can be characterized as a LOVE PROJECT. Provision of *exercise aficionados* with the *iPod* by Apple Inc. was a Love Project, a solution to the problem of not been able to have a variety of their best music available to them, this while they walked, jogged, or cycled outdoors.

♣ People who become part of the Experiment are not inputs, rather are PARTICIPANTS who stand to benefit from success of the experiment.

♣ Within context of *experiments that subsist in the workspace*, advance preparation, such that, upon winding down of an experiment that has run it's course, Participants have opportunity to, with some preparation, move seamlessly into new opportunities that already are arriving. Remember, POWERS FOR CHRIST develop capacity for *Conception* of love projects that are to be *formulated* and *implemented* in future.

Why would the Little Scroll be sweet in the mouth, yet bitter in the stomach?

An important misconception of the original 12 Apostles, a misconception that remained even after ascension of our Lord Jesus Christ, is the misconception that part of the objective of the reign of Jesus Christ is establishment of a Physical Kingdom on earth. In this respect, with full recognition of the fact that the exchange to follow between Jesus and the Apostles transpired subsequent to His resurrection, consider the following words in Acts 1:4-8.

And being assembled together with them, He commanded them not to depart from Jerusalem, but to wait for the Promise of The Father, which, He said, "you have heard from Me; for John truly baptized with water, but you shall be baptized with the Holy Spirit not many days from now." Therefore, when they had come together, they asked Him, saying, "Lord, will You at this time (*at timing of baptism of The Holy Spirit*) restore the kingdom (*reign*) to Israel?" And He said to them, "IT IS NOT FOR YOU TO KNOW TIMES OR SEASONS WHICH THE FATHER HAS PUT IN HIS OWN AUTHORITY. But you shall receive power when the Holy Spirit has come upon you; and you shall be witnesses of Me in Jerusalem, and in all Judea and Samaria, and to the end of the earth."

Prophecy Principle 108 *If The Lord Jesus Christ says those who have faith in Him are not to seek to know times or seasons, which The Father has put in His own authority, He cannot at the same time provide a prophecy whose objective is knowing of exactly those times or seasons.*

Prophecy Principle 109 *In Acts 1:4-8, we have additional confirmation for the truth that I have espoused since the Preface of this book, which is, the Book of Revelation is not, and per the words of Jesus Christ Himself, cannot be about timing of His Second Coming.*

Prophetic Lessons 33 *Rather than worry about times and seasons that The Father holds in His own authority, our Lord Jesus Christ commands that you focus on how to proceed from a Neophyte to a Power for God; it is Powers for Christ who are best able to witness to reality of faith in the Name of Jesus Christ. Amen. Hallelujah!!!*

While the apostles received correction from The Lord Jesus Christ, given Jesus did not, in His response, rule out restoration of the reign of the heavens to nation of Israel, they, it would seem continued to believe such a restoration resided somewhere in the future. In the characterization of Christians as PILGRIMS OF THE DISPERSION by Apostle Peter in 1Peter 1:1-2, there seems to be expectation of a nation that would be symbolic of spiritual Israel. With full knowledge that this was not the plan of Himself and His Father, but with the understanding that the disciples would not understand (John 16:12), The Father and The Son decided to demonstrate to the disciples, once and for all, dangers inherent in coalescing of Church and State into one entity.

Historical Spiritual Nugget 26 *The experiment that serves to demonstrate, for all time, dangers of coalescing of Church and State into one entity is the* CHRISTIAN BYZANTINE EMPIRE, *the* EASTERN ROMAN EMPIRE.

But did The Father do any evil, or plan any evil for the Christian Byzantine Empire?

Absolutely Not!!!

THE CHRISTIAN BYZANTINE EMPIRE IS CONSIDERED ONE OF THE GREATEST CIVILIZATIONS THAT THE EARTH EVER HAS WITNESSED. If The Father informed you ahead of time of such an experiment, would you choose not to be part of it? Would you decline such an offer? If you would be considered a *serf* everywhere else in the world, that is, a person farming lands and keeping less than 50% of the produce for himself or herself, but you had opportunity to be a *free small farmer* in the BYZANTINE EMPIRE, keeping 100% of whatever you produce, would you decline participation in the experiment?

But whenever there was war, did the free small farmer not have to provide one member of his family to fight in the king's army, you counter?

WELL THEN, TRUE AS THAT MAY BE, THE REAL QUESTION TO ASK IS:

Was it only free small farmers who died during a war? If Nobles also die during wars, which is fact, is the free small farmer treated any worse than Nobles of the land?

By the way, whenever there was war, the *serf* who keeps less then 50% of what he produces also still is drafted by force to fight for the king.

Love of Truth 46 *No one in their right mind would decline participation in an experiment designed to produce one of the greatest civilizations of all time, an experiment within which those who have the least have enough, are as free as the rich, and are 'MORE FREE' than anywhere else in the world.*

Love of Truth 47 *If those who die during fighting of wars equally are inclusive of free small farmers and Nobles, the free small farmer is not treated any worse than the rich Noble. In ancient times, children of Nobles were raised to consider serving in armies of their kings the most noble of efforts to which they could apply themselves.*

Remember our prior discussions about the Christian Byzantine Empire, how the Empire sought to validate itself via seeking of recapture of the earthly Jerusalem? In the push for recapture of the earthly Jerusalem, the Christian Byzantine Empire sought to reassure itself that it was representative of God's Church on earth.

BUT COULD THIS BE TRUE? NATURALLY NOT.

"*By this, all we know you are my disciples, if you have love one for another*"

is declaration of our Lord and Savior Jesus Christ. In the focus on earthly grandeur, and worldly reassurances, the Christian Byzantine Empire lost it's way, engaged in a rivalry with what had become the second most prevalent religion on earth, Islam. We already have discussed how this was a mistake, because The Father demands that we not engage in any rivalries whatsoever, not with siblings, friends, enemies, parents, not with anyone.

The danger inherent in coalescing of Church and State into one entity?

Prophecy Insight 69 *An earthly kingdom typically seeks earthly grandeur for self validation, and can be seized by an usurper. This state of affairs actually transpired in the Christian Byzantine Empire. Abuses of free small farmers, and loss of spiritual perspective commenced about 1056 AD, only after the reigning house (*THE MACEDONIAN DYNASTY*), which was steeped in Christian traditions, could not produce an heir for the throne.*

Prophecy Insight 70 *The* REIGN OF OUR LORD JESUS CHRIST, *a reign that, in entirety, is spiritual thrives on* SPIRITUAL GRANDEUR, *cannot ever be seized by usurpers, for only those who attain to* POWERS FOR CHRIST, *only those who earn The Father's trust ever make it into the reign of Jesus Christ.*

Prophecy Insight 71 *The sweetness of the* LITTLE SCROLL *in Apostle John's mouth is symbolic of commencement of the* CHRISTIAN BYZANTINE EMPIRE, *an event the apostles desired in their hearts. The bitterness of the* LITTLE SCROLL *in Apostle John's stomach is symbolic of ultimate failure of the Christian Byzantine Empire to abide by principles of Jesus Christ.*

In Revelation 10:11, the messenger who had held the LITTLE SCROLL in his hand declares as follows to Apostle John.

> And he saith to me, It behoveth thee again to prophesy about peoples, and nations, and tongues, and kings - many.

In the words above, the messenger informs Apostle John that time would proceed subsequent to demise of the CHRISTIAN BYZANTINE EMPIRE, that there yet would be many peoples, and nations, and tongues, and kingdoms. Since that time (about 100 AD), the world has discovered tongues, such as *Yoruba, Spanish, Portuguese, Mexican* etc. Since that time, the world has witnessed formation of new and perhaps, formerly great nations, such as the UNITED STATES OF AMERICA, BRITAIN, SPAIN, FRANCE, NETHERLANDS etc. Since that time, we have had many famous kings, such as RICHARD THE LIONHEART (*1157-1199 AD*), and KING JAMES I (*1603-1625 AD*) who provided funding for production of the *King James Version (KJV)* of the Bible etc., rule over regions of the world, such as ENGLAND.

Prophecy Insight 72 *In the SSGLAE, Apostle John prophesies about tongues, people, nations, and kings that would arrive in time. This is evident in the fact that whether righteous, or evil, responses of all tongues, people, nations, or kings are accounted for in formulation of the SSGLAE.*

Prophetic Word 6 *If nations start off with civil laws that have the Love of our Lord Jesus Christ as their foundation, then move away from that foundation, if they think the glory that accrued from the earlier righteous decision will remain, they kid themselves. If any country pays lip service to the Love of*

God as foundation for civil laws, and societal interactions, it will not escape destruction. If 'WE BELIEVE ALL MEN ARE CREATED EQUAL' becomes mere talk, mere whimsy, becomes an anachronism, the United States of America toys with destruction of it's foundations.

11.2 Revelation 11: The Two Witnesses

In Revelation 11:1, Apostle John is instructed to '*measure the sanctuary of God, and the altar, and those worshipping in it*'. To measure is to assess, meaning arrival at a Grand Judgment of the SANCTUARY, the ALTAR, and THOSE WORSHIPING in the sanctuary. We know from inspiration of the Holy Spirit that Apostle John had right of an assessor. This is evident in the following words by Apostle Paul in 1Corinthians 6:2-3.

> Have ye not known that the saints shall judge the world? and if by you the world is judged, are ye unworthy of the smaller judgments? have ye not known that we shall judge messengers? why not then the things of this life?

In the preceding chapter, we discussed how it is persecution of the church is predicated on failure of the Church to remain in unity, to arrive at a perfect man, with outcome there is arrival at an APOSTATE CHURCH, or on resurgence of the Church back to it's former love for arrival at a RESURGENT CHURCH, but with nations refusing to acquiesce civil laws to the Love of God. Within context of a RESURGENT CHURCH, in 303 AD, the first *official* persecution of the Church commenced under Emperor Diocletian.

Prophecy Interpretation 32 *Persecution is one instrument via which The Father generates truths that enable assessments of genuineness of faith within His Church within context of either of an APOSTATE, or RESURGENT Church.*

In this respect, consider these words by our Lord Jesus Christ in Matthew 13:20-21.

> As for what is sown on rocky ground, this is he who hears the word and immediately receives it with joy; yet he has not root in himself, but endures for a while, and when tribulation or persecution arises on account of the word, immediately he falls away.

With *303 AD* as commencement of measuring of genuineness of faith within the Church, *42* months translates into *1,260* prophetic days for arrival at a time period *1,260* years. We have then that the *1,260* years for which the two witnesses of Revelation 11:2-3 are to prophesy ends in *1563* AD. First, however, note that Apostle John is not to measure the court outside of the sanctuary because it was given to the nations.

What does it mean that the court outside of the sanctuary is given to the nations?

In the sanctuary system, only the priests enter into the Holy Place, or the Most Holy Place, with outcome, they only have opportunity for experiencing and acquiring the glory of our Lord Jesus Christ. In His death on the cross, our Lord Jesus Christ established you and I as priests unto Him, meaning we now, all of us are able to enter into the Holy Place, and the Most Holy Place (1Peter 2:9). The Holy Place consists of the BREAD (not Christ Himself, but the body of Christ, see John 6:25-58) and the OIL (the Holy Spirit). We have then that if you want to experience the fullness of the Godhead - Father, Son, and Holy Spirit - you must transition from the Holy Place into the Most Holy Place. The Most Holy Place consists of the mercy seat, which rests on the ark of the covenant, as such is symbolic of the throne room of God. The Scriptural Evidence?

> But you are a chosen race, a ROYAL PRIESTHOOD, a holy nation, God's own people, that you may declare the wonderful deeds of Him who called you out darkness into His marvelous light (1Peter 2:9).

> And I saw, and lo, in the midst of the throne, and of the four living creatures, and in the midst of the elders, a Lamb hath stood as it had been slain, having seven horns and seven eyes, which are the Seven Spirits of God, which are sent to all the earth (Revelation 5:6).

> And He (God) who searches the hearts of men knows what is the mind of the Spirit, because the Spirit intercedes for the saints according to the will of God (Romans 8:27).

> But as it is written, "What no eye has seen, nor ear heard, nor the heart of man conceived, what God has prepared for those who love Him," God has revealed to us through the Spirit. For the Spirit searches everything, even the depths of God. For what person knows a man's thoughts except the spirit of the man which is in him? So also no one comprehends the thoughts of God except the Spirit of God (1Corinthians 2:9-11).

Love of Truth 48 *Scriptures are unequivocal, while the Holy Spirit is one essence with The Father and The Word (1John 5:7), the Holy Spirit is not The Father or The Word.*

If you ever are to enter into the Most Holy Place, you first must pass through and experience the Holy Place. This means you must experience the body of Christ, and the Holy Spirit. Remember how the body of Christ is united in the same *Right Recognition of Christ (RRC)*? Well, arrival at the same *RRC* demands arrival at common interpretation of Scriptures in so far as they relate to the truth of God. In this respect, the words of Jesus in John 14:6; 6:63 apply.

> Jesus said to him, I am the way, the truth, and the life. No one comes to The Father except through me (John 14:6).

> The spirit it is that is giving life; the flesh doth not profit anything; the sayings that I speak to you are spirit, and they are life (John 6:63).

Prophetic Lessons 34 *With symbolism of the sanctuary at play, it is normative that if you are to pass through the Holy Place, and have opportunity for fellowship of The Father and The Word, that you either know Scriptures for yourself, or are taught it within the body of Christ, with outcome you arrive at a Right Recognition of Christ.*

Prophetic Lessons 35 THE GOAL OF ALL OF CHRISTIAN SCRIPTURES CAN BE SUMMED UP AS GOD'S REVELATION OF THE *Right Recognition of Christ.*

If you are to enter into fellowship with The Father and The Son, you must press on, must choose to enter with boldness into the Most Holy Place for experiencing of fellowship with The Father and The Son.

The Condition for entry into the Most Holy Place?

Prophetic Lessons 36 *Well, your willingness to, and exertion of effort towards growth in your capacity for love. Remember, the growth comes from The Father as reward for your willingness and genuineness of effort.* YOU ARE NOT TO DREAM UP OF CHALLENGES OF LOVE FOR YOURSELF. *Any challenges of love that are of The Father will come to you naturally in course of your normal daily living.*

Prophetic Lessons 37 *You are saved by virtue of your entrance into the Holy Place. For arrival at revelational knowledge of Father and Son, however, you must proceed into the Most Holy Place.*

For reiteration, the way into the Most Holy Place?

FAITH THAT WORKS BY LOVE (GALATIANS 6:6).

> Jesus answered him, "If a man loves me, he will keep my word, and my Father will love him, and we will come to him and make our home with him (John 14:23).

He who has my commandments and keeps them, he it is who loves me; and he who loves me will be loved by my Father, and I will love him and manifest myself to Him (John 14:21).

A new commandment I give to you, that you love one another; even as I have loved you, that you also love one another. By this all mean will know that you are my disciples if you have love for one another (John 13:34-35).

Be watchful (*be thankful to God in all things*), stand firm in your faith, be courageous, be strong, *let* ALL *that you do be done in love* (1Corinthians 16:13-14).

Spiritual Insight 86 *If you want to experience eternal life here on earth, you trust our Lord Jesus Christ that* LOVE NEVER FAILS, *and no matter what comes your way, commit yourself to continuance in the* LOVE OF GOD. *When The Father, and our Lord Jesus Christ become convinced of your commitment to the* LOVE OF GOD, THEY MANIFEST TO YOU AND REVEAL THEMSELVES TO YOU IN YOUR SPIRIT, *with outcome your spirit arrives at fellowship, not only with the Holy Spirit, but with The Father, and The Son. You begin then to experience the* PEACE OF GOD THAT SURPASSES UNDERSTANDING, *and* INEXPRESSIBLE BOTTOMLESS JOY *that only are outcome of actualization of the Presence of Christ in your spirit.*

Spiritual Insight 87 *If you want to find out more about Faith that works by Love, and how to progress from* NEOPHYTE *to* POWER FOR CHRIST, *pick up copies of my books,* In Jesus Name, *and 'True Sanctification'. Amen.*

The nations who are in the outer courts are people who subscribe to morality, but for whatever reason do not arrive at faith in Jesus Christ. We already have discussed The Father's provision for salvation of such people. For ease of remembrance, these are not people who, regardless of conviction in their hearts, reject Jesus as Lord and Savior. Rather, these are people who, for one reason or the other, never were presented with conviction of heart in respect of the person and work of our Lord Jesus Christ. These people are in the outer court because all they know is their conscience. Whenever their conscience has pricked them, they have been willing to acknowledge their sins, being willing to reform (turn away) from their sins, and being willing to choose righteous courses of actions. Since these people are not part of the Church, and since judgment was starting in the Church, these people were not to be measured.

The Scriptural Evidence?

All who have sinned without the law will also perish without the law, and all who have sinned under the law will be judged by the law (Romans 2:12).

When Gentiles who have not the law do by nature what the law requires, they are a law to themselves, even though they do not have the law. They show that what the law requires is written on their hearts while their conscience also bears witness and their conflicting thoughts accuse or perhaps excuse them on that day when, according to my gospel, God judges the secrets of men by Christ Jesus (Romans 2:14-16).

For the time has come for judgment to begin with the household of God; and if it begins with us, what will be the end of those who do not obey the gospel of God (1Peter 4:17).

Prophecy Insight 73 *The nations consist of people who live and are judged in relation to eternal principles of right and wrong - thou shall give honor to whom honor is due; thou shall not steal; thou shall not commit murder; thou shall not commit adultery; thou shall not bear false witness against thy neighbor; thou shall not covet your neighbors' spouse or property. These persons were not at any time during their earthly lives convicted of the person and work of our Lord Jesus Christ by the Holy Spirit.*

Prophecy Insight 74 *We already have discussed how it is that identification of the righteous, that is, judgment of The Church (3rd* SEAL *of the SSGLAE) precedes Grand Judgment of those who love and do evil (4th* SEAL *of the SSGLAE).*

The two witnesses prophesy for 1,260 years, which as we have seen spans the period, *303 to 1563 AD.* The year *303 AD* marks onset of the first official persecution of Christians. The year *1563 AD*? The year during which all of the heresies of apostate Papal Rome were reiterated as Church Canon. By this time, the Church of The Reformation already was in full swing. Up until *1563 AD*, persecution of reformers and their adherents had yet to become official policy of Papal Rome. Subsequent to *1563 AD*, however, persecution of reformers and their adherents became official policy of papal Rome.

With respect to identity of the witnesses, Revelation 11:4 declares that the two witnesses are LAMP-STANDS. From Revelation *chs. 1 through 3*, we already know that *lamp-stands* are representative of Churches. In the imagery that lamp-stands are the same as olives, we arrive at the inference that olives also are symbolic of Churches.

Prophecy Interpretation 33 *It is unequivocal that the* TWO WITNESSES *of Revelation ch. 11 are* CHURCHES. *Olives have the same symbolism as lamp-stands, are symbolic of Churches.*

What then did the two witnesses prophesy? The two witnesses prophesied that Papal Rome is an apostate Church. The CHURCH OF THE BYZANTINE EMPIRE established this witness in *867 AD*. In context of the CHURCH OF THE REFORMATION, Martin Luther and other reformers established the same witness in the first half of the *16th Century AD*. Rightness of this witness was verified via reiteration of heresies of papal Rome, such as the doctrine of the Eucharist, selling of indulgences, and worship of idols in *1563 AD*.

> The Church of the Byzantine Empire declared, in writing, that the pope does not have authority over believers, and that obeisance to statues is idolatry.

> In the doctrinal evidence that INDULGENCES ARE UNSCRIPTURAL, the Church of the Reformation prophesied that papal Rome cared more about money than about truth.

Once the witness was completed, the Church of the Byzantine Empire DIED IN THE EAST, as did the Church of the Reformation IN WESTERN EUROPE. Both Churches are killed by a beast which rises out of the abyss. In Bible symbolism, a BEAST is symbolic of an entity that refuses to give credence to reasonings, that deems reasonings irrelevant for decision making. In essence, an entity that only believes in demonstration of power. The beast then, typifies persons who give in to such a spirit. Consistent with the symbolism, having failed to convert the papal Church to the truth with reasonings, the Byzantine Church went on to adopt papal Rome's *power rubric* for survival, an exercise that was doomed to fail, for Jesus will not allow His glory to be associated with wanton demonstrations of power. With respect to the Church of the Reformation, no amount of debate could get the papal Church, or some of it's proponents to consider falsity of their positions on matters of faith. So then, while it was clear that it was the reformers who were right, it simultaneously was the outcome that the more powerful entity, the papal Church persecuted the CHURCH OF THE REFORMATION out of Western Europe.

Prophecy Principle 110 *At formation of the* CHRISTIAN BYZANTINE EMPIRE *in 325 AD, there did not exist any schism between the* CHURCH OF THE BYZANTINE EMPIRE, *and the* CHURCH OF THE WESTERN ROMAN EMPIRE. *There also was not any pope in the Church of the Western Roman Empire. Due to the fact that the Western Roman Empire would not give up it's pantheon of Gods, gradually the Church of the Western Roman Empire gave up sanctity of the Gospel for maintenance of it's relevance to politics of the Western Roman Empire. This drift from sanctity of the gospel was recognized in writing by the* CHURCH OF THE BYZANTINE EMPIRE *in 867 AD. Many years before our Lord Jesus Christ had declared that 'you cannot have each of God and money be* *primary motivations in your life (Luke 16:13)'. In the choice of earthly wealth and splendor over purity of the gospel, papal Rome chose money over our Lord Jesus Christ, and ended up corrupting the gospel. The two witnesses testified to the sad reality that papal Rome is an apostate Church.*

Prophecy Principle 111 *No matter the apostasy of which papal Rome is representative, we are called to love all men, meaning you cannot hate Catholics, papal Rome, or the pope. All that The Father requires is that you do not compromise purity of the gospel in order to love Catholics, papal Rome, or the pope.*

Prophecy Principle 112 *The CHURCH OF THE BYZANTINE EMPIRE was killed off by papal Rome, this via sacking of Constantinople in 1204 AD. The Christian Byzantine Empire never really recovered from this sacking, an event that led eventually to overthrow of the Empire by Turks in 1453 AD. The Church of the Reformation was killed off in Western Europe by persecution of papal Rome, persecution which commenced in 1563 AD. We arrive then at the inference that papal Rome typifies an entity that functions on basis of power, as opposed to reasonings.*

What then about location of the death of the witnesses, and their resurrection?

Revelation 11:8 declares that, SPIRITUALLY SPEAKING, the two witnesses are killed where our Lord Jesus was crucified, that is, in Sodom and Gomorrah. We know for a fact that our Lord Jesus Christ was killed in Jerusalem, meaning, consistent with assertions of our Lord Jesus Christ, that the earthly Jerusalem has spiritual characterization as Sodom and Gomorrah. In this respect, Romans 9:29, Jeremiah 23:14, and Matthew 11:23-24 declares as follows.

> And as Isaiah said before, Unless the Lord of Sabaoth had left us a seed, we would have become like Sodom, and we would have been made like Gomorrah.

> And in prophets of Jerusalem I have seen a horrible thing, committing adultery, and walking falsely, yea, they strengthened the hands of evil doers, so that they have not turned back each from his wickedness, they have been to me - all of them - as Sodom, and it's inhabitants as Gomorrah.

> And you, Capernaum, who are exalted to heaven, will be brought down to Hades; for if the mighty works which were done in you had been done in Sodom, it would have remained to this day. But I say to you that it shall be more tolerable for the land of Sodom in the day of judgment than for you.

Prophecy Interpretation 34 *In Scriptures,* SODOM *and* GOMORRAH *are symbolic of giving in of an entire city, and it's leaders, spiritual or administrative to sin and evil.*

Historical Spiritual Nugget 27 *In 1095 AD, the leadership of the Christian Byzantine Church, and Empire gave in to evil, chose evil over what is good, decided to partner with a church - papal Rome - which she had, herself recognized to be an apostate Church. The Byzantine Empire had, by this time begun maltreatment of free small farmers, maltreatment, which, as we have seen, commenced about 1056 AD. In 1563 AD, the kings of Western Europe gave in to evil, chose persecution of law abiding people merely because they disagreed on matters of faith with papal Rome.*

With respect to the *three and a half days* during which the two witnesses lay dead, we already have established that, prophetically, *a day equals a year*, with outcome, the two witnesses each lay dead for three and a half years. Starting from *1095 AD*, $3\frac{1}{2}$ years takes us to *1099 AD*, the year during which the forces of the Christian Byzantine Empire recaptured Jerusalem. Starting from *1563 AD*, $3\frac{1}{2}$ years takes us to *1567 AD*, the year during which Protestants began to revolt against the edict of *1563 AD* by papal Rome. While the earthly Jerusalem does not any longer have any spiritual relevance for Christians, the death of the Byzantine Church having been evident in the request for help from papal Rome, the victory over Muslims in context of the quest for recapture of the earthly Jerusalem restored some semblance of life to the Church. By this, our Lord Jesus Christ declares that while the Church was mistaken in it's undertaking of a rivalry with Islam, the mistake was a honest one, not an intentional revolt against our Lord and Savior Jesus Christ. The intentional mistake resided in the partnership with papal Rome. In the choice of the partnership, the Byzantine Empire devolved even more into adoption of a '*might is right*' rubric, as opposed to the Love of God for management of interactions within society. Perhaps even more importantly, the Byzantine Empire declared an earthly focus - the Jerusalem on earth - as opposed to a heavenly focus - the Jerusalem above, which is mother of us all (Galatians 4:26).

Non-arrival at Friendship implies Non-arrival at Unity

Regardless of comfort that is represented by two churches which each stood up to apostasy of papal Rome, there is symbolism to presence of 2, as opposed to 3 witnesses. Remember that the number 2 signifies COMPANIONSHIP OF PURPOSE, the number 3, an INNER CIRCLE OF FRIENDSHIP, formed around purpose. While each of the *Church of the Byzantine Empire,* and *Church of the Reformation* stood up to papal Rome, in principle, the two did not arrive at agreement. Note for example, that while the Byzantine Church rejected idolatry evident in worship of, equivalently, reverence for statues, the Lutheran Church practices such liturgy. So then, whereas the Byzantine Church fought against each of idolatry and authority of the pope, but not perfectly, the Church of the Reformation only fought against authority of the pope, did not arrive at objection to idolatry. We arrive then at an important insight, which is, while reformers, such as *Huldreich Zwingli* (*1484-1531*), and *Carlstadt*, who initially was an associate of Martin Luther, fought against both idolatry and authority of the pope, the view of the reformation that survived, that of Martin Luther, was the view that continued to validate idolatry of papal Rome. We have then that while there was *companionship* of opposition to Rome, there was not arrival at an *inner circle of friendship*. Given non-agreement meant non-arrival at unity of the faith, the Church of Western Europe did not arrive at a PERFECT MAN, did not arrive at a measure of the stature of the fullness of Christ.

Having not arrived at willingness to be perfected, the two Churches experienced persecution, that is, passed through a 4th SEAL, a 4th SEAL that culminated in killing of the two witnesses by the beast. In response, as stipulated in context of the 4th SEAL, The Father orders death and hades to kill, and 7 THOUSAND die. The 7 THOUSAND is symbolic of Completeness of judgment of persecution of the two witnesses, meaning absent any future persecution, there would not be imposition of future judgments for the exact same persecution. Simultaneously, the 7 THOUSAND is symbolic of Commencement of new Grand Judgments that are premised on assessments of willingness of the Nations to base civil laws, and societal interactions on the Love of God. In this respect, note that until all of Western Europe arrived at Constitutions that celebrated equality of mankind, from *1563 to 1945 AD*, all that Western Europe would experience is *wars*, *wars*, and *yet more wars*. In the celebration of individual humanity that was the LEAGUE OF NATIONS, eventually, Western Europe became afraid and gave glory to the God of heaven (Revelation 11:13).

Prophetic Lessons 38 *The Father will not allow any nation to get the best of Him. When His True Church is ejected from a Nation, The Father continues to demand that civil laws and societal interactions be premised on the Love of Christ. If a Nation continues to fail the test, it continues to be judged for rebellion against it's maker. It took about 400 years for The Father to bring all of Western Europe to it's knees. But what is 400 years to a God for whom a 1,000 years of man's time, is as a day gone by (2 Peter 3:8)?*

In Revelation 11:1, the SANCTUARY OF GOD equates to the spiritual state of the Church as a whole (Ephesians 2:19-22); THE ALTAR is representative of the extent to which believers are willing to both consecrate their bodies as living sacrifices to The Father, and allow their minds to be renewed by the Holy Spirit (Romans 12:1-2; Philippians 2:5-11; Ephesians 4:23-24); in this respect consider that only those who make it past the altar gain entrance into the Holy Place; the altar symbolizes the extent to which the spiritual atmosphere in Church incentivizes believers towards all of the 'willingnesses' of sanctification; and BELIEVERS WORSHIPPING IN THE SANCTUARY equate to individual believers in the name of Jesus Christ (Romans 12:5; 1Corinthians 12:27). If the altar passes, the sanctuary must pass. If the sanctuary of God, and the altar pass (the BP7 or GP7 PATHS), and you as an individual worshipper fail the Grand Judgment, it would be clear that while surrounded by righteousness, you loved evil; you then are characterized as a CHARLATAN. If the altar and sanctuary fail (the RP7 PATH), but you pass the test, in presence of a Church characterized primarily by FLESHLY NEOPHYTES and/or CHARLATANS, you, a SPIRITUAL NEOPHYTE or POWER FOR GOD were sidelined from leadership. So then, you pass. If the altar and sanctuary fail (the RP7 PATH), and you also fail the test, The Father focuses on your sincerity, on the sincerity of your efforts at love. So then, you either pass or fail.

Prophecy Interpretation 35 *Revelation 11:1-14 depicts* SWEETNESS IN THE MOUTH - *Churches who prophesy for 1,260 years, yet, simultaneously depicts* BITTERNESS IN THE STOMACH - *Churches that are killed by the beast out of the abyss, that is, Churches that are not perfected.*

The Things That Are 70 *The spiritual reality that* GRAND JUDGMENT OF THE CHURCH *encompass (i) the state of the Church as a whole; (ii) the willingness of the Church, as a whole, to be perfected; and (iii) the state of individual members of the Church is an eternal truth, a thing that always was, always is, and always will be.*

The Things That Are 71 *Having not been perfected, the invitation to the 2* CHURCHES *that they* 'COME UP TO HEAVEN' *is consistent with a 5th* SEAL *that transpires in context of the RP7* PATH, *the path on which the Church does not arrive at* MATURITY OF RIGHTEOUSNESS, *as such, is not perfected. On the RP7 path, upon arrival at the 5th* SEAL, *the souls of the saints are seen in heaven, under the altar of the sanctuary that is in heaven.*

> But how could each Church be faithful to God, yet not be able to agree?

Consider these words by our Lord Jesus Christ in John 16:12-13.

> I have yet many things to say to you, BUT YE ARE NOT ABLE TO BEAR THEM NOW and when He may come - the Spirit of truth - He will guide you to all the truth, for He will not speak from Himself, but as many things as He will hear He will speak and the coming things He will tell you.

Why were the disciples of Jesus not able to hear, that is, to understand things He wanted to say, but on which He had to hold back?

BECAUSE THEY HAD 'HONEST BLINDERS' ON THEIR MINDS AND HEARTS.

Prophecy Insight 75 *Whenever Churches have* HONEST BLINDERS *on, and the blinders are not intentional, are relics of which The Church has yet to arrive at conviction of their falsity, sincerity of faith and love is sufficient for salvation of The Church.*

Prophecy Insight 76 *While the* PAPAL CHURCH *was apostate due to love of money and power, mistakes made by the* CHURCH OF THE BYZANTINE EMPIRE, *and* CHURCH OF THE REFORMATION *were 'honest' mistakes, mistakes that, perhaps transpired because there were false shepherds who sought to impede progress of those Churches towards* MATURITY OF RIGHTEOUSNESS.

Whenever the minds and hearts (spirits) of those who have faith in Jesus Christ are blinded by any of *traditions, cherished interpretations of Scripture,* or *substitution of zeal for love,* there always are things The Father wants to teach, but of which no one is ready or able to hear, that is, able to understand. Each of the two churches had it's own specific blinders, as such could not perceive truths that would have generated unity of the faith. Rather than arrive at friendship, the two merely complemented each other, merely arrived at companionship.

Prophecy Insight 77 *Whenever the Church of today builds on truths of yesterday, such that there are not any new errors introduced into the Church, and such that old truths are maintained, there is not only companionship, there is arrival at friendship, and feasibility of progression to* MATURITY OF RIGHTEOUSNESS, *equivalently, feasibility of arrival at a* PERFECT MAN.

Prophecy Principle 113 *Whenever those who have faith in Jesus Christ are characterized by any of 'magnification of traditions over the sayings of Jesus Christ', 'cherished interpretations of Scripture that are not true', or 'substitution of zeal for love', the Church has blinders on, and is unable to arrive at* MATURITY OF RIGHTEOUSNESS.

Prophecy Principle 114 *If the Church ever is to be perfected, the* SAYINGS *(commandments, or declarations) of The Father, and of our Lord Jesus Christ must be magnified over all else, and all must submit their selves to the sayings of Father, Son, and Holy Spirit.*

11.3   The Woman of Revelation 12

The woman of Revelation 12 is the Church. The Church clothes herself with Christ (Romans 13:14), meaning the sun is symbolic of our Lord Jesus Christ, the *Sun of Righteousness* (Malachi 4:2). The moon derives it's light from the sun, but is not the sun, meaning the moon represents the Scriptures, which testify of Christ (John 5:39-40). At timing of the birth of our Lord Jesus Christ, The Church, which means 'THE CALLED OUT ONES' consists of Joseph and Mary, the earthly parents of our Lord Jesus Christ. While Jesus still was an infant, Joseph and Mary are instructed to relocate to Egypt (Matthew 2:13-15) - which then was essentially part of Asia - and relative to intellectualism of Western Europe, Egypt then was more of an intellectual wilderness. Joseph and Mary relocate to Egypt, which would become part of the Christian Empire that was the Byzantine Empire, because the devil *(the dragon)* through Herod sought to kill the baby Jesus (Matthew 2:16). We have then that right from the year of birth of our Lord Jesus Christ, the church sought refuge in what would become the Byzantine (Christian) Empire. Our Lord Jesus Christ of course would ascend back to His Father, as such, upon completion of His earthly ministry, was caught up to the throne of God (Revelation 12:5; 3:21).

When Herod sought to kill Jesus, it was a messenger who appeared to Joseph to direct him to take Mary and Jesus, and escape to Egypt. Note this was in *4 BC*, at least 616 years prior to emergence of Islam in Arabia. Revelation 12:6 declares that subsequent to giving birth to Jesus, the woman fled to the wilderness, to a place prepared for her by God where she is nourished for 1,260 days, which as we already know, implies 1,260 calendar years. The event that best fits commencement of the 1,260 years then is the birth of our Lord Jesus Christ in *4 BC*, and subsequent escape to Egypt by Joseph, Mary, and the Lord Jesus Christ (Matthew 2:13-15). Note that whereas Joseph, Mary, and Jesus returned physically to Judea (Matthew 2:19-23), nourishment of the woman in Egypt, equivalently, Asia is spiritual, not physical. From *4 BC*, 1,260 years of nourishment takes us to *1255 AD*.

> Do we then have any evidence for nourishment of the Church in Asia for 1,260 years?

ABSOLUTELY!!! When Apostle Paul was converted, this of course shortly after *27 AD*, as such 585 years prior to emergence of Islam, the Holy Spirit led him into ARABIA (Galatians 1:17) where he received revelations of the person of Christ. We see then that the Church, as represented by Apostle Paul, is nourished out of Asia. Subsequent to institution of official persecution of the Church under Emperor Diocletian, persecution, which commenced in *303 AD*, and that was ended officially in *324 AD* by Constantine the Great, in presence of resistance of Rome to abandonment of it's pantheon of gods for monotheism of faith in Christ, in the establishment of Constantinople and the Christian Byzantine Empire in Asia, the Church again would find succor, that is, nourishment via location in Asia. Given the CHRISTIAN BYZANTINE EMPIRE continued until at the very least *1260 AD*, at which point it transitioned to Greek Orthodoxy, as at *1255 AD*, the Church still could be regarded as being nurtured in Asia.

Prophecy Insight 78 *From Mary finding refuge and succor in Egypt, that is, in Asia about* 4 BC *to* 1255 AD *is exactly* 1, 260 *years. There is good evidence that the Church, as represented by* MARY, APOSTLE PAUL, *and the* CHRISTIAN BYZANTINE EMPIRE, *found spiritual refuge and nourishment in Asia between* 4 BC *and* 1255 AD.

The Reign of Jesus Christ

Revelation 12:5 declares that the woman, Mary, who is symbolic of the Church *"brought forth a child, who is about to rule all the nations with a rod of iron,"* and that the child was caught away unto God and His throne. Clearly then, the child did not begin to reign at timing of birth, that is, commencement of the reign of the child, commencement of the reign of our Lord Jesus Christ still yet was in the future.

Consistent with Revelation 12:5, all of the Gospels declare that what Jesus taught, and what He commanded His disciples to teach was that:

The reign of the heavens is at hand.

In this respect, Jesus severally declares as follows.

From that time Jesus began to preach, saying, "Repent, for the kingdom (*reign*) of heaven is at hand (Matthew 4:17)."

Not every one who is saying to me 'Lord, lord', shall come into the reign of the heavens; but he who is doing the will of my Father who is in the heavens (Matthew 7:21).

Jesus answered, verily, verily, I say to thee, if any one may not be born of water, and the Spirit, he is not able to enter into the reign of God (John 3:5).

From perspective of the preaching and teachings of Jesus Christ on the Reign of God, we again arrive at the insight that, in context of faith in Jesus Christ, believers either are NEOPHYTES - believers who have yet to enter into the Reign of God; or POWERS - believers who, by showing themselves worthy of the grace of God, have been ushered into the Reign of God.

The following are evident from the preceding Scriptures.

✠ At timing of ministry of Jesus Christ, the REIGN OF GOD still was in the future.

✠ Only those who have been washed with water, and baptized of the Holy Spirit are able to enter into the REIGN OF GOD. Since the command to be washed in water, and baptized of the Holy Spirit come from Christ, a person who does the will of God is washed with water, and baptized of the Holy Spirit. So then, only those who are washed with water, and baptized of the Holy Spirit - Neophytes, have opportunity for entrance into the REIGN OF GOD, have opportunity for arrival at the PRESENCE OF CHRIST, have opportunity to become Powers for Christ.

Prophecy Insight 79 *A person who adopts the* LOVE OF GOD *as* WAY OF LIFE *is in the will of God. This person is a* LOVING CITIZEN OF THE NATIONS, *and is in the Acceptable Will of God. A person who adopts the* LOVE OF GOD *as* WAY OF LIFE, *but who also is born of water and the Spirit is in the will of God. This person is a* NEOPHYTE, *and is in the Good Will of God. A person who adopts the* LOVE OF GOD *as* WAY OF LIFE, *who is born of water and the Spirit, and who attains to the* PRESENCE OF CHRIST *is in the will of God. This person is a Power for Christ, and is in the Perfect Will of God.*

Revelation 12:7-9 declare that subsequent to His resurrection, and ascension to heaven, that there was war in the heaven, at end of which the devil and his messengers were cast out of the heaven, as such cast forth to the earth. Upon this casting out, and casting forth, the Reign of God is announced to have fully arrived. Note that it is not the case that the Reign of God did not exist between the ascension of Christ to heaven, and the announcement in Revelation 12:10 that '*now is the reign of our God, and the authority of His Christ*'. Rather, it is the case that relative to man's spiritual cognition or capacity, there was work that remained to be done, work that was completed post ascension of Christ back to the heaven. Essentially, it would seem that man and messengers had to become convinced to give up their belief that success of the Gospel required coalescing of Church and State. Until this blindness was cured, it was difficult for the Presence of Christ, equivalently, the Reign of Christ, which is spiritual, to be fully realized in the spirit. It was not until the time of the Church of the Reformation that the Gospel would take on an *individual character*, would take on character of *individuality of faith*, as opposed to acceptance of faith of a monarch.

> And I heard a great voice saying in the heaven, "Now did come the salvation, and the power, and the reign, of our God, and the authority of His Christ, because cast down was the accuser of His brethren, who is accusing them before our God day and night (Revelation 12:10)."

Prophecy Insight 80 *The* REIGN OF GOD *did not fully arrive until Jesus had ascended back to His Father in the heaven. For the* REIGN OF GOD *to fully arrive, the devil and his messengers had to be cast out of the heaven, and cast forth to the earth.*

Prophecy Insight 81 *The essence of the* REIGN OF CHRIST *resides in the spiritual reality that, absent any contact with the Church, a man can arrive at fellowship with Christ. With the Church dichotomized from the Nations, fellowship with Christ is dissociated not only from the Church, but also from the Nations.*

Prophecy Insight 82 *In the command to those who truly have faith in Jesus Christ to come out of Babylon, to come out of an Apostate Church in Revelation 18:4-5, our Lord Jesus Christ declares that those who truly are faithful to Him - * NEOPHYTES, *or* POWERS *- can be commanded to eschew fellowship, which transpires in context of an Apostate Church, that is, in context of a Church, which deliberately has chosen the RP7* PATH.

When Lazarus fell ill (John 11:1-4), Jesus waited four days (John 11:17), this so he could die, and so everyone would know he was raised from the dead, not from a coma. Given the blood continues to pump in bodies of people in a coma, the bodies of people who fall into a coma do not stink. This is evidence they remain alive, but are brain dead. Lazarus already was stinking (John 11:39-40) before he was brought back to life. Yet, Jesus had declared the miracle four days earlier (John 11:11). When it comes to the promises of God, friend, the admonition from The Father is:

> And Jehovah answereth me and saith: "Write a vision, and explain on tables, that he may run who is reading it. For yet the vision is for a season, and it breatheth (*gathers strength*) for the end, and doth not lie, if it tarry, wait for it, for surely it cometh, it is not late. Lo, a presumptuous one! Not upright is his soul within him, and the righteous by his steadfastness liveth (Habakkuk 2:2-4)."

Prophecy Principle 115 *When God declares that "It is Finished", and yet it appears as if "It is not yet Finished", trust God, for the vision surely does not lie, surely will come to pass.*

How did the saints overcome the devil?

> And they did overcome him (the devil) because of the blood of the Lamb (*willing participation in their own sanctification*), and because of the word of their testimony (*the choice not to, in presence of persecution, deny their faith in Christ*), and they did not love their

life - unto death; because of this be glad, ye heavens, and those in them who do tabernacle; wo to those inhabiting the land and the sea, because the devil did go down unto you, having great wrath, having known that he hath little time (Revelation 12:11-12).

When you received Jesus as Lord and Savior, your life became hid with Christ in God (Colossians 3:1-3), with outcome your life resides in the heavens with Christ. This is the reason your spiritual citizenship is in the heavens (Philippians 3:20), and the reason you are seated in the heavenly places in Christ Jesus (Ephesians 2:6). So then, the devil has come down to earth, but your life is in the heavens in Christ, and in Christ you have opportunity to become part of the reign of the heavens. So then, obey your Lord and Savior Jesus Christ, and do what?

Rejoice, Friend, Rejoice and Be Glad, that your life is tabernacled in the heavens (Revelation 12:12; 1Thessalonians 5:16).

Prophecy Principle 116 *You overcome the devil by the blood of our Lord Jesus Christ (that is, via willing submission to cleansing from all unrighteousness of body, soul, and spirit), and via witness of your faith in Christ, both in word (testimony) and actions (character, and essence) and by willingness to die, if necessary for your faith in Christ.*

Prophecy Principle 117 *Your life is in the heavens with our Lord Jesus Christ, so rejoice, and again I say to you, rejoice.*

Prophecy Principle 118 *If you seek to know how to apply the blood of Jesus Christ so you are able to overcome the devil, pick up a copy of my book, True Sanctification, today.*

Revelation 12:15-16 declares that it was the devil who flushed the Church out of the Byzantine Empire, resulting in birth of the Church of the Reformation in Western Europe. The devil poured out water as a river out of his mouth, such that the woman could be carried away by the water, but the land came to the aid of the woman, swallowed up the river, meaning a new home was found for true believers, which in this case was the United States of America - the land to which most of those persecuted by papal Rome and other Churches of the Establishment were banished because of their faith. We already have established, using typology from the Scriptures, that a river symbolizes peace. Using this typology, the devil attempted to carry the Church away via producing of a 'FALSE PEACE', a peace that is not rooted in unity of faith in Jesus Christ. In the rejection of such peace by Protestants, in the willingness to be persecuted for maintenance of their understanding of what it means to have faith in Jesus Christ, the plan of the devil failed. In response, papal Rome and the Anglican Church, and other Churches, which had been adopted by their States, expelled Protestants from all across Western Europe to life in the USA.

Prophecy Insight 83 *Whenever the Church seeks to become fused with the State, this always is rooted in desire for* EARTHLY GRANDEUR, *not desire for* SPIRITUAL GRANDEUR.

Prophecy Insight 84 *Should a society ever persecute those who, regardless of their religion, treat others right?*

The dragon then went off to make war, not with the woman, that is, not with the Church herself, but "*with the rest of her seed, those keeping the commands of God, and having the testimony of Jesus Christ (Revelation 12:17).*" In these words, our Lord Jesus Christ intimates us that persecution now inherently is at level of the individual, as opposed to level of the institution. Our Lord Jesus Christ declares that the devil does not any longer focus on the Church as an institution, but on those within the Church who keep the commands of God, that is, who adopt the Love of God as Way of Life, and have the testimony of Jesus Christ, which as we already have severally established is, the Reality of the Presence of Christ. Persecution then is targeted primarily at those who seem to have capacity for, or who already have attained to the Presence of Christ, that is, believers who have capacity for, or who already have become Powers for Christ.

Prophecy Insight 85 *Is the world on either of the GP7 or RP7* PATHS? *This is easily deducible from actions of leaders and people, and character of the Church in a specific region. It is straightforward to see that just about every nation of the world has been on the RP7 SSGLAE path. In presence of the evidence, the teaching by popular pentecostal, or protestant pastors that absence of trouble in this world is evidence that your faith is working is rooted in the devil, is in entirety, a teaching of demons who seek to prevent you from aspiring to, or becoming a Power for Christ. If these pastors are sincere in their teachings, they are sincerely heretical, sincerely misleading, sincerely wrong.*

The Scriptural Evidence

These things I have spoken to you, that in Me, you may have peace. In the world (*because Jesus foresees choices of the nations in relation to His original 12 apostles*) you will have tribulation; but be of good cheer, I have overcome the world (John 16:33).

Happy are ye whenever THEY MAY REPROACH YOU (the word, 'MAY' implies *conditionality*, implies *choice* of the nations to embark on the GP7 PATH), and MAY PERSECUTE, and MAY SAY ANY EVIL THING AGAINST YOU FALSELY for my sake - rejoice ye and be glad, because your reward is great in the heavens, for thus did they persecute the prophets who were before you (Matthew 5:11-12).

Yes, and all who desire to live godly in Christ Jesus will (*in presence of either of the RP7* PATH) suffer persecution (2Timothy 3:12).

| Those keeping the Commandments and Testimony of Jesus Christ |

We already have seen that our Lord Jesus Christ gave only one command, which is, to love as He has loved us. There exists yet another command, however, one that, in entirety, is spiritual, that is, not directly observable. Given it is spiritual, it is not direct evidence for faith in Jesus Christ, rather is a RESOURCE. In so far as evidence that we are followers of Christ is concerned, there is only one incontrovertible evidence - practice of the Love of God.

Spiritual Insight 88 *The faith whose motive is love, and that is evident in decisions and actions that have quality of the* LOVE OF CHRIST, *is the only incontrovertible evidence that you and I are disciples of Jesus Christ.*

But then I just mentioned 'faith', declared that faith is grounded in love. We love then not in our own power, but via receipt, by faith, of the love of God, such that the love is not a matter of will, but a matter of who we already are in Christ. When you will to do something, that thing is not inherent in you, is something that you have to produce. When you are something, that thing is inherent in you, is part of you. When you exert your will, your effort is directed at producing something. When you manifest something that you already are, your effort is directed at maintenance of who you are. This distinction is subtle, yet profound, and those who truly seek to understand will ask the Holy Spirit for discernment and understanding, and their prayer shall be heard. This is why the righteousness of Christ is a righteousness of faith, not a righteousness of works. In Christ, we exert effort to maintain, and experience increase in context of what we already have become. The effort then is not to ingratiate ourselves with God, for we already are in Him. Rather, the effort is to maintain who we already are in Christ.

Spiritual Insight 89 *If you seek to ingratiate yourself with The Father by recommending your efforts as sufficient for your salvation, you recommend your will and your strength to God, none of which, combined, are sufficient for your salvation. The Father always rewards good works, that is, works of love, but works that are not purified by the blood of Jesus Christ, that are not sanctified by the Holy Spirit never are pure enough for attraction of the* PRESENCE OF CHRIST.

So then, we have two commands that are absolutist for identification of a disciple of Jesus Christ. These two commands are enunciated in all of the Epistles, but are stated profoundly by Apostle John in *1John 4:23*. The source of the Love is expressed in Romans 5:5.

And this is His command, that we may believe in the name of His Son Jesus Christ, and may love one another, even as He did give command to us.

And the hope doth not make ashamed, because the love of God hath been poured forth in our hearts through the Holy Spirit that hath been given to us.

Spiritual Insight 90 *Only persons who seek first to become sons of God by faith in the name of Jesus Christ, who then exert effort towards maintaining who they already have become by faith in Christ have capacity for pleasing God with their Love, for their Love has quality of the Love of God.*

Spiritual Insight 91 *If you do not want to be poor in the midst of spiritual plenty, if there is one thing you must seek for as a disciple of Christ, it is to receive the Holy Spirit from The Lord Jesus Christ. Without the Holy Spirit, you attempt to create the Love of God out of your own human strength and will, both of which, combined are as* ROPES MADE OUT OF SAND.

Prophecy Insight 86 *The commands of God are to have faith in the name of Jesus Christ, to love one another, and to love all men as we have example in our Lord and Savior, Jesus Christ. If you subscribe to any teaching, which draws you away from either of these three integrated commands, you are drawn away by some heresy.*

What then is the testimony of Jesus Christ?

WELL, HOW DID JESUS SAY HIS DISCIPLES WILL BE IDENTIFIED? By their Love.

HOW IS THE LOVE OF GOD RECEIVED? Through the Holy Spirit.

WHAT IS THE SEAL THAT YOU BELONG TO CHRIST? The Holy Spirit

Prophecy Insight 87 *So the testimony of Jesus Christ is evidence that you are filled with the Holy Spirit, which is, your capacity for walking in love towards fellow believers in Jesus Christ, and the world in general.*

Prophecy Insight 88 *The testimony of Jesus Christ is evidence that you have attained to a* POWER FOR CHRIST; *that you have actualized The* PRESENCE OF CHRIST. *The* QUALITY *of the Love of God that you demonstrate is evidence for your faith in Christ. The* FAITH *is intangible, but is essential for receiving the* RESOURCE *without which you cannot become a Power for Christ, that is, the Love of God. When the Love of God grows in you, such that it attains to some minimum known only to Father and Son, the Love of God in you blossoms into actualization of the Presence of Christ.*

Supporting Scriptures that the testimony of Christ is a life filled with the Holy Spirit?

> And I fell before his feet, to bow before him, and he saith to me, See - not! fellow servant of thee am I, and of thy brethren, those having the testimony of Jesus; bow before God, for the testimony of Jesus is the spirit of the prophecy (Revelation 19:10).

> This first knowing, that no prophecy of the Writing doth come of private exposition, for not by will of man did ever prophecy come, but by the Holy Spirit borne on holy men of God spake (2Peter 1:20-21).

> "If there arises among you a prophet or dreamer of dreams, and he gives you a sign or a wonder, AND THE SIGN OR WONDER COMES TO PASS, of which he spoke to you, saying, '*Let us go after other gods*' - which you have not known, - '*and let us serve them,*' YOU SHALL NOT LISTEN TO THE WORDS OF THAT PROPHET OR THAT DREAMER OF DREAMS, for the Lord your God is testing you to know whether you love the Lord your God with all your heart and with all your soul. You shall walk after the Lord your God and fear (love and reverence) Him, and keep His commandments and obey His voice; you shall serve Him and hold fast to Him. BUT THAT PROPHET OR THAT DREAMER OF DREAMS SHALL BE PUT TO DEATH, BECAUSE HE HAS SPOKEN IN ORDER TO TURN YOU AWAY FROM THE LORD YOUR GOD...(Deuteronomy 13:1-5)"

Prophecy Insight 89 *A spirit (prophet) who truly has received prophecy from The Father will not attempt to turn disciples of Christ away from the commands that are central to discipleship, namely, faith in the name of Jesus Christ, and love for all men.*

Prophecy Insight 90 *The testimony of Jesus Christ is the* LOVE WALK, *and* LOVE ESSENCE *of Christ that is produced in you by the Holy Spirit.*

Prophecy Insight 91 *If you are to be saved, you must endure unto the end (2Timothy 2:12).*

11.4   The Two Beasts of Revelation 13

It is with much happiness, peace, and joy that I declare to you the prophetic truth that the symbolism of 2 BEASTS implies the beasts only are able to arrive at Companionship of Purpose (CP), are unable to arrive at an Inner Circle of Friendship (CF). By this symbolism, The Father declares that evil

NEVER will mature to rule over this earth. Remember that rejection of the LOVE OF GOD as foundation for civil laws and societal interactions in context of a 1ˢᵗ Seal always leads to *killing of each other* by the Nations. In presence of this outcome, which is, a natural spiritual consequence of choice of HATRED over LOVE, in context of choice of the GP7 PATH, the Nations never are able to arrive at an Inner Circle of Friendship. We rigorously established this result in our discussions of the 2ⁿᵈ, 3ʳᵈ, and 4ᵗʰ TRUMPETS of the 7ᵗʰ Seal. Note it is not God who punishes the nations under the 2ⁿᵈ Seal, rather it is the case that, the nations having chosen hatred over love, progress to manifestation of that hatred towards one another.

Prophecy Interpretation 36 *On the GP7 PATH, the choice of hatred in context of the 1ˢᵗ TRUMPET produces* COMPANIONSHIP OF PURPOSE (CP) *in context of the 2ⁿᵈ TRUMPET, but NEVER is able to arrive at an INNER CIRCLE OF FRIENDSHIP (CF).*

Prophecy Interpretation 37 *The consistency between symbolism of 2 BEASTS, and symbolisms of the 2ⁿᵈ, 3ʳᵈ, and 4ᵗʰ TRUMPETS of the 7ᵗʰ Seal ought to reinforce your confidence that all of the 66 Books of the Bible are inspired by one Spirit, the Spirit of The Father.*

While the partnership between the 2 BEASTS and BABYLON momentarily creates CF on the RP7 PATH, in the certainty that the Nations always will betray the friendship and destroy the flesh of Babylon with fire (Revelation 17:16), there is guarantee, from The Father that the CF, which is rooted in choice of hatred and evil, and which transpires *only in context of the* RP7 PATH, does not produce any sort of maturity, as such inherently is incapable of producing a 5ᵗʰ SEAL for evil. Prevention of the CF that is attained to in context of the RP7 PATH from arrival at any sort of maturity is essence of outpouring of the 7 VIALS of the WRATH OF GOD. On the RP7 PATH, only those who love righteousness are able to arrive at a 5ᵗʰ SEAL.

Prophecy Interpretation 38 *On the RP7 PATH, the choice of hatred by both the Church and the Nations in context of the 1ˢᵗ SEAL produces CP in context of the 2ⁿᵈ SEAL, and CF in context of the 3ʳᵈ SEAL, but is unable to generate any 5ᵗʰ SEAL for those who love evil. In this guarantee from The Father, we have assurance that evil never will arrive at maturity.*

To all of this, you and I ought to say, Hallelujah!

Prophecy Principle 119 *With the knowledge that* COMPANIONSHIP OF EVIL *never will mature, always will self destruct, The Father promises that, if you continue in the* FAITH THAT WORKS BY LOVE, *you are guaranteed to overcome.*

Prophecy Insight 92 *It is important, however, that you arrive at a realization of a tool of the beasts that is applied to seduction of those who truly seek to worship The Father. If you already are seduced, The Father asks that you to reform. If you are not yet seduced, you arrive at knowledge, which protects purity of your faith in Christ.*

Revelation 13: Events on an RP7 Path

Events in *Revelation ch. 13* relate to a world - individuals, The Church, and The Nations - which has ended up on an RP7 PATH. Given overcoming that is achieved in context of the 1ˢᵗ SEAL must be achieved by those who have faith in Jesus Christ (Revelation 2:7,11,17,26; 3:5,12,21), the messenger of the 1ˢᵗ SEAL in *Revelation 6:2* is a person who has faith in Jesus Christ. Given this messenger is explicitly stated to be GIVEN a Crown, this messenger did not always have a Crown, that is, is on basis of worthiness (*worthiness also is translated as 'virtue'*; Philippians 4:8; 2Peter 1:5; 2Thessalonians 1:5; Revelation 3:4), awarded *a Crown*, this because he or she arrived at a Perfect Man. The Church ends up on the RP7 PATH, because in context of the 1ˢᵗ SEAL, she refused to submit to her Lord and Savior, Jesus Christ, that is, rejected the witness and testimony of those within The Church whom her Lord and Savior put forth as *Powers* for magnification of His name. Regardless of evidence of overcoming of sin, the world, and the devil from Powers for Christ, regardless of evidence of character, regardless of evidence of good works in the secular space, regardless of evidence of miracles and signs, The Church refused to submit to her Lord and Savior Jesus Christ. Like the Pharisees and Sadducees, while The Church is supposed to celebrate righteousness, upon arrival of the righteousness, which evidently is produced by The Lord and Savior Jesus Christ, The Church declares that earthly circumstances of The Powers for Christ are not sufficiently grandiose for sensibilities of The Church. Given our Lord Jesus Christ was, in His earthly circumstances, and prior to His ministry, a Carpenter (Matthew 13:55; Mark 6:3), we arrive at an irrationality, which is, a Church which professes to worship a Lord and Savior who eschews pomp, but which herself now only respects pomp, not righteousness. The Church then refuses to be perfected, because she practices respect of persons, not respect for her Lord and Savior Jesus Christ. Overarching importance of perfection of The Church as objective of our Lord and Savior Jesus Christ is evident in the following words from Scripture.

> The husbands! love your own wives, as also The Christ did love the assembly (Church), and did give Himself for it, that He might sanctify it, having cleansed it with the bathing of the water in the saying (*words spoken by The Father and The Son*), that He might present it to Himself the assembly in glory, not having spot or wrinkle, or any of such things, but THAT IT MAY BE HOLY AND UNBLEMISHED (Ephesians 5:25-27).

The Things That Are 72 *The overarching objective of our Lord Jesus Christ is perfection of His Church (His assembly).*

Prophecy Principle 120 *The Church is able to choose the RP7* PATH, *because overcoming that is achieved in context of a 1ˢᵗ* SEAL *always is entrusted to Powers for Christ. Whenever The Church rejects the witness, testimony, and evidence produced by Powers for Christ, with outcome she refuses to be perfected by Christ, she actualizes the RP7* PATH.

Prophecy Principle 121 *Credibility of* POWERS FOR CHRIST *is attested to by evidence for: overcoming of sin, the world, and the devil; righteousness of character; capacity for demonstration of the Love of God; absence of any hatreds whatsoever; Godliness; evidence of good works in the Church, and in the secular space; The Father working miracles in response to their faithfulness.*

In presence of rejection of the work of her Lord and Savior, The Church arrives at a 2ⁿᵈ SEAL, arrives at COMPANIONSHIP OF REJECTION of her Lord and Savior Jesus Christ. Given The Father, in His Justice cannot allow such companionship arrive at an INNER CIRCLE OF FRIENDSHIP (CF) within The Church, *in of herself, The Church is unable to arrive at an Inner Circle of Friendship.* Relative to The Church then, the 3ʳᵈ SEAL is about a sealing of those, in The Church, who remain faithful to Christ. The Church having chosen evil, and The Nations having not received any meaningful witness from The Church, the dragon, that is, the devil raises up the 2 BEASTS. Combined, the 2 BEASTS, and the now apostate Church, which is depicted as BABYLON THE GREAT, arrive at an INNER CIRCLE OF FRIENDSHIP. Whereas then a CF, which subsists in context of the BP7 PATH revolves around *pursuit of Love Projects* that benefit all of society, in context of the RP7 PATH, CF revolves around persecution of the righteous. In presence of focus on evil, and abdication from projects of Love, there is choice of hatreds, killing of one another, and society arrives at loss of welfare.

Prophecy Principle 122 *In presence of choice of a path of hatreds - the RP7* PATH, *over a path of Love Projects - the BP7* PATH, *as already articulated, events that transpire in context of the 2ⁿᵈ through 4ᵗʰ* SEALS *are natural spiritual consequences of evil choices arrived at in context of the 1ˢᵗ* SEAL.

Within context of the RP7 PATH, the 2ⁿᵈ & 3ʳᵈ SEALS are characterized by hatreds within nations, the nations fighting each other, and persecutions of those who are faithful to the name of our Lord and Savior Jesus Christ. Having demonstrated their faithfulness in context of the 1ˢᵗ & 2ⁿᵈ SEALS, those who are faithful to Christ are, in context of the 3ʳᵈ SEAL, sealed for salvation. Once sealed, The Father does not allow them to be overcome by any temptation or trial. Once the faithful are sealed in context of the 3ʳᵈ

SEAL, there is arrival at the 4th SEAL. As I already have discussed in the preceding chapter, during the time of the 4th SEAL, those who have yet to arrive at faith in Jesus Christ, but who already had chosen the Love of God as WAY OF LIFE find it difficult to arrive at faith in the name of Jesus Christ (the life of Christ - Wheat or Barley - is in scarce supply, but yet still is attainable).

Prophecy Interpretation 39 *With a rejection of her Lord Jesus Christ in context of a 1st SEAL implied, or embedded, with outcome there is arrival at the RP7 path, Revelation ch. 13 depicts events, which transpire in context of the 2nd & 3rd SEALS of Revelation ch. 6, events that devolve into the 4th SEAL.*

SO THEN, EVENTS WHICH TRANSPIRE IN CONTEXT OF THE 2nd & 3rd SEALS. The institutions of the world - The Church, and The Nations - having chosen evil, the whole world is under control of the devil. By this, our Lord Jesus Christ signifies withdrawal of natural protections afforded operation of civil institutions from the devil. Only individuals now are protected by The Father.

> According as I said to you: My sheep my voice do hear, and I know them, and they follow me, and life age-during I give to them, and they shall not perish - to the age, and no one shall pluck them out of my hand; my Father, who hath given to me, is greater than all, and no one is able to pluck out of the hand of The Father; I and The Father are one (John 10:27-30).

Prophecy Interpretation 40 *In context of the 2nd & 3rd SEALS, only spirits of individuals come under protection of The Father. The Church, and The Nations having chosen evil, these institutions do not enjoy spiritual protections from the devil that are afforded by The Father. So then, those whose names are not in the Lamb's Book of Life worship the dragon, the beast, and the image of the beast, that is, begin to relish, and rejoice in desires fostered by the spirits represented by the dragon, and the beasts.*

Prophecy Interpretation 41 *Worship of the dragon and the beast refers to a relishing, and rejoicing in desires that are fostered by spirits represented by the dragon, and the beasts.*

Prophecy Interpretation 42 *The devil comes to steal, to kill, and to destroy (John 10:10). With full knowledge that people's constitutions are destroyed by choice of homosexuality, lesbianism, and transsexuality, the devil induces people into such behaviors. People delight in stealing from others, hatred for others, and attempts at destruction of others. Within context of the 2nd & 3rd SEALS, man, rather inexplicably and irrationally destroys things that already are established, things that are good for society.*

Prophecy Interpretation 43 *The FIRST BEAST induces people to believe in superiority of one group over another. So then, society is rife with conflict and oppression. The SECOND BEAST (the FALSE PROPHET) induces people to delight in falsehoods, and deceptions.*

The Church having apostasized, the Beast makes war with the saints and is allowed to overcome them.

> Why is the Beast allowed to overcome the saints?
> Two important reasons.

Prophecy Interpretation 44 *First, in the allowing of the Beast to overcome the saints, The Father demonstrates genuineness of their faith. Second, once the saints are revealed, The Nations are able, in context of the 4ᵗʰ SEAL, to turn on the apostate Church for consuming of her flesh with fire (Revelation 17:16).*

For our benefit, The Father provides an illustration of a 2ⁿᵈ & 3ʳᵈ SEAL period that is conditioned on rejection of her Lord Jesus Christ by the papal Church, the Church that gave birth to Protestantism (the rest of her seed - Revelation 12:17). In the preceding section, the section, which discusses *Revelation ch. 12*, we arrived at the inference that, officially, it was in *1563 AD*, that the papal Church rejected testimony of the two witnesses of *Revelation ch. 11*. We arrive then at rejection of testimony of Powers for Christ by the papal Church in context of a 1ˢᵗ SEAL. We already have seen that Thomas Aquinas (*d. 1274 AD*) was a Power for Christ whose testimony was rejected by the papal Church. If the papal Church had accepted his testimony, it would not have gone on to insist that, regardless of testimony of their conscience, believers had to obey the pope.

In Revelation 13:5, our Lord Jesus Christ informs Apostle John that the 2ⁿᵈ & 3ʳᵈ SEALS activated by this rejection would last for *42 months*, which is, 1,260 *days*, which translates into 1,260 *calendar years*. We arrive then at the inference that persecution of Protestants by the papal Church, persecution that is well documented, would span *1563 AD through 1823 AD*. It is well documented that, simultaneously, this period was characterized by continuity of conflict and warfare between nations of Europe, and by conflicts between the papal Church, and the Nations.

Historical Spiritual Nugget 28 *The war between Spain and coalition of England and Netherlands (THE CONFLICT) transpired between 1584 and 1609 AD. The 30 years war (1618-1648 AD) between nations of Europe, which resurrected THE CONFLICT on a large scale to include more nations, the French Revolution (1789 AD), which simply created a secular, as opposed to a divine Emperor (1799 AD), and conflicts, which transpired between Napoleon Bonaparte, that is, France and the rest of Europe (1795-1815 AD) all transpired in context of the period, 1563 through 1823 AD.*

Historical Spiritual Nugget 29 *The French Revolution was preceded by centuries of mistreatment or ignoring of the people by their king and their nobles. So then, while the people rejoiced in ejection of Protestants from France, they themselves were mistreated by the very same institutions responsible for persecution and ejection of Protestants.*

Historical Spiritual Nugget 30 *When hatred becomes a principle, in reality, with respect to the things of this life, those who rejoice in persecutions that are rooted in hatreds fare worse than those who are persecuted for faith in the name of Jesus Christ.*

For historical relevance of *1823 AD*, it is important to establish that, upon their decision not to give up their faith, the papal Church resorted to physical excommunication of the saints from all over Europe to what would become known as the United States of America. Consider then that in *1824 AD*, that the United States passed a law - the MONROE DOCTRINE, which refused to continue to tolerate physical excommunication of the saints from Europe to it's shores (*HWE, pg. 462*). In corresponding evidence from backdrop of time for relevance of the year, *1823 AD*, we find corroboration for satisfaction of the prophecy in course of time.

Historical Spiritual Nugget 31 *Evidence provided by our Lord Jesus Christ that is meant to reassure our faith in relation to spiritual reality of the SSGLAE bears up under scrutiny, reveals governance of the SSGLAE in life and affairs on earth.*

Let us then turn our attention to the matter of the Image of the Beast.

The Image to the Beast

The 2 BEASTS attempt to cheat their way to friendship via making of an image to the first beast, and giving of a spirit to the image of the first beast. As we shall see, *Revelation chs. 17 & 18* demonstrate that this attempt at cheating did not work. HALLELUJAH!!!

But then I digress.

We already have discussed why exactly it is worship of images, even images of Jesus Christ is idolatry. For ease of remembrance, since *you and I are supposed to be the* IMAGE OF CHRIST (Romans 8:29), worship of pictures or statues of Jesus Christ, Angels, or saints is, plain and simple, idolatry. This sort of idolatry is one of the great sins of papal Rome, and was part of what led to the schism between the PAPAL CHURCH, and the CHURCH OF THE BYZANTINE EMPIRE. But the Church of the Byzantine Empire was not totally pure in this regard, for while it disallowed worship of statues, it did allow for drawings of religious objects to be considered sacred.

So then, I ask you, what does Jesus look like?

Well, if you are *conformed to the image of Jesus Christ*, if CHRIST IS (SPIR-ITUALLY) FORMED IN YOU, if you have arrived at a PERFECT MAN, if you have arrived at *a measure of the stature of the fullness of Christ*, if you have arrived at a RIGHT RECOGNITION OF CHRIST, you are the image of Jesus Christ.

> IF YOU ARE BLACK, THE IMAGE OF JESUS IS BLACK. IF YOU ARE WHITE, THE IMAGE OF JESUS IS WHITE.

So then, CHRIST IS ALL, AND IN ALL (Colossians 3:11), and there is not any *picture*, *statue*, or *painting* that is representative of image of Jesus Christ.

Spiritual Insight 92 *There does not exist any picture, statue, or painting that is representative of image of Jesus Christ. Every person in whom the glory of Jesus already is formed is image of Jesus Christ.*

The Evidence from Scriptures?

First, note that subsequent to His resurrection, Mary the Magdalene could not recognize Jesus (John 20:11-18). We have then that His features no longer were what they might have looked like prior to His crucifixion. Since the body of sin that hung on the Cross had to die, for cursed is any-one who hangs on a tree (Galatians 3:13), this exactly is what we should expect, that the Holy Spirit would fashion a new body for our Lord Jesus Christ. We arrive then at an important corroborating truth.

The Things That Are 73 *Whatever Jesus looked like prior to His crucifixion, He does not look like anymore.*

NOW THEN, CONSIDER THE DESCRIPTION OF OUR LORD JESUS CHRIST IN REVELATION CH. 1.

Is there any discussion of features of His face?

Can you tell whether His face is angular, chiseled, or robust?

Can you tell whether or not He has a beard?

Does the record say he looks Middle Eastern, Hispanic, Asian, White, or Black?

WELL THEN, LET US READ THE RECORD FOR OURSELVES IN REVELATION 1:12-16.

And I did turn to see the voice that did speak with me, and having turned, I saw seven golden lamp-stands, and in the midst of the seven lamp-stands, ONE LIKE TO A SON OF MAN, clothed to the foot, and girt round at the breast with a golden girdle, and HIS HEAD AND HAIRS WHITE, as if white wool - as snow, and HIS EYES AS A FLAME OF FIRE; and His feet like to fine brass, as in a furnace having been fired, and His voice as a sound of many waters, and having in His right hand seven stars, and out of His mouth a sharp two-edged sword is proceeding, and HIS COUNTENANCE IS AS THE SUN SHINING IN IT'S MIGHT.

✠ FIRST, Jesus has the likeness (form) of a man, is not characterized as a man. This distinction is of critical importance.

✠ SECOND, there does not exist any race whose entire *head is White*. The label 'White Man' serves for distinguishing of Caucasian Men from non-Caucasian Men. THERE DOES NOT EXIST ANY WHITE MAN WHOSE HEAD IS WHITE. By the same token, there does not exist any man, White or otherwise, whose hairs are as WHITE AS SNOW.

✠ THIRD, there does not exist any race whose eyes are as a *flame of fire*.

✠ FOURTH, there does not exist any race whose feet are as *fine brass*.

✠ FIFTH, There does not exist any race whose countenance (face) is as the *sun shining in it's might*.

✠ SIXTH, there is not any discussion of the shape of His face - angular, chiseled, robust - we do not have any idea of the shape of His face. There is not any stipulation of presence, or absence of a beard, or of presence or absence of '*side burns*'.

✠ CONCLUDING INFERENCE: There does not exist any human countenance that is representative of our Lord and Savior Jesus Christ.

Prophecy Insight 93 *If we are to be true to our faith in Jesus Christ, there does not exist any human countenance (face or color) - White, Black, Yellow, or otherwise - that is representative of our Lord Jesus Christ.*

So then, was Jesus a man, or was Jesus God taking on likeness (physical form) of a man?

WELL THEN, WHAT DO THE SCRIPTURES SAY?

For what the law was not able to do, in that it was weak through the flesh, God, HIS OWN SON HAVING SENT IN THE LIKENESS OF SIN-FUL FLESH, and for sin, did condemn the sin in the flesh (Romans 8:3).

Who being in the form of God, thought it not robbery to be equal to God, but did empty Himself, the form of a servant having taken, IN THE LIKENESS OF MEN HAVING BEEN MADE, and in fashion (in living of life) having been found as a man, He humbled Himself, having become obedient unto death - death even of a cross (Philippians 2:6-8).

But when the time had fully come, GOD SENT FORTH HIS SON, BORN OF WOMAN, born under the law (Galatians 4:4).

"How that God was in Christ - a world reconciling to Himself...(2Corinthians 5:19)."

So also it hath been written, The first man Adam became a living creature, the last Adam is for a life-giving spirit (1Corinthians 15:45).

Prophecy Insight 94 *Jesus* NEVER *referred to Himself as* 'A MAN', *only as* 'SON OF MAN'. *By this, He implied that whenever God manifests physically on earth via* BIOLOGICAL BIRTH, *He manifests as a* SON OF MAN', *not as God. So then,* SON OF MAN' *is God in form of man, living as a man, but yet not a man.*

Prophecy Insight 95 *Jesus was God living amongst us in likeness (form) of man. It is unwise then to think of Jesus as a man. Wisdom dictates that you see Jesus as God coming to earth in likeness of man, and demanding that you relate with Him as with any other man, with* REASONING, WHATEVER HONOR HE DESERVES, *and* LOVE. *The disciples of Jesus honored Him, not because He told them that He was God, an event that in fact did not transpire, but rather because* HE WAS A GREAT TEACHER OF THE TRUTH.

Prophecy Insight 96 JESUS IS A LIFE-GIVING SPIRIT. *If you see Jesus as a man, yet are supposed to become like Him, how exactly are you to become what He is, which is, a life-giving spirit?*

Prophecy Insight 97 *You are a* NEW CREATION *in Christ, because while you retain the form of a man, you no longer are a man, you now are a son of God, who lives in form of a man. It is our Lord Jesus Christ who makes this possible. A* SON OF GOD *is a man who arrives at true nature of Christ, which is, a son God living in form of a man. You then cannot be characterized as a Son of Man, or son of Man,* FOR YOU ARE MAN TRANSFORMED INTO SON OF GOD.

Prophecy Insight 98 *Having created a process for transformation of 'man' into 'son of God',* THERE NEVER AGAIN WILL BE A 'SON OF MAN' ON FACE OF THIS EARTH. *Jesus stated this explicitly when He declared in Matthew 24:23,26: "Then if anyone may say to you, 'Lo, here is the Christ!' or 'here!' ye may not believe;" "If therefore they may say to you, 'Lo, in the wilderness he is,' ye may not go forth; 'lo, in the inner chambers,' ye may not believe."*

Consider, at this point in time, that contrary to Scriptures, Christians have crafted a well defined physical representation (*face*) for The Lord Jesus Christ. This face that has been christened '*the face of Jesus*' is the face that is depicted in every MOVIE, PICTURE, PAINTING, or STATUE. This face has become so synonymous with Jesus that for a lot of people, this is the image of Jesus that they carry about in their mind. If you do a search online using the phrases, '*Pictures of Jesus Christ*', and '*Pictures of Salah al-Din*', and compare the pictures or statues that come up, you will find facial representations that are produced eerily similar. The only difference, contrary to the other two sets of pictures, the features of Jesus Christ appear to have arrived at *softened features of a refined* WHITE MAN. So then, Jesus is an Oriental (Jewish) man whose features have, *via contact with the* WHITE MAN, become refined. For a sample of such pictures, see the APPENDIX section at end of this book.

> Can you imagine, or do you perceive the sacrilege of which this is representative?

Contrary to Scriptures, not only have Christians come up with a WHITE MAN image for Christ, they simultaneously have rendered Jesus a, '*thanks to the* WHITE MAN', refined version of an erstwhile leader of Muslims.

Love of Truth 49 *Crafting of a* WHITE MAN *image for Jesus Christ is contrary to Scriptures, is assertion of a falsity, is sacrilege.*

Now note this important fact, which is, from the CATHOLIC CHURCH to EVERY DENOMINATION OF CHRISTIANS - inclusive of *Seventh-day Adventists*, a denomination which believes the Catholic Church to be one of the two beasts of Revelation Chapter 13 - every Church adopts this very same image for depiction of the person of Jesus Christ. Now, add to this the fact that similar features are applied to depiction of *Salah al-Din*, the Saracen leader of Muslims who took over Jerusalem in 1187 AD after it initially had been captured in 1099 AD by the First Christian Crusade, and we arrive at the realization that Jesus has been conferred with features that simultaneously are conferred on leaders of Muslims.

Consider then the declaration of Scriptures in respect of the image to the beast in Revelation 13:14-15.

And it leadeth astray those dwelling on the land, because of the signs that were given to it to do before the beast, saying to those dwelling upon the land to make an image to the beast that hath the stroke of the sword and did live, and there was given to it to give a spirit to the image of the beast, that also the image of the beast may speak, and that it may cause as many as shall not bow before the image of the beast, that they may be killed.

Prophecy Insight 99 *If when you ponder the person of Jesus Christ you have the image in question at back of your mind, you are committing idolatry, you are, rather unconsciously, worshipping the image created by the beast.*

Prophecy Principle 123 *Jesus is a Spirit - the eternal Spirit - The Word - who tabernacled on earth in human form. When you think of Jesus Christ, think of Him as the eternal Word of God (Revelation 19:13).*

The Scriptural Evidence?

So also it hath been written, The first man Adam became a living creature, the last Adam (JESUS) is for a life-giving spirit, the first man is out of the earth (*has a physical body*), the second man is the Lord out of heaven; as is the earthy, such are also the earthy; and as is the heavenly, such are also the heavenly; and according as we did bear the image of the earthy, we shall bear also the image of the heavenly (IF YOU RELATE TO CHRIST AS SPIRIT, YOU WILL BECOME LIKE HIM) - 1Corinthians 15:45, 47-49.

So that we henceforth have known no one according to the flesh, and even if we have known Christ according to the flesh, yet now we know Him no more (KNOW HIM NO MORE ACCORDING TO THE FLESH, RATHER ACCORDING TO SPIRIT) - 2Corinthians 5:16.

Love has been perfected among us in this: that we may have boldness in the day of judgment; because as He is (*which is, Spirit*), so are we (*spirit*) in this world - 1John 4:17.

And to the messenger of the assembly in Sardis write: These things saith He (OUR LORD JESUS CHRIST) who is having the Seven Spirits of God...(Revelation 3:1).

And I saw, and lo, in the midst of the throne, and of the four living creatures, and in the midst of the elders, a Lamb hath stood as it had been slain, having seven horns and seven eyes, which are the Seven Spirits of God, which are sent to all the earth (Revelation 5:6).

Friend, is Jesus a Lamb, or a Lion, or a Root (Revelation 5:5-6), or a man? Clearly Not!

Prophecy Insight 100 *Jesus can take up just about any form He chooses. The form of a man merely is for our benefit, for ease of companionship and friendship.* JESUS IS SPIRIT, IS THE ETERNAL WORD OF GOD.

Prophecy Principle 124 *If you think of Jesus as an earthy man, as a man with a physical body much like yourself, much like Adam, this is all you will have capacity for becoming - an earthy man. But if you consider The Lord Jesus Christ to be Spirit, then you are able to bear His image, the image of the Lord out of heaven. You become a spirit who interacts with the physical universe through his or her body.*

Prophecy Principle 125 *You and I are the image of Christ to the world. If you rather worship drawings or sculptures, which purport to be representative of Christ, but which normatively cannot be representations of Christ, you give up the right and opportunity to be the image of Christ to the world.*

Generalization of avoidance of worship of the beast and it's image

More generally, worship of the beast and it's image involves placing of anything ahead of love for Jesus Christ. In this respect, consider these words by Apostle Paul in 2Thessalonians 2:3-4.

> Let not any one deceive you in any manner, because - if the falling away may not come first, and the man of sin be revealed - the son of the destruction, who is opposing and is raising himself up above all called God or worshipped, so that he in the sanctuary of God as God hath sat down, shewing himself off that he is God - the day (*of institution of the Presence of Christ on earth*) doth not come.

> But seek ye first the reign of God and His righteousness, and all these shall be added to you (Matthew 6:33).

In 2Thessalonians 2:9, Apostle Paul makes clear that the MAN OF SIN, equivalently, MAN OF LAWLESSNESS is an apostate Christian entity. As we already have discussed, in it's declaration, in *867 AD*, that it can force doctrines on people who have faith in Jesus Christ, the papal Church asserted itself as the MAN OF SIN. In this respect, the papal Church received push back in writing from the Church of the Byzantine Empire. This rendered the Church of the Byzantine Empire the first witness of *Revelation ch. 11*. In *1563 AD*, in response to the CHURCH OF THE REFORMATION, the papal

Church again reiterated itself as the MAN OF SIN, as the agent seeking to extol itself above Jesus Christ, as such above God. In this respect, an entity, which professes faith in Jesus Christ, but yet declares the right to ignore explicit commands of The Lord Jesus Christ, attempts to lift itself above Christ, as such attempts to lift itself above The Father. In the repudiation of the claims of the papal Church, the Church of the Reformation became the second witness of *Revelation ch. 11.* In the evidence provided by the 2 WITNESSES, necessity of availability of the Presence of Christ directly to each and every individual was established. We have then that the Presence of Christ arrived on earth, that is, became directly available to individuals at commencement of the time of the CHURCH IN LAODICEA (*1454 AD to ∞*). With printing of the Bible by Gutenberg having commenced in the same *1450s AD*, The Father already was providing resources that would enable individuals arrive at revelations of the Person of Christ, revelations that would lead to ACTUALIZATION of the Presence of Christ.

What exactly are (some of) the idolatrous claims of the papal Church?

꙳ THAT BELIEVERS IN JESUS CHRIST CAN WORSHIP STATUES, PAINTINGS ETC. We know for a fact that this is contrary to teachings of our Lord Jesus Christ (John 4:24), and the apostles (Romans 1:23; Acts 15:20).

꙳ THAT IT CAN FORCE IT'S TEACHINGS ON THOSE WHO HAVE FAITH IN JESUS CHRIST. Neither of our Lord Jesus Christ (Matthew 28:19-20; Revelation 22:18-19), nor the apostles (Acts 18:13, 26:28; 2Corithians 5:11; Colossians 1:28, 3:16) taught or practiced this belief. By this assertion, the Church can command a believer in Christ to disobey his or her Lord and Savior.

꙳ THAT IT'S TRADITIONS ARE JUST AS IMPORTANT AS SCRIPTURES. In the implication that the papal Church can, in presence of conflict between Scriptures and tradition, choose tradition, the papal Church provides itself with a *carte blanche* check for non-submission to Christian Scriptures. Our Lord Jesus Christ made explicitly clear that whenever tradition runs contrary to Scriptures, that such traditions must be abandoned in favor of truth (Matthew 15:3-9).

꙳ THAT THE BREAD AND WINE PHYSICALLY ARE TRANSFORMED INTO THE BODY AND BLOOD OF CHRIST. We know for a fact that this is not true. When we celebrate the Lord's Supper, we confess spiritual reality of the High Priestly work of Jesus Christ. Given we are in the presence of The Father, and have fellowship with the blood of Christ, and with Christ (Hebrews 12:22-24; 1Corinthians 10:16), we celebrate what already is a spiritual reality, do not create any new reality. The work is Christ's not ours.

Love of Truth 50 *If you notice one commonality in the preceding list, note this, that every tradition of the papal Church that I have enumerated obviates either of (i)* REALITY OF PERSON OF CHRIST, *or (ii)* REALITY OF THE PRESENCE OF CHRIST, *or (iii)* REALITY OF THE WORK OF CHRIST *in our behalf. So then, these are not mere doctrinal disagreements, rather these are direct affronts to authority of The Father over those who receive Jesus as Lord and Savior.*

Love of Truth 51 *In essence, while professing faith in Jesus Christ, simultaneously, the papal Church attempts to substitute itself in the role of our Lord Jesus Christ. This is the very worst sort of idolatry.*

Love of Truth 52 *As we already have discussed, if you seek to avoid spiritual deception, you need to develop and arrive at Love for the Truth.*

> Jesus, therefore, said unto the Jews who believe in Him, "If ye may remain in my word, truly my disciples ye are, and ye shall know the truth, and the truth shall make you free." "If then the son may make you free, in reality ye shall be free. (John 8:31-32, 36)."

> him, whose presence is according to the working of the Adversary, in all power, and signs, and lying wonders, and in all deceitfulness of the unrighteousness in those perishing, *because the love of the truth they did not receive for their being saved,* and because of this shall God send to them a working of delusion, for their believing the lie, that they may be judged - all who did not believe the truth, but were well pleased in the unrighteousness (2Thessalonians 2:9-12).

Prophecy Insight 101 *If you do not now learn to love the truth, this, so you are free indeed in The Lord Jesus Christ, you set yourself up for the possibility of arrival at love for deceptions, and loss of your salvation.*

> Well then, how exactly do you place love for Jesus ahead of everything else?

"By this, all men will know that you are my disciples (*equivalently, that you place me first in your lives*), when you have love one for another," is declaration of our Lord Jesus Christ. So then, if you place Jesus first by sticking to the way of love, via refusal to give in to hatred in your relationships with others, is this self aggrandizement on the part of our Lord Jesus Christ?

CLEARLY NOT!!!

Love of Truth 53 *Only a person who is totally deluded in his or her mind, only a person who is totally depraved can declare that it is self aggrandizement for a father to either (i) be upset that neither of His children is willing to take initiative of love in respect of the other; or (ii) be upset that someone intentionally sets out to hurt one of His children.*

Love of Truth 54 *The demand from our Lord Jesus Christ that He be placed first in our love is the demand that you and I treat each other with love. If Jesus turned relations between you and I into a 'free for all', into a 'cage fight', would you construe such an arrangement to be love? If Jesus said all are to love others, but excludes you as a person to be loved, would you consider Jesus to be Love? The absoluteness of the demand of love for each and every fellow man is the evidence that Jesus is Love.*

Love of Truth 55 *It is in your willingness and effort to relate to others with love that you demonstrate placing of Jesus first in your life.*

Wherever there is idolatry, there also are sins that are sexual in nature. Each of the Churches with which Jesus found some fault - as opposed to stating that the church was dead (*Sardis*) or lukewarm (*Laodicea*) - either was characterized by idolatry, or each of idolatry and sexual immorality. These were the Churches at *Ephesus*, *Pergamum*, and *Thyatira*. Consistent with association of idolatry with sins that are sexual in nature, it is common knowledge that Catholic priests have been guilty, on an ubiquitous scale, of sexual molestations of children. That people continue to flock to the Catholic Church reveals there is a LOVE OF LIES principle at work in society, a LOVE OF LIES that perhaps is rooted in political influence of which the Catholic Church is representative.

Love of Truth 56 *If you seek not to be deceived by the two beasts, and the image of the beast, do not allow yourself to be seduced by either of sexual immorality, or tolerance for hatred in your heart towards anyone.*

Love of Truth 57 *Ahab and Jezebel hated only one man (1Kings Chapter 21), and both, and all of their descendants paid a heavy price for that hatred (2Kings Chapters 9 &10). A just Father and almighty God must ensure that hatred for only one man is sufficient for derailment of salvation, for always people only choose to hate persons whom, relative to themselves, they consider to be weak.* WHETHER SUCH PERSONS TURN OUT, AFTER THE FACT, TO BE WEAK, IS ANOTHER MATTER IN ENTIRETY.

Love of Truth 58 *People pander to bosses whom they detest in their hearts, this because, to some extent, their economic welfare depends on good graces of such bosses. Whenever people allow hatreds in their hearts, it always is targeted at people whom they deem inconsequential to their welfare. A just God always ensures such hatred is, to the glory of His holy name, self defeating. In Jesus Name. Hallelujah!!! Amen!!!*

What is required of disciples of Jesus Christ in respect of those who are weak?

And we ought - we who are strong - to bear the infirmities of the weak, and not to please ourselves (Romans 15:1).

See that none of you repays evil for evil, but always seek to do good to one another and to all (1Thessalonians 5:15).

Spiritual Insight 93 *Among disciples of Christ, it is persistence in love that is strength, and giving in to evil that is weakness.*

What response is required of you in respect to the two beasts, and the image to the beast?

THEREFORE SUBMIT TO GOD. RESIST THE DEVIL and he will flee from you (James 4:7).

Be sober, vigilant, because your opponent the devil, as a roaring lion, doth walk about, seeking whom he may swallow up, WHOM RESIST, STEADFAST IN THE FAITH, having known the same sufferings (*the same demand for resistance to attacks from the devil*) to your brotherhood in the world to be accomplished (1Peter 5:8-9).

For walking in the flesh, not according to the flesh do we war, FOR THE WEAPONS OF OUR WARFARE ARE NOT FLESHLY, BUT POWERFUL TO GOD for bringing down of strongholds, reasonings bringing down, and every high thing lifted up against the knowledge of God, and bringing into captivity every thought to the obedience of the Christ (2Corinthians 10:3-5).

Spiritual Insight 94 *The weapons of our warfare are* REASONING *and* CHARACTER *weapons that, in their origins, are spiritual. If you read Christian Scriptures carefully, in every Book, The Father attempts to reason truths with you, attempts to convince you of some important truths. Accompanying all of such reasonings are demonstrations of His Goodness, Mercy, Love, Righteousness, and Power.*

FOR AN EXTENSIVE DISCUSSION OF THE WEAPONS OF OUR WARFARE, PICK UP A COPY EACH OF MY BOOKS, In Jesus Name, and True Sanctification.

Prophetic Lessons 39 *You are not called to passivity in respect of persecution of the beasts, you are called to* ACTIVE SUBMISSION TO GOD, *and* ACTIVE

RESISTANCE TO THE DEVIL. *Your weapons, first and foremost, are spiritual, not earthy, but yet, much like The Father raised up Constantine the Great to fight for His cause with earthy sword and shield in 312 BC, so also it is not impossible that The Father can adopt earthy swords and shields for the good fight of the faith, but only alongside the spiritual armor of our Lord and Savior Jesus Christ.*

What then are the identities of the two beasts of Revelation 13?

Friend, what does it matter? If you continue in faith in Jesus Christ, if you love the truth as it is in Jesus Christ, if you walk in love that you receive through the Holy Spirit towards all men, particularly those who share your faith in Jesus Christ, if you refuse to believe that sexual immorality is permissible, you will not fall under the deception of the two beasts, or their image.

What then do you care about the identities of the two beasts? They are two in number, they cannot mature their evil, they are doomed to fail and be destroyed by our Lord Jesus Christ.

What then do you care? Glorify Christ.

Prophecy Insight 102 *The specific identities of the two beasts are immaterial to your capacity for avoidance of their deception, for maintenance of your faith in Christ. Only knowledge of their strategies, and your willingness and efforts directed at remaining faithful to our Lord Jesus Christ - Love of the Truth, Knowledge of the Truth, and Sanctification of the Holy Spirit, all of which facilitate infusions of the Love of Christ from The Father - are important. Hallelujah! Glory and praise and adoration to The Father, and to the Lamb who sits upon the throne. Amen!!!*

Alright then, lest you assume it is a question to which I do not have an answer, but yet a question whose answer you deem important, here then is identity of the two beasts. There will be more to say on this in our discussion of *Revelation ch. 20.*

Prophecy Interpretation 45 *The First Beast* IS A SPIRIT, WHICH DOES NOT BELIEVE IN JESUS CHRIST, AND WHICH HATES THOSE WHO BELIEVE IN JESUS CHRIST. *It is straightforward to see that a spirit that hates a leader, and followers who love their fellow man is an irrational spirit.* IS IT NOT TRUE THAT GOOD CITIZENS OF A COUNTRY CONSIST OF THOSE WHO DO NOT SET OUT TO HARM THEIR NEIGHBORS?

Prophecy Interpretation 46 *The Second Beast* IS A SPIRIT, WHICH INFILTRATES THE CHURCH, BUT WHICH IN REALITY DOES NOT BELIEVE IN JESUS

CHRIST; *a spirit in Church which pretends to love Jesus Christ, but which hates those who have faith in Jesus Christ. This is the reason this 2ⁿᵈ* BEAST *is referred to as the* FALSE PROPHET *(Revelation 16:13; 19:20; 20:10). It is this spirit, which points out to the First Beast those within The Church who have potential to, or who already have become* POWERS FOR CHRIST.

Prophecy Interpretation 47 *Know this for a spiritual fact, the 2* BEASTS *are not physical entities. The 2* BEASTS *are spirits. While it is true that they work through* ORGANIZATIONS, INSTITUTIONS, CHURCHES, *or* NATIONS, *they are spirits not physical entities.*

You see then that I speak the truth, that the 2 BEASTS do not have any specific institutional identity, that all that matters is your capacity for recognition of their workings, and your commitment to obeying our Lord and Savior Jesus Christ.

The promise from our Lord Jesus Christ is, if you are faithful to Him, with outcome your name is written in The Lamb's Book of Life that you will not worship the Beast, or it's image (Revelation 13:8; 17:8).

Hallelujah!!!

11.5   Revelation 14:1-13 - Additional Confirmation for the SSGLAE

We already established, in *Chapters 7 and 8*, that the worship of the 24 EL-DERS, and the 4 LIVING CREATURES occurs on earth, is embodied in the fact that they live to the praise of the glory of God. By the same token, given the 144,000 are in assembly with the 24 ELDERS, and the 4 LIVING CREATURES, they are on earth, but spiritually speaking simultaneously, have just, in con-text of a transversing of Seals 1 through 3, attained to Powers for Christ, as such have gained entrance into Mount Zion. It is this arrival at designation as Powers for Christ that is celebrated in *Revelation 14:1-5*.

Prophecy Interpretation 48 *The 24* ELDERS *are representative of believers in Christ who previously had attained to* POWERS FOR CHRIST. *The 144,000 are representative of believers in Christ who, in context of the immediately preceding Seals 1 through 3 of an SSGLAE, have attained to recognition from The Father as* POWERS FOR CHRIST.

Prophecy Interpretation 49 *The numbers, 24 and 144,000 are symbolic. Symbolism is evident in the fact that they are multiples of 12. There are 12* TRIBES, *12* DISCIPLES, *12* GATES *into the* NEW JERUSALEM, *12* MONTHS *in a year, etc.*

Prophecy Interpretation 50 *In presence of applications of the number 12, the* ELEMENT *12 is symbolic of* PERFECTION OF PURPOSE. *So then, the 144,000 all belong to one of the 12* TRIBES *of Israel (Revelation 7:1-8; 21:12), with outcome all who believe in Jesus Christ now are the Israel of God (Galatians 6:15-16).*

Prophecy Interpretation 51 *Presence of 24* ELDERS *is consistent with creation of only 2* AGES *by our Lord Jesus Christ - 12* ELDERS *for each of the* AGE OF THE MESSENGERS, *and the* AGE OF THE PRESENCE OF CHRIST. *Using the same principle, 144,000 sealed out of all of mankind is suggestive of, in total, 12* CYCLES *of SSGLAE. But then, it is The Father who is counting.*

Prophecy Interpretation 52 *If The Father is counting down to the 12*th ITER-ATION *of the SSGLAE, given just about all nations of the earth remain on the RP7* PATH *of the SSGLAE, in absence of any reformation, it is the case, perhaps, that it is failure of the 12*th *SSGLAE, which ushers in the* SECOND COMING OF CHRIST.

We already have engaged in extensive discussions of Hebrews 12:22-24. In the Scripture, while physically you remain on earth, spiritually, you are assembled in Presence of The Father on Mount Zion, which is the same thing as the New Jerusalem. Note that the 144,000 are on Mount Zion, meaning it is not just that they are assembled to Mount Zion, but rather have become part of the spiritual assembly that is gathered on Mount Zion. In this respect, it unequivocally is the case that they have transformed into '*just men whose spirits already are perfected*', this while they remain alive on earth. That the phrase '*bought from the earth*' refers to saints who physically are on earth is evident as follows.

> FOR YE WERE BOUGHT WITH A PRICE; GLORIFY, THEN, GOD IN YOUR BODY AND IN YOUR SPIRIT, which are God's (1Corinthians 6:20).

> Having known that, not with corruptible things - silver or gold - were ye redeemed (*bought*) from your foolish behavior delivered by fathers, but with precious blood, as of a lamb unblemished and unspotted - Christ's (1Peter 1:18-19).

So then, the 144,000 are bought out of the persecution, are sealed with the Holy Spirit, yet remain on earth, with outcome what is expected next is judgment of the nations in context of the 4th Seal.

In the discussion of the declarations of the three messengers of *Revelation ch. 14* to follow, note that the messengers are not numbered, merely that they total three in number. Given they are not numbered, the NU-MEROLOGY OF THE FATHER does not apply. Consistent with arrival at the 4th

Seal, in Revelation 14:6-7 a messenger flies in mid-heaven proclaiming the good news that the judgment of The Father has arrived. In context of the judgments of The Father, people are advised to:

> "...fear God and give glory to Him, for the hour of His judgment has come; and worship Him who made heaven and earth, the sea and springs of water (Revelation 14:7).

Following on the first messenger, another messenger declares that Babylon (*all Churches that substitute falsehoods for the truths of the gospel*) has fallen, she who made all nations drink of the wine of the wrath of her fornication. The message of the second angel of Revelation 14 alludes to the fact that Churches, which were supposed to be faithful to Christ, had deviated into falsehoods, idolatry, and whoredom. We have then that consistent with insights developed in the preceding chapter, that the 144,000 are sealed in context of an apostate Church system. Condemnation of Babylon implies those who are perfected in context of a new 1st Seal period come out of Babylon for forming of a new Church that has feasibility of arrival at a perfect man. Consistent with presence of an apostate Church in context of Seals 1 through 3, Revelation 14:8,9-10 declares as follows.

> And another messenger did follow, saying, Fall, fall, did Babylon, the great city, because of the wine of the wrath of her whoredom she hath given to all nations to drink.

The third messenger that follows in Revelation 14:9-12, discusses persecution that erupts in response to arrival of new life in the Church, and warns people not to worship the beast and his image else they will drink of the wine of the wrath of God. The third messenger concludes with the two most important characteristics of disciples of Jesus Christ.

> And a third messenger did follow them, saying in a great voice, If any one the beast doth bow before, and his image, and doth receive a mark upon his forehead, or upon his hand, HE ALSO SHALL DRINK OF THE WINE OF THE WRATH OF GOD, that hath been mingled unmixed in the cup of His anger, and he shall be tormented in fire and brimstone before the holy messengers, and before the Lamb (Revelation 14:9-10).

> Here is the endurance of the saints: here are those keeping the commands of God, and the faith of Jesus (Revelation 14:12).

Following on these words, those who die in the Lord Jesus from that point on are declared to be blessed, meaning some saints die as part of their testimony to reality of faith in our Lord Jesus Christ. But they die only to rest from their labors, and their works (*the white garment of the saints*) follow them. Simultaneously, there is a promise of the WRATH OF GOD on all those who worship the beast, and the image of the beast.

Prophecy Insight 103 *Those who die in the Lord are blessed (Revelation 14:13) because they die for their faith in Jesus Christ, as such have rest from the persecution that is inflicted on the Church by Babylon the Great.*

What are the sources of the Wrath of God?

And I saw another sign in the heaven, great and wonderful, seven messengers having the seven last plagues, because in these was completed the WRATH OF GOD (Revelation 15:1).

And one of the four living creatures did give to the seven messengers seven golden vials, FULL OF THE WRATH OF GOD, who is living to the ages of the ages; and filled was the sanctuary with smoke from the glory of God, and from His power, and no one was able to enter into the sanctuary till the seven plagues of the seven messengers may be finished (Revelation 15:7-8).

Prophecy Interpretation 53 *On the RP7 PATH - the only path on which the 2 BEASTS and BABYLON are encountered - following on the 4th SEAL, there is arrival at the 7 VIALS of the Wrath of God. Given the Seal that follows the 4th SEAL is the 7th SEAL, a Seal whose last segment coincides with the 6th SEAL, The Lord Jesus Christ declares that, on the RP7 PATH, there is substitution of the 7 VIALS of the Wrath of God for the 7 TRUMPETS. The necessity of this substitution soon will be clear.*

The dynamics of the SSGLAE from the 4th SEAL, and onwards are as follows. The Nations and Babylon persecute those who have faith in Jesus in context of the 4th SEAL. Naturally, the 5th SEAL consists in entirety of the saints asking The Father for vengeance. We arrive then at simultaneity of the 7th SEAL, and the 6th SEAL. Within this context, there must be a transversal of the WRATH OF GOD prior to arrival at simultaneity of the 7th VIAL. of the Wrath of God, and the 6th SEAL. So then, whereas the 6th SEAL is simultaneous with the 7th TRUMPET of the 7th Seal in context of the GP7 PATH, On the RP7 PATH, the 6th SEAL is simultaneous with the 7th VIAL of the 7th Seal.

11.6   Revelation Chapters 15, 16, & 19 - The 7 Vials of the Wrath of God

Revelation *ch. 15* introduces the 7 VIALS of the wrath of The Father. Revelation *ch. 16* details the wraths. These wraths from The Father are poured out on Babylon and The Nations for persecution of His saints. These wraths, equivalently, plagues, complete the wrath of The Father, and are represented as 7 VIALS that are poured out by 7 MESSENGERS. Consistent with the assertion that the 7 VIALS follow on the 4th SEAL, as such transpire in context of the 7th SEAL, Revelation 15:2-4 declares as follows.

> And I saw a sea of glass mingled with fire, and THOSE WHO DO GAIN THE VICTORY OVER THE BEAST, AND HIS IMAGE, AND HIS MARK, AND THE NUMBER OF HIS NAME, standing by the sea of glass, having harps of God, and they sing the song of Moses, servant of God, and the song of the Lamb, saying, "Great and wonderful are thy works, O Lord God, The Almighty, righteous and true are thy ways, O King of saints, who may not fear thee, O Lord, and glorify thy name? Because Thou alone art kind, because all the nations shall come and bow before Thee, because thy righteous acts were manifested."

FIRE is representative of the cleansing work of the Holy Spirit (Matthew 3:1; Mark 9:49; Luke 3:16; Acts 2:3; 1Corinthians 3:5-15; Hebrews 12:29). GLASS is symbolic of all those who, through the ages, have become conformed to the image of our Lord Jesus Christ. Glass mingled with fire then is symbolic of all believers who, as evident in their cleansing from sins and weaknesses, have through time reflected the glory of Christ. In this respect, consider the following Scriptures.

> That the proof of faith - much more precious than of gold that is perishing, and through fire (*the cleansing work of the Holy Spirit*) being approved - may be found to praise, and honor, and glory, in the revelation of Jesus Christ - 1Peter 1:7.

> And we all, with unvailed face, the glory of the Lord beholding in a mirror (*in a glass, that is, in a reflection, not directly*), to the same image (*into the same sort of reflection*) are being transformed, from glory to glory, even as by the Spirit of the Lord (2Corinthians 3:18).

> For we see now through a mirror (*glass*) obscurely, and then face to face; now I know in part, and then I shall fully know, as also I was known (1Corinthians 13:12).

> Therefore, we also having so great a cloud of witnesses (*a cloud of* REFLECTIONS) set around us, every weight having put off, and the closely besetting sin, through endurance may we run the contest that is set before us, looking to the author and perfecter of faith (*making sure to focus on Jesus, the one of whom all reflections testify*)... - Hebrews 12:1-2.

Prophecy Insight 104 *We see through a* GLASS (MIRROR) *darkly because when we believe in Jesus, typically all we have available to us is the witness of those who precede us in the faith. The clarity with which we see depends on how well those who precede us, with whom we are in fellowship, got to know Christ.*

Prophecy Insight 105 *The believers depicted in Revelation 15:2-4 do not themselves become mirrors (images) of Christ, rather by seeing through images of Christ arrived at faith in Christ, but not at conformity with the image of Christ (Romans 8:29). So then, all of the believers depicted in Revelation 15:2-4 are* NEOPHYTES *who, during the 4ᵗʰ* SEAL, *maintain faith in Jesus Christ.*

Can a Church having Powers for Christ choose the RP7 path?

Well then, WAS JESUS A POWER FOR GOD, and was He able to induce The Church of that time - the Jewish Nation - to choose the BP7 PATH? How then about ELIJAH, ELISHA, ISAIAH, JEREMIAH, EZEKIEL, and DAVID, is it not true that each of this men was a Power for God? But were they successful at inducing the Church of that time - the Jewish Nation - to choose the BP7 PATH? You see then that The Father already has provided us with numerous instances of Powers for Christ who, regardless of their efforts, could not induce The Church to choose the BP7 PATH.

Prophetic Lessons 40 *Regardless of their best efforts, The Church can refuse to respond to* POWERS FOR CHRIST, *as such deliberately choose, and arrive on the RP7 PATH.*

Prophetic Lessons 41 NEOPHYTES *who still are beset by sinful pride, lusts of the flesh, and lusts of the eyes can resist the Right Recognition of Christ of which* POWERS FOR CHRIST *are representative.*

Prophetic Lessons 42 *Whenever* POWERS FOR CHRIST *are not part of institutional leadership of The Church, that is, are not regarded as leaders by believers in the name of Jesus Christ, leadership of The Church consists either of* NEOPHYTES *who resist the Right Recognition of Christ of which Powers for Christ are representative;* CHARLATANS, *equivalently,* FALSE PROPHETS; *or a mix of* FLESHLY NEOPHYTES *and* CHARLATANS.

Whenever The Church refuses to respond to Powers for Christ, Powers for Christ experience persecution from each of CHARLATANS and FLESHLY NEOPHYTES within The Church, and The Nations. We have then that those who best reflect Jesus - POWERS FOR CHRIST - are persecuted by The Church, and The Nations. The Father remedies, such injustice in context of VIALS 1 through 6 of the 7ᵗʰ Seal.

Prophetic Lessons 43 *Whenever The Church finds herself on either of the BP7 or GP7* PATHS, *it is guided either by* POWERS FOR CHRIST, *or a mix of* SPIRITUAL NEOPHYTES *and* POWERS FOR CHRIST. *In presence of a mix in leadership of The Church,* NEOPHYTES *willingly have bought into the Right Recognition of Christ of which Powers for Christ are representative.*

Prophetic Lessons 44 *On the GP7* PATH, *unity of The Church portends destruction of The Nations, as such, The Nations are unable to be effective in their persecution of The Church. Since* POWERS FOR CHRIST *look out for the weak within The Church, The Nations are unable to succeed at targeting of weak believers, that is, are unsuccessful at targeting of* SPIRITUAL NEOPHYTES *within The Church. If there exist* CHARLATANS *in The Church in context of the GP7* PATH, *they are destroyed in context of the 1ˢᵗ* TRUMPET *of the 7ᵗʰ Seal and The Church continues triumphantly towards the 7ᵗʰ* TRUMPET *of the 7ᵗʰ Seal.*

The Vials, and Numerology of The Father

In *Chapter 6*, we established the NUMEROLOGY OF THE FATHER. We have seen how the NUMEROLOGY has been consistently satisfied in context of the 7 SEALS, and the 7 TRUMPETS. If the NUMEROLOGY continues to be robust to interpretation of the prophecies entrusted to Apostle John, with caveat to follow, they must be applicable to interpretation of the 7 VIALS. The caveat, which must be borne in mind in interpretation of the 7 VIALS resides in characterization of the Vials as PLAGUES which punish the beasts and those who worship the beast and his image, with hope they reform from evil. If people are to reform from evil, companionship and friendship built around evil must be unwound, with outcome evil no longer is profitable. Consistent with proposed typology, in Scriptures, a VIAL contains an item, such as *oil*, which has a specific characteristic or purpose. In the specific context under consideration, it is explicitly stated that the VIALS contain the Wrath of God, meaning they serve for destruction of capacity for evil, equivalently, for unwinding of capacity for evil.

> And Samuel taketh the VIAL OF THE OIL, and poureth on his head, and kisseth him, and saith, "Is it not because Jehovah hath appointed thee over His inheritance for leader (1Samuel 1:1).

> And Elisha the prophet hath called to one of the sons of the prophets, and saith to him, "Gird up thy loins, and take this VIAL OF OIL in thy hand, go to Ramoth-Gilead (2Kings 9:1).

Prophecy Interpretation 54 *In Christian Scriptures,* A VIAL *always has character only in context of whatever it is it contains, meaning a Vial is defined by it's contents.*

IN PRESENCE OF THE CONTEXT, THE Numerology of The Father HAS APPLI-
CATION AS:

- ♣ ELEMENT 1: New Beginnings of Pain.

- ♣ ELEMENT 2: Unwinding of Companionship of Purpose around evil.

- ♣ ELEMENT 3: Unwinding of Inner Circle of Friendship built around evil.

- ♣ ELEMENT 4: Grand Judgment of those who could be considered to have been deceived by the beasts.

- ♣ ELEMENT 5: Arrival at Incapacity for Righteousness.

- ♣ ELEMENT 6: Execution of Judgment.

- ♣ ELEMENT 7: Completion of Judgment, and Commencement of a New Age characterized by Righteousness.

Prophecy Interpretation 55 *Whereas* TRUMPETS *serve for destruction of Charlatan Christians, and prevention of those who love evil from arrival at* INNER CIRCLE OF FRIENDSHIP, *this on the GP7* PATH, VIALS *serve for unwinding of Inner Circles of Friendship already arrived at in context of the RP7* PATH *of the SSGLAE.*

The 7 Vials of the Wrath of God

The 1ˢᵗ Vial that is poured out goes on the land, resulting in grievous sores on those who have the mark of the beast, and those who bow down to the image of the beast (Revelation 16:1-2). As already discussed, men are likened to TREES or GRASS, both of which require LAND for existence. Pouring of the 1ˢᵗ Vial on the land implies pouring of the wrath of God on nutrients in the land required for nourishment of men, resulting in sores - bad and grievous - on men. It is clear that in presence of sin, The Father commands the land to produce what is hurtful to man. In essence, disease can be outcome of the wrath of God poured on the land, with outcome what is produced by the land becomes hurtful to man's constitution, resulting in creation of new diseases.

Prophecy Insight 106 *In the pouring out of the 1ˢᵗ Vial, The Father promises man that one of the consequences of rebellion against His Love as foundation of civil laws is manifestation of diseases within populations of men. Only in presence of refusal to eat anything at all can man who rebels against God avoid this punishment for sin. Given the diseases come out of the land, neither of the* REBELLIOUS VEGETARIAN *nor* REBELLIOUS MEAT EATER *are able to avoid punishment meted out by The Father.*

Numerology 12 *The pouring of the 1st Vial on the land represents a NEW BE-GINNING, represents Commencement of Pourings that, for those who worship the beast, destroy substance of life on earth.*

The 2nd Vial is poured out to the sea. As already discussed, the sea represents trouble. In the pouring out of the 2nd Vial on trouble, there is a quelling of the trouble that is directed at those who have faith in the name of Jesus. The pouring out kills off not only the trouble, but also all who are sources of the trouble (Revelation 16:3). In respect of this, the Holy Spirit has this to say (through Apostle Paul):

> We ought to give thanks to God always for you, brethren, as it is meet, because increase greatly doth your faith, and abound doth the love of each one of you all, to one another; so that we ourselves do glory in you in the assemblies of God, for your endurance and faith in all your persecutions and tribulations that ye bear; a token of the righteous judgment of God, for your being counted worthy of the reign of God, for which also ye suffer, since IT IS A RIGHTEOUS THING WITH GOD TO GIVE BACK TO THOSE TROUBLING YOU - TROUBLE (2Thessalonians 1:3-6).

Spiritual Insight 95 *Apostle Paul reiterates the fact that increase of faith is evident in increase of love towards one another. When people claim that their faith increases, while yet their love grows cold, they assert that the faith of which they speak is not the faith of Jesus Christ.*

Prophecy Insight 107 *People who trouble those who have faith in Jesus Christ receive trouble in return, and perish in the trouble. The trouble outlined affects the blood, makes the blood like that of a man who is dead. In this, The Father perhaps refers to all sorts of diseases that affect well functioning of the blood.*

Numerology 13 *In context of Digestion, FOOD and BLOOD are 'Companions'. Without Blood, Food cannot be digested. In the pouring out of the 2nd Vial, such that Blood ceases to function right, way before science arrived at the insight, The Father revealed Companionship of Purpose inherent in relation between INGESTED FOOD and BLOOD.*

The 3rd Vial is poured out on the rivers and the fountains of waters. We already know that rivers and fountains represent, respectively, peace and life. On pouring out of the 3rd Vial, there came blood. By this symbolism, The Father, who is Father of spirits (Hebrews 12:9) demonstrates that He, Father of all spirits has power for killing off of spirits, which, contrary to His will, were supplying life and peace to living souls whom He killed off in context of the 2nd Vial. In this respect, the Scriptures declare as follows.

And will you profane Me among My people for handfuls of barley and for pieces of bread (will you profane me so you can have access to pittance of life), killing people who should not die, and keeping people alive who should not live, by your lying to My people who listen to lies (Ezekiel 13:19).

Because with lies you have made the heart of the righteous sad, whom I have not made sad; and you have strengthened the hands of the wicked, so that he does not turn from his wicked way to save his life. Therefore you shall no longer envision futility nor practice divination; for I will deliver My people out of your hand, and you shall know that I am the Lord (Ezekiel 13:22-23).

Prophecy Insight 108 *The 3ʳᵈ* VIAL *destroys lying spirits who have been keeping the wicked alive, and who have been attempting to pain the hearts of the righteous, such that they despair of life, and seek to die.*

Numerology 14 LIVING SOULS *that are sources of trouble for the righteous having been killed off in context of the 2ⁿᵈ* VIAL, *the 3ʳᵈ* VIAL *targets* LYING SPIRITS, *which enabled the persecutions,* LYING SPIRITS, *which propelled* LIVING SOULS *to rebellion against The Father. The 3ʳᵈ* VIAL *completes destruction of the Inner Circle of Friendship consisting of* LIVING SOULS *and* LYING SPIRITS, *which were responsible for persecution that transpired in context of the 4ᵗʰ* SEAL.

The 4ᵗʰ Vial is poured out on the sun, resulting in scorching of men with fire, and great heat. In presence of the scorching, men spoke evil of the name of God, and refused to reform, refused to give Him glory. Note that, with living souls that were sources of the trouble having been killed off, and with lying spirits, which produced the deceptions that were sources of the persecutions destroyed, other than the righteous, people who are left are those who worshipped the dragon, the beast, and the image of the beast. With those who deceived them out of the way, those who worshiped the beast reveal that they themselves love evil, as such refuse to repent.

The sun is given to man for ruling of the day, with outcome man finds healing in the rays of the sun (Malachi 4:2). Medically, this is evident in association of mild rays of the sun with accruement of Vitamin D in the body. In presence of persecution of faith in Christ, the sun becomes a scorcher of men, resulting in diseases, as opposed to healing. MELANOMAS OF THE SKIN, which are one of the five fastest growing cancers in the United States, and other diseases that are outcomes of exposure to sunlight, perhaps are outcomes of outpouring of the 4ᵗʰ Vial. Increases in temperatures, increases that have been known to be fatal in the sense of leading to deaths also can be outcome of pouring out of the 4ᵗʰ Vial.

Prophecy Insight 109 *The 4ᵗʰ* Vial *turns the rays of the sun, which ought to bring healing to man, into a source of discomfort, pain, and disease.*

Numerology 15 *The 4ᵗʰ* Vial *produces a Grand Judgment of those -* Hateful Citizens of the Nations *- who worshipped the dragon, the beast, and the image of the beast. In the decision not to reform and give glory to The Father,* Hateful Citizens of the Nations *reveal that the deception worked only because they also love evil.*

The 5ᵗʰ Vial is poured out on the throne of the beast, resulting in his kingdom becoming darkened, resulting also in pains and sores. With Maturity of Righteousness depicted as the 'righteous shining as the sun', Element 5 of the *Numerology of The Father* is symbolic for *Maturity of Righteousness*. In context of plagues, which destroy capacity for evil, Element 5 must have characterization of incapacity for shining as the sun, hence, must be symbolic of arrival at darkness. We arrive then at evidence for applicability of Numerology of The Father. Upon arrival of the darkness, with the tongue symbolic of evil speaking (Revelation 16:11), the first beast, and the second beast (false prophet), both of whom are spirits whom eventually are cast into the lake of fire (Revelation 20:10), and those who worship the beast and his image gnaw their tongues from pain.

Numerology 16 *The 5ᵗʰ* Vial *conforms with Numerology of The Father that is established for the* Element *5.*

The tongue is supposed to be guarded from evil (1Peter 3:10), and be a source of loving words to others (1John 3:18). When it is only the tongue that speaks, with outcome the words do not come from within a man, this is evidence for Sophistry, for Artifice of interactions (1John 3:18). In this respect, those who have the faith of Jesus Christ are admonished to speak to one another only words that edify the hearers, only words that build up (Romans 14:19; Ephesians 4:29), for words that build up never can be words that are rooted in artifice or sophistry. When people choose love for evil over love for good, they apply their tongues to speaking of evil (1Peter 3:10), that is, to declarations of faithlessness (1Timothy 1:4), with outcome they cease to love life and to have good days (1Peter 3:10). In midst of cessation of love for life and good days, they are convicted of the Holy Spirit, and the Holy Spirit seeks for them to burst out into the declaration that Jesus is Lord. In order to avoid confession that Jesus is Lord (Philippians 2:11), they gnaw their tongues and choose to remain in pain, as opposed to confession that 'Jesus Christ is Lord to the glory of God.' That they choose not to acknowledge truth of which they have become cognizant is evident in the assertion that '*they did not reform from their (evil) works.*'

Prophecy Insight 110 *Men gnaw their tongues because while they are convicted in their hearts that Jesus Christ is Lord, they choose to refuse to give in to the Spirit of God, choose to remain in evil, choose to continue to worship the beast and it's image. For avoidance of the confession that 'JESUS CHRIST IS LORD' TO THE GLORY OF GOD, they rather gnaw on their own tongues, such that they continue in pain.*

Concerning gnawing of tongues, such as not to acknowledge Jesus as Lord, that is, such as to remain in darkness, our Lord Jesus Christ, Apostle John, and Apostle Paul declare as follows in John 3:19-20, 1John 1:7, and 1Corinthians 12:3.

> And this is the judgment, that the light hath come to the world, and men did love darkness rather than light, for their works were evil; for every one who is doing wicked things hateth the light and doth not come unto the light, that his works may not be detected.

> But if we walk in the light as He is in the light, we have fellowship with one another, and the blood of Jesus Christ His Son cleanses us from all sin.

> Wherefore, I give you to understand that no one, in the Spirit of God speaking, saith Jesus is anathema,, and no one is able to say Jesus is Lord, except in the Holy Spirit.

Prophecy Interpretation 56 *Whenever men choose to cling to evil, they love darkness, and refuse to come to the light. In context of the 5ᵗʰ VIAL, The Father eliminates all possibility of repentance from the spirits of the beast and the false prophet, and from those who choose to worship the beast, and the image of the beast. Given all of these spirits and men explicitly refused to repent in context of the 4ᵗʰ Vial, casting of the beasts and those who worship the beast and his image into darkness is righteous and just.*

The 6ᵗʰ VIAL is poured out on the great river, the Euphrates, which then dries up so the way of the kings who are from the rising of the sun may be made ready (Revelation 16:12). We already know that a river symbolizes peace, so then, the great river, the Euphrates symbolizes a Great Peace that dries up, that turns into conflict. Since the sun rises in the east, the kings come out of Asia. Upon seeing that the great river is dried up, three unclean spirits - spirits of demons - are released by the dragon, the beast, and the false prophet. These demonic spirits bring together the kings of the earth together to the battle of that great day of God the Almighty.

The 6ᵗʰ VIAL is tantamount to our Lord Jesus Christ saying to Judas Iscariot (I paraphrase), "what you believe you must do, do quickly (John 13:27)." The 6ᵗʰ VIAL makes it easy for the kings and their nations to come together for engaging our Lord Jesus Christ in battle. Combined, a coming out of kings from Asia for conflict, and an assembling of all the kings of the earth for battle with our Lord Jesus Christ signals that the kings of the earth simultaneously are fighting each other, and characterizing Jesus as their common enemy. So then, as currently seems to be the case, while they fight each other, Homosexuals, Muslims, Buddhists, Atheists, Agnostics etc. simultaneously are ganged up against those who have faith in Jesus Christ.

The Response of The Father?

Why have nations tumultuously assembled? And do peoples meditate vanity? Station themselves do kings of the earth and princes have been united together, against Jehovah, and against His Messiah: Let us draw off their cords, and cast from us their thick bands (*let us set ourselves free from their demand that we love one another*) - Psalms 2:1-3.

HE WHO IS SITTING IN THE HEAVENS DOTH LAUGH, THE LORD DOTH MOCK AT THEM. Then doth He speak unto them in His anger, and IN HIS WRATH HE DOTH TROUBLE THEM. And now, O kings, act wisely, be instructed, O judges of the earth. Serve ye Jehovah with fear, and rejoice with trembling. Kiss the Chosen One, lest He be angry, and ye lose the way, when His anger burneth but a little, O the happiness of all trusting in Him - Psalms 2:4-5, 10-12.

Prophecy Insight 111 *The 6th VIAL sets the stage for the warfare between our Lord Jesus Christ and His messengers, and the kings of the earth, warfare that transpires in context of pouring out of The 7th VIAL.*

We already established that the Numerology of The Father is an exercise in symbolisms, symbolisms, which are not necessarily sequential. In this respect, in context of the 7 SEALS, we saw that the 7th TRUMPET of the 7th Seal coincides with the 6th SEAL. We also know that on the BP7 PATH, there is a jump from the 1st SEAL to the 7th TRUMPET of the 7th Seal. We further know that the ELEMENT 6 symbolizes each of Commencement and Execution of Justice. In context of the 7 Vials, the 6th VIAL symbolizes *Commencement of Execution of Justice*, execution that is *Completed* in context of the 7th Vial.

Numerology 17 *The 6th VIAL is symbolic of COMMENCEMENT OF EXECUTION OF JUSTICE by The Father, as such is consistent with Numerology of The Father.*

The 7th VIAL ushers in execution of judgment of the nations and their kings in context of warfare between our Lord Jesus Christ and His messengers, and the kings of the earth. This warfare is discussed in *Revelation ch.*

19. In this respect, *Revelation chs. 17 & 18* serve as an interlude, provide some details on the relationship between Babylon, the Nations, and the saints of God. The question here is,

"Is the battle depicted in Revelation ch. 19 literal or spiritual?"

First, a cursory reading of Revelation 6:12-17 demonstrates that the 7th VIAL that is poured out coincides with the 6th Seal. As with the Trumpets then, the 7th VIAL of the 7th Seal coincides with the 6th Seal.

We arrive then at insights that are of extreme importance.

Prophecy Interpretation 57 TRUMPETS *1 through 7 of the 7th Seal, and Vials 1 through 7 of the 7* VIALS *are substitutes.*

Prophecy Interpretation 58 *On the GP7* PATH, *subsequent to the 5th Seal, Life and Affairs on earth experience* TRUMPETS *1 through 7 of the 7th Seal. The 6th Seal coincides with the 7th* TRUMPET *of the 7th Seal.*

Prophecy Interpretation 59 *On the RP7* PATH, *the Church having not arrived at Maturity of Righteousness, there is not arrival at Maturity of Righteousness, and the 7th Seal consists of Vials 1 through 7; the 7th Vial of the 7th Seal coincides with the 6th Seal.*

Prophecy Interpretation 60 *We already know that on the BP7* PATH, *there is transition from the 1st* SEAL *directly to the 7th* TRUMPET *of the 7th Seal. On the BP7* PATH, *the 6th Seal never is activated.*

Symbolism of Removal of Every Mountain

In Christian Scriptures, Mountains signify TRUTH, RIGHTEOUSNESS, or HOLINESS (Zechariah 8:3; Psalms 26:6; Jeremiah 31:23). When a person's sense of righteousness is inflated, the person's righteousness has characterization as a MOUNTAIN OF PRIDE (Luke 3:5). When righteousness is genuine, it is a MOUNTAIN THAT IS IMMOVEABLE, that is, steadfast, and unwavering (Matthew 17:20; 21:21). When people's sense of righteousness is tied to a specific location, Worship of God is tied to a specific Mountain (John 4:20-21). When a person faces a challenge that tests their capacity for maintaining righteousness, RIGHTEOUSNESS IS A MOUNTAIN in need of scaling, or in need of transformation into a plain (Zechariah 4:7). In Scripture, Islands symbolize VULNERABILITY (Isaiah 23:2,6).

Fleeing of every mountain implies that, upon revelation of the righteousness of our Lord Jesus Christ, every righteousness that is contrary to the righteousness of our Lord Jesus Christ is unable to stand. Fleeing of every mountain further implies failure of every alternate form of worship of God, failure of the pride of the nations, and arrival of a challenge, which is, what to do in presence of imminent spectre of destruction. In this respect, consider Micah 4:1-3; and Revelation 6:15-17.

It shall come to pass in the latter days that the mountain of the house of the Lord shall be established as the highest of the mountains, and shall be raised up above the hills; and the peoples shall flow to it, and many nations shall come, and say: "COME, LET US GO UP TO THE MOUNTAIN OF THE LORD, TO THE HOUSE OF THE GOD OF JACOB; THAT HE MAY TEACH US HIS WAYS AND WE MAY WALK IN HIS PATHS." For out of Zion shall go forth the law, and the word of the Lord from Jerusalem.

And the kings of the earth, and the great men, and the rich, and the chiefs of the thousands, and the mighty, and every servant, and every freeman, hid themselves in the dens, and in the rocks of the mountains, and they say to the mountains and to the rocks, "Fall upon us, and hides us from the face of Him who is sitting upon the throne, and from the anger of the Lamb, because come did the great day of His anger, and who is able to stand?"

Upon pouring out of the 7th VIAL, every truth that man thought he knew, every prior standard of holiness is shown for what it is, that is, nothing but ROPES MADE OUT OF SAND, nothing but filthy rags (Isaiah 64:6). All of mankind arrives at the realization that the only thing that does not fail is the Love of God. It is not only that secular knowledge fails, but also that Prophecies, Tongues, and knowledge that is not rooted in the Love of God, all of which are elements that are specific to Christianity, fail (1Corinthians 13:8).

In this respect, consider Ephesians 3:17-19, and 1Corinthians 13:10.

So that Christ may dwell in your hearts through faith. And I pray that you, being rooted and established in love, may have power, TOGETHER WITH ALL THE SAINTS, to grasp how wide and long and high and deep is the love of Christ, AND TO KNOW THE LOVE THAT SURPASSES KNOWLEDGE - THAT YOU MAY BE FILLED TO THE MEASURE OF ALL THE FULLNESS OF GOD.

And when that which is perfect (attainment to the LOVE OF GOD, to a PERFECT MAN, to a MEASURE OF THE STATURE OF THE FULLNESS OF CHRIST, to a RIGHT RECOGNITION OF CHRIST, to a POWER FOR CHRIST) may come, then that which is in part (*prophecy, other sorts of knowledge, tongues* etc.) shall become useless.

Prophecy Principle 126 *To arrive at* KNOWLEDGE OF THE LOVE OF OUR LORD JESUS CHRIST *is to arrive at* A FORM OF KNOWLEDGE *that surpasses* ANY OTHER FORM OF KNOWLEDGE. *In presence of knowledge of the Love of God, all other knowledge becomes 'useless', are shown to be inferior to knowledge of the Love of God.*

Prophecy Principle 127 Knowledge of the Love of God, *equivalently, Knowledge of the Love of Christ, is a specific form of knowledge, a knowledge that surpasses any other.*

Simultaneous with fleeing of every mountain out of it's place, those who have faith in our Lord Jesus Christ, those who were thought to have become vulnerable, who are regarded as having become islands surrounded on all sides by the enemy, all of a sudden are thus no longer. All of a sudden are the victors. So then, the assertion,

"If God be for us, who can be against us (Romans 8:31)?"

proves to be true. That the righteous still are on the earth in context of the 7ᵗʰ VIAL is evident in Revelation 16:15, which states:

Lo, I do come as a thief; happy is he who is watching, and keeping his garments, that he may not walk naked and they may see his unseemliness.

Prophecy Insight 112 *If believers still have to remain faithful in order to be saved, they remain on earth during the time of the 7ᵗʰ VIAL, which coincides with the 6ᵗʰ SEAL.*

With respect to spiritual nature of the 7ᵗʰ VIAL or 6ᵗʰ Seal, consider Psalms Chapter 2. In Psalms 2:1-3, the nations and their kings gather against The Father and our Lord Jesus Christ. In Psalms 2:4, The Father laughs at the foolish boldness that makes the nations gather against Him and His Messiah. In Psalms 2:5-9, The Father gives His anointed permission to crush the nations and their kings, and to rule over them with a sceptre of iron. But then the nations remain afterwards, meaning the rule is spiritual, for in Revelation 19:14-16, we have as follows:

And the armies in the heaven were following Him upon white horses, clothed in fine linen - white and pure; and out of his mouth doth proceed a sharp sword, that with it He may smite the nations, and He shall rule them (the nations) with a rod of iron, and He doth tread the press of the wine of the wrath and anger of God The Almighty, and He hath upon the garment and upon His thigh the name written, King of kings, and Lord of lords.

Consider now the promise of our Lord Jesus Christ to those who have faith in Him in Revelation 2:25-29.

But that which ye have - hold ye, till I may come; and he who is overcoming, and who is keeping unto the end my works, I will give to him authority over the nations, and he shall rule them with a rod of iron - as the vessels of the potter they shall be broken - as I also have received from my Father; and I will give to him the morning star. He who is having an ear - let him hear what the Spirit saith to the assemblies.

Remember that we have established three groups of people whose spirits are saved, namely POWERS FOR CHRIST, NEOPHYTES, and LOVING CITIZENS OF THE NATIONS (LCN). As already discussed, spiritually speaking, *Neophytes* are no different from *Loving Citizens of the Nations*, as such are classed together as the saved who are standing next to the sea of glass in Revelation 15:2. We established this equivalence in *Chapters 7 & 8*.

Prophecy Interpretation 61 *So then, these three groups - Powers, Neophytes, and LCN - have spirit from God.*

With respect to the rest of the people, the two beasts experience the second death in the lake that burns with fire and brimstone (Revelation 19:20). The spirits of all those who worshipped the beast then are killed by our Lord Jesus Christ. These people have opportunity, in context of a next SSGLAE, for choice of righteousness. Clearly the victory of our Lord Jesus Christ is spiritual, and is domiciled in those who maintain faith in Him unto the end. This is the reason our Lord Jesus Christ always is leading us in triumph, and through us spreading the fragrance of His knowledge everywhere (2Corinthians 2:14). In presence of the Scriptures cited, it is conclusive that the war that transpires in context of the 6th Seal is a spiritual war whose victories are passed on to those who are faithful to Christ, who then rule over the nations with a rod of iron. Note that the rod of iron does not signify slavery or mistreatment, rather signifies absence of tolerance for any form of evil within the nations and among their kings.

Prophecy Interpretation 62 *Commencing with the original 1st* SEAL, *and counting the 1st* SEAL *made possible by our Lord Jesus Christ, we arrive at two iterations of the SSGLAE for arrival at the spiritual resolution in Revelation ch. 21 (see Chapter 15). If, upon arrival at that spiritual resolution, the Church and the Nations choose the more glorious resolution that accompanies the BP7* PATH - *the spiritual resolution in Revelation ch. 22 (see Chapter 16) - we arrive at, in total three SSGLAEs.*

Prophecy Insight 113 *The victory that our Lord Jesus Christ wins in context of the 7th* VIAL *of the 7th Seal, equivalently, in context of the 6th Seal, is passed on to those who keep His works unto the end, that is, to those who let 'ALL*

THAT THEY DO BE DONE IN LOVE' *unto the very end. We have then confirmation of the declaration in 1Corinthians 13:8, which asserts that* IT IS LOVE THAT NEVER FAILS. *Given faith is for producing of love (Galatians 6:6), and the hope of our calling is the hope of acquiring the glory of Christ, which is His Love (2Thessalonians 2:13-14; 1John 4:8; John 13:35), Faith and Hope are embedded in the Love of God.*

Prophecy Insight 114 *So then, there abides* FAITH *(which is rooted in knowledge),* HOPE *(which expects to become like God in Love), and* LOVE *(essence of The Father), and the greatest of these is* LOVE *(the Love of God).*

11.7   Revelation 17 & 18: The great prostitute and the beast

The great whore of Revelation *ch. 17* is '*Babylon the Great, the mother of the whores, and the abominations of the earth (Revelation 17:5).*' The great whore is full of abominations (idolatry), uncleanness (whoredom), and the beast on which she sits is characterized by evil-speaking. We already have discussed idolatry and whoredom. EVIL-SPEAKING IS FAITHLESS SPEAKING, is speaking of words that portend lack of faith in brotherhood of mankind, lack of faith in the fact that we all are created by one God, as such are equal. For an extensive discussion of evil-speaking, check out *Chapter 14* of my book, True Sanctification. For our purposes here, it is sufficient to cite the following words by Apostle Paul in 2Thessalonians 3:1-3.

> Finally, brethren, pray for us, that the word of the Lord may speed on and triumph, as it did among you, and THAT WE MAY BE DELIVERED FROM WICKED AND EVIL MEN; FOR NOT ALL HAVE FAITH. BUT THE LORD IS FAITHFUL; HE WILL STRENGTHEN YOU AND GUARD YOU FROM EVIL.

Prophetic Lessons 45 *A society, which functions on* EVIL SPEAKING - *the practice, as opposed to the statement that '*ALL MEN ARE NOT EQUAL*', functions on a philosophy that is direct antithesis of the Love of God.*

Prophetic Lessons 46 *While countries, such as the United States of America assert that '*ALL MEN ARE CREATED EQUAL*', ubiquity of racism, and ubiquity of hatred from those who are targets of racism, is evidence the practice - interactions within the society - run contrary to the assertion that '*ALL MEN ARE CREATED EQUAL*'.*

Prophetic Lessons 47 *People who assert that some men are 'animals', this so they can be considered less than they, degrade themselves, become whatever they assert others, who evidently are created in the same likeness as they, to be.*

The Things That Are 74 SCIENCE, *which man seeks to exalt in place of God, declares, all who have the likeness of man, are man.* BIOLOGY, GENETICS, HISTORY, *and* ANTHROPOLOGY *all attest to this scientific fact.* SCIENCE AGREES WITH OUR LORD JESUS CHRIST THAT ALL MEN ARE CREATED EQUAL. *It is straightforward then that when a man declares another who has the same likeness as himself or herself to be less than a man, that he or she declares himself or herself* SCIENTIFICALLY IRRATIONAL.

It is straightforwardly clear from words of Apostle Paul that wicked and evil men are men who lack faith, who as such seek to do evil to men who love righteousness. Given God has declared all men equal, evil speaking is rebellion against God, is an attempt at setting up of a throne that is higher than God's. We see then that the two beasts of Revelation *ch. 13*, whom also are characterized by evil speaking, the beast of Revelation *ch. 17*, and the man of sin of 2Thessalonians *ch. 2* all have the same spiritual essence.

Prophecy Insight 115 *The two beasts of Revelation ch. 13, the scarlet beast of Revelation ch. 17, and the man of sin of 2Thessalonians ch. 2 all seek to exalt their throne above God's, all seek to actualize a world within which all men are not equal. Clearly, all are manifestations of essence of that great dragon, the devil.*

Prophecy Insight 116 *Every society that already functions on basis of some stratification of intrinsic worth of different men already is ruled by the beasts.*

Prophecy Insight 117 COMMUNISM, *which entrusts fates of a lot of other men into the hands of a few, is a condensed version of societies that function on basis of stratifications of intrinsic worth.*

Prophecy Insight 118 *Every religion or Church organization within which* LAITY *are regarded as inferior in spiritual worth to* CLERGY *already is infiltrated by the beasts of Revelation.*

Love of Truth 59 *Apostles* PETER, JAMES, *and* JOHN *were fishermen, never enrolled in any theology programs, at timing of ascension of Jesus to The Father did not even yet know how to read and write (Acts 4:13), yet their words have generated thousands of books, articles, and blog posts by people who obtain PhDs from seminaries, colleges, or universities. By this* SPIRITUAL PRECEDENT, *it is* IMPOSSIBLE *for a PhD in theology or religion to be superior to direct spiritual revelation arrived at in context of fellowship with The Father, Son, and Holy Spirit.*

Love of Truth 60 *Apostle* PAUL *declared that in order to know Christ, he first had to jettison everything else that he already knew (Philippians 3:3-11). So then, it is was not Apostle Paul's seminary training at the feet of Gamaliel*

(Acts 22:3) that made him wise unto salvation (2Timothy 3:15), rather it was spiritual revelations that he received from The Father, Son, and Holy Spirit (Galatians 2:2; Ephesians 3:3). Apostle Paul's intellectual preparation only enabled a phrasing of spiritual revelations in philosophical language. We again arrive at the insight that a PhD in theology or religion is not superior to direct spiritual revelation arrived at in context of fellowship with The Father, Son, and Holy Spirit.

11.7.1   The Context

Revelation 17:1 states very clearly that the messenger who shows Apostle John *the great whore who is sitting on many waters* is one of the messengers having the 7 Vials. Clearly then, the visions to follow elaborate on character of Babylon, the Great Whore who is partner in commerce with the kings of the Nations (Revelation 18:3) and partner with same kings with respect to persecution of those who have faith in the name of Jesus Christ. Remember, given Babylon only can subsist in context of an Apostate Church, *Life and Affairs on Earth* are domiciled on the RP7 path of the SSGLAE. Consistent with a vision premised on an intermission between the 4th and 7th Seals, Revelation 17:6 declares as follows.

> And I saw the woman drunken from the blood of the saints, and from the blood of the witnesses of Jesus, and I did wonder - having seen her - with great wonder.

> Why did Apostle John wonder? Because Babylon appeared beautiful, yet was full of evil.

Concerning Babylon, Revelation 17:15-17 declares as follows.

> And he saith to me, the waters that thou didst see, where the whore doth sit, are peoples, and multitudes, and nations, and tongues; and the ten horns that thou didst see upon the beast, these shall hate the whore, and shall make her desolate and naked, and shall eat her flesh, and shall burn her in fire, for God did give into their hearts to do it's mind, and to make one mind, AND TO GIVE THEIR KINGDOM TO THE BEAST TILL THE SAYINGS OF GOD MAY BE COMPLETE.

It is very straightforward from Revelation 17:15-17 that:

♣ Babylon the Great is a spirit that cuts across nations, tongues, tribes, multitudes and peoples. Clearly, there is reinforcement of characterization of the two beasts as spirits that also manifest in individuals and/or institutions.

♣ Babylon is a spiritual system, a suite of philosophies, not a system of nations.

♣ Until His sayings are complete, The Father places it in the heart of the Nations to choose to persecute Christians, that is, to give themselves over to the Beast, as opposed to Babylon, which only wants to kill the saints. You see then that the Beast and Babylon are competing spiritual philosophies. They are able, initially, to arrive at an INNER CIRCLE OF FRIENDSHIP, because both consider true followers of Christ their enemies.

When are the sayings of God complete?

Whenever the Church arrives at a perfect man, at a measure of the stature of the fullness of Christ.

Revelation 17:15-17 declares that the kings of the earth will, subsequent to their partnering with Babylon, HATE BABYLON, MAKE HER DESOLATE, EAT HER FLESH, AND BURN HER WITH FIRE. This course of action is placed in their hearts by The Father, with outcome the kings choose the beast over Babylon until the words of The Father are fulfilled.

What then is the difference between Babylon and the Beast?

Well, while Babylon is drunken with the blood of those who have faith in Jesus Christ, meaning she kills those who have faith in Jesus Christ, the beast seeks to prevent those who have faith in Jesus Christ from participation in economic activities of life. In Revelation 17:15-17, The Father declares that He never will allow killing of those who have faith in Jesus Christ to proceed in any sort of wanton manner, that the apostate Church, which seeks to kill off genuine faith always will be check mated.

Prophecy Interpretation 63 *Those who have faith in Jesus Christ, and who give their lives for their faith in context of persecution, which transpires in course of the 4*th *SEAL are blessed (Revelation 14:13). The Father does not allow such outcomes - death for the sake of the name of Jesus Christ - to wipe out faith in Jesus Christ from the face of the earth. So then, only some believers are allowed to pay the ultimate price for their faith in the name of Jesus Christ.*

Prophecy Interpretation 64 *Do not assume that The Father has called you to give your life for sake of your faith in the name of Jesus Christ. Do not then seek death for sake of your faith in the name of Jesus Christ. SUBMIT TO GOD, AND RESIST THE DEVIL (James 4:7; 1Peter 5:8-11) is the command from The Father, meaning if you are to die for Christ, this occurs contrary to your resistance. You have precedent of resistance to martyrdom by Apostle Paul in this regard (2Timothy 4:17).*

Prophecy Insight 119 MARTYRS FOR CHRIST DO NOT SEEK OUT DEATH FOR SAKE OF THE NAME OF JESUS CHRIST. MARTYRDOM FOR CHRIST ARRIVES REGARDLESS OF THEIR DESIRE TO CONTINUE LIVING FOR CHRIST.

Prophecy Interpretation 65 *If you have faith in the name of Jesus Christ, and experience economic hardships, which seemingly do not make any sense, know that this is evidence of workings of the beast in affairs of life on earth. In presence of this additional testament to your faith, our Lord Jesus Christ declares that you are to rejoice in the evidence that you are counted worthy of the name of Jesus Christ (Matthew 5:11-12).*

By characterization of Babylon as a system that seeks to put witnesses to Jesus to death, *Revelation ch. 17* declares that papal Rome and the Church of England, both of which have in past intensely persecuted people on basis of their faith in Jesus Christ, all have in past submitted to influence of Babylon. Every Church that has become institutionalized in any country, which then persecuted those who have faith in Jesus Christ, has participated in, or been influenced by Babylon.

Prophecy Interpretation 66 *Any Church, which persecutes fellow believers, this because of disagreements as to interpretation of Scriptures, is an Apostate Church.*

Prophetic Lessons 48 *The Church cannot persecute fellow believers on basis of morality. Morality is not persecuted, rather is judged in the open, with outcome those accused are able to defend their actions, with outcome there is arrival at justice.*

11.7.2   Babylon - A Trader in Bodies and Souls of Men

Revelation 18:13 declares that Babylon the Great IS A TRADER IN BODIES AND SOULS OF MEN. By this, our Lord Jesus Christ declares that every system within which slavery - trading in bodies of men - is tolerated or celebrated is part of Babylon the Great.

Historical Spiritual Nugget 32 *These words about Babylon the Great have been available to us in Scriptures from about 100 AD, thousands of years prior to foray of the White man into slavery.*

Love of Truth 61 *Our Lord Jesus Christ asserts to all men, who then can choose to listen, or not listen, for their own salvation or damnation, that whenever His Church appears to justify slavery, that it only is because it is an apostate Church. If, regardless you accuse Jesus of justification of slavery, you consign your own soul to damnation.*

The Things That Are 75 *It is* UNEQUIVOCAL *that our Lord Jesus Christ and Christian Scriptures* DENOUNCE SLAVERY, *declare that any system rooted in slavery or demarcations of society by social strata are antithesis of faith in Jesus Christ.*

In addition to trade in bodies of men, BABYLON THE GREAT TRADES IN SOULS OF MEN. What exactly does this mean? Part of the answer resides in Revelation 18:3, which declares that "THE MERCHANTS OF THE EARTH FROM THE POWER OF HER REVEL WERE MADE RICH." Consider what this means, which is, in the systems designed by Babylon for her revel, the merchants of the earth derive profit and riches. We have then that systems that, in entirety, are designed for facilitation of revel are designed for profit of Babylon and merchants with whom she trades in souls of men.

Prophecy Insight 120 *Every activity that consists, in entirety, of revel is designed for trading of souls, is designed primarily for benefit of Babylon and merchants with whom she trades in souls of men.*

Prophecy Insight 121 *Revel consists of activities which, regardless of your participation, do not embed any possibility of development of relationships. Such activities serve only for facilitation of* MIRTH, LAUGHTER, *or* PLEASURE.

11.7.3   What activities are designed, in entirety, for revel?

♣ Comedy that makes jest of different classes of people. Whenever a comedian tells jokes about fat people and a slim person laughs, the goal just might be a seeking for an excuse to condemn the slim man, a seeking of an excuse for trading in the soul of the slim man.

♣ Any activity that is designed primarily for facilitation of non-relationship based sex is an activity that subsists solely for facilitation of revel. In Proverbs 2:16-19 and Proverbs 5:1-23, Proverbs 6:23-29, Proverbs 7:4-27, Proverbs 30:20 sexual consorts with strange women can lead to *loss of soul, loss of strength and honor,* or both. A society that today glorifies ONE NIGHT STANDS does not realize that it is involved in trading of soul, strength, and honor for no more than 30 minutes, or a whole night of revelry in sex.

♣ Activities that are designed primarily for facilitation of FACILE interactions - interactions, which by intention do not lead to development of relationships - subsist solely for facilitation of revel. Activities that are premised on deception, such as the following shows: 'Survivor', 'Big Brother', 'Real Housewives' all are exercises in glorification of revelry, for no one seeks to build relationships around deception.

11.7.4   Clarification: Popular activities that are not by design exercises in Revel

Every movie or novel is a parable. Watching a movie, or reading a novel is no different from sitting by the fireside at night to listen to stories about the TORTOISE and the HARE. While either of the tortoise or the hare, but yet typically the *tortoise* can do things that are wrong, introduction of things that are wrong serves for illustration of importance of choosing right over wrong. It is for this reason that Christian Scriptures are filled with evil outcomes for evil done by evil people, and good outcomes for good done by righteous people. In presence of the evidence, you are encouraged to choose right over wrong. In the parable of the GOOD SAMARITAN, Jesus depicts both loving and unloving behavior, then encourages His listeners to be people who love their neighbors, that is, people who are able to love total strangers (Luke 10:29-37).

Love of Truth 62 *In the parable of the Good Samaritan, Jesus declared that the definition of a* NEIGHBOR *is a* TOTAL STRANGER, *is a person who previously was unknown to you. So then, if you only love those whom are known to you, those who already love you, Jesus declares you do not as yet love your neighbor.*

Prophecy Insight 122 *Based on characterization of a* NEIGHBOR *by our Lord Jesus Christ,* AMERICANS *are supposed to love* CHINESE *people whom they have never met;* CHINESE *people are supposed to love* NIGERIANS *they have never met; and* NIGERIANS *are supposed to love* OTHER NIGERIANS *who are unknown to them.*

The Things That Are 76 IT IS UNEQUIVOCAL, IF YOU ONLY LOVE THOSE WHOM YOU KNOW, IF YOU ONLY LOVE THOSE WHO ARE LIKE YOU IN THEIR MANNER-ISMS, BELIEFS, OR COLOR OF SKIN, IN SO FAR AS JESUS IS CONCERNED, YOU DO NOT AS YET LOVE YOUR NEIGHBOR.

In the story of David, and his foray into sin, there is depiction of adultery, murder, and punishment from God (*2Samuel chs. 11 & 12*), with outcome The Father warns that you to depart from all appearance of evil, that you do not believe you are able to get away with doing of evil to another who is weaker than yourself.

Love of Truth 63 MOVIES AND NOVELS ARE PARABLES. *It is what you take away from the reading, or the watching that matters, that can define you.*

If you consider movies or novels entertainment that reinforces your love for what is good, and your hatred of what is evil, you use movies the right way. In presence of such an attitude, neither of watching of movies, or reading of novels can be characterized as participation in revel. If you watch a movie or read a novel that glorifies an evil ending, denounce that ending in your mind, and use that as an opportunity for reaffirming of your love for what is good, of your love for triumph of righteousness over evil. Remember, if your heart rejoices in an evil ending, this is evidence that there as yet remains in you some love for evil. In presence of such evidence it is best to seek out the blood of our Lord Jesus Christ for your cleansing from sin and iniquity. When you judge yourself in this manner, you avoid having to be judged by our Lord and Savior Jesus Christ, this so you do not die in the iniquity of your soul (1Corinthians 11:31-32). If you use movies and novels right, they are not activities rooted in revel, are parables that reinforce your hatred of evil and love for what is good.

Life Nugget 5 *It is not the details of a movie or novel that are of utmost importance; rather, it is the* PREMISE, ETHOS, *or* SUBLIMINAL *message in the movie that is of utmost importance. Typically, the* PREMISE, ETHOS, *or* SUBLIMINAL *in a movie is evident in the ending of a movie. The only caveat? If a movie or novel depicts evil throughout, such that good is consigned only to the end of the movie or novel, the* PREMISE, ETHOS, *or* SUBLIMINAL *in such a movie or novel likely is* EVIL.

Life Nugget 6 *David committed adultery and murder are details of his story. Overall, however, David paid a huge price for the adultery and murder, yet was rewarded by God for his overall faithfulness. So then, the lesson? If you do not want the rewards you accrue from The Father to be tainted with evil, depart from every appearance of evil (1Thessalonians 5:22), hate what is evil, love what is good (Job 1:1,8; Romans 12:9).*

Every song that debases your view of men and women is rooted in revelry, is a song you should not desire to keep in your music library. When a song depicts women merely as sexual beings it debases the glory of God in woman.

Woman is supposed to represent purity, virtue, dignity.

When a song characterizes women merely as creatures for sex and pleasure, it debases this glory of which woman is supposed to be representative. When a song depicts a man as nothing more than a person who *trawls around for sex*, this also is a debasing of the glory of God in man. More generally, any song that debases the glory of God in man, woman, and interactions between men and women and children ought not to be in the music library of a person who has faith in the name of our Lord and Savior Jesus Christ.

You may wonder then how exactly to react to depictions, in movies, of activities that are debasing to women, such as pole dancing or stripping. In this respect, trust your standing with God and guidance of the Holy Spirit. If such a scene makes you desire to abandon the movie, this is right and good for you. Remember, however, that a woman who engages in prostitution, pole dancing, or stripping is not sinning against God, rather uses her body in a manner not in accordance with God's stipulations, as such only sins against her own body.

Life Nugget 7 Economic Prostitution, Pole Dancing, *or* Stripping *are not sins against God, are sins against the body of the person engaging in such activities. Why does The Father deems this so? If men or women were not themselves perverse, there would not be any demand for* Economic Prostitution, Pole Dancing, *or* Stripping. *Since none of the activities -* Economic Prostitution, Pole Dancing, *or* Stripping *- hurt anyone else, The Father does not consider these activities to be sin.*

Life Nugget 8 *Women or Men who engage in Prostitution, this because they are evil, as such seek to hurt others, are judged, not for the Prostitution itself, but for the evil intent that is hidden in the Prostitution. Such Men or Women sin against The Father.*

Life Nugget 9 *If you have faith in Jesus Christ, The Lord Jesus Christ declares that, for you, the decision to consort with prostitutes, a decision that is contrary to your faith in Jesus Christ, is sin.*

If you are able to get through scenes involving Prostitution, Pole Dancing, or Stripping etc. without desire for masturbation, or without your mind becoming flooded with sensual thoughts, if you are able to maintain your righteousness through those scenes, and if you watch such scenes primarily because you do not want to miss out on an important piece of the story, there is not any sin in watching such scenes. In this respect, judge yourself and act accordingly. Note, however, that if you seek out movies or novels that have seedy scenes, such as pole dancing or stripping, this is evidence that there exists a craving in you that needs to be fixed in power of the Holy Spirit. You would be wise to submit such cravings to the cleansing power of the blood of Jesus Christ, and sanctifying power of the Holy Spirit. Remember, only those willing to give up not just sins, but also weaknesses or imperfections are able to reign with our Lord Jesus Christ (Hebrews 12:1-2).

What then about Christian Comedy?

When done right, Christian Comedy can be a blessing. When a comedian points out that the church bulletin reads:

Sister Amelia is taken ill, let us hold her leg up to the Lord in prayer, he or she points out the unintended imagery that is outcome of a poor choice of words. When the next church bulletin reads:

> Sister Nadee is taken ill, let us anoint her with oil of healing in our prayers,

the comedy has produced a good outcome.

Life Nugget 10 *Ideally,* CHRISTIAN COMEDY *enables, in context of lightness of banter, a pointing out of things that can be improved within the community of believers in Christ. Whenever* CHRISTIAN COMEDY *has such a focus, it is not an exercise in revel, it is rooted in desire for righteous outcomes. Amen.*

Life Nugget 11 *Any television show, radio program, movie, novel, or music that does not have a righteous subliminal, a core message of righteousness is an exercise in revelry.*

For illustration, consider the comedy, 'Martin', which originally ran on Fox for five seasons from 1992 through 1996. The role 'Martin' is a bumbling, African American guy who acts brash to cover up insecurities. Standing by Martin and all of his bonehead ideas is his common law wife, equivalently, fiancee *Gina* who, no matter what, stands by him. In the depiction of a woman who, come what may, stands by her 'husband', the show attempts to encourage women to, no matter what, do their best to stand by their husbands. In the fact that it is obvious Martin hides insecurities under a veneer of indifference and brashness, the show hopes men in similar situations are able to look inwards, are able to desire, and exert effort for arrival at better versions of themselves. The show Martin may have been imperfect, but for those who watch television for the right reasons, it was a show fit for Christian sensibilities.

11.7.5   All Apostate Church Systems are Part of Babylon

In Revelation 18:4-5, God's people are advised to come out of Babylon. With this loving command, The Father declares that it is possible for genuine believers to, at some initial point, be participants in spiritual activities, which subsist in Babylon. The fact that all Protestants were, at some point in time, members of the papal Church is sufficient for demonstration of feasibility of participation of those who genuinely have faith in Jesus Christ in Babylon. In the illustration, you perhaps see how exactly genuineness can be linked with Babylon, which is, ignorance of the truth on the part of those who genuinely have faith in Jesus Christ. In respect of power of ignorance of the truth, and importance of a righteous response to arrival of truth, which eliminates ignorance, consider the following Scriptures.

The times of ignorance God overlooked, but now commands all men everywhere to repent (Acts 17:30).

My people are destroyed for lack of knowledge. BECAUSE YOU HAVE REJECTED KNOWLEDGE, I ALSO WILL REJECT YOUR FROM BEING PRIEST FOR ME; because you have forgotten the law of your God, I also will forget your children. The more they increased (prospered), the more they sinned against Me; I will change their glory into shame (Hosea 4:6-7).

Beware that you do not forget the Lord your God by not keeping His commandments, His judgments, and His statutes which I command you today, lest - when you have eaten and are full, and have built beautiful houses and dwell in them; then you say in your hear, *My power and the might of my hand have gained me this wealth.* AND YOU SHALL REMEMBER THE LORD YOUR GOD, FOR IT IS HE WHO GIVES YOU POWER TO GET WEALTH, that He may establish His covenant which He swore to your fathers, as it is this day. Then it shall be, *if you by any means forget the Lord your God*, and follow other gods, and serve them, I TESTIFY AGAINST YOU THIS DAY THAT YOU SHALL SURELY PERISH (Deuteronomy 8:11-12, 17-19).

The Things That Are 77 *Whenever The Father addresses ignorance with arrival of revelational knowledge, and the new knowledge is rejected, for those who reject, destruction always is outcome.*

The Things That Are 78 *Whenever prosperity induces people to spurn God, to raise their face towards God, and declare, "who is God that we should honor Him, after all is this not prosperity of our very own creation" they exchange their glory for shame.*

In order for Babylon to emerge, she has to adopt philosophies that are alien to faith in Jesus Christ. Typically, all of these philosophies revolve around speaking of evil, that is, the declaration that all men are not created equal. In this spiritual sense, Babylon encompasses not only apostate Churches, but also all philosophies, which espouse inequality of men, that is, EVIL PHILOSOPHY. Babylon then is, in entirety, a system of philosophies and spirituality that contradicts the Love of God as essence of interactions within Church and Society at large. This is evident in the following declarations.

An in her blood of prophets and of saints was found, and of all those who have been slain on the earth (Revelation 18:24).

And he did cry in might - a great voice, saying, "Fall, fall did Babylon the great, and she became a HABITATION OF DEMONS, and a HOLD OF EVERY UNCLEAN SPIRIT, and a HOLD OF EVERY UNCLEAN AND HATEFUL BIRD (Revelation 18:2)."

Prophecy Insight 123 *Every killing that is predicated on hatred, that is, on inequality of mankind, on direct opposition to the Love of God is domiciled in Babylon. So then,* BABYLON *consists not only of* APOSTATE CHURCHES, *but all* EVIL PHILOSOPHY.

Prophecy Insight 124 *Babylon the Great hates those who have faith in Jesus Christ, seeks to put them to death. The kings of the earth seek control of men for their own prosperity. So long as Christians are not in the way, the kings of the earth are happy. But preaching of the gospel makes men free, decreases control of the kings of the earth, with outcome they seek to place Christians in situations within which they are less obstructionist to control agenda the kings design for their own personal enrichment, and enrichment of their partners or cronies.*

Prophecy Insight 125 *The Father declares that the beasts of Revelation will fail, that equality of men, which is essence of the gospel of Christ, will triumph over attempts at building of hierarchical societies.*

Prophecy Insight 126 *For understanding of the distinction between the spiritual truth that all are equal before God, yet all can attain to different realizations of merit, check out my books,* Divine Meritocracy, *and* True Sanctification.

With respect to destruction of Babylon, Revelation 18:20, & 18:5,8 declares as follows:

Be glad over her, O heaven, and ye holy apostles and prophets, because God did judge your judgment of her (Revelation 18:20).

Because her sins did follow - unto the heaven, and God did remember her unrighteousness. Because of this, in one day, shall come her plagues, death, and sorrow, and famine; and in fire she shall be utterly burned, because strong is the Lord God who is judging her (Revelation 18:5,8).

In Revelation 17, the kings of the earth hate Babylon, burn her with fire. In Revelation 18, it is The Father who acts on judgments of His holy apostles and prophets to judge Babylon. These judgments are achieved in context of the 7 VIALS of *Revelation chs. 15 & 16*, and events, which transpire in context of the 7th VIAL in *Revelation ch. 19*. Combined, we arrive at the conclusion that God can place enmity between two sets of evil persons for arrival at His judgments.

Prophecy Principle 128 *Just as enemies of Israel were confounded to turn their swords on one another (Judges 7:19-23), resulting in destruction of one another, so also The Father sets enmity between people who previously did evil together for judgment of one or the other.*

Prophecy Insight 127 *Events in life that seemingly are random can be judgments instituted by The Father, yet with The Father remaining seemingly anonymous.*

Prophecy Insight 128 *Just because The Father does not announce His interventions does not mean He is silent, doing nothing.*

Have Believers in Christ Ever Really Come out of Babylon?

We already have discussed how each of the Church of the Byzantine Empire, and the Church of the Reformation did not really arrive at a perfect man. We know also that much the same as the Corinthian Church, the *Church of the Tongues Movement* got so focused on spiritual gifts that it did not arrive at maturity in Christ. The Evidence? The Church of the Reformation was splintered, did not arrive at any unity of the faith. The Church of the Tongues Movement is order of magnitude more splintered than the Church of the Reformation. So then, have believers in Christ ever really come out of Babylon? What seems to be the sad answer?

> No, it would seem believers in Christ never really have come out of Babylon.

> Church organizations or traditions continue to remain more important than purity of faith in and obedience to commands of Jesus Christ.

Prophecy Insight 129 *The historical record suggests believers in Christ never really have come out of Babylon. The Father of our Lord Jesus Christ declares that should the Church ever really come out of Babylon, that there will be arrival at the 7ᵗʰ* VIAL *of the 7ᵗʰ* Seal.

11.8   Revelation 19:1-16

We already have established that, on the RP7 PATH, VIALS 1 *through* 6 of the WRATH OF GOD are substitutes for TRUMPETS 1 *through* 6 of the 7ᵗʰ Seal. TRUMPETS 1 *through* 6 of the 7ᵗʰ Seal are specific then to the GP7 PATH of the SSGLAE. We further have established that Vials 1 *through* 6 are designed for UNRAVELING of power of evil on the earth, with outcome the faith of the righteous is strengthened, and the righteous are protected from evil. Given those who pretended to profess faith in Jesus Christ, but who worshipped the Beast already are identified at timing of pouring out of the 1ˢᵗ VIAL, all those who pretended to love Christ, but who secretly were part of Babylon already are identified, as such cannot any longer be considered part of the BODY OF CHRIST. In presence of necessity of exclusion of *pretend believers* who worshipped the beast, THE CHURCH is *reconstituted* in context of the 1ˢᵗ VIAL. In the preceding chapter, I characterized this *Reconstitution of The Church* as an intermediate SSGLAE #C2, which spans VIALS 1 through 6, such that in context of the 7ᵗʰ VIAL of the 7ᵗʰ Seal, the Church becomes seed for another NEW BEGINNING (1ˢᵗ SEAL), that is, SSGLAE #C3.

Schematically, for The Church, and The Nations, we arrive at the following outcome, which is implied in summaries of the RP7 PATH that I provide in the preceding chapter.

SSGLAE	Item	Sub-Item	The Church	The Nations
SSGLAE _1	1st Seal	NA	#C1	#C1
RP7 Path	2nd Seal	NA	#C1	#C1
	3rd Seal	NA	#C1	#C1
	4th Seal	NA	#C1	#C1
	5th Seal*	NA	#C1	#C1
	7th Seal	1st Vial	#C2	#C1
		2nd Vial	#C2	#C1
		3rd Vial	#C2	#C1
		4th Vial	#C2	#C1
		5th Vial	#C2	#C1
		6th Vial	#C2	#C1
SSGLAE_2		7th Vial, 6th Seal, & 1st Seal of SSGLAE_2	#C3	#C3

Choice of Path up
to Church & Nations

The 5th Seal is notional. There is not arrival at Maturity of Righteousness

The INTERMEDIATE SSGLAE in the preceding chart, SSGLAE #C2 is necessary, because as articulated in the preceding chapter, the newly reconstituted Church would be formally inaugurated as The Church of SSGLAE #C3 in context of the MARRIAGE OF THE LAMB. The Marriage of The Lamb represents official inauguration of the Reign of our Lord Jesus Christ (Revelation 19:6). In this respect, Revelation 19:6-7 declares as follows.

And I heard as the voice of a great multitude, and as the voice of many waters, and as the voice of mighty thunderings, saying,

Alleluia! because REIGN DID THE LORD GOD - the almighty! may we rejoice and exult, and give the glory to Him, because come did the marriage of the Lamb, and His wife did make herself ready.

Our Lord Jesus Christ REIGNS because every spirit that remains at play in *Affairs of Life* on earth is a righteous spirit, a spirit, which delights in the LOVE OF GOD. While man remains capable of choosing evil, choice of evil is not predicated on presence of evil spirits, is predicated, in entirety, in man's decision to disobey God, to choose evil over what is good. To ensure that any devolution into evil is, in entirety, on basis of choice made by man, the devil is bound for a thousand years. A THOUSAND here signifies, '*for as long as man chooses to keep the devil at bay via choice of what is good over what is evil*'. I establish this interpretation of the 1,000 *years* in discussion of *Revelation ch. 20*.

Prophecy Insight 130 *The people who are invited to the Marriage of The Lamb are* NEOPHYTES, *and all those who have characterization as* LOVING CITIZENS OF THE NATIONS, *all of whom did not worship the beast, or the image of the beast in context of the 4ᵗʰ* SEAL.

Prophecy Insight 131 *While* NEOPHYTES *are part of the Church of SSGLAE #C3, they are not yet mature enough to be married to Christ.*

For additional evidence that there exists a process from faith in Jesus Christ to arrival at marriage to Jesus Christ, consider the following Scripture.

> Therefore, my brethren, you also have become dead to the law through the body of Christ, THAT YOU MAY BE MARRIED TO ANOTHER - to Him who was raised from the dead, that we should bear fruit to God (Romans 7:4).

> And now, having been freed from the sin, and having become servants to God, ye have your fruit - to sanctification, and the end life age-during (Romans 6:22).

> And this is the life age-during, that they may know Thee, the only true God, and Him whom thou didst send - Jesus Christ (John 17:3).

Prophecy Insight 132 *Only those who are sanctified arrive at life age-during. Simultaneously, only those who get to know Jesus arrive at life age-during. We have then that only those who are sanctified arrive at knowledge of Christ. Knowledge of Christ implies Marriage to Christ. So then, only those who arrive at knowledge of Christ, who arrive at the Presence of Christ arrive at marriage* *to Christ, as such, are part of the Bride of Christ. Only those who have been recognized by The Father as Powers for Christ have arrived at knowledge of Christ.*

Prophecy Insight 133 *A* NON-REVELATIONAL *reading of Scriptures suggests that life that is age-during - eternal life - is, upon confession of faith in Jesus Christ, automatic. This is not true. Sometimes, as in John 3:16, the Scriptures focus on specification of the ideal outcome, do not delve into reality of inter-vening of* SANCTIFICATION *between* JUSTIFICATION *and arrival at* LIFE THAT IS AGE-DURING. *The evidence in Scriptures is unambiguous, however, only those who, subsequent to justification, allow themselves to be sanctified, arrive at eternal life, are recognized by The Father as* POWERS FOR CHRIST.

It is because of immense importance of sanctification, and the revelation from the Holy Spirit that The Church has lost sight of real spiritual meaning of 'sanctification', and 'Godliness', and the inter-action between Godliness and Love, that the Holy Spirit impressed upon my heart to pen the book, 'True Sanctification'. I implore you in Christ that you pick up copies of True Sanctification not only for yourself, but for those whom you love.

Consistent with simultaneity of a 7th VIAL of the 7th Seal with Commence-ment of a new 1st Seal period, our Lord Jesus Christ goes forth on a white horse conquering in Revelation 19:11. Let us juxtapose then, Revelation 6:1-2, and Revelation 19:11-14.

And I saw when the Lamb opened one of the seals, and I heard one of the four living creatures saying, as it were a voice of thun-der, Come and behold! and I saw, and lo, a white horse, and he who is sitting upon it is having a bow, and there was given to him a crown, and he went forth overcoming, and that he may overcome.

And I saw the heaven having been opened, and lo, a white horse, and He who is sitting upon it is called Faithful and True, and in righteousness doth He judge and war, and His eyes are as a flame of fire, and upon His head are many diadems (a crown with diadems) - having a name written that no one hath known, except Himself, and He is arrayed with a garment covered with blood, and His name is called, The Word of God. And the armies in the heaven were following Him upon white horses clothed in fine linen - white and pure.

Clearly, Revelation 19:11-14 refers to a 1st Seal period. Note that our Lord Jesus Christ engages in war with messengers in tow. The dichotomy, however, is as follows.

Prophecy Interpretation 67 *While an SSGLAE #C1 is, as symbolized by receipt of a Crown from The Father, entrusted to a messenger for Christ, due to the fact that an SSGLAE #C3 coincides with outpouring of the 7ᵗʰ Vial, that is, judgment of those who loved evil in context of SSGLAE #C1, conquering, which occurs in context of SSGLAE #C3 always is led by our Lord and Savior Jesus Christ, The Word of God.*

11.9   Revelation 20

Revelation *ch. 20* introduces visions on THE MILLENIUM, that is, the 1,000 YEARS during which the devil is bound; the defeat and casting of the devil into the lake of fire; and the GREAT WHITE THRONE JUDGMENT.

11.9.1   The Millenium

For arrival at the right interpretation of the 1,000 years during which Satan is bound, we first have to recognize that the ELEMENT, 1,000 is symbolic, not literal. First, let us, absent any association with TIME, derive symbolism of the ELEMENT 1,000 from outside of the Book of Revelation. In this respect, consider the following Scriptures.

> For the Lord has driven out from before you great and strong nations; but as for you, no one has been able to stand against you to this day. One man of you shall chase A THOUSAND, for the Lord your God is He who fights for you, as He promised you (Joshua 23:9-10).

> There fall at thy side A THOUSAND, and a myriad at thy right hand, unto thee it cometh not nigh (Psalms 91:7).

> And thou hast known that Jehovah thy God He is God, the faithful God, keeping the covenant, and the kindness, to those loving Him, and to those keeping His commands - to A THOUSAND generations (Deuteronomy 7:9).

> O seed of Israel, His servant, O sons of Jacob, His chosen ones! He is Jehovah our God, in all the earth are His judgments. Remember ye to the age His covenant, the word He commanded - to A THOUSAND generations (1Chronicles 16:13-15).

> He remembers His covenant forever, the word which He commanded, for A THOUSAND generations, the covenant which He made with Abraham, and His oath to Isaac, and confirmed it to Jacob for a statute, to Israel as an EVERLASTING COVENANT (Psalms 105:8-10).

They have made Me zealous by no-god, they made me angry by their vanities; And I make them zealous by no-people, by a foolish nation I make them angry. For a nation lost to counsels are they, and there is no understanding in them. How doth one pursue A THOUSAND, and two cause a myriad to flee! If not - that their rock hath sold them, and Jehovah hath shut them up (Deuteronomy 32:21,28,30)?

In Joshua 23:9-10, whenever Israel is faithful to The Father, one man - one person who has faith in Jesus Christ - chases a thousand enemies AWAY. But then, if a person who maintains faith in Jesus Christ chases a thousand enemies AWAY everyday, the day never will arrive during which the thousand he has power to chase AWAY are able to remain. We have then that the 1,000 that are chased away are symbolic of victory for the people of God. Psalms 91:7 echoes the symbolism that the 1,000 is symbolic of victory, is symbolic of the spiritual reality that those who are faithful to The Father 'more than conquer' in Jesus Christ (Romans 8:37). Deuteronomy 7:9, 1Chronicles 16:13-15, and Psalms 105:8-10 render the symbolism emphatic, associate 1,000 with eternity, with outcome the ELEMENT 1,000 is, in entirety, symbolic of spiritual victory, equivalently, spiritual reality, such as covenants with The Father, which last for all time. Deuteronomy 32:21,28,30 chastises Israel, declares that if they would be faithful to The Father, they would not experience defeat at hands of their enemies. In the adoption of the Element 1,000 as symbolism for defeat, we arrive at what can be referred to as reverse confirmation for the inference that, for those who have faith in Christ, conditional on faithfulness, or unfaithfulness to Christ, the ELEMENT 1,000 is symbolic of either of victory, or arrival at spiritual defeat.

Application to the Millenium & the SSGLAE?

Prophecy Interpretation 68 *In presence of perpetuity of faithfulness to The Lord Jesus Christ, the* ELEMENT *1,000 is symbolic of perpetuity of spiritual victory. In presence of departure from faithfulness to Christ, the* ELEMENT *1,000 is symbolic of spiritual defeat at hands of enemies.*

Prophetic Lessons 49 *If those who make it into SSGLAE #C3 do not choose evil, if they* ALWAYS *choose what is right, the devil remains bound, meaning they, in perpetuity keep the devil at bay from* AFFAIRS ON EARTH. *In presence of maintenance of the victory via doing of what is right, there is not any pain, or tears, or misery.* LIFE AND AFFAIRS ON EARTH *are characterized by Righteousness, Peace, and Joy.*

Prophetic Lessons 50 *If those who make it into SSGLAE #C3 choose evil, do not do what is right, they provide the devil with opportunity, once again, to deceive the nations and their kings. This results in preponderance of* EVIL, PAIN, *and* MISERY *on earth.*

Suppose then that we consider associations of the ELEMENT 1,000 with time. In this respect, let us consider the following two Scriptures.

> And this one thing let not be unobserved by you, beloved, that one day with the Lord is as a thousand years, and a thousand years as one day (2Peter 3:8).

> For a thousand years in thine eyes are as yesterday, for it passeth on, yea, A WATCH BY NIGHT (Psalms 9:4).

Concerning what it means to watch, through Apostle Paul, The Holy Spirit admonishes as follows in 1Corinthians 16:13-14.

> Be watchful, stand firm in your faith, be courageous, be strong.
> Let all that you do be done in Love.

Prophecy Interpretation 69 *If 1* DAY *with the Lord is a 1,000* YEARS, *and a 1,000* YEARS *as 1* DAY, *clearly, a 1,000* YEARS *is symbolic of some phenomenon, cannot be literal.*

Prophecy Interpretation 70 *1Corinthians 16:13-14 provides corroboration for all of the preceding Prophetic Lessons, declares that whenever a 1,000* YEARS *is* AS A WATCH BY NIGHT, *that it is so because those who have faith in Christ watch by ensuring* ALL THAT THEY DO IS DONE IN LOVE, *that is, by ensuring they always choose to do what is right.*

In our discussion of the 7 VIALS of the WRATH OF GOD, we saw that the spirits of all those who worshipped the beast, and the image of the beast are destroyed, with outcome these persons now are devoid of spirit, as such, as in the parable of Jesus are, in sense of spirituality, representative of a void (Matthew 12:43-45; Luke 11:24-26). Let us refer to these persons, people who were deceived by the beast, and the false prophet in course of SSGLAE #C1 as CITIZENS OF THE NATIONS (CTN). If CTN are not to immediately be bent towards evil, they must receive spirit for their guidance. Given they are not eligible for the Holy Spirit, how exactly are they to arrive at spirit, which enables them, along with those who have faith in Jesus Christ, stay on the right track?

> Glory to our Lord Jesus Christ, for there is provision made in Christ for CTN.

The phrase, '*they did live and reign with Christ the thousand years*' in Revelation 20:4 refers to a spiritual rising again, to a reign of the heavens. In respect of this, The Father and our Lord Jesus Christ declare as follows:

Happy those persecuted for righteousness' sake - because theirs is the reign of the heavens (Matthew 5:10).

Prophecy Insight 134 *Believers in Christ who 'live and reign with Christ the thousand years' in Revelation 20:4 are those who died in context of persecution, which subsisted in context of the 4ᵗʰ Seal, who then experience a spiritual rising again that enables them participate in the reign of the heavens with our Lord Jesus Christ.*

The Provision?

Prophetic Lessons 51 *The spirits of all of the saints who died in context of the 4ᵗʰ SEAL of SSGLAE #C1 are resurrected, and made available to CITIZENS OF THE NATIONS. It is in this sense that those who died in Christ in context of the 4ᵗʰ SEAL of SSGLAE #C1 resurrect to reign with Christ.*

Prophetic Lessons 52 *The resurrection depicted in Revelation 20:4-6 does not have anything to do with the SECOND COMING of Christ. Resurrected spirits reign with Christ in the sense that it is their spirits that are made available to The Nations. If The Nations do not submit to these spirits for choice of good over evil, the symbolic 1,000 YEARS end. If The Nations submit to these spirits for choice of good over evil, the 1,000 YEARS do not end.*

If CTN do not allow themselves to be guided by these blessed and holy spirits, these spirits cannot again die, cannot be hurt by the second death. In presence of the provision made by our Lord Jesus Christ, obedience of CTN to the Love of Christ is not conditioned on witness of the perfected Newly Reconstituted Church, rather is conditioned on submission of CTN to holy and blessed spirits that are furnished them for their spiritual guidance. Note that given CTN can choose not to allow themselves to be guided by resurrected spirits of the saints, there is not any robotization here, for power of choice is not controverted. Access to resurrected spirits of the saints is no different from access to the Holy Spirit for POWERS and NEOPHYTES.

Revelation 20:7 opens as follows, "*And when the thousand years may be finished.*" The word, '*may*' indicates, consistent with conditionality of evolution of the SSGLAE that arrival at end of the 1,000 YEARS is not a given, meaning the 1,000 YEARS may extend ad infinitum in the sense that the nations having acquiesced to guidance of a perfected Church, and resurrected spirits of the saints, the devil is not loosed. If the nations continue to love evil, the 1,000 YEARS is, at some point in time, truncated, and the devil is loosed.

Prophetic Lessons 53 *The 1,000 YEARS in Revelation 20:2&6 is symbolic. If either of NEOPHYTES, or CITIZENS OF THE NATIONS devolve into evil, they declare that their hearts inherently are evil.*

Prophetic Lessons 54 *Our Lord Jesus Christ declares that perfection of the Church in context of SSGLAE #C2 buys The Nations a symbolic 1,000 YEARS during which they reveal the true state of their hearts towards God.*

11.9.2 The loosing and defeat of the devil

If the devil is loosed, it is only because, regardless of spiritual resources made available by The Father, that CITIZENS OF THE NATIONS choose evil over what is good. So then, much like Judas Iscariot was commanded by Jesus Christ to hasten arrival of the evil that he cherished in his heart, so also the devil is released, such that the evil chosen by the Nations can arrive as quickly as possible, as such be dealt with by our Lord Jesus Christ as quickly as possible. Clearly, the release of the devil serves for protection of the righteous. You see then that release of the devil is not an evil, rather is for hastening of INSTITUTIONAL arrival at new heavens, new earth, and New Jerusalem in which righteousness dwells (2Peter 3:13).

Prophetic Lessons 55 *The loosing of the devil, which is conditioned on choice of evil by Citizens of the Nations, this regardless of spiritual resources, which enable choice of what is good, is a Righteous, Just, Wise, and Merciful action on the part of The Father, an action that hastens* INSTITUTIONAL *arrival at* NEW HEAVENS, *and* NEW EARTH, *and* NEW JERUSALEM *in which righteousness dwells.*

If the devil is loosed, he goes on to deceive the nations, and they gather to fight a war that they cannot win against our Lord Jesus Christ (Revelation 20:8-9). Note that the nations are devoured, that is, destroyed by fire, not cast into the lake of fire (Revelation 20:9-10). The devil then is cast into the lake of fire and brimstone where he, the beast, and the false prophet are tormented day and night - to the ages of the ages. Given the nations are not cast into the lake of fire, rather are devoured by fire from our Lord Jesus Christ out of heaven, clearly men and women who choose to disobey God are not tormented in fire, rather have been killed. Having already established that the beloved city, the camp of the saints, which is, Mount Zion, the New Jerusalem is a spiritual city, clearly, the attack on the city is spiritual, and the destruction of the Citizens of the Nations, and casting of the devil into the lake of fire and brimstone are spiritual. In the assertion that the beast and the false prophet already were in the lake of fire prior to casting of the devil into the lake of fire (Revelation 20:10), we arrive at additional confirmation that events portrayed occur subsequent to the pouring out of the 7 VIALS.

What then is Essence of the Millenium and loosing of the devil?

THE MILLENIUM is representative both of The Father's Mercy, and The Father's Justice. Regardless of their decision to worship the beast, and the image of the beast, The Father has mercy on those who are not perpetrators of the evil, on those who only submitted to the evil, provides these *Citizens of the Nations (CTN)* with spiritual resources that enable them to choose what is right. Since the devil is bound, CTN are not tempted by the devil.

So then, if they choose evil, they reveal that their hearts are settled into rebellion against the Love of Christ. Now then, The Father destroys them with fire, yet the righteous spirits provided them survive, do not die. What then is destroyed? In so far as the spiritual realm is concerned, in presence of loosing of the devil, CTN become dead to the spiritual realm, are no longer able to participate in the spiritual realm, lose sensitivity to reality of the spiritual realm. In the casting of these persons into the lake of fire and brimstone, such that they no longer are able to affect the course of actions on earth, The Father ensures that arrival of New Heavens, New Earth, and New Jerusalem are not consigned to certainty of futility of conflict between the perfected Church and The Nations.

Prophecy Insight 135 THE MILLENIUM, *and if necessary, loosing of the devil, are evidence that The Father loves all, that He does not delight in stripping man of spiritual capacity, but that when all opportunities provided man for choosing of the Love of God over Hatred are spurned, that He, The Father is not averse to implementation of* JUDGMENTS *that are Righteous, Just, and Merciful to the Righteous.*

11.9.3   The Great White Throne Judgment

In Revelation 20:11, the earth and the heaven flee from the face, that is, from the presence of our Lord and Savior Jesus Christ, and there was not any place found for them, meaning the heaven and earth are placed in what can be referred to as a SPIRITUAL LIMBO, an addressless location in realm of the spirit. Then the dead are judged out of the scrolls of records of works, and the scroll of the life. Note that the scroll of the life only records those who are saved, but that it is the scroll containing records of works, which determines rewards, which accrue to each person who is saved. Once the work of judgment is completed, death and hades, and all those whose names are not found in the scroll of the life are cast into the lake of fire. Note that rewards ascertained, are not yet awarded, rather are to be awarded subsequently. The Great White Throne Judgment serves then for ridding all spirits who love evil ETERNALLY out of the presence of Christ.

11.9.4   Torment in the Lake of Fire

Persons who deem themselves rational have questioned how exactly a righteous Father can torment people eternally in a LAKE OF FIRE. If you truly have understood interpretations of the visions entrusted to Apostle John, if you truly have ascertained extent of The Father's patience, love, and mercy, I am confident you do not ask yourself, such a question. When The Father has rendered possible the BP7 PATH, a path that does not demand relationship with Jesus, only obedience to His Law of Love; when upon embarkment on the RP7 PATH, there is opportunity for repentance in context of the 7 Vials of the Wrath of God, and opportunity for choice of the Love of Christ in context of a *devilless* MILLENIUM, and people continue deliberately to choose evil, continue to deliberately mistreat their fellow man, how exactly is The Father unjust to design a LAKE OF FIRE for those who love evil?

Necessity of Grand Judgments 7 *How exactly is a man who attempts to destroy his or her neighbor justified in criticism of existence of a* LAKE OF FIRE *in which he or she is to be tortured for wantonness of attacks on his or her neighbor?*

> But yet again, the torment in the Lake of Fire is a symbolism, interpretation of which is as follows.

THE FATHER DOES NOT TORMENT ANYONE. The term 'Torment' refers to the spiritual reality that having been cast off from His Presence, those who remain on the heaven and earth for which there does not exist any place (the Old Heaven and Earth), those who have been consigned to spiritless existence in the sense that their capacity for living as spirits has been destroyed, are, by design of The Father, harried with TROUBLES OF LIFE, such that, in of themselves, they do not even have time for reflection, which reveals the true nature of their spiritual state. This is the first sort of torment. The command from The Father through Apostle Peter that is source of His Justice?

> For he who is willing to love life, and to see good days, let him guard his tongue from evil (*from stating he or she is intrinsically superior to any other person*), and his lips - not to speak guile (*let him or her not pretend to love, only so as to have opportunity to hurt another*); let him turn aside from evil (*let him or her cease to plan or implement evil*), and do good (*let him or her replace evil with good*), let him seek peace and pursue it; because the eyes of The Lord are upon the righteous, and His ears - to their supplication, and the face of The Lord is upon (*against*) those doing evil (1Peter 3:10-12).

Prophetic Word 7 *The Father has promised that whenever people refuse to guard their tongue from evil, and their lips from guile, as such choose evil and conflict over what is good and peaceable, that He will take away their love of life, and capacity for seeing good days.*

Prophetic Lessons 56 *Friend, did God anywhere in the words in 1Peter 3:10-12 demand prayer to Jesus Christ, or faith in Jesus Christ? If the nations delight in love of life, if they seek to see good days, all that The Father demands is right treatment of one another.*

Prophetic Lessons 57 *While The Father does not demand prayer to Jesus, or faith in Jesus, when man finds himself or herself unable to love his or her neighbor in his or her own power, yet repugns help offered by The Father through Jesus Christ, he or she confesses that the incapacity is a delight, that he or she only pretends to seek to love his or her neighbor.* A PERSON WHO TRULY DESIRES HELP DOES NOT REPUGN HELP THAT IS OFFERED.

Love of Truth 64 *Is this too much for The Father to ask of His own creation, that man love his or her fellow man? Can it ever be rational that man considers this too much to ask?*

Have you ever wondered how it is with all of the understanding of *Economics* and *Finance*, and *Business* in the world that some nations remain PERPETUALLY UNDERDEVELOPED? It is because the people have been stripped of capacity for functioning as spirits? Whenever nations who, spiritually speaking, are domiciled on the OLD HEAVEN AND EARTH speak of, or plan economic development, The Father ensures that their designs, plans, and execution fail. The Father Himself sets His face against their agenda, ensures that every agenda fails. If The Nations will not acknowledge His Love, the cost from The Father is Troubles of Life. It is this setting of His Face against every good agenda, such that all such agenda fail that is characterized as torture of the beast, the false prophet, the devil, and all those who, eventually in context of the second death, are cast into the Lake of Fire. In this respect, The Father declares as follows.

> Righteousness exalts a nation, but sin is a reproach to any people (Proverbs 14:34).

> The face of The Lord is against those who do evil, to cut off the remembrance of them from the earth (Psalms 34:16).

Prophetic Lessons 58 *The Father* NEVER *will allow any nation, which repugns love for fellow men as basis for civil laws and societal interactions, which practices inequality of intrinsic worth of fellow men, to arrive at any meaningful* ECONOMIC DEVELOPMENT.

Prophetic Lessons 59 *If countries, which hitherto had been characterized by presence of men who put forth best efforts towards love for all men, men who put forth best efforts towards directing others towards equality of love for all men, countries, such as produced men like* WILLIAM WILBERFORCE, *devolve into practice of institutional inequalities, their choice of hatreds and conflicts will eat out all of the economic development made possible by exaltation, which always had been received, from The Father.*

Whenever Nations reject the Love of God as basis for civil laws, and societal interactions, they lose capacity for functioning as spirits, and are cast into the Lake of Fire. Note that it is not the case that they are not in touch with their spirit, but rather, The Father has destroyed whatever original capacity that He, The Creator placed in them. Such persons can no more will spirit into play in their lives, than they can continue breathing in presence of a filling of their house with smoke. Whenever such persons encounter a person who has spirit, they consider that it is that person who is an anomaly, not themselves. This then is the problem with democracy, which is, when a nation becomes filled with people who have lost capacity for functioning as spirits, democracy becomes what one eccentric, yet brilliant musician (Fela Anikulapo Kuti) referred to as,

'Demonstration of Crazy', or 'Crazy Demonstration'. Supporting evidence from Scriptures?

Since it is a righteous thing with God to give back to those troubling you - trouble, who shall suffer justice - destruction age-during (*destruction that never ends until a new 1ˢᵗ Seal is made possible by a Power for Christ*) - from The Face of the Lord, and from the glory of His strength (2Thessalonians 1:6,9).

For we - willfully sinning after the receiving the full knowledge of the truth - NO MORE FOR SINS DOTH THERE REMAIN A SACRIFICE. Fearful is the falling into the hands of a living God (Hebrews 10:26,31).

Prophetic Word 8 *It is a dangerous thing for a nation to reject the* LOVE OF GOD *as basis for civil laws, and societal interactions; for it is a dangerous thing for a nation to fall into the hands of The Living God. Where there is deliberate rejection of what is good and right, The Father sets aside merits of the sacrifice of Jesus Christ. All of the merits of the sacrifice of Jesus Christ are, in such situations, guaranteed to be lost to such Nations.*

Prophetic Word 9 *When democracy is operated by, as such filled with people who have lost capacity for functioning as spirits who live in a body, democracy becomes a curse, as opposed to a blessing.*

Whenever a person who, somehow is drawn to The Father, who somehow loves and seeks The Father arises in Nations, which are domiciled in the OLD HEAVEN AND EARTH, when such a person is recognized by The Father as a Power for Christ, The Father provides such Nations with opportunity for yet another 1ˢᵗ SEAL, with yet another opportunity for escape from the LAKE OF FIRE, from the OLD HEAVEN AND EARTH, for making alive of their spirit, for arrival at meaningful economic development. If the Nations respond, they arrive at opportunity for meaningful progress. If they do not, relative to their prior situation, their situation worsens, deteriorates.

Prophetic Lessons 60 *Every Nation that has rejected the Love of God as basis for civil laws and societal interactions remains in the heaven and earth that flee from the presence of our Lord and Savior Jesus Christ, whose place cannot be found (the* OLD HEAVEN AND EARTH*). These nations do not have opportunity for spiritual engagement with Christ at all, are barred from His Presence. Whenever, somehow a person in such nations truly connects with Christ, that person experiences the Presence of Christ personally, and through him or her, such nations have opportunity for reconnection with the Presence of Christ. In presence of a choice of the Love of God in context of a new 1*st* SEAL, such nations arrive at opportunity for spiritual translation of their Nations from the* OLD HEAVEN AND EARTH, *into the* NEW HEAVENS, NEW EARTH, AND NEW JERUSALEM IN WHICH RIGHTEOUSNESS DWELLS.

11.10   Chapter Summary

Friend, you can see how neatly and nicely all the passages discussed in this chapter fit into the SSGLAE. In this respect, it is important to note that *Revelation chs. 15 through 20:1-10* pertain only to the RP7 PATH of the SSGLAE, do not pertain to either of the GP7, or BP7 PATHS. Revelation *ch. 20:11-15* pertains to each of the GP7 and RP7 PATHS, but not to the BP7 PATH. On each of the RP7 and GP7 paths, the Great White Throne Judgment enables reconstitution of the Nations, such that those who are in rebellion are cast out of the Presence of Christ, and those who are LOVING CITIZENS OF THE NATIONS are reconstituted into Nations who are able to enter into the New Jerusalem.

Upon arrival at the 5th SEAL in context of the GP7 PATH, there is transition, not to the 1st Vial of the 7th SEAL, but to the 1st TRUMPET of the 7th Seal. So then, while each of the BP7 and GP7 paths end up at the 7th TRUMPET of the 7th Seal, on the RP7 PATH, the 7th Vial of the 7th SEAL is the equivalent of the 7th TRUMPET of the 7th Seal. In absence of blowing of any trumpets on the RP7 PATH, and the declaration of our Lord Jesus Christ that trumpets will accompany His Second Coming (Matthew 24:31; 1Corinthians 15:52; 1Thessalonians 4:16), it is unequivocal that, at end of a specific iteration of the 7th SEAL, there is not any Second Coming of Christ on the horizon. On the RP7 PATH, the Nations either submit to the reign of the heavens by RESURRECTED SPIRITS OF THE SAINTS via voluntary choice of the Love of God as basis for civil laws, or societal interactions, or the outcome is a spiritual sequestering of the Nations on the OLD HEAVEN AND EARTH, with outcome there is demand for New Heavens and New Earth for those who are saved by the grace of our Lord Jesus Christ. So then, the 1st SEAL that is outcome of a transversing of the RP7 PATH involves New Heavens, New Earth, and a New Jerusalem, and is depicted in *Revelation ch. 21*.

Prophecy Interpretation 71 *At end of transversal of one iteration of the RP7 PATH of the SSGLAE, we either arrive at reign of the heavens by spirits of dead saints that are resurrected to life, or we arrive at sequestering of rebellious nations on the* OLD HEAVEN AND EARTH *- whose place cannot be found, and descent of New Heavens, New Earth, and the New Jerusalem for the saved. By these outcomes, which ensure there is not any benefit to those who love evil from subversion of His Church, The Father declares that He will not tolerate subversion of His Church by those who love evil. The Father warns those who love evil to stay out of His Church, to not make any attempt to pervert His overarching objective of perfection of His Church.*

Prophecy Interpretation 72 *Upon completion of any iteration of the RP7 PATH of the SSGLAE, there does not exist any likelihood of the Second Coming of Christ.*

Prophecy Interpretation 73 *The institutional spiritual equilibrium that is outcome of the RP7 PATH is depicted in Revelation ch. 21.*

Prophecy Interpretation 74 *Subsequent to the Great White Throne Judgment, the Church and spiritually reconstituted Nations transition to the Utopia that is depicted in Revelation ch. 22.*

Prophecy Interpretation 75 *A BP7 PATH produces Utopia of Revelation ch. 22 on Earth.*

So then, on to exposition of *Revelation chs. 21 & 22*. First, however, a few stops over the course of the next three chapters. In the next chapter, I provide evidence from the Old Testament that The Father does not punish people who love their neighbors, but who do not pray in His name. In the chapter after the next, I provide some historical spiritual anecdotes, which provide additional support for fit of some of the details of the 7 TRUMPETS into the SSGLAE. In the chapter after that, I discuss the transition from co-rulership of the heavens by each of the SSGLAE and TIME in context of the Old Covenant, to sole rulership of the SSGLAE since time of the CHURCH IN LAODICEA.

CHAPTER 12

Saved without Praying in the Name of Jesus Christ

Throughout this book, I have provided evidence that The Father has deemed things, such that a person who adopts Love as Way of Life, who is not required of The Holy Spirit to arrive at a decision in respect of faith in Christ, is saved. I have referred to such persons as Loving Citizens of the Nations (LCN). I believe the Scriptural evidence that I have provided for salvation of LCN, which is sprinkled through all of this book, is conclusive. For concreteness, however, I provide you with an illustration from Scriptures, an illustration that is mediated by The Father Himself, an illustration in context of which The Father provided LCN with salvation, yet did not demand that they offer their prayers to Him.

I have, somewhere in this book, discussed the fact that, with exclusion of 3 TRIBES - *Judah, Simeon, and Levi*, which collectively were referred to as NATION OF Judah, that all of the people who made up the 10 TRIBES of the NATION OF Israel were taken into captivity to Assyria (2Kings 17:1-18). For the record, note that with the TRIBE of Joseph split into 2 TRIBES - *Ephraim* and *Mannaseh* - for inheritance, by decree of The Father, there in fact were, in total, 13 TRIBES. Given the *tribe of* LEVI was not provided with land inheritance of it's own, however, and given Jehovah Himself was their inheritance (Numbers 18:20-21), in so far as the civil life of the descendants of Jacob was concerned, there only were 12 TRIBES. In the declaration that He, Jehovah was their inheritance, The Father declared that the tithe from the people was allocated to the TRIBE of Levi as an inheritance. So then, we arrive at the inference that if you seek to honor Jehovah (The Father) with your substance, that Jehovah is pleased by a giving of OFFERINGS to a person who is a good *teacher* or *minister* of the things of Christ (1Timothy 5:17). If you seek to know why I believe TITHING is not a Christian principle, check

357

out *Chapter 8* of my book, True Sanctification. The testimony in respect of spirituality of the NATION OF Israel is damning.

> So they left all the commandments of the Lord their God, made for themselves a molded image and two calves, made a wooden image and worshiped all the host of heaven, and served Baal. And they caused their sons and daughters to pass through the fire, practiced witchcraft and soothsaying, and sold themselves to do evil in the sight of the Lord, to provoke Him to anger. THEREFORE THE LORD WAS VERY ANGRY WITH ISRAEL, AND REMOVED THEM FROM HIS SIGHT (PRESENCE); THERE WAS NONE LEFT BUT THE TRIBE (NATION) OF JUDAH ALONE (2Kings 17:16-18).

> Until the Lord removed Israel out of His sight (*His Presence*), as He had said by all His servants the prophets. So Israel was carried away from their own land to Assyria, as it is to this day (2Kings 17:23).

Historical Spiritual Nugget 33 *In the account in the Book of 2Kings ch. 17, we arrive at a historical spiritual anecdote, which provides support for our discussions in the preceding chapter, an anecdote which corroborates the inference that whenever nations stubbornly cling to* HATREDS AS WAY OF LIFE, *that eventually The Father removes them from participation in* HIS PRESENCE. *Since The Father is Father of all spirits (Hebrews 12:9), removal from His Presence implies absence of capacity for functioning as spirits who live in a body.*

Subsequent to taking of ISRAEL people into captivity, the Assyrian king repopulated regions formerly populated by Israel with ASSYRIANS (2Kings 17:24). These Assyrians came into the region with their evil tendencies, with their propensity for mistreatment of one another (2Kings 17:25). Note these Assyrians were not mistreating Judah, rather were mistreating one another. So then, The Father sent LIONS into their cities. Consider, however, that this was strange, for lions do not delight in coming into cities. Typically, lions delight in their command of the wild. During this specific time, however, quite unexpectedly, lions began to love to come into the cities for killing of humans. Given the lions were not eating their kills, meaning the killing was not done out of hunger, or a desire to eat, it became apparent that there was some hidden spiritual meaning to a phenomenon that typically ought not to transpire.

Wisely, the people informed their king, the king of Assyria of their predicament, who then wisely commanded that a priest who formerly lived in the land be brought back to teach the people how to fear Jehovah (2Kings 17:26-28).

The outcome?

JEHOVAH THEY ARE FEARING, and their gods they are serving, according to the custom of the nations whence they removed them. AND THESE NATIONS ARE FEARING JEHOVAH, AND THEIR GRAVEN IMAGES THEY HAVE SERVED, both their sons and their sons' sons; as their fathers did, they are doing unto this day (2Kings 17:33,41).

What does it mean that these people feared Jehovah?

Well, using the response of the Assyrian king to the preaching of Jonah in capital of Assyria, which was Nineveh, let us consult the Assyrians' understanding of what it means to fear Jehovah, and let us also explore the response from The Father (Jehovah).

And he caused it to be proclaimed and published throughout Nineveh by the decree of the king and his nobles, saying, "Let neither man nor beast, herd nor flock, taste anything; do not let them eat, or drink water. But let man and beast be covered with sackcloth, and cry mightily to God; yes, LET EVERY ONE TURN FROM HIS EVIL WAY AND FROM THE VIOLENCE THAT IS IN HIS HANDS. Who can tell if God will turn and relent, and turn away from His fierce anger, so that we may not perish (Jonah 3:7-10)?

THEN GOD SAW THEIR WORKS, THAT THEY TURNED FROM THEIR EVIL WAY; and God relented from the disaster that He had said He would bring upon them, and He did not do it (Jonah 3:11).

Several things are noteworthy, namely:

♣ There is not any mention of praying in the name of Jehovah, equivalently, praying in the name of Jesus Christ.

♣ The king commands his people to turn from their evil ways, does not make any mention of praying in the name of Jehovah.

♣ It was in their turning away from their evil ways that The Father was induced to exhibit mercy towards Nineveh.

Concerning prayer, The Father Himself, and our Lord Jesus Christ declare as follows:

When you spread out your hands, I will hide my eyes from you; EVEN THOUGH YOU MAKE MANY PRAYERS, I WILL NOT HEAR. Your hands are full of blood. Wash yourselves, make yourselves clean; put away the evil of your doings from before mine eyes. CEASE TO DO EVIL (Isaiah 1:15-16).

Not everyone who is saying to me, 'Lord, lord', shall come into the reign of the heavens; but he who is doing the will of my Father who is in the heavens (Matthew 7:21).

Historical Spiritual Nugget 34 *In the account in the Book of Jonah, we arrive at historical evidence, once again, that it is actions - works - that please The Father, not a calling upon His name in prayer. So then, when the account declares that the people feared Jehovah, the account declares that they repented of their evil ways.*

Historical Spiritual Nugget 35 *Regardless of the fact that the people continued to pray to idols that they brought along from their nations, the decision to fear Jehovah, the decision to treat each other right, was sufficient for turning away the anger of The Father.*

The Things That Are 79 *It is not that The Father does not desire people to pray to Him. Rather, it is the case that The Father does not punish anyone for not praying to Him, only punishes people for mistreating others who also are created in His image.*

The Things That Are 80 *The Father desires that people pray to Him. It is not, however, prayer that pleases The Father, rather it is the doing of His will on earth, as it is in Heaven. Whenever prayer to God is not accompanied by doing of His will, our Lord Jesus Christ explicitly declares that neither He, nor The Father know any such persons.*

In the cessation of the killing of the people by lions, The Father demonstrated His principle, which is, having given man the right to choose *'to be'*, or *'not to be'* in relationship with Him, He does not punish anyone for the decision not to delight in fellowship with Himself, The Word, and the Holy Spirit. Regardless, however, of whether a Nation is HINDU, BUDDHIST, MUSLIM, or CHRISTIAN in it's orientation, *The Father makes clear that He never will abdicate His right, both as Creator and Redeemer of mankind, to specify that no one is given power to mistreat another on the face of the earth.* So then, when Buddhists (or Christians, or Muslims, or Hindus) mistreat Buddhists (or Christians, or Muslims, or Hindus), The Father punishes the offending Buddhists (or Christians, or Muslims, or Hindus).

Prophecy Insight 136 *Should a Buddhist (or Christian, or Muslim, or Hindu) hate a God who, so long as the Buddhist (or Christian, or Muslim, or Hindu) treats others right, accepts him or her? Should a Buddhist (or Christian, or Muslim, or Hindu) who himself or herself seeks to be treated right, desire to mistreat others?*

The Things That Are 81 *In their capacity as Creator and Redeemer, The Father and The Word have declared that they will not tolerate mistreatment of anyone, that whoever mistreats another intentionally and maliciously suffers both consequences (2ⁿᵈ* SEAL *events), and punishments (*VIALS *1 through 7, or* TRUMPETS *1 through 7) that are evidences of the wrath of The Father.*

The Kicker?

Do you realize that when the Scriptures, and our Lord Jesus Christ refer to 'SAMARITANS' in the *New Testament*, that they refer to descendants of Assyrians who, by virtue of their relocation to lands formerly occupied by Nation of Israel, made themselves partakers of a promise that was supposed to belong only to Judah? A people who lacked any prior knowledge of Jehovah - SAMARITANS - arrived at a higher stature of righteousness than the 10 TRIBES whose forefathers, and themselves experienced the saving power, and glorious miracles of Jehovah. With respect to inclusion of themselves in the hope of the Jews, consider the following words between Jesus and the woman famously described as the '*Woman at the Well*' in John 4:6-7,9,25-26,40-42).

> And there was there a well of Jacob. Jesus therefore having been weary from the journeying, was sitting thus on the well; it was as it were the sixth hour; there cometh a woman out of Samaria to draw water. Jesus saith to her, "Give me to drink;" the Samaritan woman therefore saith to Him, "How dost thou, being a Jew, ask drink from me, being a Samaritan woman?" for Jews have no dealing with Samaritans.
>
> The woman saith to Him, "I HAVE KNOWN THAT MESSIAH DOTH COME, WHO IS CALLED CHRIST, when that one may come, He will tell us all things;" Jesus saith to her, "I AM HE, WHO AM SPEAKING TO THEE."
>
> When, then, the Samaritans came unto Him, they were asking Him to remain with them, and He remained there two days; and many more did believe because of His word, and said to the woman - "no more because of thy speaking do we believe; for we ourselves have heard and known that this is truly the Savior of the world - The Christ".

It was in respect of people, such as Samaritans, and such as you and I, that, The Father declares through Prophet Isaiah.

> I have been inquired of by those who asked not (*by those who were not aware of my existence*), I have been found by those who sought me not, I have said, 'Behold Me, behold Me', unto a nation

not calling in My name. I have spread out My hands all the day unto an apostate people (*Judah*), who are going in the way not good, after their own thoughts (Isaiah 65:1-2).

Life Nugget 12 *In English, there is a form of writing referred to as Hyperbole. An Hyperbole is a 'SEEMING IMPOSSIBILITY', or 'EXTRAVAGANT EXAGGERATION'. When an idea is expressed as an Hyperbole, the extravagant exaggeration that it embeds highlights Profundity of what typically is not expected to be. So then, The Father does not state an irrationality, rather, in context of a demonstration that HE IS ORIGIN OF ALL LANGUAGES, demonstrates His command of intricacy of expression of a thought.*

Life Nugget 13 *When a man declares to his female lover that, 'WITHOUT YOU, THE SUN DON'T SHINE' he expresses himself in an hyperbole, for in reality, even in presence of divorce, the sun continues to shine. What the man expresses, however, which can be true, and when true is profound, is that in absence of his lover, being in the sun does not feel quite as exhilarating as it feels in presence of his lover. For MAXIMUM IMPACT, the man states the thought as an Hyperbole. What then does The Father imply by His Hyperbole? In His Hyperbole, The Father declares that while people whom He had loved for hundreds of years had become apostate, people whom had yet to acquire a personal experience of His Love found it in themselves to arrive at an appreciation of His Godhead. For MAXIMUM IMPACT, The Father states the thought as an Hyperbole.*

It was partly because Samaritans attempted to inject themselves into promises made to Judah that they were despised by Jews. In so far as the Jews were concerned, being not descendant from Jacob, the Samaritans, who continued to worship idols, but yet continued to fear Jehovah, did not have any business attempting to inject themselves into the promises of Jehovah. The parable told by Jesus, about the GOOD SAMARITAN was premised on age old hatred of Jews for Samaritans, on the fact that, in the '*not doing of what is good*' by a PRIEST or LEVITE, the '*doing of what is good*' by a SAMARITAN to a total stranger highlights the fact that The Father is not a respecter of persons (Acts 10:34-35); highlights the fact that a total stranger qualifies as a neighbor. So then, when Jesus tells the crowd listening to Him to go and do likewise (Luke 10:37), He tells them that their NEIGHBOR can be construed to be a total stranger.

The Things That Are 82 *If, on basis of the expectation that he or she is hated, a BLACK (or African American) man or woman hates WHITE people, he or she cannot be justified before The Father, for JESUS HAS DEFINED THAT SUPPOSEDLY HATEFUL WHITE MAN OR WOMAN AS HIS OR HER NEIGHBOR.*

The Things That Are 83 *A* WHITE *man or woman* WHO SEEKS TO RETAIN *a sense of intrinsic superiority over other races cannot arrive at the Presence of Christ, is, by declaration of Jesus Christ excluded from Presence of Christ.*

The Things That Are 84 A WHITE MAN OR WOMAN WHO SEEKS SPIRITUAL CHANGE, WHICH FREES HIMSELF OR HERSELF FROM CLUTCHES OF FEELINGS OF RACISM, OR INTRINSIC SUPERIORITY IS WELCOME INTO THE *Presence of Christ*, CAN, VIA SUBMISSION TO THE CLEANSING POWER IN THE BLOOD OF JESUS CHRIST, AND THE HOLY SPIRIT, ACTUALIZE THE *Presence of Christ.*

The Things That Are 85 *With respect to* RACISM, *The Father asks all people who are looked down upon to believe that the only weapon against racism, the only weapon which never fails, is the Love of God. A White man or woman raised to be racist will, if willing, find healing in Christ. A Black man whose heart is filled with hatred for White people, this because of all of the racism he or she has endured or witnessed, will, if willing, find healing in Jesus Christ.*

Now then, look what The Father has done.

Not only are Samaritans part of the promises of Jehovah to Abraham by faith, but so also are all nations who are not direct descendants of Jacob (Galatians 3:13-14). AND WHAT IS ESSENCE OF THE PROMISE TO ABRAHAM?

The Fellowship of the Holy Spirit.

Not faith in Jesus Christ, not salvation, rather, fellowship of the Holy Spirit. Faith in Jesus Christ, and salvation merely are stop-overs on your way to fellowship of the Holy Spirit, and fellowship of Father, Son, and Holy Spirit.

Life Nugget 14 *If you are headed to* CALIFORNIA, *and there are two stop-overs in* PHILADELPHIA *and* OHIO, *if you disembark in either of* PHILADELPHIA *or* OHIO, *it is definite that your journey is, as yet, not completed.*

If you stop at faith in Jesus Christ, if you only care about being saved, you do not proceed to fellowship of The Holy Spirit, you do not, in reality, arrive at the promise to Abraham, you do not arrive at the promise to faith in Jesus Christ. So then, you are a Neophyte, a believer in Christ whose capacity for relationship with the Holy Spirit, and a higher trust relationship with Father, Son, and Holy Spirit has yet to be established. If you are to be trusted by The Father, this only can transpire in context of your relationship with Him, The Lord Jesus Christ, and The Holy Spirit. The Father desires that you pass, that you not only are called by Him, but that you arrive at being chosen by Him, such that you are recognized by Him as a Power for Christ.

Prophetic Lessons 61 *Jews, who looked down on other nations, ended up not having capacity for beholding The Christ. Let him who thinks he stands, take heed, lest he fall (1Corinthians 10:12; 2Peter 3:17) is the admonition from the Holy Spirit to all those who think anyone else undeserving of the grace of our Lord and Savior Jesus Christ.*

Prophetic Lessons 62 *If you seek to become all Jesus desires you to be, you desire to arrive at fellowship of the Holy Spirit, then onwards to a higher trust fellowship of Father, Son, and Holy Spirit.*

Let him (or her) who has an ear to hear, let him (or her) hear what the Spirit says to those who desire love of life, and good days.

CHAPTER 13

The SSGLAE: Additional Evidence from History

As we already have established, the SSGLAE is a continuing eternal system for spiritual governance of life and affairs on earth. We have then prediction of multiple resets of the SSGLAE, and have identified *six* at the very least, namely:

1. The SSGLAE of the Church of the Apostles.

2. The SSGLAE of the Church that Survived the Apostles.

3. The SSGLAE of the Church of the Byzantine Empire.

4. The SSGLAE of the Church of the Reformation.

5. The SSGLAE of the Church of the Tongues Movement.

6. The SSGLAE that coincides with the writing of this book under inspiration of the Holy Spirit.

Since the SSGLAE of the Church of the Byzantine Empire, it does not appear as if The Church has been perfected. While The Church of the Byzantine Empire was not apostate, it simultaneously was not perfected. Ditto The Church of the Reformation, and The Church of the Tongues Movement. While I count six, I do not know whether The Father has counted in exactly the same manner. It could be for instance that The Father did not begin to count until the time of the Church in Laodicea, until the time of the Presence of Christ. Or perhaps yet, The Father only is about to begin counting, this because in the commissioning of the works entrusted to me, for perhaps the very first time, the entire Gospel - JUSTIFICATION, SANCTIFICATION, AND GLORIFICATION - is placed in proper perspective.

Historical Spiritual Nugget 36 *Evidence for* ABSENCE OF LOVE *or* LACK OF UNITY OF THE FAITH *within The Church is sufficient for establishing of absence of willingness to be perfected. Denominations that are unwilling to engage themselves in discussions for arrival at the most Excellent and Truthful Recognitions of Christ do not love Jesus Christ above all else.*

But if the Church of the Apostles, and The Church that Survived the Apostles were perfected, why would time continue? Why did The Father not activate the Second Coming of Jesus Christ?

There are several interrelated answers to these questions. First, remember how that we established The Father has given the earth to man, and desires that the earth continue to be inhabited? Well then, the Second Coming of Christ is not an objective of The Father, rather is an interjection that destroys life on earth. Subsequent to perfection of the CHURCH OF THE APOSTLES, and The CHURCH THAT SURVIVED THE APOSTLES, there still remained spirits to be witnessed to, and there still remained many love projects to be pursued in context of partnerships that would subsist between The Church and The Nations. In this respect, consider that:

ဢ Gutenberg developed the PRINTING PRESS because he was thinking about how the Bible could be made available in large quantities to all those who have faith in Jesus Christ. Absent development of the PRINTING PRESS, Formal Western Education would be nigh impossible. So then, the GUTENBERG PRESS is a love project produced in context of The Church of the Reformation, a Church that was not perfected.

ဢ Galileo Galilei's, and Isaac Newton's research were, respectively made possible by funding from an apostate Church - the papal Church, and a Protestant Church. It is reprehensible that some scientists and historians deceptively characterize Christianity as anti-science. It is matter of fact that most of the scientific discoveries of the Renaissance era, which is, *1400 through about 1800 AD* were funded, at least in part by The Church. Robert Boyle, FATHER OF CHEMISTRY was a practicing Christian.

I COULD GO ON, BUT THE POINT OF THE ILLUSTRATIONS?

Prophecy Insight 137 *The Father is not desirous of cessation of life on earth. Cessation of life on earth will occur only under the most extreme sorts of disobedience on part of The Church, and The Nations.*

Prophecy Insight 138 *In context of partnerships, which subsist between The Church and The Nations, The Father delights in all of the beautiful knowledge and applications that are produced by* INTERSECTION *of faith, reason, evidence, intelligence, and wisdom of* NEOPHYTES, POWERS, *and* LOVING CITIZENS OF THE NATIONS.

Prophecy Insight 139 *Since there always are new children being born, there always are new spirits in need of spiritual maturity.*

Prophecy Insight 140 *With The Father supplying* NEWNESS *in every manner imaginable, and with arrival of* NEW CHILDREN, *physical death of* INCUMBENT POWERS, *necessity of creation of* NEW POWERS, *and necessity of creation of* NEW NEOPHYTES *creates demand for loops of the BP7* PATH *of the SSGLAE. A world that loops the BP7* PATH *will, in partnership with* LOVING CITIZENS OF THE NATIONS, *always be filled with righteous activity and joy.*

With respect to The Father's delight in salvation of all, Apostle Paul declares as follows.

First of all, then, I urge that supplications, prayers, intercessions, and thanksgivings be made for all men, for kings and all who are in high positions, that we may lead a quiet and peaceable life, godly and respectful in every way. This is good, and it is acceptable in the sight of GOD OUR SAVIOR, WHO DESIRES ALL MEN TO BE SAVED AND TO COME TO THE KNOWLEDGE OF THE TRUTH (1 Timothy 2:1-2).

Prophecy Principle 129 *The Father, The Word, and The Holy Spirit delight in transversing eternity with man, do not delight in cessation of life on earth. Since The Father always will be inspiring man to* NEW THINGS, *to* NEW IDEAS, *to* NEW ABILITIES, *to* NEW SKILLS, *to* NEW KNOWLEDGE *etc. a transversing of eternity with The Father, The Word, and The Holy Spirit always will be filled with righteous activity and joy.*

On then to a discussion of the Historical Context for the expositions to follow.

The Historical Context

Constantine the Great had to found CONSTANTINOPLE and the EASTERN ROMAN (CHRISTIAN BYZANTINE) EMPIRE, because Rome and it's Senators would not subscribe to Christian principles as foundation of civil laws, and societal interactions. Founding of Constantinople and the Byzantine Empire provided Constantine with the opportunity to impound his new found faith in Jesus Christ into civil laws of an Empire. As already discussed, this purpose of founding of civil laws on the Love of God was continued up until later Emperors began to substitute personal aggrandizement for implementation of righteous laws that are founded on the Love of God. We have then that, as represented by Rome, which would go on to become the capital of the WESTERN ROMAN EMPIRE, that the nations rejected the Love of God as foundation of civil laws. The WESTERN ROMAN EMPIRE had then to experience both consequences (2nd SEAL), and punishments (the first 6 TRUMPETS of the 7th Seal).

Given The Church was willing to be perfected - as evidenced by founding of *Constantinople* and the CHRISTIAN BYZANTINE EMPIRE, and presence of Unity of the Faith between the Byzantine Church and the Church of the Western Empire - at timing of founding of Constantinople in *325 AD*, there would be *two Churches*, both of which were, at that time, faithful to Christ. Faithfulness of both Churches is evident in the fact that both Churches were able to arrive at agreement on spiritual matters at the *Council of Nicaea* held in Constantinople in *325 AD*. There also now were two nations, The EASTERN ROMAN EMPIRE, and the WESTERN ROMAN EMPIRE. Given faithfulness of the two Churches could not be independent of their willingness to walk in love towards one another, continuation of walking in love towards one another is an important continuing yardstick of their willingness to be perfected. Note, however, that while The EASTERN ROMAN EMPIRE was, alongside the Byzantine Church, embarking on a new 1st SEAL period, and while the The Church of the Western Empire (a *Newly Reconstituted Church*) also was embarking on a new 1st SEAL period, this because none of the three entities had, hitherto had a separate existence, having refused to base civil laws and societal interactions on the LOVE OF GOD, the WESTERN ROMAN EMPIRE was embarking on a 2nd SEAL period.

Prophecy Principle 130 *The* ELEMENT *of the 7* SEALS *that is pertinent to either of The Church, or The Nations, can, conditional on past choices, not be coincident.*

Prophecy Principle 131 *The* BYZANTINE EMPIRE, *and the Church of the Byzantine Empire both commenced a new 1st* SEAL *period in 325 AD. The Church of the Western Empire, a Church that hitherto did not exist, commenced a new 1st* SEAL *period in 325 AD. Having, subsequent to execution of Emperor Licinius in 321 AD, rejected a basing of civil laws, and societal interactions on the Love of God, the* WESTERN ROMAN EMPIRE *had consigned itself to a transversing of the GP7* PATH *of the SSGLAE.*

Emperors *Diocletian* and *Licinius*, the two Emperors who persecuted Christians between, at the very least, *303 AD* and defeat of *Licinius* in *321 AD* are, physically speaking, representative of the *Beast*, which persecutes those who have faith in Jesus Christ. Note, however, that as already established, and as is The Father's Sovereign right, the CHURCH IN SMYRNA, which experienced this persecution, was perfect. So then, this persecution cannot be located in context of the 4th SEAL of the SSGLAE.

Prophetic Lessons 63 *Whenever The Father throws a spanner in the works of the SSGLAE, there always is a righteous objective to be achieved.*

In the raising up of Constantine the Great for defense of Christians in *312 AD*, resulting in *9 years* of war, and with execution of *Emperor Licinius* in

321 AD as backdrop, it would appear that The Father demonstrates mercy, that is, interlocutes with HIS EXECUTIVE INTERVENTIONIST AUTHORITY which gives up His Right to Punish, with outcome Rome and her Senators had opportunity to arrive at a new 1st SEAL period. Roman Senators having, regardless of the mercy, rejected the Love of God as basis for civil laws, and societal interactions, went on to arrive at the 2nd SEAL of the GP7 PATH.

Given the Church of the Western Empire did not exist at timing of the decision by the Western Roman Empire to reject the Love of God, her SSGLAE had to evolve independent of that of the Western Roman Empire. Further, with Christianity the official religion of the Western Roman Empire, the Church of the Western Empire could not experience any persecution. We arrive then at additional confirmation for dichotomy of evolution of SSGLAEs for The Western Church, and the Western Empire. We further arrive at the inference that the Church of the Western Empire would be judged in context of her willingness to walk in the Love of God towards the Church of the Byzantine Empire. By the same token, the Church of the Byzantine Empire would be assessed on basis of her willingness to walk in love towards the Church of the Western Empire.

Prophecy Insight 141 *Given the* WESTERN ROMAN EMPIRE *had adopted Christianity as official religion, rejection of the Love of God as basis for civil laws, and societal interactions could not be deciphered from treatment of The Western Church. So then, the SSGLAE for The Western Church, and The Western Empire had to be dichotomized.*

Prophecy Insight 142 *Just because a country claims to be 'Christian' does not imply that it consciously and actively is basing civil laws, and societal interactions on the Love of God. It is not words or labels that matter with The Father, rather it is actions. If a Church can be apostate, it is self evident that a Nation, which claims to be Christian can, itself be apostate.*

Prophecy Insight 143 *The* BYZANTINE EMPIRE *also having adopted Christianity as official religion, but having based civil laws, and societal interactions on the Love of God, could be judged on basis of it's adherence to maintenance of the Love of God within it's borders.*

Prophecy Insight 144 *Given the* BYZANTINE EMPIRE *had, in truth, christened itself a Christian Empire, willingness of The Byzantine Church to be perfected could not any longer be deduced from interactions with a Nation in need of conversion. Given the Church of the Western Empire was in exactly the same situation, willingness of the* TWO CHURCHES *to be perfected would be assessed in context of their love walk in relation to one another.*

So then, the Western Roman Empire finds itself in the 2nd SEAL of the GP7 PATH. Note a 2nd SEAL is a CONSEQUENCE SEAL, does not embed any punishments for evil done in context of persecution that was quelled by *Constantine the Great.* The Father had sought to forgive the persecution, but the Roman Senators chose otherwise. Given there is not any demand for a sealing of believers, because the Church is willing to be perfected, and there is not any risk of persecution from the Nation, there is not any demand for a 3rd SEAL. Given identification of the righteous must precede a 4th SEAL, obviation of the 3rd SEAL induces obviation of the 4th SEAL. Given the SSGLAE for the Church is dichotomized from that for the Nation, arrival of the Church at MATURITY OF RIGHTEOUSNESS is not inferred in context of relations with The Nation. We have then that there is a skipping of the 5th SEAL for arrival at the 7th Seal. We arrive then at the inference that the GP7 PATH for the WESTERN ROMAN EMPIRE consists of the 2nd and 7th SEALS. Given the 7th Seal involves meting out of Judgments of The Father, combined, the 2nd (*Consequence*) and 7th (*Punishment*) Seals enable arrival at justice. Given both Seals are characterized by hurt and death, are consequences of, or punishments for rejection of the Love of God, both Seals can overlap, collapse into each other in time, as such can run simultaneously.

Prophecy Insight 145 *For the* WESTERN ROMAN EMPIRE, *the GP7* PATH *consists of the 2nd and 7th* SEALS, *all of which run simultaneously.*

The Western Roman Empire

What then do we find? Do we find any evidence for fulfillment of the 2nd and 7th Seals subsequent to 325 AD in context of the Western Roman Empire?

In *Chapter 9*, we discussed the 7 Trumpets that are blown in context of the 7th Seal period. Two out of the 7 Trumpets are associated with time periods. The hurt that occurs in context of the 5th Trumpet lasts for 150 days, which using the '*a day for a year*' prophetic principle translates into 150 years of hurting. The hurt that transpires in course of the 6th Trumpet lasts for an *hour*, a *day*, a *month*, and a *year*. A year equals 360 days; a month is tantamount to 30 days; and an hour is a fraction ($\frac{1}{24}$) of a day. In total, we arrive at $391\frac{1}{24}$ days of hurting, which, using the prophetic principle of a day for a year translates into $391\frac{1}{24}$ years of hurting.

Using the time established for the 5th Trumpet of the 7th Seal? Absolutely.

Most if not all historians agree that the WESTERN ROMAN EMPIRE was deceased no later than *476 AD* (*HWE*, pg. 137). The first sack of Rome by it's enemies occurred in *454 AD*, but yet it could be argued that the Empire was able to continue, albeit in a much weaker state. By *476 AD*, however, the last Roman Emperor was deposed (*HWE*, pg. 137), with outcome it is unambiguously the case that the Roman Empire had ceased to exist. Friend, from *326 AD* to *476 AD* is exactly 150 years. Why is this significant?

Prophecy Insight 146 *The time of the 5ᵗʰ* TRUMPET *of the 7ᵗʰ Seal is exactly 150 years.*

Prophecy Insight 147 *Starting about 337 AD, and until 476 AD, the* WESTERN ROMAN EMPIRE *was tormented by the Visigoths.*

We already have discussed how it is that the time of the 6ᵗʰ Trumpet of the 7ᵗʰ Seal lasts for $391\frac{1}{24}$ years. Do we find any evidence for such a time period subsequent to 325 AD?

AGAIN, ABSOLUTELY. The historical record states clearly that it was starting in 716 AD that onslaught of the Visigoths and the Muslims on Western Europe was stemmed by Charles Martel, who, ironically had to escape from prison in order to stem onslaught of the Visigoths and Muslims (*HWE*, pg. 194). As typically can be the case, charges had been trumped up, and Charles Martel had been consigned to prison so a Queen Mother, *Plectrude* could preserve the throne for her infant children (*HWE*, pg. 194). Never mind that if the Visigoths and Muslims had their way, there perhaps would not be any kingdom for her infant children to inherit. Charles Martel being son of a concubine of Charles' father, PEPIN, was not considered a legitimate heir to the throne of his father.

From *325 AD* to *716 AD* is exactly 391 *plus some fraction* total number of years. We can trust The Father then and accept the fraction to be $\frac{1}{24}$ years for arrival at a total of $391\frac{1}{24}$ years. We find then that the 150 years of the 5ᵗʰ Trumpet coincide with commencement of the 391 years of the 6ᵗʰ Trumpet. On basis of the evidence, the 2ⁿᵈ and 7ᵗʰ SEALS did, indeed collapse in time, run simultaneously.

Prophecy Insight 148 *Invasion of Western Europe by Islam is part of the judgments that occurred in context of the 6ᵗʰ* TRUMPET *of the 7ᵗʰ Seal. The description of the hordes on horses that would inflict judgments of the 6ᵗʰ* TRUMPET *in Revelation 9:16-19 matches well descriptions of the ferocity of the Islamic hordes of those times.*

Prophecy Insight 149 *From 325 AD to 716 AD is right about $391\frac{1}{24}$ years. So then, we see that the 2ⁿᵈ Seal, and* TRUMPETS *1 through 6 of the 7ᵗʰ* SEAL *all ran concurrently.*

Additional Corroborating Evidence?

Charles Martel, a forebear of the GERMANS, was in essence a king of ancient Germany, a people who, since that time have acted as if they believe they ought to rule over Western Europe. The two World Wars that have engulfed the entire world? Occasioned by Germany's belief in some God given right to rule over all of Western Europe. This belief can be seen to stem from the view that with Charles Martel representative of Germany, that it was Germany which seized mantle of rulership of Western Europe from the Western Roman Empire. If in addition, Germans see themselves as having fulfilled ancient prophecy, this adds to the notion of some sort of divine right for rulership of Western Europe. Starting about the *13th Century*, PRUSSIA, an ancient forbear of Germany was for many centuries a powerful empire in Europe, a powerful empire that was instrumental to demise of ANCIENT POLAND.

The Two Churches

As I already have stated, with the Byzantine Church and the Church of the Western Empire willing to recognize the most compelling, most excellent, most true articulation of nature of God in context of the Council of Nicaea, the two churches demonstrated several qualities that are evidence of willingness of the Church to be perfected, namely:

1. Love of the Truth

2. Desire for a United Front

3. Respect and Love for One Another

Subsequent to demise of Roman Emperors in *476 AD*, the Church of the Western Empire chose to scrap with nations of Western Europe, and threats to those nations, such as the Visigoths, and the Muslims. As always is the case whenever a Church chooses to hold on to worldly glory at all costs, it was inevitable that eventually the once pure Church of the Western Empire would devolve into apostasy. In pursuit of worldly power, and for cohesion of it's organization, in *590 AD*, GREGORY I was instituted as the first Pope (*HWE, pg. 194*). During the *750s AD*, as part of it's attempts at holding on to worldly glory, the Church of the Western Empire, which now had transformed itself into the PAPAL CHURCH presented the matter of worship of statues to the Church of the Byzantine Empire for discussion. The Church of the Byzantine Empire refused to accede, likely put forth excellent Scriptural rationales for heresy of worship of statues. Rather unfortunately, the Byzantine Church did not simultaneously recognize that production of paintings, which attempt to depict Jesus Christ, also constituted a departure from purity of the gospel. Given they did not bow to these paintings, however, the distinction was subtle, was lost to their spiritual sensibilities. The papal

Church did not budge, devolved into worship of statues. This was the first schism between the two Churches. In presence of availability of Christian Scriptures to all and sundry in today's world, it is straightforwardly clear that the Byzantine Church was right, that the papal Church wrong. In the unwillingness to listen to her counterpart Church, the papal Church was first to break ranks on *Items 1 and 2 above*, namely, LOVE OF THE TRUTH, and DESIRE FOR A UNITED FRONT. The final spiritual break transpired in *867 AD*. In an attempt at justifying her heresies, the papal Church declared that her pope has final authority over all other Christians and on all spiritual matters. By this, the papal Church declared that the Church of the Byzantine Empire no longer was considered an equal, clearly and in context of the Gospel of our Lord Jesus Christ, an heresy. Rightly, The Byzantine Church disagreed. The papal Church did not budge. With Respect and Love for the Byzantine Church now sacrificed for worldly splendor, the papal Church now was in full heresy.

Prophecy Insight 150 *By 867 AD, the Church of the Western Empire, which now had transformed into the* PAPAL CHURCH *had chosen not to be perfected, as such had embarked on the 2ⁿᵈ* SEAL *of an RP7* PATH.

Having chosen not to be perfected, clearly, the papal Church would transition to a 2ⁿᵈ SEAL of the RP7 PATH. By *1056 AD*, the Byzantine Empire began to not any longer protect it's free small farmers from exploitation. By *1099 AD*, in the choice of worldly splendor over the glory of Christ, the Byzantine Empire would embark on it's own version of the 2ⁿᵈ SEAL of the RP7 PATH. THE ONLY DIFFERENCE? The path undertaken by the Byzantine Church was not a path of intentional disobedience, was rooted in a misundertanding of the Gospel, the misunderstanding that the reign of Christ is rooted in earthly kingdoms. In light of the ignorance nature of the sins of the Byzantine Church, the mercies of Christ would cover arrival on the RP7 PATH. All that remained then was for the Church to be deactivated, to be called up to heaven as one of the two witnesses of *Revelation ch. 11.*

Prophecy Insight 151 *The* CHURCH OF THE BYZANTINE EMPIRE *lost it's way on basis of ignorance. It's effectiveness having been compromised, it was deactivated totally, called up to heaven as one of the two witnesses of Revelation ch. 11.*

What then about the papal Church? Due to the fact that the papal Church gave birth to the Church of the Reformation, there was arrival at a Newly Reconstituted Church, with outcome the papal Church transformed into an apostate system that is cast out of the Presence of Christ. This is what the Scriptures imply when they state that the devil "went away to make war with THE REST OF HER SEED, those keeping the commands of God, and having the testimony of Jesus (Revelation 12:17)."

By this, the Scriptures declare existence of an apostate church *not comprised of the rest of her seed*, as such not comprised of people who keep the commands of God, and have the testimony of Jesus. You see then that Christians who declare that they never pass through any challenges, never have to make any stand for Christ, likely are CHARLATANS who are part of the apostate system, as such do not attract any attacks from the devil. But they will not escape, for they will be judged by the almighty God. Tis the reason judgment begins in the household of God (1Peter 4:17).

Prophecy Insight 152 *If you envy supposed Christians (inclusive of Church pastors) who seem to have it easy, who are able to stand up and boast in Church meetings of their cars, houses, and financial prosperity, you just might be envying CHARLATANS whose goal is to induce you to indulge in lust of the eyes, lust of the flesh, and pride of life, people who are after your soul, people who, in context of Babylon, seek to trade in your soul.*

Missionaries from the United States and Western Europe have attempted with lots of zeal to evangelize Asia. None of those attempts have produced any stable, progressive success. In China, a country that used to be heavily Christian in ancient times, faith in Jesus Christ was successfully persecuted out of the country. Today, China has a state run Christianity, which as you can imagine, cannot afford to glorify Jesus Christ - such glorification eats directly at foundation of it's Communist Ideology.

In Revelation 2:13, our Lord Jesus Christ declares that ASIA IS THRONE OF THE ADVERSARY, that is, throne of the devil. In Revelation 2:24, He declares that some in the CHURCH IN THYATIRA sought to know the depths of the Adversary, that is, sought to taste evil to it's utmost. By the time of the CHURCH IN SARDIS in *Revelation 3:1*, the Church of the Byzantine Empire was declared, by her Lord and Savior to be spiritually dead. The timing of commencement of the CHURCH IN SARDIS - as established in *Chapter 5, 1100 AD*, right after choice of earthly splendor over spiritual splendor in *1099 AD*. In the failure of the Church of the Byzantine Empire, spirits domiciled in Asia chose hatreds over the Love of Christ. This was real essence of failure of the Byzantine Church, which is, the people themselves demonstrated preference for a hierarchical society, as opposed to a society within which all men were deemed equal. But they were not the first to embark on such a path. Thousands of years before, during the time of Samuel, who was High Priest and Prophet, descendants of Jacob chose servanthood to an earthly king over equality of all, and leadership of a High Priest and Prophet (1Samuel 8:10-22).

What is it that makes mankind arrive at deliberate choice of foolishness over wisdom, at deliberate choice of inequality over equality?

The Things That Are 86 THE ANSWER MY FRIEND REALLY IS SIMPLE. THE FATHER DECLARES THAT LOVE OF SIN MESSES UP MAN'S COGNITION. IF ONLY WE KNEW JUST HOW MUCH.

The Things That Are 87 *The only answer to man's choice of foolishness over wisdom is* LOVE FOR RIGHTEOUSNESS, LOVE FOR WHAT IS RIGHT, *love for the truth that with respect to intrinsic worth,* ALL MEN ARE EQUAL *in sight of The Father.*

Prophecy Insight 153 *Dearth of true faith in Jesus Christ in Asia is, in part, outcome of unwillingness of individuals to participate in the Presence of Christ. When the Presence of Christ arrived in 1454 AD, only Christians in Western Europe would respond. There was not any meaningful response in Asia.*

With respect to the papal Church, friend, outside of the worldly splendor of the Vatican City, do you see any evidence for the Glory of Jesus Christ in the Nation of Italy?

Life Nugget 15 *Italy is known for* THE MAFIA, CORRUPTION, PROSTITUTION, *and* SOCIALISM *bordering on* PSEUDO COMMUNISM. *Does this sound anything like the Glory of Christ?*

If we extend the evidence to all of the countries, which reasonably can be characterized as 'CATHOLIC', such as the countries of Latin or South America, do we see any real success stories? Can we consider any of MEXICO, NICARAGUA, COLOMBIA, HONDURAS etc. to be success stories? The only country, which seems to have made some progress, Chile, *piggybacked* that progress on adoption of more of a secular state.

The Things That Are 88 *It is not possible for a Church that is apostate in her teachings about Jesus Christ Himself to remain in the Presence of Christ.*

Prophecy Insight 154 *I have enunciated heresies taught about Jesus Christ Himself by the papal Church in discussion of the two beasts of Revelation ch. 13 in chapter 11 of this book.*

Consider, however, the United States of America (USA), the country that became home for most Protestants. In the history of the USA, we observe some Glory for Christ. Rather sadly, the USA it would seem has progressed on a path, which seems set on extinguishing all of the Glory of Christ for which it has been known. If the USA thinks becoming like *Mexico, Italy, Nicaragua,*

Colombia, Honduras etc. will be fun, it is in for one of the rudest shocks known to man, for TO WHOM MUCH IS GIVEN, MUCH IS EXPECTED *(Luke 12:48).* If the USA thinks it will be no worse than these sorts of countries, which never really experienced the Glory of Christ, it will find that the amount of Glory that is repugned will reflect in the depth to which a country will sink. If the USA continues determinedly on it's path to destruction of the Glory of Christ that is domiciled in her history, by the time all is said and done, she will not be able to look even Honduras in the eye.

Prophetic Word 10 *In the history of the United States of America, however dim, we see evidence for the Glory of Christ. If the USA insists deterministically on a path set for extinguishment of that glory, a path it commenced on in 1958 when it decided, against all scientific evidence, to teach evolution as a fact, as opposed to a hypothesis for origin of life on earth, it will discover what happens when Glory that is Great is repugned on altar of 'WHO IS GOD, AND JESUS CHRIST TO DEMAND THAT WE LOVE THE TRUTH, AND LOVE ONE AN-OTHER?' Absent repentance and reformation, the USA is headed for a great destruction.*

Plea from the Holy Spirit that you Love The Truth

Friend, if you as yet are not convinced that the SSGLAE system resides at core of visions revealed to and penned by Apostle John in the Book of Revelation, I ask that you seek the Holy Spirit for eyesalve to see, or for an alternate, better, more consistent, and rational explanation for visions of Apostle John. I did not conceive the SSGLAE in my mind, it has been revealed to me by the Holy Spirit. Granted, I had to wrestle it out in the Spirit in the sense that I had to begin to arrange all of the revelations, such that it all could make sense and fit together. Inspiration for that exercise came, however, from the Holy Spirit. From the time that I received Jesus by faith in 1990, with the seeming import then that The Father did not want me to become an expert in interpretation of prophecy, but rather wanted me to focus on teaching of the principles of faith in Jesus Christ, the Holy Spirit bid me to not attempt to understand and interpret the Book of Revelation. The real reason the Holy Spirit guided me away from an attempt at understanding the Book of Revelation, a reason I then would not have been able to understand? I HAD NOT EXPERIENCED ENOUGH OF CHRIST. If I had attempted to understand revelations entrusted to Apostle John at that point in time, this prior to my arrival at the Presence of Christ, I probably would have made exactly the same mistakes as all of those interpretations out there, which assume the Presence of Christ pertains to the SECOND COMING OF CHRIST. Having, by the grace of our Lord Jesus Christ arrived at the Presence of Christ sometime in 2016, however, in terms of spiritual preparation, I was prepared for arrival at a right interpretation of the Book of Revelation. It is a righteous principle of faith in Jesus Christ that our capacity for understanding of truth is progressive, that there are truths for which we require some more of spiritual maturity if we are to properly understand (John 16:12).

Life Nugget 16 *Friend, I cannot tell you the exact or precise time in 2016 that I arrived at the Presence of Christ. But then if I could, I would be a fraud, for then it would be my work, not Christ's. When you arrive at the Presence of Christ, you become aware of a* GOOD CHANGE *in your fellowship with Father, Son, and Holy Spirit, and as a wise son of God, you simply rejoice in what The Lord Jesus has done.*

Life Nugget 17 *If The Holy Spirit initially restrains you from a path, there always is a greater glory planned in context of the restraint, both for yourself, and for the good news of our Lord and Savior Jesus Christ.*

Sometime in 2016/2017, for the very first time, the Holy Spirit directed me to a reading of the entire Book of Revelation. Do you know friend that I came away from that reading with only one revelation, but yet a revelation that would become crucial for my understanding of the revelations entrusted to Apostle John. During that reading, the Holy Spirit provided me with the insight that succor provided the woman of *Revelation ch. 12*, who is representative of the Church, was provided in context of the CHURCH OF THE BYZANTINE EMPIRE. I searched around then, could not find anyone else who had such insight into interpretation of the 1,260 days of *Revelation ch. 12.*

In 2018, the Holy Spirit again directed me to a study of the Book of Revelation, and in my spirit made me realize that I would be sharing revelations that I would receive with fellow believers in Christ. In 2019, my spirit again was directed to a study of the Book of Revelation. During that study, and in midst of attempts at resolving my confusions, the Numerology of The Father, which lies at heart of the SSGLAE was revealed to me. Therein was born the insight that the Seals of *Revelation chs. 6 & 8* are, first and foremost, symbolic. Friend, would you know that other than revelation of the Numerology of The Father, most of the insights I thought I had arrived at in course of that third study did not turn out to be as accurate as I initially had thought. The SSGLAE was revealed to me only whilst and after I had written *Chapter 6* of this book, which is on Numerology of The Father. I say all of this so you can be assured this is not some pre-conceived interpretation of Scripture.

Life Nugget 18 *Apostle Paul revealed that it was not his wisdom that produced his understanding of the grace of God, that it was by revelation of Father, Son, and Holy Spirit (Galatians 1:12, 2:2; Ephesians 1:17, 3:3). Where there is* TRUE HUMILITY, *and* MEEKNESS OF WISDOM, *Powers for Christ are not ashamed to acknowledge that they did not start the journey having it all together, that it was Father, Son, and Holy Spirit who perfected their revelation,* *their insight, their knowledge, their wisdom, and their practice of the grace of God.*

Prophetic Encouragement 7 *It is the meek, those who believe The Father that all are equal in intrinsic worth, who as such do not attempt to lift themselves above others, who do not interpose themselves between those who learn from them, and their Lord Jesus Christ, who direct attention to Christ, not themselves, who inherit the earth.*

Friend, this book is inspired by the Holy Spirit, is a gift to you, and the Church, and The Nations through me from the Father, Son, and Holy Spirit. If you doubt still, I commend you to the grace of our Lord Jesus Christ, and pray that He, our Lord Jesus Christ will grant to you a spirit of wisdom and of revelation in your reading of this book and the Book of Revelation. I pray that you receive discernment, and that you go on to know the truth as it is Jesus Christ. The grace of our Lord Jesus Christ be with your spirit in Jesus name. Amen.

Because of this I also, having heard of your faith in the Lord Jesus, and THE LOVE TO ALL THE SAINTS, do not cease giving thanks for you, making mention of you in my prayers, that the God of our Lord Jesus Christ, the Father of the glory, may give to you a spirit of wisdom and revelation in the RECOGNITION OF HIM (*in the recognition of the truth, for our Lord Jesus Christ is embodiment of all truths that are eternal*) - Ephesians 1:15-17.

FOR THE LAW WAS GIVEN THROUGH MOSES; grace and truth came through Jesus Christ (John 1:17).

Jesus saith to him, I AM THE WAY, AND THE TRUTH, AND THE LIFE, no one doth come unto The Father, if not through me (John 14:6).

Prophecy Insight 155 *Knowledge of the SSGLAE, and it's ramifications, and arrival at a realization of just how much THOUGHTFULNESS, LOVE, CARE, and TIME The Father has invested in your welfare and mine, a realization that ought to produce adoration of The Father, are the truths that The Father seeks to bring to your spiritual understanding, are the reasons for this book.*

Prophecy Insight 156 *The SSGLAE provides knowledge, revelations, and insights, which enable you arrive at a Right Recognition of Christ (RRC). Remember, only those who arrive at RRC have opportunity for recognition from The Father as Powers for Christ.*

CHAPTER 14

Importance of 'Time' Prior to Institution of the SSGLAE

In *Chapters 5, 9* and *11*, we established that, starting with arrival of the CHURCH IN LAODICEA about *1454*, evolution of time became, in entirety, a function of the SSGLAE. With some preliminary evidence in tow, I further asserted that prior to arrival of the Church in Laodicea, spiritual events were governed both by time and the SSGLAE, with outcome sanctification of people, that is, protection from consequences of sin, and feasibility of rightness with God were function of interaction of the SSGLAE and timed events. As already discussed, this interaction was necessary because the advent of our Lord Jesus Christ had to occur in time, so also timing of initial arrival of the Presence of Christ on earth. Upon arrival of the Presence of Christ on earth in course of the time of the Church in Laodicea, response to the Gospel became, in entirety, an individual matter. In light of this spiritual reality, time no longer is co-ruler with the SSGLAE, rather serves as backdrop for the SSGLAE. In this respect, in *Chapter 11*, we saw how the LITTLE SCROLL was sweet in the mouth of Apostle John, but bitter in his belly. This was symbolic of setting up, initial success, and eventual failure of the CHURCH OF THE BYZANTINE EMPIRE. For ease of remembrance, the Church of the Byzantine Empire commenced with the Church in Pergamum, ended with the *Church in Philadelphia*, that is, four of the seven Churches of *Revelation chs. 2 & 3*. In order to provide His Apostles and early believers with evidence that the Reign of Christ had to be, first and foremost spiritual, some timeline had to be incorporated into early implementations of the SSGLAE, timelines that we have explored and verified in several of preceding chapters. So then, we arrive at an SSGLAE within which, with the reign of our Lord Jesus Christ spiritual, it is the body of Christ, which, hopefully coincides with The Church, that manifests the Presence of Christ to the Nations. Given Powers for Christ have attained to more of spiritual maturity, existence of Powers for Christ is critical for the witness of The Church. This is evident in the spiritual reality that, given The Father demands much only from those whom He has given much, in absence of Powers for Christ, there are demonstrations of the Reign of Christ for which there are none who can be trusted. Clearly, this is not a desirable situation, hence, The Father's desire that you mature, that if you currently are a Neophyte, that you exert effort which enables you become a Power for Christ. Given there does not exist any believer who is recognized as a Power for Christ, who was not at some point in time, a Neophyte, there is not any shame in being a Neophyte, for all at some point or another are Neophytes.

Prophetic Lessons 64 *At the point at which every believer confesses faith in Jesus Christ as Son of God, Lord, and Savior, all each and every believer can be is a Neophyte. There is not any person who has faith in Jesus Christ who, absent initial characterization as a Neophyte, becomes a Power for Christ.*

Prophetic Lessons 65 *In order for The Father to provide some deep revelations of Christ to the Nations, The Father needs* NEOPHYTES *who are willing to be transformed into the image of Christ, who are willing to become* POWERS FOR CHRIST. *The progression from* NEOPHYTE *to a* POWER FOR CHRIST *requires voluntary spiritual participation in process of sanctification, the process absent which, none are able to become* POWERS FOR CHRIST.

> But what then about the time of the Old Covenant? Is there evidence that sanctification was a function of the SSGLAE and timed events in context of the Old Covenant?

I already have, in preceding chapters, and particularly in *Chapter 10* demonstrated existence of the SSGLAE in context of the OLD COVENANT. In this chapter, I provide evidence that sanctification also was a function of timed events in context of the Old Covenant. Importance of time for sanctification of the people was most evident in context of the weekly seventh-day Sabbath. In this respect, consider the following words from Exodus 31:13-17.

> Speak also to the children of Israel, saying: 'SURELY MY SAB-
> BATHS YOU SHALL KEEP, for it is a sign between Me and you through-
> out your generations, THAT YOU MAY KNOW THAT I AM THE LORD
> WHO SANCTIFIES YOU. You shall keep the Sabbath, therefore, for
> it is holy to you. Everyone who profanes it shall surely be put to
> death; for whoever does any work on it, that person shall be cut off
> from among his people. Work shall be done for six days, but the

seventh is the Sabbath of rest, holy to the Lord. Whoever does any work on the Sabbath day, he shall surely be put to death. Therefore the children of Israel shall keep the Sabbath, to observe the Sabbath throughout their generations as a perpetual covenant. It is a sign between Me and the children of Israel forever; for in six days the Lord made the heavens and the earth, and on the seventh day He rested and was refreshed.'

It is very clear from the Scripture that the weekly Sabbath was special. Out of all of the Sabbaths (*days on which Israel did not do any work*) Israel was commanded to observe (Leviticus Chapter 23), only observance of the weekly Sabbath signifies that it is The Father who sanctifies Israel. Note, however, that the commandment in Exodus 31:13-17 does not say anything about a holy convocation (*a physical assembly of believers*). Neither does the rendition of the Sabbath Matter in Exodus 20:8 associate the weekly Sabbath with a holy convocation. So then, while abstinence from work was spiritual, was a sign that Israel considered itself sanctified by The Father, convocations that were commanded were part of the ceremonial rites of Israel. This is evident in the fact that convocations are commanded only in context of enunciation of the other 6 ceremonial convocations in Leviticus Chapter 23. In this respect, consider the following words in Leviticus 23:1-3; 4-8.

> And the Lord spoke to Moses, saying, "Speak to the children of Israel, and say to them: 'THE FEASTS OF THE LORD, which you shall proclaim to be holy convocations, THESE ARE MY FEASTS. Six days shall work be done, but THE SEVENTH DAY IS A SABBATH OF SOLEMN REST, A HOLY CONVOCATION. You shall do no work on it; it is the Sabbath of the Lord in all your dwellings.

> THESE ARE THE FEASTS OF THE LORD, HOLY CONVOCATIONS which you shall proclaim at their appointed times. On the fourteenth day of the first month at twilight is THE LORD'S PASSOVER. And on the fifteenth day of the same month is THE FEAST OF UNLEAVENED BREAD to the Lord; seven days you must eat unleavened bread. On the first day you shall have a holy convocation; you shall do no customary work on it. But you shall offer an offering made by fire to the Lord for seven days. The seventh day shall be a holy convocation; you shall do no customary work on it."

The Father went on to enumerate Five other feasts in the rest of Leviticus Chapter 23, namely, THE FEAST OF THE FIRSTFRUITS; THE FEAST OF NEW GRAIN; THE FEAST OF TRUMPETS; THE DAY OF ATONEMENT; and THE FEAST OF TABERNACLES.

Prophecy Insight 157 *In so far as 'holy convocations' were concerned, the weekly 7th day Sabbath was on an equal pedestal with the 7 ceremonial once-a-year Sabbaths.*

The evidence that it was not the holy convocations that were evidence of adherence to the weekly Sabbath, that rather it was celebration of God as Creator, with the celebration evident in abstinence from evil towards neighbors?

> Blessed is the man who does this, and the son of man who lays hold on it; who keeps from defiling the Sabbath, and keeps his hand from doing any evil (Isaiah 56:2).

> Bring no more futile sacrifices; incense is an abomination to me. The new moons, THE SABBATHS, and the calling of assemblies - I cannot endure iniquity and the sacred meeting. Your new moons and your appointed feasts my soul hates; they are a trouble to me, I am weary of bearing them (Isaiah 1:13-14).

> When you spread out your hands, I will hide my eyes from you; even though you make many prayers, I will not hear. Your hands are full of blood. Wash yourselves, make yourselves clean; put away the evil of your doings from before my eyes. Cease to do evil, learn to do good; seek justice, rebuke the oppressor; defend the fatherless, plead for the widow (Isaiah 1:15-16).

In Isaiah 56:2, Jehovah links observance of the Sabbath - abstinence from work (Exodus 31:13-17) - with abstinence from evil, meaning observance of the Sabbath signified the belief that all men are created by God, with outcome doing of evil to another could not be justified. In Isaiah 1:13-16, The Father declares that 'supposedly' holy convocations, which are not rooted in abstinence from evil, that comprise of people who practice evil towards others, are an abomination to Him, that He is not in midst of such supposedly holy convocations. Note that The Father explicitly defines evil as actions towards others, as unrighteous actions that are directed at fellow men - male or female, neighbor or foreigner, White or Black.

Prophecy Principle 132 *Sabbath keeping that is pure and undefiled before The Father, Son, and Holy Spirit is demonstration of the faith that we all are of one blood, that we all are created by one God who is Father of all. Being of one blood, we are equal in essence, none is superior to the other, hence, none can justify direction of evil at another.*

It is clear from the two contrasted passages that holy convocations are ceremonial, that it is abstinence from work on the 7th day Sabbath, which signifies belief that all men are created equal in sight of God. Whenever Israel observed the Sabbath in their hearts in sense of belief in their intrinsic equality, they proclaimed that The Father is sanctifier of their souls.

Prophecy Insight 158 *Holding of holy convocations on the weekly Sabbath was part of Israel's ceremonial spiritual system. This is evident in the fact that a holy convocation for a ceremonial Sabbath could coincide with the holy convocation for a weekly Sabbath (see chart to follow).*

With the assumption that the 14th day of the 1st Month, which is, the first feast of every year - THE PASSOVER - falls on a *Sunday (S)*, and with the following notation for days of the week - *Monday (M), Tuesday (T), Wednesday (W), Thursday (R), Friday (F), Saturday (Sa)* - and with NS signifying '*50 days from the* FEAST OF THE FIRSTFRUITS' that is, a set time, the design of the feast days runs as follows.

| | | | Day of the Week | | | | | | |
Feast	Month	Day	Yr 1	Yr 2	Yr 3	Yr 4	Yr 5	Yr 6	Yr 7
Passover	1	14	S	W	Sa	T	F	M	R
Unleavened Bread	1	15	M	R	S	W	Sa	T	F
	1	21	S	W	Sa	T	F	M	R
Feast of Firstfruits	NS	NS	S	S	S	S	S	S	S
New Grain	NS	NS	S	S	S	S	S	S	S
Feast of Trumpets	7	1	Sa	T	F	M	R	S	W
Day of Atonement	7	10	M	R	S	W	Sa	T	F
Feast of Tabernacles	7	15	Sa	T	F	M	R	S	W
	7	22	Sa	T	F	M	R	S	W

The beauty of the system of ceremonial Sabbaths?

Prophecy Insight 159 *With a year consisting of 12 months of 30 days each, over the course of every 7* YEARS*, inclusive of Sunday, it was guaranteed* *that each day of the week was, at some point, declared to be a day holy to The Father in context of each and every feast. So then, Completeness of sanctification of every day of the week in context of the feast system required 7 years of time.*

Prophecy Insight 160 *We already have established that in The Father's numerology, 7 signifies completeness and commencement. In the feast cycle established by The Father for Israel, we again find confirmation for association of the number 7 with completeness and commencement, in this case completeness of sanctification of days of the week, and commencement of the process all over again.*

Prophecy Insight 161 *While it is days of the week whose sanctification are completed in context of the number 7, it is the Church that is perfected in context of the SSGLAE that now governs evolution of time.*

How are we sanctified, and how do we know we are sanctified in Christ in context of the New Covenant?

And we - we ought to give thanks to God always for you, brethren, beloved by the Lord, that God did choose you from the beginning to salvation, in SANCTIFICATION OF THE SPIRIT, and belief of the truth (2Thessalonians 2:13).

Peter, an apostle of Jesus Christ, to the choice sojourners of the dispersion of Pontus, Galatia, Cappadocia, Asia, and Bithynia, according to a foreknowledge of God The Father, IN SANCTIFICATION OF THE SPIRIT, to obedience and sprinkling of the blood of Jesus Christ: Grace to you and peace be multiplied (1Peter 1:1-2).

And this is His command, that we may believe in the name of His Son Jesus Christ, and may love one another, even as He did give command to us, and he who is keeping His commands, in Him he doth remain, and He in him; and in this we know that He doth remain in us, from the Spirit that He gave us (1John 3:23-24).

In whom (that is, our Lord Jesus Christ) ye also, having heard the word of the truth - the good news of your salvation - in whom also having believed, ye were SEALED WITH THE HOLY SPIRIT of promise (Ephesians 1:13).

And make not sorrowful the Holy Spirit of God, in which YE WERE SEALED TO A DAY OF REDEMPTION (Ephesians 4:30).

Prophecy Principle 133 *It is very clear from the preceding verses that we are sanctified by the Holy Spirit, that only those who believe in the name of Jesus, and who evince their faith in love for others are sanctified of the Holy Spirit. Submission to sanctification in the Spirit attracts the seal of God, which is the Holy Spirit.*

Clearly, sanctification has nothing to do with observance of a day, and neither can it, else Christ died in vain (Galatians 2:21; 3:4). This is evident as follows. When you received Jesus, when you believed in His name, you were justified in the blood of Jesus, and you received the Holy Spirit by faith. Having received the Holy Spirit you are sanctified. Given you are sanctified, with the necessary assumption that you do not engage in willful sin, all that you do, and every day in which you participate, already is sanctified, for all that you do is done in the Spirit. You see then that your sanctification is spiritual, not earthy, as such cannot consist in any observances. To drive this point home, suppose you did not believe in Christ, but you are moral, meaning you do not commit adultery, do not steal, do not commit murder, do not covet, do not bear false witness, and honor your parents. Based on declarations of the Holy Spirit, could you be sanctified in Christ? The answer of course is a resounding No!! So then, if treating your neighbor right cannot sanctify you, how exactly can God be so wicked as to allow others to be sanctified merely by gathering in some building claiming to praise His name? Can a God who refuses to sanctify you because you treat others right ever be just if others are sanctified merely because they sing and pray? In addition to Scripture already cited from Isaiah Chapter 1, which show none can be sanctified by singing or praying to God, consider words spoken by our Lord Jesus Christ in Matthew 15:8-9, and Mark 12:38-40.

> This people honors with their lips (*with their singing and pray-ing*), but their heart is far from me; IN VAIN DO THEY WORSHIP ME, teaching (*while congregating in holy convocations*) as doctrines the precepts of men.

> And in His teaching He said, "Beware of the scribes, who like to go about in long robes, and to have salutations in the market places and the best seats in the synagogues and the places of honor at feasts, who devour widows' houses and FOR A PRETENSE MAKE LONG PRAYERS. They will receive the greater condemnation."

Prophecy Principle 134 *If prayer can be hypocritical, can be an attempt at appeasing God, none can by attending holy convocations sanctify themselves before God. If holy convocations can be filled with iniquity (Isaiah 1:11-20), attendance at holy convocations cannot induce sanctification from God. If lips that are singing can be far from God, this because the heart, the spirit, is far* *from God, as such not filled with His Spirit, singing cannot commend anyone to God.*

To sum it all up?

Formerly, when you did not know God, you were in bondage to beings that by nature are no gods; but now that you have come to know God, or rather to be known by God, how can you turn back again to the weak and beggarly elemental spirits whose slaves you want to be once more? YOU OBSERVE DAYS, AND MONTHS, AND SEASONS, AND YEARS! I AM AFRAID I HAVE LABORED OVER YOU IN VAIN (Galatians 4:8-11).

Prophecy Insight 162 *The Holy Spirit makes clear that faith in Jesus, and resulting infilling of the Holy Spirit does away with necessity of observances of time.*

In addition to the Sabbaths, there were laws of time in respect of agriculture - land was to be sown for 6 years, then left to fallow in the seventh year (Leviticus 25:3-4), and fruit from newly planted trees was not supposed to eaten until the fourth year (Leviticus 19:23-25). If a man indentured himself to service to another, he had to be freed at the end of the sixth year (Deuteronomy 15:12-15). Every 50 years was a year of jubilee, a years for cancellation of debts, a year during which if you sold your ancestral property it had to be given back (Leviticus 25:8-17). Evolution of history of the Jews then was tied to events that were rooted not only in the actions of the people, but in time.

Prophecy Principle 135 *The principles enunciated, namely celebration of God's blessings via convocations, provision of land that is farmed with opportunity for rest, being patient for soil to acquire the nature of fruit that is planted on it prior to eating of the fruit, setting of people free so they can prosper, declarations of jubilee etc. all remain good purposes. In these times, however, application of these principles no longer is rooted in time, is rooted in a determination as to what is right to do at any point in time as guided by the Holy Spirit.*

Whoever knows what is right to do and fails to do it, for him it is sin (James 4:17).

With The Father, Purpose is more important than Time. But so rationality dictates, for there are men who live only to be 40, but are remembered, and there are men who live to be 90 and soon are forgotten.

Prophecy Insight 163 *In so far as The Father is concerned, time without purpose is meaningless. Time exists only because there are purposes to be achieved. So long as there are purposes to be achieved, time is not binding, serves merely as backdrop for pursuit of purposes.*

Prophecy Insight 164 *Whereas Time had served as Guardian of Purpose up until the time of the* CHURCH IN LAODICEA, *from the time of the Church in Laodicea and onwards, Time now serves merely as backdrop or canvas for pursuit of Purpose.*

Prophecy Insight 165 *The reign of our Lord Jesus Christ having fully commenced at timing of the* CHURCH IN LAODICEA, *time no longer is arbiter of affairs on earth, The Father has instituted the SSGLAE as arbiter of life and affairs on earth.*

CHAPTER 15

New Heavens, New Earth, & New Jerusalem

The SSGLAE is designed to run in context of these existing heavens and earth, exists for governance of affairs on this earth. In Revelation 20:11, the SSGLAE having been on the RP7 PATH, this earth and it's heaven flee away from the face of the Father of our Lord Jesus Christ and there was not any place anymore found for these existing heavens and earth. Note that unrighteous persons who reject the Love of Christ as foundation for civil laws and societal interactions remain on the OLD HEAVEN AND EARTH. So then, as is evident in the Scriptures, it is not that the OLD HEAVEN AND EARTH cease to exist, rather it is the case that there is not any place in Presence of Christ for the *Old Heaven and Earth*.

The Supporting Scriptural Evidence?

And Jehovah kicketh against all the seed of Israel, and aflicteth them, and giveth them into the hand of spoilers, till that He hath CAST THEM OUT OF HIS PRESENCE (2Kings 17:20).

Till that Jehovah HATH TURNED ISRAEL ASIDE FROM HIS PRESENCE, as He spake by the hand of all His servants the prophets, and Israel is removed from off it's land to Asshur, unto this day (2Kings 17:23).

If any one may not remain in me (*if anyone repugns love as way of life*), he was cast forth without (*outside of the Presence of Christ*), and was withered (*loses capacity for functioning as spirit*), and they gather them, and cast to fire, and they are burned (John 15:6).

THE SPIRIT IT IS THAT IS GIVING LIFE; THE FLESH (*mind and body*) DOTH NOT PROFIT ANYTHING; the sayings that I speak to you are spirit, and they are life (John 6:63).

Prophecy Interpretation 76 *In ancient times, the Nations were judged by their right treatments of one another, were allowed to pray to whatever god of whom they claimed to have revelation. For casting out of Israel out of His Presence, The Father needed only to cast them out of their promised land.*

Prophecy Interpretation 77 *In these times, our Lord Jesus Christ having gained reign of the heavens, that is, reign over life and affairs on earth, the only way that those who love evil can be cast out of His Presence is if, spiritually, absent any change in location, they lose capacity for functioning like Jesus Christ; that is, function only in context of their mind and body, lose capacity for functioning as spirit.*

Prophecy Insight 166 *As our Lord Jesus Christ, so those who believe in Him and become like Him (Powers for Christ), which is, spirits who, through their bodies, interact with the physical universe.*

The righteous dead having being identified, the unrighteous dead, the devil, the beast, and the false prophet having been cast into the lake of fire, Babylon having being destroyed, and the current heavens and earth having fled away, the stage is set for institution of new heavens and a new earth. We have then that *Revelation ch. 20* set the stage for necessity of new heavens and a new earth. Enter then NEW HEAVENS, NEW EARTH, and a NEW JERUSALEM in *Revelation ch. 21*.

On the BP7 PATH, the nations align with The Church, premise civil laws, and societal interactions on the *Love of Christ*. In light of this outcome, they are not any Nations to be domiciled on an OLD HEAVEN AND EARTH. So then, as already highlighted, *Revelation ch. 20* does not apply to the BP7 PATH, only applies to the RP7 PATH. In presence of this insight, the earth is filled with the righteousness of Christ, with outcome it cannot be the case that the current heaven and earth flee from the face of our Lord Jesus Christ. In absence of fleeing of the current heaven and earth in context of the BP7 PATH, there is demand for NEW HEAVENS and NEW EARTH only in context of the RP7 PATH. On the BP7 PATH, there only is demand for arrival at an institutional, that is, church wide New Jerusalem, which aggregates spiritual realities of all those who are perfected in Christ.

With respect to the GP7 PATH, the nations having refused to repent in context of the 6th TRUMPET of the 7th Seal, while the Church is perfected, disobedient Nations are cast out of the Presence of The Father. LOVING CITIZENS OF THE NATIONS continue, however, to have opportunity for gaining entrance into the New Jerusalem. The GP7 PATH produces then what is

referred to as a Separating Equilibrium. The Church having chosen to be perfected right from the 1ˢᵗ SEAL, with outcome she merely was delayed by the
Nations, arrives at Church level institutionalization of the New Jerusalem.
The DISOBEDIENT NATIONS are cast off on the *Old Heaven and Earth*, that
is, out of the Presence of Christ. The Church having already been perfected,
however, there is not any demand for New Heavens and New Earth.

So then, we arrive at the inference that it is only in context of the RP7 PATH
that there is demand for, and institution of New Heavens, New Earth, and
New Jerusalem. The reasoning is as follows. On the RP7 PATH, the *Newly
Reconstituted Church* having yet to prove herself, requires, inclusive of spirits
of those who died in context of persecutions orchestrated by the Beast and
Babylon, assistance of spirits of just men that already are perfected. New
Heavens and New Earth render this spiritual assistance possible.

Prophecy Interpretation 78 *Institution of* NEW HEAVENS, *and* NEW EARTH
*only transpires as part of the resolution of an iteration of the RP7 PATH of the
SSGLAE. All SSGLAE paths - the BP7, GP7, and RP7 paths - are characterized
by the* NEW JERUSALEM. *Remember, reality of the New Jerusalem in the life
of every Power for Christ is the spiritual reality that connects all of the 7* SEALS
of the Book of Revelation.

Prophecy Interpretation 79 *All of Revelation ch. 21 pertains to righteous
resolution of an iteration of the RP7 PATH of the SSGLAE.*

Prophecy Interpretation 80 *All of Revelation ch. 22 pertains to righteous
resolution of an iteration of the BP7 or GP7 PATHS of the SSGLAE.*

The Evidence that *Revelation chs. 21 & 22* do not depict the same resolution of Life and Affairs on Earth?

> And the city hath no need of the sun, nor of the moon, that
> they may shine in it; for the glory of God did lighten it, and the
> lamp of it is the Lamb (Revelation 21:23).

> And night shall not be there, and they have no need of a lamp
> and light of a sun, because the Lord God doth given them light,
> and they shall reign - to the ages of the ages (Revelation 22:5).

In Revelation 21:23, THE LAMP OF THE NEW JERUSALEM IS THE LAMB,
THAT IS, OUR LORD JESUS CHRIST. We know that in Christ, a Lamp enables
those who love Jesus Christ avoid stumbling - mistakes or sin - in the race
of faith. So then, in Revelation 21:23, our Lord Jesus Christ keeps those
who love Him from stumbling in their walk with Him. This is consistent with
Jude 1:24-25, which exults in The Father as follows.

AND TO HIM WHO IS ABLE TO GUARD YOU, NOT STUMBLING, and to set you in the Presence of His Glory unblemished, in gladness, to the only wise God our Savior, is glory and greatness, power and authority, both now and to all the ages! Amen.

Consider, however, Revelation 22:5. In Revelation 22:5, there is not any need of a lamp, because the Lord God Himself gives light. Note that it is not the case that there is not a lamp present, rather that '*there is not any need of a lamp*'. Highlighted contradiction, *presence of a lamp*, vis-a-vis '*they have no need of a lamp*' is sufficient for establishing that the spiritual resolutions that are depicted in *Revelation chs. 21 or 22* are not the same. This much the Scriptures state to be fact.

The Things That Are 89 *The Scriptures are unequivocal in their declaration that spiritual resolutions of* LIFE AND AFFAIRS ON EARTH *that are depicted in Revelation chs. 21 & 22 do not pertain to the exact same resolution, pertain to two different resolutions of Life and Affairs on Earth.*

By revelation of the Holy Spirit, I have provided you with concrete evidence for two different SSGLAE paths in context of which The Church and The Nations make the same choices, that is, the RP7 or BP7 PATHS. The GP7 PATH picks the equilibrium for the Church from the BP7 PATH, and the equilibrium for the disobedient nations from the workout of the RP7 PATH. In what follows, in this chapter, and the next I provide you with concrete evidence that *Revelation chs. 21 & 22* are resolutions for, respectively, the RP7 and BP7 PATHS of the SSGLAE.

Revelation ch. 21 pertains to Righteous Resolution of the RP7 Path: The Rest of the Evidence

We already have established that the only command from our Lord Jesus Christ is that His disciples love one another as He has loved them (John 13:34-35). While disciples of Jesus Christ are called to also love other men, loving of other men, men who do not share purity of the faith of Jesus, is to be done with wisdom (Matthew 10:16). Clearly, setting Jesus as your standard of Love acknowledges His divinity (John 1:1-3; 3:16), His sojourn on earth in human form (John 1:14), the fact that you no longer are to think of Jesus as a man (2Corinthians 5:16), but as Lord and Savior (*Revelation chs. 4 & 5*), with outcome you are committed to the Love of Christ as WAY OF LIFE (1John 3:23-24).

Suppose then that you obey our Lord Jesus Christ, acknowledge Him as Lord and Savior, and with acknowledgement of your dependence on the Holy Spirit exert effort for loving your fellow believer and all men.

What then is the promise from The Father and our Lord Jesus Christ?

> He who is having my commands, and is keeping them, that one it is who is loving me, and he who is loving me shall be loved by my Father, and I will love him, and will manifest myself to him (John 14:21).

> Judas (not Iscariot) said to Him, "Lord, how is it that You will manifest Yourself to us, and not to the world?" Jesus answered and said to him, "If anyone loves Me, he will keep my word; and my Father will love him, and we will come to him and make Our home with him (John 14:22-23).

Our Lord Jesus Christ makes two promises. First, only those who obey His commands (as already highlighted) receive spiritual manifestations, equivalently spiritual revelations of His person. Second, if a believer obeys His commands, He and The Father will, in a spiritual sense, make their home with that believer.

> Friend, if The Father and The Son make their spiritual home with you, would you need to go for a church service in order to encounter or experience Father, Son, and Holy Spirit?

Consistent with domicile of the gospel in hearts of individuals in context of the CHURCH IN LAODICEA, our Lord Jesus Christ declares that His presence in your life is not dependent on His presence in the life of any other person. If you seek to receive manifestations or revelations of Jesus Christ, if you seek Father and Son to be with you in some spiritual sense, only your own actions matter, not actions of any church body, pastor, apostle etc.

The Things That Are 90 *The Father and the Son promise that they manifest (reveal) themselves and make their spiritual home with disciples of Jesus Christ right here on this current earth. This is essence of arrival at life that is age-during (John 17:3). It is those who qualify for manifestations of Jesus and His Father who arrive at life that is age-during (eternal life) here on earth.*

The Things That Are 91 *We already have established that* THE WORTHI-NESS, *which enables arrival at The Presence of Christ is well specified, as such is a meritocracy. That condition, that worthiness is your capacity for persisting in the conditioning of your words and actions on the Love of God, and the reality that you are* FILLED WITH *the Love of God, that is, have the capacity for implementation of words and actions that are premised on the Love of God.*

The Things That Are 92 *Your capacity for arriving at the Presence of Christ is not conditioned on your Church Pastor, your spouse, your children, your parents, your neighbors, or anyone else. Your capacity for arrival at the Presence of Christ is conditioned, in entirety, on your choices and actions. This is essence of arrival of the Presence of Christ on earth in context of the Church in Laodicea.*

Friend, no one perhaps ever has said this to you about Revelation ch. 21, but the truth of the matter?

Prophecy Insight 167 *The New Heavens, New Earth, and New Jerusalem of Revelation ch. 21 are spiritual, not physical. While they are spiritual, they are devoid of 'trouble', as such are 'new'. The 'new heavens' and 'new earth' are new precisely because all sources of trouble - all spirits that are rebellious to living by the Love of God - are removed from spiritual atmosphere of the new heavens and new earth. This, we established in Chapter 11.*

Prophecy Insight 168 *In the new heavens and new earth, all spirits that are available either are The Holy Spirit of The Father, which is available to all who have faith in Jesus Christ, and the resurrected spirits of saints who died physically in context of persecution, which transpired during the time of the 4*[th] *SEAL. This, also we established in Chapter 11.*

Perhaps you wonder at this interpretation, ask how it can be when Revelation 21:1 states very clearly that there is not any *sea* in the new heavens and new earth. But friend, did we not come to the conclusion, using Scripture that in the Book of Revelation, sea stands for 'trouble'? Consider then this rendition of Revelation 21:1.

And I saw a new heaven and a new earth, for the first heaven and the first earth did pass away, and the 'TROUBLE' is not any more (Revelation 21:1).

Alright then, you wonder, even if you concede that 'sea' signifies trouble, how about the holy city, the New Jerusalem, which comes down from God out of heaven in Revelation 21:2. Well then, let us again consider what is described as being in the New Jerusalem that comes down out of heaven in Hebrews 12:22-24, a Scripture which, in light of it's importance, we already have analyzed in detail in this book, that is, in *Chapter 3*.

But, ye came to Mount Zion, and to a city of the living God, to the heavenly Jerusalem, and to myriads of messengers, to the company and assembly of the first-born in heaven enrolled, and to God the judge of all, and to spirits of righteous men made perfect, and to a mediator of a new covenant - Jesus, and to blood of sprinkling, speaking better things than that of Abel!

Friend, every entity in the heavenly (new) Jerusalem is spiritual, not physical. The Father is Spirit, Jesus is Spirit, the first-born enrolled in heaven are spirit, the spirits of righteous men made perfect are spirit, the blood of our Lord Jesus Christ eminently is spiritual, and messengers in the heavenly Jerusalem are spiritual. If you become a POWER FOR CHRIST, you become one of the entities in the New Jerusalem, obviously, either of a spirit made perfect, or a first-born. If you are a NEOPHYTE at timing of resolution of an RP7 PATH, you are in the New Jerusalem, but you are as yet not incorporated into the New Jerusalem.

> While you are, by virtue of your faith in Christ, in the New Jerusalem, you may have yet to be incorporated into the spiritual structure of the New Jerusalem.

A very simple illustration of the immediately preceding spiritual assertion establishes reasonability of the spiritual design of The Father. When, like I did in the year 2000, a person enrolls in a *PhD program*, he or she is enrolled as a PHD STUDENT. Subsequent to passing of all required exams, but prior to commencement of a *PhD Dissertation*, as was my experience in 2002, a PhD Student is redesignated a *PhD Candidate*. If a PhD Candidate completes his or her DISSERTATION, which to a large extent is dependent, in entirety, on his or her efforts, as was my experience in 2005, he or she is awarded a *PhD Certificate*. If he or she does not complete a Dissertation, he or she does not arrive at a PhD Certificate.

So then, the interpretation. A *PhD Student* is a person who desires to live by the Love of God. On basis of this desire, in His mercy, and as demonstration of His Goodness, The Father has chosen to admit, such a person into His Love. This is to be interpreted to mean that, anonymously, The Father provides such a person with spiritual power for achieving desired objective of loving of others. So then, all who desire to love are born of God.

> This is the person we previously have characterized as a LOVING CITIZEN OF THE NATIONS (LCN).

Whenever an LCN arrives at faith in Jesus Christ, he or she not only is admitted into the Love of The Father, but now also receives the Holy Spirit. Whereas then, the Holy Spirit had been an external agent influencing an LCN, now an LCN has opportunity for arrival at fellowship of the Holy Spirit.

> We previously have characterized such a person a NEOPHYTE IN CHRIST.

Consider then the following travesty, which is, an LCN who arrives at faith in Jesus Christ, but who does not arrive at fellowship of the Holy Spirit.

Rather than having transformed from an LCN to a Neophyte, for all practical purposes, he or she remains an LCN who prays in the Name of Jesus Christ. You see then importance of receipt of, and fellowship of the Holy Spirit, which is, absent receipt of, and fellowship of the Holy Spirit, arrival at sonship, arrival at characterization as a Power for Christ is not attainable. Apostle Paul states this eloquently in three Scriptures, which I believe we already have utilized, but which bear reiteration.

> For as many as are led (*guided*) by the Spirit of God, these are the sons of God (Romans 8:14).

> Christ did redeem us from the curse of the law, having become for us a curse, for it hath been written, 'Cursed is every one who is hanging on a tree,' that TO THE NATIONS THE BLESSING OF ABRAHAM MAY COME IN CHRIST JESUS, that the promise of the Spirit we may receive through the faith (Galatians 3:13-14).

> That He (The Father) MAY GIVE TO YOU, according to the riches of His glory, WITH MIGHT TO BE STRENGTHENED THROUGH HIS SPIRIT in regard to the inner man, THAT YE MAY BE IN STRENGTH TO COMPREHEND, with all the saints, what is the breadth, and length, and depth, and height, TO KNOW ALSO THE LOVE OF THE CHRIST that is exceeding the knowledge, that ye may be filled - to all the fullness of God (Ephesians 3:16,18-19).

The Things That Are 93 *Friend,* ONLY THOSE WHO ARE IN STRENGTH, *that is, who are in fellowship with the Holy Spirit have capacity for arrival at* COMPREHENSION *and* KNOWLEDGE *of the Love of Christ.*

The Things That Are 94 *Friend, the Scriptures make very clear that only those who receive strength through the Holy Spirit are able* TO COMPREHEND AND KNOW *the Love of Christ, meaning only those who have the Holy Spirit have any chance whatsoever of becoming sons of God. In light of importance of the Holy Spirit, The Father has characterized The Holy Spirit as the blessing promised to Abraham, a blessing which only can be received via faith in Jesus Christ. So then, only those who receive, and enter into fellowship with the Holy Spirit, as such are guided by the Holy Spirit have capacity for arrival at* SONSHIP TO GOD.

Prophetic Lessons 66 *As I have articulated throughout this book, it is not salvation that is predicated on faith in Jesus Christ, rather it is capacity for arrival at* RELATIONAL KNOWLEDGE OF GOD *that is predicated on faith in Jesus Christ. While a person who is convicted in his or heart, but yet rejects faith in Jesus Christ cannot be saved, a person who adopts the Love of God as* WAY OF LIFE, *who never rejects conviction of faith in Jesus Christ, but who,* *simultaneously, in an imperfect world is not drawn to Christ is, in mercy of The Father, saved. Since such a person must demonstrate the Love of God to qualify for salvation, and since the Love of God is evidence of discipleship to Christ, there is not any cheating of the way into salvation. A person who claims desire to live by the Love of God, but who in reality does not, cannot be saved by The Father. If such a person were truthful in their desire, they would ask for, and receive spiritual power from God.*

Prophetic Lessons 67 *To all those who ever have accused The Lord Jesus Christ of bigotry, this because He declares "no one can come to The Father, except through Him (John 14:6)," The Father demands repentance from times of ignorance.* THE FATHER MAKES CLEAR THAT ALL WHO TREAT THEIR NEIGHBOR RIGHT, THAT IS, WITH THE LOVE OF GOD, ARE ACCEPTED OF HIM. *Much like there is protocol to be respected, if a person is to gain audience with the President of a Country, however, The Father has declared that all who seek His audience, all who seek to relate directly with Him must pass through His Son. If CEOs, and Presidents who are nothing but men can institute such protocol, it is irrational to declare that The Creator does not have any right to stipulate protocol for arrival at audience with His Person.*

Prophetic Lessons 68 *The Father commands His Church to get her teachings right, to stop implying that, except a person becomes a believer in Jesus Christ, that he or she cannot expect to be rewarded by God for living by the Love of God.*

Upon arrival at evidence that a NEOPHYTE obeys the Holy Spirit, that is, is unwilling to compromise love in dealings with others, and delights in fellowship of the Holy Spirit, there is evidence for putting Jesus above all else, as such arrival at a revelation of Jesus Christ and His Father. At this point, with qualification earned, in entirety, in context of personal merit, but with such a person cognizant of conditioning of acquired merit on the Grace and Love of The Father, there is arrival at recognition as a Power for Christ, as such arrival at the Presence of Christ.

Prophetic Lessons 69 *It is straightforward to see, from the preceding illustration that, absent arrival at a Right Recognition of Christ, a* NEOPHYTE *cannot be transformed into a* POWER FOR CHRIST. *This is evident in the spiritual reality that arrival at a Power for Christ is conditioned on arrival at a revelation of The Person of Christ. A revelation of the Person of Christ, which by design is spiritually manifested by our Lord Jesus Christ Himself (Matthew 11:27) must produce a Right Recognition of Christ.*

Consider then the following Scripture, which again, I believe I have introduced elsewhere in this book.

And we - we ought to give thanks to God always for you, brethren, beloved by the Lord, that God did choose you from the beginning to salvation, in *sanctification of the Spirit*, and BELIEF OF THE TRUTH, to which He did call you through our good news, *to the acquiring of the glory of our Lord Jesus Christ* (2Thessalonians 2:13-14).

Prophetic Lessons 70 *A person who does not develop* LOVE OF THE TRUTH *cannot believe in the truth, as such cannot get to know Him who is the Way, the Truth, and the Life, as such cannot arrive at a revelation of The Person of Christ, as such cannot arrive at a Right Recognition of Christ, as such cannot acquire the glory of Christ, as such cannot ever be recognized as a Power for Christ.*

Prophecy Interpretation 81 *The coming down of the New Jerusalem signifies then a spiritual unification of everything on earth that is in Christ, and everything in the heavens that are in Christ. Since The Father is in Christ (John 10:38; 14:10; 14:11), this is inclusive of The Father.*

The Scriptural evidence that there exists a spiritual version of your self in the new Jerusalem, and evidence that spiritual unification is an objective of The Father?

If then you have been raised with Christ, seek the things that are above, where Christ is, seated at the right hand of God. Set your minds on things that are above, not on things that are on earth. FOR YOU HAVE DIED, AND YOUR LIFE IS HID WITH CHRIST IN GOD. When Christ how is our life appears, then you also will appear with Him in glory (Colossians 3:1-3).

For He has made known to us in all wisdom and insight the mystery of His will, according to HIS PURPOSE WHICH HE SET FORTH IN CHRIST as a plan for the fullness of time, TO UNITE ALL THINGS IN HIM, THINGS IN HEAVEN AND THINGS ON EARTH (Ephesians 1:9-10).

Prophecy Insight 169 *The coming down of the New Jerusalem signifies uniting of the spiritual with the natural, with outcome we are able to have fellowship with The Father, our Lord Jesus Christ, and the Holy Spirit in course of our normal daily activities. The New Jerusalem is filled with spirits, as such, in entirety, is a spiritual entity.*

Friend, the reason that the New Jerusalem will not come down to this current earth until the Church is perfected is because your self that is hidden in Christ, and your self that is here on earth must be spiritually compatible. If the Church is not perfected, it does not arrive at *a measure of the stature of the fullness of Christ*, meaning she does not value the Love of God above all else. If the New Jerusalem comes down to an earth within which the Church does not value the Love of God above all else, the unification of heavens and earth that is sought by The Father remains unattainable. Since The Father does not practice self deceit, the new heavens and new earth, and the descent of the heavenly Jerusalem do not occur until the Church is perfected in Love.

Prophecy Principle 136 *Individual believers who pay the price, who attain to a measure of the stature of the fullness of Christ experience unification with the heavenly Jerusalem on this current earth.*

Prophecy Principle 137 *What is the minimum size of aggregate numbers of Powers for Christ that are required if the Newly Reconstituted Church is to induce descent of the New Jerusalem? Well, ideally, the answer, 1. For the* ELEMENT *1 signifies New Beginnings, and only one rider who is given a crown (Revelation 6:1-2), that is, only one* POWER FOR CHRIST *is required for arrival at New Beginnings.*

In Chapter 11, I enunciated that institution of New Heavens, and New Earth, and the New Jerusalem is predicated on the fact that the new 1st SEAL that is activated by the Newly Reconstituted Church has our Lord Jesus Christ Himself as the one who goes forth conquering and to conquer.

Prophecy Principle 138 *But the reality, in the Newly Reconstituted Church, The Lord Jesus Christ* DOES NOT FIND ANY POWERS FOR CHRIST; *so He Himself leads the conquest that is required for commencement of New Beginnings in context of a new 1st* SEAL.

In the time of Elijah the Prophet, The Father found one POWER FOR CHRIST. While there were 7,000 NEOPHYTES praying for his success in the shadows (1Kings 19:18), Elijah was the only Power for Christ available in his time (1Kings 19:14). Singlehandedly, Elijah produced a NEWLY RECONSTITUTED CHURCH, one which ushered in a new 1st SEAL period. Yet, it was a NEO-PHYTE, PROPHET ELISHA who would do the work made possible by arrival, via mercy of The Father, of a new 1st SEAL period. We arrive then at validation of the spiritual principle enunciated in *Revelation ch. 21* that resolution of the RP7 PATH devolves into a Newly Reconstituted Church that is lacking in Powers for Christ. In the request that he have a double portion of the spirit of Elijah (2Kings 2:9-10), who then was been taken to heaven (2Kings 2:1), Elisha recognized that Elijah had arrived at the PRESENCE OF CHRIST, had been recognized as a Power for God. Rightly and wisely, Elisha opined that if he started with a double portion of Elijah's spirit, that he would do just fine. For concreteness, The Father provided Elijah with three objectives to achieve (1Kings 19:15-17), yet allowed him pass on two of the objectives to his successor, Elisha (2Kings 8:7-13; 9:1-10). In this, The Father validated Elisha as carrying on the work of Elijah. So then, inclusive of the popular story about healing of Naaman the initially leprous Syrian General (*2Kings ch. 5*), Elisha went on to produce odes of miracles in context of a new 1st SEAL for the rebellious NATION OF ISRAEL. Note that Elijah could have had an easier life as Prophet to the NATION OF JUDAH. Rather, Elijah chose the much more difficult route of Prophet to the Nation of Israel. The Nation of Israel would go on to reject the Love of God as basis for civil laws, and societal interactions resulting in famines and wars, which led Israelites to kill and eat their very own children (2Kings 6:26-31; 8:1).

The Things That Are 95 *As I have severally demonstrated, the SSGLAE is an eternal principle which always has been, but now explicitly is revealed to us through visions entrusted to Apostle John.*

With respect to unification of spiritual things in heaven and earth in context of New Heavens, New Earth, and the New Jerusalem, Revelation 5:9-10 reads as follows.

> And they sang a new song, saying: "You are worthy to take the scroll, and to open it's seals; for you were slain, and have redeemed us to God by Your blood out of every tribe and tongue and people and nation, AND HAVE MADE US KINGS AND PRIESTS TO OUR GOD; AND WE SHALL REIGN ON THE EARTH.

Prophecy Insight 170 *Since the saints reign on earth, New Heavens, the New Earth, and the New Jerusalem all are spiritual phenomena that are established on earth. We have then that newness of the heavens, newness of the earth, and descent of the New Jerusalem all are spiritual, not physical phenomena.*

Necessity of Powers for Christ

In 2Peter 1:7, believers who arrive at Godliness, at becoming like Christ and The Father are admonished to next focus on developing 'brotherly kindness'. *Brotherly kindness* is the capacity for understanding FOIBLES, WEAKNESSES, and IMPERFECTIONS of fellow believers who have yet to arrive at Godliness. Clearly, a person who has attained to Godliness has become recognized by The Father as a Power for Christ. In context of a 1st SEAL period, a Power for Christ embeds the capacity for

✠ Encouragement of those among Neophytes who are weak;

✠ Leading in context of development of Love Projects that, regardless of their spiritual maturity, incorporate all believers;

✠ Understanding of why exactly it is those who have yet to arrive at godliness lag behind, and addressing of such weaknesses with love, kindness, and compassion;

✠ Teaching Neophytes the things they need to be doing if they are to arrive at the Presence of Christ;

✠ Defense of the Gospel to those who misunderstand essence of faith in Jesus Christ.

In presence of understanding of what is lacking, those who have attained are able to help those who lag behind, with outcome all eventually arrive at a measure of the stature of the fullness of Christ. Absent infusion of Godliness with Brotherly Kindness, those who attain to godliness are unable to help others arrive at the same spiritual state, rather become judgmental. But if those who lag behind are not perfected, if they are discouraged with judgmental attitudes, the cost is a discouraged church that is not able to respond to perfection overtures of Father, Son, and Holy Spirit. In presence of a Church that is not able to respond to overtures for her perfection, that is, a Church lacking in Powers for Christ, the Church always will end up on the RP7 PATH of the SSGLAE. You see then that whenever church leadership become judgmental, with outcome the saints are discouraged, they in reality shoot themselves in the foot, consign their own lives to futility of an RP7 PATH of the SSGLAE, to a path that, for arrival at any resolution, always will require formation of a Newly Reconstituted Church.

Prophecy Principle 139 *Whenever believers in Christ are judgmental in their relationship with other believers, they shoot themselves in the foot, shortcircuit willingness of the Church to arrive at maturity and perfection, with outcome there is arrival at an RP7* PATH *of the SSGLAE.*

Prophecy Principle 140 *Whenever pastors rejoice in the fact that their congregations are spiritually dependent on them, with outcome they give lots of tithe in context of idolatry of asking for spiritual protection from their pastor, they shoot themselves in the foot, increase probability of arrival at an RP7* PATH *of the SSGLAE.*

Prophecy Principle 141 *Only a Church filled with brotherly kindness, and love for truth, and that is willing to be sanctified of the Holy Spirit can arrive at a measure of the stature of the fullness of Christ.*

Absence of Trouble, Wiping of Tears, Absence of Pain etc.

Here then, we probably arrive at one of your concerns, which is, if indeed the New Heavens, New Earth, and New Jerusalem are, in entirety, spiritual, with outcome, with the caveat they have lost capacity for functioning as spirits, there still exist evil persons on earth, how exactly then to interpret Revelation 21:3-4, which declares as follows.

> And I heard a great voice out of heaven, saying, "Lo, the tabernacle of God is with men, and He will tabernacle with them, and they shall be His peoples, and God Himself shall be with them - their God, and God shall wipe away every tear from their eyes, and the death shall not be any more, nor sorrow, nor crying, nor shall there be any more pain, because the first things did go away."

Friend, first remember that whenever the *sea* forments TROUBLE, that is, *billows*, trouble is formented either by The Father or the devil. In context of Revelation 21:1, clearly, absence of sea means, 'ABSENCE OF TROUBLE THAT IS FORMENTED BY THE DEVIL'. We already applied this interpretation of sea in Chapter 9. In absence of trouble that is formented by the devil, there is not any sea anymore, as such there is not sorrow, crying, pain, or death anymore, and all tears are wiped away by the actions of The Father, by actions, which consign all of those who delight in evil to the OLD HEAVEN AND EARTH, with outcome they are unable anymore to trouble, in their spirits, those who have faith in Jesus Christ. For ease of the exposition to follow, I commence with the Prophetic Meaning of the words in Revelation 21:3-4, then articulate the supporting Scriptural evidence.

Prophecy Interpretation 82 *Revelation 21:3-4 is to be understood as follows. In presence of New Heavens, New Earth, and New Jerusalem that is populated only by the Holy Spirit, or resurrected spirits of the saints, those who love evil lose the capacity for troubling of the spirits of the saints. It is not then that those who choose evil cannot target evil at the saints, but having lost their capacity for functioning as spirits, they lose capacity for troubling of the spirits of the saints. The saints having put to death the desires of the flesh, persons who love evil are unable to appeal to their flesh, with outcome the spirit of the saints do not experience any trouble.*

Let us start with a discussion of the phrase, 'THE FIRST THINGS DID GO AWAY'?. What exactly are these first things? Well, we have the following answers from Scriptures.

> So also it hath been written, *The first man Adam became a living creature, the last Adam is for a life-giving spirit*, BUT THAT WHICH IS SPIRITUAL IS NOT FIRST, BUT THAT WHICH WAS NATURAL, AFTERWARDS THAT WHICH IS SPIRITUAL. The first man is out of the earth, earthy; the second man is the Lord out of heaven; as is the earthy, such are also the earthy; and as is the heavenly, such are

also the heavenly, and ACCORDING AS WE DID BEAR THE IMAGE OF THE EARTHY, WE SHALL BEAR ALSO THE IMAGE OF THE HEAVENLY (1Corinthians 15:45-49).

Ye are to put off concerning the former behavior the old man, that is corrupt according to the desires of the deceit, and to be renewed in the spirit of your mind, and to PUT ON THE NEW MAN, which, according to God, was created in righteousness and kindness of the truth (Ephesians 4:22-24).

Wherefore having girded up the loins of your mind, being sober, hope perfectly upon the grace that is being brought to you in the revelation of Jesus Christ, as obedient children, NOT FASHIONING YOURSELVES TO THE FORMER DESIRES in your ignorance, but according as He who did call you is holy, ye also, become holy in all behavior (1Peter 1:13-15).

As all things to us His divine power (the things pertaining unto life and piety) hath given, through the acknowledgement of Him who did call us through glory and worthiness, through which to us the most great and precious promises have been given, that through these ye may become partakers of a divine nature, HAVING ESCAPED FROM THE CORRUPTION IN THE WORLD IN DESIRES (2Peter1:3-4).

Ye are of a father - the devil, and THE DESIRES OF YOUR FATHER YE WILL TO DO; he was a man-slayer from the beginning, and in the truth he hath not stood, because there is no truth in him; when one may speak the falsehood, of his own he speaketh, because he is a liar - also his father (John 8:44).

It is very clear that 'THE FIRST THINGS' are the desires that come with the nature of Adam, the FIRST MAN, behaviors that have characterization as FORMER DESIRES, or FORMER BEHAVIORS. So then, the first desires also are the former desires, or former behaviors. What does it mean then that the 'THE FIRST THINGS DID GO AWAY', or equivalently, that 'THE FIRST THINGS DID PASS AWAY'? Well then, let us again consult Scriptures.

So that if any one is in Christ - he is a new creature; *the old things did pass away, lo, become new* have the all things (2Corinthians 5:17).

The consensus of all of the Scriptures?

Prophecy Interpretation 83 *The first things are the former, first, or old things, equivalently, the former, first, or old desires, desires that are of the nature of the devil, desires that corrupt the spirit of man.*

Prophecy Interpretation 84 *That the first things did go away means the first, former, or old desires do not any longer have any hold on those who have faith in Jesus Christ. Hallelujah!!!*

Prophecy Interpretation 85 *The former, first, or old desires do not any longer have a hold on those who have faith in Jesus Christ, because they have become partakers of a divine nature, that is, have become* SONS OF GOD, *equivalently, have arrived at a measure of the stature of the fullness of Christ, equivalently, have arrived at a* PERFECT MAN, *equivalently, have become* POWERS FOR CHRIST.

What does it mean then that there shall *not be sorrow*, nor *crying*, nor shall there be any more *pain*, because the first things did go away? Well then, a couple more Scriptures.

Happy the poor in spirit - because theirs is the reign of the heavens (Matthew 5:3).

Happy the mourning - because they shall be comforted (Matthew 5:4).

Happy those hungering and thirsting for righteousness - because they shall be filled (Matthew 5:6).

To console those who mourn in Zion, to give them beauty for ashes, the oil of joy for mourning, the garment of praise for the spirit of heaviness; that they may be called trees of righteousness, the planting of The Lord, that He may be glorified (Isaiah 61:3).

Prophecy Interpretation 86 *It is straightforwardly clear. Our Lord Jesus Christ declares that there will not any longer be any sorrowing for sin because the saints have learnt how to overcome; that there will not be any mourning for weaknesses, for the weak have received strength for overcoming of weaknesses; that there will not be any more paining of the heart from regret of sin, because the saints have become trees of righteousness, the planting of the Lord. Hallelujah!!!*

God Himself

What then about the declaration that God Himself shall be with them - their God, and God shall wipe away every tear from their eyes, and the death shall not be any more? Well then, let us remind ourselves of exact wording of the relevant Scripture, which is, Revelation 21:3-4.

"And I heard a great voice out of the heaven, saying, Lo, THE TABERNACLE OF GOD IS WITH MEN, AND HE WILL TABERNACLE WITH THEM, and they shall be His peoples, and God Himself shall be with them - their God, and God shall wipe away every tear from their eyes..."

Well then, what does it mean that "God will tabernacle with them?"

Have ye not known that ye are a sanctuary of God, and the Spirit of God doth dwell in you (1Corinthians 3:16).

Then, therefore, ye are no more strangers and foreigners, but fellow citizens of the saints, and of the household of God, being built upon the foundation of the apostles and prophets, Jesus Christ Himself being the chief cornerstone, in whom all the building fitly framed together doth increase to an holy sanctuary in the Lord, in whom also ye are builded together, FOR A HABITATION OF GOD IN THE SPIRIT (Ephesians 2:19-22).

In behalf of Christ, then, we are ambassadors, AS IF GOD WERE CALLING THROUGH US, we beseech, in behalf of Christ, be ye reconciled to God (2Corinthians 5:20).

Blessed is God, even The Father of our Lord Jesus Christ, The Father of mercies, and GOD OF ALL COMFORT, who is comforting us in all our tribulation, for our being able to comfort those in any tribulation through the comfort with which we are comforted ourselves by God (2Corinthians 1:4).

And may our Lord Jesus Christ Himself, and our God and Father, who did love us, and did give comfort age-during, and good hope in grace, comfort your hearts, and establish you in every good word and work (2Thessalonians 2:16-17).

And the Comforter, the Holy Spirit, whom The Father will send in my name, He will teach you all things, and remind you of all things that I said to you (John 14:26).

Prophecy Interpretation 87 *Whenever, as is the case with the Newly Reconstituted Church,* THE CHURCH *coincides with the* BODY OF CHRIST, *then God is, in The Church, tabernacled on earth, and through either of the Holy Spirit, or ministration of one believer to another, provides comfort to The Church in context of the good fight of the faith, that is, the fight against evil.*

Prophecy Interpretation 88 *The promise that God Himself will wipe away their tears is, in entirety, spiritual, not physical.*

Revelation 21:5-9

A careful reading of Revelation 21:5-9 reveals that the declarations of our Lord Jesus Christ in Revelation 21:5-8 are pronounced prior to a pouring out of the 7 Vials of the WRATH OF GOD. In this, we again have confirmation that the spiritual resolution that is depicted in *Revelation ch. 21*, which is, New Heavens, New Earth, and the New Jerusalem pertains solely to the RP7 PATH of the SSGLAE. With this reiteration in perspective, it is clear that the invitation from our Lord Jesus Christ in *Revelation 21:6* to those who are thirsting to come drink of the water of life is given at a time in course of which all who truly desire life that is age-during are able to receive the Holy Spirit. By the same token, the promise that he who is overcoming will inherit all things is given for encouragement of the saints who are experiencing persecutions. Consistent with discussions in *Chapter 11* then, there is opportunity for repentance, and demonstration of Love for God in context of a pouring out of VIALS 1 *through* 5 of the WRATH OF GOD. We know for instance that subsequent to a pouring out of the 4th and 5th Vials, those who reject the Love of God as way of life stubbornly refuse to repent.

Prophecy Interpretation 89 *The words in Revelation 21:5-8 are spoken, not at timing of descent of the* NEW JERUSALEM, *but prior to a pouring out of the 7* VIALS *of the* WRATH OF GOD. *If the* VIALS *still are full (Revelation 21:9) they cannot as yet have been poured out.*

With respect to the water of the life, there is the misconception that the water is received freely. Clearly, this is a mischaracterization of the words of our Lord and Savior Jesus Christ. Our Lord Jesus Christ does not declare that the water can be received freely, rather declares that He gives the water freely. That the water is given freely means, for arrival at a drinking of the water of life, our Lord Jesus Christ does not demand anything that every human being does not have to give. When an item has a price, it is possible that some are unable to afford such an item. When an item is offered freely, it is in power of all to arrive at receipt of such an item. In the demand that all those who seek to qualify for drinking of the water of life love their neighbor (John 8:31), there is a cost to qualification for the water of life. The cost, however, is within reach of everyone, for everyone has capacity for choosing of what is good - Love, over what is evil, hatred. With respect to symbolism of the water of life, we know that the water of the life is the Holy Spirit.

> "It hath been done! I am the Alpha and the Omega, the Beginning and the End; I, TO HIM WHO IS THIRSTING, WILL GIVE OF THE FOUNTAIN OF THE WATER OF THE LIFE FREELY; he who is overcoming shall inherit all things, and I will be to him - God and he shall be to me - the son (Revelation 21:6)."

Whoever believes in me, as the Scripture has said, streams of living water will flow from within him. BY THIS HE MEANT THE SPIRIT, whom those who believed in Him were later to receive. Up to that time the Spirit had not been given, since Jesus had not yet been glorified (John 7:38-39).

Prophecy Insight 171 *Our Lord Jesus Christ offers the water of the life freely only in the sense that the price of the water - willingness and effort at loving neighbors, that is, total strangers, particularly those who differ from you in their backgrounds - lies within reach of everyone, does not pose a higher cost to either of the rich, or the not-so-rich.*

The Things That Are 96 *Only those who, upon receipt of the water of the life go on to overcome, become sons of God.*

Prophecy Insight 172 *In the words of our Lord Jesus Christ in Revelation 21:5-8, we again have description of two groups of those who respond to Christ, namely, NEOPHYTES who receive of the water of the life (the Holy Spirit), and POWERS who transform that water of the life into capacity for overcoming of self, sin, the world, and the devil.*

In Revelation 21:8, our Lord Jesus Christ addresses those who choose evil over what is good, those who either are not willing to be perfected in Christ (*Believers in Christ*), or those who reject the Love of God as foundation of civil laws, and societal interactions. In this respect, the FEARFUL, and UNSTEDFAST are those who, in presence of persecution, deny their faith in the name of Jesus Christ. The Scriptures are very unequivocal, if we, in context of persecutions, deny the name of Jesus Christ, He also will deny us. In this respect, our Lord Jesus Christ declares as follows.

Therefore whoever confesses Me before men, him I will also confess before My Father who is in heaven. But whoever denies Me before men, him I will also deny before My Father who is in heaven (Matthew 10:32-33).

Then said Jesus to His disciples, if any one doth will to come after me, let him disown himself, and take up his cross, and follow me, for whoever may will to save his life shall lose it, and whoever may lose his life for my sake shall find it (Matthew 16:24-25).

Prophetic Lessons 71 *If you seek to be saved, if you seek to overcome, such that you become a Power for Christ, you cannot be fearful of man, you cannot become unsteadfast in your faith in Christ. If you are to arrive at life that is age-during in Christ, you must be willing to lose your life for sake of the name of Christ.*

The ABOMINABLE, and MURDERERS are those who, deliberately, and as an act of rebellion against The Father, choose *hatreds* as way of life. WHORE-MONGERS choose to live by the desires of the flesh, but arrive at this outcome via deliberate rejection of the Love of God as way of life.

> It is straightforward that a whoremonger cannot love the women whom he accrues to himself as whores.

SORCERERS and IDOLATERS reject the Love of God as *Way of Life*, because they feel that the Love of God smacks of teachings of Christians. LIARS reject the Love of God because they hate all those who, via demonstration of LOVE FOR TRUTH, and LOVE FOR GOD have arrived at wisdom, intelligence, and the meekness of wisdom (James 3:13). All of the enumerated spirits are cast into the lake that is burning with fire and brimstone, which is a second death. With respect to importance of love for truth, and love for God in context of development of intelligence, the Scriptures declare as follows.

> Because, having known God they did not glorify Him as God, nor gave thanks, but were made vain in their reasonings, and their unintelligent heart was darkened, professing to be wise, they were made fools (Romans 1:21-22).

> The beginning of wisdom is fear of Jehovah, Good understanding have all doing them, His praise is standing for ever! (Psalms 111:10).

> Be not wise in your own eyes, fear Jehovah, and turn aside from evil. Healing it is to thy navel, and moistening to thy bones (Proverbs 3:7-8).

Life Nugget 19 *The Scriptures are very clear. One path to arrival at* UNINTEL-LIGENCE *is a conscious decision to misinterpret or reject evidence for existence of God. Once the mind embarks on such an objective, arrival at unintelligence and* VANITY OF REASONING - *reasoning that is not sound, that is not cognitive - is guaranteed. A person who seeks to be wise practices the* FEAR OF GOD, *that is, in the decision to love his or her neighbor, obeys the declaration from The Father that all men are created equal.*

Consistent with destruction of all spirits that are evil in their tendencies, in Revelation 21:8 spirits of *fearfulness, unstedfastness,* spirits that revel in *practice of abominations, murderous spirits, whoremongering spirits, spirits of sorcery and idolatry,* and *lying* spirits all are cast in the lake of fire and brimstone, all suffer the second death. As I already have enunciated, casting of the spirits into the lake of fire means, having rejected the Love of God as way of life, they are not part of the New Heavens, New Earth, and the New

Jerusalem. In addition, those who held on to such spirits arrive at loss of capacity for functioning as spirits. Note again, that it is not the case that they have spirit, but are not aware of their spirit man, but rather that The Lord Jesus Christ who is their Creator destroys their capacity for living as spirits who have a body. This distinction is of critical importance.

> The danger inherent in loss of spiritual capacity, the danger that induced demand for a new heart from The Father as solution to sin?
>
> CROOKED IS THE HEART ABOVE ALL THINGS, AND IT IS INCURABLE - WHO DOTH KNOW IT (Jeremiah 17:9)?

> And I have given to you a new heart, and a new spirit I give in your midst, and I have turned aside the heart of stone out of your flesh, and I have given to you a heart of flesh. And My Spirit I give in your midst, and I have done this, so that in My statutes ye walk, and My judgments ye keep, and have done them (Ezekiel 36:26-27).

Prophecy Insight 173 *It is not the case that people who reject the Love of God as* WAY OF LIFE *have spirit, but are not in touch with their spirit. Rather, it is the case that The Lord Jesus Christ destroys their capacity for functioning as spirits.*

Prophetic Lessons 72 *Whenever a society deliberately and consciously repugns the demand from The Father that they love one another, with outcome they arrive at loss of capacity for functioning as spirits, they do not know the depths of depravity that they unleash on their very own society.*

In light of importance of avoidance of the second death, let us enumerate on the spirits that are listed in Revelation 21:8.

Fearfulness

A person who is FEARFUL is a person who, in face of possibility of repercussions from evil men for doing of what is right, chooses to participate in evil. If you develop the habit of conditioning doing of what is right on the extent to which persons who love evil will target you, will seek to hurt you, you are fearful, and in danger of placing yourself in the population that will participate in the lake of fire and brimstone.

Unsteadfastness

When a person is UNSTEADFAST, they give up on doing of what is right, deviate into doing of evil. The standard set by The Father is, he who endures to the end is saved. If you seek to be alive in spirit in context of institution of new heavens, new earth and the new Jerusalem, you have to endure unto the end. In this respect, consider the following words in Ezekiel 33:13; and Revelation 2:10.

> Though I say to the righteous that he shall surely live, yet if he trusts in his righteousness and commits iniquity, none of his righteous deeds shall be remembered; but in the iniquity that he has committed he shall die.

> "...Be faithful unto death, and I will give you the crown of life."

Practice of Abominations

Sexual relations that are pronounced to be abominations, such as incest, sodomy, or any other sexual perversion fall within this group. Like Apostle Paul would say, one cannot even begin to find words to describe some of these sex related perversions, which qualify people for participation in the second death.

Murderous Spirits

Do you realize that murder has become an expected part of the evening news in the United States of America. In a news article I read of recent, it was celebrated that deaths from murder had dropped from over 2,000 to just about 500 in *New York City*. Imagine a society celebrating the fact that not more than 500 people lost their lives to murderous rage in a particular year.

> Outside of crime, which must be dissuaded, what is the source of this murderous rage in the United States of America?

The answer my friend is simple. The United States of America gave in to the concept of SURVIVAL OF THE FITTEST. In context of *survival of the fittest*, it is best to eliminate the competition in entirety than have to compete all through life.

So then,

♣ Frustrate your 'intelligence', 'ability', or 'skill' competition with your economic power; then

♣ While they struggle with their economic situation, use the police and all sorts of snares to target your competition.

♣ If you succeed in getting your competition to be sent to prison, when the competition comes out of jail insist that their mistakes prevent them from being able to secure jobs or continue with their lives.

♣ When they get three strikes in some states, you arrive at finality of elimination of the competition.

What then happens? When people who go through such oppression do not have saving knowledge of Christ, sometimes the oppression drives them to rage, and rage is expressed as murder. All of the talk about regulating guns is nothing but a smokescreen. Until the police and legal system in America no longer are tools of oppression against those whom others consider competition in respect of the things of this life, murderous rage and homicides are here to stay in the United States of America.

Since people who set traps for others must themselves fall into their traps, those who oppress others lose capacity for functioning as spirits - become spiritually dead, as such are liable to fall into murderous rage themselves, or become prone to DEPRESSION or SUICIDE. When their dependencies induce divorce, and divorce is made difficult, they pick up guns and kill ex wives or children or both. So then the murderous rage multiplies. Until the Love of God becomes foundation of civil laws and foundation of enforcement of civil laws in America, gun violence is here to stay. Guns do not kill people. People who feel oppressed, or people who subscribe to a spirit of oppression pick up guns and kill others. Society may villify those who pick up guns because they are oppressed, yet in the eyes of the Father they may receive mercy because they were pushed to the wall by the self same society that turns around to judge them. If you feel yourself under pressure from society, trust in Jesus Christ, ask for strength and wisdom for directing your energies towards good works, and ask The Father for a way out of the temptation and trial. The promise from our Lord Jesus Christ is (*paraphrase*):

> You are not called to anger, but to acquiring of salvation in Jesus Christ (1Thessalonians 5:9).

> Know this, my beloved brethren, let every man be swift to hear, slow to speak, slow to anger, for the anger of man does not work the righteousness of God (James 1:19-20).

Whoremongering Spirits

A WHOREMONGER is a person who consorts with whores. In absence of whoremongers, there would not be demand for whores. In the Old Testament, a father who refused to find a husband for his daughter, with outcome she became a whore was deemed to be a wicked man, was deemed a man who seeks to consign society to wickedness (Leviticus 19:29). The Father warns that if such men are successful, society will be filled with prostitution and wickedness. The Father declares that spirits of men who, because of their desire for whoremongering seek to fill society with whores are destined for the lake that burns with fire and brimstone, are destined for the second death.

Spirits of Sorcery and Idolatry

We already have discussed IDOLATRY. Idolatry is more pervasive than you probably imagine. Every Church organization which holds on to some pet doctrine that, on basis of objective evidence can be shown to be unscriptural, has given itself to a spirit of idolatry. By this characterization of idolatry, which is scriptural, a pet doctrine that is false is an image that is put in place of God, with outcome most Christian denominations are filled with idolatrous beliefs, practices, and spirits. It is in light of this idolatry that The Father commands all those who remain true to Him to 'come out of Babylon'.

Illustrations of pet doctrines in Christian denominations that are false are:

♣ It is okay to bow down to or worship statues or pictures of Jesus Christ. I already have shown, in Chapter 11, that this is a false, heretical, and apostate teaching.

♣ The evidence of infilling of the Holy Spirit is speaking in tongues. TONGUES are a gift, in fact one of the least of the gifts of the Spirit, not a fruit of the Spirit (1Corinthians 12:7-11; Galatians 5:22-23). Jesus declared explicitly that it is fruit - love, joy etc. - that will identify those who truly are His disciples (Matthew 7:16,20; John 13:34-35). The only evidence that we are filled with the Holy Spirit is walking in the Love of our Lord Jesus Christ. We receive the Love of our Lord Jesus Christ, the Love of God through the Holy Spirit (Romans 5:5). This erroneous teaching that tongues are evidence for infilling of the Holy Spirit, a teaching that scuttled necessity of emphasis on Love as outcome of infilling of the Holy Spirit, contributed significantly to scuttling of objective of perfection of the Church of the Tongues Movement. The Father now is calling all Pentecostal churches to admit their error and repent.

♣ The belief that observance of days or feasts can make us acceptable before God. Denominations which assert that there is salvation in any sorts of observances practice idolatry (Galatians 4:8-11). I have shown, in Chapter 11, that the Lord's Supper has spiritual significance only because spiritually, and with our location on Mount Zion, we are in fellowship with our Lord Jesus Christ (His Body), and the Blood of our Lord Jesus Christ (Hebrews 12:22-24). Baptism saves us only because we signify willingness to die a death like Christ's, this so we are able to experience a resurrection like Christ's (Philippians 3:10-11).

If you value the traditions of your church organization over commands of your Lord Jesus Christ you hold on to a spirit of idolatry. This spirit of idolatry will participate in the second death and then you will be devoid of spirit in entirety.

Consider then the spirit of SORCERY. Nowadays, sorcerers have their own syndicated shows on television into which millions of people tune. When a person who has faith in Jesus Christ visits a fortune teller (sorcerer) he or she enters into a competition with the spirit of the sorcerer, for the sorcerer must endeavor to bring to pass that which he or she has foretold. Enter then unnecessary conflict between you and the Holy Spirit on one hand, and the spirit of the sorcerer on the other. When a person who is supposed to have faith in Jesus visits a sorcerer, he or she declares, in his or her actions, that he or she does not consider The Father to be trustworthy. In presence of such lack of faith, there is a grieving of the Holy Spirit. If the lack of faith persists, the Holy Spirit can abandon such a believer to the spirit of the sorcerer. Sorcery, which consists in attempts at manipulation of events in the present or the future, will be destroyed in the lake that burns with fire and brimstone, will be part of the second death.

Lying Spirits

The devil is father of FALSEHOODS (John 8:44). If you have faith in Jesus Christ, you are explicitly commanded not to lie to your brother or sister (Colossians 3:9-10). Rather, are admonished to speak the truth in love (Ephesians 4:15-16). For a discussion of the sorts of lies that The Father in His mercy overlooks (lies that, inclusive of yourself, have zero probability of producing hurt for anyone, as such cannot be construed to be false witness, with evidence from Scriptures), check out my book, In Jesus Name. For illustration, when, in course of the Second World War, a Dutch man or woman lied to the Gestapo that he or she was not hiding any Jews, this regardless of the fact there were 20 Jews hidden away in a carefully constructed and hidden section of the house, while The Father does not approve of lying, He pragmatically is aware of the reality that, in a world populated by some men who are evil, sometimes righteous objectives of those who do the will of God are facilitated by lies told to men who are evil. In Scriptures, The Father allowed the Prophet Samuel tell one such lie (1Samuel 16:1-3). Note that in this case, a lie does not qualify as false witness. FALSE WITNESS is a lie that is intended for, or that can cause harm to a neighbor. If you hold on to a spirit of lying, meaning you delight in capacity for deceiving others, you eventually will find yourself bereft of spirit in entirety.

15.1   The New Jerusalem

In order for Apostle John to see the New Jerusalem from a good perspective, he was carried by a messenger to the top of a very high mountain. Given the former heavens and earth have passed away (Revelation 21:1), the '*mountain*' of necessity is in the new earth. Using Christian Scriptures, we already have established that a '*mountain*' signifies righteousness. In this imagery, our Lord Jesus Christ declares that only those who excel in righteousness will be able to see the New Jerusalem, only they will be able to enter into the New Jerusalem. In this respect, consider the following Scripture.

> In that day sung is this song in the land of Judah: We have a strong city, SALVATION HE DOTH MAKE WALLS AND BULWARK. 'Open ye the gates, that enter may a righteous nation, preserving steadfastness (Isaiah 26:1-2).

> And opened have thy gates continually, by day and by night they are not shut, to bring into thee the force of nations, even their kings are led. For the nation and the kingdom that do not serve thee perish, yea, the nations are utterly wasted (Isaiah 60:11-12).

> Lift up, O gates, your heads, and be lifted up, O doors age-during, and come in doth the king of glory! Who is this - the king of glory? Jehovah - strong and mighty, Jehovah, the mighty in battle. Lift up, O gates, your heads, and be lifted up, O doors age-during, and come in doth the king of glory! Who is He - this king of glory? Jehovah of hosts - He is the king of glory! Selah (Psalms 24:7-10).

> And answer did one of the elders, saying to me, "These, who have been arrayed with the white robes - who are they, and whence came they?" and I have said to him, "Sir, thou hast known;" and he said to me, "These are those who are coming out of the great tribulation, and they did wash their robes, and they made their robes white in the blood of the Lamb; because of this are they before the throne of God, and they do service to Him day and night in His sanctuary, and He who is sitting upon the throne shall tabernacle over them; they shall not hunger any more, nor may the sun fall upon them, nor any heat, because the Lamb that is in the midst of the throne shall feed them, and shall lead them unto living fountains of waters and wipe away shall God every tear from their eyes (Revelation 7:13-15)."

Prophecy Interpretation 90 *These words from Revelation 7:13-15 reiterate rightness of exposition of the words that 'God shall wipe away every tear* *from their eye' in Revelation 21:4. "He who is sitting upon the throne shall tabernacle over them; they shall not hunger any more, nor may the sun fall upon them, nor any heat, because the Lamb that is in the midst of the throne shall feed them, and shall lead them unto living fountains of waters and wipe away shall God every tear from their eyes."*

It is very clear from Scripture that *walls* signify '*salvation*', and *gates* signify '*praise*'. Given those who have the faith and testimony of Jesus Christ now are the sanctuary of God, there is not now any need for a physical building that serves as sanctuary of God. Note then that if you consider the building in which you congregate for fellowship with other believers in Christ to be the sanctuary of God that you practice idolatry, are part of Babylon. Given believers continually utter praises to God, the gates of the New Jerusalem always are open for ushering in of the nations into salvation of our great God and Savior Jesus Christ. Much the same then as Constantine the Great brought the glory of the Roman Empire into establishment of a physical Christian Empire - the Byzantine Empire - so also in a spiritual sense the kings of the earth will bring their glory into the spiritual reign of our Lord and Savior Jesus Christ. Naturally, this glory is enshrouded in willingness of the nations to found civil laws on the Love of our Lord and Savior Jesus Christ. In the sense that they are consigned to futility, Nations who refuse to acquiesce civil laws to the Love of God perish off of the face of the earth. This is a warning from God of inevitability of reign of righteousness on this earth, the warning that all nations who seek to enforce laws that are unrighteous, or who seek to enforce laws unrighteously (on the wrong persons) will, in a spiritual sense, perish, that is, not find a place in the new heavens and new earth.

15.2   The Stones That Make Up the New Jerusalem

The broad places of the New Jerusalem are paved with gold that is as clear as glass. In Christian Scripture, gold signifies faith. In this respect, the Holy Spirit declares through Apostle Peter as follows in 1Peter 1:3-7.

> Blessed is the God and Father of our Lord Jesus Christ, who, according to the abundance of His kindness did beget us again to a living hope, through the rising again of Jesus Christ out of the dead, to an inheritance incorruptible, and undefiled, and unfading, reserved in the heavens for you, who, in the power of God are being guarded, through faith, unto salvation, ready to be revealed in the last time, in which ye are glad, a little now, if it be necessary, being made to sorrow in manifold trials, that the proof of your faith - much more precious than of gold that is perishing,

and through fire approved - may be found to praise, and honor, and glory, in the revelation of Jesus Christ.

When our Lord Jesus Christ invites the Church in Laodicea to come buy of Him GOLD fired (purified) by fire, He invites those who believe in Him to come buy of Him faith that is genuine, faith that stands the test of time, temptations, and trials. Faith that loves God first and foremost for who He is, that loves God because God is Creator and God is Love. Whenever a person who believes in Jesus Christ maintains faith through manifold trials, our Lord Jesus Christ is revealed, and revelation of our Lord Jesus Christ produces praise, honor, and glory to God.

Prophecy Insight 174 *The gold of which the broad places of the* GREAT CITY, *the* NEW JERUSALEM *is paved is the genuine faith of the saints. Absent this faith, talk less of an entry into, the nations are unable to make their way to the New Jerusalem.*

With respect to the stones of which the foundations and walls of the New Jerusalem are made, these stones represent different facets of those who have faith in the name of Jesus Christ. Remember, however, that only those who become Powers for Christ attain to gold that is as clear as glass. We saw in Chapter 11 that Neophytes and Loving Citizens of the Nations only are able to stand by the sea of gold that is as clear as glass (Revelation 15:2), are themselves not part of the sea of gold, which being clear as glass also is depicted as a sea of glass. If you seek to be part of the gold of the New Jerusalem, you desire to arrive at a PERFECT MAN, at a Power for Christ. In this respect, consider the following words inspired by the Holy Spirit and penned by Apostles Peter and Paul in 1Peter 2:6.

> Therefore it is also contained in the Scripture, "Behold, I lay in Zion a chief cornerstone, elect, precious, and he who believes on Him will by no means be put to shame."

Prophecy Principle 142 *Our Lord Jesus Christ is the Chief Cornerstone of His Sanctuary. The* PROPHETS *and the Original 12* APOSTLES *are stones that help complete the foundation of the Sanctuary of God. If you will allow your-self to be perfected in Christ, you and I are stones in the Sanctuary of God, are part of the secondary foundation for the walls, and part of the walls of the Sanctuary of God.*

The wall of the New Jerusalem is made of Jasper, and the foundations of the wall are adorned with 12 different STONES, namely (descriptions from associated pages on *Wikipedia*, or other alternative online sources):

- Jasper: Opaque Quartz Stone made up of silica that also is inclusive of Iron (III) that typically is *Red, Yellow, Brown,* or *Green* in color, RARELY BLUE.

- Sapphire: A precious gemstone, with traces of iron, titanium, chromium, copper, or magnesium. Comes in *Yellow, Brown, Green, Blue, Black, White, Purple, Pink, Grey, Orange.*

- Chalcedony: A cryptocrystalline form of silica, composed of quartz and moganite. Presence of MOGANITE differentiates from Jasper. Comes in *Yellow, Brown, Green, Blue, Black, White, Purple, Pink, Grey, Orange,* RED.

- Emerald: Emerald is a gemstone, a variety of the mineral Beryl that is colored green by traces of chromium, and perhaps vanadium. ONLY COMES IN Green.

- Sardonyx: A variety of the silicate mineral Chalcedony. ONLY COMES IN Black or White.

- Sardius: A RED precious gemstone.

- Chrysolite: A YELLOWISH-GREEN or BROWNISH variety of olivine, used as a gemstone.

- Beryl: A gemstone that is not an onyx or a quartz stone, and that comes in *Yellow, Brown, Green, Blue, White, Purple, Pink, Orange, Red.*

- Topaz: A silicate mineral consisting of aluminium and fluorine; comes in *Yellow, Brown, Green, Blue, White, Purple, Pink, Orange, Red,* GREY.

- Chrysoprasus: A cryptocrystalline form of silica that contains small quantities of nickel; comes in APPLE-GREEN or DEEP GREEN.

- Jacinth: An ORANGE-RED transparent variety of zircon used as a gemstone. Zircon is a zirconium silicate mineral.

- Amethyst: A precious stone consisting of a VIOLET or PURPLE variety of quartz.

The 12 Stones can be broken down as follows:

Stones with unique colors: EMERALD (*Green*); SARDONYX (*Black* or *White*); CHRYSOLITE (*Yellowish-Green* or *Brown*); CHRYSOPRASUS (*Green*), JACINTH (*Orange-Red*), SARDIUS (*Red*), AMETHYST (*Violet* or *Purple*).

ℑ Sources of Black: *Sapphire, Chalcedony, and Sardonyx (3)*

- ꙅ Sources of Gray: Sapphire, Chalcedony, and Topaz (3)

- ꙅ Sources of Blue: *Sapphire, Chalcedony, Beryl, and Topaz (4)*

- ꙅ Sources of Pink: Sapphire, Chalcedony, Beryl, and Topaz (4)

- ꙅ Sources of Yellow: *Sapphire, Chalcedony, Beryl, Topaz, and Jasper (5)*

- ꙅ Sources of Orange: Sapphire, Chalcedony, Beryl, Topaz, and Jacinth (5)

- ꙅ Sources of White: *Sapphire, Chalcedony, Beryl, Topaz, and Sardonyx (5)*

- ꙅ Sources of Purple: Sapphire, Chalcedony, Beryl, Topaz, and Amethyst (5)

- ꙅ Sources of Brown: *Sapphire, Chalcedony, Beryl, Topaz, Jasper, and Chrysolite (6)*

- ꙅ Sources of Red: Sapphire, Chalcedony, Beryl, Topaz, Jasper, Jacinth, Sardius (7)

- ꙅ Sources of Green: *Sapphire, Chalcedony, Beryl, Topaz, Jasper, Jacinth, Sardius, Emerald, Chrysolite, Chrysoprasus (10).*

Prophecy Interpretation 91 *Symbolism of 12 different* STONES *is as follows: While we all are of one Spirit, and of one Father, and saved by one Lord, we are not exactly alike. While we are one in spirit, we maintain some uniqueness in relation to one another. In presence of unity of faith and Spirit, we do not become uniform, unity does not imply uniformity, is consistent with uniqueness.*

Prophecy Interpretation 92 *All it takes for The Father to make you unique is addition of one quality, ability, skill, personality, gift etc. to your constitution. Addition of nickel to Silica creates Chrysoprasus.*

Prophecy Interpretation 93 SARDONYX *comes in only black or white, not black but not white, and not white but not black. There is a lesson in this for those who are wise, or who seek to be wise.*

Prophecy Interpretation 94 *The difference between each of* YELLOW, OR-ANGE, WHITE, *and* PURPLE *is no more than an exchange of one out of five stones for another stone.*

Prophecy Interpretation 95 BLUE, *which is considered the color for men, and* PINK, *which is considered the color for women both are produced by exactly the same stones. So then, let men be men, and women be women, and let all be celebrated for who they are.*

Prophecy Interpretation 96 *There is not any* COLOR, *which comes in all 12* STONES. *By this, The Father instructs that none are deemed absolutely perfect. So then, let all seek to honor one another, and let none seek to put others down. There is not any stone that cast itself in it's colors. All receive their colors from The Father. If you come in only one color, interpret as uniqueness. If you come in many colors, The Father seeks that you be different things to different men. Look for the blessing in your gift.*

15.3   The Glory of God

We already have, earlier on in this chapter, established that God is tabernacled among men implies presence of those who have faith in Jesus Christ in the New Jerusalem. I already have established in *Chapter 7*, that the Glory of God is the works of the saints. For ease of remembrance, I cite again two of the relevant Scriptures.

> And Jesus having heard, said, "This ailment is not unto death, but for the GLORY OF GOD, that the Son of God may be glorified through it (John 11:4)."

> Whether, then, ye eat, or drink, or do anything, do all to the Glory of God (1Corinthianss 31:10).

You see then consistency of tabernacling of The Father in context of presence of Powers for Christ, and the declaration that it is the Glory of God, that is, the works of the saints that lighten the New Jerusalem. With respect to importance of works of the saints, our Lord Jesus Christ admonishes as follows in Matthew 5:14-16.

> Ye are the light of the world, a city set upon a mount is not able to be hid; nor do they light a lamp, and put it under the measure, but on the lamp-stand, and it shineth to all those in the house; so let your light shine before men, that they may see your good works, and may glorify your Father who is in the heavens.

Friend, remember that a lamp-stand is representative of The Church (*Revelation chs. 1 & 2*). By the imagery of His words, our Lord Jesus Christ declares that The Church is supposed to be a platform from which works of the saints are positioned to be seen by men, by the world. In this assertion, our Lord Jesus Christ declares that a Church which seeks to hide light being created by a person who has faith in Jesus Christ is an apostate Church. With works of the saints as the glory of God, our Lord Jesus Christ declares that The Church must consciously magnify light that is created by those who have faith in Jesus Christ.

The Travesty in today's world?

While historically, The Church has been a platform for scientists such as KEPLER, GALILEO, FRANCIS BACON, ISAAC NEWTON etc. to demonstrate intelligence that is fostered by the Spirit of Christ, in today's world, The Church consciously and actively characterizes herself as running universities or colleges which focus on teaching, as opposed to pursuit of discovery of truth in context of the most *intelligent, articulate,* and *demanding* agenda for research. The Church has become so infiltrated with evil, she declares that she has left off discovery of truth to a world that is characterized by absence of integrity or honesty, and willingness to provide research support for just about anything in return for money. Regardless of preponderance of evidence for fraud in context of scientific research, The Church continues to assert it's preference for teaching the next generation, as opposed to discovery of truth. But if the Church has to teach what is claimed to be truth that is discovered by others, how exactly can it teach the truth in it's universities and colleges?

Love of Truth 65 *The Church has become so infiltrated with evil, it has left off discovery of truth to those who do not have any regard for truth. Rather than a source of light for science, The Church has become a co-conspirator for darkness.*

Prophecy Interpretation 97 *It is not The Father Himself who lightens the New Jerusalem, rather, it is the works of the saints - their love for every man, male or female, and their grand projects of Love, grand projects that simultaneously ensure everyone is loved - that lighten the New Jerusalem.*

With respect to the sun and moon, the sun and moon are lights, which light up nature, such that the glory of God can be discerned. Revelation 21:23 declares that it no longer will be the case that man depends on nature for discerning of God; that henceforth, man will discern God from His sanctuary, from those who already have faith in the name of Jesus Christ. So then, while we are not God or Jesus Christ, in the domicile of His Spirit in us, through us, The Father reveals Himself to the nations. As declared by our Lord Jesus Christ then, we now are the light of the world (John 8:12; 9:5; Matthew 5:14), yet with the recognition that we reflect the light that is in the face of our Lord and Savior Jesus Christ (2Corinthians 3:18). Given we reflect our Lord Jesus Christ, the nations see Christ in us, as such see God in us. I reiterate, however, that it is important to note that we are not God. But just as mistreatment of an ambassador from *Country A* to *Country B* is regarded as mistreatment of the President and people of *Country A*, so also the glory that the nations see in those who have faith in Jesus Christ is glory of The Father, not our own glory. It is as if then that God Himself is the sanctuary, and those of us who believe in Him, His agents, messengers, ambassadors, or emissaries. This is confirmed in the following Scripture.

> And the king (our Lord Jesus Christ) answering, shall say to them, verily I say to you, inasmuch as ye did it to one of these my brethren - the least - to me ye did it (Matthew 25:40).

> In this made perfect hath been the love with us, that boldness we may have in the day of judgment, because even AS HE (JESUS) IS, WE - WE ALSO ARE IN THIS WORLD (1John 4:17).

Prophecy Principle 143 *While* NEOPHYTES *glorify God in their good works, they have yet to become mirrors of the Glory of Christ. You see then the difference. While the good works of Neophytes glory God, the character and works are not yet perfected to the point at which others are able to discern true essence of faith in Christ from totality of their witness for Christ.*

Prophecy Principle 144 *When Scriptures speak about a mirror through which we are changed from one degree of glory to another, if you become a Power for Christ, you become a mirror through which Christ is reflected, through which others arrive at a Right Recognition of Christ.*

Prophecy Principle 145 *Spiritually speaking, while* POWERS *are not The Lord Jesus Christ, in so far as the nations are considered, they are reflections of Christ, as such are as Christ to the world. The testimony is, "As He (Jesus) is, so are we (Powers) in this world."*

How can Jesus be the Lamp, and His Powers, sources of the Glory of God?

In the same Revelation 21:23 within which those who have faith in Christ, particularly those who are Powers for Christ are declared to be sources of the Glory of God, our Lord Jesus Christ, The Lamb slain from the foundation of the world, is declared to be The Lamp of the New Jerusalem. Given it is the Glory of God, which lightens the New Jerusalem, and given a Lamp cannot be deemed to be brighter than light, Revelation 21:23 seems to suggest that the works of those who have faith in the name of Jesus Christ outshine the light produced by our Lord Jesus Christ Himself. This interpretation of Light and Lamp is, however, not the right interpretation, does not enable arrival at a Right Recognition of Christ.

Prophecy Insight 175 *If you base your comparison of Light and Lamp on what occurs in the natural, it would appear that a Light is greater than a Lamp. In the things of the spirit, however, this would not be true.*

For characterization of Lamp and Light, let us consider two Scriptures.

For Thou - Thou lightest my lamp, Jehovah my God enlight-eneth my darkness (Psalms 18:28).

From thy precepts I have understanding, therefore I have hated every false path! A lamp to my foot is Thy word, and a light to my path (Psalms 119:104-105).

For a lamp is the command, and the law a light, and a way of life are reproofs of instruction (Proverbs 6:23).

For with Thee is a fountain of life, in Thy light we see light (Psalms 36:9).

Remember how it is that, Powers for Christ are defined by three spiritual qualities, which can be reduced to two, namely:

1. LOVE OF GOD FOR FELLOW BELIEVERS IN CHRIST. The demand that the weak must be loved just as much, or perhaps much more than the strong. In this respect, Jesus declares that He came to save those who are sick, and those who are lost (Matthew 9:12, 18:11; Mark 2:17; Luke 19:10).

2. LOVE OF GOD FOR ALL MEN. While this encapsulates *Love for fellow believers*, absent expatiation, the demand that *Powers for Christ* be gentle and compassionate, that is, empathetic in building up of *Neophytes* is not obvious.

3. GODLINESS, which is, capacity for *Conception, Formulation,* and *Implementation* of *Love Projects*?

If we reduce the three qualities to two, we arrive at Love of God for all men, and Godliness. Now then, consider LAMP and LIGHT. A *Lamp* enables guidance in context of your immediate environment. If you walk a path and carry a Lamp, a Lamp provides *Light* for guidance of your feet. If you are in a room and set up a Lamp, a Lamp provides Light. So then, a Lamp is a source of Light. If a Lamp is SELF SUBSISTING, it does not itself require any fuel for producing of Light, with outcome such a Lamp is an Origin of Light.

Consider then LIGHT. *Light* always must have a source. When our Lord Jesus Christ declared, *"Let light be, and light is"* in Genesis 1:3, His words, which carried spiritual energy for accomplishment of His purpose, were origin of the Light that was created. In this respect, Hebrews 1:3 declares that our Lord Jesus Christ (paraphrase) *"upholds all of creation with the saying (word) of His might."* Consider then, that a *self subsisting* Lamp, a Lamp that is Origin of Light must be greater than the Light that it produces. Since the GLORY OF GOD is the *works of the saints*, and since the works of the saints are received from The Lamp (Ephesians 2:10), ultimately, all of the light in the New Jerusalem comes from our Lord and Savior Jesus Christ.

With respect to the two qualities of *Powers for Christ*, which are the LOVE OF GOD, and GODLINESS, the Love of God is known for what it really is, that is, is known in truth, only because it is understood in the Light that is produced by the Lamp (Psalms 36:9). Having properly understood the Love of God in context of the Light from our Lord Jesus Christ, Powers transform that Light into works. Given the Nations have yet to arrive at a proper understanding of the Lamp, but are able to appreciate WORKS OF LOVE, it is the works of Love that lighten the New Jerusalem, such that the Nations are able to appreciate the Person of our Lord and Savior Jesus Christ. So then, "*the nations of the saved in it's light shall walk (Revelation 21:24),*" because the light - the works of Love - is all they currently are able to appreciate. The light in which the Nations walk is received, however, from the Lamp, is received from our Lord and Savior Jesus Christ.

Prophecy Interpretation 98 *Our Lord Jesus Christ is* THE LAMP *from whom the saints receive the* LIGHT *(works of Love) that lightens the New Jerusalem, this so the Nations of the world are able to see. So then The Lamp, our Lord Jesus Christ, is Greater than the Light.*

Prophecy Insight 176 THE LAMP *enables us arrive at a Right Recognition of Christ (RRC), which then enables us arrive at a Right Recognition of the Love of God (RRLG). Upon arrival at RRLG, we are able to translate RRLG into* WORKS OF LOVE, *that is,* LIGHT *that the Nations can understand, Light that has capacity for drawing the Nations into the New Jerusalem.*

15.4   The Mystery that is Incorporation of the Nations into the Gospel

Incorporation of the nations into the gospel was deemed a mystery by Apostle Paul, the apostle who best understood the notion that the nations now were included in the gospel. With Daniel 2:44 and Isaiah 60:1-12 in tow, in Ephesians 3:4-6, Colossians 1:25-27, and Romans 16:25-27, Apostle Paul declares as follows.

In regard to which ye are able, reading it, to understand my knowledge in the secret of Christ, which in other generations was not made known to the sons of men, as it was now revealed to His holy apostles and prophets in the Spirit - THAT THE NATIONS BE FELLOW-HEIRS, AND OF THE SAME BODY, AND PARTAKERS OF HIS PROMISE IN THE CHRIST, THROUGH THE GOOD NEWS.

Of which I - I did become a ministrant according to the dispensation of God, that was given to me for you, to fulfil the word of God, the secret that hath been hid from the ages and from the generations, but now was manifested to His saints, to whom God did will to make known what is the riches of THE GLORY OF THIS SECRET AMONG THE NATIONS - WHICH IS CHRIST IN YOU, THE HOPE OF GLORY.

And to Him who is able to establish you, according to my good news, and the preaching of Jesus Christ, according to the revelation of the secret, in the times of the ages having been kept silent, and now having been made manifest, also, through prophetic writings, according to a command of the age-during God, HAVING BEEN MADE KNOWN TO ALL THE NATIONS FOR OBEDIENCE OF FAITH - to the only wise God, through Jesus Christ, to Him be glory to the ages. Amen.

And in the days of these kings raise up doth the God of the heavens a kingdom that is not destroyed - to the age, and it's kingdom to another people is not left: it beateth small and endeth all these kingdoms, and it standeth to the age.

And opened have thy gates continually, by day and by night they are not shut, to bring into thee the force of nations, even their kings are led. For the nation and the kingdom that do not serve thee perish, yea, the nations are utterly wasted.

So then, are New Heavens, New Earth, and the New Jerusalem instituted during or after The Millenium?

To this ambiguity, the Scriptures provide an unequivocal answer that the New Jerusalem already is on earth in context of The Millenium. This is evident as follows in Revelation 20:9.

And they did go up over the breadth of the land, and DID SURROUND THE CAMP OF THE SAINTS, AND THE BELOVED CITY, and there came fire from God out of the heaven, and devoured them.

Suppose, consistent with discussions in Chapter 11, that upon arrival at The Millenium that the Nations choose to be guided by *resurrected spirits of the saints*, with outcome they live by the Love of God, and participate in Love Projects that improve lot of mankind. Well then, this exactly is the spiritual resolution that is depicted in Revelation ch. 21. Suppose, however, that subsequent to institution of the resolution, which then would be on the pre-existing Earth, that the Nations rebel, choose not to live by the Love of God. This leads to loosing of the devil, casting of the devil in the lake of fire, and destruction of capacity of the Nations for functioning as spirits

(Revelation 20:9-10). We arrive then at the Great White Throne Judgment, in context of which those whose capacity for living as spirits now are destroyed are restricted to the OLD HEAVEN AND EARTH by The Lord Jesus Christ, with outcome the Old Heaven and Earth no longer is able to remain in Presence of Christ. With this separation of the wicked from the righteous, the spiritual domicile of the saints and those of the Nations who choose to live by the Love of God becomes NEW HEAVENS, NEW EARTH, AND THE NEW JERUSALEM. Consistent with this transformation, consider carefully the words of Apostle John in Revelation 21:1, and the fact, evident in Revelation 21:9-10, that Apostle John's vision of the New Jerusalem occurred prior to a pouring out of the 7 VIALS of the Wrath of God.

> And I saw (*like a scene changing*) a new heaven and a new earth; for the first heaven and the first earth did pass away (*the preceding scene depicting rebellion to Christ did pass away*), and the sea (*trouble of wicked people*) is not any more.

> And there came unto me one of the seven messengers, who have the seven vials that are full of the seven last plagues (*if the vials still are full, they are not yet poured out*), and he spake with me, saying, Come, I will shew thee the bride of the Lamb - the wife, and he carried me away in the Spirit to a mountain great and high, and did shew to me the GREAT CITY, the holy Jerusalem, coming down out of the heaven from God.

Friend, note that incidence of the Great White Throne Judgment at end of the Millenium is consistent with the notion that the *Millenium* feasibly can continue ad infinitum. If the Nations premise civil laws, and societal interactions on the Love of God, and allow themselves to be guided by *resurrected spirits of the saints*, the devil remains bound, as such, is judged in isolation. This is evident in the following words.

> And he cast him to the abyss, and did shut him up, and put a seal upon him, that he may not lead astray the nations any more, *till the thousand years* MAY *be finished*; and after these it behoveth him to be loosed a little time (Revelation 20:3).

> And *when the thousand years* MAY *be finished*, the Adversary shall be loosed out of his prison (Revelation 20:7).

Prophecy Interpretation 99 *Friend, the word 'May' means,* CONDITIONAL, *as such implies it is possible that* THE THOUSAND YEARS MAY NOT FINISH. *So then, if the thousand years do not finish, this because the Nations are willing to live righteously, the devil remains bound.*

If the devil remains bound, the Millenium, in essence, transforms into New Heavens, New Earth, and New Jerusalem. If the nations disobey God, the devil is loosed, amasses the Nations, who then are judged, and cast, spiritually on the OLD HEAVEN AND EARTH that cannot find a place in the Presence of Christ. Simultaneously, the saved arrive, spiritually, at NEW HEAVENS, NEW EARTH, AND A NEW JERUSALEM. You see then that *limit-lessness* of the Millenium is compatible with *cessation* of the Millenium for creation of New Heavens, New Earth, and a New Jerusalem.

Prophecy Insight 177 *Limitlessness of time that is embedded in the Millenium is compatible with cessation of the Millenium. Given the scenario within which the Millenium does not end only produces New Heavens, New Earth, and the New Jerusalem, as such does not encapsulate the scenario that generates* OLD HEAVENS AND EARTH, *the Scriptures focus on the scenario that generates both outcomes.*

In order for Apostle John to see the New Jerusalem, he had to be carried away in the Holy Spirit to *a* MOUNTAIN *great and high*. We already know that a mountain symbolizes righteousness. In this carrying away to a mountain great and high, The Lord Jesus Christ signifies that absent His grace, such that the New Jerusalem descends to the level of righteousness attained to by the best of His saints (*Powers for Christ*), a gradual descent, which makes the New Jerusalem available at the lowest height attained to by Powers at commencement of The Millenium, all fall short of His glory, with outcome none are able to be saved. Given the sacrifice of our Lord Jesus Christ accrues to us His perfect life, however, regardless of shortcoming of *any measure of the stature of the fullness of Christ* to which Powers for Christ attain, entry into the New Jerusalem is rooted in the MERCY, GRACE, and JUSTICE of The Father. In this respect, we have Noah as an analogy. First, Noah could be picked by The Father only because he found grace in the sight of The Father (Genesis 6:8). Given Grace means 'FAVOR THAT IS NOT MERITED', we arrive at the truth that he was not really perfectly worthy, but was the best that was available. Second, if they had responded to his teachings and preaching, The Father would have saved men who had been evil, but who on hearing of the preaching of Noah were willing to believe God and enter the ark. You see then, that willingness of The Father to work with the best that is available, and to forgive and grant a second chance to those who previously had loved evil (*those who worship the beast, and the image of the beast*) is rooted in His CHARACTER, His GLORY, His ESSENCE.

We see imagery of salvation of previously evil men in Revelation 7:13-17, a passage that depicts fulfillment of the promise of our Lord Jesus Christ of fountains of living water in Revelation 21:6. In Revelation 7:17, NEOPHYTES arrive in the heavens hungry and thirsty, as such are in need of being filled with the water of life, and are lacking in the body of Christ. Given the fact that they are hungry means they are not fed on the word of God, and given the fact that they are thirsty means they do not yet have the Holy Spirit, NEOPHYTES represent persons who have just been saved from their sins, persons who have recognized their sinfulness, and washed themselves in the blood of Jesus Christ (Revelation 7:14) in context of reprieve offered to those who worshipped the beast and the image of the beast and have chosen the Love of God as rubric for life. The declaration in Revelation 21:27 that those who defile (*those who seek to cause others to be corrupted, or to sin*), or do abominations, or delight in lies are unable to enter into the New Jerusalem reiterates the characterization in Revelation 7:14 that those who gain access into the New Jerusalem are repented of their sins.

Prophecy Insight 178 *Revelation ch. 21 depicts a glorious 1st Seal period,* THE MILLENIUM, *that is outcome, of perfecting of the Church in context of the 7th* VIAL *of the Wrath of God, as such is spiritual resolution of the RP7* PATH *of the SSGLAE. With caveat of exclusion of the Nations who refuse still to premise civil laws, and societal interactions on the Love of God to the Old Heaven and Earth, which is unable to remain in Presence of Christ, with outcome the spiritual resolution transforms into New Heavens, New Earth, and the New Jerusalem.*

Prophecy Insight 179 *If the Nations do not, in context of* THE MILLENIUM *choose the Love of God as basis of civil laws, and societal interactions, the devil is loosed and cast into the lake of fire, and capacity of the Nations for functioning as spirits is destroyed by our Lord and Savior Jesus Christ. Consequent on this destruction, rebellious Nations are consigned to the* OLD HEAVEN AND EARTH, *which does not have a place in Presence of Christ. Given The Father has declared that "it is righteousness that exalts a nation (Proverbs 14:34)," and that "progress of nations is not by power, nor by might, but by His Spirit (1Samuel 2:9; Zechariah 4:6)," it must be impossible for Nations that are consigned to the Old Heaven and Earth to escape from* FUTILITY OF INCAPACITY *for economic development.*

Prophecy Insight 180 *Preponderance of* INCAPACITY *of Nations of the Earth at escape from clutches of underdevelopment is evidence that the Nations of the Earth have been refusing to premise civil laws, and societal interactions on the* LOVE OF GOD.

CHAPTER 16

UTOPIA

In the preceding chapter, I provide unambiguous evidence that the spiritual resolution depicted in *Revelation ch. 21* differs from the spiritual resolution that is depicted in *Revelation ch. 22*. This was evident in the fact that while The Lord Jesus Christ is THE LAMP of the New Jerusalem in *Revelation ch. 21*, it is explicitly stated in *Revelation 22:5*, that 'THERE IS NOT ANY NEED FOR a Lamp' in the spiritual resolution that is depicted in *Revelation ch. 22.* It is straightforward then, that it is not I who assert the difference, but rather, our Lord Jesus Christ Himself, the Giver of the Prophecies. Whoever resists this insight, resists not I, who by the grace of our Lord Jesus Christ am given to His Church as an APOSTLE, that is, AS A REVEALER OF HIDDEN THINGS OF THE CHRIST TO THE CHURCH AND THE NATIONS, rather resists our Lord Jesus Christ Himself. Remember, cursed is everyone who *intentionally*, *deliberately*, and *stubbornly* insists on their private interpretation of prophecies that come to us from our Lord and Savior Jesus Christ (Revelation 22:18-19).

By the anointing and revelational insights that are provided me by the Holy Spirit, I have provided you with evidence that the spiritual resolution depicted as New Heavens, New Earth, and the New Jerusalem in *Revelation ch. 21* is spiritual resolution of the RP7 PATH of the SSGLAE. So then, *Revelation ch. 21* depicts a new 1st SEAL that is outcome of a transversing of the RP7 PATH of the SSGLAE. By the same anointing of The Holy Spirit, I now go on to provide you with evidence that the spiritual resolution that is depicted in *Revelation ch. 22* pertains to the BP7 PATH of the SSGLAE. First, however, let us discuss that important notion of 'a measure of the stature of the fullness of Christ' that is introduced by Apostle Paul in Ephesians 4:13.

Perfect Man: Measure, Stature, and Fullness of God

For ease of recollection, I reproduce the Scripture passage below.

> Till we may all come to the unity of the faith and of the recognition of the Son of God, to a perfect man, to a measure of the stature of the fullness of Christ.

Friend, first, 'a measure' does not have interpretation as 'the measure'. A measure means there can be more than one of such measures. Second, the phrase, 'a measure' qualifies the word 'STATURE', which itself is an adjective, as such qualifies the phrase, 'fullness of Christ'. With worthiness the most spiritual of the three variants, the word STATURE signifies 'accomplishment', 'achievement', or 'worthiness'. Combined then, 'A MEASURE OF THE STATURE' implies, 'a particular level of accomplishment, achievement, or worthiness'. With qualification of the phrase, 'FULLNESS OF CHRIST' imposed, Ephesians 4:13 can be paraphrased as follows.

> Till we may all come to the unity of the faith and of the recognition of the Son of God, to a perfect man, to any of several possible levels of worthiness that subsist in relation to the fullness of perfection of which our Lord Jesus Christ is representative.

Consider then, that a Perfect Man does not have just one characterization, that a Perfect Man can be any of several possible levels of WORTHINESS that subsist in relation to the fullness of perfection of which our Lord Jesus Christ is representative. Consider also that arrival at any of several levels is predicated on a RIGHT RECOGNITION OF THE SON OF GOD, with outcome that, as already discussed, the foundation for perfection is unity of Right Recognition of The Son of God.

For analogy and concreteness, while a *4-cylinder Toyota Camry LE* is a CAMRY, that is, fully qualifies as a CAMRY, a *6-cylinder Toyota Camry LE*, the sort of which I leased between 2007 and 2011, equally is a CAMRY, yet *is a more powerful* CAMRY. In Chapter 2, I applied the analogy that *Lt. Generals, Major Generals, Brig., Generals,* and *Generals* all are 'GENERALS'. Friend, there is a minimum stature required for qualification as a POWER FOR CHRIST. Above that minimum, however, there perhaps are infinitely many levels that yet can be attained. The '*minimum*', of which, rightly, only The Father has calibration, is all The Father demands if you are to attain to recognition as a Power for Christ. In this respect, note that in Mathematics, it is mathematically sound for a SET to have a minimum, referred to specifically as an 'INFIMUM', but yet not have a definite maximum. In this case, the maximum is set to equal infinity (∞). Since The Father must be deemed to be an Infinite Entity, it makes sense that the maximum, that is, supremum that is possible to attain to in context of the fullness of Christ is set to infinity. A set, such as I have described, qualifies as what is referred to as a mathematical 'SPACE', that is a continuum that supports every feasible form of Mathematics. For illustration, the set, $[5, \infty)$, qualifies as a space that supports every feasible form of Mathematics.

The Things That Are 97 *A Perfect Man, that is, a Power for Christ is a person who has faith in Jesus Christ, and who has attained to any of several possible levels of worthiness that subsist in relation to the fullness of perfection of which our Lord Jesus Christ is representative.*

What then is the overarching litmus test for discerning validity of the interpretation of the spiritual resolution in Revelation ch. 22 as pertaining to the BP7 path?

Prophecy Principle 146 *Since the BP7* PATH *is a Glorious Path, a path characterized by choice of righteousness by each of The Church (willingness, and effort towards perfection) and The Nations (premising of civil laws, and societal interactions on the Love of God), the Glory that is revealed in Revelation ch. 22 must be Greater than the* GLORY *that is revealed in Revelation ch. 21.*

Do we have any evidence for higher attainments to Glory in context of Revelation ch. 22?
Absolutely!!!

> Presence of The Father: Tabernacle vis-a-vis Throne

While it is only the TABERNACLE OF GOD that is present in the spiritual resolution that is depicted in *ch. 21*, an imagery we already know to imply presence of Powers for Christ, in *ch. 22*, the spiritual resolution is inclusive of the throne of God and of the Lamb. This implies that while Powers that subsist in context of *ch. 21* actualized The Presence of Christ, Powers that subsist in context of *ch. 22* actualized the Presence of Christ, and Presence of The Father. This of course implies worthiness attained to by Powers in context of *ch. 22* exceeds that attained to in context of *ch. 21*. That knowledge of our Lord Jesus Christ does not imply knowledge of The Father is evident in the following Scriptures uttered by our Lord Jesus Christ Himself.

All things were delivered to me by my Father, and none doth know The Son, except The Father, nor doth any know The Father, except The Son, and he to whom The Son may wish to reveal Him (Matthew 11:27).

And this is the life age-during, that they may know Thee, the only true God, and Him whom thou didst send - Jesus Christ (John 17:3).

I write to you, fathers, because ye have known Him who is from the beginning (our Lord Jesus Christ); I write to you, young men, because ye have overcome the evil. I write to you, little youths, because ye have known The Father (1John 2:13).

Jesus answered and said to him, If any one may love me, my word he will keep, and my Father will love him, and unto him we will come, and abode with Him we will make (John 14:23).

Prophecy Interpretation 100 *Our Lord Jesus Christ makes clear that while He and The Father are one essence, that knowledge of Him does not necessarily equate to knowledge of The Father. Our Lord Jesus Christ declares that after a person has gotten to know Him, He then decides whether such a person is worthy of a revelation of The Father.*

RP7 vis-a-vis BP7 Resolution 1 *In ch. 21, it is spirits of the saints who, in a spiritual sense, come down to earth in context of the New Jerusalem. In ch. 22, it is the throne of The Father that, in a spiritual sense, comes down to earth.*

RP7 vis-a-vis BP7 Resolution 2 *While The Father is not Himself spiritually present on earth in ch. 21, He is, in ch. 22 spiritually present on earth. So then, while only The Lord Jesus Christ is spiritually present in ch. 21, in ch. 22, both Father and Son are spiritually present.*

Reign of resurrected spirits vis-a-vis reign of the living

In *Chapter 11*, I highlighted the spiritual reality that, as part of resolution of the RP7 path, it is spirits of saints who gave their lives for Christ that are resurrected, such that they reign with The Lord Jesus Christ. There is not any allusion to spirits of the living participating in the reign. These spirits reign with Christ, and are designated PRIESTS OF GOD AND OF THE CHRIST (Revelation 20:4-6), as such are kings and priests unto Christ. Note, however, that these kings and priests are not inclusive of any members of the Newly Reconstituted Church who remain alive in New Heavens, New Earth, and the New Jerusalem.

RP7 vis-a-vis BP7 Resolution 3 *None of the living saints who are in the New Heavens, New Earth, and New Jerusalem are kings and priests unto Christ. Only spirits of resurrected saints reign with our Lord and Savior Jesus Christ. On the RP7 PATH then, none of the believers who make it into the Millenium have characterization as kings and priests unto Christ.*

Consider, however, Revelation 22:5, 11:15-16, which states:

And night shall not be there, and they have no need of a lamp and light of a sun, because the Lord God doth give them light, and they shall reign - to the ages of the ages.

And the seventh messenger did sound, and there came great voices in the heaven, saying, "The kingdoms of the world did become those of our Lord and of His Christ, and He shall reign to the ages of the ages!" and the twenty and four elders, who before God are sitting upon their thrones, did fall upon their faces, and did bow before God, saying, "We give thanks to Thee, O Lord God, the Almighty, who are, and who wast, and who art coming, because thou hast taken Thy great power and didst reign (Revelation 11:15-17)."

RP7 vis-a-vis BP7 Resolution 4 *In ch. 22, the living saints reign with Christ to the ages of the ages. Hallelujah!!! In ch. 21, none of the living saints reign with Christ, rather it is resurrected spirits of the saints who reign with Christ. Clearly, the spiritual resolution depicted in ch. 22 is more glorious than that in ch. 21.*

RP7 vis-a-vis BP7 Resolution 5 *Note that at timing of welcoming of the reign of Christ in Revelation 11:15-17, that believers who have spiritual likenesses of a* MAN, *a* CALF, *an* EAGLE, *and a* LION *are nowhere to be found in the throne room of The Father. By this, the Holy Spirit declares that only those who become Powers for Christ (as represented by the 24 Elders) do not stand any risk of being surprised by arrival of the reign of Christ.*

We already have discussed, in the preceding chapter that Jesus describes two sets of believers, those whose spirits die, but which then are resurrected, and those whose spirits do not die, that is, those whose spirits acquire life that is age-during here on earth. Consistent with arrival at life that is age-during here on earth in *ch.* 22, there is A TREE OF LIFE in the broad place that is in front of the throne of The Father.

RP7 vis-a-vis BP7 Resolution 6 *In ch. 21, there is not any mention of a tree of life, and only* RESURRECTED SPIRITS OF THE RIGHTEOUS *reign with Christ. In ch. 22, symbolizing arrival at life that is age-during, there is a tree of life, and those who reign with Christ, those whose spirits have acquired life that is age-during,* ARE ALIVE ON EARTH, *and reign with Christ on earth.*

Comfort vis-a-vis Presence

In *ch.* 21, men receive comfort from ministry of the saints. This is of crucial importance. The saints are the tabernacle of God on earth, and they minister comfort to all men. While our Lord Jesus Christ guides His saints, meaning there is guidance of The Holy Spirit, His Presence is not domiciled in the New Jerusalem. We arrive then at the inference that the saints in ch. 21 only have fellowship of the Holy Spirit. Concerning guidance of the truth as work of the Holy Spirit, and the spiritual reality that The Holy Spirit is agent for our Lord Jesus Christ, Scriptures declare as follows.

> And when He may come - the Spirit of truth - He will guide you to all the truth, for He will not speak from Himself but as many things as He will hear He will speak, and the coming things He will tell you; He will glorify Me because of mine He will take, and will tell to you (John 16:13-14).

> For as many are led (guided) by the Spirit of God, these are the sons of God (Romans 8:14).

> And ye are not in the flesh, but in the Spirit, if indeed the Spirit of God doth dwell in you; and if any one hath not the Spirit of Christ - this one is not His (Romans 8:9).

The Things That Are 98 *It is not our Lord Jesus Christ who guides you, rather it is His Spirit, The Holy Spirit who guides you. So then, for all practical purposes, with The Holy Spirit as representative of Jesus on earth, you are guided by The Holy Spirit. We already have established, in preceding Chapters (see for example, Chapter 3), that guidance of The Holy Spirit does not equate to arrival at The Presence of Christ.*

Consider, however, ch. 22. In ch. 22, the saints see the face of The Father and have His name on their foreheads, meaning they arrive at a measure of the stature of the fullness of Christ and have fellowship of The Father. Remember that the 144,000 who follow Christ wherever He goes also have the name of His Father, our Father in heaven written on their foreheads. Concerning the fact that they see the face of God, consider the following Scriptures.

> My soul thirsted for God, for the living God, when do I enter (*into the throne room of God, which is spiritual*) and see the face (*Presence*) of God - Psalms 42:2.

> Happy the clean in heart - because they shall see God (Matthew 5:8).

> Rise doth God - scattered are His enemies! And those hating Him flee from His face. As the driving away of smoke Thou drivest away, as the melting of wax before fire, the wicked perish at the

PRESENCE OF GOD. And the righteous rejoice, they exult before God, and they joy with gladness (Psalms 68:1-3).

Seek ye Jehovah and His strength, seek ye His face (*Presence*) continually - Psalms 105:4.

And now, appease, I pray thee, the face (*Presence*) of God, and He doth favor us; From your own hand hath this been, doth He accept your appearances? Said Jehovah of Hosts (Malachi 1:9).

For this is he of whom it hath been written, Lo, I do send My messenger before Thy face (PRESENCE & PURPOSE), who shall prepare they way before thee (Matthew 11:10).

And The Lord Jehovah giveth help to me, therefore I have not been ashamed, therefore I have set my face (PRESENCE & PURPOSE) as a flint, And I know that I am not ashamed (Isaiah 50:7).

The Things That Are 99 *In Scriptures, Face is symbolic of Presence and Purpose. So then, when the saints are described as* SEEING *The Face of God, they are conscious of His Presence and His Purposes.*

RP7 vis-a-vis BP7 Resolution 7 *In ch. 21, the saints are focused on* MINISTRATION TO THE NATIONS, *meaning their witness to the Nations matters significantly. In ch. 22, the saints are focused on experience of The Presence of Christ, and discernment of His Grand Purposes for the earth. Clearly, the saints in ch. 22 have attained to a higher measure of the stature of the fullness of Christ.*

RP7 vis-a-vis BP7 Resolution 8 *In ch. 21, the saints' work is focused on producing of light for guidance of the Nations. In ch. 22, the saints' work is focused on discernment of purposes of our Lord Jesus Christ. The difference? In ch. 21, it is the individual character of the saints that is source of light for the Nations. In ch. 22, there are Grand Purposes of Love that are discerned and initiated by the saints.*

RP7 vis-a-vis BP7 Resolution 9 *In ch. 21, the Nations walk in the light that is produced by the good works of the saints. In ch. 22, The Father provides light for both the saints and the Nations.*

RP7 vis-a-vis BP7 Resolution 10 *Those of the Nations who walk in the Love of God enter into the New Jerusalem, such that they can receive authority for partaking of the* TREE OF LIFE. *Note that authority is received upon entry, meaning if they are to have access, the Nations must satisfy some conditions, namely faith in Jesus Christ, and arrival at the Presence of Christ. Clearly, the Nations must have premised civil laws on the Love of God, else they would not have access into the beloved city. So then, we arrive at confirmation that ch. 22 pertains to the BP7* PATH *of the SSGLAE.*

RP7 vis-a-vis BP7 Resolution 11 *With the Nations dependent on the saints in ch. 21, clearly, the Nations are in the New Heavens and New Earth only by the mercies of The Father. So then, evidence for the RP7* PATH *of the SSGLAE. In the lower glory of the saints in ch. 21, we arrive at evidence for a* NEWLY RECONSTITUTED CHURCH, *that is remnant of a Church that initially, along with the Nations, chose evil over what is good. In depiction of Babylon, and the command to the saints to come out of her, we have confirmation for the RP7* PATH *of the SSGLAE.*

RP7 vis-a-vis BP7 Resolution 12 *In aggregate, we arrive at confirmation that ch. 21 pertains to the RP7* PATH *of the SSGLAE, and ch. 22 to the BP7* PATH *of the SSGLAE.*

The following words in Revelation 22:14-15, & 22:16-17 straightforwardly demonstrate that the depiction of the *throne of God, water of life, tree of life,* and *leaves* of the tree of life in Revelation 22:1-5 is spiritual, not in the natural.

> Happy are those doing His commands that the authority shall be theirs unto the tree of the life, and by the gates they may enter into the city; and without are the DOGS (sexual perverts, and men or women who love and practice whoredom), and the SORCERERS (those who consort with demons), and the WHOREMONGERS (men who love to consort with whores), and the MURDERERS (those who practice hatreds, see 1John 3:15), and the IDOLATERS (those who place anything or anyone before God their Creator), and everyone who is loving and doing a lie.

> I, Jesus did send my messenger to testify to you these things concerning the assemblies; I am the root and the offspring of David, the bright and morning star! And the Spirit and the Bride say, Come; and he who is hearing - let him say, Come; and he who is thirsting - let him come; and he who is willing - let him take of the water of life freely.

> Violence is not heard any more in thy land, spoiling and destruction in thy borders, and THOU HAST CALLED SALVATION THY WALLS, AND THY GATES, PRAISE. To thee no more is the sun for a light by day, and for brightness the moon giveth not light to thee, and Jehovah hath become to thee a light age-during, and thy God thy beauty. And THY PEOPLE ARE ALL OF THEM RIGHTEOUS, to the age they possess the earth, a branch of my planting, a work of my hands, to be beautified. The little one doth become a chief, and the small one a mighty nation, I, Jehovah, in it's own time do hasten it (Isaiah 60:20-22).

Revelation 22:14-15 makes the following explicitly clear, namely:

♣ There are still people doing evil who are outside of the New Jerusalem, but who by virtue of their love for their sinful nature do not have access to the New Jerusalem.

♣ Those who are outside of the New Jerusalem, but who hunger and thirst for righteousness, those who are uncomfortable with their sinful nature gain access into the New Jerusalem.

♣ Out of those who gain access into the city, only those who do the commands of The Father gain access to the tree of life.

As I have reiterated throughout this book, and as I again have to reiterate, there are two commands given to those who choose to have relationship with Christ.

The first command is to believe in the name of our Lord Jesus Christ (1John 3:23, first part). This command makes sense only if it is directed at those who have yet to be saved alongside those who already are saved. In order to arrive at relationship with Christ, you have to demonstrate faith in the name of Jesus Christ, then maintain that faith throughout the rest of your life.

The second command is to love as Christ has loved (1John 3:23, second part; John 13:34). Clearly, only those who have chosen to believe in the name of Jesus Christ can fulfill this command. In this respect, Apostle John declares as follows in 1John 3:15.

> Everyone who is hating his brother - a man-killer (*murderer*)
> he is, and ye have known that no man-killer hath life age-during
> (*eternal life*) in him remaining.

Note the consistency between the passages from the Books of Revelation and 1John, which is if you confess Jesus as Lord and Savior, but do not eschew hatred and embrace love, you will not arrive at life that lasts forever, that is, will not inherit eternal life. It is very clear then that if you gain entrance into the city via confession of Jesus as Lord and Savior, but do not obey the command to love your neighbor and brother and sister, as such do not eschew hatred of any man, that you will not gain access to the tree of life. This is unequivocal, non-debatable. If you do not demonstrate respect and love for the commands of God after you gain entry into the city, you will not arrive at life that is eternal, at life that is enduring, at life that brings light, peace, and joy.

Prophecy Principle 147 *The Father is unequivocally clear; if you will not obey the command to love your brother and your neighbor, access into the New Jerusalem will not translate into access to the tree of life. If you enter* *into the New Jerusalem via confession of faith in the name of Jesus Christ, and walk in the love of God, you receive authority - the right, and right comes with power for maintenance of right - to the tree of life.*

Prophecy Principle 148 *We arrive then at this conclusion, that in The Father's perspective, only those who already have made up their mind to do things His way have interest in gaining access into the New Jerusalem. Repentance then is not just about confessing past sins, but also about a turning away from a mind that functions on hatreds to a mind that functions by the love of God.*

> The importance of repentance from worldly philosophies for embracing of God's philosophy of the faith that works by love (Galatians 5:6)?
>
> And be not conformed to this age, but BE TRANSFORMED BY THE RENEWING OF YOUR MIND, for your proving what is the will of God - the good, and acceptable, and perfect (Romans 12:2).

> For, LET THIS MIND BE IN YOU THAT IS ALSO IN CHRIST JESUS, who being in the form of God, thought it not robbery to be equal to God, but did empty Himself, the form of a servant having taken, in the likeness of men having been made, and in fashion having been found as a man, He humbled Himself, having become obedient unto death - death even of a cross, wherefore, also, God did highly exalt Him, and gave to Him a name that is above every name (Philippians 2:5-9).

> And INCREASE YE IN GRACE, AND IN THE KNOWLEDGE OF OUR LORD AND SAVIOR JESUS CHRIST; to Him is the glory both now, and to the day of the age! Amen (2Peter 3:18).

> "...And we - WE HAVE THE MIND OF CHRIST (1Corinthians 2:16)."

And THIS IS THE LIFE AGE-DURING, THAT THEY MAY KNOW THEE, THE ONLY TRUE GOD, AND HIM WHOM THOU DIDST SEND - JESUS CHRIST (John 17:3).

Prophecy Principle 149 *Friend, if you do not get to know Christ, if your mind is not renewed, such that you are able to arrive at knowledge of Christ; if your mind is not renewed, such that you love the things of which Christ is representative - faith that works by love; if you do not arrive at some measure of the stature of the fullness (love) of Christ, you are unable to arrive at life that is age-during, you are unable to arrive at life that lasts for all time.*

Those Who Love and Live (Do) a Lie Do Not Gain Access

A group of people who will not gain access to the New Jerusalem, who will not have opportunity to partake of the grace of our Lord and Savior Jesus Christ is 'any' group of people who love and practice a lie.

Prophecy Principle 150 *Whoever declares evil to be good, and good, evil loves and practices a lie. Whoever punishes the righteous, and rewards evildoers with good, loves and practices a lie. None of such persons have opportunity for gaining entrance into the New Jerusalem.*

16.1   Those who seek to trade in souls of the righteous love and practice a lie

With remembrance that one of the sins of Babylon the great whore is 'TRADING IN THE SOULS OF MEN' (Revelation 18:13), The Father declares as follows in course of His revelations to Prophet Ezekiel in Ezekiel 13:18-19; 20-21; 22-23.

> And say, Thus says the Lord God: "Woe to the women who sew magic bands upon all wrists, and make veils for the heads of persons of every stature, in the hunt for souls! Will you hunt down souls belonging to my people, and keep other souls alive for your profit? You have profaned me among my people for handfuls of barley and for pieces of bread, PUTTING TO DEATH PERSONS WHO SHOULD NOT DIE AND KEEPING ALIVE PERSONS WHO SHOULD NOT LIVE, BY YOUR LIES TO MY PEOPLE, WHO LISTEN TO LIES."

> "Wherefore thus says the Lord God: Behold, I am against your magic bands with which you hunt the souls, and I will tear them from your arms; and I will let the souls that you hunt go free like birds. Your veils also I will tear off, and deliver my people out of your hand, and they shall be no more in your hand as prey; and you shall know that I am the Lord."

> "Because you have disheartened the heart of the righteous falsely, although you have disheartened him, and you have encouraged the wicked, that he should not turn from his wicked way to save his life; therefore you shall no more see delusive visions nor practice divination; I will deliver my people out of your hand. Then you will know that I am the Lord."

Prophecy Insight 181 *Any person who seeks to keep evildoers alive for profit, and who seeks to murder the righteous so the land is filled with evildoers will not gain entry into the New Jerusalem.*

Prophecy Insight 182 *Every nation within which evildoers are systematically rewarded with good, and those who live righteously are systematically rewarded with evil will not gain entry into the New Jerusalem.*

16.2   Those Who Teach Evolution as Fact, Love and Practice a Lie

One of the biggest lies that is being practised today is the lie that evolution is a fact, with outcome Christians are considered to be irrational. The hypocrisy? Muslims and Jews who believe in the Torah also do not believe in evolution, yet they are deemed to be rational. Or do they speak with their mouths, yet not believe in their hearts, as such are in collusion with the devil?

The truth of the matter? There is not any credible or reputable scientist worth his or her salt who, if asked the following pointed question can provide a 'Yes' answer. That question is:

> With recognition of science as consisting of sound mathematical theory and replicable evidence, has science proved evolution to be a fact?

The tools of science are theory and evidence. In science, credible theory is not deduced from experiences, rather is formulated mathematically. While our senses reveal the sun as *'rising in the east'* and *'setting in the west'*, suggesting that the sun revolves around the earth, formal tools of mathematics have demonstrated that interactions between the sun and the earth cannot be interpreted on basis of what seems to be experienced, on basis of what seems to be perceived by the senses.

Prophecy Insight 183 *The proof that the earth revolves around the sun is mathematical, not based on observation. Copernicus (1473-1543 AD), Johannes Kepler (1571-1630), and Galileo (1564-1642 AD) all proved mathematically that the earth and the planets had to revolve around the sun (HWE, pgs. 341,342). The senses - what is observed - suggest exactly the opposite, that the sun revolves around the earth. Science has proved the mathematics to be correct.*

In so far as scientific evidence is concerned, evidence that is credible and normative can be replicated a million times and yield exactly the same outcome. Consider this friend, that outside of fossils of people that are dead, starting from the earliest writings known to man, there is not any shred of historical or contemporaneous evidence for evolution. None of the ancient writings document any such phenomenon, and there does not exist any scientist, dead or alive who documented evidence for evolution. The deduction that existence of different sets of bones is evidence for evolution is a hypothesis - a potential, yet non-exclusive interpretation of evidence. In presence of evidence for false interpretations of fossils in past, interpretation of the evidence by scientists has been proven to be patently unreliable. In this respect, it is well documented that bones that previously were interpreted to be that of a beastly ancestor of man have turned out to be bones of an elderly man whose spine was deformed. This is evidence that is acknowledged by foremost scientists. We arrive then at a normative truth, which is, existence of different types of bones is not evidence for existence of different types of man. In presence of this normative, it is a truism that the assertion, to wit different sets of bones are evidence for evolution is a hypothesis, has yet to be proven to be fact.

But can the hypothesis ever be proven to be fact?

In order for science to prove that two sets of bones lying beside each other were progressions of one kind of man to another, there must be evidence that SET OF BONES 1 *gave birth to* SET OF BONES 2. In absence of any documentation of such a progression in any of historical writings, absent contemporaneous evidence, evolution only is a hypothesis, cannot be accepted as fact. So then, evidence for evolution only can be contemporaneous. BUT HOW DO DOCTORS INTERPRET SPINAL CONTUSIONS? Well, Doctors interpret spinal contusions as malformations, that is, as departures from normality. If Doctors do not consider spinal contusions to be evolution, rather consider them malformations, science declares that whenever the spine does not align with what is normal, it does not see evolution, that rather all it sees is contusions and malformations. Until man gives birth to another man who does not walk erect on two feet - that feat having already been accomplished - who perhaps has wings and flies, and with the wings natural parts of his or her body, evolution will remain no more than a hypothesis, albeit a highly speculative hypothesis.

Prophecy Insight 184 *The only evidence that exists for evolution is existence of different sets of bones, which then are interpreted as evidence for different types of man. In the retraction of at the very least two of such interpretations for bones that look different, science agrees and asserts that existence of different types of bones cannot unambiguously be interpreted as evidence for existence of different types of man.*

Regardless of stated normative, people who believe in Creationism are being labelled as stupid, fools, incapable of reasoning, and evolution is taught as if it were fact to unsuspecting children in developed economies of the world.

Prophecy Insight 185 *Teaching of theory of evolution as fact is one of the biggest lies that is loved and practiced in today's world. All who are aware that teaching of evolution as fact is a lie, but who yet love and practice this lie, are unable to gain entrance into the New Jerusalem.*

If evolution is taught as what it is, a theory of life, as opposed to a fact, so long as scientific merits of Creationism as theory of life also are taught side by side, the teaching of it ceases to be a lie, for it merely is presented to the mind for evaluation. Consider, however, that we continue to have evidence for Creationism in contemporaneous life. All it takes is one single piece of evidence to demonstrate reasonableness of Creationism as theory of life, and absurdity or preposterousness of evolution as theory of life.

Prophecy Insight 186 *From the earliest writings of man, which come to us from about 3,000 BC to this day, a human pregnancy is recorded as requiring 9 MONTHS of gestation in the womb. The right amount of time never has been less then 9 MONTHS, never has been higher than 9 MONTHS. In this normative of human experience, there is clear evidence for intentional design (consistency of amount of time required for formation of a child in the womb), and clear evidence against 'chance' and 'randomness'. Evolution cannot embed chance and randomness, yet over the course of 6,000 YEARS require exactly the same amount of time for gestation of a child.*

Prophecy Insight 187 *If scientific merits of Creationism are taught alongside scientific merits of evolution, there hardly is any rational child who will not be able to see that while one theory is consistent with human experience, the other consists majorly of 'a waving of hands' over CIRCUMSTANTIAL EVIDENCE THAT NEVER HAS BEEN CONTEMPORANEOUSLY OBSERVED. This must be the reason evolution is taught as fact, as opposed to theory; that is, the realization that juxtaposition of scientific merits of theory of evolution with scientific merits of Creationism reveals theory of evolution to be no more than 'A WAVING OF HANDS'.*

16.3   The fruits and leaves of the tree of life

We already have established that the river of water of life refers to the Holy Spirit (John 7:37-39). Clearly then, the twelve fruits that are yielded by the river of water of life refer to fruits of the Spirit. In this respect, it is important to distinguish between the FRUIT OF THE SPIRIT, and fruits of the Spirit.

In Christian Scriptures, the fruit of the Spirit is one integrated fruit consisting of all the attributes, equivalently qualities that are produced by the Holy Spirit. Consider then Galatians 5:22-23, and John 15:1-2,16-17.

And the fruit of the Spirit is: *Love, joy,* peace, *long-suffering* (modern language would substitute *patience* or *endurance*), *kindness,* goodness, *faith,* meekness, *temperance:* against such there is no law.

I am the true vine, and my Father is the husbandman; every branch in me not bearing fruit, He doth take it away, and every one bearing fruit, He doth cleanse by pruning it, that it may bear more fruit. Ye did not choose out me, but I CHOSE OUT YOU, AND DID APPOINT YOU, THAT YE MIGHT GO AWAY, AND MIGHT BEAR FRUIT, and your fruit might remain, that whatever ye may ask of The Father in my name, He may give you. These things I command you, that ye love one another.

Christian Scriptures are very clear. Every good quality that is expected of a Christian, that is produced with help of the Spirit is part and parcel of one fruit, not a separate fruit. The reasoning is simple, which is, a Christian who is meek, but who lacks capacity for love is an anachronism, as is a Christian who loves others, but is lacking in meekness. In order for a person who has faith in Jesus Christ to be complete, lacking in nothing, he or she must have all of the qualities that are produced by the Holy Spirit. It is normative then that all of the qualities expected of those who have faith in the name of Jesus Christ make up one fruit.

Prophecy Principle 151 *All of the qualities expected of a person who has faith in Jesus Christ, all of the qualities that are produced by the Holy Spirit constitute one fruit only. By this, The Father declares that if you seek not to develop any of the qualities, if you resist the Holy Spirit in respect of any of the qualities, it is tantamount to not having any of the other qualities.*

> If Love is Kind, Why is Love listed alongside Kindness as Fruit?

This question is an important essence of my book, 'In Jesus Name'. Romans 5:5 and 1John 4:7 make clear that we receive the LOVE of God through the Holy Spirit, whom only those who have faith in Jesus Christ can receive. Consequent on receipt of the Love of God, we are empowered for demonstration of love to our fellow man. In light of this expatiation, and in spirit of an amplified reading of the Scriptures, Galatians 5:22-23 can be rephrased as follows.

And the fruit of the Spirit is: the LOVE OF GOD, which first you receive from the Holy Spirit. This LOVE, which you only can receive through the Holy Spirit, produces in you - *joy,* peace, *long-suffering* (modern language would substitute *patience* or *endurance*), *kindness,* goodness, *faith,* meekness, *temperance:* against this LOVE, and *qualities of this* LOVE, which is received from The Father, through the Holy Spirit, whom only can be received in Jesus Christ, there is not any contrary law.

The Things That Are 100 *The Fruit of the Spirit is the* LOVE OF GOD, *equivalently, the* LOVE OF CHRIST, *a quality of Love, which only can be received from The Father, through the Holy Spirit, but only by those who are in Christ. In Galatians 5:22-23, and 1Corinthians 13:4-8, Apostle Paul enumerates characteristics of the Love of God.*

Now then, fruits of the Spirit. In all of the New Testament Scriptures, the word *fruits* is utilized in context not of different types of fruits, but *quantities of the same kind of fruit.* For evidence, consider Matthew 7:17-20; and 2Corinthians 9:10.

So every good tree doth yield good fruits, but the bad tree doth yield evil fruits. A good tree is not able to yield evil fruits, nor a bad tree to yield good fruits. Every tree not yielding good fruit is cut down and is cast to the fire: therefore from their fruits ye shall know them.

And may He who is supplying seed to the sower, and bread for food, supply and multiply your seed sown, and increase the fruits of your righteousness.

It is self evident that good or bad, a single tree yields only one kind of fruit (Matthew 7:19). Our Lord Jesus Christ declares, however, that while it may not be discernible to you or I, that while every fruit on a tree looks alike, they in fact can differ in some respects. So then, a tree yields only one kind of fruit, yet that one kind of fruit can be associated with many different varieties. We have then that a person who has faith in Jesus Christ, who already has the fruit of the Spirit, can accrue more of the same fruit, or different varieties of the same fruit. The apple perhaps is the best illustration of this truth. The same tree can bear green apples, yet all the apples are not of exactly the same shade of green. By the same analogy, an apple tree can bear red apples, yet all of the apples are different shades and patterns of red. So then, while the word fruit applies to a particular type of fruit, e.g fruit of the Spirit, the same fruit appears in different combinations within the body of our Lord Jesus Christ.

Prophecy Principle 152 *The fruit of the Spirit is all of the qualities that we develop with help of the Holy Spirit. When the fruit of the Spirit increases in us, the fruits of our righteousness experiences increase.*

Prophecy Insight 188 *The* TREE OF LIFE *refers our Lord Jesus Christ. The 12* FRUITS *refer to the 12 different shades of the same fruit of the Spirit that are borne by those who have faith in our Lord Jesus Christ.*

The Leaves of the Tree of Life

The leaves of the tree of life are said to be for the healing of the nations. In this respect, consider Jeremiah 17:7-8; Psalms 1:1-3; Ezekiel 47:12; Proverbs 11:28.

> Blessed is the man who trusts in the Lord, whose trust is the Lord. He is like a tree planted by water, that sends out it's roots by the stream, and DOES NOT FEAR WHEN HEAT COMES, FOR IT'S LEAVES REMAIN GREEN, and is not anxious in the year of drought, for it does not cease to bear fruit.

> O the happiness of that one, who hath not walked in the counsel of the wicked. And in the way of sinners hath not stood, and in the seat of scorners hath not sat; But in the law of Jehovah is his delight, and in His law he doth meditate by day and by night: And he hath been as a tree, planted by rivulets of water, that giveth it's fruit in it's season, and IT'S LEAF DOTH NOT WITHER, and all that he doth he causeth to prosper.

> And on the banks, on both sides of the river there will grow all kinds of trees for food. THEIR LEAVES WILL NOT WITHER NOR THEIR FRUIT FAIL, but they will bear fresh fruit every month, because the water for them flows from the sanctuary. Their fruit will be for food, and THEIR LEAVES FOR HEALING.

> He who trusts in his riches will wither, but THE RIGHTEOUS WILL FLOURISH LIKE A GREEN LEAF.

Prophecy Insight 189 *Just as the 12 fruits are produced by those who already have faith in Jesus Christ, so also the leaves of the tree of life are representative of the righteous. We have then that the righteous, those who have faith in the name of Jesus, and who are walking in the faith that works by love are sources of healing to those in the nations who choose to walk in the Love of God.*

Prophecy Insight 190 *If the nations had access to the fruits of the tree of life, they would not need any healing. So then, only those who have yet to know Christ, who have yet to have access to life that is age-during have need of healing, have need of the leaves of the tree of life. The leaves of the tree of life are symbolic of the righteous.*

16.4   Absence of Curses is Spiritual, not Linked to any Physical City

Absence of any curse in the city is straightforwardly spiritual. In this respect, Galatians 2:13-14, and declares as follows:

> Christ did redeem us from the curse of the law, having become for us a curse, for it hath been written, Cursed is every one who is hanging on a tree, that to the nations the blessing of Abraham may come in Christ Jesus, that the promise of the Spirit we may receive through the faith.

> Who did rescue us out of the authority of the darkness, and did translate us into the reign of the Son of His love, in whom we have the redemption through His blood, the forgiveness of sins.

When the nations receive Jesus by faith, they are redeemed from the curse of the law - from the authority of darkness - and translated into the reign (*new heavens and new earth*) of our Lord and Savior Jesus Christ. During His earthly ministry, our Lord Jesus Christ declared that this reign was imminent (Matthew 3:2; 4:17). Daniel 2:1-45, and all of what we have discussed from the Book of Revelation establish that the reign of our Lord Jesus Christ as sole ruler over affairs of earth commenced during the time of the Church in Laodicea.

Prophecy Insight 191 *The New Heavens, New Earth, and the New Jerusalem, and all that is in the New Jerusalem are representative of the spiritual reign of our Lord and Savior Jesus Christ. While this reign is perpetual, and always is, the experience of it by man depends significantly on the state of The Church, and The Nations. Revelation ch. 22 depicts the spiritual reality of the Reign of Christ that is actualized by His Church as outcome of the BP7 PATH of the SSGLAE. If The Church, and The Nations are to remain on the BP7 PATH, both continue to demonstrate righteous responses to The Father.*

16.5   Climate Change

There yet is another dimension to the declaration that the heat of the sun will not fall on the righteous, which is, as the heat of the sun increases over time, such that it scorches those are love evil, those who love righteousness will, miraculously be shielded from such scorching heat. The increase in the heat of the sun is a witness against man's new found sinful pride - sinful pride that, in presence of some achievements of science, makes man want to stride around as god on the face of the earth. If with all of their pronouncements against God, scientists are powerless to prevent the heat of the sun from increasing, should they not become truly humble and acknowledge that proof of existence of God lies outside of questions that can be answered by science? Whenever a scientist declares that on basis of science he or she has concluded that God does not exist, he or she commits the highest form of fraud for it normatively is impossible for science to yield any factual evidence about existence or non-existence of God. So long as scientists continue to run their mouths at God, and society allows itself to be guided into foolish ways because it knowingly places it's trust in such scientists, nature will continue to embarrass the scientific world. Never mind that in face of all of the evidences for presence of fraud in science, all we observe in academia is inertia of *'things continuing as ever they have been'* without any credible signal of meaningful change.

Prophecy Principle 153 *If society seeks a solution to climate change, it needs to stop applauding fraudulent scientists who claim that it is possible to infer non-existence of God from their scientific endeavors. It normatively is impossible for anyone to infer existence or non-existence of God* AS FACT *from scientific endeavors. When Einstein declares that he infers existence of 'God' from the arrangements of the heavens, he declares* BELIEF THAT IS PREDICATED ON THE EVIDENCE, NOT FACT.

Prophecy Principle 154 *It is impossible to infer as factual, non-existence of God from an observation of nature. Evolution of the sort thought possible in plants or man* NEVER *has been witnessed by any scientists whatsoever. So then, we apply the only scientific knowledge that is available, which is, wherever we see order, typically there exists a Creator. It was this scientific fact that Einstein applied for arrival at the belief that there must be a God who is source of the universe.*

Prophecy Principle 155 *A person who chooses not to believe in existence of God cannot premise this on any scientific fact, for all of nature, and man's existence functions on a creator-creation paradigm. Suppose there exists two mutually exclusive events, 'A' and 'not A'. Let 'A' denote 'God exists', and 'not A', 'God does not exist'. If the probability that 'A' is true is greater than 50%, science never is able to recommend 'not A', only can recommend 'A'.* IN PRESENCE OF THE EVIDENCE, THE ONLY BELIEF THAT SCIENCE CAN RECOMMEND TO MAN IS, *'A', God exists.*

16.6 The Unrighteous, Filthy, Righteous, & Sanctified

Revelation 22:11 identifies *four classes* of persons who subsist in context of the Utopia that is outcome of a transversing of the BP7 PATH of the SSGLAE. These four classes of persons are declared to maintain their spiritual states into the very next SSGLAE. Remember, in context of the BP7 PATH, that, *institutionally*, that is, as a collective, The Church was willing to be perfected, and The Nations chose to premise civil laws, and societal interactions on the LOVE OF GOD. While The Church, and The Nations do the right things at an institutional level, there remains room, *at the level of the individual,* for rebellion, against either of the demand that The Church progress to perfection, or the demand that societal interactions be premised on the Love of God. So then, regardless of confluence of right actions at the institutional level, with outcome most of the Church, and most of The Nations comply, there still can be believers in Christ, and Members of the Nations (MTN) who choose not to align with rightness of directionality of efforts within The Church or The Nations.

Remember, the demand that The Church progress to perfection is a higher demand than the demand that The Nations premise civil laws, and societal interactions on the Love of God. While an MTN who premises societal interactions on the Love of God need not experience any spiritual growth in order to be saved, a NEOPHYTE who resists growth that is demanded of the Holy Spirit gives up on his or her faith in Jesus Christ, and, as natural consequence of his or her own actions, may arrive at no other choice, but rejection of the Love of God as basis for societal interactions. The reasoning is fairly straightforward. The call to growth in Christ is a call to a higher revelation of what exactly it means to love a neighbor (Ephesians 3:14-19). When a NEOPHYTE resists this call from the Holy Spirit, he or she falls out with Christ, falls out of the grace of God. We have then that only NEOPHYTES who reject the call to a higher revelation of the Love of God fall out of Christ. I ask then, how exactly can a person, who has rejected a call to a higher revelation of Love, who then transforms into an MTN, become a person who, simultaneously seeks to premise interactions with neighbors on love? It is not that The Father prevents such a person from having a desire to love his or her neighbor, but rather, as natural fallout of rationality of the decision to resist the Holy Spirit, such a person arrives at incapacity for choice of Love of God, rationally arrives at choice of hatreds as basis for societal interactions.

Prophecy Insight 192 *If a* NEOPHYTE *transforms into an* MTN, *it is because he or she rejects a call of the Holy Spirit to a higher revelation of the Love of God. In light of essence of such a transformation, it is unlikely that such a transformation produces an* MTN *who seeks to premise civil laws, and societal interactions on the Love of God.*

The four classes of individuals that are identified in Revelation 22:11 are:

✠ The Unrighteous

✠ The Filthy

✠ The Righteous

✠ The Sanctified

Friend, right away, our Lord Jesus Christ reemphasizes the dichotomy between those who are declared Righteous - NEOPHYTES, and those who not only are declared righteous, but who also have attained to a Perfect Man, that is, POWERS FOR CHRIST.

Hallelujah!

Prophetic Encouragement 8 *If, up until this point, you had doubted this dichotomy, it is important that now, in presence of this evidence, you put your doubts aside, believe this truth, and reevaluate all of the evidence that I have presented for dichotomization of those who have faith in Jesus Christ into* NEOPHYTES *and* POWERS FOR CHRIST.

For aiding, if necessary of your reevaluation of the evidence, consider the following. If THE RIGHTEOUS are exactly the same as THE SANCTIFIED, then the command that they remain as they are merely is repetitive. The most reasonable interpretation regards, the righteous, and the sanctified to be two different groups of believers, and this exactly is representation of Scriptures. In order to be declared Righteous, a person need only declare faith in Jesus Christ (Romans 3:24). Only a person who declares faith in Jesus Christ can participate in sanctification, for the Holy Spirit only is agent of sanctification (2Thessalonians 2:13; 1Peter 1:2), and is available only to those who have faith in Jesus Christ (Galatians 3:13-14). So then, a person who is sanctified is a person who has faith in Jesus Christ, and has been sanctified by the Holy Spirit. It is straightforward then that the Righteous are those who have faith in Jesus Christ, but who have yet to become sanctified by the Holy Spirit, not because they are rebellious, but because of natural process of time, that is, only because there as yet is needed more time for perfecting of their sanctification.

Spiritual Insight 96 *There is not any person who has faith in Christ who will be condemned, because his or her sanctification still is in process. It is the willingness to be sanctified, and the obedience to the Holy Spirit in context of sanctification that keeps a believer in Jesus Christ Righteous in Presence of The Father.*

We arrive then at necessity of discussion of the UNRIGHTEOUS, and the FILTHY. The Filthy are the LOVING CITIZENS OF THE NATIONS (LCN), that is, all those who premise societal interactions on the Love of God, but whose righteousness, in sight of The Father, is no more than filthy rags. In respect of this, consider the following Scriptures.

Whoever knows what is right to do and fails to do it, for him it is sin (James 4:17).

Little children, let no one deceive you. He who practices righteousness is righteous, just as He is righteous (1John 3:7).

But we are all like an unclean thing, and all our righteousnesses are like filthy rags; we all fade as a leaf, and our iniquities (*natural propensities towards sin, as opposed to acts of sin*), like the wind, have taken us away (Isaiah 64:6).

Prophecy Insight 193 *Those who are Filthy are those of The Nations who premise civil laws, and societal interactions on the Love of God, that is,* LOVING CITIZENS OF THE NATIONS. *Having not been covered with the righteousness of Christ, while they are saved by the grace of The Father, relative to the righteousness of Christ, their righteousness is as filthy rags. The Father does not attempt to derogate, merely does not find any other word that conveys essence of stated truth.*

Having characterized all other three groups, the last one, the Unrighteous becomes very easy. The Unrighteous are those of The Nations who reject the Love of God as basis for civil laws, and societal interactions. We already have characterized these persons as HATEFUL CITIZENS OF THE NATIONS (HCN). I already have shown, in the preceding, that those who fall out of faith in Christ typically become hateful citizens of the nations.

Prophecy Insight 194 *The Unrighteous are those of The Nations who reject the Love of God as basis for civil laws, and societal interactions, that is,* HATEFUL CITIZENS OF THE NATIONS.

In the declaration that every group is to remain as they are, The Father declares that He is not an *absolutist*, that He is *pragmatic*, that He considers a BP7 PATH the best possible equilibrium. But what then about all of those Unrighteous persons who remain? Well, *all else equal*, with the Unrighteous a small segment of the population, natural attrition rates, that is, deaths, and earlier timing of deaths for the Unrighteous continuously propel the equilibrium towards a more righteous society. The caveat, ALL ELSE EQUAL is necessitated by the spiritual reality that children who are born in context of the very next SSGLAE, or who were, at culmination of the preceding BP7 PATH, not yet of spiritually responsible age can, in context of the very next SSGLAE choose not to remain on the BP7 PATH.

Prophecy Insight 195 *The declarations: "He who is unrighteous - let him be unrighteous still, and he who is filthy - let him be filthy still, and he who is righteous - let him be declared righteous still, and he who is sanctified -*

let him be sanctified still," are uttered at culmination, that is, completion of every BP7 PATH *of the SSGLAE. By this declaration, people on earth maintain their spiritual states into the very next SSGLAE, an SSGLAE whose character is influenced by actions of those whose spiritual states were not ascertained in context of the preceding SSGLAE.*

Prophecy Insight 196 *Societies, which seek to remain on the BP7* PATH *of the SSGLAE must exercise efforts for investing in their children, for if their children do not themselves, voluntarily arrive at choice of the BP7* PATH, *their parents will not be immune from the pain that is created. But children are to be guided, not controlled, and allowed to arrive at their own choices, for it is impossible for the Love of God to be premised on control from another.*

If a society, which continues to produce children is to remain on the BP7 path of the SSGLAE, and continue to progress in righteousness, such a society must emphasize and reward:

✠ Parental guidance of children, not control, guidance. Women who have children ought to feel empowered to be STAY-AT-HOME moms, and ought not to feel, upon their children turning 12, any shame at seeking of entry or reentry, on basis of their qualifications, into the job market. UNIVERSAL BASIC INCOME that is independent of number of children (*this prevents an association of raising of children with income*) for *stay-at-home* moms is a righteous initiative of Nations who premise civil laws, and societal interactions on the Love of God.

Prophetic Encouragement 9 UNIVERSAL BASIC INCOME *for all stay-at-home moms, income that is dissociated from number of children, is a righteous initiative that is consistent with the Love of God.*

Prophetic Encouragement 10 *A society within which women who choose to raise their own children, who then, as such enter or reenter the job market much later in life are not shamed, rather are celebrated for having the strength to do what they felt was right for them, and their children, celebrates the Love of God.*

Prophetic Encouragement 11 *For women who choose not to be stay-at-home moms, availability of Daycares and Preschools that are premised on demonstration of the Love of God is the next best alternative. It is godly then for Churches to consider Daycares and Preschools as initiatives, which help foster the Love of God in children.*

✠ Importance of written documentation that espouses merits of faith in Jesus Christ. I am not talking here about spiritual merits of Jesus Christ, which of course, is of primary importance, but about what typically has been neglected, which are, intellectual merits of Jesus Christ. By this, I refer to (among other things):

♣ With illustrations from NATURE and/or SCIENCE reasonableness of Triuneness of God

♣ Historicity of birth, life, ministry, and death of Jesus Christ

♣ Reasonableness of a Resurrection, that is, reasonableness of something that never had happened before (evidence that there once was a world devoid of cars, trains, or aeroplanes ought here to suffice)

♣ Evidence that, absent waging of warfare against other men, and with persecution of the faith along the way, within 300 years, faith in Jesus Christ conquered all of the then known world, resulting in the CHRISTIAN BYZANTINE (EASTERN ROMAN) EMPIRE, *the Empire best known, during it's time, for demonstration of Love towards the powerless within it's society.* It should be noted that it was not until subsequent to the demise of the Roman Emperors in 476 AD, that the CHURCH IN WESTERN EUROPE, which hitherto had remained pure, metamorphosed into an apostate papal system with institution of *Gregory I* as Pope.

♣ Intellectual superiority of the belief that man and all of creation is created by God, Father of Jesus Christ

Prophetic Encouragement 12 *The Church needs to develop material, targeted at adolescents, that is, kids of High School age, and beyond, which focus on exposition of intellectual merits of faith in Jesus Christ. This is a matter of paramount importance. By engaging with children on such intellectual questions, believing parents and The Church reinforce in their minds the fact that faith in Jesus Christ is not superstition, is founded on evidence that is possessing of intellectual merits.*

Prophetic Encouragement 13 *Importance of attitudes, choices, decisions, and documentation that celebrate capacity for Love as evidence for either of manliness, or womanliness, that is, as evidence for* STRENGTH OF CHARACTER. *A society that seeks to foster Love in context of societal interactions, but which characterizes Love as evidence for a* WEAK CONSTITUTION *cannot sustain Love as rubric for either of civil laws, or societal interactions.*

Prophetic Encouragement 14 *If Love is to be fostered as a desirable, it must come across to children, and young adults as evidence for strength of character.*

16.7   Chapter Summary

By the grace of our Lord Jesus Christ, I believe I have established, beyond any reasonable doubt, that while the SPIRITUAL RESOLUTION that is domiciled in *Revelation ch. 21* pertains to the RP7 PATH of the SSGLAE, that the spiritual resolution domiciled in *Revelation ch. 22* pertains to the BP7 PATH of the SSGLAE.

Remember the Smoking Gun?

Prophecy Interpretation 101 *If the New Jerusalem in ch. 21 has need of a Lamp, with outcome the Lamb is The Lamp, but the New Jerusalem in ch. 22 does not have any need of a Lamp, clearly, spiritual resolutions depicted in either of the two chapters cannot be descriptive of the exact same spiritual resolution. It is fact then that the Book of Revelation puts forward two different spiritual resolutions of Life and Affairs on Earth. With this caveat in mind, I have proved to you, beyond any reasonable doubt, that the resolution in ch.21 pertains to the RP7 PATH, and that in ch. 22 to the BP7 PATH of the SSGLAE.*

Prophecy Insight 197 *It is important to note that, The Nations having acquiesced civil laws and societal interactions to the Love of God in context of the BP7 PATH, there is not any* OLD HEAVEN AND EARTH *consisting of Nations who repugn God that flees away from the face of our Lord Jesus Christ, meaning there is not any need for* NEW HEAVENS AND NEW EARTH. *New Heavens and New Earth are, as we have seen, spiritually required only in context of the RP7 PATH of the SSGLAE. On the BP7 PATH, the BP7 VERSION of the New Jerusalem, which does not have need of a lamp, as such cannot be identical to the RP7 VERSION, makes her appearance on earth, such that the Nations are blessed.*

What then does Revelation ch. 22 have to say about any future coming of Christ, or does it state that Christ already has come?

Well, as already established in the PREFACE to this book, it is unequivocal that, in *ch. 22*, and at end of *ch. 22*, our Lord Jesus Christ and Apostle John emphatically declare that the Second Coming still is in the future. In this respect, our Lord Jesus Christ declares severally as follows.

"Lo, I COME QUICKLY; happy is he who is keeping the words of the prophecy of this scroll." And "lo, I COME QUICKLY, and my reward is with me, to render to each as his work shall be (Revelation 22:7,12)".

In the very last two verses of *Revelation ch. 22*, Apostle John reiterates future nature of the coming of Christ as follows.

he saith - who is testifying these things - "Yes, I come quickly! Amen!" "Yes, be coming, Lord Jesus!" The grace of our Lord Jesus Christ is with you all. Amen.

It is unequivocal that, at end of all of the revelations that are entrusted to Apostle John, that each of our Lord Jesus Christ, and Apostle John declare that the COMING of Christ remains in future. Given *Revelation ch. 21* is, in entirety, silent on the coming of Christ, a perusal of that chapter neither adds nor detracts from the inference, from *ch. 22*, that the coming of Christ remains in future. In presence of the silence, one perhaps might infer that a coming of Christ is feasible only if Life and Affairs on Earth end up on the BP7 PATH of the SSGLAE. At this point, however, this is mere conjecture, not a statement of proven evidence. What exactly then are we to infer about the COMING of Christ? For that, my friend, you just are going to have to turn the leaf until the next chapter.

Prophecy Insight 198 *Revelation ch. 22 ends with the second coming of Christ still in the future. It is unequivocal then, that none of the events in Revelation chs. 21 & 22 pertain to the Second Coming of Jesus Christ.*

Prophecy Insight 199 IF WE ARE TO INFER ANYTHING THAT IS SPECIFIC TO TIMING OF THE SECOND COMING OF JESUS CHRIST, IT CANNOT BE FROM THE BOOK OF REVELATION.

Prophecy Insight 200 *Outside of the Book of Revelation, our Lord Jesus Christ declares that even if His disciples pay attention to signs, they still would not know the timing of His SECOND COMING (Matthew 24:42,44). The Lord's original apostles agree, declare that the only way to prepare for the Second Coming of Christ is to live a life that is committed to demonstrations of the Love of God that is received by faith in Jesus Christ (1Thessalonians 5:1-11; 2Peter 3:8-13). So then, our discussion of the Second Coming of Christ in the next chapter focuses on what it is about, why it transpires, and what it means for all of the different paths of the SSGLAE, which as you now realize transpire here on earth.*

Prophecy Insight 201 *Friend, remember it is those who do not make effort to ensure they love the truth, and arrive at knowledge of the truth, who either lose their salvation in Christ, or as Hateful Citizens of the Nations, end up under condemnation of God. Of you friend, I am confident of better things.*

CHAPTER 17

The SSGLAE & You

In the preceding chapter, we established *three feasible paths* for The Church and The Nations. Since The Church is made up of individual believers, clearly, the three feasible paths on which the SSGLAE can progress have implications for individuals within The Church. By the same token, the three feasible paths have implications for individuals in The Nations. In this chapter, I explore some of the important implications of SSGLAE paths that are chosen by confluence of The Church and The Nations for believers in Christ, and individuals in The Nations. As already discussed, the three feasible paths for THE CHURCH and THE NATIONS are:

- ℘ The BP7 PATH: The Church is willing to be perfected, and The Nations acquiesce to premising of civil laws, and societal interactions on the Love of God. For concreteness, I refer to this path as the 'Rational' Path.

- ℘ The GP7 PATH: The Church is willing to be perfected, but The Nations do not acquiesce to premising of civil laws, and societal interactions on the Love of God. On this path, it is The Nations that come under judgment. For concreteness, I refer to this path as The Deviant Nations' Path.

- ℘ The RP7 PATH: The Church is not willing to be perfected, and naturally, The Nations do not acquiesce to premising of civil laws, and societal interactions on the Love of God. On this path, it is The Church that comes mostly under judgment. For concreteness, I refer to this path as The Renegade Church Path.

In presence of the three feasible paths, conditional on membership in The Church, and your spiritual state, which we have characterized as either of Neophyte or Power, there exist several feasible outcomes. While there exists a third characterization, Charlatans - *Pretend Christians*, equivalently, False Prophets - I assume that you, the reader, do not belong to this group.

Hallelujah!!!

The GP7 (Deviant Nations') path and You

In presence of unity of The Church, and choice of the GP7 path by The Nations, The Nations are not able to be effective in their persecutions of The Church. During such times, The Nations can, in attempts at intimidation of The Church, adopt *executions* of Powers for Christ as instrument of persecution. This perhaps is the rationale that, at timing of resolution of an RP7 path, there do not exist any Powers in the Church. The outcome of such executions for the Western Roman Empire? From onset of executions of Apostles sometime after *70 AD* by the Western Roman Empire to the deposing of the last Emperor of the Western Roman Empire in *476 AD* is less than 400 years. The Eastern Roman Empire, the Christian Byzantine Empire would continue to wax strong up until about *1056 AD* when it began to take political, as opposed to spiritual decisions for it's welfare.

Prophetic Lessons 73 *It is true that The Nations can, in presence of a united Church, adopt executions of Apostles for attempts at intimidation of The Church. It also is normatively true, however, that they gain nothing, for upon embarkment on such a quest, they compromise their very own prosperity, freedoms, liberty, and self rule.*

Prophetic Lessons 74 *For individuals within the Church or Nations, The Deviant Nations' Path, the GP7* path *is a path that leads to the second worst current and future outcome for society. If you infer a GP7* path, *expect attenuation of prosperity, freedoms, liberty, and self rule. Also expect magnification of conflicts, rumors of impending wars, and incidence of wars both within and between nations.*

The RP7 (Renegade Church) path and You

Babylon, and the two Beasts come into play only on the Renegade Church path. Babylon loves to kill the saints, but itself is burnt by fire by the same kings of the earth with whom she committed harlotry. So then, note the very first object lesson that you should provide you with encouragement.

Prophecy Insight 202 *If Charlatans in Church who point out those who are faithful to Christ for persecution, who themselves persecute those faithful to*

Christ, think that all will be high and dry with them, they are grossly deluded. The same kings with whom they committed harlotry shall burn them with fire, and then shall come the righteous judgments of The Father.

Prophecy Insight 203 *Those who are faithful to Christ experience economic hardships in context of the mark of the beast, and Babylon always is seeking for opportunity to kill them. The pouring out of the Vials of the Wrath of God put an end to the persecutions.*

Prophetic Lessons 75 *For individuals within The Church, or Nations, The Renegade Church path, the RP7* PATH *represents the worst current and future outcome for society. Relative to the GP7* PATH, *expect more of attenuations of prosperity, freedoms, liberty, and self rule. Relative to the GP7* PATH, *there is less of conflicts, rumors of impending wars, and incidence of wars both within and between nations, this because all can focus on persecution of those who are faithful to Christ. But there is more of diseases, particularly, diseases which relate to failure of blood at serving as source of life. Naturally, this is more of a cost on individuals.*

Prophetic Lessons 76 *The GP7* (DEVIANT NATIONS) PATH *is costlier for nations, than it is for individuals. The RP7* (RENEGADE CHURCH) PATH *is as costly, or perhaps even costlier for individuals than it is for nations.*

The BP7 (Rational) path and You

Even for the self proclaimed atheist, the BP7 PATH is the rational path for evolution of Life and Affairs on Earth. Never mind that the term, 'ATHEIST' is somewhat of a misnomer.

Faith AND Rationality 4 *If the probability that God exists is at least 51%, and all of nature, science, and man's own activities attest to this normative, how exactly can anyone be an Atheist? An Agnostic? Feasibly. An Atheist? Totally Unscientific. But then again, Atheism is no more than a play on words.*

The BP7 PATH collapses all of the 7 SEALS into the 7th TRUMPET of the 7th Seal, into the Utopia of *Revelation ch. 22.* Naturally, upon arrival at that Utopia, and unless a generation emerges, whose choices induce either of DEVIANT NATIONS, or a RENEGADE CHURCH, the SSGLAE is, essentially, in hibernation. The way to think about this is as follows. *Generation X* comes along. *Generation X* that is in Church chooses to be perfected in Love. *Generation X* that is in the Nations chooses to premise civil laws, and societal interactions on the Love of God. So then what happens? Every 1st SEAL is collapsed into the *Utopia* of *Revelation ch. 22,* with outcome the Utopia never is broken. So long as the Church continues to delight in being perfected, and the Nations continue to premise civil laws, and societal interactions on the Love of God, only judgments of individual actions remain to be actualized, for there is not any necessity of Grand Judgments. We arrive then at fulfillment of the words by Apostle Paul in 1Corinthians 13:8.

> "THE LOVE (OF CHRIST) DOTH NEVER FAIL; AND WHETHER THERE BE PROPHECIES, THEY SHALL BECOME USELESS..."

Prophecy Insight 204 *If, in context of a BP7* PATH, *a believer in Christ continues to look for emergence of the Beasts, and Babylon, he or she acts on prophecy that, on basis of superiority of the Love of Christ - Love that never fails - has become useless. This is the reason those who have faith in Christ are supposed to live by faith, that is, by the Love of Christ, not by prophecies.*

The Kicker?

In the Utopia of *Revelation ch. 22*, as I shall establish in the next two chapters, Jesus gives rewards to those who have faith in Him, rewards that translate into new abilities, skills, and knowledge that induce new types of products on earth. These are abilities, skills, and knowledge that transform not only the Church, but in partnership with the Nations, transform all of society. These are not the sorts of abilities, skills, and knowledge that can be hidden away in one corporation. These are abilities, skills, and knowledge that transform business, the arts, science, technology, and education; that transform every sphere of life and affairs on earth. In presence of new abilities, skills, and knowledge, life is not at a standstill, rather, there is societal-wide progression in abilities, skills, and knowledge.

Prophecy Insight 205 *For all and sundry - Agnostic, Deist, Muslim, Hindu, Buddhist, New Age Scientist, or believer in the name of Christ, the BP7* PATH - *the* RATIONAL PATH - *is the only path that makes sense.*

CHAPTER 18

The Coming of Jesus Christ

Whenever a person who has faith in Jesus Christ holds on to The Father for newness of life in context of a time during which the Church is apostate, this much like Jacob would not let go of the heavenly messenger until he was blessed (Genesis 32:26), this is what is referred to by our Lord Jesus Christ as '*violent men seizing the reigns of the heavens by force*' (Matthew 11:12). The reign of the heavens is seized by force because absent actions of such men, the Church does not deserve a *totally new iteration of the* SSGLAE. This is evident as follows. Whenever the Church and the Nations repugn the Love of The Father, eventually, the earth finds itself wallowing in the 4th SEAL, that is, in punishment of the nations by The Father, and persecution of those who remain faithful to Christ by The Nations and Babylon. As already discussed, believers who are faithful to Christ, and who die in Christ, go on to become part of the reign of the heavens with Christ. Remember, on the RP7 PATH, only those who die in Christ in course of the 4th SEAL become part of the reign of the heavens with Christ. This is typical resolution of the RP7 PATH of the SSGLAE. Suppose, however, that in course of a 4th SEAL that rather unexpectedly, there are some men who hold on to God until there is release of new anointing from God, new anointing that is evident in new realizations of righteous character, new revelations from The Father, and contrary to an RP7 PATH, evidence for Love Projects entrusted to such Powers by The Father. Just as Jacob wrested a blessing from the heavenly messenger with physical violence, so also via genuine striving for knowledge of The Father and Son (John 17:3), such men wrest a blessing for the earth from The Father, Son, and Holy Spirit. In this context, THE REIGN OF THE HEAVENS IS SEIZED BY FORCE BY THE LIVING, with outcome *righteousness, justice,* and *mercy* of The Father demands that He releases new grace for feasibility of a

459

new 1st Seal period that is commencement of a new SSGLAE, within which, if The Nations respond to said Powers, there is feasibility of truncation of the remainder of the RP7 PATH, and relocation of spiritual state of the earth to the BP7 PATH of the SSGLAE. Remember that, typically, subsequent to the 7 Vials of Wrath, with the devil bound, the *Newly Reconstituted Church* and the saved of the Nations coexist until there is a giving in to the devil that triggers destruction of those who love evil, and resurrection of spirits of the saints to reign with Christ. *This is the spiritual resolution that is domiciled in Revelation ch. 20* and expounded upon in *Revelation ch. 21.* Within context of manifestation of Powers who receive new revelations of Christ, and Love Projects from The Father in context of a 4th SEAL period, however, a phenomenon that is not supposed to occur, in His mercy, justice, and righteousness, The Father provides the earth with opportunity for avoidance of the normal spiritual resolution of the RP7 PATH, with outcome there is opportunity for arrival, not at the spiritual resolution in *Revelation ch. 21,* but at the more glorious spiritual resolution that is in *Revelation ch. 22.* So then, the earth has opportunity to break free from the RP7 PATH, for transition to, were the opportunity to be seized, the BP7 PATH of the SSGLAE.

If the Nations do not repent, with The Church reconstituted around said Powers for Christ, there is arrival at the *Separating Equilibrium* that is the GP7 PATH of the SSGLAE. As already discussed, the GP7 path resolves as follows. The Church ends up, by itself, and along with *Loving Citizens of the Nations (LCN)* in the Utopia of *Revelation ch. 22.* The DEVIANT NATIONS remain on OLD HEAVENS AND EARTH that, of necessity, flee from the Presence of Christ. Until, somehow, some people located in the Deviant Nations lift up their eyes for recognition of Sovereignty of The Father (Daniel 4:34), the Deviant Nations remain on Old Heavens and Earth. Simultaneously, for as long as the Church continues to choose to be perfected, she remains in the UTOPIA of *Revelation ch. 22.* The effect of this separating equilibrium?

Prophetic Lessons 77 *The Father does not any longer make any concerted effort to win Deviant Nations to Himself, meaning the Church focuses on ministering to individuals. If Deviant Nations are to regain consciousness of God at an institutional level, it will have to be because some rise up among them who seize the reign of the heavens by force.* BUT IS THAT NOT EXACTLY THE OPPORTUNITY THAT THEY REPUGNED, THAT GOT THEM ON OLD HEAVENS AND EARTH IN THE FIRST PLACE?

Prophetic Lessons 78 *Remember, on Old Heavens and Earth, man who loves evil is, by the work of His Creator, placed in a spiritual state characterized by incapacity for functioning as a spirit.*

An illustration of a man who, in midst of great darkness in respect of what exactly it means to have faith in Jesus Christ, received revelations from The Father is Francis Schaeffer - author of the book, 'True Spirituality'. In midst of not arriving at experience of what is promised in the gospels - *peace and joy in the Holy Spirit* - Francis Schaeffer refused to doubt, set his heart to seek The Father for revelation of what was wrong with His Christian experience. In his decision to cling to The Father and not let go, he received the revelation that is *True Spirituality*, a book that would change my life, a book that enabled me arrive at the answers I was searching for when I, much like Francis Schaeffer, could not relate my experience of Christ with what is promised to faith in Jesus Christ. My book, 'In Jesus Name' starts off where *True Spirituality* leaves off, is not a duplication of *True Spirituality*. *True Spirituality* helps a believer understand how to demonstrate faith in Christ. My book, IN JESUS NAME helps a believer understand meaning of '*faith in the name of Jesus Christ*' as a concept, in of itself; how it is that faith has to be applied, first and foremost, to receipt of the Love of God, this through The Holy Spirit; and the things he or she has to do if that love is to be actualized, if that love is to become part of himself or herself. My book, True Sanctification helps a believer arrive at a better understanding of what exactly the Father means when He says He has prepared beforehand good works in which believers are supposed to participate (Ephesians 2:10). *True Sanctification* shows how, absent submission to, and participation in The Father's will, as set forth in whatever He already has prepared, a believer is not able to arrive at the very best version of his or her own self. In essence, *True Sanctification* reveals to believers the following truth which is, it is only via submission to, and participation in The Father's pre-ordained will, which is designed for his or her sanctification, that a believer is able to fully actualize his or her own self. My book, Divine Meritocracy reveals to believers an important truth which is, equality of intrinsic worth before God does not imply equality of regard from The Father. The book goes on to reveal to believers the keys to accruing of merit in presence of Father, Son, and Holy Spirit. As you already have seen, this book reveals deep things of the Spirit, with outcome believers arrive at new appreciation for the love and thoughtfulness of The Father in respect of those who are heirs of salvation. In the institution of the SSGLAE, The Father has ensured that your actions and mine have power for influencing of affairs on earth. The Father and our Lord Jesus Christ have, via careful thought, planning, sacrifices, and victories ensured your faith and mine are not just abstracts on earth, have ensured your faith and mine have power for moving of mountains, have power for changing of the course of the earth.

Prophetic Encouragement 15 *I know, in my spirit, that my books, '*TRUTHS THAT CREATE OR ENHANCE, LOVING RELATIONSHIPS*', '*IN JESUS NAME*', '*TRUE SANCTIFICATION*', '*DIVINE MERITOCRACY*', and this book that you currently read are revelations from Father, Son, and Holy Spirit designed for ushering of the earth into a new iteration of the SSGLAE that is rooted in knowledge of how* *exactly to arrive at the Presence of Christ. But has the message already been rejected by The Church and The Nations in the spirit (the work may already have been sensed in the spirit, and already been rejected), or is that new iteration of the SSGLAE still feasible? Regardless, friend, when you rejoice in, and practice truths that you encounter in my books, you set yourself in the good graces of our Lord and Savior Jesus Christ. Remember, there are three levels of judgment, INDIVIDUAL, CHURCH, and NATION. In presence of judgment of the Church, and Nations as evil, you still are +able to arrive at salvation in Christ.*

If it is self aggrandizement you and I seek, it would be easier to achieve such an objective via alignment of ourselves with an apostate Church, or via alignment with a world that refuses to function on basis of love. Only those who are truly are meek, who then inherit the land (Matthew 5:5), are willing to strive for knowledge of God that brings with it anointing for ushering of the earth into new beginnings.

Prophecy Principle 156 *It is a grave (important), yet joyous and loving responsibility or opportunity that The Father has made available to you and I in context of institution of the SSGLAE.*

The Coming of Christ

Friend, I have shocking news for you that I have reserved until this time. I have reserved it until this time, because all that you needed to know, such that you are able to absorb the shock, such that you are able to recognize the truth for what it is, I first had to present. In this respect, we already have established that:

♣ The PRESENCE OF CHRIST, equivalently, REIGN OF CHRIST is, in entirety, spiritual, not physical.

♣ The Father has made allowance for the THREE PATHS (*BP7*, *GP7*, or *RP7*) that, conditional on choices of the Church, and the Nations, feasibly could subsist in all of eternity. Note that, outside of these three paths, there do not exist any others that are feasible.

♣ The SSGLAE exists in perpetuity, that is, forever, for guidance of evolution of Life and Affairs on Earth.

♣ God has given the earth to man, and absent some extreme realizations of disobedience from either of the Church, or the Nations, desires that life continue on earth, in perpetuity.

♣ Conditional on it been chosen in perpetuity, the BP7 PATH of the SS-GLAE makes possible a glorious perpetual Utopia for Life and Affairs on Earth.

What then is the shocking news?

✠ First, what you may construe to be 'NOT-SO-GOOD' NEWS, but which in reality is good news which is: The Coming of our Lord Jesus Christ is, in entirety, spiritual, not physical.

✠ The evidence that the SHOCKING NEWS is, in actuality, 'GOOD NEWS'? Jesus will appear spiritually on earth for your salvation as many times as are deemed necessary by The Father of our Lord Jesus Christ.

✠ You see then, that in entirety, I bring you 'SHOCKING GOOD NEWS'.

Talk is cheap. On then to the Evidence

I commence at the most credible point, which is, with some of the very last words spoken by our Lord Jesus Christ to Apostle John in context of the revelations that are recorded for your benefit and mine in the Book of Revelation. The words in question can be found in Revelation 22:12, which declares,

> Lo, I come quickly,; happy is he who is keeping the words of the prophecy of this scroll. And lo, I come quickly, and my reward is with me, to render to each as his work shall be.

In their lack of understanding of the meaning of the phrase, 'ACCORDING AS HIS WORK SHALL BE' in the original text, the *NKJV* and *World English Bible (WEB)* truncate the phrase, interpret it as:

> 'according to his work'.

In their assumption of a SECOND COMING of Christ, the *RSV* and *NIV* interpret the phrase as:

> 'according to what he has done.'

With focus on faithfulness to the original text, yet perhaps with acknowledgment in his heart of a rendition that must have been puzzling, the *Webster's Bible (WBS)* interprets the phrase correctly as:

> 'according as his work shall be'

We already have established, in previous chapters that our Lord Jesus Christ will not, again, in a bodily form, step foot on the earth (Matthew 24:23-26). Well then, if Jesus says He is Coming, and that He will distribute rewards that facilitate new work on earth, meaning, subsequent to His Coming, work continues on earth, the only feasible interpretation of the word Coming is spiritual.

Prophecy Insight 206 *It is unequivocal, when our Lord Jesus Christ refers to His Coming in the Book of Revelation, He refers to a spiritual event, which induces distribution of rewards that facilitate good works on earth, that is, that facilitate Love Projects.*

What then about all other texts that declare 'Coming' of Jesus Christ in the Book of Revelation?

John to the seven assemblies that are in Asia: Grace to you, and peace, from Him who is, and who was, and who is coming, and from the Seven Spirits that are before His throne (Revelation 1:4).

I am the Alpha and the Omega, beginning and end, saith the Lord, who is, and who was, and who is coming - the Almighty (Revelation 1:8).

"Holy, holy, holy, Lord God Almighty, who was, and who is, and who is coming (Revelation 4:8)."

We give thanks to Thee, O Lord God, The Almighty, who art, and who wast, and who art coming, because Thou hast taken Thy great power and didst reign (Revelation 11:17).

In the two Scriptures in which it is persons in the visions who declare that Jesus is He who was, who is, and who is coming, the persons engaged in the declarations are the 24 ELDERS and 4 LIVING CREATURES. We already have established that the 24 ELDERS and 4 LIVING CREATURES reign on earth (Revelation 5:8-10), as such are on earth. So then, we have confirmation that Jesus comes to earth, conducts transactions on earth, yet does not appear in bodily form on earth, with outcome His Coming is, in entirety, spiritual.

Prophecy Insight 207 *All of the Scriptures in the Book of Revelation, which relate to the Coming of Christ imply His Coming is spiritual, not physical.*

What then about all other texts in which Jesus declares, 'I come to thee' in the Book of Revelation?

Remember, then, whence thou hast fallen, and reform, and the first works do; and if not, I COME TO THEE QUICKLY, and will remove thy lamp-stand from its place - if thou mayest not reform; He who is having an ear - let him hear what the Spirit saith to the assemblies: TO HIM WHO IS OVERCOMING - I WILL GIVE to him to eat of the tree of life that is in the midst of the paradise of God (Revelation 2:5,7).

Reform! and if not, I COME TO THEE QUICKLY, and will fight against them with the sword of my mouth. He who is having an ear - let him hear what the Spirit saith to the assemblies: TO HIM WHO IS OVERCOMING, I WILL GIVE to him to eat from the hidden manna, and will give to him a white stone, and upon the stone a new name written, that no one knew except him who is receiving it (Revelation 2:16-17).

LO, I COME QUICKLY, be holding fast that which thou hast, that no one may receive thy crown. HE WHO IS OVERCOMING - I WILL MAKE him a pillar in the sanctuary of my God, and without he may not go any more, and I will write upon him the name of my God, and the name of the city of my God, the new Jerusalem, that doth come down out of the heaven from my God - also my new name (Revelation 3:11-12).

Prophecy Principle 157 *Jesus promised 'a Coming' to only three of the seven Churches in Revelation chs. 2 & 3. It is evident then that a 'Coming' of our Lord Jesus Christ is premised on satisfaction of certain conditions.*

In *Revelation 2:5,7*, speaking to the somewhat backslidden CHURCH IN EPHESUS (*100 to 280 AD*), our Lord Jesus Christ emphatically declares *conditional* imminence of a spiritual visit in future. Friend, we know that the time of the Church in Ephesus ceased no later than *302 AD*, and perhaps earlier at *280 AD*. We know, however, that the Church in Ephesus reformed, transformed into the Church in Smyrna, which was a healthy Church that was not lacking in any particular. It would seem then that the conditional spiritual visit was not triggered.

In *Revelation 2:16-17*, speaking to the CHURCH IN PERGAMUM (*325 to 1055 AD*), our Lord Jesus Christ again warns that if the Church does not reform, He would come to them quickly. Given the Church that followed after, that is, the *Church in Thyatira*, found itself in a worse spiritual situation, clearly, the Church in Pergamum did not reform. Absence of reformation is evident in the fact that while the Church in Thyatira is guilty of the same sins as the Church in Pergamum, in addition, the Church in Thyatira tolerates a teacher who is openly promoting idolatry and whoredom in the Church in Thyatira. Well then, what transpired in *1056 AD*? The line of the Macedonian Dynasty, which had ruled over the Byzantine Empire with ethos of teachings of Jesus Christ died off without an heir to inherit the throne. From *1056 AD* onwards, would mark downslide of the Christian Byzantine Empire. We arrive then at the inference that our Lord Jesus Christ did manifest spiritually for judgment of the Church in Pergamum.

Historical Spiritual Nugget 37 *There is evidence in history that the* CHURCH IN PERGAMUM *experienced a spiritual visit - a Coming of - The Lord Jesus Christ, a spiritual visit predicated on necessity of imposition of a judgment.*

In *Revelation 3:11-12*, speaking to the CHURCH IN PHILADELPHIA (*1188 to 1453 AD*), a Church that was weak, but yet faithful to Christ, our Lord Jesus Christ promises a spiritual visit that is premised, in entirety, on their faithfulness to Him. The spiritual visit would be, in entirety, for conferring of rewards on those who are overcoming. It would seem that the sack of Constantinople by the 4th CRUSADE in *1204 AD* is premised on the spiritual visit of our Lord and Savior Jesus Christ. Note that it is only to the Church in Philadelphia that our Lord Jesus Christ declares that He will write on them the name of the city of His God, the New Jerusalem. By this, our Lord Jesus Christ declared that Christianity would not any longer be defined by a city on earth - Constantinople - but by the heavenly Jerusalem. THE CONFIRMATION? As we already have discussed, in the message to the CHURCH IN LAODICEA, our Lord Jesus Christ declares individualization of the Gospel, with outcome from then henceforth, a Christian would be defined as a person who has fellowship with the Spirit of Jesus Christ. Consider then this fact, which is, ALL OF THE REFORMERS, such as *Zwingli* (*1484-1531*), *Martin Luther* (*1483-1546*), *Carlstadt* (contemporary of Martin Luther, timing of birth not known), *Heinreich Bullinger* (*1504-75*), and *John Knox* (*1513-72*) WERE BORN SUBSEQUENT TO 1453 AD. It would seem then that they had access to spirits who had been qualified for reign of the heavens in context of the preceding six Churches.

The resulting inference?

Prophecy Interpretation 102 *Our Lord Jesus Christ manifests spiritually in sense of a 'Coming' whenever there is either of* DISCIPLINE *(punishments or deterrents) to be imposed, or* REWARDS *to be conferred on a Church.*

> What Then is Essence of 'Coming' of Jesus Christ?

Alright then, what about all of that discussion in Matthew ch. 24? Surely, this interpretation cannot hold up can it?

I already have, in Chapter 3, demonstrated that the word, in Matthew 24:3, that is translated, 'COMING' in all other translations, is more accurately rendered, 'PRESENCE' in the *Young's Literal Translation* of Christian Scriptures. In that chapter, I went on to demonstrate that the word, PRESENCE does not have the same connotation as the word, COMING. We went on from that Chapter to establish that the Presence of Christ means spiritual realities of the Gospel operate solely at the level of the individual.

Prophetic Lessons 79 *In addition to dichotomization of 'Presence' from 'Coming', with exception of the phrase, 'Coming with the Clouds', I demonstrated, in Chapter 3, that as used in Matthew ch. 24, the word 'COMING', has, in entirety, a* SPIRITUAL MEANING, *does not imply any sort of physical appearance.*

SOME SCRIPTURE FOR JOLTING OF THE SPIRIT?

To whom coming - a living stone - by men, indeed, having been disapproved of, but with God choice, precious, and YE YOURSELVES, AS LIVING STONES, ARE BUILT UP, A SPIRITUAL HOUSE, a holy priesthood, to offer up spiritual sacrifices acceptable to God through Jesus Christ (1Peter 2:4-5).

Then, therefore, ye are no more strangers and foreigners, but fellow-citizens of the saints, and of the household of God, being built upon the foundation of the apostles and prophets, Jesus Christ Himself being chief cornerstone, in whom all the building fitly framed together doth increase to an holy sanctuary in the Lord, *in whom also ye are builded together, for a habitation of God in the Spirit* (Ephesians 2:19-20).

Prophecy Insight 208 *The* NEW JERUSALEM *is, in entirety, made up of spirits of the saints.* THERE IS NOT A CHURCH STONE. *All of the Stones are representative of individual believers in the name of Jesus Christ.*

Prophecy Insight 209 *The Church serves as aggregator and facilitator of enhancement of spiritual realities attained to by individual believers in the name of Jesus Christ. Facilitation of enhancement transpires in context of* MUTUAL UPBUILDING *of one another (iron sharpening iron, Proverbs 27:17; Hebrews 10:24-25; Romans 15:14; Colossians 3:16). If individuals do not attain, the Church does not attain. If individuals attain, and The Church recognizes, the Church attains.*

I already have established that our Lord Jesus Christ ushered in His Presence in context of the endless time of the CHURCH IN LAODICEA, the Church of our times. Clearly, COMING simultaneously means, 'not Present, then Appearing'. By the same token, if PRESENCE has arrived, then COMING cannot any longer be construed to mean 'not Present, then Appearing'. Using the messages of our Lord Jesus Christ to the seven Churches, and the immediately preceding discussion, clearly, up until the time of the CHURCH IN PHILADELPHIA, Jesus was *Coming*, meaning He was *not Present*, but, as necessary, was *Appearing*. But then, His Presence arrived in context of the time of the Church in Laodicea, with outcome the word COMING cannot any longer be interpreted as not Present, but, as necessary, Appearing.

We already have established the answer.

In the preceding, we established that our Lord Jesus Christ applies the word COMING to manifestations of His Presence for execution of JUDGMENT, or REWARD of the righteous. Now that His Presence already is with us, the word Coming implies only the actions to be executed, that is, GRAND JUDGMENTS, or GIVING OF REWARDS TO THE RIGHTEOUS.

Prophecy Interpretation 103 *Given The Presence of our Lord Jesus Christ already is with us, the word Coming connotes actions to be executed, namely, 'EXECUTION OF GRAND JUDGMENTS', or 'AWARDING OF REWARDS TO THE RIGHTEOUS'. This was exactly our conclusions in exposition of Matthew ch. 24 in Chapter 3.*

Prophecy Interpretation 104 *In Chapter 6, in the Numerology of The Father, with execution of* GRAND JUDGMENTS *(GJ) domiciled in context of the 6th* SEAL *and* REWARD OF THE RIGHTEOUS *(CC) domiciled in context of the 7th* SEAL, *GJ and CC transpire at the same time. We already have, in preceding Chapters confirmed this to be true.*

The validating words from our Lord Jesus Christ?

In the original text, and in the Gospels, our Lord Jesus Christ used the word, 'Coming' in context of an 'appearance' of Himself only in Matthew 24:30; 26:64. The words in those texts are replicated in Mark 13:26; 14:62, and Luke 21:27.

> And then shall appear the sign of the Son of Man in the heaven; and then shall all the tribes of the earth smite the breast, and they shall see the Son of Man coming upon the clouds of the heaven, with power and much glory; and He shall send His messengers with a great sound of a trumpet, and they shall gather together His chosen from the four winds, from the ends of the heavens unto the ends thereof (Matthew 24:30-31).

> And Jesus was silent. And the chief priest answering said to Him, "I adjure thee, by the living God, that thou mayest say to us,

if thou art the Christ - the Son of God." Jesus saith to him, "Thou hast said; nevertheless I say to you, hereafter ye shall see the Son of Man sitting on the right hand of the power, and coming upon the clouds, of the heaven (Matthew 26:63-64)."

In all of the preceding chapters, we have seen that right interpretation of prophecies is rooted in right understanding of symbolisms. The key to understanding of the two texts above, which unequivocally are used by Christ in context of giving of prophecies to his disciples, is understanding of the symbolism. From *Revelation chs. 21 & 22*, we arrived at the understanding that the SUN and the MOON are not literal, are symbolic of LIGHT and TIME. In respect of their symbolism of TIME and LIGHT and their capacity for ruling over affairs of earth, The Father Himself declares as follows in Genesis 1:14,15-16.

> And God saith, "Let luminaries be in the expanse of the heavens, to make a separation between the day and the night, then *they have been* for SIGNS, and for SEASONS, and for DAYS and YEARS.

> And they have been for luminaries in the expanse of the heavens to give light upon the earth. And it is so. And God maketh the two great luminaries in the expanse of the heavens to give light upon the earth. And God maketh the two great luminaries, the great luminary for the rule of the day, and the small luminary - and the stars - for the rule of the night.

Prophecy Insight 210 *A Luminary is not just a Light; a Luminary does something that is not characteristic of all lights, that is, produces Insights. So then, The Sun and Moon always had been created to provide not just* PHYSICAL LIGHT, *but also Insight into Seasons and Essence of the Time.*

Friend, what does our Lord Jesus Christ state about the New Jerusalem that is outcome of the RP7 PATH in *Revelation ch. 21*, or outcome of the BP7 PATH in *Revelation ch. 22*?

> And the city hath no need of the sun, nor of the moon, that they may shine in it; for the glory of God did lighten it, and THE LAMP OF IT IS THE LAMB (Revelation 21:23).

> And night shall not be there (*so no need of a moon*), and THEY HAVE NO NEED OF A LAMP and light of a sun, because the Lord God doth give them light, and they shall reign - to the ages of the ages (Revelation 22:5).

Throughout this book, I have been asserting, and providing evidence that, commencing with arrival of the Presence of Christ in context of the CHURCH IN LAODICEA, that The Father has suspended time as *Arbiter* of *Life and Affairs on Earth*. By The Father's own words, the Sun and Moon were set as arbiters of Time, such that they were arbiters of Life and Affairs on Earth. It was this 'power' given to the Sun and Moon that led ancient peoples to, with recognition of the Sun as the '*greater light*', worship the Sun. Naturally, if they did this in ignorance, with outcome they treated one another right, The Father did not hold this against them.

BUT THEN, I DIGRESS.

In the declaration that the New Jerusalem of the RP7 PATH does not have need of the light of the Sun or the Moon, and the declaration, as we have seen in *Chapter 16*, that the WORKS OF THE SAINTS are the light of the New Jerusalem, The Father declares suspension of Governance of Life and Affairs on Earth by either of the Sun or the Moon. So then, the Sun and Moon are symbolic of Governance of Life and Affairs on Earth, equivalently, symbolic of Time.

Prophecy Interpretation 105 *On the RP7* PATH *of the SSGLAE, the works of the saints supersede the* SUN *and* MOON *as Arbiters of Evolution of Life and Affairs on Earth. So then, those who look to the* SEASONS, *or to* TIME *for guidance as to what to do are unable to live in the will of The Father.*

With respect to the BP7 PATH, in the declaration that the light of the sun is not needed, our Lord Jesus Christ declares that it is not that there is not DAY (demand for the Sun), but rather that the light from The Father renders the light from the Sun unnecessary. We arrive then again at declaration of suspension of Governance of Life and Affairs on Earth by the Sun. So then, the Sun is symbolic of Governance of Life and Affairs on Earth, equivalently, symbolic of Time.

Prophecy Interpretation 106 *On the BP7* PATH *of the SSGLAE, the Light from The Father supersedes the* SUN *as Arbiter of Evolution of Life and Affairs on Earth.*

Corroborating Evidence?

For yourselves have known thoroughly that the day of the Lord as a thief in the night doth come, for when they may say, 'Peace and surety,' then sudden destruction doth stand by them, as the travail doth her who is with child, and they shall not escape; and *ye, brethren, are not in darkness*, that the day may catch you as a thief; all YE ARE SONS OF LIGHT, AND SONS OF DAY; *we are not of night, nor of darkness,* so then, we may not sleep as also the others but watch and be sober (1Thessalonians 5:2-6).

And this is the message that we have heard from Him, and announce to you, that God is Light, and darkness in Him is not at all; if we may say - we have fellowship with Him, and in the darkness may walk, we lie, and do not the truth; and IF IN THE LIGHT WE MAY WALK, as He is in the light - we have fellowship one with another, and *the blood of Jesus Christ His Son doth cleanse us from every sin* (1John 1:5-6).

The night did advance, and the day came nigh; let us lay aside, therefore, the works of the darkness, and let us put on the armor of the light; AS IN DAY-TIME, LET US WALK BECOMINGLY; not in revellings and drunkennesses, not in chamberings and lasciviousnesses, not in strife and emulation; but put ye on the Lord Jesus Christ, and for the flesh take no forethought - for desires (Romans 13:12-14).

And risen to you, ye who fear My name, hath the SUN OF RIGHTEOUSNESS - and healing in it's wings, and ye have gone forth, and have increased as calves of a stall (Malachi 4:2).

Arise, be bright, for come hath thy light, and the honor of Jehovah hath risen on thee. For, lo, the darkness doth cover the earth, and thick darkness the peoples, and ON THEE RISE DOTH JEHOVAH, AND HIS HONOR ON THEE IS SEEN. And come have nations to thy light, and kings to the brightness of thy rising (Isaiah 60:1-3).

Prophecy Insight 211 *Whenever The Church is in obedience to her Lord and Savior, Jesus Christ, The Church is in the Light, The Church walks as in the Day, The Church does not know Night, as such does not have any need of a Moon. Yet, however, the Light from The Father renders the light of the Sun unnecessary, with outcome Time is superseded by The Father's agenda for cleansing of His Church, such that she becomes a perfect Bride for Christ.*

Having now established that natural phenomena, such as Sun and Moon have spiritual symbolism, what exactly is spiritual symbolism of 'Clouds?'

O Jehovah, in the heavens is Thy kindness, Thy faithfulness is unto the CLOUDS (Psalms 36:5).

For great unto the heavens is Thy kindness, and unto the CLOUDS Thy truth (Psalms 57:10).

Ascribe ye strength to God, over Israel is His excellency, and His strength in the CLOUDS (Psalms 68:34).

Who is laying the beam of His upper chambers in the waters, Who is making thick CLOUDS His chariot, Who is walking on wings of wind (Psalms 104:3).

Drop, ye heavens, from above, and CLOUDS do cause righteousness to flow, Earth openeth, and they are fruitful, Salvation and righteousness spring up together, I, Jehovah, have prepared it (Isaiah 45:8).

And there is a word of Jehovah unto me, saying: Son of man, prophesy, and thou hast said: Thus said the Lord Jehovah: Howl ye, ha! for the day! For near is a day, near is a day to Jehovah! A day of CLOUDS, the time of nations it is (Ezekiel 30:1-3).

Using Symbolisms in the Scriptures, Clouds are symbolic of INVISIBLE SPIRITUAL ENERGY, which likely are spirits given birth to by The Father, that are sources of GASES, which produce *Clouds*. So then The Strength of The Father is evident in CLOUDS. In absence of a storm, Clouds, which consist of gaseous matter formed around air particles, can force a plane to alter it's path of travel. So then, the Truth that life was created out of nothing that already was physical, is evident in the CLOUDS, for gases that are sources of Clouds are invisible to the naked eye. When we observe the CLOUDS, much like the *rainbow*, The Father reminds us of His faithfulness to maintenance of life on earth. When The Father moves through space and time, the invisible spiritual energy that is His creation, that is source of CLOUDS, is His Chariot. When CLOUDS are thick, there is omen of Judgment. Science concurs, declares that all of life came out of GASES in the atmosphere. So then, what is seen, CLOUDS, appear out of what is not seen, the *Invisible Spiritual Energy*, that itself is created by The Father, He who is source of life on earth.

All allusions to CLOUDS in the Book of Revelation are consistent with the foregoing characterization. In *Revelation 10:1*, a 'strong messenger' out of heaven is clothed with a CLOUD (*strength*, *faithfulness* of The Father to maintenance of life on earth, the *truth* that what is, came out of what does not appear), and has a rainbow on his head (*assurance* of continuation of life on earth), and his face is as the sun (*light*). In *Revelation 11:12*, the two messengers go up to heaven in a CLOUD, that is, with assistance of invisible spiritual energy. In Revelation 14:14-16, a CLOUD has symbolism of a *Chariot* that enables reaping of the earth. Further, in the symbolism that the earth is reaped while our Lord Jesus Christ sits on a white cloud, there is assurance of *faithfulness* of The Father to maintenance of life on earth.

Additional Corroborating Scriptural Evidence?

By faith, we understand the ages to have been prepared by a saying of God, in regard to the things seen not having come out of things appearing (Hebrews 11:3).

Lo, He doth come with the CLOUDS, and *see him shall every eye*, even those who did pierce Him, and wail because of Him shall all the tribes of the land. Yes! Amen (Revelation 1:7).

YOUR EYE IS THE LAMP OF YOUR BODY; when your eye is sound, your whole body is full of light; but when it is not sound, your body is full of darkness. Therefore BE CAREFUL LEST THE LIGHT IN YOU BE DARKNESS. If then your whole body is full of light, having no part dark, it will be wholly bright, as when a lamp with it's rays gives you light (Luke 11:34-36).

Prophecy Interpretation 107 *The declaration that, 'ALL EYES WILL SEE JE-SUS WHEN HE RETURNS TO EARTH', is a spiritual declaration, meaning the return of Jesus to earth is spiritual, not physical.*

Prophecy Interpretation 108 *When Jesus declares that He comes with the* CLOUDS, *He declares that His Spiritual Appearance for* EXECUTION OF JUDG-MENT *and* AWARDING OF REWARDS *will be evident in the atmosphere of life on earth. So then, His Coming, His arrival for judgment and salvation will be seen to all the ends of the earth, for all of earth lives in atmosphere, that is, in contact with the invisible spiritual energy that is source of* INVISIBLE GASES, *and their product,* CLOUDS.

Prophecy Interpretation 109 *Now that the Presence of our Lord Jesus Christ has been on Earth since timing of the Church in Laodicea, His Coming only is symbolic of* EXECUTION OF JUDGMENT *and* AWARDING OF REWARDS.

Prophecy Interpretation 110 *We already have established that Rewards are given only so the Righteous are able to continue with* CONCEPTION, FORMULA-TION, *and* IMPLEMENTATION *of Love Projects in context of the Utopia that is the New Jerusalem's interactions with the Nations.*

Prophecy Interpretation 111 *Allocation of Rewards, such that Love Projects are possible occurs only in context of spiritual resolution of the BP7* PATH *of the SSGLAE.*

Prophecy Interpretation 112 THE PRESENCE OF JESUS ALREADY IS ON EARTH. JESUS ALREADY HAS APPEARED SPIRITUALLY, PERHAPS MANY TIMES OVER, FOR SALVATION OF THOSE WHO WAIT FOR HIM *(1 Corinthians 16:22; Hebrews 9:28).*

Hallelujah!!!

What then about some of those prophecies by our Lord Jesus Christ in Matthew ch. 24; how exactly do those fit into the characterization of 'Coming' of Christ?

✠ Breaking down *Matthew 24:1-14* in relation to the SSGLAE

♣ *vs. 3*: The disciples of Jesus ask - *"What is the sign of Thy Presence, and of the full end of the age?"*

♣ *vs. 5*: In context of the 4th SEAL of the RP7 PATH, a false prophet (Second Beast) prophesied to emerge. By the way, note that in Scripture, 'A BEAST' is a spirit, which stubbornly refuses to apply it's *cognition*; a spirit which stubbornly refuses to acknowledge that it has a mind capable of reasoning.

♣ *vs. 6*: The 2nd SEAL, which pertains to each of the GP7 and RP7 PATHS, is characterized by wars. Consider the explicit admonition from Jesus in *vs. 6* - *"See, be not troubled, for it behoveth all these to come to pass, but the end is not yet."*

♣ *vs. 7*: In context of the 4th SEAL, The Father unleashes death and hades, which naturally adopt famines, pestilences, rising of nations against one another, earthquakes etc. for unleashing of death on man. Note again the words of our Lord Jesus Christ in *vs. 8* - *"And all these are the beginning (not ending) of sorrows."*

♣ *vs. 9-14*: The consistency that has been missing in all of those prior interpretations that assumed 'Coming' was physical? With focus on the RP7 PATH of the SSGLAE, our Lord Jesus Christ next delves into arrival of persecution that is aided by false prophets in context of the 4th SEAL. Then our Lord Jesus Christ prophecies the *love of many will run cold*, meaning, THE CHURCH BECOMES LARGELY APOSTATE. But then the Church is newly reconstituted (in context of the 7 Vials of the WRATH OF GOD), and the Newly Reconstituted Church preaches the *Good News of Christ* as a testimony to the nations (The Millenium) and then, the end comes - The Great White Throne Judgment, the fleeing of the Old Heaven and Earth, and constitution of New Heavens, New Earth, and the New Jerusalem.

Prophetic Lessons 80 *It is unequivocally true. In Matthew 24:3-14, our Lord Jesus Christ provides a description of events that transpire between the 1st SEAL of the SSGLAE, with movement through the GP7 PATH, which transforms into an RP7 PATH, then culminates in the spiritual resolution, New Heavens, New Earth, and New Jerusalem of Revelation ch. 21.*

Prophetic Lessons 81 *If we assume that the devolution from the GP7 path to the RP7 path, eventually transforms into the BP7 path, we arrive at two sequential resolutions that take us from one degree of glory to another; that is, we experience each of the spiritual resolutions in Revelation chs. 21 & 22.*

✠ Breaking down *Matthew 24:15-28* in relation to the SSGLAE

♣ Prophecy about the destruction of Jerusalem.

♣ Reiteration of emergence of false Christs, which as we know from writings of the Apostles, transpired in time of the Apostles.

♣ Reiteration of the truth that He, Jesus will never again set foot on earth.

♣ Advancement of the truth already discussed, that all will become aware of His Presence.

✠ Breaking down *Matthew 24:29-31* in relation to the SSGLAE

♣ The sun being darkened, and the moon not giving her light, and the stars falling from the heaven, and shaking of the powers of the heavens all are spiritual, not physical. Since the sun, moon, and stars are supposed to be luminaries, note that Jesus declares that those who look to the sun, moon, and stars for guidance will not find any meaningful guidance. We already have discussed this in the preceding.

♣ Jesus comes on the CLOUDS, that is, His Presence arrives. In Matthew 24:15-28, Jesus merely introduced the notion of arrival of His Presence. We already have discussed this extensively.

♣ Jesus sends His messengers to gather His chosen from the four winds, from the ends of the heavens. Note, not from the ends of the earth, from THE ENDS OF THE HEAVENS, meaning the gathering is of spirits, not persons.

♣ It is straightforward that all of the discussion in this section continues elaboration of the RP7 path of the SSGLAE. Confirmation to follow in sections to follow.

✠ Breaking down *Matthew 24:36-51* in relation to the SSGLAE

♣ Only The Father knows the day and hour. None will be able to predict the timing of arrival of the Presence of Jesus Christ.

♣ Jesus declares that it is His Presence that arrives, meaning He states clearly that His coming on the CLOUDS is spiritual, not physical, hence there is not any contradiction to stating He will not any longer step physically on the earth.

♣ Two will be in the field, *one is taken*, and *one is left* means a *Hateful Citizen of the Nations* ends up on the OLD HEAVENS AND EARTH, and a *Power, Neophyte,* or *Loving Citizen of the Nations* is, in a spiritual sense, translated into New Heavens, New Earth, and the New Jerusalem, all of this, of course spiritual. Clearly, the spiritual resolution of the RP7 PATH that is domiciled in *Revelation ch. 21.*

♣ *Believers in Christ that are prepared for arrival of the Presence of Christ, who, spiritually are translated into New Heavens, New Earth, and the New Jerusalem?* SPEND THEIR TIME NOURISHING FELLOW BELIEVERS WITH TRUTH, ENCOURAGEMENT, AND LOVE.

♣ Believers who spend their time pointing fingers at other believers, who spend their time hating other believers, transform into *Hateful Citizens of the Nations,* end up on the OLD HEAVENS AND EARTH.

Prophetic Lessons 82 *It is unequivocal, in Matthew ch. 24, our Lord Jesus Christ devotes time to characterization of events that would transpire if, first the Nations, then the Church end up in unrighteousness, with outcome Life and Affairs on Earth transform from the GP7* PATH *to the RP7* PATH *of the SSGLAE.*

Prophetic Lessons 83 *If you start off with the awareness that Jesus discusses arrival of His Spiritual Presence, and that reaping is of the heavens, that is, of spirits that are in the heavens, meaning spirits of righteous saints that have died, and understand all of the discussions in this book, you arrive at the realization that* MATTHEW CH. 24 *is extremely* CLEAR, LUCID, LOGICAL, *and* SPIRITUAL.

Prophetic Lessons 84 *If you seek to be saved, looking to the Sun, Moon, or Stars for signs, seasons, days, or years, will not help, only your willingness, and effort for walking in the Love of God will matter.* SO THEN, STOP SEARCHING FOR SIGNS, AND SPEND THE TIME LEARNING HOW BEST TO WALK IN THE LOVE OF GOD.

Prophetic Lessons 85 *In so far as mankind is concerned, The New Heavens, New Earth, and New Jerusalem consist of men and women who have put on a 'new' nature, the nature of God, which is Love. Only those who have love for the nature of God are able to enter through the gates into the holy city.*

✠ Breaking down *1Thessalonians 4:13-18* in relation to the SSGLAE

♣ *vs. 14:* Our Lord Jesus Christ will bring with Him those who have fallen asleep, that is, the resurrected spirits of the saints.

♣ *vs. 15:* Those who are living remain over to the Presence of the Lord, and domicile of their spirits in the New Jerusalem does not precede domicile of those who have fallen asleep.

♣ *vs. 16*: Elaboration on *vs. 14*. The dead in Christ are the same as those who have fallen asleep.

♣ *vs. 17*: Elaboration on *vs. 15*. Caught up in CLOUDS spiritually to be with Jesus Christ in the New Jerusalem.

✤ Breaking down *2Peter 3:8-13* in relation to the SSGLAE

♣ *vs. 8-10*: The timing of arrival of the Presence of Christ cannot be predicted.

♣ *vs. 11-13*: The Old Heavens and Earth becomes devoid of life giving energy because the elements, the invisible spiritual energy that enable man function as spirit are, in a spiritual sense, burnt up with fire. This is inclusive of any of the invisible spiritual energy domiciled in Hateful Citizens of the Nations.

♣ *vs. 11-13*: The spirits of the saints are translated into New Heavens, New Earth, and the New Jerusalem. Through agency of the Holy Spirit, they remain connected, not with their own spirits, but with The Father and The Son. Think about it, which is better, to be connected with your own spirit, which is held in safe keeping for you by our Lord Jesus Christ until your physical death, or to be connected with The Father and Son, and with all of the spirits that The Father can make available for your help as necessary?

Prophetic Lessons 86 *The Coming of Christ, or equivalently, the Appearing of our Lord Jesus Christ a 'second' time (second here signifying, 'as many times as deemed necessary' is, in entirety, spiritual, already has transpired, and will continue to transpire. You see then, that The Father expects you, as a person who has faith in Jesus Christ, to make the most of your time on earth, to not spend your time thinking about escaping earth, rather, to spend your time Loving the earth, that is, your neighbor, your fellow man into the will of The Father.*

End-of-Chapter Encouragement for You, my Friend

Friend, remember how we read in the Book of Isaiah that The Father formed the earth to be inhabited, and that He has given the earth to man? Well, The Father declares that His original intent remains in force, that all of the rescuing of man from clutches of sin, and clutches of evil persons is spiritual, and will be effective. It will be effective, because The Father's eternal power guarantees so it will be.

Prophetic Word 11 *The Father guarantees that His spiritual interventions will have materiality, will have impact on day-to-day living on earth, will have a beneficial impact on your success in terms of the things of this life.*

The cost of this truth that you now encounter is the need for giving up the sincere teaching that has engulfed the Church that you are to expect Jesus to physically return to earth to establish a kingdom. This perhaps, may feel like somewhat of a dampener. As we have seen, however, suffering on earth is created by man. When man insists on greed and avarice, such that others suffer, this is not God's doing, rather is rebellion against God and His Love. The Father having given man power of choice, all that The Father can do is what He has promised, which is, judge the decision to engage in acts that create suffering until evil becomes so costly to those who engage in it, they have to desist. Simultaneously, if you remain in the Love of The Father, The Father promises you protection from judgments that are targeted at those who love and do evil.

Consider then the pragmatic, or practical day-to-day import of this teaching, which is, while you were focused on heaven as resolution of Life and Affairs on Earth, it encouraged you to sigh, lift up your hands in exasperation, and leave the dealing with evil in the hands of God. Now that you have become aware of perpetuity of life on earth, you cannot anymore just sigh and wait for God, rather, The Father declares that if you will engage with Him, such that you become a Power for Him, that together, you and Him and all others like you, like me, can affect the course of events on this earth, can make a beneficial difference, can increase the chance that the will of The Father is done on earth as it is in heaven.

Prophetic Lessons 87 *When your mind is set on an end-time event that resolves everything, you are not able to fully engage with life on earth. You are not able to exert all of the energy, ability, skill, promise, righteousness, Love, and courage that already is in you towards making this world as good a place as it possibly can be.*

Prophetic Word 12 *The Father declares to you that He has something better in store for you, that if you will desire to, and exert effort towards becoming a Power for Christ, that you need not any longer just sigh about state of Life and Affairs on Earth, that together, you and Him, and others like you and me can work for fulfillment of the will of The Father on earth, as it is in Heaven.*

Prophetic Lessons 88 *It is better to live with purpose on earth, and participate in intermittent spiritual interventions of The Father, than to 'sigh to the grave' hoping, and waiting for some end-of-time intervention that, absent your participation, brings about the end of the world.*

Prophetic Lessons 89 *Remember, arrival of intermittent spiritual interventions by The Father cannot be less effective than one end-of-time intervention that occurs at end of time. It is unequivocal then, that the system of repeated interventions that is domiciled in the SSGLAE, and the Presence of our Lord*

Jesus Christ on earth is guaranteed to be a better spiritual outcome, and a better outcome in context of the things of this life than some end-of-the-world cataclysmic event.

The Father urges you, encourages you, asks you to pray for spiritual strength that will enable you abandon your cherished thoughts about an *end-of-the-world* CATACLYSMIC EVENT, and embrace the truth of His spiritual interventions in time. The Father asks you to request of Him more of His Spirit, and more of His Love so you are able to arrive at love for His truth. In this respect, these words, which are set to song, and of which you are aware are appropriate.

More Love, More Power
More of you Lord Jesus in my Life
More Love, More Power
More of you O Lord in my Life

I will worship you with all my heart
I will worship you with all my mind
I will worship you with all my strength
For you are the Lord of my Life
The Lord of my Life

More Love, More Power
More of you Lord Jesus in my Life
More Love, More Power
More of you O Lord in my Life

In Jesus Name. Amen.

He who has an ear, let him hear what the Spirit saith unto the Churches.

But you, brothers, are not in darkness so that this day should surprise you like a thief. You are all sons of the light and sons of the day. Be joyful always; pray continually; give thanks in all circumstances, for this is God's will for you in Christ Jesus (*1Thessalonians 5:4-5; 16-18*).

May God Himself, the God of peace, sanctify you through and through. May your whole spirit, soul, and body be kept blameless at the coming of our Lord Jesus Christ. The one who calls you is faithful and He will do it (*1Thessalonians 5:23-24*).

CHAPTER 19

Jesus, Father of The Ages, Father of Eternity

In the preceding chapter, I established that, in all of the Bible, there is not any such thing as a second physical appearance on earth of Jesus Christ for salvation of those who repose faith in Him. Consistent with all of the other preceding chapters, I established that the '*second appearance*' of Jesus Christ is, in entirety, spiritual, already has transpired, and, as necessary, continues to transpire.

Hallelujah!!!

In this chapter, I demonstrate to you that an important source of the confusion that is, teaching of a physical second appearance of Christ, an appearance in context of which He would not arrive on earth, with outcome believers in His name are physically caught up to meet Him in the air, is a misunderstanding of what is meant by the phrase, '*the age to come*'. I aim to demonstrate to you that the phrase, '*the age to come*' refers to an age that was yet to arrive on this earth, not a domicile in heaven. With this clarification, I am confident that your mind will be cleared of confusion, that you will fully arrive at the recognition that the '*second appearance*' of our Lord and Savior Jesus Christ is, in entirety, spiritual, not physical.

Prophetic Lessons 90 *In the past, Christian theologians have interpreted the phrase* 'THE AGE TO COME' *to refer to a domicile in heaven. This was and is a misconception.*

What perhaps are the most important Scripture that are responsible for misinterpretation of the phrase '*the age to come*' derive from words spoken by our Lord Jesus Christ Himself.

And Jesus answering said, Verily I say to you, there is no one who left house, or brothers, or sisters, or father, or mother, or wife, or children, or fields, for my sake, and for the good news, who may not receive an hundredfold now in this time, houses, and brothers, and sisters, and mothers, and children, and fields, with persecutions, and in the age that is coming, life age-during; and many first shall be last, and the last first (Mark 10:29-31).

And He said to them, Verily I say to you, that there is not one who left house, or parents, or brothers, or wife, or children, for the sake of the reign of God, who may not receive back manifold more in this time, and in the coming age, life age-during (Luke 18:30).

Prophetic Word 13 *Our Lord Jesus Christ made it very clear to his disciples that there was an age to come, an age that still was in the future, and that they, His disciples, would not attain to eternal life until that age which was coming, comes into play.*

Alright then, now let us consider a couple of additional Scriptures.

And this is the life age-during, that they may know Thee, the only true God, and Him whom Thou didst send - Jesus Christ (John 17:3).

All things were delivered to me by my Father, and none doth know the Son, except The Father, nor doth any know The Father, except the Son, and he to whom the Son may wish to reveal Him (Matthew 11:27).

That ye may be in strength to comprehend, with all the saints, what is the breadth, and length, and depth, and height, to know also the love of The Christ that is exceeding the knowledge, that ye may be filled - to all the fullness of God (Ephesians 3:18-19).

And He gave some as apostles, and some as prophets, and some as proclaimers of good news, and some as shepherds and teachers, unto the perfecting of the saints, for a work of ministration, for a building up of the body of Christ, till we may all come to the unity of the faith and of the recognition (knowledge) of the Son of God, to a perfect man, to a measure of the stature of the fullness of Christ (Ephesians 4:11-13).

Love of Truth 66 *If we are not, in this life, able to arrive at recognition, that is, knowledge of the Son of God, and The Father, then life that is age-during is not possible in this life, meaning our Lord Jesus Christ makes a promise about eternal life that only can be fulfilled after we die.*

Love of Truth 67 *If eternal life comes from knowledge of The Father and The Son, and is unattainable in this life, then we are unable to arrive at a measure of the stature of the fullness of Christ, and are unable to arrive at the fullness of God. But if these objectives are unattainable, how are we to be motivated to attain them? If they are to be conferred upon our resurrection from the dead, physically, what is the point of striving while we remain alive? Surely, our Lord Jesus Christ would not usher us into such futility of striving.*

But is this true, can it be that age-during life is possible only after we die physically? For if it is true that we are unable to attain, except upon physical resurrection after death, then our Lord Jesus Christ declares a contradiction, declares that while we remain alive, it is impossible for us to arrive at knowledge of Himself, and His Father. Jesus be praised, for we are set for better things, not set for futility, but set for a striving that can produce the desired outcome, which is, life that is age-during, that is, arrival at a Right Recognition, equivalently, Knowledge of Christ.

THE SCRIPTURE EVIDENCE?

> Jesus said to her, I am the rising again, and the life; he who is believing in me, even if he may die, shall live; and every one who is living and believing in me shall not die - to the age (John 11:26-27).

Thankfully, our Lord Jesus Christ provides the answer Himself, declares, as I have exposited in *Chapter 8*, that, prior to physical death, there exists two sets of believers - NEOPHYTES who have yet to arrive at life that is age-during, and POWERS FOR CHRIST who have arrived at life that is age-during. When NEOPHYTES die, their spirits rest in Christ until commencement of a new age, then their spirits are resurrected to reign with Christ. When POWERS die, having already attained to life that is age-during, their spirits begin to reign with Christ immediately, meaning, prior to their physical death, their spirits had become known to Christ and The Father. Remember, Neophytes are not in rebellion towards their Lord and Savior, rather it is the case that they do not arrive at progress sufficient for arrival at life that is age-during prior to incidence of physical death.

The Things That Are 101 *As I have enunciated throughout this book, arrival at life that is age-during, this while we remain physically alive in this world, is goal of faith in, and love for Jesus Christ.*

The Things That Are 102 *Those to whom our Lord Jesus Christ reveals Himself, those whom He then introduces to His Father, these attain to life that is age-during in Christ.*

The Things That Are 103 *Attainment to life that is age-during in Christ is not by lottery. As I have enunciated throughout this book, it is your willingness to love with the love of Christ, and your efforts towards loving with the love of Christ that qualify you for a personal revelation of Jesus Christ. First, however, via infilling of the Holy Spirit, you need to be filled with a love essence that only can be received from The Father.*

Having arrived at confirmation from our Lord Jesus Christ Himself, that we are able to arrive at life that is age-during while we remain physically alive in this life, let us consider some Scriptures, which allude to feasibility of knowledge of The Father, and The Son.

> For I decided not to know any thing among you, except Jesus Christ, and Him crucified (1Corinthians 2:2).

> And we have known that the Son of God is come, and hath GIVEN US A MIND, THAT WE MAY KNOW HIM WHO IS TRUE, and we are in Him who is true, in His Son Jesus Christ; this one is the true God and the life age-during! (1John 5:20).

> Because of this, we also, from the day in which we heard, do not cease praying for you, and asking that ye may be filled with the full knowledge of His will in all wisdom and spiritual understanding, to your walking worthily of the Lord unto all pleasing, in every good work being fruitful, and INCREASING TO THE KNOWLEDGE OF GOD (Colossians 1:9-10).

> And INCREASE YE IN GRACE, AND IN THE KNOWLEDGE OF OUR LORD AND SAVIOR JESUS CHRIST; to Him is the glory both now, and to the day of the age! Amen (2Peter 3:18).

The Age to Come - In Heaven or on Earth?

Let us commence our discussion with a definition of 'AN AGE', and 'AGES'. Two Scriptures enable us arrival at definitions for an 'AN AGE', and 'AGES'.

> In many parts, and many ways, God of old having spoken to the fathers in the prophets, in these last days did speak to us in a Son, whom He appointed heir of all things, THROUGH WHOM ALSO HE DID MAKE the ages (Hebrews 1:1-2).

> *Jesus Christ yesterday and today the same, and to the ages (Hebrews 13:8).*

> And He (Jesus) answering said to them, "He who is sowing the good seed is the Son of Man, and the field is the world, and the

good seed, these are the sons of the reign, and the darnel are the sons of the evil one, and the enemy who sowed them is the devil, and THE HARVEST IS A FULL END OF THE AGE, and the reapers are messengers. As then, the darnel is gathered up, and is burned with fire, SO SHALL IT BE IN THE FULL END OF THIS AGE, the Son of Man shall send forth His messengers, and they shall gather up out of His kingdom all the stumbling-blocks, and those doing the unlawlessness, and shall cast them to the furnace of the fire; there shall be weeping and the gnashing of the teeth. Then shall the righteous shine forth as the sun in the reign of their Father. He who is having ears to hear - let him hear (Matthew 13:37-43).

What then do we establish? First, the ages are created by our Lord Jesus Christ, meaning there is intention and purpose to every age. Second, there are multiple ages, meaning there is transition from one age to another. Third, Jesus Christ, our Lord and Savior remains to the ages, as such is able to forever intercede for us, and oversee intention and purpose of every age. Fourth, the spiritual reaping of the righteous, and execution of judgment on the wicked marks the end of every age. THIS FOURTH POINT IS CRUCIAL.

Prophecy Principle 158 *The full end of an age is indicated by a spiritual reaping of the righteous, and execution of judgment on the wicked.*

The Things That Are 104 *It is straightforward; our Lord Jesus Christ declares that any iteration of the SSGLAE, which arrives at reaping of the righteous, and execution of judgment on the wicked, that is, at either of the spiritual resolutions in Revelation chs. 21 or 22 constitutes an age.*

The Things That Are 105 *While there exist two broad ages, the* AGE OF THE MESSENGERS, *and the* AGE OF THE PRESENCE OF CHRIST, *the phrase, 'to the ages of the ages' provides us with the insight that each of those broad ages is sub-divided into several sub-ages also referred to as ages.*

The Things That Are 106 *Our Lord Jesus Christ, already, in eternity has created multiple ages for man to experience, meaning there is intention and purpose to every age. Since our Lord Jesus Christ lives forever, He is able to oversee intention and purpose of every age.*

With respect to importance of arrival at an understanding of the intention and purpose of every age, through Apostle Paul, the Holy Spirit admonishes as follows.

And be not conformed to this age, but be transformed by the renewing of your mind, for your proving what is the will of God - the *good*, and *acceptable*, and *perfect* (Romans 12:2).

Look carefully then how you walk, not as unwise men but as wise, making the most of the time, because the days are evil. Therefore do not be foolish, but understand what the will of the Lord is (Ephesians 5:15-17).

Prophetic Lessons 91 *In light of importance of plugging into intentions and purposes of our Lord Jesus Christ, the Holy Spirit admonishes you and I to make efforts to arrive at a firm understanding and assurance of what exactly constitutes the will of God, that is, the grand purpose of The Father for the times in which we live.*

Prophetic Lessons 92 *It is a righteous initiative for a son of God always to be in thought as to how to make the most of the time. Since Godliness consists in* CONCEPTIONS, FORMULATIONS, *and* IMPLEMENTATIONS *of Love Projects, spending of the time in contemplation of loving things to do, and in doing of loving things conforms with making the most of the time.*

In respect of the will of God, Apostle Paul dichotomizes between the 'GOOD WILL' of God, the 'ACCEPTABLE WILL' of God, and the 'PERFECT WILL' of God. We already know that the *perfect will* of God is the perfection of His Church, such that she arrives at a Perfect Man, at 'a measure of the stature of the fullness of Christ.'

Prophetic Lessons 93 *Any and all specific agenda, which tie into perfection of The Church are part of the perfect will of The Father. So then, any specific efforts you exert, in context of guidance and validation of the Holy Spirit, towards enablement of arrival or maintenance of the Church on the BP7* PATH *of the SSGLAE reflects understanding of, and participation in the perfect will of The Father.*

Prophetic Lessons 94 *With respect to* LOVE PROJECTS, *the only difference between the BP7 and GP7 paths is, while Love Projects primarily are domiciled in* CHURCH *in context of the GP7* PATH, *in context of the BP7* PATH, *they equally are likely to be partnerships with the Nations.*

How then about the 'GOOD WILL' of God? In context of the spiritual resolution of the RP7 PATH of the SSGLAE in *Revelation ch. 21*, there are not any Love Projects from The Father in the offing. On the contrary, in *Revelation ch. 22*, our Lord Jesus Christ promises, in context of spiritual resolution of the BP7 PATH, arrival of Love Projects that are premised on arrival of the Church at a Perfect Man (Revelation 22:12). In context of spiritual resolution of the RP7 PATH, as we already have established, it is the good works of the saints that provide light to the nations.

Prophetic Lessons 95 *Whenever the Church, through no fault or contribution of yours, finds herself on the RP7* PATH *of the SSGLAE, the good works that you do individually, the good works into which you are guided by the Holy Spirit, provide evidence that you understand, and are participating in the* GOOD WILL *of The Father.*

Prophetic Lessons 96 *The specific works that glorify The Father in context of the RP7* PATH *of the SSGLAE, or the Love Projects that glorify The Father in context of the BP7* PATH *of the SSGLAE are context specific, are adapted to the specific purposes of our Lord and Savior Jesus Christ.*

What then can be the 'ACCEPTABLE WILL' of God? Well, the acceptable will of God is non-participation in sin, that is, love for the fellow man. So then, Loving Citizens of the Nations (LCN) are representative of the acceptable will of The Father. Note, however, that an LCN who receives a revelation of Christ, who is convicted of spiritual reality of person of Christ, but who rejects the conviction, as such refuses to confess Jesus as Lord and Savior violates the acceptable will of God.

Why is this?

Prophetic Lessons 97 *Because on this earth, in time and space, Jesus made sacrifices so an LCN can be saved. When an LCN is convicted of such sacrifice, yet refuses to honor Christ, he or she practices hatred,* REPAYS LOVE WITH HATRED, *as such falls short of the acceptable will of The Father.*

Prophetic Lessons 98 *It is straightforward to see that the acceptable will of God pertains to all possible ages. The Father has made it to be so, because whenever each of The Church and The Nations are in rebellion against His will, all that the righteous may be able to do is live their lives in quiet, in departure from evil, and in love towards others that is pure and sincere (1 Thessalonians 4:9-12).*

Subsequent to defining THE FULL END OF AN AGE, our Lord Jesus Christ explicitly declares that the age ushered in by His Life, Death, and Resurrection, the age shepherded by His Apostles, would devolve into an age marked by presence of STUMBLING-BLOCKS, and presence of people doing the LAWLESSNESS.

A person who is a STUMBLING-BLOCK is a person who attempts to prevent, or resist entrance of people into the reign of our Lord and Savior Jesus Christ. Jewish believers who attempted to impose circumcision of the flesh on non-Jewish believers in Christ were regarded as stumbling-blocks (Acts 15:1-34; Galatians 2:1-5; 5:11-12). Believers in Christ who do not practice brotherly kindness towards less mature fellow believers are characterized as stumbling-blocks (1Corinthians 8:9; Romans 14:12-13). A LAWLESS person is a person who, in the decision to consider himself or herself superior to all other men, lifts himself or herself above the throne of The Father. In the regarding of themselves as superior to non-Jewish believers, some Jewish believers characterized themselves as *Lawless* persons. As we already have discussed, in the declaration that the Pope is intrinsically spiritually superior to all other believers in Christ, the papal Church practices *Lawlessness*, as such is the 'man of sin' prophesied to arise from within The Church in 2Thessalonians 2:1-12. We already have discussed that it was not until institution of *Gregory I* in *590 AD*, that the Church of Western Europe transformed herself into the '*man of sin*'. Lest other Churches become prideful, in their decisions to hold on to one pet doctrine or the other, which, on basis of disinterested, Holy Spirit examination, can be shown to be heretically false, other Churches have not performed much better at maintenance of Purity of the Gospel. When some individual Churches in America do not say,

> "regardless of sexual orientation, we love all, but uphold standards of our Lord and Savior Jesus Christ,"

rather, declare that

> "there is not any command against sexual immorality, such as homosexuality or lesbianism,"

they perhaps act worse than the papal Church. Note that with the Presence of our Lord Jesus Christ arriving subsequent to *590 AD*, that is, in context of the making available of the Scriptures to individual believers upon commencement of the CHURCH IN LAODICEA in *1454 AD* (this aided by the invention of the Gutenberg Press), the prophecy by Apostle Paul that the Presence of Christ would not arrive until the man of sin is revealed, is fulfilled.

Prophetic Lessons 99 *Our Lord Jesus Christ declared prophetically, that the Church that would be anchored by His original 12* APOSTLES *would resist perfection, with outcome the Church of that age would end up on the RP7* PATH *of the SSGLAE. In the raising up of Apostle Paul for defense of purity of the Gospel, however, but with the Nations not premising civil laws on the Love of God, The Father provided opportunity for immediate relocation to a BP7* PATH *of the SSGLAE.*

Prophetic Lessons 100 *Regardless whether a Church has become apostate, or engages in teachings that can be regarded to be heretical, without resort to arguments, or an argumentative spirit, but with a minding of yourself, such that your spiritual garments do not become spotted, The Father compels you to walk in love towards members and leaders of apostate Churches.*

Is there any evidence that the Apostles expected some spiritual realities to be domiciled in later ages?

WELL, IN THIS RESPECT, CONSIDER THE FOLLOWING SCRIPTURE.

Let no one, then, judge you in eating or drinking, or in respect of a feast, or of a new moon, or of sabbaths, WHICH ARE A SHADOW OF THE COMING THINGS, and the body is of The Christ (Colossians 2:16).

And God being rich in kindness, because of His great love with which He loved us, even being dead in the trespasses, *did make us to live together with The Christ* (by grace ye are having saved), and did raise us up together, and did seat us together in the heavenly places in Christ Jesus, THAT HE MIGHT SHOW, IN THE AGES THAT ARE COMING, the exceeding riches of His grace in kindness toward us in Christ Jesus, for of Him we are workmanship, created in Christ Jesus to good works, which God did before prepare, that in them we may walk (Ephesians 2:4-7,10).

Friend, since you already are seated in the heavenly places in Christ Jesus, 'THE AGES THAT ARE COMING' cannot be about a *'going to heaven'*, rather must relate to life on this earth. As confirmation, Apostle Paul goes to associate 'THE AGES THAT ARE COMING' with performance of good works, which God already has prepared that we should walk in them. In Colossians 2:16, through Apostle Paul, the Holy Spirit declares that the feasts of the Old Testament, such as the weekly sabbath or Passover were, at his point in time, *shadows of things to come in the future*. The CHURCH OF THE BYZANTINE EMPIRE, the Church that was fusion of Church and State, likely is one fulfillment of this prophecy from Apostle Paul. We already have established beyond any doubt that the commencement of the Church of the Byzantine Empire signified commencement of a new SSGLAE for the Church, as such commencement of a new age created by our Lord and Savior Jesus Christ.

Prophetic Lessons 101 *Friend, there are good works, which The Father has prepared for this age, and there are good works that are prepared for ages that are coming. If you do not do the work that is set in front of you by the Holy Spirit, if you pine for more glorious work, and yet that work is set for another age, you lose opportunity to become whatever The Father has prepared you to be.*

Prophetic Lessons 102 *In the declaration that The Father has good works planned for different ages, The Father provides assurance that life on earth always will be meaningful, always will be filled with righteous purpose that produces joy in life and affairs on earth.*

The abundance of the faithfulness of The Father of our Lord Jesus Christ is New every morning - Lamentations 3:23.

Our Lord Jesus Christ is Father of the ages, is Father of Eternity (Hebrews 1:1-2; Isaiah 9:6). The ages that our Lord Jesus Christ has established in time are for our benefit, are meant to be experienced in context of life on earth. We arrive then yet again at confirmation of the SHOCKING GOOD NEWS that we discovered in the preceding chapter, which is, for your good and mine, every spiritual intervention of The Father is designed for producing of a new age for which He already has made preparation on this earth.

Prophetic Lessons 103 *The ages are created by our Lord Jesus Christ, and subsist on this earth.*

The Father having prepared ahead of time, there is the confidence that our spiritual needs, and our needs of the things of this life are secure in Him. In this respect, Apostles Peter and Paul declare as follows.

His divine power has given to us all things that pertain to LIFE (*all of the good stuff that make life on earth enjoyable*) and GODLINESS (*the spiritual blessings that, conditional on our willingness and effort, guarantee our spiritual success*), through the knowledge of Him who called us by glory and virtue (2Peter 1:3).

Command those who are rich in this present age not to be haughty, nor to trust in uncertain riches but in THE LIVING GOD, WHO GIVES US RICHLY ALL THINGS TO ENJOY (1Timothy 6:17).

Blessed is the God and Father of our Lord Jesus Christ, who did bless us in every spiritual blessing in the heavenly places in Christ (Ephesians 1:3).

In any age within which you find yourself, The Father already has made provision for your spiritual and material success. If you will trust Him, you will find that living righteously is righteous fun, for all of the good works He prepares for you are, for you and those who are blessed by them, sources of righteous joy. In Jesus Name. Amen.

CHAPTER 20

Epilogue

In the Preface to this treatise on visions and revelations that were entrusted to Apostle John by our Lord Jesus Christ, I declared to you that the Book of Revelation is not about timing of a physical Second Coming of Jesus Christ.

Friend, I have delivered on that promise.

While I did not divulge it in the Preface, I have gone on to establish that, in so far as it relates to the notion of the SECOND COMING of Christ, that you need to have your mind renewed. The demand for renewal can be encapsulated as follows.

✠ In place of a looking forward to a SECOND COMING of Christ, you are to arrive at the recognition that The Lord Jesus Christ seeks that you become a Power for Him, such that you influence His Church towards willingness to be perfected, and influence the Nations towards willingness to acquiesce societal interactions, civil laws, and implementations of civil laws to the Love of Christ.

✠ When you expend your efforts and energies towards becoming a Power for Christ: If The Church were to be disobedient to her Lord and Savior, your ethos and actions remain the same. If The Nations were to stubbornly resist that which is good for them, which is love for one another, your ethos and actions remain the same. If The Church and The Nations respond with love to their heavenly Father, your ethos and actions remain the same. Season in, Season out, you always are in the will of The Father, always are pleasing to Him. You see then, that when you desire to become a Power for Christ, you no longer are guided by time, rather time, in response to it's Creator, for whom you are an ambassador or emissary, and in whose interests you act, responds to you in Christ. It is to this inducement of a response from time in obedience to it's Creator, our Lord Jesus Christ, that The Lord Jesus refers to as 'a seizing of the reign of the heavens by force (Matthew 11:12).'

✠ Whenever The Church and/or The Nations stubbornly refuse to respond with love to their heavenly Father, you are to expect spiritual interventions from The Lord Jesus Christ, spiritual interventions, which generate spiritual resolutions on earth that create peace in your earthly circumstances. When you focus on becoming a Power for Christ, you are positioned for taking advantage of such spiritual resolutions, for making the most of the opportunities created, and the time.

✠ What it takes to become a Power for Christ?

♣ Faith in, and Love for Jesus Christ that is evident in Love for all men

♣ Infilling of the Holy Spirit

♣ Infilling of the Love of God

♣ Arrival at Godliness, that is, capacity for spending the time in CONCEPTIONS of Love Projects for the future; FORMULATIONS of Love Projects for the present; and IMPLEMENTATION of Love Projects that were conceived in past.

♣ BROTHERLY KINDNESS - the capacity for Gentleness and Understanding in dealings with fellow believers in Christ who have yet to attain to the spiritual stature to which you have attained.

♣ Love for all men, particularly, strangers, and those who, in their *racial*, ethnic, *religious*, or other make ups are starkly different from you.

✠ How then are you to become, and yet not become proud if your attention is fixed on becoming a Power for Christ?

♣ You focus only on the objective, which is, a demonstration to Father, Son, and Holy Spirit that your commitment to loving everyone around you with the Love of God is unwavering. When you are able to maintain this commitment to love, The Father and The Lord Jesus provide you with personal spiritual revelations, and usher you into actualization of The Presence of Christ. Remember, while you always are in the Presence of Christ; at the point in time during which you are recognized as a Power for Christ, however, you arrive at a spiritual actualization of this reality.

♣ The importance of your commitment to the Love of God? Watch ye, stand in the faith; be men, be strong; let all your things be done in Love (1Corinthians 16:13-14).

Prophetic Lessons 104 *Friend, as you can see, only those who are able to die to self, such that they become fully alive to Christ are able to become Powers for Christ. You see then that it is impossible to pretend your way into this Grace of The Father. If you are to attain in Christ, there cannot be any hypocrisy, there cannot be any delight in self aggrandizement, only those who truly are meek are able to become Powers for Christ. Remember, you do not declare yourself a Power for Christ, rather it is The Lord Jesus Christ who, in His relationship with you, recognizes you as a Power for His glory.*

With respect to The Church, and The Nations, I have demonstrated that it is absence of willingness to be perfected in Christ, equivalently, absence of willingness to be perfected in Love that causes the Church to go round and round in circles. I also have demonstrated that it is unwillingness at premising of societal interactions, civil laws, and implementations of civil laws on the Love of Christ that causes the nations to go round and round in circles. Most importantly, I have shown that just about all of the suffering in the world is man-made, is produced either by unwillingness of the Church to be perfected in Love (*persecutions of those who truly love Christ*), or unwillingness of the nations to acquiesce societal interactions, civil laws, and implementations of civil laws to the Love of Christ.

Prophetic Lessons 105 *When you and I do our part faithfully, when we put forth efforts towards walking in the Love of God towards all, we increase the chance that neither of The Church, nor The Nations will walk in stubborn rebellion towards The Father.*

But then, I also promised that there were some truths that our Lord Jesus Christ sought to reveal to you, some truths that would enhance your relationship with Him, that would make you stand in awe of the wisdom, goodness, graciousness, thoughtfulness, faithfulness, justice, and righteousness of our great God and Savior Jesus Christ. As you already can see, all of those truths revolve around the SSGLAE, the 'Seal System for Governing of Affairs on Earth' (SSGLAE).

Prophetic Lessons 106 *In the SSGLAE, The Father demonstrates that He is quick to reward delight in righteousness, and that He will not allow evil grow in this world to the point where you and I despair with respect to our decision to live righteously. In the SSGLAE, we see evidence from The Father of* THOUGHTFULNESS, LOVE, *and* CAREFUL PLANNING *for our welfare.*

Friend, The Father does not just want you to be saved, He wants you to know Him. He wants you to know just how much He cares for you. Just how much He has thought in advance about your welfare. He wants you to appreciate the wisdom with which He has set up the SSGLAE for your protection from evil, for your sanctification, for your glorification. In the knowledge of how much He has put into setting up the SSGLAE for your welfare, He hopes to reap an outflowing of Love and appreciation, an intimacy that brings you into the most Holy Place, the place within which He and our Lord Jesus Christ can, through agency of the Holy Spirit, make a spiritual home with each and every believer. The Father seeks for you to understand the SSGLAE so you can arrive at importance of Love for well functioning of affairs of the Church and of the world in general. Now that you understand the primaryness of the Love of Christ for well being of life on earth, the Father hopes that you will go forth and share what you know, as gently and aptly as possible with others, for as more and more people become aware of the SSGLAE, it becomes more likely that the Church, which now is so splintered that any thought of it being perfected seems ridiculous, can begin to make her way back to her Lord and Savior Jesus Christ.

But, with God, nothing shall be impossible - Luke 1:37.

Prophetic Word 14 *It is true that the Church is so splintered, one wonders whether unity will, as was the case in 325 AD, ever again be possible. The Promise from The Father? "And Jesus, having looked upon them, saith, 'With men it is impossible, but not with God; for* ALL THINGS ARE POSSIBLE WITH GOD *(Mark 10:27).'"*

Friend, the next time someone tells you to look out for *the signs of the times* so you do not miss out on the Second Coming of Christ, ask them to tell you this one thing, which is:

> If Jesus Himself declares that manifestations of His Presence for EXECUTIONS OF JUDGMENT or AWARDING OF REWARDS, manifestations that signal 'end of an age' would catch those who believe in Him unawares, what exactly is the point of paying attention to signs of His Presence?

For emphasis, let us revisit the words of our Lord Jesus Christ in Matthew 24:3,36,40,42,44.

> And when He is sitting on the mount of Olives, THE DISCIPLES CAME near to Him by Himself, SAYING, TELL US, WHEN SHALL THESE BE? and what is the sign of thy presence, and of the full end of the age? And concerning that day and the hour no one hath

known - not even the messengers of the heavens - except my Father only. Then two men shall be in the field, the one is received, and the one is left; two women shall be grinding in the mill, one is received, and one is left. WATCH YE THEREFORE, BECAUSE YE HAVE NOT KNOWN IN WHAT HOUR YOUR LORD DOTH COME; because of this also ye, become ye ready, because IN WHAT HOUR YE DO NOT THINK, THE SON OF MAN DOTH COME.

Prophecy Principle 159 *Our Lord Jesus Christ Himself declares that the only way to prepare for manifestations of His Presence for* EXECUTIONS OF JUDGMENT, *and* AWARDING OF REWARDS *is to watch, that is, to watch for traps that are set for tempting you away from faith, hope, and love.*

You, of course my friend know now why exactly the signs are irrelevant, which is, the signs are characteristic of any SSGLAE that proceeds beyond the 1st Seal. Whenever the nations do not acquiesce civil laws to the Love of Christ, arrival at the 2nd, 3rd, 4th, 5th, and 7th seals implies wars and rumors of wars (2nd Seal), persecution of The Church, and killing of the Nations (4th Seal), and injuries on the nations (7th Seal). If the Church is not perfected, the SSGLAE resets to a 1st Seal. If again the nations do not submit civil laws to the Love of Christ, there again are wars and rumors of wars, and on and on it goes. We have then that all of the signs given by our Lord Jesus Christ will continue for as long as either of The Church or The Nations remain in rebellion towards our Lord and Savior Jesus Christ.

For concreteness, consider the words of our Lord Jesus Christ in Revelation 3:3, and the admonition in respect of how to prepare for manifestations of The Presence of our Lord and Savior Jesus Christ in 1Thessalonians 5:1-4; 6-9.

Remember then, how thou hast received, and heard, AND BE KEEPING, AND REFORM: if then, thou mayest not watch (*if then, you choose not to reform, choose not to walk in faith, hope, and love*), I will come upon thee as a thief, and thou mayest not know what hour I will come upon thee.

And concerning the times and the seasons, brethren, ye have no need of my writing to you, for yourselves have known thoroughly that the day of the Lord as a thief in the night doth so come, for when they may say, PEACE AND SURETY, then sudden destruction doth stand by them, as the travail doth her who is with child, and they shall not escape; and ye brethren are not in darkness, that the day may catch you as a thief; all ye are sons of light, and sons of day; we are not of night, nor of darkness.

So then let us not sleep, as others do, but let us keep awake and be sober. For those who sleep sleep at night, and those who get drunk are drunk at night. But, since we belong to the day, let us be sober, and put on the breastplate of faith and love, and for a helmet the hope of salvation. For God has not destined us for wrath, but to obtain salvation through our Lord Jesus Christ.

Our Lord Jesus Christ Himself declares that it is by reforming yourself, that is, by forsaking evil and loving what is good that you prepare for manifestations of His Presence. The Holy Spirit through Apostle Paul reiterates the same admonition, declares that you prepare for manifestations of The Presence of Christ by putting on the breastplate of faith and Love, and the helmet of the hope of salvation. CAN IT BE SAID ANY CLEARER THAN THIS? If you love the Lord Jesus, you will choose His words over those of men who merely seek to entangle you in their traditions and idolatry, as opposed to helping you arrive at the true freedom that is available in our Lord and Savior Jesus Christ.

Friend, my book, 'In Jesus Name' introduces you to how to receive and grow in the Love of Jesus Christ. The book demonstrates that if you do not nurture the Love of Jesus Christ in your spirit, you do not grow in the Love of Christ. The book concludes with several chapters on applications of the Love of Christ in different sorts of contexts.

My book, 'True Sanctification' introduces you to the how of becoming a KING AND A PRIEST unto The Lord and Savior Jesus Christ. A Person who becomes a KING AND A PRIEST to Christ, is a person who arrives at a *Right Recognition of Christ*, that is, at a *Perfect Man*, that is, at 'a Measure of the Stature of the Fullness of Christ'. True Sanctification introduces you to the demands placed on your faith (willingness, *reasoning*, and honest responses) by the process of sanctification, the only process via which you are transformed into a Power for Christ. At about *480 pages*, True Sanctification gets into the NITTY GRITTY of your Sanctification, all of which is intended for actualization of your peace and joy. If you ever read a book on *Sanctification* that ever made you feel MOROSE? Well, True Sanctification is the ANTIDOTE produced for you by The Holy Spirit.

In my book, Divine Meritocracy, I introduce you to The Father's standards of meritocracy. While we are equal in intrinsic worth before The Father of our Lord Jesus Christ, just as Peter, James, and John emerged as leaders of the Apostolic Church by merit, so also today The Father seeks to qualify those who have faith in Jesus Christ for different works by merit. Divine Meritocracy introduces you to how exactly to gain entry into the merit books of our Lord and Savior Jesus Christ.

Brother, Sister, Friend, if you do not find yourself yet appreciating the beauty of the SSGLAE, such that you have arrived at new found appreciation for LOVE and THOUGHTFULNESS of The Father, Son, and Holy Spirit, I ask that you read through this treatise at least one more time, or get in touch with me with your concerns. I will be more than happy to engage with you, such that with help of the Holy Spirit whatever constitutes a spiritual stronghold in your mind can be pulled down and destroyed. For my contact information, refer to the '*Declarations*' section, which is placed right after the *Acknowledgments* section for this treatise on the Love of The Father, Son, and Holy Spirit.

Prophetic Lessons 107 *The SSGLAE is designed with your welfare and happiness in mind, it ought to bring you joy. If it does not, something is wrong somewhere and with help of the Holy Spirit, it can be discerned, pulled down, destroyed.*

Why should the SSGLAE bring you joy?

You have arrived at the realization that Jesus never again will manifest on earth biologically as Son of Man.

The Reason?

Having set up a '*production process*', which produces exactly what He was, but which He refused to declare to men, which is son of God, albeit, *the only begotten* Son of God, Jesus manifesting on earth biologically obviates the very same process He Himself has set up. For illustration, suppose you and I, have, via faith in Jesus Christ, become *sons of God*, as such, have become Powers for Christ. Enter then the manifestation, in likeness of human form of the only begotten Son of God, Jesus Christ. Given it must be the case that the spiritual stature of Jesus Christ towers above ours, if men flock to any son of God at all, they flock to the only begotten Son of God, with outcome you and I become redundant. So then, Jesus manifesting on earth biologically undos the very work that He came to earth to accomplish *2,000 plus* years ago, which is, revelation of truth of God's existence and essence here on earth via transformation of men into sons of God. So then, Jesus Himself declares to the disciples that He never again will be seen on this earth (Matthew 24:23). From time of His ascension back to heaven, it would be those who allow themselves to be transformed into sons of God, who allow themselves to be transformed into Powers for Christ, who would reveal Jesus to the world.

Just thinking about the trust and glory that has been reposed in us makes me shout, perhaps yet even holler, 'Hallelujah!!!'

Being rational, The Father, Son, and Holy Spirit have declared that you and I are the only representations of Jesus Christ that the world will encounter. Imagine then the trust that The Lord Jesus Christ reposes in you and I. In the SSGLAE, Jesus declares your importance, declares He is depending on you for manifestations of His Presence, for manifestations of His Glory. In this respect, note that since commencement of the time of the CHURCH IN LAODICEA, while the earth remains physically the same, spiritually, with our dwelling domiciled in the NEW JERUSALEM, you and I live in NEW HEAVENS, and NEW EARTH. Just as you remain the same physically, yet have been transformed into a NEW CREATION in Jesus Christ (2Corinthians 5:17), so also it is the case that while the earth remains physically the same, for you and I, and for The Nations who choose to participate, we live in the NEW JERUSALEM that is domiciled in NEW HEAVENS, and NEW EARTH or in UTOPIA.

Prophetic Lessons 108 *The SSGLAE should bring you joy. In it, Father, Word, and Holy Spirit declare that they trust you, declare that they entrust to you revelations of the* PRESENCE, GLORY, ESSENCE, *and* CHARACTER *of Christ to the world.*

Hallelujah!!!

Now to Him who is able to keep you from stumbling, and to present you faultless before the presence of His glory with exceeding joy, to God our Savior, who alone is wise, be glory and majesty, dominion and power, both now and forever.

The Grace of our Lord Jesus Christ be with your spirit, in Jesus Name.

Amen.

CHAPTER 21

Appendix

Jesus is not a man, only came in likeness of a man. Comparisons of artistic depictions of Jesus with those of *Salah al-Din* reveal the implicit heresy that worship of pictures or statues of artistic representations of Jesus is tantamount to idolatry, is tantamount to worship of some look alike fellow man. None of the idolatrous representations of Jesus Christ presented on the next page depict anything close to what is described by Apostle John. More importantly, Jesus is a Spirit (The Word, who is God), who took up the form of a man, as such is not a man, as such cannot be depicted as a man.

Depiction of Salah al-Din I

Depiction of Salah al-Din II

Depiction of Jesus I

Depiction of Jesus II

Printed in Great Britain
by Amazon

22358029R00295